P9-EIE-695

New York, Chicago, Los Angeles

Janet L. Abu-Lughod

NY
CHI
LA

New York, Chicago, Los Angeles

AMERICA'S GLOBAL CITIES

University of Minnesota Press
MINNESOTA
Minneapolis — London

The University of Minnesota Press gratefully acknowledges the generous assistance provided for the publication of this book by Furthermore, the publication program of The J. M. Kaplan Fund.

The University of Minnesota Press gratefully acknowledges financial assistance provided for the publication of this book by the McKnight Foundation.

This book was published with assistance from the Margaret S. Harding Memorial Endowment honoring the first director of the University of Minnesota Press.

Published by the University of Minnesota Press
111 Third Avenue South, Suite 290
Minneapolis, MN 55401-2520
http://www.upress.umn.edu

Library of Congress Cataloging-in-Publication Data

Abu-Lughod, Janet L.
New York, Chicago, Los Angeles : America's global cities / Janet L. Abu-Lughod
p. cm.
Includes index.
ISBN 0-8166-3335-5 (hc.). — ISBN 0-8166-3336-3 (pb.)
1. Cities and towns—United States—History Case studies. 2. Metropolitan areas—United States—History Case studies. 3. New York (N.Y.)—History. 4. Chicago (Ill.)—History. 5. Los Angeles (Calif.)—History. 6. International economic relations—History.
I. Title.
HT123.A613 1999
307-76′0973—dc21 93-20766

Printed in the United States of America on acid-free paper

11 10 09 08 07 06 05 04 03 02 01 00 99 10 9 8 7 6 5 4 3 2 1

Contents

Acknowledgments

In the five short years during which this book was researched and written, I have accumulated many debts, and these are in some ways the easiest to recall and identify. Two universities gave direct assistance during this period: the Graduate Faculty of the New School for Social Research, where I taught for the past eleven years; and the University of California at Los Angeles, which graciously extended periodic invitations to affiliate as a visiting scholar, making available the full resources of that remarkable institution.

At the New School I not only had an ideal base from which to study New York but the opportunity to teach several research seminars on New York, Chicago, and Los Angeles as global cities. To many of the students in those seminars I am indebted, not only for their patience in exploring ideas that were at first somewhat disorganized and inchoate, but for the direct research they did in locating sources, analyzing findings, and sharing ideas and enthusiasm. Two students in particular made significant contributions: Alex Foti, a graduate student in economics who helped assemble much of the current material on Chicago; and Christopher Williams, a graduate student in sociology who patiently explored a variety of arcane sources, looking for ways to measure the degree to which globalization influences urbanization processes. Leaves of absence were also generously granted from my teaching responsibilities at the New School, including a one-semester paid sabbatical to supplement fellowships from other sources.

In New York I also benefited from colleagues at Columbia University. Kenneth Jackson's magisterial *Encyclopedia of the City of New York* came out just in the nick of time to verify remaining details. Peter Marcuse, by his continual interest in "how it was coming along," gave me encouragement when energy lagged; I am especially grateful for the close reading he gave the penultimate draft of this book, which allowed me to correct some errors in time. And I count myself lucky indeed to have enjoyed the friendship of Saskia Sassen, whose innovative work on globalization and the global city served as both the inspiration and the goad I needed to explore the applicability of general propositions to "my" three cases. I never turned down any of the frequent opportunities to appear on panels with her as we debated and clarified our positions, because I knew I would always learn from her. I thank the New York Regional Plan Association for lending me two original maps from its *Region at Risk,* and when a third one could not be located in the files, Steven Weber of the RPA graciously generated a replacement from the association's computerized database.

The Planning Program at UCLA extended its hospitality to me during the two summers and one semester that I was in residence there, and I always found its secretary, Marsha Brown, the essence of efficiency and kindness. These periodic visiting appointments offered me access to a superb library on Los Angeles, a convenient office, and, most important, a wonderful set of colleagues from whom I learned much about the city. From these it is difficult to single out just a few, but my dear friends John Friedmann and Edward Soja stand out from the rest for offering their expertise and stimulation, as well as good company. John and I had been members of the first student cohorts of a then-new approach to planning being honed at the University of Chicago in the late 1940s and 1950s. I always followed his later work with deep interest, and to some extent the initiating ideas for this book came from his pioneering (and now classic) 1982 article on world cities. Edward Soja and I had been colleagues at Northwestern University many years ago, where we had then been drawn together by our common interest in Third World cities, he in Africa, I in the Middle East. Our paths would again cross when we met on the grounds of Los Angeles, doing thoroughly collaborative work facilitated by a grant from the Getty Foundation. He warrants special thanks because he carefully read and critiqued what I was writing about Los Angeles, corrected errors, suggested additional sources, and shared his own as yet unpublished manuscripts on that city. At UCLA I had the advantage of studying the published and not yet published books of Allen J. Scott, who was also generous with his library and source suggestions, as were Paul Ong, Alan Heskin, and the members of the UCLA poverty study program (John Johnson, Mel Oliver, and Larry Bobo). Sociologist Georges Sabbagh, whom I had first met decades ago because of our shared interest in North Africa, was, by the time of my Los Angeles sojourns, working to untangle the complex racial and ethnic demography of Los Angeles. He as well as Roger Waldinger and Mehdi Bozorgmehr, who were leading a group of scholars in preparing a collective work on "ethnic Los Angeles," made available their as yet unpublished manuscripts.

In the ten months I spent in Los Angeles I did a "crash course" on the city itself, often using the public transportation eschewed by so many Angelenos. Although it is rare to single out a car rental agency in an acknowledgment, I want to note here that I am forever indebted to Enterprise Rent-a-Car's weekend special rate (only thirty-three dollars for three days!), because it disciplined me to spend only every other weekend exploring all parts of the L.A. region. Enterprise's cars also facilitated my work in San

Marino at the Huntington Library, with its outstanding collection of historical documentation in books, papers, photographs, and maps of Los Angeles. A reader's card at that institution gave me access not only to the library's collections but to the grounds, which were a welcome change from urban smog. At a later time I returned and was helped to locate appropriate maps and illustrations by archivist Alan Jutzi and photography curator Jennifer Watts. The Midnight Special Book Store in Santa Monica was another essential if expensive research site, because there was no recent book on the city that it failed to stock and that I could resist buying.

In preparing for this book I needed to spend much less time in Chicago because I had already devoted some twenty-five years (five as a student of sociology and planning at the University of Chicago and later, two decades as a professor of urban sociology at Northwestern University) getting to know the city intimately. Updating my material was made possible through numerous return visits; I am grateful for the hospitality of Louise Cainkar and Arlene Daniels in making those visits such a pleasure, and to the superb collections at the University of Chicago, Northwestern University, the Chicago Historical Society, and the Newberry Library for access to materials not available on either coast. I was also fortunate to track down the clippings files of the Municipal Reference Library, which in my absence had been moved to the new and elegant Chicago Public Library building. I also benefited from the excellent statistical analyses done at the University of Illinois and at NIPC, and found the publications of the Chicago Urban League a mine of useful information, as were those issued by Metro Chicago Information Center. I am especially grateful to D. Garth Taylor (former research director at the League and now director of Metro Chicago Information Center) for making available to me a number of the original maps from his studies. I also owe a debt of gratitude to Jeffrey Morenoff, who so generously (and laboriously) retrieved his data files to provide me with computer-generated maps of the distribution of African Americans and Hispanics in Chicago in 1970 and 1990.

Funding for much of the time devoted to preparing this book came from the Getty Foundation's Senior Collaborative Grant Program (shared with Edward Soja), supplemented by a grant from the American Council of Learned Societies. Without the released time and travel these grants permitted, this book would have taken a quarter of a century to write! I would have been hard-pressed to spend as much time in Los Angeles as I did, or to return to Chicago to complete the necessary research on that city.

My experience with the University of Minnesota Press, which shepherded this long and complex book into print, was remarkably pleasant, thanks to the enthusiasm, warm support, and professional competence of Carrie Mullen, the Press's acquisition editor, the strong guiding hand of Laura Westlund, its managing editor, and the meticulous and informed copyediting of Judy Selhorst, a woman of rare and unflappable stamina. I hope they share with me the pride in the finished product.

Those are the "short-term" acknowledgments so easy to recall. It is harder to trace my debts accumulated in the half century that I have been obsessed with cities. From the very first term paper I ever wrote in urban sociology (in 1948 at the University of Chicago, on the Ida B. Wells housing project), I knew that I would spend my life trying to understand cities. Chicago was, for a very long time, both the exemplar and the intellectual tool I carried with me, even though I realized early on how narrow a view one obtained from a single case. Nevertheless, for the twenty years I taught urban sociology at Northwestern University, I could not fail to use that city, as I had been taught, as a "laboratory" for research. Literally hundreds if not a thousand undergraduates there were my eyes and ears on that city. And yet the most valuable experiences for me were periodic opportunities to "escape" the time- and place-boundness of the field, so tied to modern Chicago. Lengthy scholarly digressions into the study of Middle East cities such as Cairo and Rabat, into cities throughout the "Third World," and even backward in time to explore how certain "global" cities organized trade and exchange in the world system of the thirteenth century convinced me of the absolute necessity to examine cities comparatively and within a deeper time frame than most urbanists do.

This has been my goal in writing the present book. It would have been a very different document without those apparent "digressions" from looking only at American cities. Perhaps this book, warts and all, will succeed if it convinces readers to follow a similar approach to studying cities, wherever they are.

Janet Abu-Lughod
New York

CHAPTER I

An Overview

THE CASES TO BE EXPLORED

This book focuses on three gigantic urbanized places that currently occupy hegemonic positions in the spatial structure, aesthetics, economy, changing demography, contentious politics, and evolving cultural meanings of American history: New York, Los Angeles, and Chicago. By the 1990s, each had become a gigantic regional constellation or galaxy of man-imposed constructions, strewn apparently like confetti over vast landscapes of terrain and encompassing the lives of seventeen, fourteen, and eight million persons, respectively.[1]

These settlements are perhaps the most impressive objects our culture has produced, and their scatterings are not random. Each urbanized region has been shaped according to inherited armatures of passage and within the confines of natural and man-made borders. In this book we shall be searching for those shapes and their causes, and we shall be trying to capture the processes whereby the three original urban settlements evolved into ever more complex forms—each contribution to which may have been "intended," but whose composite whole was never planned nor could have been fully anticipated.

These three urbanized regions offer a particularly fertile arena for investigating the nature of global cities and for tracing not only the role they play in the international community today, but also the ways in which their changing embeddedness in an evolving world system and their unique responses to those challenges over time have created significant variations within the general category of global cities.

THE CONCEPT OF GLOBAL CITIES

The theme of "global cities" has recently captured the imagination of urbanists, but as I shall argue, much of this exciting literature has been remarkably ahistorical, as if contemporary trends represent a sharp break from the past, if not an entirely new phenomenon. Furthermore, both the general descriptions of "world cities" and the accompanying causal analyses that attribute their commonalities to general forces residing at the highest level of the international economy neglect variations in global cities' responses to these new forces.

Contemporary scholars, trying to define the "global city," imply that it is a relatively *new* phenomenon that has been generated in the present period by the development of an all-encompassing world system—variously termed late capitalism, postindustrialism, the informational age, and so on.[2] Among the hallmarks of this new global city are presumed to be an expansion of the market via the internationalization of commerce, a revolution in the technologies of transport and communications, the extensive transnational movement of capital and labor, a paradoxical decentralization of production accompanied by a centralization of control over economic activities, and the increased importance of business services, particularly evident in the growth of the so-called FIRE economic sector—finance, insurance, and real estate. Accompanying these changes, and often thought to result from them, is a presumed new bifurcation of the class structure within the global city and increased segregation of the poor from the rich.

The value of such insights cannot be denied, but it is questionable whether the phenomenon is as recent as is claimed. As I shall argue in the coming chapters, *all of these characteristics,* at least in embryo form, had already made their appearance in New York City before the last quarter of the nineteenth century, when that city was clearly recognizable as a "modern" global city. And even though the pace and scale of today's globalized economy—and thus of the global cities that serve as its "command posts"—are faster and vaster, and the mechanisms of integration more thoroughgoing and quickly executed, I contend that the seeds from which the present "global city" grew were firmly planted in Manhattan during the middle decades of the nineteenth century. Chicago and Los Angeles would eventually (and sequentially) follow that model with time lags of thirty and sixty years, respectively, although they would naturally do so in a changed world context and under revised regimes of production, circulation, and consumption, as well as politics.

Examining the earlier histories of these three cities, then, should help to identify in each the origins of its global functions and embeddedness, albeit acknowledging that these have become more pronounced and widespread in our day. But this book is not merely a comparative urban history that singles out economic and institutional variables solely for the purpose of predicting global functions. Although it treats economic and political structures, it also takes space seriously, in the manner that urban geographers do, and for very sociological reasons. In the current literature on global cities, space has almost disappeared as a focus. And yet one of the major differences obvious to anyone who has ever visited the three cities is their unique spatial arrangements and, related to those characteristics, the ways of life and social relations within them. Spatial patterns are deeply associated with variations in social life and the relationships among residents, and it is these social relations that yield differences in the patterns of urban living that give to each city its quintessential character.

THE LOGIC OF GLOBAL CITY COMPARISONS

Generalizations about the nature and functions of global cities in the contemporary era tend to underplay variations that arise from the unique national institutions that serve as the context for their development. Because so many disparate cases are included in the comparative study of global cities, it is difficult to untangle the mechanisms that operate within them and to trace how these mechanisms yield quite different spatial configurations on the ground. Because the built environment is itself the accumulated product of past forces, it is impossible to differentiate present effects from past residual influences, much less to distinguish between those that have been shaped by local social and physical conditions and those generated at the international level.

The challenge of comparing global cities has furthermore been compounded by the varying depths of their historical heritages. Most megalopolitan agglomerations that today serve as "world" or "global" cities—for example, London, Paris, Amsterdam, Tokyo—have developed over many centuries. They thus contain accretions of successive types of settlements that have layered, one upon the other, vastly different patterns of development and reconstruction, until the composite whole becomes difficult to grasp. Not only are their landscapes difficult to "read," but they are not easily compared with one another, because the national and cultural contexts in which they developed are so different.

These difficulties are somewhat eased in a more controlled comparison of the three largest global cities of the United States, each of which was essentially built on a tabula rasa of terrain and imposed upon a preurban tradition that was for all practical purposes irrelevant to the uses to which European newcomers would put their sites. Furthermore, the physical development of each is only a century or two old, having been formed almost exclusively within the so-called modern period of mercantile/industrial capitalism and within a world system that for some five centuries was dominated by the hegemonic powers of western Europe and then their Atlantic offspring. Although there were dramatic changes over time in both the systems of economic production and the levels of technology, the sources of these transformations came essentially from within the same general framework of cultural and economic evolution. And although the political context shifted, as the United States changed from a primarily rural/agrarian society to an urban/industrial one, all three cities developed within that common, albeit changing, legal framework.

Nevertheless, the three urbanized regions, although similar in their overarching economic, technological, social, and political contexts, offer enough significant variations to make comparisons among them a fertile source for new insights into the processes of urban change in the contemporary era. If all are, in one way or another, to be placed in the category of global cities, the variations among them should offer a better chance to differentiate between global and local causes.

The three differ in fundamental ways with respect to, inter alia,

1. their natural geographic settings, as defined by climate, resources, and terrain, which set significantly different parameters for their growth and functions;
2. their spatially specific links to an external world whose contours have shifted dramatically over the more than two centuries of their existence;
3. their original economic functions, political sponsorships, and first settlers, which to some extent helped to define cultural patterns that left lasting marks;
4. the moments of their most dramatic physical expansion (what I shall call *cohort* or *generation*), during which the basic template for the future form of the particular city was established;
5. the timing of their growth spurts and the changing sources of their in-migrant populations, which framed their subsequent racial and ethnic compositions and their persisting political structures and practices;
6. the technologies of transport during initial phases that generated armatures of passage in the three urbanized regions in radically different ways;
7. the social and technological organization of production and communication over time that shaped the imperatives of land, location, and scale in unique ways; and
8. the interclass and political relations that gave to each region its own modus vivendi: characteristic patterns of power relations, conflict, and modes of conflict resolution—what I shall refer to as its distinctive *civic culture.*

By tracing *how* these differences have resulted in the unique variations on the "global city" phenomenon that we find today in the metropolitan regions of New York, Chicago, and Los Angeles, I intend to shed light on the mechanisms that yield both the common and special qualities of global cities.

CONCEPTUAL FRAME

Before looking more closely at the three cities, however, we need to step back from the purely urban, because cities, interesting as they may be in their own right, are not independent forces so much as they are physical manifestations of larger economic and political space. No statement could be less accurate than the oldest cliché in city planning—the one that compares American cities to Topsy (who "just grow'd"). The built environment is *not* organic, although it may often appear chaotically unplanned. It has been created and is continually being re-created, albeit by collectivities of social actors engaged in complex dances of successive and symbiotic interactions. These interactions continually weave together nature, materials, techniques, socioeconomic processes, and cultural forms to generate the urban fabric—a transitory expression in space that, like any work of art, derives its meanings more from observers' responses than from creators' intentions.

To admit that outcomes in the built environment are often not exactly what individual contributors intend is not to deny the city its status as a "work" (oeuvre) of "art" (skilled creation). But unlike the often ephemeral matter of more transient art forms, the built environment persists, the *armature* of its *passages* often outlasting even the enduring stones out of which individual structures may be built.[3] In addition, natural albeit potentially shiftable *borders* (edges between plains and highlands, between waters and coastal littorals) and, even more important, proprietary *boundaries* (walls, property lines, easements, ethnic turf, distinctive land uses) delineate spaces in the city, creating persistent units or *templates* that not only sketch the outlines of present forms but shape future uses.[4]

Built environments are more than brute matter, however. Their human occupants endow environments with symbolic significance, with meanings. Places, and the concrete constructions that are implanted on them, are envalued by their inhabitants through associations and emotions of awe, love, attraction, fear, hate, revulsion, and even banal indifference.[5] They are frequently sites of competition and contest, but not only over material interests. Because places stand for ideas and ideologies as well as serve more practical ends and uses, places constitute a system of semiotics, a text that encodes messages potential users must "read" and interpret. But the invitations and exclusions so signified need not be heeded; users may acquiesce to the restrictions or they may choose to risk sanctions by violating them.[6]

THE ORGANIZATION OF THIS BOOK

This introductory chapter surveys the broad physical and social conditions of the United States over the past few hundred years to generate a schematic chronology of long economic cycles that have influenced patterns of American urbanization. The development of each of the cities is located within that framework. Later chapters examine these temporal phases in greater detail, to show how city building in all of the regions was not only affected by these common causes but given unique forms through their differentiated responses to them. The degrees of freedom the cities enjoyed for response were, of course, partially determined by the condition each had reached at the moments of impact. This approach will allow us to explore the continuing dialectic between past and future urban forms—as mediated by the preexisting built environment and the social environment formed by culture, social organization, and political precedents.

The Temporal Frame

Historians of American urbanization have divided the close to four hundred years of "New World" settlement into four major periods, beginning with the first colony established at Jamestown in 1607 and ending somewhere near our present era, perhaps in the late 1960s or early 1970s.[7] More recently, some scholars have suggested that a dramatically new fifth cycle has begun, the major outlines of which are still being explored and debated.

Naturally, any temporal division into cycles is somewhat arbitrary. Does one measure from low point to low point or from high point to high point, or does one try to identify a few critical "turning points" that have theoretical significance? Whichever strategy one adopts (and I favor the last), dates will be only approximate. Historical "breaking points" between eras can seldom be located with precision, because transformative moments are usually spread out over a decade or more, although dramatic economic crashes pinpoint more precise dates. In addition, long after crucial turning points occur, elements from older social formations live on within the new. The coexistence of lead and lag elements blurs any neat divisions that may be adopted for the sake of narrative coherence. And this is particularly true with respect to the built environment, which acts as a significant drag on immediate adaptation to changing conditions.

It is helpful to think of New York, Chicago, and Los Angeles as about a generation apart in their developmental trajectories, but what a difference these short gaps make. To place the three in comparative perspective, one need only consider *when* each city reached the one hundred thousand mark in population, because it was during the four or five decades *after* each city reached this benchmark that it experienced its most significant era of change, establishing the basic characteristics that even today continue to define its special spatial and economic nature.

As we shall see in Chapter 2, New York (then really only Manhattan) had achieved that total by 1820. During the subsequent half century, as recounted in Chapter 3, New York underwent its most dramatic change in functions and proportional increase in size (especially if one ignores, as one must for the moment, the effects of boundary expansions).[8] In the subsequent period, covered in Chapter 4, it established its dominance over not only its hinterlands but indeed the nation. It has retained that position of dominance, despite images of decline.

By 1860, Chicago's population had reached this benchmark, and in the ensuing half century Chicago would grow faster than any city had ever done before, laying down its economic base in heavy industry and fracturing its social life and spatial pattern along sharp cleavages based on class, ethnicity, and race. These cleavages continue to haunt the city to this day. This story is recounted in Chapter 5.

History would repeat itself in Los Angeles some scant forty years later, when, by 1900, its population approached one hundred thousand. After that, it not only took over from Chicago the position of America's fastest-growing major city, but it established the hegemonic position of white native-born elites within a sprawling region. These two characteristics, the evolution of which is the subject of Chapter 6, created L.A.'s greatest promise and shaped its problems for many years to come.[9]

Although differing by generations, during the final decades of the nineteenth century and the earliest decades of the twentieth, all three cities would develop *within* a common context of American trends, although these trends affected each of them somewhat differently.

The National Context

One of the most important of these national trends was a marked decline in the proportion of the labor force needed to work in agriculture—down from about half in 1870 and 1880 to 36 percent by 1890 and 1900, and then to only a quarter by 1920.[10] Second, there was a commensurate growth of employment in manufacturing, which, whereas it had accounted for only 17 percent of the labor force in 1870, had risen to 20 percent by 1890 and even higher by 1900.[11] Far more significant than the actual proportion of workers engaged in manufacture, however, were the fundamental changes in the nature of that sector, which was increasingly characterized by large, capital-intensive "heavy" enterprises, dependent upon steam power and mobilizing workers of lower skill on assembly lines.[12]

The third contextual trend was demographic: at first, the flood of new foreign immigrants from the 1880s on—which, as we shall see, coincided exactly with the rising demand for unskilled labor in Chicago's heavy industry—and later, toward the end of the period, the opening phase of the massive movement that would eventually relocate most African Americans from farms in the South to major urban centers in the North.

However, the specific ways these forces affected each of the cities depended in part on the preexisting legacies of the built environment and the traditions of governance as these had evolved to that date. It is this that makes "generation" a crucial variable.[13] But the effects also depended in part upon the specific political responses the cities made to these new challenges, which makes an analysis of local power structures and civic culture so central to this discussion. A constructed historical narrative useful for our purposes is as follows.

Cycle 1: The Founding of the Colonies to about 1820

The first cycle may be thought of as encompassing a mercantile period of "preindustrial" colonialism/decolonization, consisting of two successive phases: a long colonizing period that stretched between 1607 and 1776, and a briefer decolonizing period of reorganization between 1776 and (roughly) the early 1820s. Of the three contemporary American world cities, only New York figured in this earliest historic cycle, which was so critical in establishing that city's dominance on the eastern seaboard.

Chicago did not begin until the second phase. It was not until 1779 that Jean Point du Sable, mulatto son of a French frontiersman and a former slave, built his fur-trader's cabin near a site that would later house the American-built frontier post of Fort Dearborn (1803) and, eventually, the city of Chicago. (Illinois was not even admitted to the Union until 1817.) And the nucleus that was to become Los Angeles was even later in its origins and incorporation. It was not "founded" until 1781 and then only as an anachronistic colonizing effort sponsored by the Spanish governor of what later became independent Mexico. For our purposes, then, we need not address these two cities until the next cycle of development.

Cycle 2: The 1820s to the Depressed Decade of the 1870s

The second cycle is conventionally thought to have begun with the opening of the Erie Canal in the mid-1820s and the first inchoate impulses toward mechanization and primitive industrialization, although as we shall see in Chapter 2, this was only one manifestation of the increasing centrality of New York in the development of the American urban system after the War of 1812. The construction of a canal between Albany (on the Hudson River) and Buffalo (on the shores of Lake Erie) anchored an expanding agricultural interior more firmly to the mouth of the Hudson River near the port of New York. A further series of reticulations and connections among the lakes and rivers that laced the intervening regions led to a dramatic expansion of the continental system to encompass most parts of what was then referred to as "the American West" (i.e., the Midwest).

This era of canal building—strengthened and, to some extent, soon superseded by an even more ambitious period of railway construction—dramatically transformed the spatial system of urbanization in the eastern third of the nation. Thanks to canals and railroads, Chicago was becoming firmly established as the critical hub of a developing continental system by the middle decades of the nineteenth century. This was also the era when faster sailing vessels began to make scheduled voyages between England and the United States; these would later be replaced by steamships. Both innovations revolutionized international travel, trade, and integration by drastically compressing the "space-time" between places.

However, growth during this second period of global restructuring was spasmodic.[14] It was punctuated by "international" economic contractions and attendant political unrest on the European continent. The Western world, including the nonsubsistence sectors of the American economy, experienced economic crises at midcentury, when Europe's highly unstable conditions spilled over to the New World. While giving evidence that their economies were thus linked, European crises then were often experienced in the United States as "mirror images," because the New World served as a sponge to absorb both the overaccumulated venture capital and the excess populations of the Old.[15] Waves of Irish peasants expelled by famine infused the eastern seaboard's urban labor force with brute strength, and waves of politically dissident German immigrants driven out by political oppression at home nurtured a nascent labor movement in their new country.[16]

By the middle of the nineteenth century, New York had consolidated its dominant position within the American system and held a virtual monopoly over the nation's relation to the world. Manhattan already had a population of more than half a million, and had taken on the classic form of metropolitanization: a densification in the core, the beginnings in that core of multifamily residential construction, increased segregation of the poor in industrial zones that were still concentrated near the center, and the development of a few upper-class suburbs that stretched along the "mass-transit" lines, established first by horse cars and then street railroads, which the elite rode to commute to their offices and stores, still concentrated in the central business district.[17]

Chicago and other midwestern towns lagged considerably behind the cities of the eastern seaboard in these changes, because they were neither as populous as New York, Philadelphia, or Boston nor as deficient, yet, in accessible space. The overbounding of midwestern cities and counties also helped avert, at least for a time, the political bifurcation between city and suburb that was already appearing in the cities of the Northeast. In addition, the weight of past construction only lightly constrained their futures. In Chicago, in particular, the weight of the past, light as it was, went up in the smoke of the Great Fire of 1871, when its mostly wooden structures burned down. The central business district was ready to be rebuilt in brick and stone.

Cycle 3: From the 1870s through the 1920s

From the 1870s on, the world system was again restructured. European imperialism shifted from competition among "private" investment firms, seeking to gain control over and ensure their supplies of raw materials from "underdeveloped" regions (admittedly with military backing from their own national governments), to the more direct occupation of vast peripheral regions and their rule by imperial powers.[18] Under these new circumstances of imperial reach, techniques of banking and finance began to be more officially controlled, more complex, and increasingly transnational in scale. Investment itself became a more abstract commodity. Large-scale monopolies proliferated and joint stock companies began to supplement the family partnerships that had previously been the most common form of ownership. Company shares, traded in stock markets in major western cities, became increasingly "international," as did the flow of loans for development. As a result, crises experienced in one part of the system inevitably reverberated in others.[19]

Ownership was also becoming separated from management in the largest enterprises, even though partnerships and family firms continued to predominate at lower levels of scale.[20] At the same time, the application of steam power to factory production concentrated capital and labor in ever larger enterprises of true and heavy industrialization,[21] whereas innovations in communications were also making possible the physical detachment of managerial offices from places of production and the separation of "headquarters" from multiple production centers.

This third cycle encompassed the period from the late 1870s through the 1920s (albeit with a critical break associated with World War I), during which the American urban system expanded all the way to the West Coast and mass production began to prepare the ground for an early "Fordist" cycle that was to follow.[22] Steam and then electric power in production, the telegraph, cable, and then the telephone in communications (the telegraph and telephone networks stretched from coast to coast by the turn of the century), and eventually cars and trucks (and the roads on which to drive them) in transportation were the three most significant technological innovations of this period.

This period also experienced the second great wave of migrations—this time from the semiperipheries of eastern and southern Europe—which provided most of the labor power for the factories and sweatshops that spread across the thriving cities of the Northeast and North Central regions (now referred to so disparagingly as the "rust belt"). As Sam Bass Warner Jr. summarizes this period, it was a time when in-line mechanized and heavily capitalized factory production came into its own, when electricity "replaced water power and surpassed steam," and when national transportation systems of railways were "supplemented locally by the electric street railway, the motor truck, and the automobile. *These were the modes of production and transportation that created the giant industrial metropolis and the related multicity manufacturing belts of the Northeast and Midwest.*" Great regions, "organized about New York and Chicago, both produced for and marketed for the nation. . . . everything tended toward giantism." The corporation became the dominant form of organization, as workers attempted to unionize. "Urban land . . . became highly specialized [and] . . . commuters clustered by class, ethnicity, and race. Colossal scale, centralization, and segregation were the telling signs of the industrial metropolis."[23] The period was crucial for all three cities, but in somewhat different ways, because of preexistent conditions.

New York consolidated its lead, but no longer so exclusively nor independently from its interior hinterland.[24] In the final years of the century, the present five-borough system of governance was established, vastly expanding the city's area. Along with this political consolidation went the construction of bridges and, in the opening decade of the twentieth century, an enlarged underground mass-transit system that began to tie the separate boroughs together. By then, the larger ocean liners, which required deeper waters, were docking (and braving the more formidable winter storms) on the Hudson shore, and additional dock facilities were proliferating on the New Jersey and Brooklyn shores as well. Although a single rail line from the mainland in New Jersey to the West Side docks at Manhattan had been constructed as early as 1840, by 1920 multiple railway bridges linked the four boroughs with Manhattan and the city into the larger regional and national system.

During the fifty years between 1870 and 1920, New York monopolized the financial institutions of the country and served as the almost exclusive "port of entry" for new immigrants, although by then many newcomers passed through the port only on their way to other settlements. During that same period the governing structure of the city was revolutionized, the functions associated with city government were expanded significantly, and a civic culture was honed in which the extant commercial patriciate, the newer ethnically based system of "rings" and "bosses," labor organizations, and a potentially volatile but highly diverse and thus divisible populace learned to negotiate deals.

Between them, Chicago and New York dominated the U.S. urban hierarchy during this period, in a synergistic relationship in which capital moved back and forth, as did capitalists and city builders. Most of the capital that was invested to construct Chicago's early infrastructure had been attracted from New York and its vicinity, and this early pattern continued on into the later period. The two giant cities were also demographically linked, with most settlers and, certainly, members of the new American-born self-made "elites" of Chicago having been drawn from the New York region or New England.[25]

In the arts of city building the two were even more closely connected. Landscape architects such as Frederick Law Olmsted, urban planners such as Daniel Burnham, and architectural firms such as McKim, Mead & White moved back and forth to execute commissions in both cities. All were heavily influenced by the beaux arts ideas of Europe, where most had been trained. The Chicago World's Fair of 1893, which represented an apex of sorts for this type of planning, was both infused with New York architects and fed back to their city in the form of ideas and personnel.[26]

During this period, Los Angeles lagged significantly behind, even within California, where San Francisco remained the only really important city. However, once the rail connections from San Francisco to Los Angeles were in place by 1875 and the city had also become the terminus of two cross-continental lines in the 1880s, all prerequisites were in place for its economic incorporation into the national system. If Chicago came into being because of infusions from the East Coast, one could say that in this post-Hispanic phase of its history (which has proven brief indeed!), Los Angeles was transformed through migrations from the Midwest.

However, the city was not yet industrial. The chief economic base remained agriculture and, above all, ranching, although the large landholdings of the former Mexican elite had been confiscated or bought for a pittance, thus laying the foundations for a newer form of mass city building—whole towns and subdivisions designed on land in single or corporate ownership. At first, the major attraction, especially for the midwestern retirees who were drawn to the city in the late nineteenth century, was the salubrious climate, a vast improvement over the harsh winters from which they escaped. The rapid influx of population had its usual effect—fueling, toward the end of the century, the same type of unfettered speculation in urban land that had characterized Manhattan in the early nineteenth century and Chicago after midcentury.

For Los Angeles, the key transformative moment came in the first two decades of the twentieth century, a period as important to Los Angeles's future as the early 1800s had been for New York and the mid-nineteenth century had been for Chicago. Although the influx of midwesterners at the end of the century, stimulated by booster propaganda displays and loss-leader subsidized rail tickets, had pushed the city's population to some one hundred thousand by 1900 (with an additional seventy thousand outside the city limits), in the first ten years of the new century the city's population increased by 211 percent, a rate higher than it would ever subsequently experience.

But an inadequate water supply, the lack of a natural deepwater port (and sheer distance from the Atlantic trade), and the absence of sources of cheap power handicapped development. These impediments were successively removed, at least for the short run, by the construction of an aqueduct to bring Owens Valley water into the metropolis (planned in 1905 but not opened until 1913); the annexation of the port of San Pedro, improved during World War I by massive infusions of federal funds;[27] the opening of the Panama Canal in 1914, which placed southern California within shorter reach of the southern and eastern coasts;[28] and, by 1917, the availability of cheap hydroelectric power from the aqueduct, which made possible a manufacturing boom.

By the 1920s, Los Angeles was poised for transformation into a world city. This touched off a second wave of speculation in land, during which many of the extant ranchos were subdivided on a massive scale to create whole "new towns," some of which felt pressured to annex themselves to the city in order to assure their water supplies but many of which resisted such pressures, thus beginning the typical Los Angeles pattern of the "fractured" metropolis of multiple home rule.[29] By 1924, Los Angeles County had become an urbanized place of one million residents, of whom less than 60 percent lived in the *city* of Los Angeles.

The economic boom had been partially fueled by oil production. Although oil strikes were first made in the 1880s and a miniboom began in 1892, it was not until 1897 that oil was being commercially extracted, processed, and marketed on any significant scale. By the early 1920s the wells of Signal Hill, Huntington Beach, and Santa Fe Springs were producing one-fifth of the world's oil supply! The chief export of the port of Los Angeles, by then its largest American terminus, was "black gold," whose effects were to prove more lasting than the yellow gold of the 1849 gold rush.

The growth of Los Angeles mirrored in extreme fashion the trends that were taking place nationwide. In the post–World War I period, the United States entered a transformative phase of enormous consequence. Cars and highways fueled suburbanization on a new and grander scale, as earlier settlements strung along rail lines to the periphery were literally surrounded and infilled by massive zones of prematurely subdivided suburbs. By the early years of the century, the nation's telephone network had reached the farthest points of the West and Southwest. The integration of a continental economy, initially formed by rail lines and telephones, had now begun to be supplemented by cars and truck transport on a reticulating road system.

The First World War had also intensified efforts at national integration by sea, which had revolutionary effects on the West Coast. Although plans long predated actual execution, the opening of the Panama Canal in 1914 and the deepening of the federally subsidized port at San Pedro, tied to oil exports, stimulated the growth of Los Angeles at the same time that the diversion of water from the Owens Valley not only secured the city's water supply but opened the enormous zone of the San Fernando Valley for more intensive agricultural and then residential developments. Air connections would soon follow. Although the first plane service between Los Angeles and New York was not initiated until 1929, the location of the nascent aircraft industry in New York and Los Angeles helped to connect the economies of both cities.[30]

Basic changes were also under way in the organization of production and in the relations between labor and capital. During World War I, especially after the belated entry of the United States, significant labor shortages had developed in northern industrial centers, the result of heightened demand at the very time that immigrant streams were blocked by war and intensified by federal restrictions on immigration (imposed in 1917, after long debates and many studies, and tightened again in 1921 and 1924). The alternative, the systematic recruitment of "surplus" black labor from the cities and farms of the South, fueled the formation of larger and increasingly segregated black quarters in a number of northern industrial centers, especially New York and Chicago. In Los Angeles, labor shortages were met primarily by an increase in Mexican immigration, because the laws restricting immigration still exempted populations entering from countries in the New World. Only a small black population was added to Los Angeles during the World War I period and its aftermath.

At the same time, increases in the scale of production sites, the separation of management offices from their factories, and the separation of managerial personnel from ownership were proceeding apace, exacerbating capital and labor tensions. Unionization, labor mobilizations, and strikes punctuated the histories of New York and, even more, Chicago during this epoch. In all this, Los Angeles again lagged behind, not only because it had yet to establish a deep industrial base, but because its elites had forestalled unionization through ruthless enforcement of an open shop policy.

Cycle 4: Restructuring of the World Economy from the Crash of 1929 to the 1970s

All these developments were cut short by a worldwide depression—which is, unfortunately, the clearest demonstration of the country's full integration into the world system and the fact that its fate would henceforth be linked to forces far beyond its borders. The worldwide industrial crisis of the late 1920s (preceded in the early 1920s by a worldwide agricultural crisis) threw all previous modalities of existence into disarray. Factory installations closed down and lay idle. Early on, unemployment rates reached astronomical heights in New York and Chicago, as well as in other cities of the Northeast and North Central regions.

Although the West Coast was not spared, the effects of the national economic crisis were felt less severely and more briefly in California, perhaps testimony to that state's lower level of integration and greater dependence upon agriculture, and because that "frontier" region was still at an early stage of the urban product cycle.[31] In most other cities construction ceased absolutely, as did population growth, as many urbanites, especially those of rural origin, abandoned the hardships of urban life for a chance to grow subsistence crops in rural areas.

Nevertheless, by the end of the 1930s, stimulated by demands from the European war theater as well as internal policies of "reconstruction" initiated under the New Deal, the United States began to pull out of the slump. Whereas this fourth cycle had begun at the low point of the Great Depression, it peaked by the post–World War II era, when America's industrial might reached its apogee. From the late 1930s through the early 1960s, America was to consolidate its position as the dominant force within the world system.

The involvement of the United States in World War II had a very different geographic imperative than had the war that preceded it, one that would transform forever the regional balance in the country. It dictated a new emphasis on the West Coast to supplement the traditional dependence upon New York's port and the Midwest's industrial base. The bombing of Pearl Harbor in 1941 signaled that war efforts would henceforth be bicoastal, even though Chicago and the Midwest in general continued to produce the heavy machines of war. New York's role, which was restricted to shipbuilding, some aircraft construction, and a few defense industries, was modest in comparison to Chicago's, and both were dwarfed by Los Angeles's role. Los Angeles became home to the most lucrative war contracts, especially in the newer technologies associated with air power.[32]

During World War II, the massive migration of southern blacks to northern cities once again transformed the demographic composition of center cities, and this time the wave also hit the West Coast, which had hitherto used "foreign" people of color—in "controlled" fashion and chiefly in agriculture. The African American population recruited to Los Angeles for the war effort, however, enjoyed privileges not extended to the Mexican and Asian populations, at least during this early phase.[33]

New York, Chicago, and Los Angeles all boomed in the postwar period, as resources deflected to wartime were free to concentrate at home. Massive new construction—of residences, industrial plants, and consumer retailing establishments—fueled a process of explosive suburbanization, and federally subsidized highway construction vastly expanded the peripheral zones that could at great profit be converted from agricultural to urban uses. Second- and third-ring commuter zones were added beyond the inlying suburbs that had been well established before the war. This was the era of the "community builders," whose customers took advantage of the new low interest rates available through mortgages underwritten by the Veterans Administration and the Federal Housing Administration to purchase single-family houses in outlying and low-density zones formerly beyond reasonable commuting distance. And this was also the era during which downtown redevelopment and slum clearance/public housing competed for the public purse, with very different results in the three cities, as we shall see in Chapters 7 through 9. The trends set in motion in the aftermath of the war—of heightened demand for housing,[34] of massive decentralization, and a related increase in racial and economic separation between center cities and their peripheries—continued along fairly predictable lines, and planners blithely projected these into the future, essentially ignoring the social cleavages these trends exaggerated. Indeed, in the late 1950s the Regional Plan Association of New York commissioned an entire set of studies to update those done in the late 1920s, predicated on the fact that the trends would continue. New York City, Chicago, and Los Angeles built their new master plans on those same assumptions—namely, that expansion would continue at the periphery but that the centers would remain strong. These turned out to be unrealistic assumptions.

Toward the end of this cycle, and certainly by the early 1970s, major changes were under way—changes in the international economy that would greatly weaken the U.S. monopoly position in the world economy and changes in the spatial configurations of places of employment that would decentralize not only the employees, as had taken place in the prior period, but the jobs themselves (offices, shops, and factories) that had formerly concentrated toward the centers of the major cities. Not only were existing urbanized areas taking on the fragmented appearance of widely scattered confetti, but there was a reconfiguration of the entire U.S. system of cities, as federally subsidized highways and air travel "hubs" contracted time costs between certain centers and stretched distance between others.[35]

This reconfiguration had differential and somewhat paradoxical effects on the three cities, making them *more* central to the national and world economies of transactions while, at the same time, undermining their monopolies over centralized residence and production. By the mid-1960s many of these changes were altering the relative positions of the three major urbanized regions and were destabilizing the internal relations among their residents. Because the two major wars fought by the United States during the period (the Korean War of the 1950s and, even more dramatically, the fruitlessly destructive Vietnam War of the 1960s) were in the Pacific arena, military-related industry on the West Coast received massive infusions of Department of Defense dollars and virtually unlimited subsidies for aerospace research and development. In contrast, these government investments not only ignored the East Coast and Midwest but actually drained resources from them. Thus, when Los Angeles and its fringe areas (including the ports of San Pedro and Long Beach and the high-tech corridor in Orange County) experienced intense development and budgetary surpluses,[36] both Chicago and New York (as well as other industrial cities of the "rust belt") witnessed real, albeit modest, drops in their populations—declines in the rate of growth of the metropolitan regions and even, by 1970, absolute decreases within central cities.

But whether local economies were growing or stagnating by the mid-1960s seemed to have had little effect on urban "peace." Of the hundreds of cities in the country that exploded racially from 1964 onward, some had large minority populations, such as Chicago, some had moderate minority proportions, such as New York, and others, like Los Angeles, had low proportions of blacks. Some were experiencing declines in industrial employment, such as Chicago and New York, whereas others, such as Los Angeles, were still expanding. Nor did past policies to assist poor minorities ensure immunity to "disorders." New York, which had a liberal welfare system and had supported the continuous construction of massive amounts of subsidized housing, was the site of the first "riot" in the new series (Bedford-Stuyvesant in 1964), but this was soon followed in 1965 by the Watts "riot" in Los Angeles, a city that had essentially rejected public housing because of its association with "socialism" in the context of McCarthyism. Chicago, with its very large and growing black population, had experienced a continuous series of racially triggered "border wars" as the extreme segregation patterns of that city led to incremental expansions of its "Black Belt," but large-scale insurgency did not surface until the city's West Side exploded in the context of nationwide uprisings after the assassination of Martin Luther King Jr. in 1968. Chicago's active program of public housing had virtually ceased when it was required to desegregate.

The instabilities that manifested themselves throughout the nation in the 1960s, albeit in slightly different form in New York, Chicago, and Los Angeles, had their deep roots in three *general* and interrelated conditions not often linked in conventional analyses: the civil rights movement, opposition to the Vietnam War, and an end to American economic hegemony in the world. The connections among these three (and their relations to a fourth development seldom discussed in this context, namely, a reversal in 1965 of the restrictive immigration laws that had been in force in the United States since the 1920s) are discussed in greater detail in Part IV of this book.

Cycle 5: Global Restructuring/Spatial Reorganization

The past few decades appear to mark a significant transitional moment of restructuring, both in the world and in America's role in it. Certainly, much has changed: the official "decolonization" of the Third World, the globalization of production, the renewed mobility of labor, and the recomposition of immigrant and "guest worker" waves. With this came the relative decline of the monopoly the United States had held over capital, the rise of Pacific Rim states, and now the awakening of the sleeping giant of China. The unification of Europe and then the end of the Cold War, which for so long had stimulated the American economy while wasting its wealth, further reordered the still inchoate design of what has been termed, inaccurately, the post-industrial society. (Most recently, events in Central and Eastern Europe have added more unknowns.)

In the process, finance and producer services became the fastest-growing segments of the economy, but the jobs so created were more than matched by the expansion of low-paid service jobs at the lower end and by the shift to "flexible" production. The latter trend has brought with it the precipitous decline of good unionized jobs, as the brief postwar Fordist pact between capital and labor has been overturned. Deindustrialization, or rather a restructuring of industrialization, has initiated a new cycle of economic transformation, the essence of which I try to capture in the last part of this book.

All of these forces are having impacts on the three urbanized regions—but not in uniform ways, and they are not met with uniform responses. Just as the earlier cycles were played out differently in the three cities, so the "post-Fordist" globalized economy of today is having very different consequences in the three regions that constitute the objects of our study. Given that explaining the developments during this most recent cycle constitutes the ultimate goal of this book and will be addressed in much greater detail in Chapters 10, 11, and 12, there is no need to reprise them here. Rather, we need to turn back to developments during the four preceding periods to establish the historic ground on which they would be played out.

PART I

First Beginnings

CHAPTER 2

The First Growth Cycle to 1820

ONLY IN NEW YORK

Any account of American urbanization must begin with the founding of New York. As Kenneth Jackson has pointed out, "Because the earlier settlements at St. Augustine (1565), Jamestown (1607), and Plymouth (1620) either disappeared altogether . . . or declined into insignificance, *New York stands as the oldest major city in what is now the United States.*"[1] And during the period covered in this chapter, New York was the *only city* of the three already in existence.

The images of New York are as old and diverse as its origins. Americans have always felt a certain ambivalence toward the city, as reflected in the figurative names they have used to refer to it; New York has been variously called "Gotham," "Baghdad-on-the-Subway," "Our Babylon," and, most recently, the "Big Apple."[2] Less laudatory images have always paralleled these affectionate terms, from the frenetic and menacing dystopia portrayed in Fritz Lang's early classic film *Metropolis*[3] to, worse yet, Manhattan as the Hobbesian penal colony, sealed off and abandoned to criminals, as portrayed in John Carpenter's *Escape from New York.*

Most, however, have tried to capture the paradoxical nature of the city, often portraying it as the clichéd prostitute with a heart of gold; wiseacre city; the city of the almighty buck; a lonely, private, and yet exciting place.[4] The two icons of the city, engraved on its most popular postcards, are the Empire State Building, symbolizing Manhattan's verticality, and the Statue of Liberty, whose horizontal beacon welcomes newcomers, promising them hope—while often exploiting them to her advantage. Although the proportions are down from the beginning of the century and most immigrants arrive by air rather than by sea, even today almost half of all immigrants to the United States pass through New York's portals.

Almost from the start, New York demonstrated certain distinctive qualities: a relative disengagement from the battles of the nation, or at least a readiness to profit from them;[5] location at a strategic harbor site, oriented more toward Europe than toward the American hinterlands and designed to connect the "New World" to a world system in which it was to become increasingly central; a magnet for a polyglot population devoted to (some say obsessed by) commerce and trade, ever ready to make deals, prepared to absorb newcomers and tolerate diversity, but almost always on its own gruff and condescending terms; and endowed with a fluid spirit of entrepreneurial adventurism and mobility, not only in goods but in politics, ideas, and culture.

WATER: THE DEFINING ELEMENT OF NEW YORK

The key to many of these characteristics lies with New York's original function as a world port. I think Jan Morris, in her poetic paean to the New York harbor, has caught something when she calls the city "a landing-stage, a conduit, a place of movement . . . [whose] character is governed always by the successive tides of energy that flood perpetually through it. Not just fissile things, but peoples, ideas, philosophies—these are and always have been the prime commodities of the port of New York, and the city's *raisons d'êtres.*"[6]

Certainly, others have long stressed the same fluidity. Walt Whitman, the quintessential bard of New York every bit as much as Carl Sandburg was Chicago's, ends his 1860 tribute "Mannahatta" with the lines, "City of hurried and sparkling waters! city of spires and masts! \ City nested in bays! my city!"[7] Later writers as well have evoked images and metaphors of water: the flow of people moving swiftly through the streets like a great river. If ever there were a consummate early example of the city as a "space of flows," which Manuel Castells seems to suggest is a *postmodern* consequence of the "new [*sic*] informational age," it has been New York.[8]

Such metaphors are telling. They hint at essence in ways that more prosaic accounts may miss, for water *is* both the matter and the semiotic of New York. Instead, then, of thinking about New York as a vast albeit fractured agglomeration of urbanized places, turn that image inside out, like reversing black-and-white responses in a Rorschach inkblot test. Consider, instead, that New York consists of a large, complexly shaped body of water, fringed with urban settlements that were once inaccessible to one another except by water.[9] No one who has approached New York by air can doubt this.

Three states fringe this watery "core," leading to the anomaly of an urbanized region that has *no overarching political system*—nor can it ever have. Indeed, the history of New York is replete with the invention of one after another political and/or economic expedient designed to overcome that fundamental fragmentation. George Carey's description captures the essence of the site:

> The area known as the New York Metropolitan Region . . . extends over those portions of the three states which adjoin where the waters of the Hudson and the Raritan Rivers mingle with those of the Atlantic Ocean, Long Island Sound, and the numerous bays, channels and kills of the port of New York and New

Figure 2.1. John Bachman(n), *New York Environs* (colored lithograph, 1859). Source: Special Collections of The New York Public Library, Eno Collection, Miriam and Ira D. Wallach Division of Art, Prints, and Photographs, The New York Public Library, Astor, Lenox, and Tilden Foundations; used by permission.

> Jersey. . . . Twenty-two counties are roughly included within this metropolitan giant—one in Connecticut, nine in New Jersey, twelve in New York. The focal point of the region is New York City, located upon a group of islands at the junction of the principal bodies of water. *Of the five counties in New York City only . . . the Bronx is principally on the mainland.*[10]

RELATIONS OF CHICAGO AND LOS ANGELES TO WATER

The contrast of New York's site with Chicago's could not be more extreme. Located on an essentially featureless plane (a true alluvial plain) at the shore of Lake Michigan, Chicago has a physical organization (and pattern of expansion, even to this day) that is stunningly simple. The symmetrical semicircular core expands almost monotonically into the featureless (plane) plain from along the lakeshore, a pattern distorted only modestly by the sectoral divisions formed by radial rivers and rail lines. The entire political entity of Chicago is contained within a single county (Cook) that also encompasses an inner ring of suburbs on the north and south. Beyond Cook County are its five "collar counties" (Lake, Will, Kane, McHenry, and DuPage), which contain the overflow in independent suburbs and satellite towns.[11] And despite the fact that parts of Chicago's extended conurbation cross state lines into Wisconsin on the north and Indiana to the southeast, the functional planning unit falls essentially within Illinois state lines.

Despite the apparently propitious site, Chicago's location had little of the obvious imperative that determined New York's. Not until about the mid-nineteenth century, when local boosters wooed and cajoled the multiple organizers of the American railroad system to concentrate their midwestern terminals in Chicago, did the city consolidate its edge over such rivals as Galena and St. Louis. And if New York's insertion in the world system was contemporaneous with its founding, the city serving from the start as the key link between the New World and the "Old" across the Atlantic, Chicago was from *its* beginning an outpost—one that connected to the world system through the intermediary *hinge* that was New York.

The contrast of New York with Los Angeles is even more striking. Despite its glorious coastline and the fact that it now boasts one of the largest and busiest international seaports in the United States, if not the world, initially Los Angeles's site was even less promising than Chicago's. Los Angeles was bred of desert and mountains, not cradled in the lapping of an ocean or even an inland lake. And it must be noted that despite its current role as the country's largest manufacturing center and a major collector of the country's agricultural wealth, Los Angeles began with none of these economic advantages. It did, however, gain an important political advantage by accident of conquest.

If New York had to leap across multiple geographic and juridical barriers to forge an essentially polynucleated, complex, and difficult-to-coordinate urbanized region with no particular boundaries (e.g., not even Boswash is completely demarcated), whereas Chicago's urbanized region flowed smoothly outward from a single center with remarkably few barriers to deflect the stream until, at its northern and southern extremities, it merged geographically but not juridically with industrial complexes in northern Indiana and southern Wisconsin,[12] the urbanized region of Los Angeles, no matter how large it grew, remained within a single state.

Nonetheless, the city's form is highly complex and *discontinuous,* because it grew by the accretion of fragments, wedged essentially into the lowlands between barren hills, wherever it was feasible to bring in water.[13] Unlike New York and Chicago, both well endowed with surface water and groundwater, that precious sine qua non of urbanism, Southern California is essentially semiarid.[14] If left in its own natural state, its land is most appropriate for cattle grazing, which is what it was used for until the terminal years of the nineteenth century. Water was the magic ingredient required to create both rural and urban life in Southern California.

Political fragmentation, however, was mostly man-made. Although the city of Los Angeles is completely contained within the larger bounds of the county of Los

Angeles, the city's actual shape is peculiar: pockmarked with holes—small local communities that either resisted annexation to the city altogether or later opted out—as well as elongated by a narrow linear tail (the so-called shoestring addition). As we shall see in Chapter 6, it was Los Angeles's municipal control and then its subsequent loss of monopoly over the water supply that determined the politics of annexation and thus the unusual shape of the city. And the strange elongation of the city's boundaries to the south serves as the umbilical cord to its originally distant and discrete port of San Pedro. Around Los Angeles are five other counties whose urbanized "spots" are equally discontinuous, interspersed by either barren hills or lush agricultural valleys.

As we shall see in later chapters, these different physical settings played significant roles in giving to each region its distinctive character.

NEW YORK'S EARLY HISTORY AS A MULTICULTURAL MERCANTILE CITY

Manhattan Island's strategic location, at the mouth of the Hudson River where it widens into the bay that joins the Atlantic, made its harbor a particularly apposite site for a maritime city. Although during the ice ages the site of Manhattan had been far inland, the melting glaciers "scoured out the great rift of the Hudson River Valley . . . [making a depression] almost as deep as the Grand Canyon." And then, as the ocean level rose, "Manhattan, once situated on a plateau at least thirty-five hundred feet above the old sea level, became a low-lying island with tidewater on every side."[15]

Demographic diversity (multiculturalism?) also characterized the city from its inception. Note, in just this brief account, the variety of nationalities involved. For hundreds of years before Giovanni da Verrazano (a *Florentine* navigator in the service of the king of *France*) entered New York's Lower Bay in 1524, the lower tip of the island had served as a neutral point where *different Indian tribes* met to trade.[16] In 1525 the mouth of the Hudson (then called Rio de San Antonio) was charted by a *Portuguese* sailor sailing under the auspices of the *Spanish* king. The next explorer to arrive, in 1609, was the *English* navigator Henry Hudson, whose ship, the *Half Moon,* sailed under sponsorship of a *Dutch* company (not until fifty years later would the river be renamed in his honor).

Despite these various claimants, it was the Dutch company that first established a fort on Manhattan in 1624, later calling it New Amsterdam. The settlement was from the start integrated into the expansive colonizing projects of the seventeenth-century world-system, whose leadership was the object of fierce contest between the English and the Dutch.[17] The first settlers were some thirty families, mostly Walloons (*French speakers* from what would later become *Belgium*), who in May 1624 were deposited at the colony—some on Manhattan Island, but most at Albany, upstream. Their ship carried a return cargo of seven hundred otter and four thousand beaver skins, indicating the early linkage between the international fur trade and the colony.[18]

Later ships carried more colonists, and in 1626 Peter Minuit, who had been dispatched by the Dutch West Indies Company as director general of the New Amsterdam colony, which was headquarters of that company's North American operation, "bought" the island of Manhattan for its legendary sixty guilders (then twenty-four dollars).[19] This was perhaps a fitting start for a place where, it is said, anything can be bought and most things are for sale, even those that have been stolen.[20] The direct commercial purpose of the Dutch West Indies Company settlements at New Amsterdam and Albany upriver was to monopolize the fur trade, but profits were initially disappointing; furs were soon supplemented by timber and farm crops.[21] By 1628 there were only about 270 settlers living around the Manhattan fort, and that number had risen only to some 1,500 by 1664, when the city was captured, without a shot, by the English.[22]

During their brief rule, however, the Dutch had made important contributions to the site. They applied their not inconsiderable skills to reclaiming land from the marshy shores around the lower end of the island, not only widening the island but improving the dock areas (all on the eastern shore at that time) for the increasing number of ships that continued to come.

> In the seventeenth century the shore line was naturally quite different from that of today. What are now Front, Water, and South streets were then covered with water at high tide. . . . What is now Broad Street in the early days was an inlet used as a canal. . . . It is not surprising that colonists from Holland, where land fill is almost a tradition, should have extended the shore line and widened the island, even at this early period.[23]

The Dutch had also begun the agricultural development of the rich lands of the Hudson Valley, which were later to produce grain and milled flour for the international market, a more successful export than furs. Their small agricultural settlements at Harlem and Brooklyn gave lasting names to nuclei that would eventually be merged into the American city.

The British may have displaced the Dutch as the titular "rulers" of the colony, but the population continued to be polyglot. A Jesuit missionary who visited New Amsterdam in 1643 had recorded that eighteen different languages were represented among the four to five hundred men in Manhattan, drawn from various sects and nations.[24] This diversity persisted.[25] The early social structure, however, evidenced a basic paradox. Although the urban population was drawn from a wide variety of nations and cultures, and social mobility was certainly greater than on the European continent, the original upper class was drawn from a more narrowly defined set. Indeed, during the pre-independence period, under both Dutch and British rule, New York was "one of the more aristocratic colonies in North America," with an elite made up of intimately connected "manorial grandees, overseas merchants, and leading lawyers."[26]

The Dutch West Indies Company had given huge land grants in the Hudson Valley to the original (and largely Dutch) patriciate, whose properties, because of primogeniture, remained largely intact over the generations, as contrasted with the partible inheritances more common in New England.[27] However, as Jaher stresses, for both nationalities rural-based fortunes and urban commercial prosperity were synergistically linked: "Agrarian aristocrats participated in commerce; conversely, leading urban businessmen frequently acquired vast up-country estates and speculated extensively in interior and city holdings, sometimes with manorial lords."[28] After the British conquest, the original Dutch aristocracy was joined by English merchants, and intermarriage between Dutch landowners and newer important merchant "families" further consolidated this class. Despite the fact that the Dutch and English predominated, the ethnic diversity of the city *"permeated the upper stratum"* in growing numbers.[29]

The intimate relationship between rural economic power and urban activities persisted after the ethnic diversification of the elite and, not surprisingly, was translated into political power at the city and state levels of government. "Virtually every great landed clan also ranked among the foremost mercantile families . . . [and their] [e]xtensive urban real estate holdings forged another tie between the landlords and the cities. Political power promoted the enterprises of the landed and mercantile magnates."[30] There was considerable nepotism as members of elite families occupied high public posts. Jaher notes that "Hudson Valley and Long Island merchant-barons and their relatives . . . also played important political roles in New York City and in Albany, thus serving their urban commercial interests."[31]

NEW YORK AND THE AMERICAN REVOLUTION

At the outbreak of the Revolutionary War, the city had fewer than twenty thousand inhabitants, concentrated at the southern tip of Manhattan. After Washington's army retreated to the mainland, the island served as the main headquarters for British forces for the next nine years. Only in the last months of 1783, when the Continental Army formally took possession of the city, was the Union Jack lowered and the British military forces withdrawn.

However, the well-entrenched and multiethnic character of New York's aristocracy guaranteed a certain stability in the class structure even in the aftermath of war. Those of Dutch descent remained, and although some upper-class New Yorkers were evacuated with the British troops, their relatives (who had chosen "the right side of the conflict") remained behind to claim their lands. According to Jaher, this "prevented a radical disruption of the upper order." And even though the Revolution did cause some limited turnover in the ruling class, such "changes in upper class composition failed to appreciably alter its habits. Overseas trade remained central to the city's commercial life."[32]

New York had been badly damaged during the war, losing "perhaps half its buildings through incendiarism, collapse, and pillage," but by 1787 it had already regained its prewar population.[33] Jackson notes: "Soon after the winning of national independence, New York began to surpass its rivals [Boston and Philadelphia]. By 1789, it was the leading city in the coasting trade. It exceeded Philadelphia in total tonnage in 1794, in the value of imports in 1796, and in exports in 1797. And early in the nineteenth century, the city on the Hudson emerged as the largest metropolis in the New World."[34] By 1800, Manhattan's population had risen to more than sixty thousand, pulling even with Philadelphia, previously the largest urban agglomeration in the United States. Ten years later, the population of Manhattan, together with its small neighbor, Brooklyn,[35] approached a remarkable one hundred thousand, for the first time surpassing Philadelphia.[36]

Such primacy did not come without a struggle, however. Independence had its costs. After the war, American ships were barred from participating in Britain's preferential trading relations with the West Indies and Europe, an exclusion that was challenged vigorously by American privateers. A British blockade coupled with the harassment of American vessels on the high seas culminated in the War of 1812, fought in part to secure an autonomous and safer role for American ships in international trade. But the wartime embargo the British imposed on American ports had one unintended consequence: it encouraged the development of import-substitute industries. "Behind the protective wall of commercial exclusion and then war, Americans began to manufacture things which they had been importing from Britain." Once the war was negotiated to an end, however,

> British manufacturers . . . [seeking] to regain their lucrative American market . . . resolved . . . to sell their products . . . at a [temporary] loss . . . , and as the hour for the peace treaty drew near they loaded ships with goods for the American market. When . . . the peace was ratified, [most of] these ships sailed . . . into New York's harbor where the goods were . . . "dumped" . . . at unusually low prices. This policy succeeded in bankrupting many American manufacturers. It also made New York particularly attractive to buyers from inland towns, who now went there in larger numbers, giving that port an obvious and fortuitous . . . advantage over the others.[37]

The selection of New York as the port in which British shippers auctioned off (dumped) their goods was an advantage that New York's astute businessmen turned to permanent advantage by innovating techniques of credit and transaction ease that facilitated a concentration there of the commercial functions for the entire northern seaboard.[38]

Jaher cites this as one of the three factors that consolidated New York's dominant position in the opening decades of the nineteenth century. The other two were the construction of the Erie Canal, which put the harbor of New York within water-transport reach of the Great Lakes (a development to be covered in more detail in Chapter 3), and the formation of the Black Ball Packet Line, which began frequent and speedy scheduled sailings between New York and Liverpool in 1817–18.[39] These sailings did more than transport goods and people. In an era when long-distance information was exceedingly sketchy, delayed, and irregular, the fact that New York's traders had even a brief "knowledge jump" on competitors in other ports meant that speculative fortunes could (and would) be made in the moments before news of international gluts and shortages diffused to other places. This too consolidated New York's advantage.[40]

But even before the War of 1812 and the expansive boom period of New York that began with the extension of its trading hinterland via the Erie Canal (see below), the basic template for the physical city, or at least the island of Manhattan, to which it was largely confined until the end of the nineteenth century, had been unequivocally established. As Edward Spann notes, the gridiron plan of Manhattan adopted in 1811, which constituted the culmination of municipal decisions initiated as early as 1804, may have represented a major break with European traditions of more elegant city planning, but certainly no break with the pattern of Manhattan that was already evident in the closing decades of the eighteenth century.[41] While the plan clearly served the commercial/real estate preoccupations that characterize the city to this day, it merely extended to much of the rest of the island the pattern that had already been established by "private" owners when they divided up their large landholdings, at first into farm plots they leased to tenants and eventually into smaller house plots for self-constructed dwellings, as wage laborer gradually displaced yeoman and slave.

Prior to the war for independence, land in Manhattan was not viewed as "scarce," and therefore had not yet become a speculative commodity. When the wealthy invested in land, it was largely to "bank" their savings and to display their respectability through country estates. Blackmar has rightly pointed out that given the volatility of long-distance trade, land was at least a relatively secure place to park one's idle capital.[42] But as population increased and the demand for building sites went up, some large landholders subdivided portions of their properties into small lots (often twenty-five by one hundred feet, which was to become the module size), which they leased to new settlers; the owners, however, were neither investors in housing nor builders. "Most leases provided that at the end of the term, tenants should remove within ten days any buildings they had added to the land. Well into the nineteenth century, aldermen complained of the nuisance caused by New Yorkers who moved houses to new locations at the expiration of their long-term ground leases."[43] As early maps of the island show, at least one large landholder, De Lancey, had subdivided his large estate just north of the shipyards in a gridiron pattern that would later become generalized. Successive maps show how this pattern was extended in a series of northward movements.

By 1811, at a time when Manhattan still had fewer than one hundred thousand inhabitants, the officially adopted subdivision of virtually the entire island as far north as Harlem provided for a future population many times that number.

> The New York Plan of 1811, the master plan of the first great American metropolis, was devised to meet the needs of a moderate-sized Atlantic port. . . . Among several influences on the Plan was the fact that New York was emphatically not a political center; in the 1790s, it had lost its earlier roles both as the nation's first capital . . . and as the capital of New York State. Henceforth, considerations of design were subordinated to the more practical concerns of a city plainly commercial in character.[44]

The design was scarcely imaginative and, indeed, was to prove remarkably ill adapted to later needs. It created, with few exceptions, an unvarying grid of narrow rectangular blocks via 155 uniformly narrow cross streets only two hundred feet apart (approximately twenty east-west streets to the mile).[45] On the other hand, the major and wider avenues traversing the north-south axis facilitated travel in those directions and were somewhat more practical, although the lack of any diagonals other than preexistent Broadway compounded the permanent difficulty of crossing between the East and West Sides.

Anticipating future traffic, however, was not the purpose of the plan. Rather, the grid was designed to facilitate the subdivision of the entire island into module lots

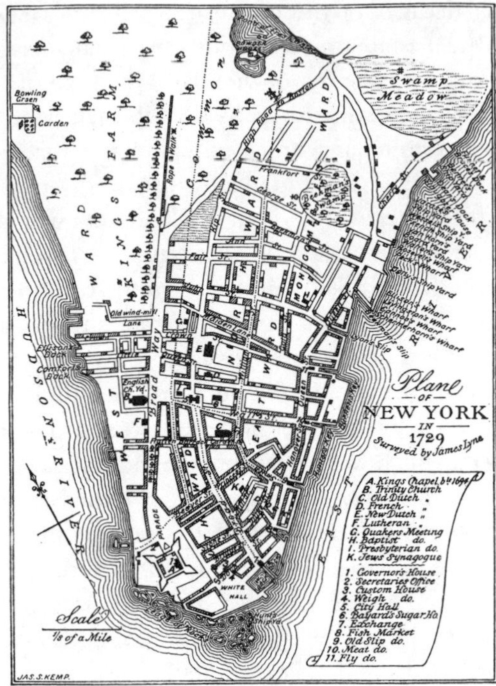

Map 2.1. Plan of New York in 1729, surveyed by James Lyne. Note the earliest organic character of the arrangement.

twenty-five feet wide and one hundred feet deep that, like coins of equal size, could be used as the currency of the realm—speculation. Imposed upon a topography far from level except at the lower parts of the island, provided with no diagonal avenue save the earlier Indian footpath of Broadway, with only a handful of public open spaces reserved (mostly in residual triangles formed by the intersection of Broadway with major avenues, in preexistent cemeteries, or on "useless" swampland), and with the streets running between the Hudson and East Rivers much too narrow to accommodate the cross-town traffic that would far exceed expectations, the plan proved shortsighted at best.

But the short-term gains were impressive. The plan facilitated a surge in urban land investments. The old alliance between the "rural" Dutch and English gentry of the Hudson Valley, the "robber barons" of the fur trade, and the merchants, shipping agents, and lawyers of Manhattan involved in international commerce was now consolidated and strengthened by urban land acquisitions.[46] German-born John Jacob Astor (who made his initial fortune in the fur trade) and his descendants would eventually become the largest landholders in Manhattan.[47]

Members of this elite alliance were simultaneously working on plans for the Erie Canal, an ambitious venture that would jump-start a boom in New York City's import and export functions, stimulate a rapid population increase, and, with it, an ex-

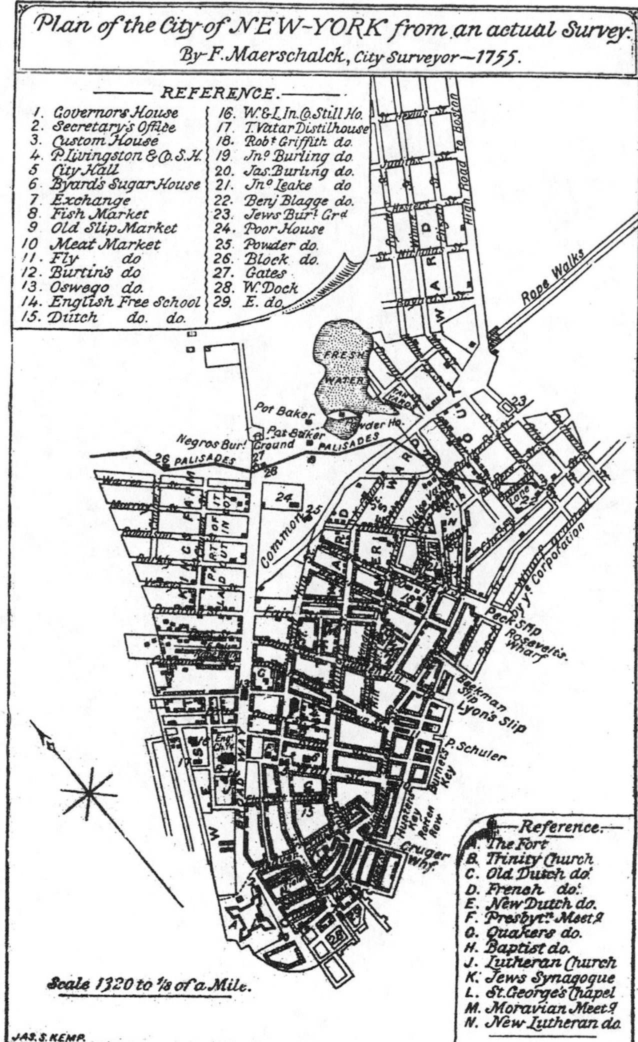

Map 2.2. Plan of New York City from an actual survey by F. Maerschalck, city surveyor, in 1755. Modest gridiron pattern develops at the edges.

plosive demand for urban lots. It would eventually lead to the founding of the city of Chicago, even though the canal's terminus at Buffalo initially fell short of drawing all the Great Lakes into New York City's trading hinterland. That would require even more investments in canals and, more important, in railroads that decisively displaced the attempts at waterborne transport.

But these developments had to await the next cycle of urbanization. Before turning to this next phase, I want to describe briefly conditions at the sites of what were to become the American world cities of the future: Los Angeles and Chicago.

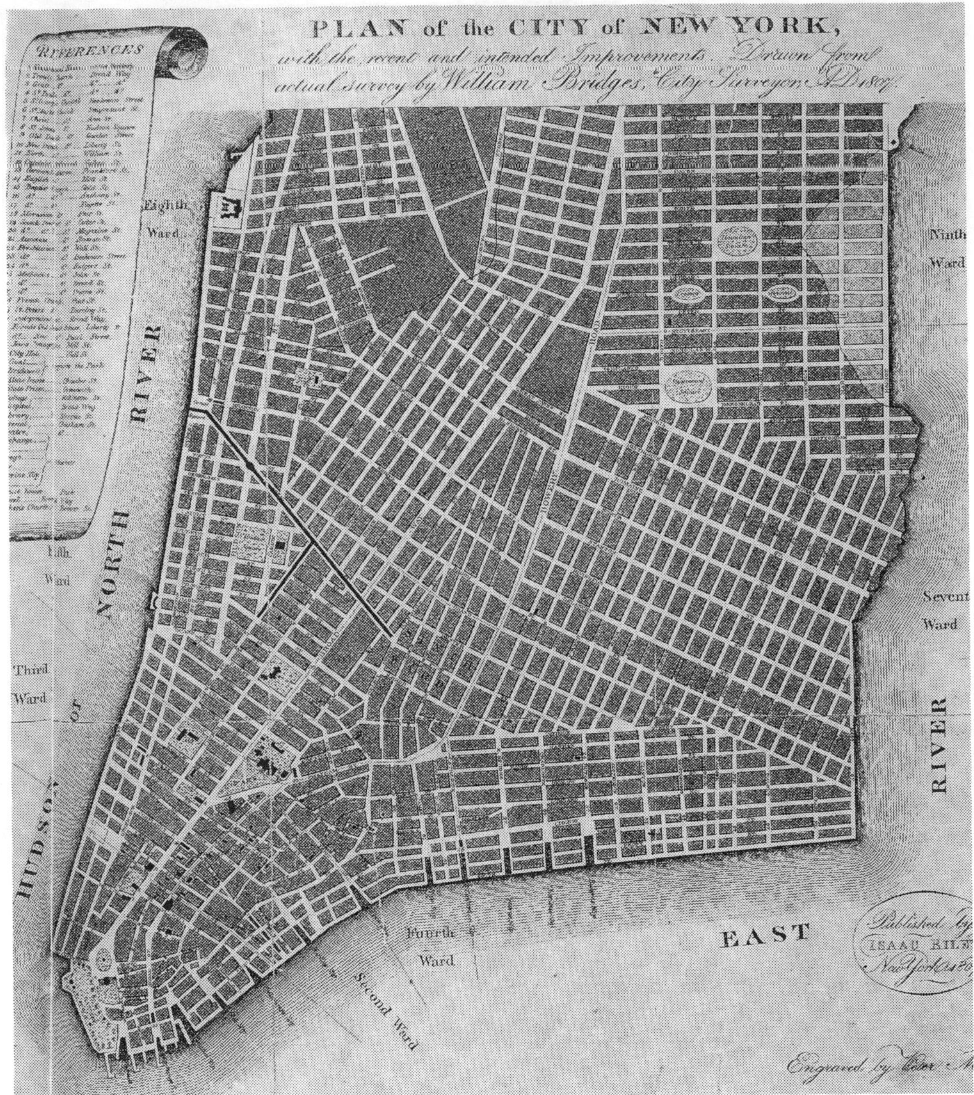

Map 2.3. Plan of New York City in 1807 with recent and intended improvements. Drawn from the actual survey by William Bridges, city surveyor, showing an intent to regularize the water edges and to unify existing grid patterns in the only portion of lower Manhattan subdivided before the 1811 plan.

LOS ANGELES UP TO THE 1820S

Few Americans would think to include Los Angeles as a "place" during this earliest phase of its history, even though the European "discovery" of the sites that were later to house New York and Los Angeles occurred almost simultaneously. Although New York was clearly *the* American city of this early period, only an Anglo East Coast-centric view of the United States can account for the fact that California is generally

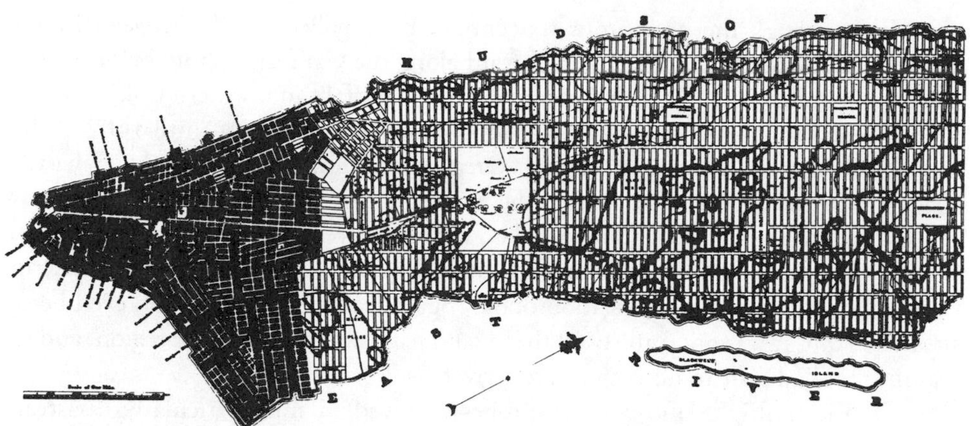

Map 2.4. The 1811 subdivision map that plots Manhattan into the greatest grid. Five years later, the scheme was extended to the unsettled upper reaches of Manhattan Island.

ignored in American history until it was acquired from Mexico by force and joined the union as a state in 1850.[48] I hope to correct this tunnel vision here.

Taking a wider worldview, we must recognize that the "great discoveries" of the sixteenth century on the Atlantic coast were paralleled by similar ones on the Pacific, and both were parts of the same European goals of that century: to gain access to the markets of India and China via routes other than the traditional and shorter ones through the Middle East, over which Europe had failed to gain control. If 1492 represents the date of Christopher Columbus's efforts to find such a route by traveling westward, and 1498 marks Vasco da Gama's circumnavigation of Africa to reach the Orient by a southern and eastern route, the date of 1520, when Magellan finally circled South America, marks Europe's efforts to continue the westward route into the Pacific.

A few years after Magellan's historic voyage and only some eighteen years after the lower Hudson was "discovered" by Verrazano in 1524, the site that would host Los Angeles also came within the ken of Europeans, albeit exclusively Spanish. Less well know than Columbus, da Gama, or Magellan was Juan Rodriguez Cabrillo, who sailed northward from New Spain (Mexico) to look for a northern route to Cathay, as well as to search for the still-elusive water passage thought to connect the Pacific and Atlantic Oceans. According to Nelson's detailed account:

> What Cabrillo found was California. . . . Cabrillo . . . was no ordinary sailing captain. He had been with Cortez during the capture of the wondrous Tenochtitlán and was one of the conquerors of Guatemala, El Salvador, and Nicaragua. . . . Cabrillo . . . left San Diego Bay October 3, 1542 and continued north along the coast for three days . . . [and] visited the islands of San Clemente and Santa Catalina. . . . On the 8th of October they came to the mainland in a large bay. . . . The following day they continued up the coast . . . [anchoring presumably in] Santa Monica Bay. . . . Cabrillo died on the voyage, but . . . his pilot reached at least Point Arena before heading back to New Spain.[49]

Even though the prosperous sixteenth-century galleon trade between Manila and Acapulco sometimes coasted northward along the California shore before setting out for the Philippines, Spanish ships rarely made landfalls in northern California and never needed to stop in southern California. It was therefore not until 1602–3 that the shoreline between Acapulco and Oregon was finally surveyed by Sebastián Vizcaíno. In the course of his studies, he entered the bay he named San Pedro (now one of Los Angeles's ports) and reported on the attractiveness of the surrounding area. But although such early accounts stressed the richness of California and these descriptions entered the Spanish navigation books, Spain was preoccupied with even better sites. And thus it was not until 1768 that a land party was sent into the region, and for reasons that had little to do with its attractiveness.[50]

Of the multiple land and sea probes involved in this particularly disastrous Spanish expedition, only a few survivors managed to link up at San Diego with Captain Gaspar de Portolá, who led them past the future site of Los Angeles on their way to the San Francisco harbor.[51] Their experiences in the vicinity of Los Angeles-to-be were scarcely benign, although they appear tragically familiar to contemporary newspaper readers. On their way northward they were terrified by a series of earthquakes, and upon their return, "as they crossed the Los Angeles River they observed evidence of a recent great flood."[52] Of the many catastrophes that have recently struck Los Angeles, only brushfires and drive-by shootings are not mentioned in Portolá's diary.

Beginning in the 1770s, the Spanish founded a number of missions in California, including one on the site of Los Angeles.

> [In 1780] Captain Rivera began recruiting an authorized twenty-four married settlers and their families for the Los Angeles settlement. They were to be offered lands in California, ten pesos a month for three years, plus a daily allowance of rations. Complete personal outfits from saddles to shoes would be furnished each settler, as well as his farming needs: two cows, two oxen, two horses, three mares, one mule, two ewes, two goats, and tools, and equipment. Repayment was to come out of future production. . . . [Despite these generous incentives] [r]ecruiting the first civilian settlers for California proved extremely difficult.[53]

In the end only fourteen families were recruited, of whom two deserted and another died of smallpox. The settler party ended up as eleven families—a total population of forty-four. Almost all of these were Indian, black, or mulatto.

Upon their arrival in 1781, the settlers followed a plan for settlement that placed them on high ground accessible to the river, established the central plaza, and even set out the dimensions of long strip-planting fields.[54] Each settler was assigned a building lot and four adjacent fields, only two of which were irrigable. *"All the rest of the land . . . [was to] be held in reserve in the name of the King . . . [to] be awarded gratuitously to later settlers."*[55] This final provision was to have long-lasting effects on the development of the metropolis that would grow from such humble beginnings.

Nelson describes Los Angeles in the years between 1781 and 1821 as a simple agricultural village living by subsistence farming, although "a few ranchos gradually developed with sizable herds of cattle and horses." By 1790, the population of the impressively named place (literally Our Lady Queen of the Angels of Porciuncula) was still only 140. This number rose only gradually, to 315 by 1800, 365 by 1810, and 650 by 1820.[56]

CHICAGO BEFORE 1820

There is even less to report on the development of Chicago during this first period, given that the first "permanent" cabin on the site dated back only to 1779, the U.S. fort only to 1803.[57] The town would not be chartered until the 1830s. If earth trembles, droughts, and an uneven flow of river water (the bed of the Los Angeles River sometimes flooding capriciously, other times drying to a narrow ditch) had made the site of Los Angeles inhospitable to settlement, too much water on the marshy bottoms along the shore of Lake Michigan would delay Chicago's settlement until the land could be stabilized by a series of canals. If in prehistoric times the site of Manhattan lay many miles inland from the ocean, the site of Chicago then lay beneath the waters of a lake much larger than now exists.

In modern times, Chicago's site had been "discovered" in the same fruitless search for a passage to the East Indies that had led earlier European adventurers to the sites of New York and Los Angeles. French "explorers" had found their way to Chicago's lakeshore by the late seventeenth century (Marquette and Jolliet in 1673 and La Salle and his associates in the 1680s), and these "discoveries" were used by the French to claim the much vaster Indian fur-trading territory around it. They were forced to concede their claim to the British in 1763, who in turn gave up their rights to the Americans in the Treaty of Paris, which ended the Revolutionary War in 1783.[58]

But such shifting "rights" were never recognized by the existing inhabitants. Throughout, the true "rulers" of the region remained the Potawamis, who occasionally camped at the site they called Checagou.[59] The real hazards to American settlement of the site, then, came not from France or England, but from the native tribes who used it. It was not until 1795 that these original occupants were forced into an agreement that ceded a six-square-mile piece of land at the mouth of the Chicago River to pioneer settlers, and it was really not until the conclusion of the Black Hawk War in 1832 that large-scale settlement became possible.

The location of Checagou was potentially of critical importance, although the site required much work to make it hospitable to settlement. The central core of what became Chicago had, in prehistoric times, been under the water of an enormous inland lake; gradually, deposits built up the shoreline, but the land abutting the lake was a marsh in which the "wild onion" (probably garlic), whose odor inspired Chicago's Indian name, was the chief growth. Depressions left by glaciers created the beds of rivers that, with brief portage zones later excavated, almost opened Lake Michigan to the drainage basin of the Mississippi.[60] With the purchase of Louisiana from the French in 1803, access to this broad midcontinental waterway, with its outlet to world trade at New Orleans, strengthened the motivation of the United States to guard Chicago's site. The construction of Fort Dearborn in 1803 was thus no coincidence.

But Fort Dearborn had not been the first "European" settlement in what was to become Chicago. Perhaps symbolic of the city's "embarrassing" origin was the fact that the first "white" settler on the spot, Jean Baptiste Point du Sable (also referred to as Point De Saible), was actually a "black" man, perhaps a fitting start for a city whose "majority" population is now made up of "people of color." Acknowledgment of du Sable's prior claim as founder was periodically resisted by Chicago's later white elite. As late as the Chicago World's Fair of 1933–34, the black community of Chicago had to fight to have a replica of du Sable's cabin included in the exhibition.[61] Although not all the facts are known, the evidence that du Sable was "founder" or at least builder of the first permanent cabin on the site in 1779 comes from "British records from the revolutionary period as well as the bill of sale for De Saible's homestead in 1800, a document completed three years before the U.S. government's Fort Dearborn was erected."[62] When du Sable left, "the locale was sprinkled with settlers." John Kinzie, the city's putative founder, did not arrive until 1804.[63]

However, it was members of the Kinzie family who were major forces in the true establishment of the city, involved from the start in the Canal Company, which prepared the site for development in the early 1830s, and in enticing the rail lines to locate their terminals at Chicago in the 1840s. John Kinzie's biography throws significant light not only on the development of Chicago in the decades to come but on the intimate connections between that history and the role New Yorkers played in creating the "Second City." Kinzie actually came to the area as the representative of the New York firm of John Jacob Astor, and his family never lost that affiliation, because one of his sons succeeded him in the post. While serving in that capacity, the son also became the "first president of the Village of Chicago, registrar of public lands, canal collector of tolls, receiver of public moneys, a large landowner," and was, as well, the founder of a savings association. Another son became "sheriff, an insurance agent, the president of the Chicago Board of Underwriters, a real estate speculator and Chicago's first auctioneer."[64]

The Kinzie family was soon joined by other leading self-made men, such as Ogden (first president of the "city" of Chicago) and McCormick (inventor of the famous reaper and owner of one of the first industrial establishments in the city); most hailed either from New York or had business connections to the investors from that city. Their story, however, belongs more properly to the next chapter. Equally important were Chicago's roles as creditor for grain and other crops and as "commodifier" for sales of these items at distant points.[65]

CHAPTER 3

Developments between the 1820s and the 1870s

MANHATTAN: AMERICA'S FIRST GLOBAL CITY

Sam Bass Warner Jr. singles out the period between 1820 and 1870 as the acme of urbanity in American cities and identifies New York as the quintessential example: "If the criterion of urbanity is the mixture of classes and ethnic groups . . . along with dense living and crowded streets and the omnipresence of all manner of business near the homes in every quarter, then the cities of the United States in the years between 1820 and 1870 marked the zenith of our national urbanity."[1] In many ways, one can claim that this pattern of urbanity still prevails in New York, at least in large portions of Manhattan, whose physical form was framed during this period.

Paradoxically, however, whereas land uses were mixed and classes and races interspersed, this did not ensure harmony in the nineteenth century—just as it does not in today's New York. A marked bifurcation of the class structure accompanied the remarkable economic advances of the nineteenth century. Warner is correct in claiming that whereas between 1776 and 1820 "America seemed to be moving toward a growing egalitarianism . . . , beginning in the 1820s . . . the benign trends reversed themselves." And as workers organized to protest this growing bifurcation, social unrest grew. "All the big cities suffered epidemics of violence; there were labor riots, race riots, native-foreign riots, Catholic-Protestant riots, rich-poor riots. New York City alone underwent a series of riots, eight major and at least ten minor, between 1834 and 1871."[2] And, we might add, as elsewhere, increased residential segregation came to be seen as one way to insulate hostile social groups from one another.

It was during the period between 1820 and 1870 that New York surged ahead of all competitors to dominate an American urban system that was spreading westward and growing more integrated. In this chapter I explore how and why this happened. My explanations are somewhat more complex than Warner's, however. As is conventional among urban geographers and historians, Warner attributes the transformation of the national urban system that occurred during this period to a revolution in the technologies of transport, which expanded the size of markets and, thanks to a shift to steam power, the size and complexity of production units. This narrative tells only part of the story; demographic infusions and social inventions in business and the state must also be seen as facilitating these transformations.[3]

BECOMING THE CORE OF A WEB OF TRANSPORT AND INFORMATION

There is no question that existing systems of transportation were revolutionized during this second period of American urban development. Between 1815 and the "Panic" of 1837, some two thousand miles of canals were constructed, at first to link the Atlantic port cities with one another and then to connect them with the Midwest. By 1840, another thousand miles of canals had been added, not only integrating markets but substantially reducing the costs of transport. "On the Erie Canal in New York, the most successful of them all, average rates for a ton-mile of goods moving from Buffalo to New York City fell from nineteen cents in 1817 to two cents and finally to one cent after some years of operation."[4] But of even greater importance were the rail lines that quickly displaced canals as the major means of interregional transport. By 1840 some three thousand lines of track connected New York with St. Louis and with the latter's fast-rising competitor, Chicago, and fifteen years later the Union Pacific and Central Pacific rail companies had completed the transcontinental route to San Francisco.[5]

Along with important English firms and banking families, New York investors played major roles in financing these expansions.

> Manorial descendants and members of the [New York] business elite participated in the creation of the new transportation system. . . . In the late 1840s New York's Old Guard and maritime-financial elite became interested in western lines. Their efforts produced the Illinois Central (1851), one of the earliest, soundest, and largest Mid-American roads. *Illinois Central was a wholly eastern creation.*[6]

Cornelius Vanderbilt, a former ferryboat deckhand, started to take over New York lines and by 1867 had gained control over the New York Central. Two years later, Vanderbilt had consolidated that line with the Hudson River Railroad and proposed the construction of Grand Central Station, a project not completed until 1871.[7]

By midcentury, then, New York City "sat like a spider in the web of the American economy, drawing resources into the metropolis, transforming them and sending them to places near and far."[8] But whereas canals and railroads explain New York's dominance over its interior hinterland, the real key to the city's hegemony remained her international role via the port, on which converged the canal and rail lines and from which radiated the Atlantic ocean trade. This nexus generated the concentration of wealth, productive capacity, business services, power, and economic control that even today define a "world city."[9]

Jackson stresses how dependent such dominance was on the port: "Throughout the first three centuries of Gotham's history, the cornerstone of [New York's] growth was commerce, and the backbone of its economy remained at the water's edge. . . . From 1820 until 1960, when Rotterdam overtook it, the Port of New York ranked as the world's busiest."[10]

Jaher concurs, noting that ever since the 1820s, when Boston clippers engaged in the Far Eastern tea trade began to dock in Manhattan, and especially since the 1850s, when the bulk of Boston's wholesale cotton trade was also marketed there, New York was clearly established not only as the nation's shipping and trade center but also as the country's chief money market. By 1860, nearly half of all American foreign commerce went through the city's port,[11] and by the 1870s one could say that New York's market influenced pricing even in those commodities in which it did not trade directly. A national economy was coming into existence, organized through an urban hierarchy headed by New York.

> Banking and wholesale trade in farm staples and some manufactured goods were controlled by the market rates and prices in [what might be termed] . . . national and international trading centers. Wheat, cotton, corn, banknotes, bonds, cloth, iron, books, and all manner of goods for which there were large markets [may have been] traded in regional centers, but *with an eye to New York and ultimately to Atlantic demand and prices.*[12]

THE FIRE SECTOR: FINANCE, INSURANCE, AND REAL ESTATE

In contemporary discussions of the "global city," the growth of one particular economic sector, FIRE, is singled out as the most significant symptom of globalization. It was during the era between 1820 and 1870 that this sector took on a specialized role in Manhattan and generated the consolidation of an upper class that increasingly began to segregate itself from the rest of the city's residents.

Finance

New York established its dominance not only in the arenas of international commerce, shipping, and "pricing," but in the all important area of finance. Originally, before commercial roles became more specialized, merchants had performed many of the functions of bankers, financiers, and insurance agents. However, these roles became more distinctly delineated by the mid-nineteenth century.[13] Although the Bank of New York had been founded as early as 1784, New York lagged behind other ports until 1824, when its capital of sixteen million dollars in thirteen banks finally surpassed that of other port cities.[14] By 1831 the capital in all New York City banks exceeded eighteen million dollars, compared with Boston's fourteen million and Philadelphia's just under eleven million.[15]

One can see dramatic proof of how early this financial centralization became established by tracing the path along which the financial (specie) Panic of 1837 quickly spread from the West to New York, and then radiated out to other cities from New York banking circles. When specie payments were first suspended on May 4, 1837, the panic spread by May 11 from New York to cities of New England (as far north as Providence) and the Mid-Atlantic (as far south as Baltimore). Between May 12 and 15, the panic had affected Montreal and Boston on the north, as far west as Pittsburgh, and as far south as Richmond and Norfolk, Virginia. By May 22, the effects were reaching Charleston, Savannah, Mobile, and New Orleans in the South, and Detroit, Cleveland, Cincinnati, Louisville, and St. Louis in the Midwest.[16]

Banking operations expanded in the 1850s, thanks in part to the involvement of European capital in financing the railroads, but also due to an infusion of specie from California's "gold rush," another indication of the nascent integration of the national economy. By 1855, more than fifty-five banks were operating in New York City;[17] in only the three years between 1854 and 1857 their deposits had increased by 70 percent.[18] But unhappily, their loans increased even faster than their capital. Overextended, such loans precipitated a financial panic in the country that in 1857 again radiated out from New York. Nevertheless, the rapid recovery of the city's banks from the second panic left New York as the unchallenged financial center of the country.[19]

Stock Exchanges

Stock exchanges and insurance and trust companies were also major sources of capital accumulation (and elite jobs) in early New York, and these, too, became more specialized in mid-nineteenth century Manhattan.

> Security dealers rapidly branched out from public securities to handling the private issues of banks, canal and insurance companies, and, later, railroads. Their activities became institutionalized through brokerage houses and the New York Stock Exchange (1792). . . . In 1816 the New York stock market overtook Philadelphia's exchange as the busiest in the country. By the 1830s Wall Street['s] . . . market quotations, reproduced in Philadelphia, Boston, Baltimore, and other places, set the standard national values, and its brokers were America's largest traders in state and federal, bank, canal, and insurance company shares, and primary promoters of new issues.[20]

By 1841, when the New York Merchants Exchange moved to its new quarters on Wall Street, the occupation of stockbroker was fully professionalized.[21] Improved communications further facilitated the centralization of the market at New York. By the late 1840s, an electromagnetic wire service made possible "almost instant telegraphic communications between New York and other large cities in the northeast."[22]

Insurance

Marine insurance, of course, has had a very long history, and so it should be no surprise that the premier port in the United States also hosted the lion's share of insurance companies. Jaher informs us that "by 1824 New York had at least thirty-four firms providing [insurance] protection against shipping and fire disasters . . . and the total capital of its [insurance] institutions" exceeded that of Philadelphia, Boston, and Baltimore combined.[23] Because the "great fire" of 1835 destroyed a large portion of downtown Manhattan, many of these firms went bankrupt, but the reformed insurance system set up afterward expanded on a somewhat firmer foundation. As today, insurance companies, along with private investors, were also involved with real estate, albeit sometimes by default.[24]

Real Estate

New York's traditional elite had always engaged in real estate ventures in both rural and urban areas, and merchants had generally used landownership as a "bank" for idle capital. As the city grew, its land was sought for its potential speculative gains, realizable through a process of quick turnover.[25] Such speculation, however, could also make investments in real estate highly volatile. In the middle and later decades of the nineteenth century, risks became greater, although over the long haul profits continued to be made as Manhattan expanded northward.

As population expanded in the 1830s, the value of lands above Canal Street shot up. During the cholera epidemic of 1832, many families had sought refuge in suburban outposts such as Greenwich Village, and in 1835 an uncontrollable fire downtown forced many more residents out of the oldest section of the city, which drove values up in peripheral areas. The properties they abandoned would later be subdivided into slum tenements (as in the Five Points area) or rebuilt for purely commercial uses.

Speculative bubbles in real estate, however, primarily mirrored more general booms and busts. In the aftermath of the 1837 Panic, for example, values temporarily collapsed. Between 1841 and 1843 mortgage foreclosures reached record levels, with lenders like John Jacob Astor foreclosing to become the city's biggest landlord.[26] But the greatest impulse toward real estate inflation came in the late 1840s, when an influx of immigrants took over downtown properties that were subdivided to accommodate them. This further encouraged the movement of the wealthy farther uptown. The newer subdivisions above 14th Street became more attractive in 1842, once the Croton aqueduct began pumping fresh water to what was then considered "upper" Manhattan. But it was "only with the recovery of prices—particularly agricultural prices—after 1844, however, [that] trade and real estate rebounded," fortunately before the largest influx of immigrants in the late 1840s.[27] Their arrival helped to fuel the pace of industrialization in the ever labor-short United States.

INDUSTRIALIZATION

One of the important ways that nineteenth-century New York diverged from contemporary global cities is that, in contrast to the deindustrialization that is today's hallmark, the city was just beginning to undergo a deep process of industrialization. However, such industries, with the exception of shipbuilding, which peaked by mid-century and then declined, would never be as large in scale, as high in capitalization, or as "heavy" in production processes as those in Chicago, for example, or even Philadelphia. Nevertheless, by the middle decades of the nineteenth century New York had become the greatest manufacturing city in the country.[28] By 1860, three principal manufacturing sectors were already well established in Manhattan: clothing making,[29] iron manufacturing, and printing and publishing. By then, almost fifty thousand workers were employed in some twelve hundred establishments in those three industrial sectors alone.[30] The number of industrial workers would more than double by 1880, even though the most significant growth period would not come until the last two decades of the century.[31]

However, manufacturing never assumed the dominance over New York's economy that it came to have in other major cities of the Northeast and Mid-Central regions, nor did it ever entirely displace the smaller-scale handwork production that continued to characterize most enterprises well into the twentieth century.[32] As Warner notes, "Often the old and new existed side by side," and there was room "in 1870 for the carpenter who followed the ancient custom of bidding on a house or two each year and doing most of the work himself, for the tailor who measured and fitted each suit individually, or for the wood carver who carried his tools from shop to shop." However, by becoming entrepreneurs and expanding the scale of their operations, they could enhance their profits. "Although the city of this period was made up of a multiplicity of small firms . . . the clustering of complementary businesses made expansion easy."[33] This coexistence of large-scale firms and a proliferation of small ones would persist into the twentieth century, as the study conducted by Pratt in 1911 documents so well.[34]

THE GROWTH OF THE PROLETARIAT FROM IMMIGRATION

Another hallmark of today's "global city" is its ethnic/racial diversity, and thus its tendencies toward an ethnic division of labor and an ethnicity-based class system. It is significant that these elements were also already in place by the 1870s, as was an associated pattern of identity-based local politics. In the period between 1820 and the 1870s, rural-to-urban migration and a massive flow of immigrants from abroad completely reshaped the class structure of New York. And these changes were eventually reflected in the redistribution of space and political power.

Rosenwaike estimates that in 1825 only "11.3 percent of the city's [Manhattan's] residents were counted as aliens, [although] as much as 20 percent of the population may have been of foreign birth."[35] By 1845, a year for which we have firmer figures, the proportion of foreign-born had risen to more than one-third, with most of the newcomers hailing from poverty-stricken Ireland.

> The story of New York's population growth in the nineteenth century is inseparable from the saga of mass migration from Europe. . . . Only eight thousand immigrants were reported to have arrived in the United States in the fiscal year ending September 30, 1820, the first for which statistics were published by the Department of State; but by 1860 some four million aliens had reached American shores.[36]

Most entered the country at New York City, and most remained there.[37]

Between 1845 and 1860 (after which there was a temporary hiatus in immigration due to the Civil War), the foreign-born population of New York almost tripled—increasing from some 135,000 to close to 384,000. And although the native-born population increased as well, the proportion of foreign-born increased from 36 percent in the earlier year to 47 percent by 1860. If we add to the foreign-born population their offspring born in the city, it is likely that two-thirds of New York's "natives" were stained with the stigmata of "ethnicity" in the 1870s, even before the next wave of immigrants arrived. In the first wave, the Irish clearly predominated. By 1845, close to 100,000 residents had been born in Ireland, and their numbers more than doubled in the subsequent fifteen years. Second in importance were persons born in the various German states (Germany was not yet "unified"). Although there were only 24,400 in 1845, their total rose rapidly thereafter, to about 57,000 by 1850, 98,000 by 1855, and more than 118,000 by 1860.[38]

Just as today, when the immigration of Mexicans to Los Angeles is eliciting an excessively defensive response among that city's "older settlers," so the enormous influx of Irish and German immigrants in the 1840s and 1850s called forth virulent nativistic reactions in the United States. Despite the facts that the country suffered from a labor shortage and the new industrialization and the accompanying ambitious public works programs undertaken would never have been possible without their contributions, immigrants were blamed for any and all troubles. The Irish in particular were stigmatized as drunkards and feared as unruly; what is worse, their Catholicism, called "Papacy," was suspected of undermining the Protestant character of American society. The Know-Nothing Party was a rallying point for these "nativist" sentiments.[39]

Repelled by the newcomers and expelled by the rising demand for older downtown housing, which was being occupied at very high densities and was consequently deteriorating rapidly, the wealthier residents of New York City were already moving northward on the island, commissioning elegant houses on high ridge lands along Fifth Avenue and its flanking streets, converting their country estates into permanent quarters and subdivisions, and starting to "commute" to their offices, still concentrated below Canal Street.

In the neighborhoods they vacated, tenement houses began to be constructed for the newly arriving working-class immigrants.[40] But still, the built-up portion of the island did not extend much beyond about 40th Street.[41] North of there were scattered small, unregulated, and low-density settlements—some like the long-standing and predominantly black "suburb" of Seneca Village, largely owner occupied and inhabited by service workers who supplemented their wages downtown through subsistence farming; others better described as noxious squatter camps where pig raising, bone boiling, and wood foraging were the sources of a marginal livelihood for recent Irish and German immigrants not yet integrated into the city's economy.[42]

Such settlements were "threatening" to the establishment in two ways: they reduced the social attractiveness of the northern parts of the island that had already been subdivided into building lots but still lacked infrastructure, not to mention permanent structures; and they inhibited rising land values based on speculative interest.

Furthermore, much of the "uptown" land in the center of the island—which would eventually be selected as the site of Central Park—was very rough, even rugged, terrain that would be prohibitively expensive to develop with roads and to install sewerage and water systems (see Figure 3.1).

This land did lend itself, however, to development as a public park, which could achieve three important goals: it would "remove" the undesirable residents who stood in the way of northern expansion; it would enhance the land values of all abutting lots, encouraging speculation on their development for "higher" uses; and it would provide New York with a public amenity it hitherto lacked—a large park suitable for bucolic retreat and fashionable promenades.

The construction of Central Park, from 1857 onward, which was the single most important development in shaping the physical form of Manhattan, cannot be understood outside the context of the growing gap between elite and proletariat, between native and foreign immigrant. Although its effects on the ecological structure of Manhattan would not be fully felt until the building boom of the 1880s and 1890 (to be treated in greater detail in Chapter 4), it is important to grasp the class divisions that partially motivated this wondrous achievement in city planning.

THE GROWTH OF THE ELITE AND THE CONCENTRATION OF WEALTH

Analysts of the contemporary global city stress the bifurcation of the urban class structure into rich and poor, with a relative decline of the middle classes. In a later section of this book I explore to what extent and why this has happened and whether considering the entire metropolitan area makes a difference to the conclusions. Here I wish only to establish the fact that one of the major characteristics of nineteenth-century New York City was the appearance of an income gap even wider than the one that prevails today. The concentrations of both wealth and poverty were extreme, and the gap between them was growing larger, even though the opportunities for social mobility at that time were more open to "self-made" fortunes than they are today.

The number of superrich was remarkably small. In 1842, Moses Yale Beach compiled a list of New Yorkers who had assets of $100,000 or more, then considered a fortune; he enumerated fewer than five hundred, including John Jacob Astor, who led the pack with $10 million.[43] According to historian Edward Pessen, in 1845 the richest 1 percent of New York's families controlled almost half (47 percent) of its noncorporate wealth, with the next three percent controlling an additional third (32 percent).[44] By 1856, about nine thousand New York families "controlled a significant share of the city's and nation's resources."[45] Who were these wealthy New Yorkers?

> Merchants were by far the most important group of the city's [mid-nineteenth century] bourgeoisie. . . . by 1855 approximately forty-one percent of all taxpayers assessed on personal and real wealth above $10,000 were engaged in mercantile undertakings. Not only were they the largest group in numbers but also among the wealthiest: An estimated seventy percent of the richest one percent of New Yorkers in 1854 were merchants, auctioneers, brokers and agents.[46]

By midcentury merchants were finally being joined by industrialists whose initial capital, amassed in trade or smaller artisan activities, was being reinvested in production. "Twenty percent of all bourgeois New Yorkers in 1856 were producing goods in one way or another."[47] This new elite was not as inbred as in earlier times, and indeed, some of the industrialists had actually risen from the ranks of artisans. Nevertheless, funds for manufacturing also came from the investment of "old" merchant capital, and both the established merchants and the newly rich families invested at least some of their money in the newer ventures of industry and railroads.[48]

By the 1850s, a new diversification within the elite was becoming evident, a fact that made it difficult to consolidate and maintain patriciate power in the city. Jaher's information on where members of the 1856 elite had been born indicates the roles that industrialization and immigration were playing in allowing "outsiders" into the top of the class structure. By then, about half of New York's wealthiest men had been born in New York City or State (down from 62 percent in 1828), whereas 30 percent had come from other states (primarily New England); one-fifth had been born abroad, primarily in Great Britain.[49] As before, intermarriage between the nouveau riche and old landed and mercantile families helped to consolidate the upper class, but there remained relatively unbridgeable fissures related to ethnicity—especially those that set off the newer German-Jewish moneyed elite from the WASP and Dutch subsets.[50]

The Civil War further fragmented class solidarity at the top, as New York City hosted both abolitionists who sought an end to slavery and cotton brokers whose fortunes were based upon it. Nevertheless, the net gains the war brought to New York merchants and industrialists greatly outweighed their losses, regardless of their ideological positions. Newer fortunes were generated in the early 1860s, when wartime profiteering and bond investments yielded windfall returns. These stimulated, inter alia, a renewed real estate boom that greatly expanded the urban fabric of Manhattan—at least until markets collapsed in the depression of 1874.

CLASS CONFLICT

Given the growing gap between rich and poor and the volatile booms that brought disastrous busts in their wake (in 1837, 1857, and again in 1874), it should not be surprising that the era was characterized by considerable labor unrest. The growing and primarily immigrant proletariat that depended upon wages was tragically affected by these cycles. When times were good, they struck for higher wages, a shorter working day, and better conditions of employment, but during periods of crisis they marched on city hall or rallied in parks to demand employment and relief. Often, their demonstrations were met with police brutality, as this was the period in which a more formalized and uniformed police force had been established to combat threats to law and order. Public works employment (including the construction of Central Park and the building of New York's infrastructure) increasingly responded to their demands for work,[51] and charitable efforts at housing reform began the long struggle against the insalubrious tenement housing that had been adapted or hastily thrown up to accommodate the new immigrants.

By the middle of the nineteenth century, when Manhattan's population exceeded half a million, the tenement house was just beginning to appear as the dominant form of new construction for the poor.[52] Philip Hone, a famous if somewhat snobbish commentator on the New York scene, had already noted with alarm that "our good city of New York has arrived at the state of society found in the large cities of Europe; overburdened with population, and where the two extremes of costly luxury . . . are presented in daily and hourly contrast with squalid misery and destitution."[53] He was particularly concerned with the proliferation of multifamily housing and overcrowding, because, as was being argued, poor housing bred both physical diseases and moral degeneracy. These concerns attracted the attention of tenement house reformers and charitable institutions such as the New York Association for the Improvement of the Conditions of the Poor (AICP), which was organized as early as 1843.[54] But such charitable impulses often masked self-interest, because the wealthy would be best served by a healthy and quiescent labor force.

Members of the immigrant working class of New York seem not to have been so ambivalent over the reforms they needed in the workplace and at home, nor so conflicted over how to respond to issues raised by the Civil War. Throughout the contentious period of the 1850s, there were various mobilizations of the working class, primarily focused on employment and relief demands. But in 1863 such conflicts came to a head over another issue of conspicuous inequality.

A lottery had been organized to determine who would be conscripted into the Union army; it was implemented in New York City in July 1863. The selection process blatantly favored the rich, given that those whose numbers were drawn were permitted to "buy" exemption from military service by paying three hundred dollars for an alternate to fight on their behalf. As this sum represented the annual salary of an ordinary workman, it was scarcely an option open to the poor. Furthermore, recent (primarily Irish) immigrants were distinctly unenthusiastic about serving in a war to which they were ideologically uncommitted and that so poorly served their interests. The gross unfairness of the plan triggered five days of rioting, during which not only were the lottery headquarters, civic buildings, and homes of the wealthy attacked, but, tragically, some of the targets of the violence proved to be black residents of the city, who were viewed as the "cause" of the war.[55] Attempts by the authorities to control the marauding bands of malcontents only served to escalate the violence.

THE INCREASE IN CLASS SEGREGATION AND DENSITIES

The ability of the crowds to mobilize and to target specific areas testifies to the fact that residential segregation by class and race had begun to take clearer shape in the city, although the relatively close juxtapositioning of wealthy and poor areas made access between the two easier than it would later be. Although land uses continued to be quite mixed, and industrial plants, with the exception of the shipyards, were still scattered at many relatively small sites, residential segregation on the basis of class and ethnicity was becoming more pronounced.

> By the 1850s, the separation of workplace and home had largely been accomplished for elite New Yorkers. . . . Beginning in the 1820s, New York's wealthy citizens moved north. . . . In 1856, the area around Washington and Union Square[s] was the most bourgeois neighborhood in Manhattan. In the four adjacent wards to this area . . . fifty-seven percent of all taxpayers assessed over $10,000 made their homes, and . . . between Fourteenth and Twenty-third Street east of Fifth Avenue—fully one quarter of all the city's merchants, industrialists and bankers lived. . . . By 1856 very few bourgeois lived south of Houston Street—a sort of social boundary between the "respectable" and working-class neighborhoods.[56]

Not only was segregation increasing, but residential densities were also, the inevitable result of the fact that by 1870 the population of Manhattan approached one million. Although horse cars had been introduced by the 1850s, no revolution had yet occurred in transportation that would have permitted an opening of vast peripheral areas for convenient settlement. While the rich continued to build lavish mansions along Fifth Avenue and the poor were resigned to living in crowded tenements, the middle class had gradually to be weaned from the assumption that single-family brownstone houses (which many could no longer afford) were the only respectable way to live.

Before this could occur, the apartment house had to be socially distinguished from the déclassé tenement, and privacy had to be redefined. A new form of multifamily housing first made its appearance in Manhattan in the late 1860s and early 1870s. These multifamily dwellings were euphemistically called French flats, in an effort to legitimate them by reference to high-status Parisian prototypes.[57] Richard Morris Hunt is credited with designing the first one, Stuyvesant Apartments, located on 18th Street near Third Avenue, and in 1871 David Haight remodeled a nearby mansion into apartments.[58] It took some time before this innovation was accepted, but eventually apartment houses, of necessity, became the most popular form of new construction. It was not until

> the end of the first decade of the twentieth century [that] apartment houses were fully established as a successful building type in New York. Whereas in 1890, 835 plans for single-family dwellings had been filed with the Buildings Department, in 1901 barely 100 were filed. Meanwhile the prices had skyrocketed from an average cost per dwelling of $16,700 in 1889 to $64,000 in 1902. Single-family houses had become so expensive in Manhattan that they had nearly ceased being built, while *apartments became the kind of dwelling every middle-class Manhattanite would expect to live in.*[59]

The land and building boom of the post–Civil War expansion lasted from 1865 to 1873, fueled by fortunes made in the war. More than 11,000 building plans were filed with the city between 1868 and 1872, as the built-up area pressed northward above 42nd Street. Construction peaked in 1871, when some 2,800 buildings were constructed, a thousand of them "first-class residences." (In contrast, only two apartment buildings went up between 1868 and 1872.) Construction declined in the depression years between 1873 and 1877, when fewer than 7,000 plans were filed. In the recovery year of 1880, however, 2,252 buildings were erected, 900 of them first-class (single-family) residences. But 516 were apartment houses, which indicated a growing dependence upon this type of housing arrangement.[60] Clearly, the "middle-class buyer . . . was being driven out of Manhattan by the speculation of the 1860s, leaving the city to the millionaire and the pauper."[61]

THE EVOLUTION OF A POLITICAL CULTURE

Between the 1820s and the 1870s, local politics underwent as dramatic a shift as did the physical form of the city. As we have seen in Chapter 2, during the earlier period there was very little conflict between the interests of rural patricians who dominated the state government and those of the interrelated urban patriciate of New York City. Politics and economics meshed well. Jaher tells us that in the early nineteenth century, as before, "the upper order manipulated government policy by entering public office or by associating with politicians. . . . Merchant-bankers were particularly active in public life because of the relationship between government and finance. The early presidents of the Bank of New York almost invariably had political backgrounds."[62] But changes gradually appeared as the monopoly over power was undermined.

By 1825 the franchise had been extended to non-property-holding males, and by midcentury, the electorate, swelled by new immigrants, grew more powerful as various officials, including the governor and the mayor, who had formerly been appointed, were now to be elected. The concerns of the elite, who deplored and feared the new immigrants and their rising power, were certainly well founded. Tammany (an old, secret "gentlemen's club" organized after the Revolutionary War by the "better classes"), which had traditionally served as local "kingmaker" for appointed offices, was gradually taken over by a new class of politicians whose power base derived from the enfranchisement of the "new ethnics." Their rise to power in the city went hand in hand with and was greatly facilitated by the expansion of government-sponsored projects and services. The hard-won "home rule" wrested from Albany conferred on these elected officers the power to borrow money in the name of the city, which enhanced their leverage with bankers and financiers and also afforded the powerful "bosses" virtually unlimited opportunities for graft. Because they controlled public jobs and could distribute them through patronage, they commanded enormous resources, which they used to consolidate their control over votes.

By the 1870s, the new form of city governance was well established. Reform movements would periodically dislodge incumbents (such as in 1871, when "Boss" Tweed was arrested for corruption),[63] and Fusion and even socialist candidates might surface from time to time, but the lock that the bosses gained over the Democratic Party and the "machine's" power not only in city but in state and even federal elections, would remain significant elements in the civic culture of the city.[64]

Although the old aristocracy and the new politically organizing "lower classes" were often at odds over the goals and functions of city government and about how public resources should be allocated, there was one project in which their aims came symbiotically together, and that was over the construction of Central Park, the nineteenth century's most significant contribution to the urban form of Manhattan.

THE PLANNING OF CENTRAL PARK

A number of upper-class New Yorkers had been traveling to Europe, where they admired the great parks of London and Paris and felt ashamed that their community, despite its world city pretensions, had almost no public spaces at all, and none suitable for those with "higher" tastes.[65] Although the original proposals by the city's movers and shakers favored an off-center park site (on land conveniently owned by some of them), by the early 1850s a decision was reached to locate this ambitiously planned embellishment to the city on the more than seven hundred acres of inhospitable wild terrain between 59th Street and 106th Street and between Eighth and Fifth Avenues. In the following year the northern limit was extended to 110th Street to encompass the marshy declivity of the Harlem Meer.

Support for the construction of a park came not only from the wealthy, who viewed the potential product as a much-needed "playground" for themselves, but from laborers, who saw it as a source of employment during the disastrous depression of 1857. However, the same depression made it difficult to sell the public bonds that were intended to finance the work. Although surveys had already been completed and the design by the team of Frederick Law Olmsted and Calvert Vaux accepted, albeit duly modified after they won the competition, it was not until 1858 that construction actually began.[66]

> Central Park was soon turned into a vast construction area with blasting teams, stone breakers, road-building gangs, masons, blacksmiths, carpenters, stonecutters, gardeners, wagon teams, and cart and wheelbarrow gangs working side-by-side. At the peak of construction in 1859 and 1860, the Board of Commissioners of the Central Park was one of the city's largest employers, hiring an average of four thousand workers each year, with as many as thirty-six hundred laborers working on a single day at the peak of construction in early 1859.[67]

As is often the case with public projects, the original estimates proved much too low. Assembling the land; grading, draining, and landscaping it; and meeting the exacting demands of Olmsted, who was put in charge—all were incredibly costly, and more and more money had to be borrowed to finance the project. It must also be acknowledged that some of the excess costs came from kickbacks and graft, as contractors raised their bids to cover payoffs to officials. Matters reached a peak with the election of William Tweed, who engaged in even greater graft than his predecessors. (He was indicted and convicted in 1871.) The leading citizens were disgusted enough to organize "'a tax and investment strike,' as the political scientist Martin Shefter describes it," one that paralleled later fiscal crises in the city when expansive public spending was curtailed, but later bailed out, by the "watchdogs" from the investment community.[68]

Thus the basic lines of New York's special "civic culture" seem to have become

Figure 3.1. The raw land of Central Park in 1858. View in Central Park, southward from the Arsenal, Fifth Avenue, and 64th Street. Photo by George Hayward. Courtesy of The New-York Historical Society, with thanks to M. Christine Boyer; copyright Collection of The New-York Historical Society.

established in general outline by the 1870s, although newer immigrant groups and, even later, the African American community would be co-opted into the system of public employment. This seems a good note on which to end the discussion of New York, for as we shall see in subsequent chapters, many of the themes raised here will appear with regularity in the periods that followed.

CHICAGO BETWEEN 1820 AND 1871

Although in 1820 Chicago did not even *exist* as a city, by 1870 it stood on the threshold of becoming a "world city," having experienced the fastest rate of growth of any city in the United States, if not the world. And yet everything before the Great Fire of 1871 must be viewed as prolegomenon. In Chapter 5 I focus on the creation and maturation of this industrial giant, but it is important to note here that the groundwork for that achievement was laid in the preceding half century.

Perhaps the best book ever written about Chicago in the nineteenth century is William Cronon's *Nature's Metropolis: Chicago and the Great West.* His thesis is a simple one—namely, the intimate and mutually dependent nature of urban and rural development. He could hardly have reached any different conclusion, given that he had decided to study Chicago, which became

> *"urban,"* spawning belching smokestacks and crowded streets, *at the same time that the lands around it became "rural,"* yielding not grass and red-winged blackbirds but wheat, corn, and hogs. Chicago's merchants and workers had built their warehouses and factories *in the same decades* that farmers had plowed up the prairie sod and lumberjacks had cut the great pine trees of the north woods. City and country shared a common past, and had fundamentally reshaped each other.[69]

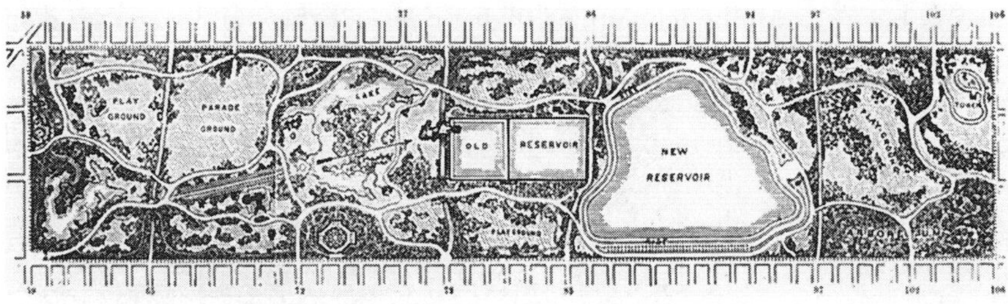

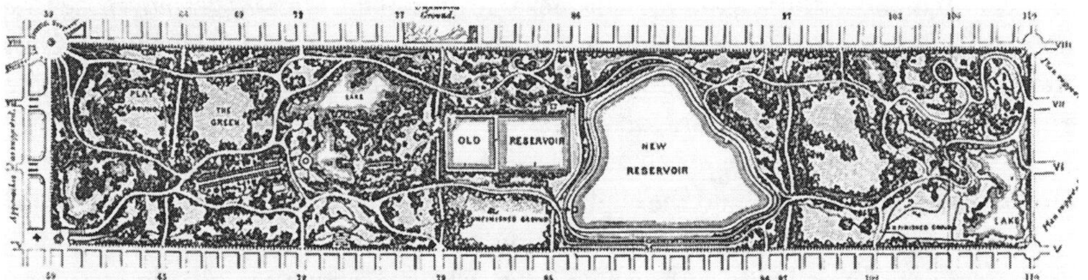

Maps 3.1 and 3.2. Two diagrams of Central Park from the pamphlet by Calvert Vaux and Frederick Law Olmsted, "Description of a Plan for the Improvement of Central Park," circa 1858, showing the northern extension of the park from 106th to 110th Streets. Courtesy of The New-York Historical Society, with thanks to M. Christine Boyer; copyright Collection of The New-York Historical Society.

And if the appropriate trope for New York is an island in the sea, and the most often invoked image of approach is that of the foreigner, sailing into the harbor and sighting (as appropriate to the time) either Indians on the shore or gathered curiously or hostilely in approaching canoes, or the torch of the Statue of Liberty beckoning him into an incomprehensible immigrant reception center, to be poked and probed and herded, the trope for Chicago is the rail terminal. At this entry point the rural hick or the perplexed Polish peasant, after a noisy train ride, enters the gates of hell, replete with fires and belching smoke, jostling crowds, and the dangers and excitement of "the big city."[70] The "docks and wharves" of Chicago were its multiple railway stations, and the seas that bordered the city were surfaced by waves of wheat and corn. One *could* approach Chicago by water, but few did, once there were trains.

Early Physical and Demographic Changes

In 1833, when Chicago was incorporated as a town, it covered less than half a square mile on either side of the main channel of the Chicago River and contained only 350 adventurous inhabitants, mostly male. There was little to recommend the settlement, for the site was still essentially uninhabitable. However, in 1833, "Congress appropriated $25,000 for major improvements in the harbor. In 1834, a channel was opened through the sand bar at the mouth of the river." Patrick Shirref, a Scottish traveler, described the city as containing "about 150 wood houses," although he also reported that "speculators have already bought up, at high prices, all the building-ground in the neighborhood."[71] By the time the city was incorporated in 1837, it was ten square miles in area; these borders were successively expanded as the city grew. According to John Lewis Peyton, although the population had risen to twenty thousand by 1848, the city still had neither paved streets nor sidewalks, and its three thousand houses were "almost entirely small timber buildings."[72]

Nevertheless, brick makers and stonemasons were busy preparing more solid building materials; blacksmiths and wagon makers were producing furiously to meet farmers' demands; and Cyrus McCormick's reaper plant already employed several hundred workers. Future expansion was eagerly anticipated, and "real estate agents were mapping out the surrounding territory for ten and fifteen miles in the interior, giving fancy names to the future avenues, streets, squares, and parks."[73]

Their preparations were well warranted, for by midcentury the population had grown to thirty thousand, and the city's potential as a transportation nexus and industrial giant was becoming clearer. "The Illinois and Michigan Canal opened in 1848 connecting the Great Lakes with the Mississippi Valley" and, after "a period of vigorous railroad building," trains entered Chicago "from almost every direction. By 1855, Chicago was . . . the focus of ten trunk lines. Ninety-six trains a day arrived or departed from the city, and on a single day the Michigan Central brought 2,000 immigrants into the city."[74]

But "the train did not create the city by itself." Rather, it allowed Chicago to become the "site of a country fair, albeit the grandest, most spectacular country fair the world has ever seen."[75] Underlying the development of this great city, at least initially, was not the industrial might associated with the "city of the broad shoulders," but the grain, lumber, and meat that farmers produced in the vast and fertile hinterland that expanded exponentially as rail lines cut the time-cost of transporting their products to market.[76] Out of these rural products would be generated both a growing manufacturing and a booming finance sector.

These sectors, however, did not have to be developed *ex nihilo.* Their technological and institutional arrangements could be imported from the East, together with many of the civic figures who would lead in the city's transformative period. Jaher draws a sharp contrast between the "important" Chicago dynasties and those of the East Coast:

> Recent origin, an interior location, and early identification with heavy industry distinguishes Chicago from Boston, New York, or Charleston. The seaboard ports exuded elegance, cosmopolitanism, cultural achievement, and pride in their historical roles and had aristocratic elements in their social structures. The midwestern metropolis *epitomized the raw and powerful adolescence of industrial America.* Even New York, the nation's *parvenu* capital, had roots in the past and an ascriptive group that influenced its upper class.[77]

Nevertheless, most members of the earliest Chicago elite came from New York and New England, albeit as "self-made men." According to Jaher, this elite "dominated the economy. Its members formed the first banks and insurance, manufacturing, and utility companies, and pioneered in retail and wholesale trade, transportation ventures, and real estate operations."[78] Jaher notes that "those with eastern connections naturally took the lead in banking and insurance since capitalists in that region [i.e., the East] constituted the main source of funds for early Chicago enterprise."[79]

Only after the Civil War did Chicago become a true manufacturing town.[80] As late as 1860, only 5 percent of the city's residents were involved in industry, a proportion that had doubled by 1870. "But by 1880 Chicago had the largest industrial force . . . west of the Appalachians."[81] Because the maximum economic growth took place during the postbellum period, I discuss this subject further in Chapter 5.

The Role of Catastrophe: The Chicago Fire of October 8, 1871

The city of Chicago, whose economic base had evolved considerably by 1870, had already taken on a physical structure that might have exercised a limiting constraint on the future had it not been "fortuitously" destroyed. It had become an overgrown, sprawling "village" whose population was expanding rapidly and whose transformation into a major industrial metropolis and midwestern center for an expanding region was beginning to occur. Mrs. O'Leary's cow was the deus ex machina that, at this turning point in the city's development, suddenly "cleared space" for the rebuilding of an urban structure more appropriate to Chicago's role as "Queen of the North and the West," as she was called in the hyperbolic words of a local poet-booster, Will Carleton:

> This is the rich and voluptuous city,
> The beauty-thronged, mansion-decked city,
> The golden-crowned, glorious Chicago.
> The Queen of the North and the West![82]

Just before the fire, Chicago's population had reached 334,000, living in an area of some eighteen square miles around the central nexus where thirteen major rail lines met. Physically, the half-circular city "was divided into three divisions by its river, which was spanned by a dozen wooden bridges."[83] The western segment was industrial, especially along the two branches of the river. Along the lakefront south of the central business district, later to be called "the Loop," were areas of fine homes, but as one moved inland from the lake, the buildings became more ramshackle and the population poorer.

The basic building material for the city, as noted above, was still flammable wood, making it a tinderbox. There were raised wooden-planked sidewalks to keep pedestrians from rain accumulations of mud, streets were paved with wood blocks, and all the bridges over the river were also made of timber. Only recently had construction in brick and stone begun to displace wood within the central business district, and the architecture of these new structures looked exactly like the beaux arts commercial structures and residential row houses of New York, on which they were modeled. The crazy stone and crenelated water tower had just been built in 1867 in the northern division to bring Lake Michigan water to city areas that had previously depended mostly on wells.[84]

And yet there had been a serious drought for several years, and fires had become more frequent; in 1870 alone, the city experienced some six hundred fires. The drought continued into 1871, when "only five inches of rain fell between July and October. . . . The rainfall in the month preceding October 8 had been less than one inch . . . [and] some twenty-seven fires struck during the first week of that month."[85] The city was therefore highly vulnerable when, on Sunday evening, October 8, a fire started at O'Leary's barn on De Koven Street, in the southern division of the city, just southwest of the central business district.[86]

The fire spread northeastward, fanned by high winds, and raged for twenty-nine hours before the flames finally subsided to smoldering embers. It leaped northward across the Chicago River, defied the firebreaks created by firefighters using dynamite, and destroyed virtually everything in its path. "$192,000,000 worth of property was wiped out. . . . Seventy-three miles of streets were swept by the flames, which destroyed 17,500 buildings, and made 100,000 Chicagoans homeless."[87] In the aftermath between October 11 and 23, the city was placed under martial law to restore some semblance of order, and a massive national charity campaign was organized to bring relief to the homeless and provisionless citizens, most of whom had taken refuge, without any possessions, in the shallow edges of the lake itself to avoid being engulfed by flames.

Although the downtown and near north were drastically razed, much of Chicago's transportation and industrial infrastructure remained unscathed. The shipping docks were intact, although the wooden grain elevators along the northern shore burned down. Most of the trunk rail lines were unharmed. And the stockyards and most of the factories in the western and southwestern quarters continued to function without interruption. The McCormick Reaper works, however, was completely destroyed.

Recovery began almost immediately.[88] Transportation was restored, with horse cars functioning in downtown only two days after the fire. Temporary wooden shacks were thrown up as an interim measure, but permanent frame buildings were outlawed and standards for new structures built of brick, stone, or stucco were established. Although property ownership lines did not change, the entire architectural appearance of the areas later known as "the Loop" and the Near North—which had borne the brunt of the destruction—was altered in one fell swoop. The heavy demand for rebuilding drove a countercyclical economic expansion in the city throughout the rest of the 1870s, even when the country's and New York's economy was depressed in a worldwide recession.

Ross Miller (a professor of comparative literature and not an urbanist) has written a remarkable evaluation of the way that the apocalypse myth of the Chicago fire insinuated itself immediately into the city's image of itself—an image that persists and that, it must be confessed, continues to infuse the "can do" (city's motto) spirit, even in the face of other less flattering images held by outsiders.[89] Some of Miller's insights are worth reproducing. He points out that the image of the phoenix rising from the ashes pervades all of the postconflagration literature:

> Chicago . . . became the only American city whose myth of founding and development was absolutely contemporaneous with its modern condition. . . . Through

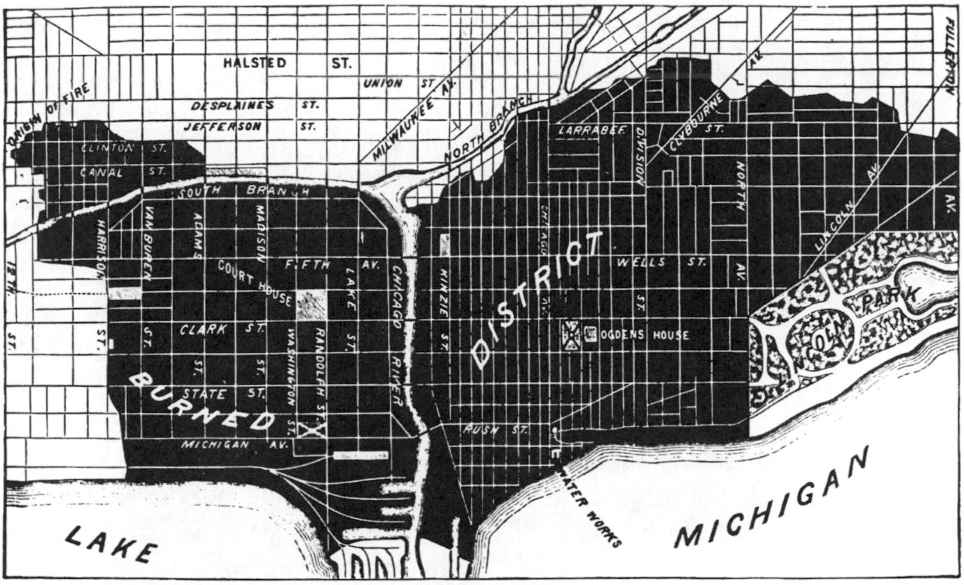

Map 3.3. The extent of the downtown area of Chicago that burned down in the Great Chicago Fire of 1871. Courtesy of the Chicago Historical Society.

> one dramatic act, the present was no longer necessarily subordinate to the past. What separates Chicago's history of emerging modernity from that of other nineteenth-century cities is the clarity of its imagery. While others suffered the modern through a host of neurasthenic symptoms . . . Chicagoans felt its freeing possibilities. Their initial view of the modern was positive. From the omnipresent engravings of the phoenix rising from the ashes to the apocalyptic talk of preachers and reporters, Chicagoans had a way to picture the way they felt.[90]

Miller also suggests a theme that I find very compelling because it resonates so completely with my own analysis of the "personality" of Chicago. He speaks of Chicago's "double identity—as both queen of the inland lakes and gritty frontier city on the make. . . . it is precisely this doubleness, even in the face of the postfire city's ever more dissonant realities, that provides modern Chicago with its character—a doubleness observed and systematically denied, that is as old as the city."[91] The *dual city,* at least with reference to Chicago, is no contemporary product of globalization. The bifurcation was there from the start.

J. W. Sheahan, a Chicagoan who published an account of the fire in 1875 in *Scribner's Monthly,* invoked the idea of a divided Chicago, but not on the basis of class:

> Sheahan noticed none of the cultural anxiety expressed in earlier accounts. Something had happened that changed the way Chicagoans presented and perceived themselves. Not that the facts were different; only the attitudes toward development had changed. *Chicago had found a way to see itself. Instead of trying to resolve its divisions like the cities of the East Coast and Europe, it would make its conflicts the basis of its identity.*

> . . . Divisions that might paralyze other places provided the very condition for Chicago's existence.[92]

I return to this theme in later chapters, where I note how the massive class and racial bifurcations of the city and the confrontational character of its political culture surface time and time again. These divisions are indeed the condition of its existence.

LOS ANGELES: DEVELOPMENTS BETWEEN THE 1820S AND 1870S

Although few Americans would consider Los Angeles a significant urban center during this period, the fifty years in question were particularly transformative in preparing the ground for its future development. Unlike the cases of New York and Chicago, where fairly steady trend lines can be identified, however, the dominant theme for Los Angeles was its political *discontinuity* during this period.

There were three distinct marker events: the success of the Mexican war of independence from Spain, which culminated in 1822, when California became a Mexican province; the gold rush of the late 1840s, which was directly responsible not only for a local boomlet but, of far more lasting significance, for motivating the conquest of southern California by the United States and the admission of that state to the Union in 1850; and (perhaps not as political, but certainly as transformative) the subsequent arrival of rail connections from other parts of the United States—at first to San Francisco in 1870 and then extended from San Francisco to Los Angeles by 1876. Direct connections from the East would not be in place until a decade later. If the half century covered in this chapter consolidated New York's lead as hegemonic city in the nation and established Chicago as a nascent industrial power, the same period was clearly only the "planting" season for a Los Angeles to come.

Nelson calls Los Angeles in the period between 1822 and 1840 still an "embryo town . . . [that was] developing an urban form typical of Mexican cities everywhere." It had a central plaza focused on the church and surrounded by the homes of the large landholders, and with agricultural land and vast dry ranches on the periphery.[93] And even though the port at San Pedro was, after Mexican independence, newly allowed to import foreign goods and ships docked there more frequently, the population of the town remained minuscule. The pueblo contained only 770 inhabitants in 1830, 1,110 in 1840, and 1,250 by 1845, with equal numbers living on ranches in the hinterlands. A primitive division of labor had barely begun to occur. The town contained a few stores, some craftsmen, and even some home manufacturing, but the economy continued to be based on cattle raising and its by-products (hides and tallow), the only objects that entered international trade.

Nevertheless, the Mexican revolution did make a difference. By 1835 the town's status was raised to that of *ciudad* (city) and Los Angeles was declared the capital of the territory, even though the government was not moved there until ten years later. Far more definitive in shaping the characteristic of the settlement, however, were the *ranchos,* because in the 1830s the Mexican government had distributed large amounts of land to its supporters, who formed a glittering, albeit rough, "elite."[94]

Map 3.4. In 1849, after the U.S. conquest was regularized, E. O. C. Ord made the first American survey of Los Angeles, preparatory to reorganizing ownership. His survey shows a primitive gridiron frontier town.

The California gold rush, although concentrated mostly in northern California, also scattered some fallout glitter on Los Angeles. Not only was some gold found in the town's vicinity as early as 1843, but the demand for southern California's meat and other food products increased significantly during the northern gold rush. Formerly useful only for their hides and tallow, cattle on the hoof were being herded northward and sold for meat at outrageous prices paid by gold miners. The gold rush also redoubled the urgency to add California to the United States. In 1846, the United States had already declared war on Mexico, and after seesaw battles in which Los Angeles changed hands several times, the city came under the control of American forces by 1847. In 1849, after conquest was "regularized,"[95] E. O. C. Ord made the first American survey of Los Angeles preparatory to revamping ownership patterns. His plan showed a primitive frontier town.

The U.S. Census taken in 1850 revealed the preponderance of the town's Mexican residents; only some three hundred of the Los Angeles population were of "American ancestry," with men outnumbering women three to one.[96] Southern California was to lag considerably behind the rest of the state in Anglofication. This had long-lasting effects on the city, as Carey McWilliams so astutely recognized:

> For three decades after 1849, while thousands of Americans were invading Northern California, taking possession of the land and establishing their institutions, Southern California remained virtually unchanged. Spanish continued to be used as the language of instruction in most communities throughout the 'sixties and 'seventies. Twenty years after the discovery of gold, Los Angeles was still a

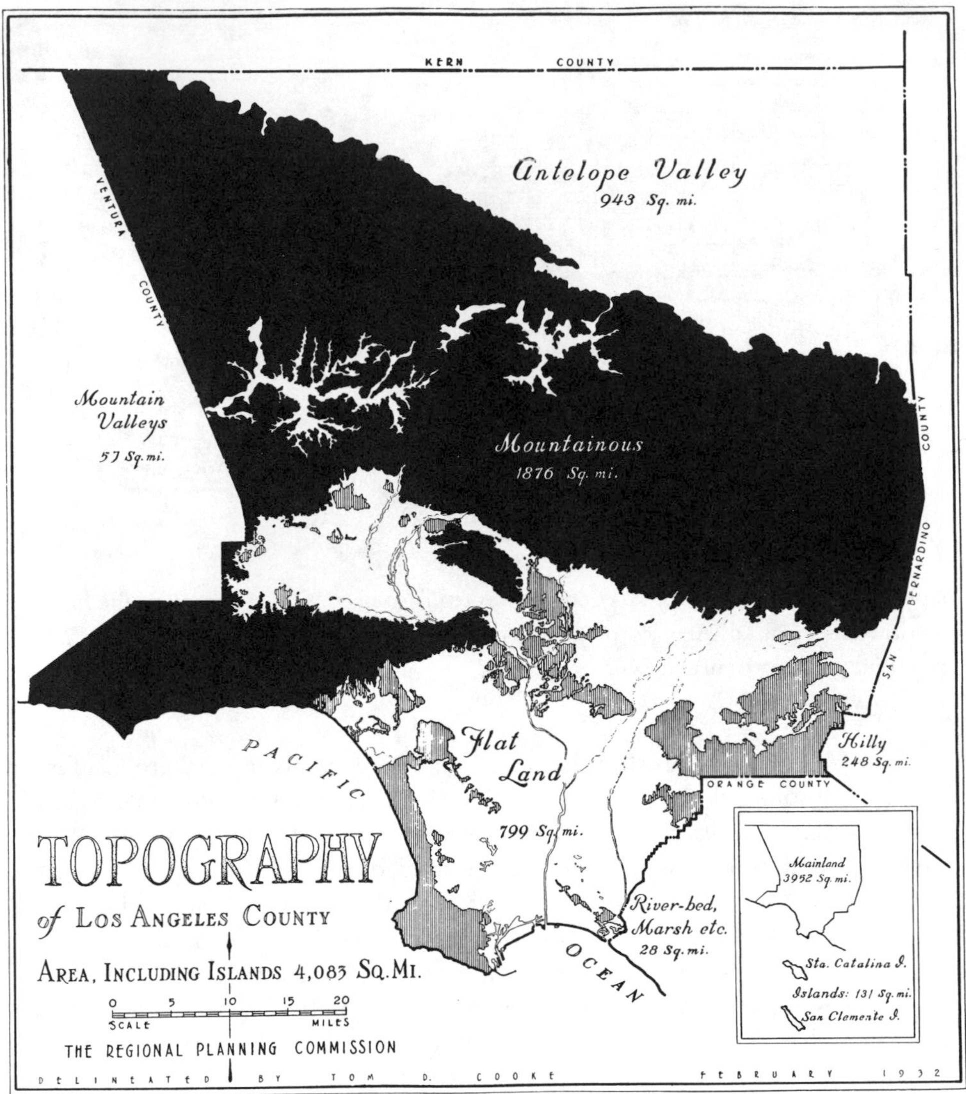

Map 3.5. Topography rules: the lay of the land in Los Angeles County. Source: Regional Planning Commission. Reproduced by permission of The Huntington Library.

> small Mexican town in which Spanish was spoken almost universally, with all official documents . . . being published both in Spanish and in English. . . . As a result of this time-lag in social change, Spanish-Mexican influences struck deeper roots in Southern California than elsewhere in the state . . . [It] was not until the great influx of the 'eighties that the Spanish influence began to decline.[97]

The term *Mexican,* however, concealed a complex social hierarchy, in which "race," social privilege, and economic class were all invoked to distinguish the self-styled "Spanish" elite (consisting of large landholders, government officials, and mili-

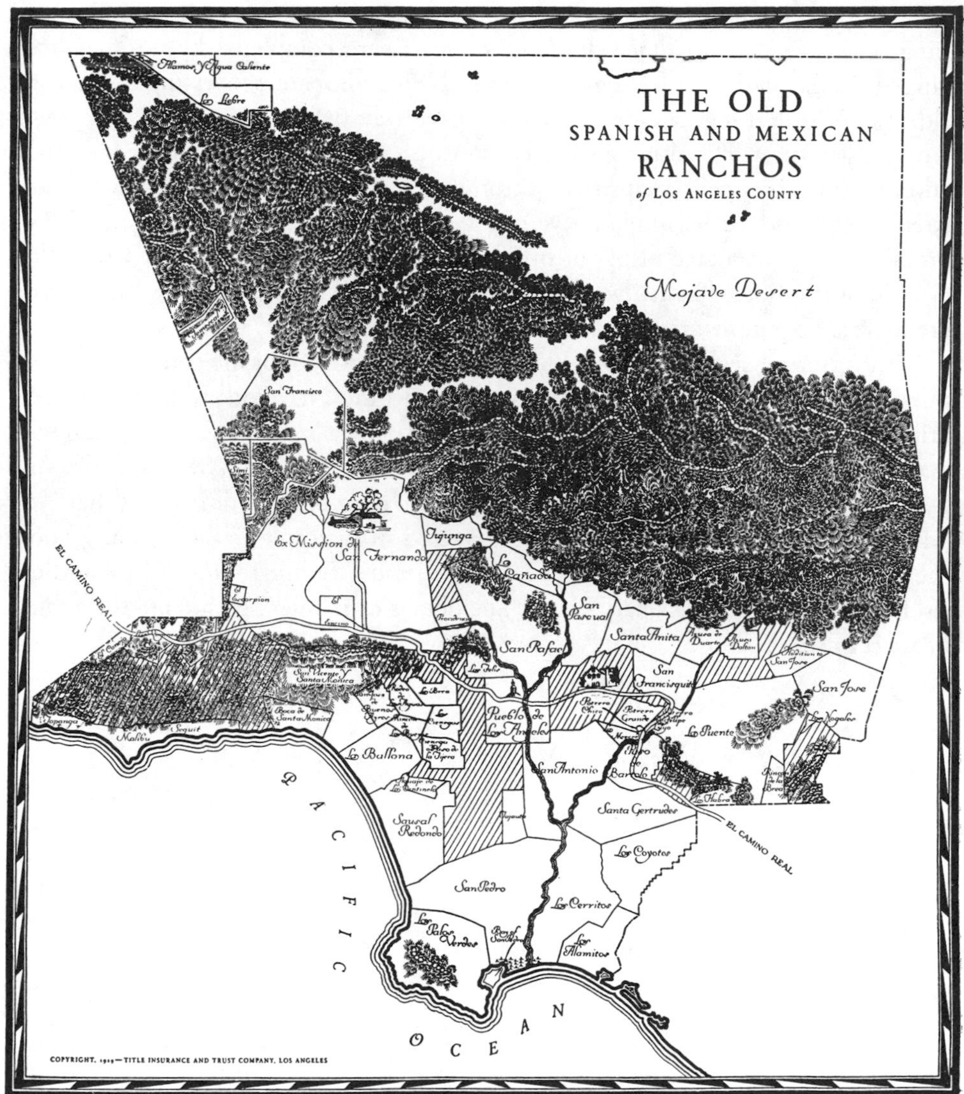

Map 3.6. The old Spanish and Mexican ranches of Los Angeles County. Reproduced by permission of The Huntington Library.

tary officers, as well as Franciscans) from ordinary Mexicans (troops, artisans, and colonists) who were mostly "mestizo."[98] Charles Dwight Willard describes the pre-American social structure as "not unlike that of the Deep South: the Indians were the slaves, the *gente de razon* were the plantation owners or 'whites,' and the Mexicans were the 'poor whites.'"[99]

Landownership was a fundamental object of dispute in the wake of the conquest. The Land Grant Act of 1851 required confirmation of titles by the Mexican owners of *ranchos,* which proved disastrous for them. "At least 40% of the land owned under Mexican grants was sold, by the owners, to meet the costs . . . involved in complying with the Act."[100] Once the land surveys were completed by 1860, parcels changed hands rapidly, with "Anglo" individuals and companies investing in extensive holdings. Within a few decades, ranching "gave way before agricultural and town-founding activities."[101] Although the censuses of 1860 and 1870 showed vintners as dominating the small "industrial" sector, some manufacturing had appeared, and entrepreneurs and businessmen arrived by sea from New England, Texas, and even Europe to take advantage of opportunities in the "new" settlement. However, they were still outnumbered by native Californians, who, because they had lost their lands, were increasingly proletarianized into wage and farm laborers.[102]

But Los Angeles still remained outside the rail network of the country and continued to be dwarfed by San Francisco, itself far behind New York and Chicago. Not until the next period, when rail lines opened—at first via San Francisco but then with direct connections to the East—would the history of modern Los Angeles begin. And when it started, it ran counter to national trends. The economic difficulties that New York experienced in the 1870s were counteracted in Chicago by the building boom engendered by the Great Fire and in Los Angeles by the migration of new settlers, who fueled its first expansionary phase. The details of the next period are the subject of Part II of this book.

PART II

The Establishment of the Triumvirate: From Stock Market Crash (1873) to Stock Market Crash (1929)

The Establishment of the Triumvirate: From Stock Market Crash (1873) to Stock Market Crash (1929)

THE INTERNATIONAL CONTEXT

There is no more sensitive indicator of the extent to which the post–Civil War economy of the United States was becoming enmeshed in the core world system—still centered in Britain and on the European continent—than the rapidity with which economic crises spread from one part of the system to another. The American crises of 1873–74 and 1893 were triggered by severe contractions in Europe, which served to "dry up" capital investments in the United States—primarily the British investments in railways that had facilitated so much of the western expansion. But the effects of the late-nineteenth-century depressions were less severe in the New World than on the European continent.[1] The reverse was true by the 1920s, when the crisis spread from the United States to Europe. That primarily American crash reverberated in Europe, albeit less severely.

These crises represented more than normal business cycles. They bracketed a much longer economic fluctuation associated with basic restructuring, a cycle first identified by the Russian economist Kondratiev.[2] As Hobsbawm astutely observes:

> The operations of a capitalist economy are never smooth, and fluctuations of various length, often very severe, are integral parts of . . . running the affairs of the world. The so-called "trade cycle" of boom and slump was familiar . . . from the nineteenth century [on] . . . [and was] expected to repeat itself . . . every seven to eleven years. A rather more lengthy periodicity had first begun to attract attention at the end of the nineteenth century, as observers looked back on the . . . previous decades. *A spectacular record-breaking global boom from about 1850 to the early 1870s had been followed by twenty-odd years of economic uncertainties* . . . and then

> another evidently secular forward surge of the world economy. . . . In the early 1920s a Russian economist, N. D. Kondratiev . . . discerned a pattern of economic development since the late eighteenth century through a series of "long waves" of from fifty to sixty years.[3]

The process of economic globalization[4] expanded dramatically from the early 1890s up to the start of the First World War; during that expansionary phase, world trade more than doubled. A period of retrenchment followed, during which "the integration of the world economy stagnated or regressed." By the late 1920s, international trade had barely recovered to its prewar level, before plummeting during the Depression, when "the international flow of capital seemed to dry up. Between 1927 and 1933 international lending dropped by over 90 per cent."[5]

These fluctuations in the international system provide the general context within which developments in American global cities must be placed, even though conditions were not exactly parallel, largely because the United States suffered considerably less than Europe (and indeed may have profited) from the disastrous effects of what, combining together the two world wars of the twentieth century, Hobsbawm calls Europe's "30 years war."[6] Chapters 4, 5, and 6 examine urban developments in New York, Chicago, and Los Angeles during the (roughly) fifty-five-year Kondratiev cycle that began in the latter nineteenth century and terminated in the Great Depression of the 1930s.

Henceforth, international events would reverberate throughout the nation, exercising a profound "common" influence on the fates of the three cities. The reluctant entry of the United States into World War I marked the end of American isolationism, even though that impulse would reappear in the late 1930s to delay the American entry into World War II.[7] In the aftermath of the second war, however, American international involvement and, indeed, at least temporary hegemony prevailed until the late 1960s or early 1970s, the final breaking point in our chronology, which marks the beginning of the fifth cycle of urbanization.

THE NATIONAL CONTEXT

In the course of the two generations between the financial collapse of 1873–74 and the Great Depression that followed the stock market crash of October 1929, New York, Chicago, and Los Angeles took on distinctive characteristics that continue to differentiate them from one another. They diverged in population composition, economic functions, and physical form, becoming more unlike one another than they would ever be again. In some ways, one might view their "convergence" as world cities after the Second World War as the "mirror image" of their divergence as regional capitals between 1874 and 1929.

Such a characterization, however, is confounded by several paradoxes. Why is it that the cities diverged in character at exactly the time the United States itself was becoming more enmeshed (and in an irreversible manner) with the European-centered world system; when the American national market was solidifying, integrating the three cities into a continental urban system that achieved virtually final form by the end of the nineteenth century; and when political policies at the national level increasingly impinged upon their own local uniqueness?

Common integration with the world was not the only thing these cities shared. It is paradoxical that the natures of the three urban regions were diverging at the very time that the U.S. system of cities had expanded to reach almost its present form. The "closing of the urban frontier" in the terminal years of the nineteenth century meant that very few cities of significance would subsequently be added to the system, although existing conurbations would expand to encompass whole regions. By the 1920s, this system of cities had become a truly completed and integrated functioning unit, producing a national economy within the context of a greatly entailed and integrated international economy. Whereas in the preceding periods, one could speak of growing connections among the three places, these intercity linkages were still supplementary to the basic core-hinterland organization that shaped each region. From the 1870s on, a national market had begun to take precedence, and by the time of the Great Depression, demographic, economic, and physical connections among the cities had become integral to the functioning of each. The cities were linked in deep symbiosis, which occasionally operated synergistically but often put them, at least in their own eyes, in zero-sum competition with one another.

In another paradox, differences in the demographic compositions of the three regions also became more marked during this crucial period, just at the time when the national government became more deeply involved in setting up uniform laws to regulate immigration. After the great "second wave" of immigration to the United States that peaked between the 1880s and World War I, the federal government placed drastic restrictions on entry to the United States.[8] After 1914, the war in Europe curtailed "natural" flows of immigrants from eastern and southern Europe to the United States; new immigrant streams were therefore unavailable to meet war-induced labor shortages in the industries of New York and Chicago. Firms in both cities engaged in active recruitment of black labor from the South, although New York drew its new labor force from the more urbanized eastern seaboard of the South and from the Caribbean, whereas Chicago depended almost exclusively on workers from rural and backward agricultural states, especially Mississippi. The 1920s, therefore, witnessed the emergence of segregated "black ghettos" in both cities: the South Side "Black Belt" in Chicago and the northern Manhattan district of Harlem.

Los Angeles, which at the start of this period had one of the most "Anglo" and native-born populations of any city in the country, was little affected by the reductions in European immigration. Although the city also attracted some African American migrants from the Midwest and Southwest, the war did not inhibit Southern California's supply of Mexican labor, either for agricultural or urban purposes, although with the exception of oil extraction and shipping, Los Angeles experienced little additional industrial demand.[9]

When World War I ended, fears of a labor surplus and a renewed surge of "nativism" led to national restrictions on immigration (in federal laws passed in 1917,

1921, and 1924).[10] These restrictions, however, had very different impacts on the three urbanized areas. Although quotas were established for all European sending countries and Asians were subject to exclusion rules (the Oriental Exclusion Laws for Chinese and the "Gentlemen's Agreement" limiting the admission of Japanese, expanded by the new laws to exclude persons from the enormous "barred zone" of Asia), immigrants from the Caribbean as well as from Central and Latin America were temporarily exempted from the restrictive quotas. This allowed significant numbers of Jamaicans to settle in New York (thus joining the extant black population of that city) and permitted Mexican immigration to cities and farms in the Southwest, including California. It even led to a modest influx of Mexicans in Chicago.

Industrialization was also a common force during this critical half century of urban transformation. Steam and then electricity had long supplanted water power as the chief energy sources in the factories of America, and the "consumption" of this inanimate energy, largely for production, increased tenfold during the period, rising from 43,000 horsepower per 100,000 persons in 1870 to 492,000 per 100,000 persons by 1920.[11] Industrial differences among the three cities, however, were marked; each city developed a unique mix of industrial enterprises, its own typical "scale" of plant, and its own pattern of industrial relations.

New York continued to concentrate on consumer products (and services) that were produced in relatively small-scale factories and workshops. Although unionization made significant progress during the period and labor mobilizations were frequent, labor organizations (with the exception of workers in the port and transport services) were faced with the challenge of unifying workers scattered in diffuse plants and workplaces. In proto-Fordist Chicago, where heavy industrial goods produced in large plants rapidly became the typical modus operandi, the scale of plantwide unionization was commensurately large and the confrontations between "capital" and "labor" more acrimonious and conflictual.

Los Angeles's industrial mix was less coherent: heavy industry was still confined to oil extraction, and in the 1920s, the city's chief "industry" had become the making of motion pictures.[12] Unionization there also followed a distinctive pattern. The late-nineteenth-century boosters of the city had advertised, among the attractions of Los Angeles, the fact that the city had an "open shop," as contrasted with the strong union mobilizations in San Francisco.[13] And whatever progress union organizing had made was undermined by the repression that followed the bombing of the *Los Angeles Times* building in 1910; thereafter, union organizers were tarred with the brush of anarchy and then communism. Furthermore, it was not until the years just before the start of World War II that Los Angeles became the recipient of "heavy industry" (automobiles, tires, and eventually aircraft) and a commensurate increase in the demands of unions.

And finally, differences emerged despite the cities' common exposure not only to an increasingly unified national urban system and the development of a national market, but to common trends in the national political system and in commonly evolving redefinitions of the functions of municipal government.

THE MUNICIPAL CONTEXT

During the last decade of the nineteenth century and the opening ones of the twentieth, all three cities underwent transformations in their internal political balances of power, as the nationwide Progressive movement, coupled with the increased complexities of providing "modern" utilities, services, and administrations to cities, led to municipal reforms and new structures for urban governance. In a world increasingly driven by technological imperatives and governed by the new ideology of reform, defined as "depoliticization," all three cities tried to substitute civil service for political appointments and placed their faith in the "technical solutions" of engineers to pressing infrastructural problems.[14] Municipal administrations throughout the country were redefined, so that running cities became increasingly like governing large corporations.

However, the political structures established before the advent of Progressivism yielded somewhat different balances of power between neighborhoods and central regimes, between patronage and civil service, and between politics and technocratism in the three cities. Although in all cases the mayor's role was strengthened, and along with that his executive/administrative apparatus for governing, the mayor's powers vis-à-vis more locality-based representation in city councils and commissioners with whom he shared power varied from city to city.

In New York, the newly consolidated Board of Estimate and Appropriations (1898), led by the presidents of the unified boroughs and the mayor, who was elected by voters in all five boroughs as *primus inter pares,* reduced the political strength of "ward heelers" and councilmen (aldermen) elected by their neighborhoods to protect and advance their (often ethnically defined) interests. In Chicago, which had by far the strongest tradition of neighborhood representation through a powerful city council, this system of local prerogatives persisted even though the mayor's office took on more and more responsibility for day-to-day administration of the increasingly complex services offered by the city. In Los Angeles, where local representation had not developed prior to the advent of the Progressive Era, the system of a limited number of council members/commissioners (now still only fifteen for the city and five for the county) precluded the development of heavily invested local representatives.[15]

Another paradox of this period was that although all three urbanized areas were forced to cope with the rapid expansion of their built-up areas beyond existing municipal limits, the special circumstances in which each found itself created unique possibilities and constraints; each city thus had to utilize a different strategy to solve the problem of spatial spread. Although, ideally, each might have preferred to unify all urbanized areas within its jurisdiction, this solution was constrained by the cities' special histories and geographies.

New York's solution, to some extent forced by the prior existence of the very large independent city of Brooklyn, was to consolidate the four adjoining counties (called boroughs; the Bronx designation as a borough came later), all located within New York State, into a federated system, with a common Board of Estimate and Appropriations, a common mayor, new officers called borough presidents, and an expanded legislative council.[16] But resistance on Long Island and the persistence of "irrational" state boundary lines prevented a wider incorporation of "fringe" areas, some of which already contained large established cities (such as Newark). And after the consolidation of 1898, no boundary adjustments occurred.[17]

At the same time, in the final decades of the nineteenth century, Chicago was engaged in a vigorous campaign to annex to the city all the remaining townships within Cook County, although many suburban towns resisted annexation.[18] Between 1869 and 1893 vast peripheral areas were absorbed into the city limits. After that, the pace of annexation virtually ground to a halt, so that by 1915 only four additional small areas had been added. Chicago's city boundaries today are virtually coterminous with those that had been established by 1915; only tiny boundary adjustments were later possible.[19]

Los Angeles presents a sharply contrasting case. By 1900 the city had annexed several small contiguous zones around its core, expanding from the twenty-eight-square-mile area established when the city was first incorporated, following the American conquest, to some forty-three square miles. Modest incremental additions were recorded up to 1912, when the annexation of Arroyo Seco brought the city's area to somewhat over one hundred square miles. The most significant of these annexations was the so-called shoestring addition of 1906, which created the umbilical cord to the distant town of Wilmington (consolidated in 1909) and facilitated the annexation of Wilmington's southern neighbor, the newly improved port of San Pedro. This established a precedent for the piecemeal expansion of the city's limits to encompass noncontiguous and scattered zones, a precedent that was dramatically unleashed in the next phase.

However, a number of the oil-producing suburbs, which enjoyed high incomes and low tax rates, continued to resist the enticements of municipal services that were offered in return for joining the city.[20] It was only after the completion of the Owens Valley Aqueduct in 1913 that, using the carrot-and-stick pressure of its monopoly over a water supply in the semiarid region, Los Angeles succeeded in annexing many communities within Los Angeles County. The most important of the postaqueduct annexations occurred in 1915, when the newly irrigated San Fernando Valley added 170 square miles to the city's boundaries. Annexations to the city continued throughout the next half century, although as early as the 1940s, even as voters in some zones exercised their option to approve annexation, other important areas (among them Burbank, Beverly Hills, and Culver City) were exercising the opposite option: detaching from the city to join other encapsulated independent towns such as Santa Monica that had never merged with the city. Once the "Lakewood option" became available in the late 1950s, making it possible for independently incorporated towns to contract their various municipal services directly from Los Angeles County, the motivation to join the city was not strong enough to outweigh the disadvantages of additional taxes and the loss of local autonomy.[21]

Therefore, before the 1920s, annexation as an adequate solution to the boundary problem had become virtually impossible in New York and Chicago; and even Los Angeles, despite its more liberal annexation possibilities, also began to come to terms with the fact that regional growth in the new type of spreading metropolis was proceeding faster than annexation could ever keep up with. By then, the vast conurbations and galaxylike metropolitan areas that were developing could no longer be logically encompassed within contiguous borders. Each region, in its own way, had to develop techniques for coordination with its hinterlands through regional plans and special-purpose administrative structures. It is not insignificant that both New York and Los Angeles tried to develop "regional plans" in the late 1920s, even though there existed no administrative mechanisms for their implementation.

THE ARTS OF CITY BUILDING

Architecturally, the appearance of the three cities also diverged during this crucial period. The years between 1874 and 1929 were particularly vital in terms of the arts of city building, in which New York and Chicago, but only to a limited extent Los Angeles, solidified in brick, mortar, and stone, their central business districts taking on characteristic appearances that persist to this day. During the final decades of the nineteenth century, both New York and Chicago began with a common heritage copied from the beaux arts revival in Europe, although by the early twentieth century their architectural styles had begun to diverge.

The vigorous "Chicago school" of skyscraper construction produced clean lines and a delicately embossed surface decor, pioneered by Louis Sullivan, whereas New York continued to follow a wonderfully chaotic juxtapositioning of European-inspired extravaganzas. Los Angeles began, in its very central "downtown" zone (now much degraded), with the architectural repertoires of both eastern and midwestern cities, constructing elaborately embossed "heavy" structures of stone and steel. But by the 1920s and 1930s, the art deco style, which saw only modest applications in New York and virtually none in Chicago, began to dominate the newer commercial zones of Los Angeles.[22]

Surprisingly enough, it was an event that took place in a city that had already been displaced at the top of the American urban hierarchy that set New York's and Chicago's model for the future: the Philadelphia Centennial Exhibit of 1876, which put beaux arts on the American architectural map and lay the foundations not only for buildings and structures but for the form and planning of cities themselves.[23] The Chicago World's Fair of 1893 and the Burnham Plan for Chicago of 1909 that grew out of it were created in part by New York architects and planners (McKim, Mead & White), and at least one participant (Charles Dyer Norton), who had been the chair of the sponsoring Commercial Club when the Burnham Plan was promulgated, went on to New York, where he later became a founder of the Regional Plan Association for that city.

By the 1920s, city and regional master plans were proliferating throughout the country, often emanating from a common set of actors and increasingly following a common model. The period was characterized by the emergence of "professional" planners (from both the older occupation of landscape architect, which assumed chief responsibility for physical planning, and the newer-style lawyers who designed the zoning and subdivision regulations that were to guide/enforce compliance). A number of these new planning professionals were itinerant consultants, moving from city to city with their wares, so that parallels are not difficult to account for.

Commonalities were also nurtured through the promulgation of "model" state enabling legislation, recommended by professional associations. These laws were designed to permit municipalities to make overall plans and to establish land-use controls through zoning ordinances and, eventually, subdivision regulations. Model local ordinances were also recommended and many cities simply adopted them. Although such regulations remained controversial, by 1926 the U.S. Supreme Court had validated the right of cities and towns to use their police powers to regulate land uses, which unleashed almost universal applications.

Although all three cities adopted such laws, the paradox here was that zoning regulations are, of course, not retroactive. This meant that whereas they could, potentially at least, be used to "good" advantage in the newer urbanized region of Los Angeles, which still had large amounts of agricultural land within its overbounded limits not yet converted to urban uses (especially in the San Fernando Valley), they and, even more, the accompanying subdivision regulations were less effective in more established cities. They had little effect on Manhattan, where built-up preexisting zones had already foreclosed the possibility of prior planning and where new subdivisions were moving beyond the city's jurisdiction.[24] And they had only slightly more influence on Chicago's development, because that city was already reaching its limits to further annexation. Therefore, "generation" and boundaries yielded very different results in the three regions.

These are some of the critical comparisons that will come out more clearly in the chapters that follow.

PERIODICITY AND ORGANIZATION

It is useful to subdivide this lengthy and crucial period into three subcycles that conform to major shifts in the economy: 1873 (a depression) to 1893 (another low point), about 1893 to 1917 (the entry of the United States into World War I), and from 1918 to the crash of 1929. The first witnessed a short-lived building boom in all three cities, during which population increased, prices rose, and new areas were opened for urban settlement. This boom soon proved temporary, as markets collapsed in all three cities from common economic pressures.

The second was a planning phase in which annexations added extensive peripheral areas to the political control of the expanded central cities and in which mass-transit lines and municipal services were extended to encompass these newly annexed zones. It ushered in a changed era in local politics as well, as reforms associated with the Progressive Era (such as the expansion of civil service) brought new elites to the fore and required new relationships between the public and private sectors.

The third period was paradoxically one of "retrenchment," of delinking from international connections and imposing restrictions on immigration, at the same time that internal economic overexpansion and an explosion in the availability of credit for speculation overheated urban growth. This phase ended abruptly with the crash of 1929.

In conformity with the conventional approach that makes the technologies of transport, energy, and communication central to understanding urban changes, I begin with these variables. However, I shall also demonstrate that social and political innovations were of equal importance in creating the three metropolises. Although one could argue that all were exposed to similar trends in transport, energy sources, and modes of communication, their approaches to integrating and controlling these capabilities were highly distinctive. And these differences are still operative, as I shall argue.

CHAPTER 4

New York Solidifies Its Character

Between the depressions of 1874 and 1929, New York experienced three significant "spirals" of growth, ones that both drove and were facilitated by major advances in transport and communications. Each was fed by its own demographic dynamic and each was accompanied by its own form of political reorganization.

The first cycle spanned the building boom bracketed between two severe economic contractions, which occurred in the early 1870s and in the early 1890s. During this growth cycle, most expansion took place on Manhattan Island itself, and the force behind it was massive immigration from abroad.[1] Stimulated by this infusion, major changes in land uses and heightened densities became evident in the already built-up portions of the island. Industrial establishments multiplied, assisted by the virtually unlimited supplies of cheap immigrant labor and fueled by the new demands for affordable housing and for an urban infrastructure that the expanding population and a redefinition of municipal functions and standards entailed.

At first, some still-existing vacant spaces were filled in, primarily on the eastern side of the island, as new tenement houses were constructed on the Lower East Side to accommodate the immigrants.[2] This immigrant "port of entry" became grossly overcrowded, as we shall see. The lower tip of Manhattan also became more densely developed, but also more exclusively commercial, industrial, and administrative, as taller structures replaced many of the brownstones and mansions formerly occupied by Gotham's movers and shakers. The wealthy were relocating to midtown and upper Fifth Avenue along the eastern borders of Central Park. There was even some expansion into the periphery, as the original farming village of Harlem was transformed into New York's "first suburb," and as the still-independent town of Brooklyn became more closely integrated with Manhattan and began to sprout its own suburbs.

The population infusions led to increased social segregation between the "classes" and even "castes" in the city.[3] And the struggles for power—between old and new elites, between old and new immigrants, and between old and new models for government—set the basic framework for New York's divisive politics, or, to put it more positively, honed the skills of multiple groups to form coalitions and to negotiate outcomes. These became parts of the political culture of the city, a civic culture that in many ways still operates in the present.

The second cycle, from the turn of the century through World War I, was marked by a maturation of New York's economy as an industrial and commercial powerhouse and by the refinement of its complex financial system, which increasingly dominated the nation. One of the most important changes in this period was the political consolidation of Manhattan with its peripheral boroughs, which, in one fell swoop, vastly multiplied the area and almost doubled the population within the city's jurisdiction. A commensurate physical unification was achieved through the construction of bridges and then of a vast subway system to supplement (and eventually replace) the elevated street railways already in use, although the last elevated line in Manhattan would not be demolished until 1958. The larger city experimented with a variety of rules, regulations on land uses, and inchoate attempts to plan future developments, casting a competitive eye on Chicago's Master Plan of 1909 but unable to replicate that feat. Toward the end of the second cycle, however, foreign immigration ceased to be the driving force of demographic growth. European immigrants were beginning to be replaced by a migration of southern-born (and Caribbean) African Americans to the city during the war-induced labor shortages that appeared during World War I.

The third cycle, which began in earnest as the war drew to a close, saw a sharp drop in immigration from abroad due to drastically restrictive changes in U.S. immigration laws, continued black migration from the South, and a new burst of explosive construction that pushed the envelope of development well beyond the city's limits, as fast-growing suburban communities began to dot the adjacent counties of Nassau, Westchester, and even Suffolk. This period also witnessed the start of a process known as residential "white flight"—at first from overcrowded Manhattan to the more expansive districts of the so-called outer boroughs, and eventually farther out into the suburban fringe.[4] In some congested zones, such as the Lower East Side, the population simply thinned out to more bearable densities; in other neighborhoods, the spaces freed up by departing residents were made available to the growing black community. It was during this third period that Harlem became the largest African American "city" in the world.

By the early twentieth century, it had become absolutely impossible to extend New York City's boundaries. This meant that its legal jurisdiction fell increasingly short of its metropolitan extent. Coordinated developments became more difficult, and different mechanisms, outside existing political structures, had to be invented. It was then that special districts and "authorities" were institutionalized to supplement and even substitute for municipal rule, and informal "regional" plans were advocated to guide a metropolitan expansion that could no longer be encompassed by city government. Because of New York's unique constellation of waterways, ports, and "inconvenient" state boundaries, this required inventiveness of the highest order.

Paralleling the process of horizontal expansion was a shift upward in the vertical scale, and here, too, the "role of the state" was central. True skyscrapers came to dominate the skyline of lower Manhattan, as steel-frame structures and elevators became the taken-for-granted clichés of new construction. Zoning, first experimented with in New York City in 1916, was adopted as a planning mechanism for controlling densities and land uses in the city.[5] It also had a forming effect on the skyline of Manhattan, as we shall see later.

THE NEW ERA BEGINS WITH IMMIGRATION

By 1880, the total population of Manhattan was approaching 1.2 million, and almost all the land south of 42nd Street had been built up. The next wave of demographic increase would push settlement uptown and would thus mark a transformation not only of the Upper East Side but of more outlying zones as well. Much of the city's subsequent growth would not have occurred without immigration, especially because, in the late nineteenth century as during the contemporary period, there may even have been a net out-migration of native-born New Yorkers from Manhattan. Their loss was more than compensated for by foreign immigrants.

The year 1881 marks the beginning of the great emigration of Jews from Russia and of Italian peasants from the *mezzogiorno*.[6] Between 1881 and 1905 some 850,000 new immigrants arrived in New York, where most of them remained. Their chief urban "port of entry" was the Lower East Side, which experienced a tremendous spurt in tenement-house construction to accommodate them.[7] Severe overcrowding accompanied this influx. Indeed, during the half century of immigration between 1855 and 1905, the population living on Manhattan's Lower East Side (below 14th Street and east of the Bowery) increased two and a half times, from just under 200,000 in 1855 to more than 518,000 by 1905. The total peaked at 542,000 in 1910, at which time almost two out of every three residents had been born abroad and the district was reputed to be the most densely settled urban quarter in the world.[8]

This immigrant labor fed the growing garment trade, which preempted more and more space in downtown loft structures, thus heightening the competition among residential, commercial, and industrial users. And it intensified the city's quintessential characteristic—its cultural and linguistic diversity. As Jackson has pointed out, New York was (and still remains)

> particularly unusual in the extraordinary heterogeneity of its citizens. Between 1890 and 1919, more than 23 million Europeans emigrated to the United States; about 17 million of them disembarked in New York. . . . as early as 1880 more than half of the city's working population was foreign-born, providing New York with the largest immigrant labour force on earth. Half a century later, the city still contained two million foreign born . . . and an even larger number of persons of foreign parentage. . . . New York [was] . . . a hodge-podge of nationalities.[9]

In the 1880s alone, the newcomer Jews from eastern Europe and Italians from southern Europe, who overwhelmed the continuing flow from the older traditional sources in central Europe and the British Isles, infused the city with almost 300,000 additional residents.[10] But it would be a mistake to confuse magnitude with proportion. In 1860, before the second migration wave struck, 47 percent of Manhattan's population of 813,669 had been born outside the United States. Thereafter, the proportion of foreign-born Manhattanites dropped gradually, to 44.5 percent by 1870, before stabilizing at about 40 percent in 1880 and 1890.[11] (The proportion of Manhattan's population that was foreign-born would peak again at 47 percent by 1910, before gently subsiding.)

Dispersal and Uneven Development

This anomaly of a stabilizing proportion of foreign-born at the very time when immigration was peaking can be understood only in the context of the wider region and, more specifically, the relationship between the "twin cities" of Manhattan and Brooklyn (which remained separate municipalities until 1898). Improved transportation connections made possible the diffusion of some heavier industry and an associated labor force from Manhattan to Brooklyn, even before the two cities were juridically joined.

By 1878 Manhattan's elevated railway system was completed, not only binding together the already built-up areas but opening up new ones, such as Harlem and the lower Bronx, for settlement.[12] And finally, in 1883, the Brooklyn Bridge accepted its first wheeled and pedestrian traffic, making it more possible to decentralize industry and residences to the eastern shore of the East River by physically joining the two cities, which, by then, were already functionally linked. This facilitated the development of immigrant "second settlement" areas in hitherto more native-born Brooklyn.[13]

Manhattan's relationship to its "sister city" of Brooklyn (the latter old and already well developed and containing a population half as large as Manhattan's by 1880) was thus changed. Brooklyn began to absorb a larger number of the more established foreign-born and their American-born children. In the two decades following the construction of the bridge, Brooklyn's population soared from about 600,000 (of whom only about 31 percent had been born abroad) to well over a million (37 percent born abroad).[14] If the figures for Manhattan and Brooklyn are cumulated, we find that foreigners constituted 45 percent of their combined population in 1860, 42 percent in 1870, 37 percent in 1880, 39 percent in 1890, and 37 percent as late as 1900. Indeed, between 1880 and 1900 the number of foreign-born residents of Manhattan and Brooklyn increased by more than 600,000 (net of those who merely passed through on their way to other places).[15]

This diffusion of the foreign-born paralleled the general decentralization of population in the metropolitan region that had been taking place since the mid-nineteenth century, but the pace picked up as population burgeoned and transit improved. The metropolitan region had even begun to overflow into the still sparsely settled adjacent counties of Queens, Richmond, and lower Westchester (later the Bronx).

Whereas in 1830 Manhattan contained 84 percent of the total population living in all five boroughs, by 1890, the last census date before their consolidation into "Greater New York City," Manhattan accounted for only 58 percent of the combined population of 2.5 million. By then, another 33 percent were living in Brooklyn. The remaining three boroughs were still very sparsely populated, with the Bronx and Queens accounting for only 3.5 percent each, and Richmond (i.e., Staten Island) containing less than 2 percent.[16] After the consolidation of the five boroughs in 1898, no new territory would be added to enlarge Greater New York's boundaries.[17]

As might therefore be anticipated, there were wide discrepancies in the residential densities of the five boroughs. Pratt points out that Manhattan, as early as 1850, was more densely settled than the other boroughs would be by 1910.[18] By the latter year, when residential densities in Manhattan had reached 166 persons per acre, Greater New York City had an overall density of only 24 persons/acre, and of the four outer boroughs, only Brooklyn, with 33 persons/acre, exceeded this average by a narrow margin.

Not only were there sharp contrasts between the island and the outer boroughs, but by the turn of the century Manhattan itself was beginning to evince more marked class, ethnic, and racial polarities, the visibility of which was heightened by greater residential segregation. As the Lower East Side and Greenwich Village came to be dominated by the new immigrants from eastern and southern Europe, the last remnants of the bourgeoisie deserted lower Manhattan; they followed the wealthy uptown. By the 1880s, "fashionable" residential districts began to appear north of 59th Street along Central Park, thus fulfilling the promises made decades earlier by the park's proponents.

But such movement was highly selective; it followed the perimeter of the park only on its eastern side.[19] The Upper West Side lagged far behind, and that zone was marked particularly by its widespread and desolate empty lots (see Figure 4.1), although development leaped over these neglected spaces to encompass Manhattan's first "true suburb," Harlem, which was opened for upper-class residence in the late 1870s when the elevated rail line was extended to it. Clearly, additional incentives were needed to attract development to the West Side.[20] Therefore, in 1889 proposals were put forth to build Riverside and Morningside Parks, in order to stimulate West Side development.

HANDLING THE BOTTLENECKS

Political Consolidation

By 1890, Manhattan, with a population of 1.4 million, was thus already embedded in a "metropolitanized" zone of some 2.5 million, accessible (as before) by ferries and now, thanks to the Brooklyn Bridge, by a limited land connection as well.[21] What it most required to coordinate its growth with that of its periphery was political unification. As early as 1874, the city had annexed the southernmost portion of Westchester County, but it was not until 1898 that Manhattan, Brooklyn, Queens, Staten Island, and additional parts of Westchester (now known as the Bronx) were consolidated into the five boroughs that today constitute the city of New York.

Figure 4.1. The isolation of the first apartment house in the Upper West Side. View south from the roof of the Dakota apartment house, Central Park West and 72nd Street. Photograph by H. B. Jackson, New York City, 1887. Courtesy of The New-York Historical Society, with thanks to M. Christine Boyer; copyright Collection of The New-York Historical Society.

In 1898, the state legislature approved a new city charter for this larger unit that, together with the amendments passed in 1901 and subsequent years, created the complex federated structure of governance for the city that operated for years to come.[22] The original 1898 charter added a second level to the executive branch headed by the commonly elected mayor—the "presidents" elected from each of the boroughs, who were responsible for local administration and public works at the borough (county) level. Coordination and financial control for the combined boroughs were exercised through a unified Board of Estimate (sometimes called the Board of Estimate and Appropriations).[23] For the legislative branch, amendments in 1901 collapsed the original bicameral Municipal Assembly and Board of Aldermen into a single Board of Aldermen, consisting of seventy-three elected representatives, one from each district in the greater city. Membership on the all-powerful Board of Estimate and Appropriations was expanded to include the presidents of the separate boroughs as well as the mayor, the comptroller, and the president of the Board of Aldermen. The major outlines of this system remained in force, with only minor modifications,[24] until a federal district court ruled, in November 1986, that the Board of Estimate system was unconstitutional because it violated the principle of "one man, one vote." This decision, upheld by the court of appeals and eventually by the U.S. Supreme Court, thus forced a charter revision in 1989 that enlarged the city council and strengthened its powers while significantly weakening the executive branch. But these changes were still in the future.[25]

By the turn of the century, then, Greater New York City had come into existence, pushing the total population to almost three and a half million. This consolidation greatly strengthened the "voice" of the city (and its Democratic machine) vis-à-vis state government and provided it with additional resources and powers to plan for a more coordinated development. Jackson calls the period that followed a "golden age" for the city, a time when the wealth of America was concentrated in its coffers and the talents of its citizens selectively concentrated there as well.

> The years between the consolidation of 1898 and the end of World War Two presented a kind of "golden age" for New York. It contained the largest concentrations of architects, bankers, lawyers, consulting engineers, industrial designers, and corporate officials on the continent. . . . Manhattan became a kind of Main Street to the nation. . . . According to an 1892 survey, New York and Brooklyn contained . . . 30 per cent of the extreme wealth holders in the United States. Another 15 per cent lived in the nearby suburbs.[26]

Physical Unification via the Subway System

Accompanying and facilitated by the political unification was a commensurate and much-needed physical transformation—the construction of a vast subway system that would eventually reach 722 miles in extent, which is about the same number of miles separating New York from Chicago.[27] This integrated the five boroughs via what is still, today, the longest rapid-transit system in the world.

New York was late in beginning this project, although not for lack of interest. It was generally acknowledged that the extant system of mass transit—the elevated railway cars that screeched above the major avenues, darkening the roadways, spewing black smoke into the air, and democratically depositing oil and cinders on the heads of pedestrians below—was totally inadequate for the region's growing needs. Various "schemes" for a subway were first proposed just after London commenced building its underground in the 1860s, but the complexity of preannexation political conditions in New York, coupled with the ongoing tensions between the commercial/business elite and the Tammany machine, as well as understandable fears of uncontrollable graft that were residues of Tweed-era scandals, led to several false starts. The problems were compounded by an ultimate indecisiveness as to how the more ambitious plans for New York could be financed and managed.[28]

By the mid-1870s there was general consensus that faster and cleaner mass transit was needed if urban growth was not to be deflected to zones that lay beyond the taxing jurisdiction of the city.[29] The controversies concerning how to finance and build this enormously ambitious system and who should own it were finally resolved in the 1890s through an arrangement that anticipated the currently much-touted "public-private partnership." The city would finance the project through bonds, but it would be built and managed by and as a business firm.

In 1900 financier and entrepreneur August Belmont[30] agreed to build, equip, and operate the line in return for a long-term lease and $36.5 million to cover land

Figure 4.2. Photograph by Berenice Abbott of the shadows cast by either the Second or the Third Avenue elevated lines. Works Progress Administration project, 1935.

acquisition and construction costs.[31] Politically enabling legislation (the Rapid Transit Act of 1891) was passed in Albany, backed by reform progressives and pushed by a sympathetic governor, and in April 1892 Belmont formed the Interborough Rapid Transit Company (IRT), appointing William Barclay Parsons as his chief engineer. Given the tricky hard schist rock of Manhattan (sometimes fiercely resistant, sometimes cracking perilously) and a terrain that sloped sharply up at the northern end of

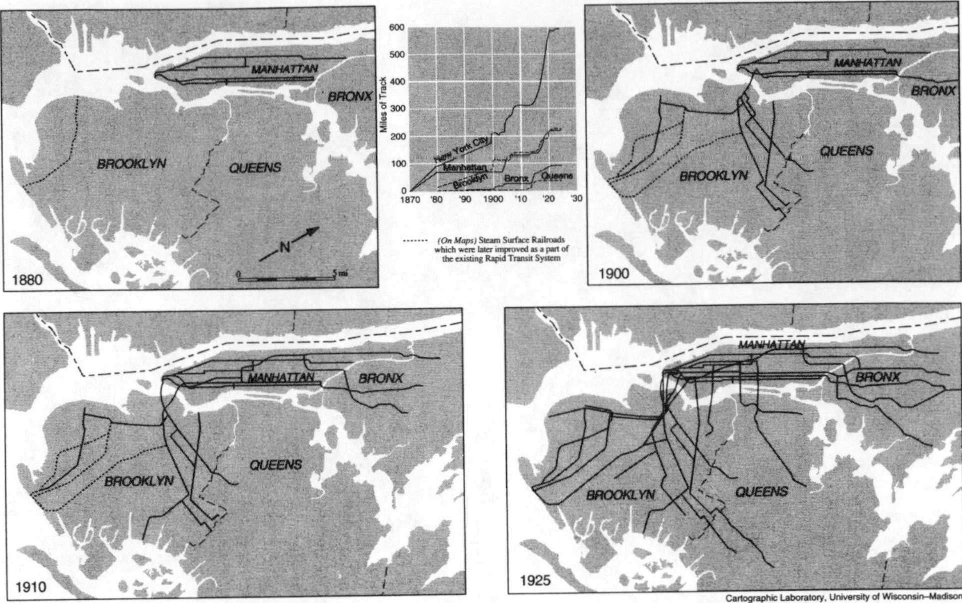

Map 4.1. Expansion of the various New York subway lines, 1880 to 1925.

the island, the engineering challenge was formidable. And, as might have been anticipated, construction took a long time, and the cost overruns were phenomenally large.

Nevertheless, on October 27, 1904, the first segment of the subway line was ceremonially dedicated and then opened to masses of users who stood in line to experience the marvel. By 1908 the IRT lines extended all the way to the Bronx and across the East River to Brooklyn, opening vast territories to urban growth. In just four years the fission of the city into its hinterlands was an accomplished fact. Between 1905 and 1920, the population of Manhattan north of 125th Street "grew 265 percent, to 323,800, and the population of the Bronx advanced 150 percent, to 430,980."[32] Population growth continually outstripped carrying capacity, however, and two other companies were organized to expand the system further: the Brooklyn Manhattan Transit (BMT) and the Independent Subway System (IND). Eventually, they would be brought under a single municipal authority.

In the 1920s and 1930s, when other major cities were favoring highways, neglecting their rapid-transit systems, or, like Los Angeles, abandoning their already proposed plans for more street railways, New York remained adamantly nonconformist. Even as late as 1990, almost half of the labor force living in the five boroughs used public transportation to get to work. Contrast this with the less than 20 percent in Cook County (including Chicago) and the 6.5 percent in Los Angeles County (including the city of Los Angeles) who depended upon mass transit for their journeys to work.[33] If one were looking for the truly basic variable that distinguishes New York from Chicago and Los Angeles and gives rise to its unique form of city building and city life, this would be it.

THE FURTHER DECENTRALIZATION OF RESIDENCES AND EMPLOYMENT

The effects on Manhattan of this revolution in transport were dramatic. The mass-transit system facilitated the separation of work from residence, the conversion of high-value land on the island to concentrated commercial uses, and the dispersal of residences to what came to be called the "outer boroughs."[34] As Jackson points out:

> The population of Manhattan reached a peak of 2.3 million in 1910. By 1940, it had declined to 1.9 million. . . . The outlying boroughs . . . exhibited a strong contrary pattern. Brooklyn . . . grew from 1.2 million in 1890 to 2.7 million in 1940. . . . Scarcely developed at all and containing only 89,000 inhabitants in 1890, the Bronx was covered with six- and eight-storey apartments . . . by 1940 when its population reached 1.4 million. Queens blossomed from less than 100,000 in 1890 to 1.3 million in 1940. . . . *about one-half of the population [of NYC] in 1905 lived within four miles of City Hall; by 1925, the percentage in this area was below 30.*[35]

THE GROWTH AND DECENTRALIZATION OF EMPLOYMENT

As we have already seen, decentralization of population had already begun as early as the mid-nineteenth century, but the pace picked up decisively after political consolidation and subway construction. Once the boroughs were united politically and physically, the locations of employment sites began to shift with these changes in the shape and functions of the metropolitan region. However, their effects were not uniform; some functions decentralized whereas others became even more concentrated at the core.

It must be emphasized that manufacturing, in general, had been increasing at a remarkable pace, both in Manhattan and in the outer boroughs. Pratt estimates that in the fifty years between 1860 and 1910 the value of manufactured products in the New York region increased from $159 million to $1.5 billion, with most of the increase occurring in the final decades of that half century.[36] In part, this reflected both the dramatic multiplication of individual firms, which rose from 4,317 in the early year to almost 26,000 by 1906, and the increased number of workers employed in manufacturing, which rose from 91,671 in 1860 to 611,738 by 1910.[37]

While such figures parallel the process of industrialization that was occurring in other major urban centers around the turn of the century, Pratt's study highlights one of the unique and continuing features of manufacturing in New York, namely, the degree to which it resisted the increases in plant scale evident in other industrial centers such as Chicago (see Chapter 5) and Philadelphia.[38] In 1860, the average number of workers per manufacturing establishment in Manhattan had been nineteen; by 1900 this had actually dropped to an average of thirteen for the five boroughs and fourteen for Manhattan alone. As we shall see, this had major implications for industrial relations and the form that unionization and labor mobilization would take in the city.

A second notable feature of New York's manufacturing sector was the persistence of lower Manhattan's dominance as an industrial district, despite the proliferation of

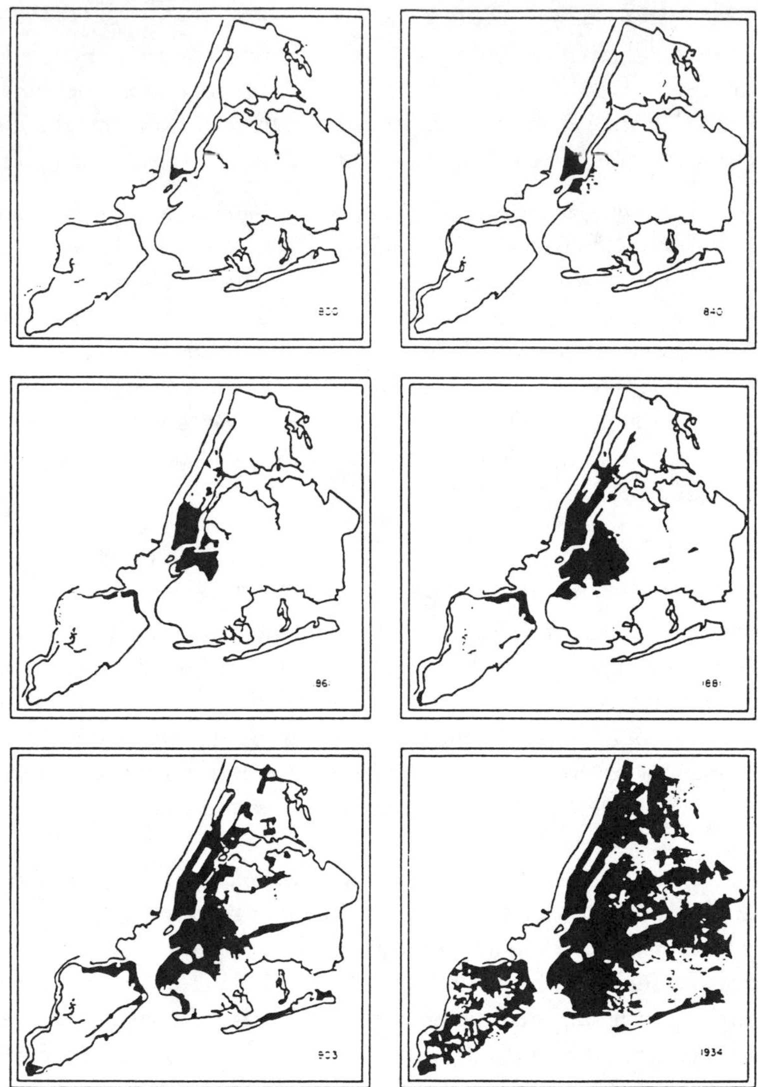

Map 4.2. The growth of settled areas of New York City, 1800 to 1934. Courtesy of the Federal Housing Administration, Washington, D.C.

plants being newly established in or moving to the outer boroughs. In 1860, Manhattan had accounted for an overwhelming 78 percent of all establishments and 85 percent of all jobs in manufacturing in the five-borough region. But even as late as 1900, 68 percent of all establishments and 75 percent of all workers in manufacturing were still on the island. The concentration was even more extreme than these figures suggest, because almost all industrial activity was found on the southern tip of the island, below 14th Street.[39]

Garment manufacturing remained concentrated in that area of Manhattan, although bundle or piecework was sent out to second-settlement immigrant areas in the

Bronx and Brooklyn. Printing also remained in the center city, as did such consumer-linked trades as baking, slaughtering, and custom furniture making. But decentralization of bulkier and more noxious industries was well under way; such firms were departing to lower-cost land, particularly because a local labor force was now available off the island. This trend was noted with approval as early as 1911, in Pratt's remarkably detailed and prescient study of the causes of Manhattan's residential congestion.

After studying the demographic developments in both Manhattan and the outlying boroughs, surveying the growth of industry in the city, and even interviewing a variety of industrialists about their decisions to remain in Manhattan or to relocate, Pratt concluded:

> There has been considerable movement of manufactures from Manhattan, which has taken two directions. First, there has been a removal of factories to the outlying or suburban districts of the metropolitan area. This is a distinct movement from the center of the city to its periphery. In the second place, there has been a movement from the city to more distant points entirely outside the industrial district of New York. The industrial history of New York City furnishes several instances of the removal of entire industries. Iron foundries have long ceased to exist in Manhattan; the stone and marble cutters found property too expensive and moved to the Long Island City waterfront; the boot and shoe industry needed air and light; it moved out of Manhattan, many factories going to Brooklyn. Some of the largest industries in the nearby Jersey towns were once located in New York City. The movement is going on slowly but steadily; factories are moving out of Manhattan and others are preparing to leave.[40]

And, as he predicted, this trend continued. By 1919 much of the electronics industry had moved to New Jersey, and by 1929, Chicago had displaced New York as the chief producer of electronics.

Compensating for the stagnation in the growth of its heavy industry, Manhattan concentrated even more on its important function as the center of "information" for the United States. By 1885, the city was already the nation's leader in publishing, having "swept past Boston as the centre of book and magazine publishing." Not only headquarters but printing establishments continued to be centralized in lower Manhattan, in part because of the availability of skilled labor, in part because of proximity to publishers and writers. "And when the new science of telecommunications developed in the 1920s, New York became the home of the major radio and television [*sic*] networks."[41]

Producer and corporate services also continued their dominance as contributors to the city's economic base, and these, too, were located almost exclusively in lower Manhattan. Stock market transactions grew many times over, as partnerships and limited companies gave way to corporate forms of organization,[42] and as ownership, in the form of stocks, was separated from the managerial functions performed by a new class of "professionals." Bankers, brokers, lawyers, and workers in insurance firms were all overrepresented in Manhattan, in comparison with both the nation and the rest of the metropolitan area.[43]

Also remaining concentrated in Manhattan, however, were a large variety of jobs at the lowest end of the class spectrum, not only in the highly exploitative garment industry, but in many of the menial occupations that served the growing consumption demands of the wealthy: domestics, janitors, hotel and restaurant workers, and the like. All of these occupations shared one characteristic. Instead of workers being congregated in large factories, which Marx had predicted would create the conditions for class consciousness and labor mobilization, they were employed in multiple scattered sites, which precluded easy contacts and solidarity. It is therefore all the more remarkable that these trades were among the first to be unionized; some of the first significant strikes in New York were mounted in these occupations.[44]

The garment trade, in particular, became increasingly subject to labor strife, given that it employed the largest number of "industrial" workers in New York. The year 1909 marks the "Uprising of the Twenty Thousand," which demonstrated the growing strength of the International Ladies' Garment Workers' Union. Especially after the disastrous Triangle Shirtwaist Company fire in 1911, agitation for better working conditions grew.[45] Mobilization spread to the fur workers and also to the hotel workers, another of the earliest occupations to organize. Both struck against their employers in 1912. Two years later, the Amalgamated Clothing Workers Union was founded, adding to the bargaining power of workers and incorporating even those who had moved to the Bronx and Brooklyn.[46]

The peculiar organization of these trades, concentrated in Manhattan but at so many small sites, may paradoxically have facilitated more labor strength. While it was true that Manhattan employers benefited from the enormous immigrant pool to obtain cheap and to some extent easily substitutable workers, employees also had the (often dubious) advantage of being able to choose among a large number of possible places of employment, which reduced their dependence upon and commitment to a single employer. In a trenchant passage, Pratt compares the trade-offs between firms located in less diversified places, where workers might be more loyal but not as easily replaced, to conditions in Manhattan:

> In a manufacturing plant in New York City it is a comparatively easy matter for employees to break away from a particular establishment, because it is common knowledge there are many other establishments engaged in the same line of business. . . . The employers, on the other hand, feel little responsibility toward any particular group of workmen. They discharge men with impunity and immediately draw anew from the overflowing labor market all around them. . . . [Because of this] the relations between employers and employees are comparatively loose and can be severed much more readily with less cost to either, unless the working force is a very large and well organized one, or the dispute is one involving an entire trade.[47]

Thus, of necessity, unions *had* to organize around given trades, rather than around specific industrial sites. In this, they were aided by ethnic affinities and communal loyalties that went beyond class solidarity.

Given the expansions in municipal functions that were also occurring at this time, however, the largest single employer of menial labor was becoming the city government itself. During the Progressive Era, many of the functions that had been performed by private utilities were coming to be incorporated into municipal ownership or regulation, and many of the expanding municipal service jobs that had fallen under the corrupt patronage of political bosses were being converted to civil service positions. This, in itself, stimulated labor mobilizations, such as the 1907 strike of New York's garbage workers.[48] Such strikes of municipal workers would become increasingly common in the later years of the city's history.[49]

THE AFRICAN AMERICAN COMMUNITY'S PLACE IN THE SOCIAL AND ECOLOGICAL STRUCTURE OF NEW YORK

In comparison to the foreign-born, the number of black residents in New York remained relatively insignificant until the labor shortage that characterized the period of the First World War and the reduced quotas restricting immigration in the 1920s. Indeed, the proportion of black residents had fallen considerably below what it had been in the early days of the colony, when black slaves and freemen may have made up 10 percent or more of the total.[50]

Slaves from Africa and the Caribbean had been a part of New York's history from the beginning. The first slaves arrived with the Dutch in 1626, and the system grew harsher under British rule.[51] However, New York was among the most liberal states in the nation (in contrast to the rampant racism evident in Illinois, to be described in Chapter 5). Its legislature recognized manumission and during the Revolutionary War even "passed an act granting freedom to all slaves who served in the army for three years or until honorably discharged."[52] The state's first constitution of 1777 extended suffrage to free blacks, provided they met the other requirements, and slavery was officially abolished by 1827. Nevertheless, of the twenty-six thousand "Negroes" in New York State counted by the first census in 1790, less than one-fifth were freemen,[53] and between 1827, when slavery was abolished in the state, and 1863, when slavery ended nationwide, "the condition of the Negro in New York City was anomalous and precarious . . . neither slave nor citizen; he had neither the protection of a master nor full equality before the law."[54] By the census of 1830, there were some forty-five thousand free "Negroes" in the state, of whom only about one-third lived in Manhattan. Those numbers remained remarkably constant throughout much of the nineteenth century. Although blacks were thus too few to constitute quarters of their own, the slum of Five Points (now the governmental zone around City Hall) contained a large concentration of very poor blacks, at least until they were displaced northward by the incoming Irish. There was a second, more "respectable," enclave in Greenwich Village, then referred to as "Little Africa," which housed a wider range of class positions, including some black tradesmen who had previously owned slaves themselves.[55]

But the position of New York's small black population deteriorated as Irish and German immigrants displaced them in many trades. And by the time the new immigrants vented their anger during the draft riots of 1863, there were still only fifty thousand blacks in the entire state, of whom fifteen thousand lived in the city.[56] After the Civil War, this population expanded significantly. By 1898 more than sixty thousand African Americans lived in Greater New York, mostly concentrated in a few zones of Manhattan.[57]

By then, Italian immigrants had virtually replaced blacks in Greenwich Village and blacks were forming new concentrations farther uptown on the West Side, at first in the "Tenderloin" (New York's red-light district) and "Hell's Kitchen" (later renamed Clinton), especially after the noise and nuisance of elevated lines there drove out whites who had more choice. These transitions were not benign. Racial violence erupted in 1900, when rampaging whites invaded the Clinton quarter in a "brutish orgy, which, if it was not incited by the police, was, to say the least, abetted by them."[58] The riot of 1900 followed a pattern that was to become "classic" and widespread throughout the United States: indiscriminate and escalating white attacks (police and civilian) upon blacks.[59] With few exceptions (e.g., in New York in 1935 and again in 1943), race riots in American cities would follow this pattern up to the 1960s.[60]

Origins of Harlem

Such hostilities, however, did not dampen migration. By 1910 the number of African Americans in Greater New York had risen to almost ninety-two thousand, of whom two-thirds lived in Manhattan, including the new district of Harlem well north of Central Park. But Harlem was not yet a ghetto. Originally a pleasant and pastoral farming community founded by Peter Stuyvesant, its population had remained remarkably stable for some two hundred years.[61] However, the farmers, faced with declining crops from the depleted soil, "simply deserted the seemingly worthless property and went elsewhere. Formerly great estates were sold at public auction." By the mid-nineteenth century, Harlem had been reduced to a poor country village of shanties, huts, and an occasional farmhouse, and poor Irish immigrants had begun to squat on its vacant land.[62]

Annexation and the extension of mass-transit lines changed the area's fate. After the 1870s, Harlem became Manhattan's first suburb, one developed primarily for the white upper-middle and upper classes. In 1873, the village was annexed to Manhattan, and between 1878 and 1881 three lines of elevated railroads were extended to 129th Street. Electric lights were installed in 1887 and telephone lines in 1889. All these developments touched off a massive wave of speculation and construction. "Rows of brownstones and exclusive apartment houses appeared overnight."[63]

The area remained a living contradiction, however. While the newer housing attracted established wealthy families from downtown, together with newer municipal "luminaries,"[64] it still contained garbage dumps and poor people, including new Italian immigrants, at its less savory fringes.[65] A small Negro population also remained, which "gradually increased in size in the late nineteenth century as colored servants worked in homes of the wealthy who moved into the neighborhood."[66]

The speculation that had fueled the first movement of the white bourgeoisie into the area in the late 1870s and 1880s was repeated again in the late 1890s, in anticipation of the subway's extension. Between 1898 and 1904, when the Lenox Avenue line opened at 145th Street, "'practically all the vacant land in Harlem' was 'built over.'"[67] Not only private buyers but large insurance companies invested heavily, as did upwardly mobile eastern European Jews seeking an escape from the Lower East Side.[68]

Rampant speculation between 1902 and 1905 drove the prices of land and buildings in Harlem to unsustainable heights. The bottom fell out of this market in the "bust" of 1904–5,[69] and it was only then, after "financial institutions no longer made loans to Harlem speculators and building-loan companies, and many foreclosed on their original mortgages . . . [that] large numbers of colored people began to settle in West Harlem. . . . Rather than face 'financial destruction' some landlords and corporations opened their houses to Negroes and collected the traditionally higher rents that colored people paid."[70] Even so, it was a long time before Harlem became predominantly black.[71] Only with the new influx of African Americans at the beginning of World War I, coupled with "white flight," did the number of African Americans in the neighborhood approach fifty thousand.[72]

As in other northern cities, the labor shortage of World War I led recruiters to comb the South, dealing directly with black workers, arranging their transportation en masse, and shipping them in consignments of hundreds and even thousands.[73] Unlike the rural cotton folk who went to Chicago, however, New York's laborers were drawn more from southern cities and towns on the Atlantic seaboard and thus were "better prepared to adapt themselves to life and industry in a great city." In addition, a sizable number of migrants came from islands in the Caribbean, and they brought with them better education than migrants from the American South. This may be why they were better received.[74]

As late as 1930, James Weldon Johnson observed that, in contrast to other large cities such as Chicago or Cleveland, where expansions of "nascent black belts" were met with bombs, this did not happen in New York:

> Although there was bitter feeling in Harlem during the fifteen years of struggle the Negro went through in getting a foothold . . . there was never any demonstration of violence that could be called serious. Not since the riot of 1900 has New York witnessed, except for minor incidents, any interracial disturbances. Not even in the memorable summer of 1919 . . . did New York, with more than a hundred thousand Negroes grouped together in Harlem, lose its equanimity.[75]

He hypothesized two reasons for the somewhat more peaceful race relations in the city. First, he noted that blacks were "employed more as individuals than as non-integral parts of a gang," which gave them "more intimate contacts with the life and spirit of the city as a whole," a fact not unrelated to the small scale of enterprises that I have described above.[76] And further, he attributed New York's greater tolerance to

> the natural psychology of a truly cosmopolitan city, in which there is always the tendency to minimize rather than magnify distinctions. . . . New York, more than any other American city, maintains a matter-of-fact, a taken-for-granted

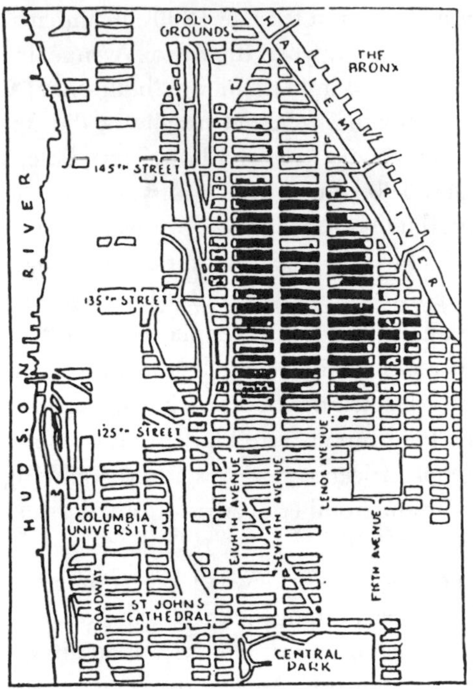

Negro Harlem 1925

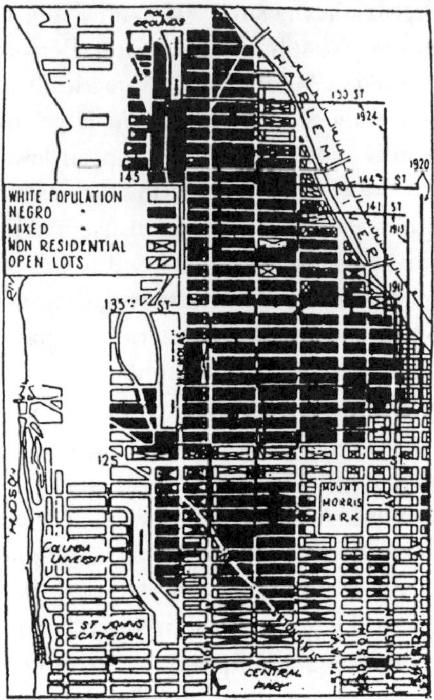

Negro Harlem 1930

Map 4.3. The growth of "black" Harlem between 1925 and 1930. Source: James Weldon Johnson, *Black Manhattan;* the map appears in this 1930 classic, opposite page 146.

> attitude towards her Negro citizens. Less there than anywhere else in the country are Negroes regarded as occupying a position of wardship; more nearly do they stand upon the footing of common and equal citizenship. It may be that one of the causes of New York's attitude lies in the fact that the Negro there has achieved a large degree of political independence; that he has broken away from a political creed based merely upon traditional and sentimental grounds. Yet, on the other hand, this itself may be a result of New York's attitude.[77]

Although in retrospect this evaluation seems overly romantic, it does capture some of the optimism of the period, when the Harlem Renaissance was flowering and an interracial culture seemed pregnant with great possibilities.[78]

The Making of the Harlem Ghetto

By 1920, at the beginning of its great cultural renaissance, Harlem was becoming a predominantly black neighborhood that housed two-thirds of Manhattan's African Americans and served as a mecca for the rest.[79] Because of the special manner in which blacks had fallen heir to this new and elegant suburb, it was unique among the urban ghettos that were forming in other northern cities. Osofsky emphasizes that "its streets and avenues were broad, well-paved, clean and tree-lined . . . [and] its homes . . . spacious . . . with . . . modern facilities." Far from being a slum, it was "an ideal place in which to live," albeit an expensive one, given that African Americans were overcharged.[80]

But despite the overly optimistic hopes of black scholars such as Johnson, the area was becoming increasingly degraded, because its boundaries could not be expanded fast enough to keep pace with its growing population. Between World War I and the Depression, most of Harlem's remaining white population left for other boroughs, their places more than taken by a massive influx of rural southern blacks. In 1910, the number of African Americans in all five boroughs was still fewer than 100,000; by 1920 this number had risen to more than 150,000, and by 1930 it stood at more than 325,000. Most lived in the expanding black "city" of Harlem. In 1930, more than three-quarters of the city's black population were migrants born outside New York State. Although most hailed from the South, a surprisingly large number had been born abroad, primarily in the Caribbean.[81] Competition for jobs and doubling up in scarce housing were already problems for New York's black population even before the Depression struck. And when it did, the Harlem of the 1920s became the segregated deteriorating zone of the 1930s, increasingly isolated from the city around it and vulnerable to even greater hardships than would be faced by other residents of New York. By then, a second area of black concentration had begun to form in the Bedford-Stuyvesant district of Brooklyn. (See Map 4.4.)

THE EXPANSION OF MUNICIPAL FUNCTIONS AND POLITICAL REFORM

"Diversity" in New York permeated not only the proletariat but the elite elements of the city as well. Although the conventional narrative of elite succession in New York's politics pits the older refined Protestant mercantile elite against the corrupt immigrant-dominated political machine in a battle for control, the actual story is far more complicated.[82] Even Jaher, who hews closely to this line, acknowledges that by the 1890s the "Old Guard" had already been "engulfed by a massive tide of [rich mostly self-made] newcomers," many of them Jewish bankers and merchants.[83] And Hammack, who has written perhaps the best analysis of the changing political structure of New York in the late nineteenth century, stresses the multiplicity of competing elites in the city by the end of the century, which opened the path to greater democratization and influence for groups other than the rich or the corrupt:

> [By] the late nineteenth century the metropolitan region's power was strongly concentrated in the hands of *competing* economic and social elites . . . so numerous, and so frequently in conflict with one another, that other groups, less wealthy but well organized, were also able to exert significant influence on their own behalf. The political party organizations were the most notable of these less wealthy groups, but on occasion others—including neighborhood economic associations, the Catholic Church, organized Jews and Protestants, and even organized labor and school teachers—were able to gain their own ends or at least to defend their own interests. . . . *Competition among the very wealthy at the end of the nineteenth century may very well have opened the way to a wider distribution of power among well organized though individually less wealthy pressure groups in the twentieth century.*[84]

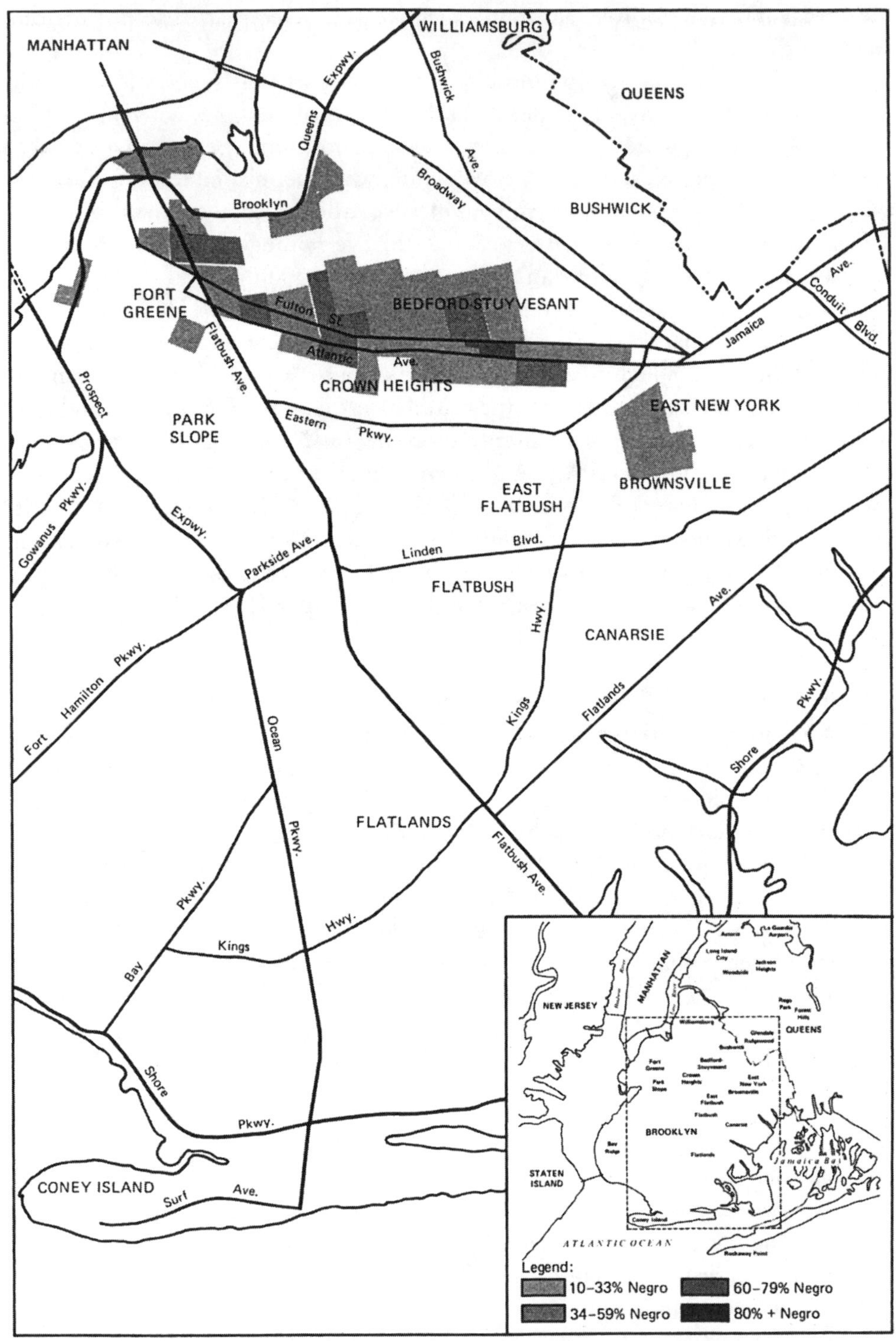

Map 4.4. The nucleus of a "second ghetto" in Brooklyn, 1930. Source: Harold X. Connolly, *A Ghetto Grows in Brooklyn;* reprinted with permission from New York University Press.

This view is shared by Teaford, who documents the remarkable capacity of governments to function in late-nineteenth-century American cities, despite their incredibly rapid growth; heightened social, ethnic, and class divisions; and the constraints on finances imposed by state governments. He chronicles the amazing accomplishments of American cities in the late nineteenth century in providing a high standard of public services such as water and sewerage systems, parks, libraries, schools, fire and police protection, street paving, bridges and tunnels, and transportation systems and demonstrates with comparative data how much better American cities were at these functions than were their European (mostly German and English) counterparts.

Teaford explores the complex system of governance that was worked out in American cities in the 1870–1900 period; he traces the evolution (and deal making) from the elite aldermanic rule that prevailed before the great migrations, to a more powerful city council, elected by ward/district, to represent neighborhoods and ethnically diverse interests when suffrage was extended, to a period of "reform" in which the roles of the mayor, his executive officers, and special commissions were strengthened and technically skilled professionals came to dominate.[85]

To understand how this transition played out in New York, one must go back to the 1870s, when Boss Tweed was unseated in disgrace. The revenue-raising powers of New York's municipal government had made possible enormous improvements in the city, including the provision of a complex water system and the construction of fabulous Central Park, but had also facilitated the growth of an equally bloated system of patronage and a perilously mounting city debt.[86] When the depression of 1873 struck, the city almost went bankrupt, opening the way to drastic "reform." The state legislature responded to the crisis by creating the Board of Estimate and Appropriations, which restricted the powers of the Board of Aldermen (the city council) over budgets, bond raising, and vis-à-vis the executive branch.[87] The new charter gave the mayor power to appoint department heads and members of various commissions, which reduced the patronage available to ward bosses.[88] This permitted a higher level of professionalization in municipal services.[89]

During the Progressive Era, both of these trends became evident. Civil service laws were passed in the 1880s and 1890s, and substantial powers were transferred to executives of various city departments and special commissions whose tenures in office often outlasted those of elected officials.[90] And because of the expanding functions taken on by the city government (public works, water supplies and sewers, libraries and schools, parks, and public health and safety, and so on), there was greater dependence upon experts such as civil engineers, landscape architects, librarians, schoolteachers, physicians, firemen, and policemen.[91] Paradoxically, it also increased the power of the economic elites to pursue their agenda to create a city conducive to the smooth operation of business and commerce. As Hammack has pointed out, "during what can be called the Era of the Swallowtails, 1872–1886 [e.g., after Tweed was thrown out], every man elected Mayor of New York City was a prominent merchant who owed his nomination to the most important politically active groups of Democrats among the merchants, bankers, and lawyers who directed the city's economy."[92]

But even between 1886 and 1903, which Hammack defines as the transitional era between domination by merchants and the Tammany-managed city of the first third of the twentieth century, business interests continued to guide policy, relatively independent of the formal governmental structure of the city. Their opportunities may have been strengthened by the fragmentation of the Democratic Party into three competing components during the 1870s and 1880s: the dignified "reformers" (called "swallowtails,"after the formal morning coats they favored), Tammany Hall, and the latter's breakaway faction, housed around the corner in Irving Hall. In any event, as Teaford puts it:

> In the last twenty years of the century . . . the distinction between commerce and civic improvement became increasingly blurred. . . . During the 1880s and 1890s New York's Chamber of Commerce entered the municipal fray as advocate of a wide variety of measures. In 1880, for example, the chamber joined the campaign for the consolidation of Brooklyn, New York City, and the surrounding suburban communities because the group perceived that metropolitan disunity was detrimental to municipal services and consequently unfavorable to local business. . . . and in 1895[93] New York's chamber even went so far as to take sides in the city's electoral struggle. The chamber resolved that its Committee on Municipal Reform, consisting of five millionaire businessmen, should join with other anti-Tammany forces in the city to . . . oppose the Democratic machine ticket.[94]

Mostly, however, their focus was on improving municipal services, especially in the crucial area of transportation. The Chamber strongly backed plans for the subway and in 1894 actually drafted for the state legislature the bill that created a new self-perpetuating rapid-transit commission and authorized it to finance the subway by issuing city bonds. Therefore, although "municipal bonds funded the construction of New York City's subways, the Chamber of Commerce was actually in charge of the project."[95] In addition, the Chamber had been a force behind the construction of the Brooklyn Bridge and later, when that became overtaxed with traffic,[96] the Williamsburg Bridge, which was opened in 1903. Other bridges were being proposed. Later, the Chamber turned its attention to zoning and planning issues, which, in the twentieth century, took on new significance.

CITY AND REGIONAL PLANNING

The business elites in New York played leading roles in the origins of planning and zoning, as they did in Chicago and Los Angeles. The extent to which developments in Chicago and New York were interrelated from the 1890s on is testimony to the fact that the two cities were experiencing similar problems, and not only trying to learn from one another, but actually employing many of the same "professional consultants" who cross-pollinated, for good or evil, similar solutions. Some of these solutions were actually imported from European precedents, suggesting that New York and Chicago had indeed become "world cities." However, U.S. cities, unlike their European counterparts, were growing faster and absorbing high proportions of foreign immigrants. This not only intensified their problems but entangled two issues—confounding the assimilation of immigrants with removing the injuries of class.

Housing

The relationship between immigrants and insalubrious overcrowded housing was acknowledged as a basic problem in both cities, in part because such immigrant zones were viewed as creating hardships for their residents and in part because bad housing was feared as a foyer of infection (in terms of both physical health and "social disorder") that could "infect" the healthier and wealthier quarters.[97] It is not an accident that immediately following the draft riots, a group of influential New Yorkers formed the Citizens' Association of New York, which undertook the first comprehensive survey of tenement housing in the city. The 1865 survey led to some municipal regulations over tenement construction, but enforcement was lacking and conditions continued to deteriorate. Exposés followed in the next decades, of which perhaps the most famous was muckraker Jacob Riis's photojournalist documentary *How the Other Half Lives.*[98]

Finally, in 1900, in response to pressures from the Charity Organization Society (another elite organization), the New York Legislature appointed its fourth Tenement House Commission, with Robert De Forest as chair and Lawrence Veiller as secretary. The results of the commission's detailed studies were made available in a two-volume work by 1903,[99] but even before its publication, its humanitarian goals and the researchers' methods were being replicated in Chicago, at Jane Addams's behest, through Robert Hunter's parallel inquiry into Chicago's housing conditions.[100] The New York legislature also passed the Tenement House Act of 1901, which mandated the so-called new-law tenements for new construction, but these proved scant improvements over the older types.[101] Ineffectual efforts at housing reform would continue throughout the early decades of the twentieth century, but it was not until the Depression of 1929 that New York initiated, even before federal involvement, its first public housing project. (See Chapter 7.)

Planning

Peter Hall, among others, has pointed out that in the United States from the beginning there was a strange divorce between housing amelioration and planning: "Early American planning . . . was dominated by the City Beautiful movement, and that was planning without social purpose—or even with a regressive one."[102] And in this divorce, Chicago played an even more important role than New York. The City Beautiful movement is often traced back to the Chicago World's Fair of 1893, when the European tradition of beaux arts entered the United States with a vengeance,[103] but it must be emphasized that architect Daniel Burnham, the chief executive of the fair, hired Frederick Law Olmsted, the father of Central Park, to lay out the fairgrounds, and that commissions for most buildings were accorded to New York architectural firms, especially McKim, Mead & White—firms that were already established purveyors of that European style.[104] The influence of these architects on American building was already deeply entrenched in showy office buildings and homes for the wealthy, as Hall's account clearly demonstrates:

Map 4.5. The location of new-law tenements in lower Manhattan circa 1903. Source: Portion of insert map in First Report of the Tenement House Department, circa 1903.

Between the 1870s and World War I, America's multimillionaires, particularly New York's robber barons, engaged in an orgy of competitive and conspicuous expenditure. Resplendent mansions and mausoleums and imposing skyscrapers symbolized their triumphs and established their credentials. . . . The foremost architect of the 1870s and '80s was Henry Hobson Richardson, a devotee of the Romanesque fashion. . . . His most famous followers were Charles Follen McKim, William Mead, and Stanford White. McKim and White were draftsmen for Richardson before going into partnership with Mead. In the 1880s and '90s the principals in the firm built Newport mansions and Manhattan townhouses for New York's premier capitalists . . . , planned the Pennsylvania Railroad station and

> the Columbia University campus . . . [and] also created the Boston Public Library edifice. . . . Although most wealthy and well-known Chicagoans preferred local talent, noted eastern architects were also sought after. . . . White helped design the summer home of Cyrus H. McCormick, Richardson constructed the Field Wholesale Building . . . and Hunt built [Marshall] Field's residence. According to renowned Chicago architect Louis H. Sullivan, Burnham, the favorite builder for the town's elite, as superintendent of construction at the World's Fair, wanted to place all the exposition work with the eastern masters. . . . Burnham became a champion of classicism and left the planning of the fair to Hunt and McKim, Mead and White.[105]

Thus the architecture of the fair and the planning of its grounds—which led directly to the Burnham-directed 1908 Plan of Chicago (sometimes referred to as the Plan of 1909, because it was not published until that year)—were not independent of New York influences; both infused New York ideas through their personnel.

I discuss the fair and the plan in more detail in the next chapter, but it is important to point out here that by the end of the nineteenth century one could no longer speak of independent developments in Chicago and New York, not only in technology and economic base, but in political mechanisms and aesthetic "superstructure." The two world cities were linked not only with one another but with European traditions and models from which, it must be confessed, they were highly derivative. And as we shall see in Chapter 6, these influences were also beginning to be felt in Los Angeles, as midwestern settlers carried the Chicago pattern to that city. By the turn of the century, one could truly speak of a common culture of architecture and city building.

But it would be a gross error simply to conflate planning developments in New York with those in Chicago. Although both were initiated by commercial and industrial elites who tended to ignore the needs of the masses in favor of themselves, New York plans were far less pretentious and more practical than those encompassed in the 1909 Chicago Plan. The analogue, New York's City Improvement Plan of 1907, focused more on such bread-and-butter issues as piers, bridges, and a regularization of streets.[106] And New York's "invention" of the zoning ordinance as a mechanism for planning was similarly concerned less with aesthetics than with the facilitation of commerce.

Zoning

In 1916, in response to growing congestion, New York passed the first citywide zoning law in the United States.[107] Its goal was to control densities, not only in the overcrowded tenement zones (which, because it never regulated existing structures and uses, it could not) but in the commercial districts, where the substitution of new skyscrapers for the lower buildings that had previously dominated was generating gridlock of wheeled and pedestrian traffic and, as we shall see, was threatening to "degrade" the social tone of "better" quarters.[108] The idea for comprehensive zoning was in direct lineage from housing reforms, although it was to have a highly regressive effect on the poor.

In 1907, Benjamin C. Marsh, the executive secretary of the Commission on Congestion of Population in New York (which grew out of De Forest and Veiller's work on tenements), and Edward M. Bassett, another New York lawyer, visited Europe and were impressed by how German cities were regulating land uses and building heights through zoning. It was this "German model of combined land-use and height zoning that was imported to New York City in its 1916 zoning ordinance," and its "main agents were Bassett . . . and his fellow New York reform politician George McAneny."[109]

But the reformers' proposals might not have been adopted had support not come from the business community, an unlikely source, and for reasons quite distinct from the concerns of tenement-house do-gooders.

> Their moment of opportunity came in 1911, when Fifth Avenue garment retailers, worried by the spread of the manufacturing workshops that served them, formed a quasi-official commission to pressure the city. . . .
>
> . . . The Fifth Avenue merchants were concerned that floods of immigrant garment workers on the noontime streets would destroy the exclusive character of their businesses and would thus threaten their property values.[110]

With the backing of commercial interests concerned with property values, the first zoning ordinance was enacted in New York City, from which the idea spread throughout the country, assisted by the promulgation of a standard state enabling act for zoning prepared in 1923 by professional planner/lawyers. This was supplemented by preparation of a standard planning enabling act, which many states adopted to foster master plans.

The legitimacy of using the police powers for zoning was contested in the courts, but was finally upheld by the U.S. Supreme Court in 1926 in the case of *Village of Euclid, Ohio et al. v. Ambler Realty Company.* As Hall has pointed out, the major defense employed by planner/lawyer Alfred Bettman, who presented the case, was that "the 'public welfare' served by zoning was the enhancement of the community's property values."[111]

Zoning played an immediate and dramatic role in creating the special skyline of Manhattan—a skyline that Carol Willis has referred to as "ziggurat" and that many other scholars refer to as "wedding cake."[112] Both terms denote the successive setbacks that the zoning ordinance specified as structures increased in height. The same regulations that sought to segregate land uses also were designed to protect the air and light of adjacent buildings—that is, their rental values as offices. The perhaps unintended consequence of these regulations was to create a maximum "procrustean bed" for the design of skyscrapers: the so-called zoning envelope within which a tall commercial building was confined.

Prior to 1916, New York City had imposed no height or lot-coverage limits (except minimal ones for tenements).

> In theory, a property owner could build straight up from the lot lines as far into the heavens as he or she desired, or as money allowed. After code approval of steel-

> cage construction in 1889, office buildings regularly began to top sixteen or more stories. . . .
>
> The passage in 1916 of New York's first zoning legislation changed the rules of the game for skyscraper design. In addition to regulating uses by districts . . . the law limited the height and bulk of tall buildings with a formula called the *zoning envelope*. Designed to protect some measure of light and air for Manhattan's canyons, it required that after a maximum vertical height above the sidewalk (usually 100 or 125 feet) a building must be stepped back as it rose in accordance with a fixed angle drawn from the center of the street. A tower of unlimited height was permitted over one-quarter of the site. The resulting "setback" or "wedding cake" massing, with or without a tower, became the characteristic form for the New York skyscraper from the 1920s through the 1950s.[113]

Given the typically small size of New York lots and the heavily built-up character of Manhattan, which made assembly of large sites virtually impossible, towers were a reasonable solution to the problem of providing sufficient light and air to offices that still lacked air conditioning and fluorescent lighting. And given the high land values of downtown and then midtown, it was economic to build structures to a height of sixty-three stories before diminishing returns set in. It was not until after 1950, when natural light and air were displaced by fluorescent lights and central air conditioning, that skyscrapers in cities throughout the United States became rather uniform, following the lines of international modern, and even using glass—without windows that open—in place of other facings. And it was not until 1960, when New York City drastically revised its zoning code, that the imperatives of ziggurat zoning were "repealed."[114]

From this discussion it is clear that the major motivation in regulating land uses and building heights was to enhance the economic value of property. Peter Hall concludes that "far from realizing greater social justice for the poor locked in the tenements of New York and Chicago, the planning and zoning system of the 1920s was designed precisely to keep them out of the desirable new suburbs that were being built along the streetcar tracks and the subway lines."[115]

Regional Planning

A similar motivation propelled the interest of the elites in regional planning. Recognizing that the forces of decentralization could not be stopped and that there was no hope of expanding the boundaries of a single jurisdiction over the vast regional complex that, even by the 1920s, encompassed some four hundred municipalities located within twenty-two counties that spread over three states, two models of regional planning were advanced: one by the Regional Planning Association of America (RPAA), and an alternate scheme by the Regional Plan Association (the RPA of New York).[116] Of the two, the former exercised maximum influence on the planning profession itself, whereas the latter, because it was promulgated by the economic and political

Figure 4.3. The search for light and air in New York's pre-Depression skyscrapers. Photographs are from the private collection of Carol Willis, which appeared in her book *Form Follows Finance: Skyscrapers and Skylines in New York and Chicago* (New York: Princeton Architectural Press, 1995). Reproduced with her permission.

power elite of New York, had more direct influence on practical action. I shall therefore concentrate on the origin and approach of the RPA.

A direct line of influence on the RPA can be traced from Chicago to New York in the person of Charles Dyer Norton, a top insurance executive who, after a brief stint in Washington as secretary of the treasury, moved to New York in 1911 as the vice president of the First National Bank and eventually became a trustee and the treasurer for the Russell Sage Foundation.[117] Norton had been a former president of the Commercial Club of Chicago, which sponsored the Burnham plan, and had worked closely with Daniel Burnham. Almost immediately after arriving in New York, he "set about the business of preparing a similar document [for New York]. . . . Collaborating with Manhattan Borough President George McAneny, Norton helped establish a Committee on the City Plan (made up of the five borough presidents) in 1914."[118] The scope, however, was recognized as woefully inadequate, given the extent to which the five boroughs were already being dwarfed by developments in the environs.

"What was to become *The Regional Plan of New York and Its Environs* had begun as no more than a gleam in Charles Norton's eye,"[119] but with the support of the Russell Sage Foundation, it grew to a voluminous set of studies and some concrete proposals (particularly with respect to transportation) that had a lasting, if not always positive, effect on the region. By 1921, Norton, by then treasurer of the Russell Sage Foundation, had convinced the foundation to sponsor the expansion of planning to the whole New York region through the newly organized Committee on the Plan of New York and Its Environs. Norton approached the British town planner Thomas Adams and asked him to conduct a survey and prepare a plan for a vast region:[120]

> Norton had called for a wide compass: "From the City Hall a circle must be swung which will include the Atlantic Highlands and Princeton; the lovely New Jersey hills back of Morristown and Tuxedo; the incomparable Hudson so far as Newburg; the Westchester lakes and ridges, as far as Bridgeport and beyond, and all of Long Island." The resulting area—over 5,000 square miles, with nearly 9 million people—was a far bigger canvas than any plan before had covered.[121]

A superb team of experts was assembled that by 1929 had published ten volumes of reports that dealt with the region's population trends, its economy, its housing, land use and zoning, and ideas for its future development. Although the scholarship was sound, the proposals were critiqued as both too visionary, given that there was no governmental unit capable of executing the plan, and too inadequate, because there was no end in sight for the process of decentralization.[122] But despite such opposition, the "New York plan went ahead, through the medium of a Regional Plan Association under business elite leadership, and [the voluntary participation of] Planning Commissions for each area: it was particularly successful in its highway, bridge and tunnel proposals, mainly because that master-builder Robert Moses was in charge."[123]

Transportation Planning under Robert Moses

The decentralization duly noted by the authors of the Regional Plan Association's studies was perhaps the most obvious trend of the 1920s, a phenomenon clearly linked to the explosive spread of motor vehicles of all kinds.[124] In the decade of the 1920s, when the proportion of residents in central cities of metropolitan areas grew by some 22.5 percent, the population in the suburban rings expanded by close to 35 percent.[125] The growing discrepancy between existing conditions and new needs generated by the automobile created two crises. First, downtown streets were becoming so overcrowded that in some cities (although not New York) "there was talk of barring cars from downtown streets."[126] The second problem related to the inadequacies of existing roads to connect city centers with their fast-growing peripheries. And in this crisis New York became a true innovator, thanks to ideas put forth by the Regional Plan Association surveys and the dynamic personality of Robert Moses, who found ways to get around existing political divisions within the New York metropolitan region to build the first highways.

Hall traces the precedent for Moses's schemes back to the parkways designed by Olmsted:

> First used by Olmsted in his design for New York's Central Park in 1858, the parkway had been widely employed by landscape architects in the planning of parks and new residential areas. . . . But, beginning with William K. Vanderbilt's Long Island Motor Parkway (1906–11), which can claim to be the world's first limited-access motor highway, and the 16-mile Bronx River Parkway (1906–23), followed by the Hutchinson River Parkway of 1928 and the Saw Mill Parkway of 1929, this distinctively American innovation was rapidly adapted . . . [to give] rapid access from the congested central city both to new suburbs and to rural and coastal recreation areas.
>
> The moving spirit was New York's . . . Robert Moses. Using a State Act of 1924, which he had personally drafted to give him unprecedented . . . powers to appropriate land, he proceeded to drive his parkways across the cherished estates of the Long Island millionaires . . . to give New Yorkers access to the ocean beaches.[127]

In Chapter 7 I offer a fuller discussion of Moses's role in re-forming New York's parks and transportation system. Opinions are much divided on this controversial figure, who, by force of personality and somewhat devious brilliance in circumventing barriers to his exercise of almost dictatorial powers, almost single-handedly imposed his vision of transportation planning on the New York region. The effects of his achievements, however, are more commonly recognized. His plans eventually contributed to bifurcating the New York region into a largely proletarian city and a more privileged set of suburban communities by facilitating an "escape from New York." Furthermore, the mechanisms whereby Moses established his own independent financial "empire" through appropriating tolls on his highways and bridges undermined the city government's capacity to control its own planning process. Here I wish only to emphasize that by 1929, after which the Depression and then the Second World War interrupted such constructions, New York was the only city of the three that had supplemented its mass-transit system with freeways to reach its suburbs.[128]

Substitutes for Metropolitan Government

Regional transportation planning, however, was not the only "invention" credited to New York in the 1920s. The city also experimented with sociopolitical inventions. Special authorities and districts were innovative mechanisms for imposing some (admittedly functionally fragmented) order on the conurbation that would always lack metropolitan government. Perhaps the most noteworthy of these was the Port of New York Authority, formed in 1921 and given special authority to bring "order" to the multiple port facilities.[129] But single-function "special districts" also proliferated, not only as a way of coordinating planning over areas larger than any one jurisdiction, but as a mechanism for bypassing state-set ceilings on city debt. These special districts could raise their own revenues by issuing tax-exempt bonds, and their operating costs could be added to local tax bills.

By the late 1950s, when the New York Metropolitan Region Study updated the

RPA studies of 1929, one of the volumes in that series focused on the 1,467 governmental and quasi-governmental units that were attempting to coordinate a region without an overarching governmental structure.[130] As author Robert Wood remarks, this was "one of the great unnatural wonders of the world: . . . a governmental arrangement perhaps more complicated than any other that mankind has yet contrived or allowed to happen."[131] One can only agree, although perhaps the qualifier "perhaps" should be dropped.

Wood distinguishes two general "sectors": local units of government (cities, counties, boroughs, towns, and villages, as well as special-purpose districts for schools, fire, water, and so on) and translocal, metropoliswide giants that involve state and federal actors, of which the Port Authority of New York and the Triborough Bridge and Tunnel Authority are singled out as examples, although the Croton Reservoir system was an even earlier prototype. Both sectors expanded enormously in the first three decades of the twentieth century. The burgeoning of public organizations took on new dimensions in the 1930s, but the institutional mechanisms for many of the New Deal programs were first "invented" in the juridical nightmare of the New York region. And as the stakes increased, the contentiousness of the struggle for power over public resources similarly intensified, presaging a continual tension between conflict and coordination outside the normal framework of local government.

One final New York innovation might be mentioned here, namely, the experiments with co-op ownership that became popular at the start of 1920 as a compromise between the (financial and psychic) benefits of home ownership, geared primarily to single-family homes or small walk-ups, and the necessities of larger apartment buildings in an increasingly dense city. New York pioneered in this form of ownership, which a generation later would become more and more widespread as rent controls made investments in rental complexes less attractive.[132] Nevertheless, New York always remained a city of renters, which distinguishes it to this day from Chicago and even more from Los Angeles.

THE END OF AN ERA

The 1920s were the most optimistic era the United States had experienced. In New York, the researchers who conducted the RPA studies foresaw continued expansion into the periphery in planned suburbs that would incorporate Perry's ideas for neighborhood units. The real estate speculators foresaw equally expansive needs for center-city high-rises. It is ironic that, just as the city and country stood on the edge of the precipice that would hurl them into the chaos of the 1930s, some of New York City's most enduring monuments to capitalism would be built. The structures that still symbolize the economic and aesthetic might of the metropolis—the crown-topped Chrysler Building and the needle-topped Empire State Building—both date from the moment of the crash.[133]

CHAPTER 5

Chicago Becomes Fordist

This chapter adopts the same three temporal divisions employed in Chapter 4, namely, from the early 1870s to about 1893–94, from the mid-1890s through World War I, and then the postwar period to the Great Depression in 1929. But we begin in the middle of this sequence, as it were, by taking a measure of Chicago, both socially and physically, in the year 1893, when the World's Columbian Exposition opened—an event its planners saw as confirmation that the city had achieved world city status.

It was a celebratory moment designed to supplant the negative symbolism of the catastrophic fire of 1871 with a new and progressive icon: the oft-repeated metaphor of Chicago as the phoenix rising from the fire's ashes.[1] It was also a moment of unconcealed competitive glee, because the honor of hosting the fair commemorating the four-hundredth anniversary of Columbus's landfall had been wrested away from New York. Furthermore, the year marked the culmination of decades of important changes in the city, some of the most radical actually linked to preparations for the fair itself.[2]

The fair, and the Burnham plan that grew organically out of it, further solidified the bifurcation of Chicago into two sharply contrasting parts: an elegant facade and a deeply shadowed backstage. It exaggerated the cleavage within the "dual city," which of course consisted not of two separate entities but was, rather, a manifestation in space of a complex division of labor—in which backstage workers created but did not share in the surplus displayed so prominently at the facade. We look first at the display and then at the system of labor that enabled it.

THE CHICAGO OF THE EARLY 1890S IN THE EYES OF ITS BOOSTERS

Hubert Howe Bancroft's commemorative volume prepared for Chicago's World's Fair of 1893 paints a glowing image of the city at this moment:

> He who would picture . . . the Chicago of to-day, must imagine the city extending for more than twenty miles along the shore of Lake Michigan, with 2,500 miles of streets, 2,100 acres of public parks, boulevards from 200 to 300 feet in width, and the whole being the centre of a railroad system including more than one-third of the mileage of the United States. In the business quarter he will pass between buildings from seventeen to twenty stories in height . . . reached by swift running elevators. . . . And the end is not yet. Great as Chicago is, the era of real greatness is yet before her. Little more than seventy years have elapsed since the site of this city was rescued from savage men and beasts; little more than twenty since she began to recover from the ruin which her conflagration wrought; yet in this brief period she has risen to a prominent rank among the commercial, industrial, and social cities of either hemisphere. Most fitting it is that an Exposition which is to represent the progress of the world in science, industry, and art, should be held amid this the most progressive of all our New World communities.[3]

Progress was certainly evident along the lakefront and in the Loop, although, as we shall see, little of that glow was reflected in the sordid zones behind them.

The Lake

The city's early developers recognized that Chicago's greatest natural asset was its location at the edge of Lake Michigan, although the struggles to preserve that sight were to be recurring issues in local politics. In 1836, a year before the city was even incorporated, the agents appointed by the State of Illinois and charged with selling the empty lots to raise funds for Chicago's new shipping canal refused to sell lakefront land, although, with the coming of the railroads, much would be lost.[4]

Nevertheless, in 1869, inspired by New York's example and only two years before the Chicago fire opened more space for its execution, the civic leaders of Chicago (more "industrial" than those of New York but no less ambitious) commissioned Frederick Law Olmsted to prepare plans for Chicago's parks and boulevards. Shoreline development was a major thrust of his effort. "Three parks districts were created in 1869, and by 1880 Chicago stood second only to Philadelphia in total park space," although by the opening of the next century, city boosters would bemoan their demotion in rank.[5] This foresight was timely. In 1870 the city had a population of perhaps 300,000 living on only 35 square miles of territory. By 1893, the city's population would exceed 1.3 million living in an expanse of 185 square miles (thanks to annexations—see below), making Chicago during this period the fastest-growing city in the history of the country, if not the world.

The function of the lake, however, was not only decorative. It was the city's lifeblood: both the major source of its water supply and, unhappily, its outlet for waste. Although the city "had a ready supply of drinking water at its front door," this supply was befouled by sewage. In the late 1850s, therefore, the city designed "one of the first comprehensive municipal drainage systems in the world."[6] In order to execute this plan, the level of many city streets had to be raised an average of ten feet, because the

Figure 5.1. Lakefront rail yards (circa 1916–17), subsequently partially covered by Grant Park and by the overpass next to the Art Institute. Photograph from the Chicago Historical Society; used with permission.

site was so flat and swampy.[7] By 1871, however, the city had installed only 140 miles of sewer lines, almost exclusively within the downtown area. In addition, the sewerage system originally drained directly into the Chicago River, and thence into the lake itself.[8] To guarantee a supply of unpolluted water, therefore, in 1864 the city began to construct a water intake tunnel (two miles offshore and sixty feet below the surface). By 1900, the municipal waterworks was pumping some five hundred million gallons of water daily, and the expanded city boasted more than fifteen hundred miles of sewers.[9] It was the central business district (CBD) and its nearby elite residential quarters that were most completely served.

The Loop

Chicago's central business district was, after the lakefront, the second "pride" of the city. The shape and extent of "the Loop," on land partially "cleared" by the Chicago Fire, was rigidly delineated when, in early 1882, cable car service copied from San Francisco's was inaugurated to serve—and to encircle—the CBD.[10] Although this mass-transit system and its extension (an elevated line first installed to give access to the fairgrounds) greatly facilitated the consolidation of shopping, hotels, and other commerce as well as banking, finance, and producers' services within one location, it would later serve as a strangling constraint on CBD expansion, essentially forcing an overconcentration of multiple functions within a single area.

> The new business center was more elaborate and ornamental and, foreshadowing Chicago's skyscraping future, substantially higher. Most new construction was four or five stories high, and a half-dozen buildings rose to eight floors. . . . The introduction of elevators made possible greater height, the use of electric lights a few years later permitted construction to go on at night, and mixing salt with the mortar allowed bricklaying in winter months.[11]

That the "skyscraper" became a "necessity" earlier in Chicago than elsewhere, and that the true pioneers in this form of architecture (e.g., Jenney, Sullivan, Root, Adler, and Burnham) concentrated their works in the Loop, is thus hardly accidental. The forerunner of the skyscraper (a construction system that depends upon a steel frame rather than bearing walls) is usually acknowledged to have been the ten-story Home Insurance Building in Chicago's Loop, designed by Jenney and completed in 1885.[12] That Chicago did not outstrip New York in creating a skyline of bristling towers is chiefly due to a municipal law that, in 1893, capped tall buildings at a maximum height of 130 feet. This limit was raised and lowered and raised again in the ensuing decades, in response to market fluctuations.[13] But if skyscrapers are defined simply as tall buildings, one notes, with Bluestone, that the boom of skyscraper building took place in Chicago between 1880 and 1895—at a time when vertical space was desperately needed to accommodate the expanding services required by the fifty thousand persons being added to the city each year.[14]

The radial mass-transit system that eventually converged on the Loop also solidified Chicago's semicircular spatial organization into the three distinct wedges initially shaped by the North (really northwest) and South (really southwest) Branches of the Chicago River and by the system of long-distance rail lines. Industry gravitated to the shores of the sluggish branches of the river, with residential quarters relegated to the interstices. The wealthy favored areas near the lake, at first south of the Loop but later, once the flow of the river's North Branch had been reversed, to the Loop's north.[15] A rapidly growing proletariat settled in what was left over, congregating especially in the vicinity of the large industrial agglomerations in peripheral locations.

The contrast with New York's spatial patterning of business is striking. If the circle and wedge set the fundamental geometry of Chicago, the geometric form that best fits Manhattan is the line. We have already seen how, up to the end of the nineteenth century, Manhattan expanded northward, the waters around the elongated island constituting their own "loop" to constrain and channel growth. Dock areas at the water's edge constricted the space available for "better" uses. Rather than having its business functions concentrated in a single centralized zone, then, New York's specialization occurred *along* several north-south ribbon strips of Manhattan. As the central business district(s) and associated elite residences moved steadily northward along these avenues, at first to Union Square, then to Madison Square, then to 40th Street,

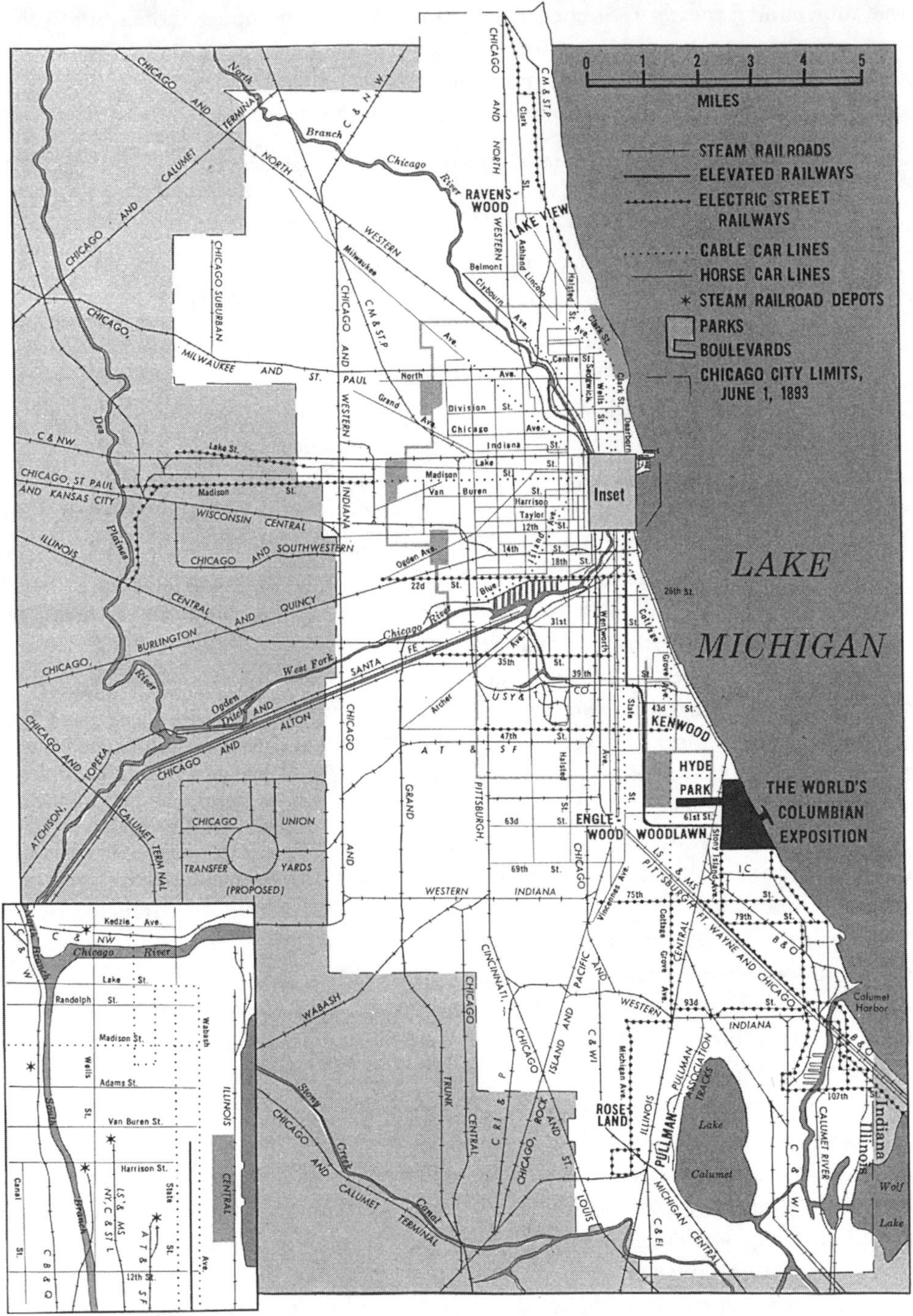

Map 5.1. The radial pattern of train and transit lines in Chicago in 1893. Source: Harold Mayer and Richard Wade, *Chicago: Growth of a Metropolis;* reproduced with permission of the University of Chicago Press.

and then as far north as 59th Street and even beyond, the lower portions of the island were successively recycled to accommodate governmental, financial, and legal institutions, along with their attendant services. Consumer commerce may have systematically followed its wealthier customers northward along the central spine of the island, with industry and tenements flanking them on both edges, but the ribbon itself evolved into a colorful sequential mosaic of small and highly specialized districts: the fashion district, the fur district, even a flower district.

Chicago from the start followed an opposite pattern of organization, its commercial core fixed in amber, at least until its modern bifurcation into a "degraded heavily minority loop" south of the Chicago River, and an "upper Fifth Avenue" zone on the northern shore. (In recent years there have been noncontiguous eruptions along highway intersections that constitute "edge city.") Because of its persisting core position, the Loop became the privileged and often exclusive domain of progress. Throughout most of the nineteenth century, however, business hours in that commercial center had been shortened by early sunsets and Chicago's relentless gray cloud cover, some of the latter arising from lake-induced condensation, but most generated by smoking gaslights and billowing steam from heating plants.[16] It was perhaps inevitable, therefore, that conversion to electrical power should have occurred first (and exclusively) in the Loop, both out of need and ability to pay.[17]

Although experiments had begun as early as 1879 with various methods of illuminating the smoke-polluted darkness, multiple inefficient systems coexisted, and costs of this duplication were high. In 1892, when Samuel Insull became president of Chicago Edison, his firm established a virtual monopoly over electrical service by consolidating Chicago's multiple utility companies and driving recalcitrant rivals out of business.[18] Insull not only electrified most of the Loop, but his efforts also lay behind the electrification of the city's mass-transit system, in which he was a major player. One of his first initiatives was to extend an electric-powered elevated transit line and electric lights to the residential zone south of the Loop (then still the most prestigious neighborhood for the elite),[19] and on to the fair itself, which was proudly dubbed "The City of Lights."[20]

The Loop also became differentiated architecturally from its surroundings during the period of rebuilding, a fact directly traced back to the fire itself, which had almost leveled the zone. Closing the proverbial stable door, fire regulations were immediately imposed, although they applied exclusively to downtown; only gradually were they extended, incompletely and piecemeal, to the rest of the city. Just after the fire, the powerful Board of Fire Underwriters threatened not to insure property in Chicago unless the fire service was depoliticized (professionalized) and equipment upgraded. "Aroused by the action of the [insurance] companies, the Citizen's Association, consisting of leading Chicago businessmen, moved quickly to force improvements."[21] And, perhaps of even greater significance, the city passed an ordinance proscribing construction of wooden buildings in the downtown area; a new form of construction had to be invented.

The task of rebuilding in brick and stone was so enormous that architects flocked to the city from everywhere to take advantage of this unparalleled opportunity.[22]

Thus, rather than a slow process of evolution, city building (or rebuilding) in the Loop was instantaneous, albeit only partial. But in the process, a sharp line was drawn between the zone covered by the new fire code and all those areas that lay outside, where cheaper old-style wooden balloon-frame buildings were still permitted. This served to solidify the dual city further—in a most obvious physical sense.

These improvements to the Loop did not come any too soon. They were absolutely essential because between 1871 and 1893 the functions of the commercial/administrative core expanded dramatically. First, it became the administrative center for a vastly expanding territory along with its resident population. And second, it experienced a growing demand for office buildings to house the professional and producers' services that it now needed, as its economy gained increased independence from its earlier subordination to New York.

ANNEXATION

In 1871, the municipal government of Chicago had jurisdiction over perhaps 325,000 residents living in an area of only 35 square miles. By 1893, the city's control had expanded to 185 square miles (almost all of Cook County except some northern and western suburban fringes, which demurred), and its total population had risen to some 1.4 million, although only about 300,000 of that increase was due directly to the expansion of boundaries.

The dramatic moment was June 29, 1889, when "voters in a surrounding 120 square miles elected to join the city," responding to offers of police and fire protection and "the chance to be served by growing and efficient water and sewage systems."[23] In the next four years a few more suburbs opted to join the city, but after 1893, annexation had, for all intents and purposes, ceased.[24] The annexations took a relatively symmetrical form of movement outward within sectors of the city's half-circular pattern, and were channeled into the same basic three wedges (defined by the river branches) that had organized space from its origins. The radial pattern of the rail lines converging on the Loop's perimeter set this pattern in an unalterable mold. In a sense, space in the city was "overdetermined." (See Maps 5.2 and 5.3.)

ECONOMIC "INDEPENDENCE" AND NEW BUSINESS FUNCTIONS

By the time of the Civil War, Chicago was already well established as the transportation and wholesale center for the "West," and by the 1870s it had already surpassed St. Louis to become the major financial fulcrum of its region.[25] But it must be emphasized that, as in any colony, much capital and control remained outside. Jaher reminds us:

> The midwestern [rail] network was built without any important contribution of Chicago capital, and before 1900 none of the great western lines with central offices in Chicago used that city's stock exchange. Even after World War I, when Chicago investment banking became more prominent, flotations still originated mostly in Wall Street . . . [and both major and local rail lines] were controlled by

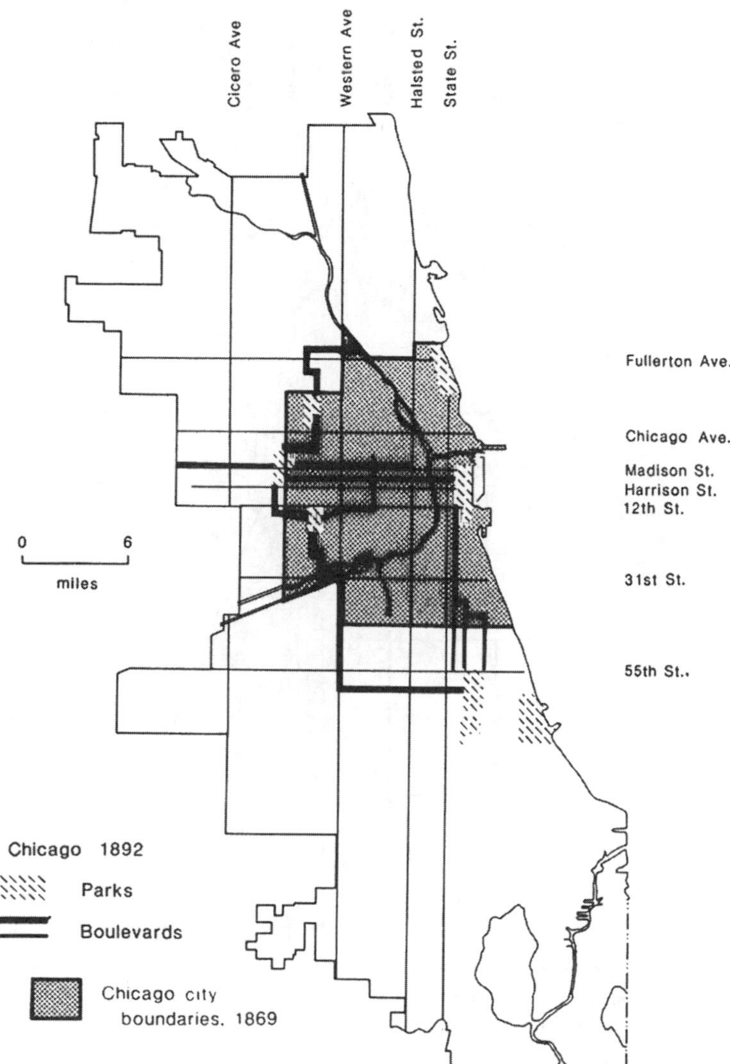

Map 5.2. The city boundaries of Chicago in 1869, in comparison to the current city limits. Source: Ann Durkin Keating, *Building Chicago: Suburban Developers and the Creation of a Divided Metropolis;* reproduced with the permission of Ohio State University Press.

> eastern, usually New York, capitalists. . . . Easterners . . . dominated the board and the executive committee [of the Chicago & Northwestern line], and financial control reposed in Manhattan even if operations were directed from Chicago.[26]

And it was not until after 1870 that Chicago began to import directly from abroad, without having to go through New York brokers.

Even Chicago's solidly expanding industrial base depended initially on outside owners and investment funds. Although meatpacking was one of the very first industries

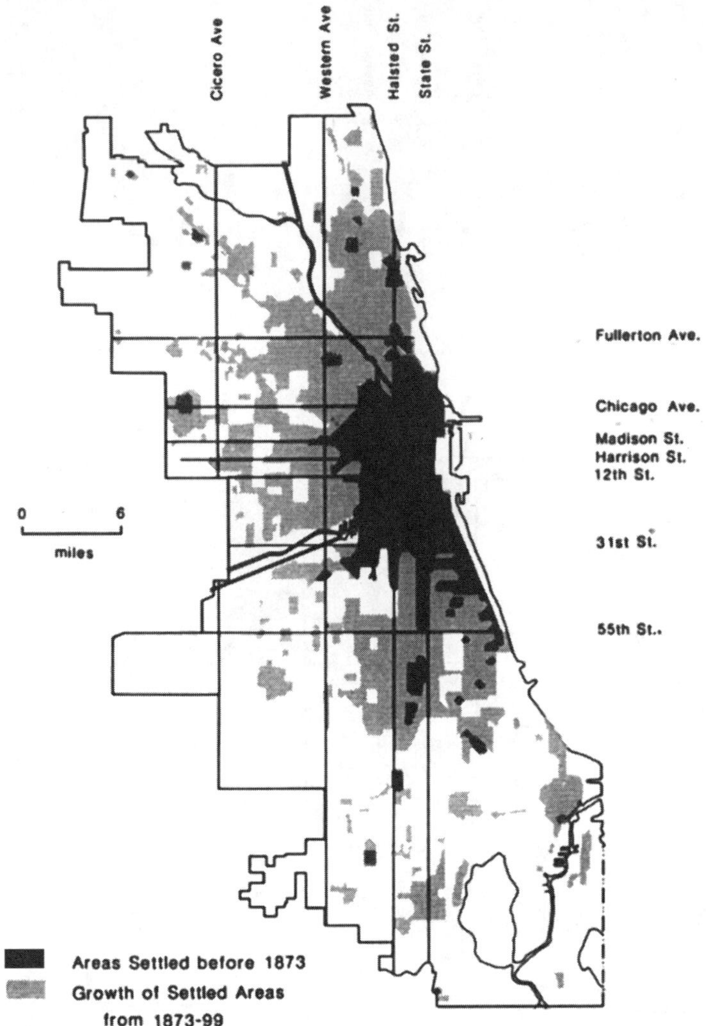

Map 5.3. The expansion of settled areas of Chicago between 1873 and 1899, the period of peak annexation. Annexations essentially end by 1915. Source: Ann Durkin Keating, *Building Chicago: Suburban Developers and the Creation of a Divided Metropolis,* based on an original map in Mayer and Wade, *Chicago: Growth of a Metropolis;* reproduced with the permission of Ohio State University Press.

to be established in the city, "as late as 1850 the largest packinghouse was a branch of a New York firm."[27] And decades after Chicago had become the nation's most important producer of agricultural implements, the country's second-largest packer/processor of meat, and the third-largest producer of freight and passenger cars for the railroads,[28] Chicago's banks still kept large balances in New York and depended heavily on that city's financial institutions. Gradually, however, Chicago's financial services were becoming magnets of their own. The Chicago Board of Trade was attracting New York investors who wanted to speculate in grain and meat futures, and independent brokerage and insurance firms were beginning by the 1880s to supplement their activities in local real estate mortgages and loans for urban transit and utilities by selling substantial amounts of securities.[29] These burgeoning activities created a strong demand for more and more banks and office buildings in the Loop, which stimulated a phenomenal expansion of office space between 1873 and 1893.[30]

THE SITE SELECTED FOR THE 1893 FAIR

Given the preoccupation with the Loop, the preference for the lakefront, and the prior existence of an elite residential quarter just south of downtown, especially along Prairie Avenue, it was perhaps inevitable that the unattractive southern fringe just beyond this quarter should have been selected as the site for the Columbian Exposition by the wealthy businessmen who sponsored the project and stood to benefit most from it.[31] Cleaning and beautifying the shoreline for the fair would enhance land values nearby and would provide the wealthy residents with a playground that, although neither as large nor as centrally located as Manhattan's Central Park, would be a worthy venue for the city's first citizens.

The nucleus for the fairgrounds already existed in Jackson Park, planned earlier by Olmsted, but it would require extensive filling and the creation of lagoons and canals to enlarge the site, which was then "a sandy waste of unredeemed and desert land, in its centre a marshy hollow, and without trace of vegetation, save for a stunted growth of oak, and here and there a tangled mass of willow, flag, and marsh grass, which served but to render its desolation still more desolate."[32] The costs of preparing the site and constructing the buildings were anticipated to be high, and indeed, they eventually mounted to twenty million dollars for grounds and buildings alone.[33] Private subscriptions totaling some five million dollars were raised from Chicago's business and industrial leaders in order to make the city eligible to bid on the fair, and these funds were eventually supplemented in 1890 by another five million dollars raised through issuance of a special municipally backed bond. (The remainder evidently came from fair exhibitors.)

The Exposition and Its Sponsors

In 1889, Mayor DeWitt C. Creiger invited several hundred prominent citizens to a meeting to secure enough financial pledges to compete for the fair. He counted not only on their philanthropic instincts but, although not made explicit, on their self-interest as well. He had a large pool of possible donors, thanks to the fortunes many of Chicago's mostly self-made (and self-congratulatory) men had amassed through industry, commerce, utilities, and, of course, shrewd real estate investments.[34]

As might be expected from the recency of the city's growth and industrialization, hardly any of the men to whom he appealed had been born in Chicago, although they were mostly American-born. Jaher's analysis of Chicago's richest men in

1863 reveals that 80 percent had been born in New England or the New York/ Middle Atlantic states. (Only a handful had been born abroad, despite the fact that, by then, half of Chicago's population was foreign-born.) Even as late as 1892, few of the more than two hundred city millionaires with known birthplaces had been born in Chicago or Illinois. New York still provided the largest number of Chicago's wealthiest residents, with Middle Atlantic and New England states accounting for most of the rest. However, by then the proportion of the rich who were foreign-born had increased to 17 percent, and a similar proportion had been born in midwestern states.[35] Despite their diverse origins, the members of this parvenu plutocracy closed ranks in support of the fair, and consistent with trends elsewhere, technically skilled engineers, architects, and lawyers came forth to mingle with the wealthy capitalists in this joint project.

Given their origins and pretensions, the sponsors and planners of the fair turned to New York architects, who in turn were still under the spell of European revivals of classical, Romanesque, and baroque styles.[36] Daniel Burnham, the local architect they selected to direct the planning and construction of the grounds, fully shared their values and was, indeed, the town's favorite builder, well connected to the industrial elite. (He was a solid member of Chicago's elite and the husband of a stockyard entrepreneur's daughter.) Maverick Louis Sullivan seems to have been the sole dissenter, complaining bitterly when Burnham awarded almost all the design contracts to the same beaux arts New York architects who had designed many of the mansions in which wealthy Chicagoans, as well as their counterparts in New York, held court. Chief among the contract recipients was the well-established firm partnership of Charles Follen McKim, William Mead, and Stanford White. (Sullivan was asked to design only the Transportation Building, which is retrospectively acknowledged to have been the single masterpiece of the fair. It has, indeed, been credited with giving birth to "modern" architecture.)

Louis Sullivan was appalled by the classical revival, which, to his mind, had undermined all the progress "honest" Chicago architecture had made: he panned the U.S. government building as incredibly "vulgar," the Illinois state pavilion as a "lewd exhibit of drooling imbecility and political debauchery," and the Palace of the Arts as "the most vitriolic of them all—the most impudently thievish."[37] In his unmeasured (and typical) style, he called the fair's style a virus that "after a period of incubation in the architectural profession and in the population at large . . . began to show unmistakable signs of contagion. There came a violent outbreak of the Classic and the Renaissance in the East, which slowly spread westward, contaminating all that it touched. . . . The damage wrought by the World's Fair will last for half a century . . . , if not longer."[38] In actual fact, at least one of the classical buildings lasted for more than a century, because the Palace of the Arts, for which he reserved his most intemperate criticism, was later "recycled" as Chicago's Museum of Science and Industry for the *next* world's fair, the Century of Progress exhibit, which would open in 1933, the city's darkest hour.

But the fair itself had only a short-lived influence on Chicago building. Instead, it was the work of John Root, Sullivan's friend and mentor, Louis Sullivan himself, and

Sullivan's most famous disciple, Frank Lloyd Wright (who began as a lowly draftsman in Adler and Sullivan's firm when they were at work on the still-standing Auditorium Theater—now the "campus" of Roosevelt University), who left the deepest and most permanent marks, at first on the architecture of Chicago, and then on the world.

THE CHICAGO PLAN, 1906 TO 1909: "MAGIC TO STIR [RICH] MEN'S BLOOD"[39]

Just as the architecture of the fair was atavistic, looking backward to a mythical age of grandeur that never was, so the Chicago Plan, although not published until 1909, was an anachronistic continuation of the fair, rather than an opening to a new era.[40] I therefore deviate a bit from chronology in order to demonstrate that it was essentially a more grandiose (megalomaniacal) version of "fair" planning, this time expanded to a region extending some sixty miles beyond the Loop, a distance then estimated to take two hours to travel by automobile.[41] It involved most of the same personnel and sponsors, pursued the same goals, and represented in words and pictures the same ideals that had been physicalized in the smaller, trial-scale version that was the fair.[42]

The Same People, the Same Ideals

One year after the fair closed, the South Park commissioners proposed to connect Jackson Park, including its fairgrounds, with Olmsted's Grant Park, just east of the Loop. Their design, first exhibited at a dinner given by the Commercial Club, was enthusiastically received; more refined versions were presented in the next few years to a Women's Club meeting at the Art Institute and a dinner of the Merchants Club at the Auditorium. In combination, these three organizations enrolled most movers and shakers of Chicago "society," and their excitement was kindled into a scheme to design a "master plan" for the entire region. It was the Commercial Club (which merged with the Merchants Club in 1907) that commissioned the plan in 1906 and hired Daniel Burnham to prepare it.[43]

It is instructive to examine the plan's front matter. The first page lists plan committee members. Many of the names will be familiar to readers who know even a little about Chicago: Charles H. Wacker (of Wacker Drive), Cyrus McCormick (of McCormick Reaper), Martin A. Ryerson (Ryerson Library of the University of Chicago), John G. Shedd (Shedd Aquarium). But even more fascinating is the list of 334 "subscribers" to the plan, which includes men (and they *were* all men) whose families had made fortunes in meatpacking or in stockyard real estate, such as Armour, Cudahy, Hammond, Hutchinson, several Joneses, Kent, Mayer (of Oscar Mayer), four Swifts, Tilden, Walker, two Porters, and two Wilsons; in manufacturing, including two Cranes, two Otises, and two McCormicks; and in commerce, including Montgomery Ward, two Fields, Pirie (of Carson Pirie Scott), and three Palmers (of Palmer House). But big "capitalists" were not the only subscribers. They were joined by the "new technocrats," who designed the engineering marvels of the city or created its infrastructure, and by the politicians who passed the legislation that empowered them.

I have checked in biographical dictionaries only the first eleven individuals whose names begin with *A*,[44] but even this peculiar "sampling" of seven (four names could not be traced) can illustrate something about the "mix," origins, and interests of Chicago's elite:

1. *George A. Adams:* A lawyer and politician (member of the Illinois Senate and then of the U.S. House of Representatives), Adams was born in New Hampshire and descended from a family dating back to 1628. He was a Harvard graduate who moved to Chicago in 1853.
2. *Owen Franklyn Aldis:* Born in Vermont, Aldis was a Yale Law School graduate. He moved to Chicago in 1877 and was the director of the 1893 Columbian Exposition.
3. *William Arthur Alexander:* Born in Mississippi, Alexander arrived in Chicago at age twenty-three and later became an important insurance executive.
4. *John Alvord:* A hydraulic and sanitary engineer, Alvord was born in Massachusetts and educated in Washington, D.C. He was the chief engineer of surveys for the Columbian Exhibition and later designed the water supply and sewerage systems for the new town of Gary, Indiana, built by U.S. Steel.
5. *Jonathan Ogden Armour:* Born in Milwaukee and educated at Yale, Armour described himself facetiously as "author" and "renegade vegetarian," but he actually became president of his father's enormous meat empire when the latter died in 1901, and he served on literally dozens of boards of directors, including the boards of grain companies, insurance companies, and railroads.
6. *Bion J. Arnold:* An electrical engineer born in Michigan, Arnold became a consultant to General Electric (1889–93) and actually built the power plant for the Columbian Exhibition and consulted on the construction of the rail line to the fair.
7. *Edward Ayer:* Identified as a "capitalist" with extensive lumber interests throughout the United States, Ayer was born in Illinois but not Chicago. He was noted for his fine Americana library and for his presidency, between 1893 and 1898, of the Field Columbian Museum.

What could these men have known of life on the other side of the tracks?

The Same Flawed Vision and Blind Spots

The Chicago Plan itself is a strange mixture of romantic history and practical prescriptions. After the first chapter, which reprises the accomplishments of the fair and acknowledges it as "model," Chapter 2 opens with pictures of the Giza pyramids and the Acropolis and makes reference in its subtitle to Babylon, Egypt, Athens, Rome, medieval cities, Paris, Germany, London, and Washington, D.C. (Burnham had just completed a "replan" of the U.S. capital).

IX. THE PYRAMIDS AT GIZEH.

CHAPTER II

CITY PLANNING IN ANCIENT AND MODERN TIMES: COMMERCE A LEADING MOTIVE IN CITY BUILDING: BABYLON, EGYPT, ATHENS, AND ROME: MEDIÆVAL CITIES: THE DEVELOPMENT OF PARIS: CITY PLANNING IN GERMANY: OVERCOMING CONGESTION IN LONDON: WASHINGTON A CITY BUILT ON A PLAN: OTHER AMERICAN CITIES

Figure 5.2. Delusions of grandeur: the Burnham plan for Chicago, 1909. This image is reproduced from the first page of Chapter 2 of the Burnham plan.

But the real text begins with Chapter 3, which shifts to a more practical agenda. It includes a proud but histrionic call to action to avert disaster, because the population of Chicago is projected (via an unrealistic straight line) to increase to thirteen and a quarter million by 1952.[45] The practical agenda is best captured, however, by the map depicting successively larger "rings" around the city's core for which circulation systems needed to be designed; by 1990, only two-thirds of this delimited region had become built-up parts of the metropolis. Chapter 4 of the plan deals with parks; Chapter 5 covers transportation, emphasizing the need to coordinate rail lines and to build centralized stations; Chapter 6 focuses on a more rational system of city streets; and Chapter 7, the most ebullient, envisages the future city center—replete with monumental civic buildings in ceremonial plazas and Hausmann-like boulevards. The five-page text of the final chapter focuses on finance, justifying the enormous expenses entailed as follows:

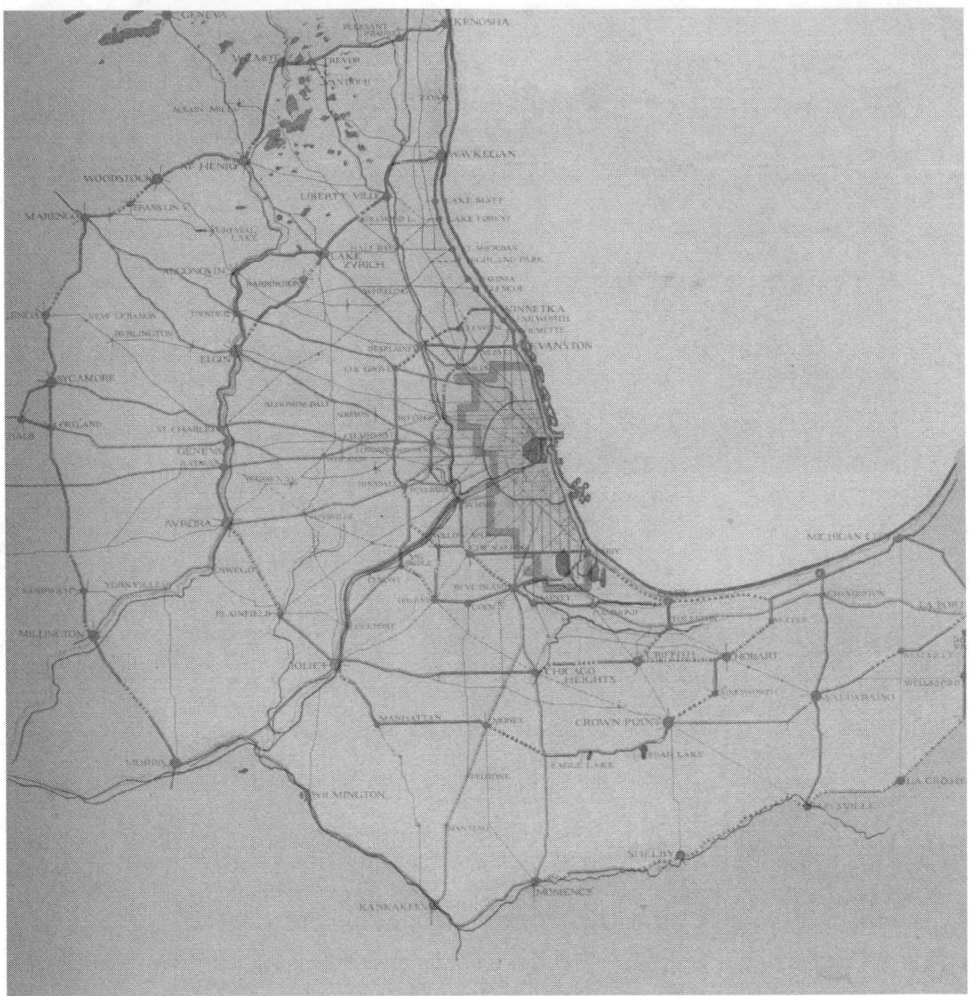

Map 5.4. Burnham's sixty-mile city, from the Burnham plan of 1909.

> [The plan's] adoption and realization will produce for us conditions in which *business enterprises can be carried on with the utmost economy . . . while we and our children can enjoy . . . life. . . . Then our own people will become home-keepers, and the stranger will seek our gates.*[46]

It would be cruel to point out that the stranger had already crashed the gates, even though he and his conditions are entirely invisible in the document.

Just as the fair had been oblivious to the social problems around it, opening in the depression of 1894, when "the air was full of revolt,"[47] so the Chicago Plan was beautifully adorned with aquatints at a time when some of Chicago's bloodiest labor uprisings were being ruthlessly repressed. Not a word in the document refers to the city's underside, however. The Chicago Plan that paid so much attention to the efficiency of transport and to the glamour of decorative civic jewels totally ignored the vast terrain of the city in which "strangers" were struggling to survive in offensive and hazardous factories and in overcrowded and degraded hovels.

ON THE BACKS OF PEASANTS

It is really remarkable that as late as 1909 the planners of Chicago should have remained so blind to their city. It was not for lack of reminders. In 1893, William T. Stead, English editor and a Christian Socialist, gave an incendiary speech exposing corruption in Chicago's government, describing the plight of workers and detailing the savage brutality against them.[48] There was some reaction, although not much from members of the Commercial Club.

> In response to the conditions that Stead revealed, . . . The Civic Federation, headed by many of Chicago's most prominent businessmen and their wives, dabbled in genteel reform. . . . [It] made noteworthy efforts to provide systematic relief for the needy, improve housing and sanitary conditions, and drive the grafters from City Hall. Among the supporters of the Federation were a group of professional reformers . . . Jane Addams, for instance.[49]

Certainly, the "peasants" were growing numerous enough to require notice and would be making every effort to call attention to themselves. Where had these "needy" come from?

If New York was already expanding into its metropolitan region in the immediate post-Civil War period, Chicago was still poised at the edge of its most important burst of growth.[50] Between 1860 and 1870, the population of Chicago (within the same boundaries) nearly tripled, rising from 109,000 to almost 300,000. Of the 190,000 residents added to the city in those ten years, only about 30,000 can be attributed to natural increase (an excess of births over deaths). The remaining growth came from migration. In that decade some 63,000 native-born whites moved to Chicago from other places in the country, especially the Northeast; another 2,700 native-born blacks came, mostly from the adjacent border states, rather than the Deep South;[51] but most of the gain came from the 90,000 newcomers who had been born abroad. Primarily Irish and German, they had either moved directly to Chicago, recruited by "labor bosses" who took them en masse from boats to train stations, or left their earlier homes on the East Coast to seek better opportunities. Although a few of these early immigrants would eventually become economic and civic "leaders," most would join the base of the bifurcating social structure becoming clearly evident by the 1890s.

During the 1870s, jobs in construction were plentiful, due to the need to rebuild Chicago after the fire. And at the same time, Chicago's heavy industries (such as the slaughterhouses, the farm machinery plants, and the factories producing railway cars) were demanding more labor. The city became a magnet not only for foreign immigrants but for workers from other parts of the United States, which had been hit more severely than Chicago by the recession of 1873–74. By 1880 the total population exceeded half a million, and of the 204,208 residents added in the preceding decade, only about 50,000 represented the difference between births and death; another 60,000 came from foreign immigration; and some 95,000 could be traced to white internal migration.[52] As before, the number of black internal migrants remained low, at about 2,800.[53] The real "takeoff" decade of growth came in the 1880s, when an increase of some 600,000 brought the population (within preannexation boundaries) up to 1.1 million. This increase clearly reflected the same surge in "new" immigration that was infusing New York, although selective sifting and sorting resulted in different mixes. Between 1880 and 1890, Chicago's foreign-born population increased by almost a quarter of a million (245,807), drawn mostly from the peasant regions of east-central Europe. Although natural increase added another 100,000 in the decade, most of these were children of the foreign-born. This influx of non-English-speaking peasants overshadowed the 144,000 native white and the 7,800 native black Americans who also flocked to the city. A similar number of new residents would be added in the last decade of the century, although the marginal contribution of the foreign-born immigrants (a net increase of only 136,446) was by then overshadowed by the 170,000 added through natural increase, the 265,000 added to the white native-born by internal migration, and the 15,879 added by black native-born migrants.[54] Nevertheless, by 1900, almost four in five Chicagoans were either foreign-born or the offspring of this first generation.

THE CONGRUENCE BETWEEN IMMIGRATION AND INDUSTRIALIZATION

Although the "Industrial Revolution" long predated the American Revolution, industry came late to the United States, because the English had forbidden the colonies to engage in any manufacturing except simple processing of agricultural products.[55] After independence, mechanized textile production began, capitalized by the profits made from the China trade or whaling, but even heavier industry was possible because, as early as 1790, "the United States . . . [produced] close to one-sixth of the world's iron."[56]

By the time of the Civil War, however, major changes in both the location and type of industrialization were well under way. Sam Bass Warner Jr. has characterized the period between 1870 and 1920 as a "giant leap forward in power, speed, energy, and adaptability," especially in steel production, after the French-designed Siemens-Martin open-hearth method of high-quality steelmaking was developed in 1862 and after 1865, when cheap Bessemer steel production was first introduced.[57]

The reticulation of the rail system made centralization of large-scale production in steel more feasible and propelled the largest and best-connected cities in the country to dominant positions in diversified manufacturing. New York, Chicago, and Philadelphia became the largest manufacturing centers in the country.[58] Not only did the scale of enterprises increase, but new ways of managing such larger firms—such as incorporation, separate management, and bureaucracies—accompanied the shift in scale.[59]

> Nowhere were these developments as sudden and complete as in Chicago. Increasingly after 1850 the city became the workshop, manufacturing goods for local and regional consumption and exporting the surplus all across the continent, and then around the world. The burgeoning steel mills, slaughterhouses, lumberyards,

> freight warehouses, mail-order establishments, and retail stores needed hands to do the lifting, hauling, slicing, stacking, selling. . . . The legend grew that if a man couldn't "make it" in Chicago, he couldn't make it anywhere.[60]

Some measure of Chicago's industrial growth can be gained from Skogan's compilation of information for the period between 1880 and 1919.[61] The number of manufacturing establishments grew from some 3,500 in 1880 to more than 10,000 by 1919, and the number of employees increased even more dramatically, from 80,000 in the early year to over 400,000 in the later year. This indicated that there was a marked increase in scale in the interval. In 1880, the average number of workers per establishment was still only 22.5, not much larger than New York's in that year, whereas by 1919, the Chicago average approached 40 workers/plant, far outstripping New York.[62]

It was into this expanding industrial sector that the "new immigrants" arriving in Chicago in the 1880s were absorbed. Their histories are inextricably interwoven with those of the largest firms, which not only determined their class position but exercised a decisive influence on where they settled. The ethnic "pecking orders" established in the firms, the peripheral locations of the largest industries, coupled with the still primitive state of mass transit in the city, help to explain the social and physical segmentation of proletarian Chicago. Job segmentation according to ethnicity hindered labor solidarity, and the formation of a multiplicity of white "ethnic ghettos" militated against political solidarity. And the immigrants' places of work and residence became increasingly isolated, socially and spatially, from the "facade" city enjoyed by the wealthy industrial magnates who benefited from this virtually unlimited supply of poor workers.

The first industries of Chicago had been linked to either agriculture/forestry or the railroads and were located near the city center.[63] Many of these industries moved farther out in the late nineteenth century. The McCormick Reaper plant, after its destruction in the Chicago Fire, was rebuilt in modernized fashion at a more distant location. The abattoirs after 1865 congregated well beyond the city limits to escape regulation, the Pullman sleeping car plant was relocated to a planned company town at the periphery,[64] and the steel plants were consolidated in the distant and desolate Calumet Harbor swamp, eventually spilling over as far as Gary, U.S. Steel's planned town in Indiana. These were among the largest employers and the most powerful protagonists in the increasingly contentious labor relations in the city. Their poorly paid workers could not afford a "journey to work" on the relatively expensive streetcars or railways; perforce, they settled near coworkers/coethnics next to the factories.

I single out here two of the largest employers of labor that came to symbolize Chicago in the period in question, the stockyards and the steel mills. In their histories we can see in microcosm many of the factors that shaped the city of the poor.

Building Big Industry: Porkopolis and the Open Hearth

Animal slaughtering/meatpacking had been one of Chicago's earliest industries, although the city was less important than Cincinnati until the Civil War, when army demand boomed and Chicago's more protected location made it the preferred source. But facilities were still small and scattered throughout the city. Health-related pressures mounted to regulate or even "expel" them. The industry favored a unified facility beyond municipal control, and in 1865 the Union Stock Yards of Chicago opened on 320 acres of marshland in the still unannexed town of Lake.[65] At that time, the site appeared well located, not only far from the city, but along the South Branch of the Chicago River, which permitted easy, if polluting, waste removal, and adjacent to rail lines that could deliver meat "on the hoof."[66]

By 1870, "the value of Chicago's beef and pork climbed to $19 million and packinghouse by-products added another $4 million," far outstripping its next ranking industrial products: lumber ($7 million), garments ($6 million), and iron and steel ($5 million).[67] Expansion was rapid, and by 1928 "the Yards" had become the largest livestock facility in the world, containing more than a hundred plants (the largest of which employed some ten thousand workers) and employing over twenty-eight thousand workers, more than any other industry in the city.

The first packinghouse workers had been Irish and German, some of the latter being highly skilled butchers. But mechanization in the 1870s, increased production, and more widespread use of refrigeration cars by the 1880s led to a change in production.[68] Many tasks were routinized via assembly lines, which permitted the substitution of unskilled (and cheaper) workers.[69] And because the work was so unpleasant, hazardous, and often irregular, "the stockyards [came to be] manned chiefly by those who had no alternative—the most recent immigrants and [later] Negroes."[70]

The steel mills developed later. Therefore, Irish and German craftsmen had little chance to entrench themselves before the great migration began; from the start the mills were highly mechanized but demanded the proverbial "broad shoulders." The North Chicago Rolling Mill Company's South Works was opened in 1880 in South Chicago, close to the mouth of the Calumet River, where four blast furnaces were constructed. Two years later a Bessemer steel mill and a rail mill were operating.

> In 1889 the North Chicago Rolling Mills Company and the Union Steel Company merged . . . and formed the Illinois Steel Company. The South Chicago plant, often referred to as the South Works, had expanded by 1898 from the original site of 74.5 acres to one of approximately 260 acres. . . . Other firms followed. . . . The industry expanded across the state line into Indiana, where after 1900 the huge United States Steel Corporation created a new town called Gary. . . . By 1900 . . . [t]he steel industry [had] expanded from the mouth of the Calumet River to cover the entire lakefront south of 79th Street.[71]

By about 1910 steel production was heavily centralized in huge plants and the industry had merged with Minnesota iron ore mining companies that assured them of steady raw material supplies.[72] Conditions of work were oppressive and very hazardous, although corporations tried to hide the extent of the fatal injuries.[73] And, as in the stockyards, a multiethnic labor force was organized via ethnic stratification, with the lowest-paid and most noxious or dangerous jobs reserved for those in the most vulnerable market position.

These two prototypical industries of Chicago, although perhaps more extreme than most in their geographic concentrations and their voracious demands for immigrant labor, help us explore two of the defining elements of Chicago during that period: first, the large-scale contentious nature of labor relations in the city, despite unions whose strength was often undermined by the manipulation of interethnic tensions; and second, the tendency to translate ethnic specialization on the job into residential segregation of workers in what Wade tells us were actually referred to at the time as "citylets"—that is, relatively self-contained quarters around the large installations.[74] The factors most responsible for the latter were the city's undeveloped mass-transit system and wage levels that were so low that workers could not afford to use the system that did exist.[75]

Confrontations at the Workplace

Given the more heavily capitalized and larger-scale industrialization that characterized Chicago's economy, it is not surprising that Chicago's labor strife should have been much more confrontational and massive than that found in New York.[76] Between 1887 and 1894, Chicago experienced some 528 strikes involving some 283,000 workers. These events reveal a common pattern: owners relied on the local police, privately hired strongmen, and, occasionally, the national guard to "discipline" workers and to guard the strikebreakers they routinely imported to keep their plants running.

A representative list would include the Haymarket Riot of 1886; a day later, the first organized march of wildcat garment trade workers; a strike at the McCormick Reaper works in the same year, where workers were also fired upon by the police; the great Pullman strike of 1894 and a major stockyard strike in the same year; machinists' strikes in 1900 and 1901; and a major steel strike in 1901, followed in 1902 by a citywide teamsters' strike and, in 1904, by a long and bloody strike by packinghouse workers, in which black scabs were first employed in large numbers.[77] Although clothing workers struck in 1910 and newspaper workers in 1912, more typical for Chicago were the recurring strikes and boycotts by machinists.[78] After the moratorium of World War I, a wave of strikes hit the city, including a major confrontation between owners and steelworkers.

Not unexpectedly, it was in the largest industrial complexes that some of the first attempts were made to form unions and mobilize for strikes.[79] One of the earliest manifestations came in the massive 1886 strike at the McCormick works, which lasted for seventy-eight days, resulted in six deaths, and not only involved the thirty thousand employees at the plant but an additional hundred thousand in citywide sympathy. Two of the most important labor actions took place in the depression of 1894: the Pullman strike, which lasted eighty-three days, involved three thousand strikers, and was put down only with the intervention of the local militia and the regular army (and which precipitated a nationwide railway strike); and an equally explosive forty-three-day strike in the Union Stock Yards. The stockyards continued to be the scene of considerable unrest. In 1902, stockyard workers struck again in sympathy with the teamsters, and in 1904, thirty thousand workers in the yards struck for fifty-seven days.[80] Looking more closely at the stockyards can give us some insight into quintessential elements organizing the city's increasingly fractured social system.

Labor Actions in the Stockyards

The availability of a virtually unlimited labor reserve army created by new immigration continuously undermined the efforts of original stockyard workers to organize for improved working conditions. In 1886, just before the Haymarket Riot, skilled butchers had negotiated an eight-hour day without loss in pay, but employers reinstituted the ten-hour day within months. In the ensuing lockout, "'Poles,' an appellation fastened on all newcomers from southern and southeastern Europe, were used as strikebreakers." Poles had entered the Back-of-the-Yards as early as 1884, but only a few had succeeded in obtaining jobs, almost exclusively in the fertilizer plants and hide cellars, the most noxious positions. However, they "soon shared in all unskilled work. *By 1894 they had fairly monopolized the jobs lowest in the scale.*"[81]

It was this split between craft unions and brute labor, which initially corresponded to ethnic cleavages, that weakened labor in Chicago.[82] And it was the close relationship between place of work and place of employment that tended to trigger ethnic succession in Chicago's neighborhoods. After the "Poles" were brought in as strikebreakers, they were kept on, and the neighborhood adjoining the yards, previously occupied by Irish and Germans, became increasingly occupied by Poles, Slovaks, and Croatians, as the earlier residents moved farther south.

"Ethnic succession" in the plants always intensified during labor disputes, which stoked intergroup hostilities.[83] But the usual pattern of retaining strikebreakers did not apply to the African American workers who were first introduced in significant numbers as strikebreakers in the acrimonious strike of 1904. For two weeks,

> trainloads of several hundred Negroes, accompanied by officers of the law, arrived daily. . . . The role of the Negro in the strike of 1904 differed from that which he had assumed in 1894. *He was at the center of attack from the moment the strike began.* . . . To the striking union men no scabs were as loathsome as the Negroes who took their jobs. . . . At the close of the struggle . . . [t]he colored deserters were herded into special trains which carried them to the Black Belt. The packers preferred white laborers and hired them to replace the Negroes whose services as strike-breakers were no longer required.[84]

It was not until the labor shortage of World War I that African Americans were finally recruited in any number in the industry, but hostilities persisted between white "ethnics" and blacks, who were discriminated against and who retained a healthy suspicion of the unions that had opposed their hiring and, indeed, at first excluded them.[85] Some of the simmering interracial hostilities that erupted in the race riot that wracked Chicago between July 27 and August 2, 1919 (to be discussed below) can be traced directly to tensions that built up in large workplaces, ostensibly over unionization.[86] Nevertheless, between 1921 and the Depression, African Americans constituted about 30 percent of stockyard workers and had begun to form separate unions.

However, by then they were already beginning to be displaced by Mexicans. Blacks were the first to be fired in the downsizing of the 1930s.[87]

Labor mobilizations came later to the steel industry and had even less success. It was not until World War I that, because of the strategic significance of steel, the federal government intervened; the War Labor Board's 1918 decision regarding the Bethlehem Steel Works in Pennsylvania confirmed the rights of labor to organize. In the national steel strike called in 1919, some ninety thousand steelworkers struck in the Chicago-Gary and other Indiana plants.[88] But "1919 marked the beginning of the end of the success of the wartime labor movement," and it would not be until late in the Depression (1937) that a major steel strike would again be mounted in Chicago.[89]

Confrontations by Residence

Because ethnicity organized the backstage neighborhoods of Chicago into minighettos, and because, unlike New York, the City Council members retained significant power as representatives of neighborhood interests, the battles at the workplace between owners and workers were often replicated in city government between members of the elected City Council, heavily weighted to the "back city," and the technocrats and elite executives and administrators who lived mostly in the city of the facade.[90] Teaford notes that although the power of municipal legislatures declined everywhere in nineteenth-century cities, Chicago was an exception:

> As late as 1898 a student of Chicago's city government concluded that "the municipal history of Chicago has emphasized . . . the supremacy of the common council during more than half a century of municipal activity." Chicago's council determined the appropriations without any strictures imposed by boards of estimate or finance commissions. Moreover, aldermanic confirmation was necessary for executive appointments. The Chicago council did have to share power with independent park and sewerage commissions; and the library and school boards, though formally subject to the council, did not kowtow to its authority. *But the formal powers of Chicago's municipal legislature generally remained intact.*[91]

As elsewhere, ward politics became the means through which immigrant communities tried to protect their interests. But "as the social and ethnocultural background of neighborhood party chiefs changed, native-born reformers and plutocratic downtown businessmen grew increasingly contemptuous of the office of ward leader."[92] They also found ways to bypass the growing power of "ethnics." In Chicago, the elite drew back from direct political participation, but as Jaher argues, wealthy Chicagoans exercised their influence through payoffs to more plebeian political bosses:

> Deference accorded to leading businessmen produced government policies advantageous to their primary concerns. The tycoons led the annexation movement in the 1880s . . . [and] the state's attorney for Cook County refused to prosecute violators of an Illinois factory law prohibiting employment of children. . . . Meat

> packers were on good terms with Chicago police, who gave them protection in labor disputes. . . . The most consistent example of the ability of wealth to manipulate government was the underassessment of real and personal property.[93]

Nevertheless, the elite of transplanted northeasterners found the toleration of gambling parlors, saloons, and brothels by machine politicians from immigrant wards as offensive as did their counterparts in New York, and they agitated against vice and for civil service and ballot reforms. They achieved their goals briefly in the 1890s, when "the police department was reorganized, gambling was curbed," and the merit system was adopted for municipal employment.[94] But their efforts were essentially undermined once "Big Bill" Thompson succeeded in taking over municipal government in 1915, leaving the Chicago Civic Federation and the Municipal Voters' League in disarray. Progressivism was short-lived in Chicago.

In all of this, whether machine politics or civic reform, the black population was essentially ignored. While Jane Addams and other social work reformers concentrated their efforts on assimilating white immigrants, Chicago's black population attracted little attention, and its few ward representatives were loyal servants of Thompson's Republican machine.[95]

AFRICAN AMERICANS IN THE SOCIAL AND PHYSICAL STRUCTURE OF CHICAGO

We have seen how the proletarian role of masses of European immigrants intersected with Chicago's rapid industrialization. The formation and distribution of ethnic communities along the industrial and railway corridors that radiated out (sometimes very far out) from the central business district—primarily along the North and South Branches of the Chicago River but also in the outlying marshlands to the south—can be largely explained by how immigrants from different origins were inserted into the industrial labor force, and thus settled near their jobs.

The distribution of blacks in the city—their persisting poverty, and their early hypersegregation in Chicago's South Side "Black Belt"—requires a very different explanation, one in which racism must be recognized as constituting a bedrock element. One must raise a serious question as to why Chicago has suffered from greater segregation and race prejudice than almost any other northern city. It was certainly not because blacks constituted an unduly large and threatening proportion of the population. In 1880 only 1 percent of the total population was black, a representation that, despite inmigration, rose only gradually: to 1.3 percent in 1890, 1.8 percent in 1900, and about 2 percent as late as 1910. Even after the great migration of southern blacks to Chicago from 1915 onward, the proportion had risen only to 4 percent by 1920 and in 1930 was still less than 7 percent.[96] Yet long before this increase in numbers, blacks were highly disadvantaged in the city.

The earliest historical precedents may hold a key, especially when these are contrasted with New York. One might begin by considering that Illinois, originally a "colony" of Virginia, shared more with its southern neighbors than with its northeastern

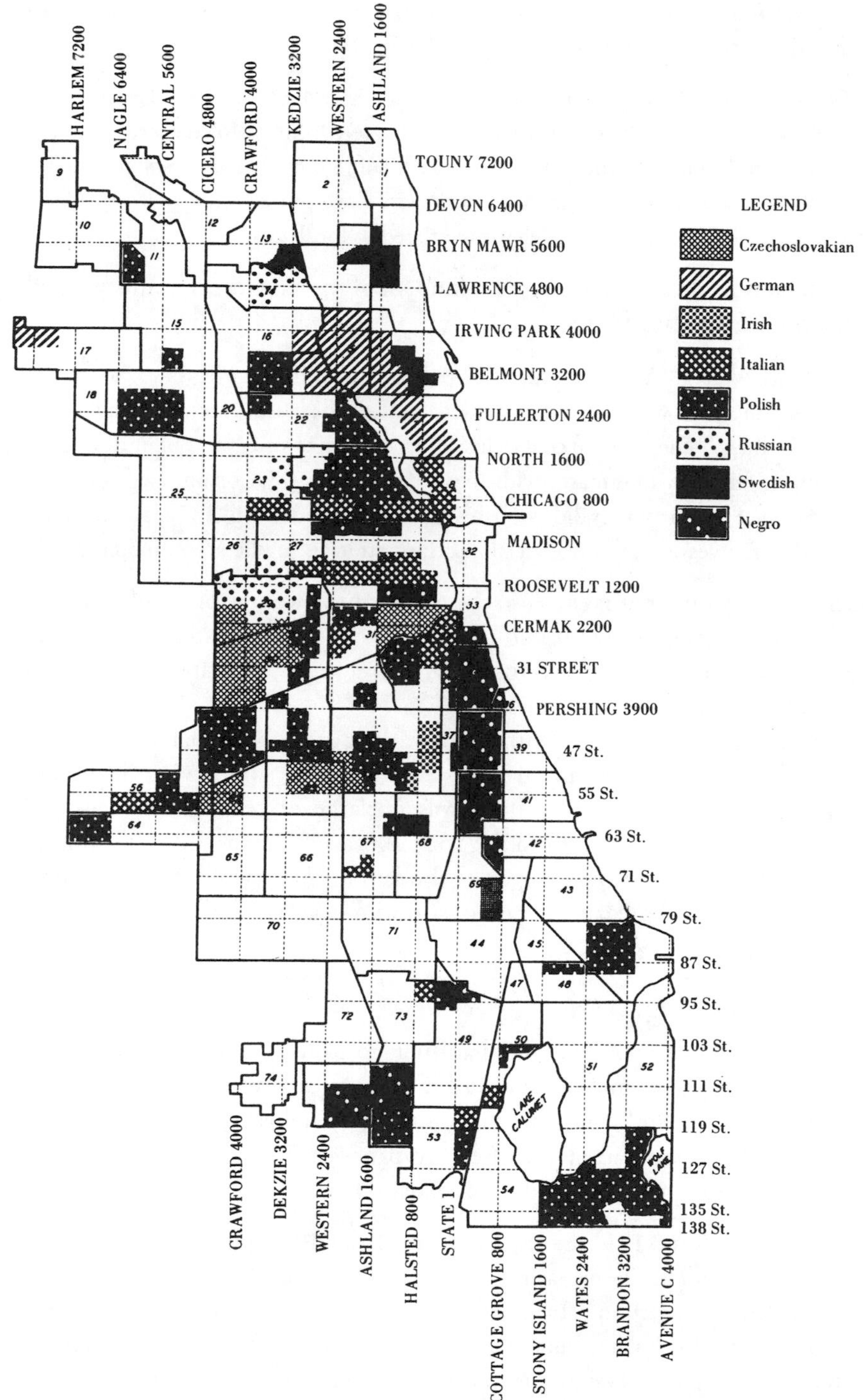

Map 5.5. The distribution of ethnic communities of Chicago in 1930. Source: Thomas Lee Philpott, *The Slum and the Ghetto;* used with permission of Oxford University Press.

ones.[97] This may be one reason that, even though Chicago's black population long preceded the arrival of immigrants, their relative status was inferior.[98]

> One year after Illinois became a state . . . it instituted severe "Black laws." Under such laws it was necessary for blacks to have a certificate of freedom to become a resident of Illinois. Failure to produce said document could have resulted in being sold for a period of one year. Blacks had very little protection under these laws. Blacks could not vote and travel was restricted to local areas.[99]

These disabilities continued into the second half of the nineteenth century. As Philpott summarizes the disadvantages:

> A state law of 1858 forbade free Negroes to enter Illinois. Negroes who already resided there or who slipped in undetected by the authorities were subject to "black codes." They had no civil rights. They could not vote, serve on juries, testify against whites, or intermarry with them. . . . It was 1870 before Negroes could vote. The State of Illinois did not ban school segregation until 1874, and it waited another ten years to prohibit racial discrimination in public accommodations.[100]

Nevertheless, within Chicago at least, the abolitionists were strong and active. In 1850 the city passed a resolution that said the police were not obligated to help recover escaping slaves; by then, two underground railway stations were operating in the city, in which blacks played important roles.[101]

But throughout the nineteenth century, their numbers remained small and most of Chicago's blacks were employed in domestic service, some living in the homes of their employers. Because of this, there was no large or centralized ghetto until the 1890s, when a new migration from the South began.[102] It was only after this that segregation intensified, and it was only after the tentative entry of blacks into industry as strikebreakers that the preexisting racism spread to the "new ethnics."

The Formation of the Black Belt

By 1900, "several of the old colonies had merged to form a long, narrow Black Belt" along State Street between 12th and 39th Streets, a quarter of a mile wide and some three miles in length and completely surrounded by railway tracks.[103] In the next few decades the black population increased from about 30,000 in 1900 to 44,000 in 1910, but the area open to them did not expand.

> Between 1910 and 1914 the district absorbed over 10,000 new migrants, but the saturation point had been reached. The area had to expand. Most of the southerners settled in the section between State Street and the Rock Island Railroad tracks to the west. This was the poorest and most run-down part of the Black Belt. . . . Rents were high . . . even before . . . the great migration. . . . Hostile whites surrounded the Black Belt.[104]

It was then that the great migration began. By 1920, the black population exceeded 109,000 and approached 234,000 ten years later. White resistance stiffened, and "the

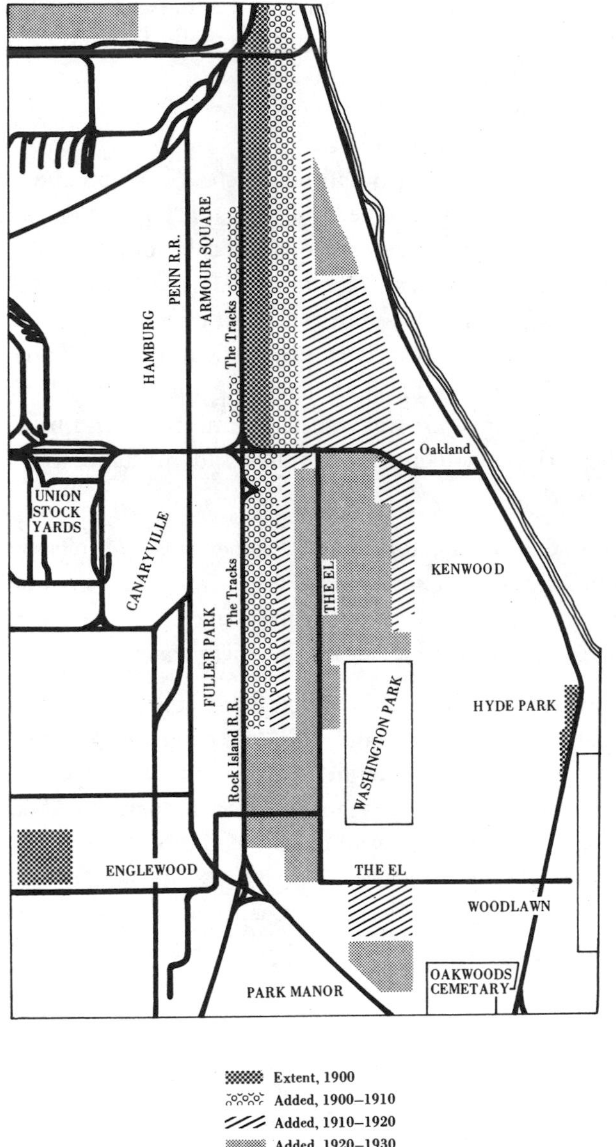

Map 5.6. The original Black Belt on Chicago's South Side. Source: Thomas Lee Philpott, *The Slum and the Ghetto;* used with permission of Oxford University Press.

black population piled up in a ghetto circumscribed as no immigrant enclave had ever been."[105]

Some 80 percent of the 30,000 native-born nonwhites in Chicago in 1890, like their white counterparts, had come to the city from elsewhere, but most hailed from "upper South" bordering states; these areas continued to provide newcomers in the decades of slow migration that followed.[106] But in the period between 1916 and 1919, the size and composition of the black community changed drastically. During these short years, some 50,000 newcomers, recruited chiefly from Mississippi, Louisiana, and Arkansas, were crowded into the existing ghetto, whose boundaries proved impermeable. By the 1920s, the Black Belt emerged as "a fully-developed Negro ghetto," from which any remaining whites had fled.[107]

The labor shortage in Chicago had become critical after the United States entered the war early in 1917, and the steel mills, foundries, and packinghouses sent recruiters south for more workers (a venture vigorously supported and assisted by the publishers of the *Chicago Defender*). The industrialization of Chicago's black population was dramatic. As late as 1910, more than half of black males had worked in domestic or personal services; ten years later, only little more than a quarter did, whereas the proportion of blacks engaged in manufacturing and trade had tripled.[108]

These economic gains were not translated into more and better housing, however. Indeed, they triggered increased hostility and resistance on the part of their neighbors and coworkers.

> Instead of expanding the boundaries of the Negro districts, the migration converted the old South Side black belt from a mixed neighborhood into an exclusively Negro area. There was remarkably little change in the areas of Negro settlement despite the 148 per cent population increase . . . [and the] sharp rise in the density.[109]

As routinely happened elsewhere, this overcrowding resulted in rapidly deteriorating housing accompanied by inflated rents. The festering slum west of State Street became even worse, and the Prairie Avenue mansions inherited from the old elite quarter were divided up and subdivided again to accommodate the "better-off."[110] Some of Chicago's earliest "border wars" were fought as the Black Belt expanded slightly at its edges into white districts, arousing white hostility and intensifying efforts to "tighten the noose" through restrictive covenants and even bombings.[111] All these served as preludes to the race riot of 1919, the bloodiest in the city's history to date.

The Race Riot of 1919

Economic developments and spatial segregation almost overdetermined that a "race war" would break out in 1919. In the postwar recession of 1919, black industrial workers suffered severe setbacks. "In the spring of 1919, the packing houses paid off 15,000 workers—a large proportion of them Negroes."[112] Although the recession was short-lived, blacks were not rehired. Even before that, racial tensions had been building. Between July 1, 1917, and July 27, 1919, the day a black swimmer was hit by an object thrown by a hostile white and drowned off a South Side beach—the immediate event that triggered the riot—there had been twenty-four racially motivated bombings, "more than half of them in the six months just prior to the race riot."[113] During the six days between July 27 and August 2, white gangs made raids on the Black Belt and battles erupted outside, wherever blacks had to travel to reach their jobs. In these occurrences, spatial patterns proved highly significant.

Some of the worst violence occurred in relation to the stockyards, because workers from the Black Belt had to go through intervening Irish quarters to get to work there. "White mobs molested blacks returning home from the stockyards . . . and after a transit strike the next day stopped violence on public transportation . . . African Americans had to walk through hostile, Irish-dominated neighborhoods in order to reach their jobs in the stockyards."[114] There were even racial clashes between workers in the livestock pens.

The National Guard was called out, and the body count at the end of hostilities stood at fifteen whites and twenty-three blacks dead. But the toll was even higher for future race relations. After the riot, the two communities withdrew more firmly within their own "borders," and the black community of Bronzeville proceeded to develop its own institutions.[115] It also became more directly involved in Chicago's politics.

Blacks had aligned themselves with the elite's bête noire, Big Bill Thompson, whose election as mayor in 1915 marked the end of Chicago's brief Progressive Era. By then,

> Negro politicians had built an organization of their own within the Republican party . . . [although t]he ward organization was still in white hands. [Blacks had, however, already elected] one of their number to the city council, acquired several attractive patronage positions, and forced white politicians to heed Negro wants and aspirations. No one better understood the importance of the Negro vote than William Hal Thompson. . . . [Even though he was a notorious symbol of Chicago as a violent, corrupt, and gangster-ridden city in the 1920s,] the majority of Chicago's Negroes never faltered in their loyalty to him, and they helped elect him to three terms as mayor.[116]

According to Spear, by the 1920s, African Americans had obtained greater political power and held more offices, both appointed and elected, in Chicago than in any other part of the country. And yet, "the gestures that the white political structure made toward the Negro community remained largely formal and ceremonial. They hardly touched the basic problems of the black belt: inadequate housing, inferior job opportunities, poverty, social disorganization, crime, and corruption."[117] These issues would surface with a vengeance during the Great Depression, which hit Chicago's Black Belt the hardest. This setback threw the African American community completely into the hands of the Democratic Party, thus solidifying that party's subsequent hold over local politics.

CITY-SUBURB CLASS SEGREGATION

Although firm racial segregation did not manifest itself until the early twentieth century, segregation by class was already becoming evident by the 1890s, especially with respect to the suburbs. In the 1870s there was still considerable "class mixing" in Chicago neighborhoods, but

> During the next two decades the outmigration of Chicago's middle class completely reorganized the settlement patterns of the city. Instead of taking up vacant

> tracts in the partially built-up fringe where the working class were also settled, as had been the practice in the past, the middle class skipped over that ring entirely and settled itself in its own districts beyond. . . . [It was assisted by the] transportation improvements during the years from 1887 to 1894. . . . In this way Chicago's residential pattern by class had been fully set by 1894.[118]

Class thus became the third axis on which the "dual city" split.[119]

In 1893, when annexation came to a virtual halt, the suburban settlements that had resisted joining the city were mostly white and middle- to upper-class. The professionals in these communities could afford to commute to the Loop by expensive rail service and, once cars became a preferred and common mode of transportation, to drive downtown. They were joined by middle-class families seeking less dense settings. More and more, poorer working-class populations were "trapped" within the city, where older "cottages" were increasingly replaced by denser two- and three-family flats.[120] By 1930, one-third of all dwelling units in the city were three-story walk-ups or nineteenth-century dwellings over stores along main streets; another third were double- and triple-decker houses. The rest were bungalows near the outskirts.

Most working-class city residents who had to commute to work were dependent upon mass transit rather than cars, although the number of cars was also increasing within the city limits.[121] The expanding role of the automobile in the twentieth century helped to reinforce the division between city and suburbs and made mass transit (and its fares) a contentious arena for both class and city-suburban conflict. Paul Barrett identifies the central dilemma: "The fundamental difference . . . was that facilities for the automobile were publicly subsidized while mass transit was regulated and taxed," and because in Chicago transit was a private enterprise, it was "expected to make a profit."[122]

Unlike New York, which had assumed public responsibility for its mass-transit system early on, in Chicago between 1900 and 1930 "the city administration and the mass transit companies were [often] at odds," because users pressured for low fares and better service while transit companies expected to run a profitable business.[123] A city council ordinance of 1907 sought to regulate mass transit (to end the so-called traction wars), to declare it a public utility and to share in the profits,[124] but municipalization under the Chicago Transit Authority was not achieved until 1947. And even then, its governing board represented business and other special interests and was "effectively insulated from public pressures."[125] This may help explain why even the modest-length subway beneath the Loop was not built until 1943.

Building Classy Suburbs

Similar to other cities of the time, suburban "development" in Cook County beyond the city limits was initially the work of real estate speculators who bought undeveloped land and held it for eventual profit, a technique sometimes called the "Astor" method, earlier used in New York.[126]

> Many [investors] remembered the spectacular increases in land values in Manhattan in the first half of the nineteenth century and saw the possibility of a similar boom

> in Chicago. Charles Butler and his New York neighbor Arthur Bronson, for example, invested heavily in Chicago through their agent, William B. Ogden. . . . His work as a Chicago booster and entrepreneur helped to assure the continued rise in property prices.[127]

But there was another model, that of actively stimulating price rises by "development." Syndicates, land companies, and improvement associations were organized for the purpose of subdividing land and, on occasion, installing basic infrastructure, such as roads and utilities. Companies of this type founded "over half the settlements between 1861 and 1880."[128] It was not usual for developers also to build houses in their subdivisions, although a few did, and the practice became more common by the end of the century. By the early twentieth century, the construction of housing had become a normal part of suburban development. By 1930, just before the bottom dropped out of the market, most subdividers were delivering houses along with land and infrastructure.[129] Class segregation in the new suburbs was generally achieved through uniform lots varying in size by location and through deed restrictions. However, there were at least a few suburbs that catered to persons whose incomes did not qualify them to buy in such elegant planned communities as River Forest or Kenilworth (the latter still reputed to be one of the "richest" suburbs in the United States).

Subsidizing Housing in the City:

Housing for the less wealthy was very slow in coming. And in this area also, Chicago lagged behind New York. What little subsidized housing was built within the city limits served middle-income tenants and was constructed by private philanthropists whose idea of "subsidy" was to accept a 3 percent, instead of the usual 6 percent, return on their investment. Quite remarkably, however, the first of these projects, Francisco Terrace, was designed by a very young Frank Lloyd Wright in 1895.[130] Garden Homes was a larger project of single-family homes subsidized by Benjamin Rosenthal in 1919 on the style of British garden cities he had admired, but it ended in bankruptcy.

Some efforts to build garden apartments for the black community were made in the expansive 1920s. Julius Rosenwald of Sears, Roebuck, a trustee of Tuskegee Institute and a major supporter of the NAACP, sponsored the Michigan Boulevard Garden Apartments, intending them for black occupancy. Built in 1929, they consisted of 421 flats in five-story walk-ups organized around a courtyard and occupying the square block between 46th and 47th and between Michigan and Wabash.[131] Soon afterward, Marshall Field III sponsored the Marshall Field Garden Apartments, also located at the edge of the Black Belt. The project, containing 628 apartments, was modeled after one that had already been built in New York by the Metropolitan Life Insurance Company. At the time of its construction it was the largest moderate-income development in the country.[132]

But all the efforts to build upward in the Loop and to expand the supply of housing, albeit for whites in the suburbs and for the "ethnic" working class or black middle class in the city, ground to a halt when the Depression hit. Heavily dependent upon an industrial base that was capital-intensive and organized into large-scale enterprises, Chicago was among the most vulnerable cities in the country when the expansionary era of the 1920s ended with a bang and *also* a whimper.

ON A LESS DISMAL NOTE

But it would be unfair to leave this account with the somber picture I have painted of the city of broad shoulders because, for all its racial, ethnic, and class cleavages and their attendant strife, Chicago during the first few decades of the twentieth century exhibited exemplary vitality and creativity. The same grim realities that accompanied its growth into a powerhouse of industrial America spawned achievements in architecture, in literature, in social amelioration, and also in the sociological study of "the city" as an object of interest in its own right, thanks to the pathfinder scholars at the University of Chicago.

Architecture

Although by 1910 both Louis Sullivan and Frank Lloyd Wright had left Chicago—the former for other parts of the Midwest, where he deposited gems in lesser places before his death in 1922; the latter for Europe and later Los Angeles, where in the 1920s his style underwent significant development as he changed building materials from wood to cement—they left legacies behind.[133] The achievements of these two geniuses are part of the pride of Chicago architecture, even though the later commercial genre of the city favored a return to the solidity of the nineteenth century. Unhappily, in the 1920s, when art deco constructions were blossoming in places such as Los Angeles and even New York, Chicago remained relatively immune to its blandishments.[134] There then followed a hiatus, until a new infusion of creativity came with the work of Bauhaus master Mies van der Rohe, beginning in the 1940s.

Literature

Just as the Chicago school of architecture divested itself gradually of European and eastern influences to create new and indigenous forms of construction and new ideals of beauty, so a Chicago school of writers and poets was honing a new literary language. The mean streets of Chicago and the city's smokestack power inspired the production of a uniquely American literature, more active, direct, and earthy than the involuted and somewhat flowery style perfected by such eastern seaboard writers as Henry James and Edith Wharton. At least this is the thesis of Hugh D. Duncan, who claims:

> The relation of word and thing, or word and action, was far more intimate in Chicago usage than in a society where a usable literary tradition existed, and where images of life were formed in written works. Chicago words and phrases

> were related to action. . . . The language of sports, business, politics, and work had to be invented. . . . newspaper writers such as George Ade and Ring Lardner were creating an indigenous urban language . . . just as Mark Twain . . . had given us the indigenous American literature of the rural Middle West.[135]

He may overstate his case, but one must admit that the comparable "people's" literature being generated in New York was geared more to growing up in an immigrant community than it was to social commentary. There is nothing in New York's literary output of the time that can compare to Dreiser's repeated attempts to write "the great American novel," or, for that matter, Mr. Dooley's ascerbic comments (in Irish dialect, admittedly) on political shenanigans in the city.[136]

The Chicago Urban Reformers and Urban Sociologists

Chicago's other great contributions during the late 1890s and the early decades of the twentieth century were in the area of research-grounded social work reform (a movement associated mostly with the work of Jane Addams and Florence Kelley at Hull House)[137] and with the more academic but not unrelated activities of a small group of men and women at the University of Chicago who initiated the so-called Chicago school of urban sociology.[138]

In the 1890s, Jane Addams had founded Hull House (modeled after London's Toynbee Hall), located on the near West Side of Chicago, which then housed a diverse population of poor European immigrants much in need of "Americanization." While many of the settlement house's activities, therefore, were oriented toward socializing this population into the ways of their adopted country, there was growing awareness that the system into which they were being initiated was in need of considerable reform. Florence Kelley, in particular, stressed the exploitative character of Chicago's industrial organizations and advocated higher wages and better working conditions, paying special attention to women in the garment industry.

The settlement house also championed the cause of better housing, recognizing that the poor health and family tensions within immigrant households were exacerbated by their overcrowded and insalubrious living conditions. This latter concern was picked up by several women (notably Edith Abbott and Sophonisba P. Breckinridge) who, excluded from faculty appointments in existing academic departments of the University of Chicago, went on to found the field of social work and their own Institute of Philanthropy, later affiliated with the university. Long before the (all-male) Department of Sociology allegedly initiated the "Chicago school of urban sociology," these women and their students had been surveying the abominable housing and working conditions of immigrant families in Chicago. Both they and Addams had a strong if seldom acknowledged influence on the developing field of urban sociology.[139]

One would never wish to minimize the contributions of all these pioneers, but there were two conspicuous omissions or "dead ends" that resulted from their work, both of which can be attributed to the particular conditions that prevailed in Chicago at the time. First, there were the premature generalizations about urban form produced by Ernest Burgess, which sent urban sociologists off on a fruitless search for parallels in other cities, without recognizing that his findings were specific to the particular topography and simplified semicircular arrangement of Chicago.[140] The second was even more serious in the long run, although one can certainly understand why it occurred, given the importance of the immigrant communities of Chicago at the time the field was being laid out. Conspicuously absent, except for some of the work of Robert Park, was any attention to the still small, but growing, community of African Americans in the city. It would not be until the University of Chicago attracted more black students that this community, which was rapidly displacing immigrants as Chicago's largest "underclass," received the attention it deserved.[141] I discuss these developments in greater detail in Chapter 8.

CHAPTER 6

Los Angeles Becomes "Anglo"

> Most of the legends about Los Angeles are true—even when they are mutually contradictory.
>
> John Russell Taylor, *Strangers in Paradise*[1]

AN IMPROBABLE METROPOLIS

Robert Fogelson prefaces his detailed history of Los Angeles between 1850 and 1930 with a quotation from an English observer who remarked in the early 1930s, "It struck me as an odd thing that here [in Los Angeles], alone of all the cities in America, there was no plausible answer to the question, 'Why did a town spring up here and why has it grown so big?' "[2]

Despite its lack of a good natural harbor, the ports that currently serve Los Angeles (including not only Los Angeles Harbor [San Pedro] but also Port San Luis, Long Beach, El Segundo, Ventura, Port Hueneme, Captain, and Morrow) now handle some of the highest tonnages of imports and exports in the country.[3]

Set in a semiarid climate zone characterized by low humidity, capricious rainfall (where torrential winter floods can alternate with long periods of drought), a river of variable flow, inadequate groundwater and few nearby lakes, the metropolitan area now sprawls over some of the richest farmland in the country, and many of its mostly single-family houses boast green lawns and year-round flower beds, as well as blossoming deciduous, cypress, and palm trees. This "unnatural" cornucopia was made possible only through the construction of complex systems of irrigation, the water delivered via aqueducts from increasingly distant sources.

Initially, Los Angeles had been part of Spain's New World empire, inherited by

Mexico after independence and populated exclusively by Spanish speakers. By the 1920s, however, the city had become one of the most "Anglo" of all American metropolises—overwhelmingly "white" and native-born. Its rapid increase had come about largely through internal migration from the farm states of the Midwest.[4]

Improbable, also, was its pattern of development, which, instead of spreading gradually outward from a single center, was fragmented almost from the start into a crazy quilt stitched out of literally dozens of small towns and independently formed subdivisions, nestling in clusters that were not necessarily contiguous. These settlements, often constructed on former large *ranchos* already in single ownership, were differentiated according to a terrain that contained at least three of the "four ecologies" that Reyner Banham identifies as "surfurbia" (the beach areas), the "foothills" (on the slopes of low mountain ridges), and the "plains of Id" (the valleys), each with its own aesthetics and engineering imperatives.[5]

It was in the period between the mid-1870s and 1930 that these "unnatural" transformations occurred, by dint of human intent and through the skilled manipulation of federal, state, and local powers that provided the significant subsidies needed—both to "create" a more hospitable natural environment and to "determine" that the unpromising site would be selected as the hub of a transportation network that connected the city by rail to the rest of the continent and by sea to the rest of the world. Without these efforts, there would be no world city on the site of Los Angeles.

In each of these developments, our general periodicity of 1873–93, 1893 through World War I, and post–World War I through the 1920s, while roughly fitting the "facts," is a less powerful analytic device in the case of Los Angeles (where turning points were often related to locality-specific events) than it is for New York or Chicago. My exposition, then, traces certain issues over the entire time period, but also shows when and how such turning points affected them. The period between 1873 and 1893 was particularly inchoate, but as we shall see, the 1890s did introduce a new phase in Los Angeles history, just as World War I was a critical moment of transition out of which new metropolitan forms and functions emerged.

CALIFORNIA AS A WESTERN STATE

To understand some of the underlying causes of Los Angeles's anomalous history, it is necessary first to grasp how developments in the Far West differed from those in the eastern or even the midwestern regions of the United States, and how, in this, California represented perhaps the most extreme case. To some extent, the West was different because the federal government, still weak when the East and Midwest were being settled, had grown more mature and was better able to accomplish its "Manifest Destiny" by the time Los Angeles began its modern period of growth. To some extent, the West was different because capitalism was already taking on a larger and more monopolistic form by the time California was "won." And in part, the West was different because, from the start, it depended heavily on a system of direct referenda to determine policy decisions that elsewhere were more likely to be made by elected or appointed officials.[6]

Arthur Schlesinger captures some of these points in an early book that remains so relevant I quote him at length:

> Economically, the Great West at the close of the [eighteen] seventies was passing out of one era into another. The older industries, mining and ranching, were being obliged to assume new forms and agriculture was about to take its dominant place in Western economy. . . . The new system required large investments of capital. . . . Already by 1880 groups of capitalists controlled . . . the richest mines in Nevada. One gigantic California company owned all the best mines near Deadwood in the Black Hills. . . . Huge cattle companies were formed, often with English and Scotch capital, and in many sections of the Western range the cowboy began to receive his orders from a boss appointed by a board of directors in New York or London. . . . By the early eighties scores of great tracts of from five thousand to a hundred thousand acres in Kansas, Dakota, Minnesota, Texas and California, had gravitated into the hands of individuals or companies, many of them absentee owners. . . . While the westward extension of the wheat and corn belts was the most striking development in Western agriculture, almost equally significant was the increasing diversification of farming through most parts of the region. California, for example, was in 1878 not only the greatest wheat-growing state in the Union, but the banner state in oil production. Sheep raising . . . [gave way to] more intensive agriculture. . . . Although fruit culture had been tried earlier, it was the decade after 1878 which, by means of irrigation and better marketing facilities, changed it from a highly speculative venture to a settled business.[7]

Many of these developments were facilitated by the federal government, which not only distributed the unclaimed lands of the West[8] and gave special concessions to major railroads, but provided subsidies to pay for elaborate infrastructural improvements. In addition, states and cities, using their bond- and revenue-raising powers, also invested in ambitious ways that not only advanced local development but preferentially rewarded the large-scale capitalists who dominated the politics of the region.

Precedents for government involvement already existed before urbanization took root. Erie reminds us that "in the 1860s, Yankees used the legal system to wrest control of the Spanish [*sic*; really Mexican] land grants from the ranchero class," and in the 1870s the business-dominated government of Los Angeles "skillfully manipulated the electoral process to secure voter approval for the large subsidy necessary to bring the Southern Pacific Railroad to Los Angeles."[9] Massive subsidies were also obtained from the federal government to improve Los Angeles's ports in Wilmington and San Pedro, and later the powers of the federal and city governments would be used to survey and then help acquire the land and water of the Owens Valley that Los Angeles needed for its reservoirs and aqueducts.[10] This close collusion between private enterprise and governmental powers in city building in the western United States gave Los Angeles's political economy its special character from the start.

EARLIEST ECONOMIC CHANGES

Between midcentury and the 1870s, Los Angeles was only beginning to be linked into the political, economic, linguistic, and transportation systems of the country that had conquered it. But even before the Civil War major changes were already occurring. Just after California's admission as a state, the first steamship from San Francisco arrived in the shallows of the San Pedro harbor, hinting at the port's future. In 1853 the first orange trees were planted, with seeds brought from Central America and Hawaii, and one year later, the first shipment of grapes was sent to eastern markets, presaging the region's future as market garden to the country. By 1860 the first telegraph communication lines connecting Los Angeles, San Pedro, and San Francisco were in place, foreshadowing a future pattern of connections by rail and eventually by modems. And in that same year, once land surveys had been completed, the transfer of land parcels began to be transacted according to American law, ushering in a building boom that, with only brief albeit frequent and sometimes deep setbacks, continued for the next 130 years.[11]

After the Civil War, Los Angeles shared in the country's postwar boom, sinking its first oil well in 1865 and establishing its first bank in 1866, but by the end of the decade there were still fewer than six thousand residents within the narrowly delineated city limits and fewer than ten thousand in the county area outside the "city." This population was a strange mixture of native (Mexican) Californians who were becoming landless;[12] more recent Sonoran immigrants, peeling off on their way back to Mexico from the thinning gold fields in the north; formerly indentured Indians huddled together in "a miserable village near the Los Angeles River"; Americans hailing from New England, Texas, and other coastal states (for they still came mostly by sea); and even a variety of northern European immigrants.[13]

Some minor manufacturing, including brick kilns to provide building materials, had begun, although vintners still dominated the economy. And the town had begun to take on a more urban appearance, boasting twenty-five gas streetlights and a new residential zone of houses set in gardens between First and Fourth Streets.[14] But it was not until the 1870s and, even more so, the 1880s that the city and county would take on true urban characteristics. That transformation awaited Los Angeles's connections to the world.

LINKING LOS ANGELES TO THE NATIONAL NETWORK BY SEA AND RAIL

As early as 1851, Phineas Banning had developed a stage and wagon service between Los Angeles and its modest southern port, San Pedro, naming his "base" Wilmington, after his hometown in Delaware. Eventually his wagon trail became the path for Los Angeles's first rail line, the Los Angeles & San Pedro Railroad, a nucleus that would eventually be extended northward to San Francisco.[15] But Los Angeles still lacked a connection to the transcontinental system.

The chief player in that system was the Southern Pacific Railroad, which initially planned to bypass Los Angeles in its cross-continental service to San Francisco, the only city of any consequence on the West Coast at that time. Recognizing the absolute necessity of a rail connection, local county officials of Los Angeles agreed to pay the Southern Pacific a handsome "bribe" to convince the company to divert its line through Los Angeles:[16]

> The agreement included a sum of $600,000, representing five per cent of the total assessed valuation of the County of Los Angeles, a right-of-way 256 feet wide, 60 acres of land for depot purposes, and the existing Los Angeles & San Pedro Railroad. . . .
>
> The total proposition was agreed to by the voters in November 1872, and the Southern Pacific Railroad, now owner of the Los Angeles to San Pedro standard gauge line, assumed a position of virtual control over all shipping to and from Los Angeles.[17]

This also made (Yankee-born) Collis P. Huntington, the head of the Southern Pacific, the real power in Los Angeles—at least until his company's monopoly could be broken.

A simultaneous effort to create a rival port at Santa Monica, with a rail link to Los Angeles, aborted before it could prove a threat, although it did produce an independent city in the region. Santa Monica's history illustrates the close relationships among ports, rail lines, and urban development. Accumulating the land, laying out a town, building a railway, and improving the port all went hand in hand. The town of Santa Monica (formed through the purchase of the 38,409 acre Rancho San Vicente, the 2,112 acres of Rancho Boca de Santa Monica, and the smaller Rancho La Ballona) was chartered in 1875, and construction of the Los Angeles & Independence Railroad and an associated wharf began in the same year.[18] Then ensued a rivalry between the ports at San Pedro and Santa Monica, in which the latter was easily defeated when, in 1876, the Southern Pacific cut its rates (temporarily, of course) and activity in the port at Wilmington-San Pedro soon outstripped its rival two to one.[19] That was the year the Southern Pacific completed construction of its line from San Francisco to Los Angeles. Service on the Los Angeles & Independence Railroad between Santa Monica and Los Angeles declined, and the Southern Pacific eventually took it over. Once the competition had ended, the Southern Pacific raised the Santa Monica rates, closed the depots, and the port functions died. The last steamer to dock at Santa Monica arrived in 1878.[20]

The Southern Pacific parlayed its control over transport into control over the city and the region. By 1885 the company owned 85 percent of all California railroad lines and exerted an "economic stranglehold" over Los Angeles. "Representing the interests of San Francisco and eastern capital, the Southern Pacific treated Southern California as a colony . . . [and] created a powerful bipartisan machine to control Los Angeles's destiny."[21] Even after the Southern Pacific lost its rail monopoly (when in the 1880s the Santa Fe Railroad decided to make Los Angeles, not San Diego, its western terminus), this still did not break Huntington's power over city government, although by the middle of that decade it did lead to a fierce if short-lived rate war between the two on the long haul from Chicago to Los Angeles.[22]

The temporary bargain rates subsidized the export of fruits and vegetables eastward and also enticed many midwesterners to explore the possibility of settling in the much-advertised healthy climate of Los Angeles. By 1885, therefore, notwithstanding San Diego's natural advantages as a port, "Los Angeles emerged as the regional metropolis . . . [becoming] the focus of the extraordinary population movement which subsequently transformed southern California into one of the nation's foremost urban centers."[23]

THE DEMOGRAPHIC EXPLOSION

During the boom unleashed by these rail connections, the volatile market in land, which had earlier fizzled, revived with a vengeance.[24] Even though as late as 1880 there were still only a little more than eleven thousand residents in the city (granted almost twice as many as had been there a scant decade earlier),[25] by 1885 almost all of central Los Angeles had been subdivided into buildable lots.[26] At the height of the land boom in 1887, prices of land in the city rose some 400–500 percent in a single year, as properties changed hands in a frenzy of speculation.[27] The bubble would soon deflate, but before it did, the population in the city had risen by 351 percent and the county by more than 200 percent in the decade between 1880 and 1890.[28]

Internal migration accounted for almost all of this increase. By 1890, less than a third of the city's native-born population had actually been born in California (and this included "Californios," i.e., the original Mexican inhabitants), whereas more than half of the remaining native-born whites (34 percent of the total) had been born in the Midwest.[29] (In contrast, 85 percent of New York City's native-born residents in 1890 had been born in New York State.) And despite the fact that the 1880s was a decade of massive foreign immigration to the United States, persons born abroad (even including Mexican immigrants) constituted only about a fifth of Los Angeles's 1890 population, compared with about 40 percent in both New York and Chicago.

The influx of settlers from the Midwest was stimulated by campaigns mounted by the Chamber of Commerce and facilitated by price wars between rail companies that at one point dropped the fare between Chicago and Los Angeles to one dollar a head. But even before the nationwide economic difficulties of 1893 spread to California, there was some falling off of migration, and with it, a collapse of many of the speculative (often waterless) ventures begun in the first orgy of optimism. Howard Nelson recounts the fate of one:

> A typical boom time "town" was Chicago Park . . . in the sands of the bed of the San Gabriel River. Here streets with names like "State" and "Dearborn" were surveyed, and plat map after plat map was filed as lots were sold off by the hundreds [to speculating investors]. . . . At one time there were reported to be "2,289 lots and one resident" in Chicago Park. Eventually, he left, too. . . .
>
> Although much of the boomtime action involved the creation of new towns, land within the city limits of Los Angeles was also subdivided at a record pace. . . .
>
> By the middle of 1888 it was clear that the boom was over; lots that had been snapped up just a few months previously were unsaleable at any price. . . . The Los Angeles County Assessor counted sixty ghost towns.[30]

The center of the city fared better than the early suburban subdivisions. Bunker Hill, with its impressive array of new Queen Anne and Victorian residences, became one of the most fashionable neighborhoods by the 1890s, traversed by new streetcar lines that extended even to a few close-in suburbs that were eventually annexed to the city.[31]

The collapse of the brief boom, however, put city leaders on notice that more efforts would be needed if growth were to be sustained and fortunes still to be made in real estate. The Chamber of Commerce, therefore, set up a permanent exhibit in Chicago in 1888, extolling the glories of Los Angeles's climate, the region's agricultural productivity, and its nascent industrial structure, boasting of six hundred (*sic*) manufacturing establishments in the city. To stimulate growth, California mounted a particularly extravagant exposition at Chicago's Columbian Exposition, seeking to lure more migrants to reignite the languishing real estate market.[32] Between 1890 and 1920, the Los Angeles Chamber of Commerce

> encouraged local farmers to participate in fairs and expositions . . . dispatched a railroad car filled with authentic southern California fruits, vegetables, and spokesmen into rural parts of America, . . . joined with local publishers to distribute Los Angeles newspapers throughout the country, worked with hotel proprietors to attract conventions, . . . circulated innumerable pamphlets, purchased immeasurable advertising space, and replied to countless inquiries about the region. During these years, largely as a result of the Chamber's activities, Los Angeles and its environs became the best publicized part of the United States.[33]

The Chamber's efforts were rewarded. By 1900 the city's population was more than one hundred thousand, with an additional seventy thousand persons residing in the county areas beyond city limits, up from the respective 1890 totals of fifty thousand within the city and an equal number in the county beyond.

But not all the growth was spurred by the Chamber's propaganda; other developments were of even greater importance in the decade of the 1890s. In 1892 an oil boom began and five years later the region was producing oil in such quantities that California had become the third most important oil-producing state in the country. This development, often equally as speculative as real estate investment,[34] not only created the potential for industrialization by reducing the costs of energy, but made Los Angeles more important for U.S. military strategies. The port through which petroleum was exported took on greater value—for commerce and shipbuilding, and as a home for the fleet.

OIL, WARS, AND THE PORT: PUBLIC SUBSIDIES FOR SAN PEDRO

Between 1871 and 1892, the port at San Pedro received close to a million dollars in federal funds for improvements to its inner harbor.[35] Although these investments certainly facilitated the export of oil in the ensuing years, they proved insufficient to accommodate the new strategic interests of the United States in the Pacific, interests that peaked in the aftermath of the Spanish-American War of 1897–98, when the United States gained control over the former Spanish colonies, not only of Cuba and

Figure 6.1. An altar to oranges: from the Citrus Fair in Los Angeles, 1898. California Chamber of Commerce.

Puerto Rico in the Caribbean, but of the Philippines.[36] It is not without significance that in the year following the war, the federal government appropriated sizable funds to construct a new breakwater and further deepen the harbor at San Pedro.[37]

These improvements certainly intensified Los Angeles's interest in annexing its greatly enhanced port. This was accomplished by 1906–7 via the so-called shoestring addition, an umbilical cord only a mile wide that attached the city to San Pedro, some twenty miles away. In 1907, the annexed port complex was placed under the supervision of the city's newly appointed Board of Harbor Commissioners. The federal Tidelands Act of 1911 transferred additional valuable waterfront properties to Los Angeles, and the city floated a three-million-dollar bond for harbor improvements.[38] The federal government subsidized even more developments for the harbor after the construction of the Panama Canal (begun in 1913), which was designed to link the Atlantic and Pacific arenas. And in 1916 it fortified the harbor and made it a home for its Pacific fleet.

Although commercial activation of the Panama Canal was slowed because of World War I, by the early 1920s some 2.5 million tons of cargo *per month* were being shipped through San Pedro, as contrasted with the 2 million tons *per year* that had been shipped in 1913.[39] Thus, even before the spurt of growth associated with World War II, there was a close relationship between war-oil-industry and Los Angeles's capacity as a port. All of these developments spurred the growth of Los Angeles.[40]

POPULATION GROWTH AND ETHNIC MIX IN THE REGION AFTER 1900

Because the city of Los Angeles took on a very fragmented and often changing shape in the decades after 1900, due to the caprices of annexation, it is preferable to gauge changes in population between 1900 and 1930 by examining the figures for Los Angeles County, whose boundaries remained constant after 1889 and fully contained the expanding city. Table 6.1 demonstrates not only the increasing scale of settlement but the relatively constant composition of the county's population during this era of dramatic growth, despite a contraction in the extent of Los Angeles County as new peripheral counties were formed out of it (see Map 6.1).

Two fairly important consequences of this demographic composition affected Los Angeles's future, at least for a time. First, Southern California "essentially missed the inpourings of the vast throngs of European immigrants that engulfed eastern and midwestern cities in the late nineteenth and early twentieth centuries . . . [and thus] Los Angeles did not experience an era of large ethnic enclaves." Furthermore, despite the "continued presence of a Mexican-American minority," this group did not influence Los Angeles "in the same way the Irish affected Boston, or the Italians San Francisco, or the Jews New York."[41] Ironically, the residents of Mexican origin

Table 6.1. Totals and ethnic/racial composition of Los Angeles County's population (including Los Angeles city), 1900–1930

Census year	1900	1910	1920	1930
Total	170,298	504,131	936,455	2,208,492
Native white	136,330	395,042	727,928	1,667,227
Foreign-born white	27,645	88,436	166,579	282,655
Negro	2,841	9,424	18,738	46,425
Mexican	—	—	—	167,024
Japanese	204	8,461	19,911	35,390
Chinese	3,209	2,602	2,591	3,572
Other	69	166	708	6,199

Note: In 1930, persons of Mexican birth or descent who were not classified as white or Indian were designated as "Mexicans." (In those days, census takers often guessed at race/ethnicity by "appearance.") In previous censuses, most of those Mexicans had been classified as white; hence the sudden appearance of this new category when it became available in 1930. It is more difficult to interpret the increase in the category "other" in 1930, but this may also represent a reclassification of the population of Mexican or Indian origin. If so, Mexicans and Mexican Americans constituted at least 8 percent of the total by 1930, more than most other scholars acknowledge. Indeed, Coons and Miller suggest an even higher estimate, more than 9 percent.

Source: Arthur G. Coons and Arjay Miller, "An Economic and Industrial Survey of the Los Angeles and San Diego Areas" (California State Planning Board, mimeo, 1941), 388, Table IX.

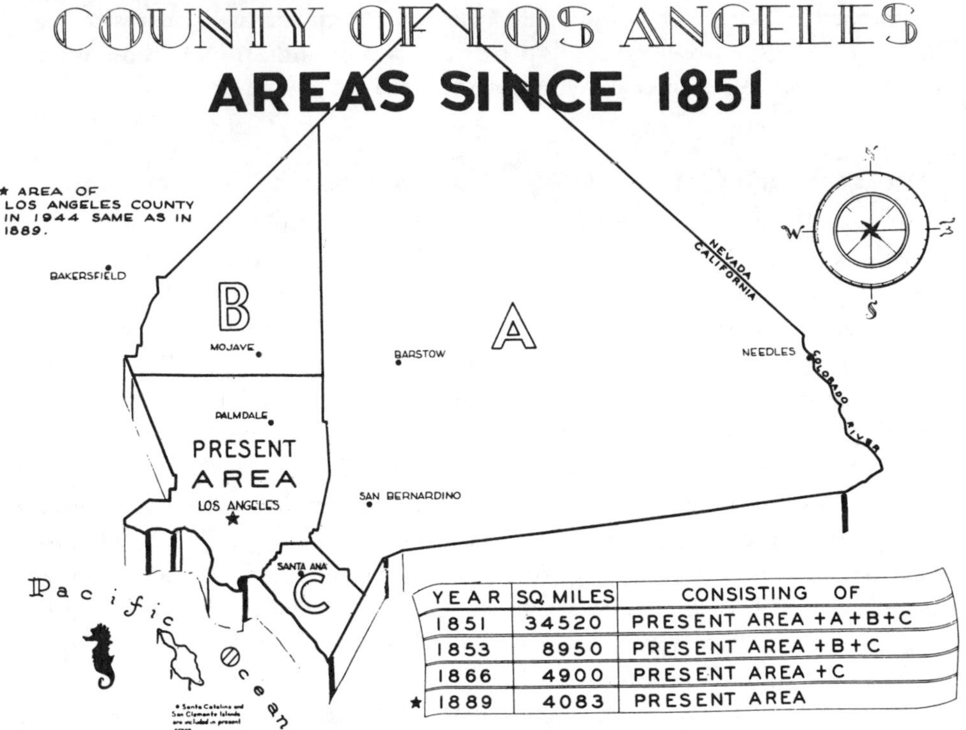

Map 6.1. The reduction in the size of Los Angeles County between 1849 and 1889. Source: Los Angeles County Surveyor.

became virtually "invisible" (through the Census Bureau's categories) at the very time the city was

> actively discovering and romanticizing its Spanish heritage . . . [and creating] a myth . . . glorifying an imaginary life of the "mission days." . . . By 1900 this movement was well underway. . . . Its style of architecture was copied widely by builders throughout southern California . . . [and] numerous cities sponsored annual fiesta days . . . seen today in a different form . . . [at] the Tournament of the Roses Parade in Pasadena each New Year's Day.[42]

I return to this irony in later chapters.

It is clear from Table 6.1 that in the thirty years after 1900, the population of the county had increased thirteenfold, growing at a simple average rate of more than 40 percent per year. It is also evident that by the turn of the century, the native-born white population had not only established its numerical dominance, but managed to maintain it up to 1930, despite some in-migration of blacks and Asians. By 1900, 80 percent of the total were classified as native-born "whites" (including persons of Californian-Mexican descent); only 16 percent were listed as foreign-born whites, and there were only tiny representations of minority racial groups (1.6 percent black and 2 percent Asian).[43] A very similar situation prevailed in the larger five-county region that now makes up most of the consolidated metropolitan statistical area of Los Angeles (consisting of Los Angeles, San Bernardino, Ventura, Riverside, and Orange Counties), as can be seen in Table 6.2.[44]

Table 6.2. Totals and ethnic/racial composition of the population of Los Angeles, San Bernardino, Ventura, Riverside, and Orange Counties, 1900–1930

Census Year	1900	1910	1920	1930
Total—five counties	250,187	648,316	1,150,252	2,597,066
Native white	201,444	507,576	894,516	1,950,071
Foreign-born white	38,842	112,389	204,225	308,818
Negro	3,443	10,745	20,493	49,386
Mexican	—	—	—	236,792
Japanese	546	11,685	23,236	38,767
Chinese	4,457	3,391	2,982	4,017
Other	69	166	708	67,199

Note: In 1930, persons of Mexican birth or descent who were not classified as white or Indian were designated as "Mexicans." (In those days, census takers often guessed at race/ethnicity by "appearance.") In previous censuses, most of those Mexicans had been classified as white; hence the sudden appearance of this new category when it became available in 1930. It is more difficult to interpret the increase in the category "other" in 1930, but this may also represent a reclassification of the population of Mexican or Indian origin. If so, Mexicans and Mexican Americans constituted at least 8 percent of the total by 1930, more than most other scholars acknowledge. Indeed, Coons and Miller suggest an even higher estimate, more than 9 percent.

Source: Arthur G. Coons and Arjay Miller, "An Economic and Industrial Survey of the Los Angeles and San Diego Areas" (California State Planning Board, mimeo, 1941), 388, Table IX.

WHERE DID THESE PEOPLE LIVE, AND WHAT DID THEY USE FOR WATER?

Land for Development

Given this enormous population growth in only a few short decades, how were the newcomers accommodated, and who provided them with transportation and utilities? The answers to these questions lie in the interrelationships among real estate developers, mass-transit companies, and the city government's eventual involvement in water and power. Initially, all of these were in the private sector.

Private mass transit, in particular, was viewed as a "loss leader," an investment that, while not economically viable, was absolutely essential if building lots in the vast peripheral zones were to be sold. As Fogelson has astutely recognized, "The expectations of prompt profits from real estate at least as much as the hopes for eventual returns from transportation stimulated the construction of local and interurban lines throughout Los Angeles after 1885."[45]

The repeated failures of the earliest horsecar and cable companies, and even of the first electrified street trolley lines toward the end of the century, attested to the fact that the low-density city would never be able to provide mass-transit accessibility beyond the city center without subsidies. These subsidies came from land developers.

A good case in point was the Pacific Electric Railway Company, organized in 1901 by Henry E. Huntington, nephew of Collis Huntington, the late head of the Southern Pacific Railroad. H. E. Huntington

> formed the Huntington Land and Improvement Company which acquired vast tracts . . . through which the Pacific Electric built its lines—and subdivided and marketed these properties. . . . Huntington not only extended the Pacific Electric throughout southern and eastern Los Angeles County, but also purchased the Los Angeles and Redondo Beach railway and its terminal townsite on the Pacific Ocean. There too returns from real estate sales compensated for the costs of railroad construction.[46]

Other developers, most with far fewer resources than Huntington, took advantage of these lines or were even forced to build access feeders if their ventures were not to abort, as had Chicago Park. "The early subdivisions on the periphery closely followed the streetcar lines of the LARY [Los Angeles Railway]. By 1914 the trolleys had opened much of the region within five miles of the downtown area. . . . So vital was transportation to these neighborhoods that developers rarely built houses more than four blocks away from a streetcar line."[47]

Regulations on Land

During those early days, California had no laws governing subdivisions, which opened the way for massive swindles. To control some of these abuses, the California State Legislature, closing the proverbial stable door in the midst of the depression of 1893, passed a law requiring subdividers to record their lots on an "officially approved" subdivision map before sales could be made. Later, reflecting the potential importance of automobiles, this law was amended in 1907 to require submission of the official map to the local governing body, which would have to certify that it accepted the streets for public dedication.[48]

Although such regulations did not end the scandals, other developments in organization, finance, and transportation helped reduce the risks to developers and purchasers entailed in opening new areas for settlement. At first, the real estate industry tried to police its own members through the California State Realty Federation, founded in 1905. It was one of the oldest and largest state associations of local realty board members and "closely allied with the major transport companies, utilities, and other large landholders."[49] And because, as Weiss points out, developers worked on a large scale since much of the land around Los Angeles still consisted of large parcels in single ownership, in the absence of other controls such as zoning, developers "established tough, enforceable deed restrictions as a fairly reliable method of controlling large, newly subdivided residential and commercial developments."[50]

Other innovations that facilitated subdivisions lay in the realm of finance. Initially, buyers paid for their lots in cash raised from savings or informal loans, but gradually they were able to borrow a portion from savings and loan associations, or even banks. By the 1920s, "mortgage bonds appeared as a major new source of financing, and mortgage guarantee insurance and secondary mortgage markets also grew in importance," easing the transition for developers from simple subdividers to large-scale "merchant builders" who put up whole communities, selling houses along with the lots.[51]

If institutional financing freed developers from the need for ready cash, the automobile freed them from the locational constraints on sites, although the full consequences of the shift to cars and trucks (and the eventual demise of mass transit, which the city had refused to municipalize) would not be felt until the 1920s and even later. The basic cause was Los Angeles's pattern of development, which depended almost exclusively on single-family homes. In 1930, 94 percent of all dwelling units in Los Angeles were in such structures, contrasted with only half in cities such as New York and Chicago.[52]

Nevertheless, when the 1920s began, Los Angeles still had "a dominant central business district and adjacent industrial area,"[53] and "as late as 1929, three-quarters of all department store sales in Los Angeles County occurred inside the city's central business district."[54] But gridlock had already set in downtown when the 1920s building boom dispersed large numbers of daily car commuters to peripheral towns and subdivisions.[55] This put downtown business interests, which favored the continuation of street railways, and suburban developers and car owners, who saw the mass-transit tracks as obstacles to their access, on a collision course, and mass transit finally capitulated. By the late 1920s department stores had begun to open branch outlets in the periphery; "within five years, 88 percent of all new retail stores were built in the suburbs."[56] Commerce had followed housing.

With the introduction of truck transport in the 1910s and especially after the invention of the pneumatic tire after World War I, just as Los Angeles was emerging as an industrial power with an excellent artificial harbor, transportation facilities, and nearby oil deposits, it also became easier for factories to decentralize. Nevertheless, most new industries, except for those near oil installations, still favored location in the original industrial quarter that had been set aside southeast of downtown, near the Los Angeles River and well served by rail lines.[57] Only much later would factories seek new ground farther out.

Water for Development

Land, whether for residential or industrial purposes, was useless without a dependable water supply, and even before the opening years of the twentieth century it was becoming apparent that a water shortage might impose the most stringent "limits to growth" for the state and its cities.[58] The manner in which Los Angeles addressed this potential problem illustrates quite dramatically the typical pattern of interactions between local and federal governments and the manner in which local elites were able to use both to execute their plans.

In 1905 the so-called water wars began when Los Angeles's plan to transport water from the Owens Valley was first revealed.[59] Under the auspices of a new municipal

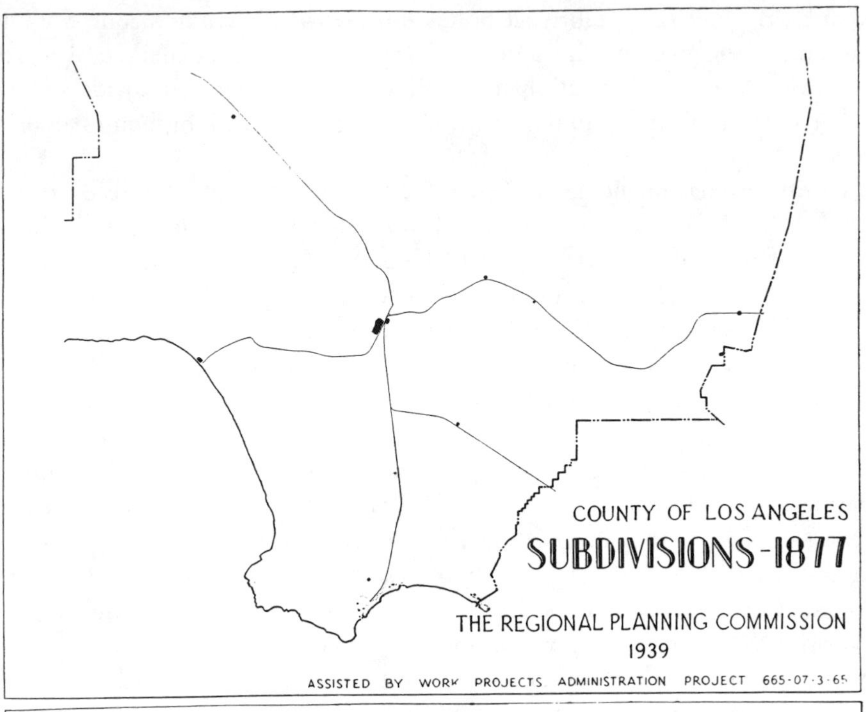

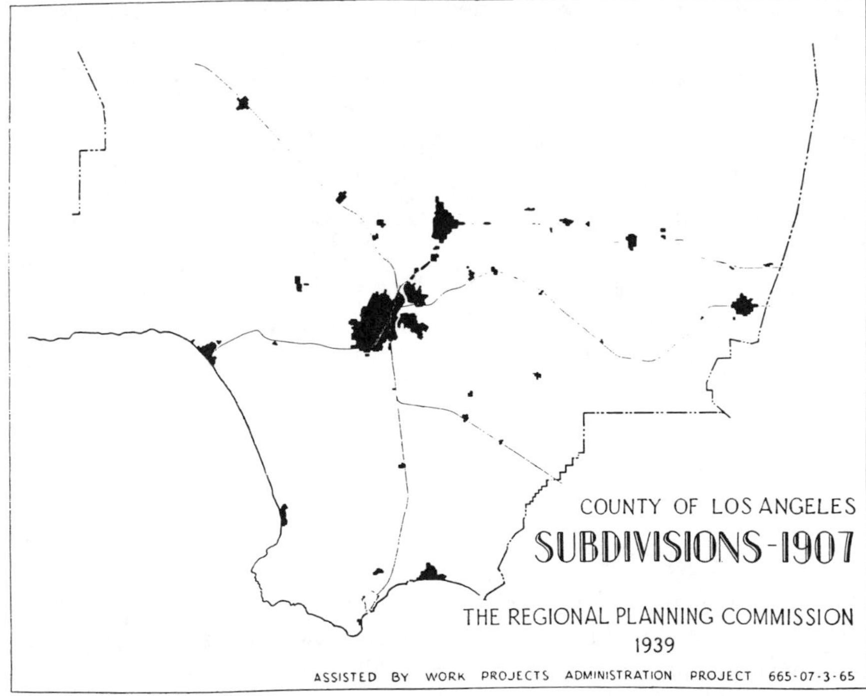

Map 6.2. The expansion of the built-up and zoned areas in Los Angeles County, 1877, 1907, 1937, and 1939. Reproduced by permission of The Huntington Library.

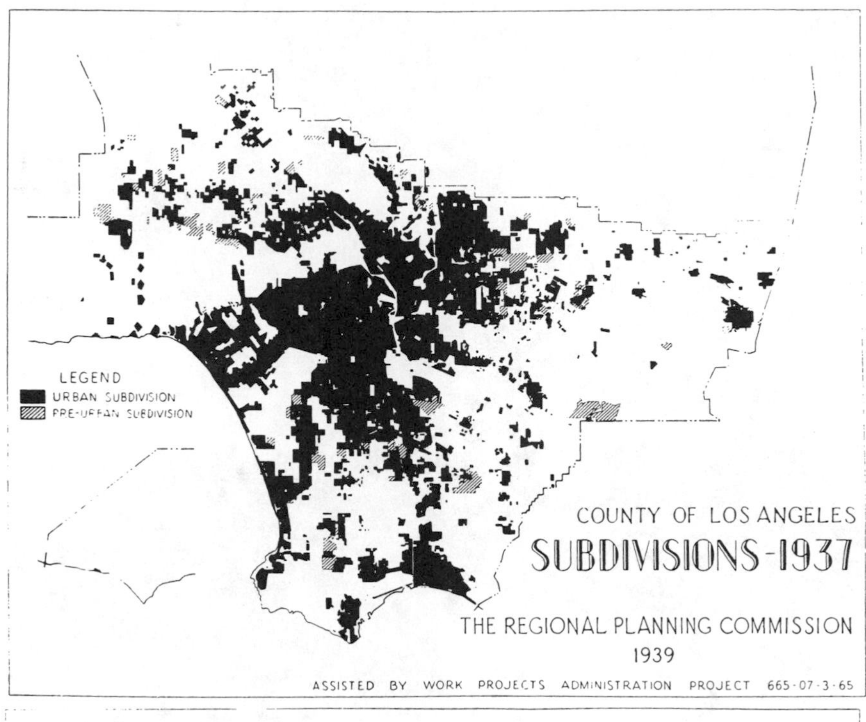
LEGEND
URBAN SUBDIVISION
PRE-URBAN SUBDIVISION
COUNTY OF LOS ANGELES
SUBDIVISIONS-1937
THE REGIONAL PLANNING COMMISSION
1939
ASSISTED BY WORK PROJECTS ADMINISTRATION PROJECT 665-07-3-65

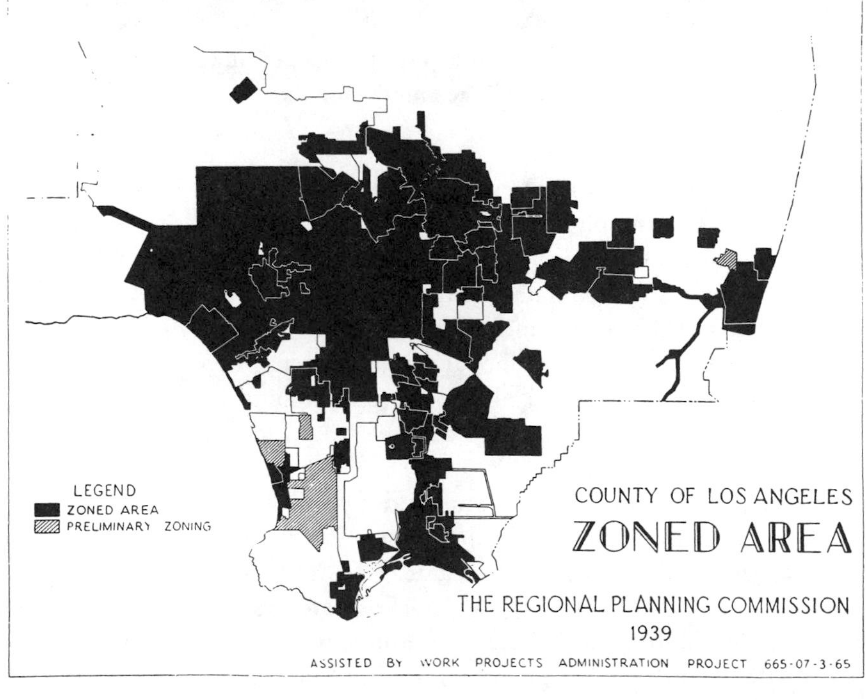
LEGEND
ZONED AREA
PRELIMINARY ZONING
COUNTY OF LOS ANGELES
ZONED AREA
THE REGIONAL PLANNING COMMISSION
1939
ASSISTED BY WORK PROJECTS ADMINISTRATION PROJECT 665-07-3-65

Figure 6.2. Street railways first, subdivisions follow: street railway lines to nowhere, 1910. Photograph reproduced by permission of The Huntington Library.

water company, an ambitiously executed aqueduct was opened in 1913, which not only increased the city's supply well beyond current demand, but transformed the San Fernando Valley into lushly irrigated farmland, ripe for eventual urban development. The system, however, stranded irate Owens Valley farmers with little water. Although the usual narrative of this achievement takes the form of a "morality play," with self-taught water engineer William Mulholland usually cast as hero, former mayor Fred Eaton as duplicitous and greedy villain, and Joseph Lippincott, surveyor for the Federal Reclamation Service, as turncoat Judas, the story, albeit with the same stars, is much more complicated.[60]

Kevin Starr's *Material Dreams* begins, and rightly so, with an emphasis on water in the history of California: its scarcity, its indispensability, and its "created" character, especially in the southern part of the state.[61] During the early days of Spanish/ Mexican rule, communal rights over Los Angeles's water resources were unquestioned, but by 1868 the still disorganized local government had so much trouble managing this that, "with almost a sigh of gratitude, the city council . . . turned over the water franchise to the Los Angeles City Water Company, which constructed a system of reservoirs and open ditches [that] clearly [proved] obsolete by the boom-era expansion of the 1880s."[62] There were growing pressures, however, spearheaded by Mayor Fred Eaton, to "remunicipalize" the facility.

> When the State Supreme Court ruled that Los Angeles held jurisdiction over the Los Angeles River watershed, which had also been claimed by the [private] Los Angeles City Water Company, the case for municipalization gained . . . momentum. . . . A bond issue was passed . . . [in] 1901 [and] by 13 February 1902, the City of the Angels [had] bought out the Los Angeles City Water Company . . . [thus translating] water into a public enterprise.[63]

From the start, it was apparent to the chief water engineer, William Mulholland (who had been inherited by the municipality because, in the absence of any map to the old system, only he carried a guide to it, "in his head"), that even an upgraded version of the extant utility would be woefully inadequate to accommodate the growth anticipated for the city.

Meanwhile, "back at the ranch" in the Owens Valley, the newly established Federal Reclamation Service was exploring a proposal to subsidize irrigation in the adjacent farming areas. It hired Lippincott, an old associate of Eaton, to conduct a full feasibility survey of the region.[64] In the next few years, Eaton and Mulholland, along with Lippincott, seem to have hatched a plan to divert the water earmarked for the Owens Valley Reclamation Service project to the city's growing needs, and to construct a reservoir at Long Valley connected to an aqueduct capable of conveying the water to Los Angeles.[65] Mulholland judged that if they could pull off this coup, there "was water enough for two million people, ten times the population of Los Angeles in 1904."[66] Lippincott was put on the payroll of the Los Angeles Water Company, and Eaton, who had been provided with the maps and surveys made for the Reclamation project, started to buy up options to land in Owens Valley.[67] The secret plan went public in 1905, and within the next two years the Reclamation Service ceded its Owens Valley claims to Los Angeles. Bonds were issued to pay Eaton back and to buy more land in Owens Valley; Mulholland designed the complex aqueduct, and more bonds were issued to raise the money to build it.[68]

Equally as ambitious as New York's construction of Central Park, the aqueduct project employed an army of more than three thousand nonunion laborers who worked around the clock. Despite tunneling setbacks and shortages of funds, by fall of 1913 construction of "235 miles of canals, conduits, tunnels, flumes, penstocks, tailraces and siphons . . . was nearing completion."

> On the morning of Wednesday, 5 November 1913, a crowd of between 30,000 and 40,000, many of them carrying tin cups to take their first drink, gathered outside the city of San Fernando at the base of the last spillway in the Los Angeles aqueduct system. . . . After a brief speech, Mulholland unfurled an American flag, an army cannon boomed, the spillway gates were raised, and the water of the Owens River cascaded down a long spillway.[69]

The aqueduct's capacity was far greater than Los Angeles needed at the time, but the municipal water company was legally restricted to using the supply for domestic purposes only. As we shall see below in the section on annexation, this restriction, along with the growing needs of suburban communities for water, created a powerful symbiosis that led in short order to the radical expansion of the city's boundaries.

Map 6.3. Territory annexed to the city of Los Angeles: the seventy-eight annexations between 1859 and 1930. Reproduced by permission of The Huntington Library.

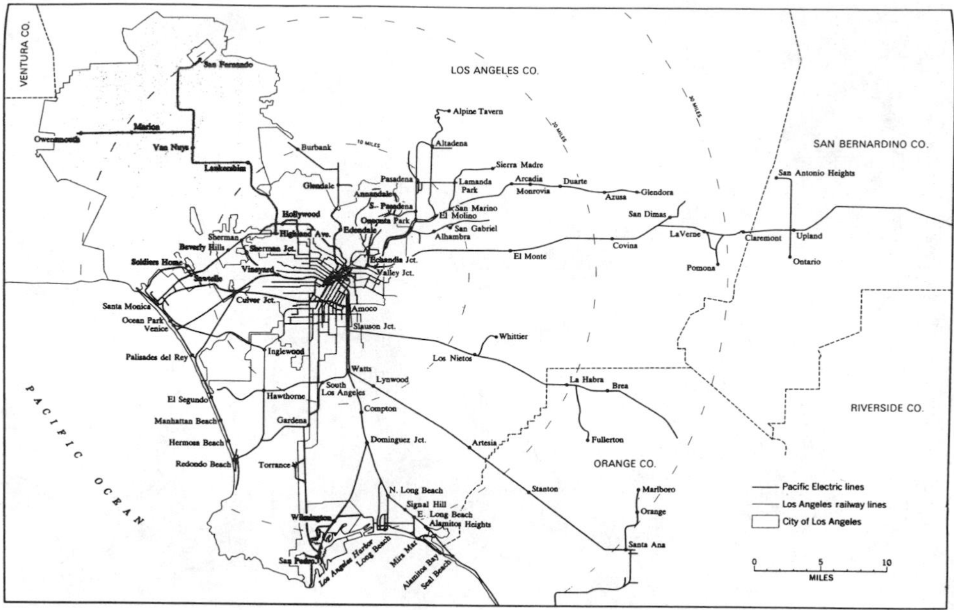

Map 6.4. Regional extent of the Los Angeles and Pacific electric railway systems, 1925.

JOBS FOR THE NEW RESIDENTS

Despite the existence of oil, a port, and industrial districts and suburbs, industrialization lagged behind in Los Angeles during the early decades of the twentieth century, although the city did have more of an economic base than the "real estate boondoggles" that wags claimed. Especially after the involvement of the United States in World War I, which stimulated shipbuilding and manufacture (the latter assisted by the availability of cheap energy from the oil fields and, from 1917 on, hydroelectric power produced from the aqueduct), there was a modest boom that peaked in 1919. Industrial firms and employment grew, as can be seen in Table 6.3.

Between 1919, when Goodyear opened its branch tire plant in Los Angeles, and the crash of 1929 (only one year after the city began to manufacture automobiles), the Los Angeles area became *the* center of the oil equipment and service industry, the second-largest tire manufacturing center, the headquarters of the western furniture, glass, and steel industries, as well as the regional center for the aircraft, automotive, chemical, and trucking industries.[70] By the mid-1920s the port of Los Angeles had become the largest American terminus for oil, thanks to the wells at Signal Hill, Huntington Beach, and Santa Fe Springs, which were producing one-fifth of the world's oil supply. In 1926, twenty-three million tons of cargo passed through the harbor, and "Los Angeles placed second only to New York in tonnage of foreign exports."[71] The demand created by oil exports led to massive improvements. The decade of the 1920s "represented the . . . greatest advancement in the history of the Port of Los Angeles prior to World War II, both in the expansion of its facilities and the scope of its commercial operations."[72] Many of the installations

Figure 6.3. The fathers of the Owens Valley Project (Mulholland at center). Courtesy of The Huntington Library.

built in the 1920 to 1930 period were still in use, duly renovated or improved, in the early 1980s.

Despite all these developments, as late as 1930 "a smaller proportion of gainful workers [in Los Angeles] was engaged in manufacturing than was characteristic of the Nation."[73] Over a tenth of the gainfully employed labor force still worked in farming and fishing (7.8 percent) or in the capital-intensive field of oil and gas (2.3 percent). Manufacturing accounted for less than a fifth of employed workers. Construction added another 7.8 percent. In contrast, fully a third of all workers were engaged in trade (24 percent) or transport (almost 9 percent), and an unusually high proportion (almost 28 percent) worked in the "service" sector.[74] This is an employment profile that more closely fits our stereotype of the "postindustrial" city than it does the era of large-scale industry.

The Movies

This conclusion is supported by the fact that the only industry of note, in addition to oil, shipbuilding, and branch manufacturing, was one that made images, not goods: the movies, an industry that rapidly diffused from New York to Chicago before settling in Los Angeles. Although by 1888 George Eastman had produced a camera that used flexible photographic film, the first 35mm viewing apparatus was not exhibited until early 1893 (at a penny arcade in New York).[75] Chicago then took up the experiment. By 1896 the first shop had opened in Los Angeles, and in 1902, the first the-

Table 6.3. Industrial establishments in the city of Los Angeles, 1889–1921 (according to the Census of Manufactures)

Year	1899	1904	1909	1914	1919	1921
Number of establishments	534	814	1,325	1,911	2,540	2,210
Total capital (in millions of dollars)	10	28	60	102	160	—
Average number of workers	5,173	10,424	17,327	23,744	47,118	42,161
Workers/establishment[a]	9.7	12.8	13.1	12.4	18.6	19.1
Value of product (in millions of dollars)	15	35	69	103	278	314

[a]My calculations.

Source: Arthur G. Coons and Arjay Miller "An Economic and Industrial Survey of the Los Angeles and San Diego Areas" (California State Planning Board, mimeo, 1941), 380, Table IV.

ater,[76] but the motion picture camera did not settle in Los Angeles until a year later. Los Angeles's first real motion picture, still silent, was made in 1904.[77]

Two explanations for why Los Angeles became the center of the new industry have been advanced, one emphasizing the natural and locational advantages of the site and the other pointing to the almost accidental movement to the city of a particularly brash and initially capital-poor group of (mostly) Jewish "greenhorn" adventurers. Both have some validity. Clarke stresses the locational advantages:

> As a result of the patent suits against the infringing companies, . . . many fly-by-night producers [came] to Southern California . . . close to the Mexican border, where they could flee with their suspect cameras if ever necessary. . . . Far more importantly, the Los Angeles area offered ideal conditions . . . plenty of sunshine, a good climate, a near ocean, desert, mountains, sylvan glades, and a lively theater. . . . A variety of buildings, Mexican streets, a great assortment of homes and gardens, surrounded by flowers and green trees the year round, were at every hand.[78]

Some support for his position is found in the fact that David W. Griffith came to Los Angeles in January 1909 in order to "escape the cold and dark winter" of New York. By spring he had finished his two-reel film version of *Ramona.* This film (and the novel on which it was based) is credited with almost single-handedly giving birth to the "mission" revival romance associated with Los Angeles.[79]

Neal Gabler takes a different perspective, focusing instead on the paradox "that the American film industry, which Will Hays . . . called 'the quintessence of what we mean by "America,"' was founded and for more than thirty years . . . [dominated by] Eastern European Jews who themselves seemed to be anything *but* the quintessence of America."[80] He credits the opportunity to "become big" on very little capital and a lot of nerve as accounting for their singular success. But that story is best kept for our discussion of Los Angeles in the 1930s and the 1940s, for it was not until then that they and the European émigrés they recruited truly ruled Hollywood.[81]

The film industry seeded a number of neighborhoods in the Los Angeles area (Brooklyn and Boyle Heights, the San Fernando Valley, Culver City, and even Santa Monica) before concentrating in Hollywood after 1915, and it provided employment for a sizable labor force that increased from the 3,000 who worked at some seventy-three companies in 1912 to the more than 21,500 employed in motion pictures by 1939, when they accounted for almost 15 percent of all persons employed in manufacturing.[82] But perhaps the movies' greatest contribution to the Los Angeles economy was that they served as a "silent Chamber of Commerce," publicizing Hollywood around the country and the world and attracting more and more people to the city.[83]

THE POLITICS OF ANNEXATION

The new developments in both water and industry reshaped the physical outlines of the city, encouraging annexation in some cases and intensifying resistance in others. In general, the offer of water induced annexation while the presence of oil served as a deterrent. Los Angeles shared with New York and Chicago the "will" to expand its boundaries by annexing large zones at their peripheries, but its circumstances gave a peculiar twist to this general process. Not only could it offer as incentives the usual powers of central cities—to finance, through the sale of bonds, the infrastructure that was becoming so necessary for modern urban development (water and sewer systems, roads and other transit services) and the public services (such as police and fire protection) that were coming to be taken for granted in urban centers—but after the completion of the aqueduct, it had surplus water to distribute to its water-scarce environs.

Wooing with Water

Thus the solution to Los Angeles's "boundary problems" at the end of the nineteenth and the opening decades of the twentieth century was different from the solutions used in either New York or Chicago. Although the caption on Map 6.5, "The city water built," is accurate, the full story, as we have seen, is one not merely of natural resources, but of human machinations and design.

The first thing that strikes the eye in this map is the irregular and, indeed, irrational boundaries of the city of Los Angeles. To the originally square shape of the 1781 land-grant town and its early enlargements, annexations after the turn of the century added two crucial and asymmetrical expanses whose locations and dimensions are explicable *only* with reference to the two missing prerequisites of the city's economic life. The creation of the deepwater port at San Pedro explains the southern extrusion referred to graphically as the "shoestring"; and the enormous elliptical addition to the northwest, the San Fernando Valley, is explicable only in relation to its role as the ultimate destination of the Los Angeles aqueduct. "In 73 separate annexation elections held between 1906 and 1930, Los Angeles voters dramatically expanded the city's boundaries from 43 to 442 square miles,"[84] and in most of these instances it was Los Angeles's promise to provide the area with a reliable water supply that tipped the decision.

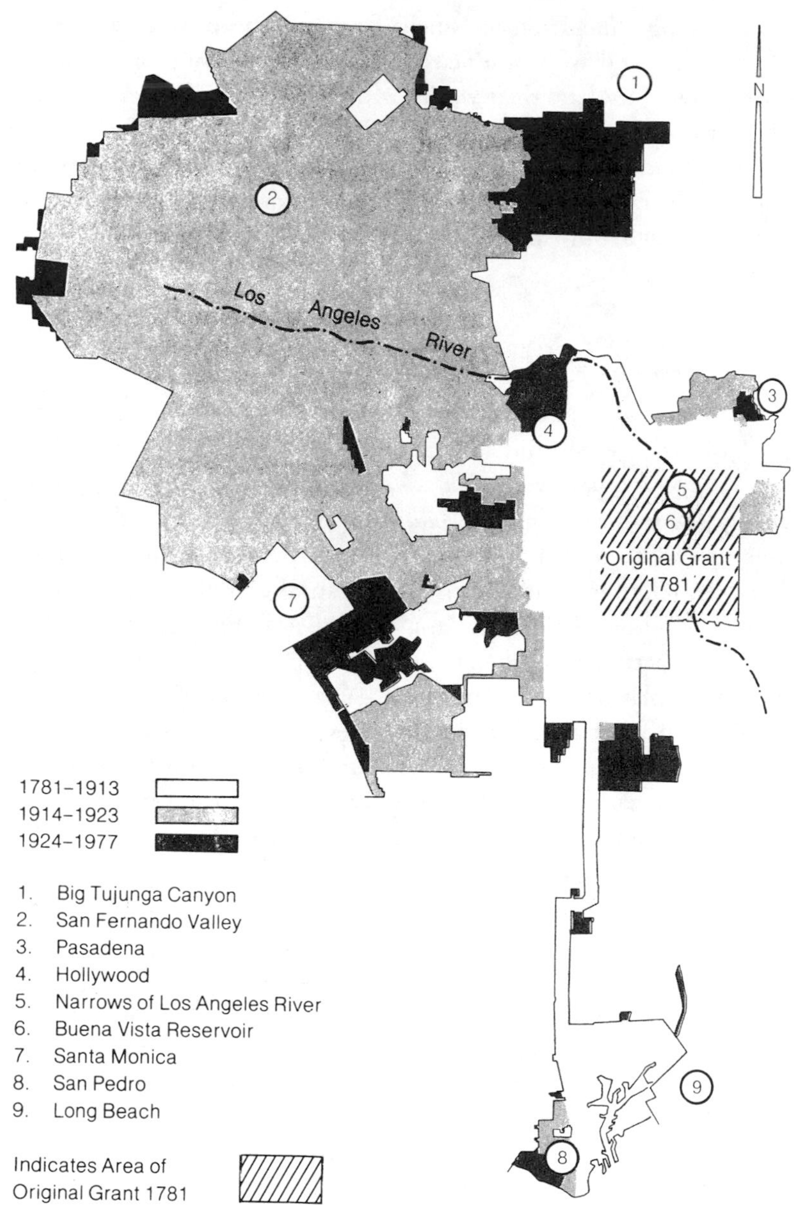

Map 6.5. The city water built. Source: William Kahrl, *Water and Power;* used with permission of the University of California Press.

If asymmetry is the most noteworthy distortion, a second equally perplexing element in the city's current boundaries is its discontinuity. Although the city of Los Angeles (though certainly not its metropolitan region) is entirely contained within the single county of Los Angeles, the county contains numerous incorporated cities as well as unincorporated areas that remain outside the jurisdiction of the city. This patchy jurisdictional pattern resulted from differential "bargaining power," with some communities seeking annexation to benefit from the cheap water only the municipality could provide, and with other communities, especially those built around oil wells, resisting having to share their wealth with the city. Much later, certain subareas actually chose to "deannex" from the city, when the "Lakewood option," available after 1958, allowed localities to contract for urban services without submerging their identities within the city. Whereas resistance to annexation had been experienced by New York and Chicago, only in Los Angeles did oil towns play a special role in fragmenting the region.

Oil Towns and Independence

Fred W. Viehe argues that although "inter-urban transportation [and, I would add, water] may have been responsible for the suburbanization of the San Fernando and San Gabriel Valleys, *it certainly does not explain suburban developments in southern Los Angeles County and northern Orange County,*" where the discovery of vast amounts of oil from the mid-1890s on led to the separate incorporation of many suburbs at the sites of oil fields, refineries, and associated industrial complexes. He notes that "by 1930, a suburban industrial network founded by the oil industry surrounded the city of Los Angeles and occupied much of the land throughout the Southland."[85] Refuting the conventional explanations that link suburbanization to the introduction of transportation systems or that attribute suburban resistance to annexation to American preferences for small-town autonomy, Viehe argues that oil was "the primary factor behind the suburbanization of Los Angeles," accounting for the rapid decline of Los Angeles's ability to annex territory in southern Los Angeles County and northern Orange County. The "dispersed location of the oil fields and refinery sites" gave their associated towns an independent taxable wealth, which allowed them to purchase the services they needed while avoiding city (and any labor) regulations.[86] Such settlements often became "company towns," effectively controlled by the biggest oil men.

Viehe presents a number of specific cases to illustrate how oil policies and annexation were interrelated. Initially, the Amalgamated Oil Company, an appendage of the vast Huntington empire, purchased a ranch west of Los Angeles to search for oil, but, when none was found, the promoters transformed their unsuccessful venture into upscale Beverly Hills.[87] Hollywood, in contrast, outlawed the extraction of oil when it annexed to Los Angeles. In 1924, the residents of Signal Hill, where the largest oil strike to date had been found, immediately incorporated to prevent their lucrative oil fields from being annexed by Long Beach, whereas Torrance and Hawthorne, after the discovery of oil in their vicinity, incorporated to keep oil derricks *out* of their residential zones.

> By 1930, a patchwork of industrial and residential suburbs spread across the Southland, and Los Angeles emerged as a fragmented metropolis. . . .
>
> . . . some suburbs incorporated to exploit the oil fields within their borders, while others incorporated to keep oil out. An oil man, for example, encouraged Montebello to secede from Monterey Park in 1920, three years after the discovery

> of the Montebello field. . . . An almost identical situation occurred east of Fullerton in 1926 when an oil man encouraged Placentia to incorporate as a "rich, little city" following the lucrative Richfield strike.[88]

SHADOW LOS ANGELES: THE WORLD OF THE EXCLUDED MINORITIES

Despite the stereotypical view that Los Angeles was inhabited by midwestern "American Gothics" (the phrase is Nelson's), the economy and the suburban lifestyles of this group depended in large part on the city's "invisible" minorities: Mexicans, blacks, and Asians.

Asians

Little information is available about the Asian communities in Los Angeles during the late nineteenth and early twentieth centuries. Given the labor shortages after 1850, large numbers of Chinese male workers were "imported" to help build the railroads; some of them patronized the block-long "Chinatown" in downtown Los Angeles that had been established in the early 1860s. "By 1870 one-third of the local Chinese population was concentrated within walking distance of that site."[89] By 1880 there may have been as many as 150,000 Chinese men in California, where they accounted for one-fourth of all workers.[90] "The latent bias [against them then] came to the surface. For Irish workers, the Chinese temporarily displaced blacks as scapegoats until congressional legislation virtually halted Asian immigration" through the Oriental Exclusion Laws, which, although they commenced as early as 1882, did not permanently and specifically exclude Chinese until 1904.[91]

A limited number of Japanese immigrants were admitted after the so-called Gentlemen's Agreement between Japan and the United States was signed in 1909. As is clear from Table 6.2, the Chinese remained a tiny minority (about thirty-five hundred in Los Angeles County and four thousand in the five-county region in 1930), while the number of Japanese increased sharply after 1909, until twenty years later the total surpassed thirty-five thousand in Los Angeles County and approached forty thousand in the five-county region, making Los Angeles host to the largest enclave of Japanese in the United States. At that time the Japanese and Chinese were more strictly segregated than were blacks or Hispanics.[92]

African Americans

Even though blacks, mulattoes, and mestizos had constituted an important element in the early Spanish settlement of Los Angeles, native black representation was insignificant by 1850.[93] It was only in the 1880s that the number of African Americans began to increase—from a scant hundred at the beginning of the decade to some thirteen hundred by the end. Ten years later, the community still numbered fewer than three thousand (less than the number of Chinese), so it should not be surprising that there were only small residential enclaves dispersed across the county. By 1920, however, this had changed; by then, three-fourths of Los Angeles's black population lived in only three of the city's twelve wards.[94] In that year,

> although the proportion of blacks to whites was no larger than it had been forty years previously, most blacks were living in a spatial ghetto . . . [that] stretched about thirty blocks down Central Avenue from the original downtown settlement. The city of Watts at this time was a small rural outlier [*sic*]. (Watts . . . was annexed by Los Angeles in 1926.) This marked change in residential pattern was due to the increased use of deed restrictions. . . . However, the ghetto itself in this decade was . . . mixed . . . with many whites interspersed among the blacks. Central Avenue with its churches and businesses became one of the most notable "Negro streets" in the country. By 1925 the main black community had reached Slauson Avenue, which was to remain an impenetrable barrier until World War II.[95]

The situation of African Americans was far from enviable, despite the surprising observations of W. E. B. Du Bois, who, when he visited Los Angeles in 1913, gushed that "Los Angeles is wonderful," averring that "nowhere in the United States is the Negro so well and beautifully housed," and predicting, echoing Los Angeles booster language as he addressed an NAACP meeting, "out here in this matchless Southern California there would seem to be no limit to your opportunities, your possibilities."[96] In all fairness, he also qualified his enthusiasm in an article in *Crisis* in which he emphasized the sharp color line that gave the lie to Los Angeles as paradise.[97]

Despite the appearance of a black professional bourgeoisie (mostly catering to the Central Avenue community), most African Americans remained servants, janitors, and porters, even after employment in the industrial sector opened to them during World War I.[98] And with every increase in numbers, the noose of restrictive covenants tightened around their settlements. As elsewhere, newcomers would gradually crowd into an unexpanding space, although Los Angeles's high rates of single-family housing and home ownership and the safety valve of Watts partially mitigated the worst difficulties, at least for a time.

Hispanics

Although Mexicans had constituted 90 percent of Los Angeles's population in 1850, the rapid growth of the Anglo population in the decades that followed reduced them to a minority of no more than 10 percent by 1930, despite further immigration and natural increase.[99]

> Not only were Mexicans and Mexican-Americans the largest minority group in southern California but they gave Los Angeles the most concentrated Latino population in the nation. Initially, the[y] . . . lived near the Plaza, the original center of Los Angeles. The rise in industrial activity, however, pushed the Mexican families into the old Jewish and Eastern European suburbs of Boyle Heights and East Los Angeles. . . . Many of the white emigrants living in East Los Angeles moved into the outlying areas once they had attained a bit of affluence. This

> flight, combined with the heavy Mexican immigration, turned the region into a bustling Hispanic enclave . . . [only two to three miles from the industrial sector of downtown]. . . . A few isolated Mexican districts sprang up along various PE [Pacific Electric] lines because the railway hired Hispanics to maintain its tracks, but these suburban labor camps remained isolated from their white neighbors.[100]

Given the Census Bureau's faulty classification and the endemic "illegal" immigration, it is difficult to get a consistent estimate over time of the Mexican American population of Los Angeles. Morales reports that in 1910 there were about nine thousand Mexicans in Los Angeles, but suggests higher "unofficial estimates" of between twenty thousand and forty thousand in the city alone, even before the major migrations occurred in the 1910s and 1920s.[101] During those later decades of growth, the population in the original central "barrios" of Sonoratown and the Plaza (sometimes called "the Pueblo") swelled to some fifty thousand (about 40 percent of the total), and new barrios to take the overflow were forming east of the Los Angeles River and southward along the railroad tracks toward Watts.[102]

Relations between Mexicans and Anglos were tense from the start.[103] Anglos were both contemptuous of those they had referred to, early on, as "greasers" and fearful that they would resist their demotion to a "minority."[104] Mexicans were resentful of new and bewildering laws, police brutality, and the double standard of justice from which they suffered.[105] The worst fears of the Mexican minority were fully confirmed after the stock market crash of 1929, when "over 80,000 Mexicans were rounded up with their household effects, domestic animals, and personal belongings, loaded into railroad cars, and shipped back to Mexico, taking with them their children, many of whom were born in the United States and were therefore U.S. citizens."[106]

THE MUNICIPAL/COUNTY POWER STRUCTURES

Regardless of numbers, minorities exercised no power in the Anglo-dominated and elite-controlled politics of the city and county, even as these underwent significant changes over time.[107] Erie has divided this period into two: from 1880 to 1906, which he characterizes as an "entrepreneurial regime," and from 1906 to 1932, when he says it became more "state centered."[108] He argues that the "elite" changed from being dominated by railroad interests, geared to national or at least nonlocal corporate interests, to being more locally based. This local elite, while including private real estate and commercial interests as well as professionals, utilized the power of the public sector, which had its own goals and mechanisms of performance. In the process, the city's regime changed from a "business-run, low-tax, caretaker government pursuing private strategies of economic development . . . to a high-tax-and-debt activist state successfully pursuing public development strategies [even] in the face of growing business opposition."[109] Erie critiques the conventional wisdom about Los Angeles's power structure (e.g., Fogelson, but also Weiss and even Logan and Molotch), which he claims overemphasizes the importance of real estate developers and rentiers and "seriously underestimates the role of the state and of public actors, particularly bureaucrats, in shaping

Los Angeles's development from the Progressive Era onward." In contrast, Erie argues "that an unusually large, powerful, and autonomous local-state apparatus—requiring voter approval at each step of the way—was constructed after the turn of the century to provide the necessary infrastructure for metropolitan growth."[110] It was this need to garner voter approval that made the publishers of local newspapers (i.e., the Otis/Chandler dynasty of the *Los Angeles Times* and to a lesser extent, Hearst's paper) so powerful: by shaping opinion, they could mold decisions.[111]

The one thing early and later elites agreed upon, however, was the need to project Los Angeles as an "open shop" (read antiunion) town in order to attract industry and compete with San Francisco. In contrast to the sometimes successful labor mobilizations that were increasing working-class power in New York and Chicago, similar attempts in less-industrialized Los Angeles were ruthlessly suppressed by the police and their "radical" leaders defanged by the "Red Squad," a 1919 precursor to the McCarthy era.[112] By the 1920s, Erie suggests, "a downsized and domesticated labor movement had been incorporated as a junior partner in the DWP [Department of Water and Power]-led growth coalition."[113]

By then, the main characteristics of Los Angeles politics had been established. Lacking the large ethnic/immigrant blocs found in New York and Chicago, it had only a small city council (with nine, then eleven, and eventually fifteen members) in which the voices of individual neighborhoods were drowned out and where minorities were for a long time mute. An even smaller set of five supervisors held even greater power in the larger county. Today, only five Los Angeles County supervisors rule a population of almost nine million.

Because the executive and administrative structures of Los Angeles had essentially been formed in the Progressive Era, when civil service was taken for granted, the political party apparatuses could never command the patronage jobs that "bosses" in New York and Chicago had used to consolidate their powers.[114] And because of the city's service economy, the narrowness of its industrial base, and the weakness of its labor unions, as well as the invisibility of its small minorities, no real counterforce existed to temper the plans of the Anglo elite. Although conditions changed in the 1930s and even more so after that, the political traditions had already been set.

ARCHITECTURE

Just as the form of the growing metropolis was patched together like a crazy quilt out of separately generated subdivisions and towns, so the built environment was formed from a variety of molds that coexisted in ecumenical eclecticism. The history of architecture in Los Angeles reveals a stumbling search for expression of the newly minted society, a search that set off in a variety of directions and left a melange of styles that still constitute uneasy neighbors. However, as Brendan Gill reminds us, "few architects took part in the building booms of earlier days; tens of thousands of houses that have survived admirably into the present were put up by one builder or another who happened to see a pretty picture in a magazine, sometimes accompanied by a floor plan and sometimes not."[115] Nevertheless, Southern California also hosted its famous architects.

The search for an "authentic" Los Angeles architectural style yielded at least five discrete "products": the craftsman cottage, the midwestern Victorian multistory house, the mission-style "hacienda," the art nouveau/art deco commercial structure, and the ranch house based on Bauhaus modern. All were derivative, but each adapted to the California climate the model from which it sprang.

Of these, the craftsman cottages contributed by the Greene brothers (Charles Sumner Greene, 1868–1957, and Henry Mather Greene, 1870–1954) were among the earliest and least probable. Arriving in Pasadena in 1893 from St. Louis—after several years of architectural training at MIT, assorted apprenticeships, and a brief stop at the Chicago World's Fair on their way—they first produced some fairly conventional houses influenced by Stanford White before settling on the form with which they are most associated. Inspiration for the last came from William Morris's English arts and crafts movement, but the affinities (use of warm wood and stained glass, an emphasis on simplicity, and high standards of craftsmanship) were already in their repertoire, and their adaptations to the climate were their own. Gradually, other elements also entered. They, like Frank Lloyd Wright, whose work theirs most closely resembles, began to draw also on the simplicity of Japanese and American Indian forms of the Southwest.[116] Although their houses are found mostly in Pasadena, their bungalow style was widely copied in Los Angeles.

The second model, the fictive "Mediterranean revival," made its appearance with the mission romance (often attributed to Helen Hunt Jackson's novel *Ramona*), through which Angelenos sought to come to terms with their conscience—by identifying with those whom they had displaced.[117] In any case, the simple walls, arched doorways and windows, courtyards, and Spanish red-tiled roofs that swept over the landscape in the building boom of the 1920s, and that perhaps reached perfection in the work of Irving Gill, not only infused California architecture but diffused from there to less likely places in the South and East.[118]

As one might have suspected, given the heavy in-migration of midwesterners, the third model was simply transplanted from the solid "North Shore" suburban architecture of Chicago, with few modifications for the new climate. One can see this influence in sections of Los Angeles such as Hancock Park, which more resembles Kenilworth, Chicago's richest North Shore suburb, than it does other parts of Los Angeles. Also of midwestern provenance (but perhaps by way of San Francisco) were the so-called Queen Anne Victorian extravaganzas originally concentrated in the Bunker Hill zone downtown.[119]

Art deco became perhaps the most popular style for commercial buildings in Los Angeles in the building boom of the 1920s and 1930s, and the city contains some dazzling examples, which makes it unique in some respects.[120] Given that this architectural form enjoyed considerable popularity in the 1920s in both New York and Los Angeles, it is puzzling that it never caught on in Chicago. One hypothesis is that less building went on in that city during the height of the craze than in New York or Los Angeles. Certainly, the 1920s and even extending into the 1930s was a period in which Los Angeles grew dramatically (especially along the newly extending commercial arteries of Sunset, Hollywood, and Wilshire Boulevards), just when the popularity of that architectural form peaked. But New York, with less construction, also experienced a miniexplosion of art deco.[121] My strongest hypotheses concern the role played by the Chicago school of architecture itself, which established an overpowering "standard" in that city for what important buildings should look like; this standard interacted with the tastes of investors and major sponsors of important buildings, causing them to reject the new genre.[122]

The final infusion came from Bauhaus architecture imported from Europe. Although Jaher dates the movement of modern architecture to the West Coast after World War I, when California "became to mid-twentieth-century architectural innovators what Chicago had been to revolutionaries of an earlier day,"[123] in fact it began earlier and flowered later. In both cases Frank Lloyd Wright was instrumental. He hired the Viennese architect R. M. Schindler in 1914, and eventually, the latter encouraged his friend, Richard Neutra, to join them. In 1923, Neutra was put on Wright's payroll. Neutra first worked in Chicago, then at Taliesen, and eventually in Los Angeles.[124] Between them, they laid the ground for modern architecture that would be transplanted en masse from Berlin to the United States when Hitler rose to power.

I have left out a sixth short-lived genre, namely, the late-nineteenth- and early-twentieth-century commercial structures on Broadway, so derivative of the skyscrapers that were going up in Chicago and New York, because these were isolated excursions that proved sterile. The Bradbury Building, with its interior court so imitative of the Chicago style, is simply the most famous of this group.[125]

Given such a rich repertoire, one would have expected Los Angeles to become a masterpiece of beauty and taste, albeit eclectic or ecumenical.[126] However, the juxtaposition of this large variety of styles, which in Manhattan often makes for interest, is primarily jarring in Los Angeles. And leaving out the isolated masterpieces, it must be admitted that most of Los Angeles is filled with far less attractive small houses and undistinguished commercial strips that deaden, if they do not offend, the senses.

URBAN PLANNING

Despite the fact that Los Angeles, because of its rapid growth, had more need of planning than any other city, it attempted neither a grand master plan, as had Chicago, nor an elaborate excursion into regional planning, as had New York.[127] Outside of some relatively primitive advances in zoning and the preparation of a 1924 master plan for transportation, advocating improved rail and mass transit, which was promptly ignored,[128] one can point to little in the way of visionary planning. Perhaps real estate interests felt that their needs were sufficiently served by subdivision regulations and deed restrictions.

In all fairness, Los Angeles did establish "America's first citywide use-zoning in 1908," and the "Los Angeles Realty Board . . . even hired their own professional city planning consultant in 1920 to write a new zoning law for the Los Angeles City Council." Furthermore, they "helped create the Los Angeles County Regional Planning Commission to facilitate suburban growth and circumvent the need for involvement of the City of Los Angeles in land-use regulation, infrastructure and service provision, and property taxation."[129]

But despite Weiss's claim that California was a major innovator in planning from the 1920s on,[130] zoning goals in the city of Los Angeles were limited to segregating land uses so as to exclude noxious industries from residential areas and to vastly overzoning the major arteries for commerce (although the first ordinance in 1908 also set aside seven industrial districts where such uses were permitted).[131] Even after more comprehensive rules were established with the passage of a new zoning ordinance in 1921, the city was so large and the City Planning Commission so recently established that at first the new zoning maps covered only a fraction of the city (Hollywood, East Hollywood, Wilshire, and West Lake).[132]

Finally, in 1929, the state passed legislation on subdivisions and planning, but by then the Depression was around the corner and real estate activity virtually collapsed. During this hiatus, a new zoning ordinance was passed and the planning commission was charged with rezoning more areas of the city.[133] This newfound power seems mostly to have led to a prosperous trade in zoning variances, when in the late 1930s several councilmen and planning commissioners were indicted for selling them.[134] It would not be until the late 1930s that decent legislation was in place.[135] These were all the more essential because, as we shall see, Los Angeles suffered less during the Depression than did New York or Chicago, and its growth, although reduced, never ceased. Indeed, while the rest of the nation's cities experienced disastrous losses in their economic bases, Los Angeles added new industries that positioned the city favorably when World War II production pulled the country out of the doldrums.

PART III

From the Depths of the Depression to Restructuring, 1930–70

From the Depths of the Depression to Restructuring, 1930–70

The American "century," at least according to some analysts, lasted only a generation or two, rising in the 1940s from a low point in the Great Depression and peaking somewhere between 1955 and 1965, before beginning its wobbling descent in the early 1970s, although none of these predicted the end of the Cold War and the unraveling of the Soviet Union, which restored American hegemony after 1989. Given the pandemic collapse that marked the early 1930s, there was, of course, no direction for the national economy to go other than up, and after the boom of the 1950s and early 1960s, none other than down, at least within the *same* cycle.[1] While predictions of decline may seem overly pessimistic, and certainly, as of the late 1990s, there has been no repeat of the plummet of the early 1930s, at least during the 1970s and 1980s we were apparently in the "B" or downward phase of the most recent Kondratiev cycle. Although it is hard to predict exactly what new trends lie hidden in the confusing decade of the 1990s, we may now be emerging from the uneven trough of the past two decades.[2]

But to speak of these fluctuations in abstract cyclical terms is to ignore the actual chain of events that precipitated these "rises" and "falls," making the analysis far more mechanistic than is warranted. And, as we shall see in this second half of the book, even a clear grasp of the larger cycles of the American economy cannot help us to see just *how* these trends were manifest in the three urbanized regions, not only because trends were played out differentially in inherited space, but also because local political responses to them have varied so radically.

The chapters in Part III explore changes in the three metropolitan regions between 1930 and about 1970, focusing on three general phases that, as we shall see, had somewhat different effects in the three sites. The first phase was, of course, the period of economic collapse in the 1930s, a disaster whose consequences were experienced more severely in the Northeast and Midwest than on the West Coast. The second phase was associated with the economic recovery engendered by World War II and its aftermath, in which America's relative immunity from destruction contrasted sharply with the devastation experienced by its European industrial "rivals." It is therefore not difficult to explain the economic hegemony of the United States in the immediate postwar period, a dominance that this nation enjoyed for at least a decade, until competition set in. All three cities benefited from this prosperity, expanding their frontiers deep into their countrysides and sustaining a prosperity that some attribute to the "Fordist" peace between large industrialists and powerful unions, which were equally devoted to sharing the fruits of their monopolies.[3]

The third phase, from the mid-1950s to the early 1970s, saw a revival of a war-geared economy, at first propelled by the "Cold War," eventually supplemented by hotter conflicts in Asia. During this phase, the three urbanized areas diverged markedly in the degree to which they benefited from the new economic stimuli. Chicago's economy (and, to a lesser extent, New York's) stagnated as federal investments in the development of defense/high technology essentially ignored the Midwest and paid scant attention to the Northeast. In contrast, such investments heavily favored the Southwest, and Los Angeles, along with much of the southwestern perimeter of the "gunbelt," received an enormous boost.

These regional discrepancies were compounded by the movement of factories in private industry to the "open shops" in the southern and southwestern regions of the United States, in part to escape union demands in what came to be known as the rust belt. The social turmoil of the 1960s intensified these trends, revealing deep fissures in the country's social structure along fault lines delineated by class, race, and ideology. By the end of the decade, Los Angeles, New York, and Chicago were very differently positioned to respond to the challenges that would determine their fates in the global restructuring of the 1970s.

Most analysts date the turning point of "restructuring" somewhere between the late 1960s and 1974,[4] and their descriptions of the symptoms (trade deficits, downsizing, subcontracting, offshoring of production via transnational corporations) are quite similar. However, there is considerably less consensus about the causes of the economic reversals that the United States was experiencing by the early 1970s. Part IV presents a fuller discussion of the developments in the post-1973 phase.

THE DEPRESSION: ITS IMPACT AND ITS "CURES"

Differential Impact

The collapse of international trade and finance in 1929 had its most profound effects on New York, as the abrupt drop in the international circulation of goods and money struck at the very heart of the city's global functions. The disappearance of demand for industrial goods hit Chicago the hardest, and the plant closings and extremely high unemployment rates there foreshadowed the beginning of a "rust belt" future. In contrast, although growth rates in the Los Angeles economy slowed almost to a halt during the opening years of the Depression, in general the effects of this period on Los Angeles were less disastrous and of shorter duration.[5] To some extent, this stronger relative position was acknowledged by the continued migration of people into the area from more severely affected zones. Indeed, whereas unemployment rose astronomically in other urbanized parts of the country, by the middle of the decade a new period of "industrialization," and thus a modest increase in jobs, was already under way in Southern California.

National "Cures"

At the national level, the Depression initiated a period of significant sociopolitical change, the legacy of which persists to this day. For the first time, the federal government, under the New Deal, instituted central allocations for poor relief and wove the first thin strands of a safety net via the 1935 Social Security Act for widows, orphans, and dependent children; it even instituted a retirement system for (some) workers. It sponsored a massive program of direct construction—from the building of schools and post offices to the creation of roads, dams, and irrigation basins and the generation of cheaper and more widely distributed electrical power. It thus created direct employment for some of those displaced by natural disasters and by plant closings.[6] Furthermore, by offering financial assistance to municipalities to clear slums and replace them with subsidized low-rent housing, it created jobs for construction workers who had been rendered superfluous by the cessation of private building. Other legislation strengthened the position of organized labor, protecting its rights to organize and to bargain collectively.

All of these program *should have* tended to level the playing field among U.S. cities. If, in the early part of the twentieth century, the three metropolitan areas were diverging in their economic bases, demographic compositions, and political structures, as I have contended in Part II, their common positions of misery by the 1930s *should have* made them similarly receptive to common programs emanating from the "center." But, as we shall see, the political cultures and institutional arrangements in each led to important variations in the ways they responded to these opportunities.

Local Responses

New York was best positioned to take advantage of the new programs, assisted by its well-honed capacity for coalition building (Fiorello La Guardia was elected mayor in 1933 on a Fusion ticket, which combined liberal democrats with reformist republicans) and by its close preexisting relations with Roosevelt, who had moved to the presidency from governorship of New York State. Political power in New York City had long been based on the regime's capacity to offer various forms of welfare—a practice established in the heyday of the Tammany machine, when turkeys or jobs may have been the local currency. The expanded resources newly available from the federal government were therefore enthusiastically plowed into programs for which widespread support, as well as institutional mechanisms for their execution, already existed.

The alacrity with which New York responded to the prospect of public housing may illustrate this point. One of President Roosevelt's earliest acts had been to inaugurate the Public Works Administration (PWA) to create employment;[7] among the options were slum clearance, the construction of affordable housing, new public works projects, parks, roads, and the renewal of aging infrastructures. New York was one of the first cities in the nation to avail itself of these opportunities.[8] Mayor La Guardia saw an immediate linkage between these possibilities and the city's long-term concerns with tenement house reform, and Robert Moses, parks commissioner, recognized a similar opportunity to expand his network of highways and parks. Both were able to use the powers and resources newly available to reshape the city, albeit not necessarily for the same, or even consistent, ends.

Chicago, along with the great belt of "Fordist" industrial cities of the East North Central region of the country, was of course hardest hit by the Depression.[9] Between 1930 and 1931, the male unemployment rate in Chicago shot up from a high 12 percent to an astronomical 31 percent, with the burden falling particularly heavily upon industrial workers: by 1931, 40 percent of male skilled workers, almost 37 percent of semiskilled workers, and 57 percent of male unskilled workers were unemployed.[10] By 1933, employment in manufacturing had dropped to half of what it had been in 1927 (the peak year), and the total payroll from manufacturing jobs was little more than a quarter of what it had been at the peak in 1929, just before the crash.[11]

The jolt was sufficient to dislodge the incumbent Republican machine that had ruled the city for some fifteen years and to replace it with a new Democratic machine controlled by "white ethnics." This machine would maintain a powerful one-party city and county regime for decades to come. But as Gosnell's superb study of 1937 reveals, this "shift" to democratic rule occurred even though the local party never embraced the "liberal" goals of the New Deal.[12] Furthermore, the growing black population was temporarily disenfranchised, even after the New Deal succeeded eventually in weaning it away from its traditional loyalty to the party of Lincoln. The relationship between blacks and working-class whites, already tense before the Depression began, deteriorated even more during hard times.

It must be acknowledged, however, that there was really very little in the New Deal program that was capable of addressing the deeper economic problems of this classic Fordist city, dependent as it was on large-scale heavy industries that not only manufactured consumer goods but supplied the machinery ordered by other factories. (Indeed, because of this multiplier effect, plant closings anywhere in the country reverberated in Chicago.) But the federal government could not reopen failed factories, nor could it reemploy skilled and semiskilled workers at their trades, and its ability to stimulate demand for producers' goods was distinctly limited. Thus it was not until the United States began to produce for Europe's war needs that the demand for steel, machine tools, army vehicles, and armaments pulled Chicago's economy out of its malaise. The federal government did offer direct income and employment-related relief, which the political "machine" doled out selectively, and it did offer some modest housing assistance. But, as we shall see, Chicago took only limited advantage of this last opportunity, in part because its most needy population was black; there was the not-unfounded suspicion that public housing might open white areas beyond the rigidly segregated Black Belt to unwelcomed neighbors.

Because of agriculture's importance to its economy, Los Angeles may have begun to experience the effects of the world decline in crop prices even before the Depression became widespread in the United States. However, by the mid-1930s large corporations were opening modern plants in the city, at the same time that aging factories were being closed down in the Midwest. In addition, Los Angeles's major "industry," producing motion pictures, was sustained by a nationwide thirst for escapist fantasies. Of the three cities, only Los Angeles increased in population during the Depression, as migrants continued to flock to it from areas in even greater economic difficulties.

Ironically, Los Angeles's industrial expansion may have been assisted by the very federal laws, introduced by New York's liberal representatives in Congress, that strengthened the rights of labor elsewhere.[13] The Wagner-sponsored National Labor Relations Act of 1935 established protections for labor, legitimating the rights of workers to unionize and to engage in collective bargaining. These reforms allowed American labor unions to triple their membership between 1935 and 1941, before wartime restrictions against strikes were temporarily imposed. Unionization took off again in the postwar period and peaked in strength in the heydays of the 1950s. Such enhancement of labor's bargaining powers in, inter alia, New York, Chicago, Detroit, and San Francisco may actually have made Los Angeles, with its more docile (or more terrorized) labor force, even more attractive to industrialists.

The Depression caused no fundamental upheavals in the power structure of Los Angeles, whose elite had long championed the "open shop" and had ruthlessly repressed any displays of labor mobilization and protest. The defeat of Upton Sinclair's radical proposals to end poverty in California (EPIC), advanced in his campaign for governor of the state in 1933–34, signaled the strength with which such "socialist" notions would be rejected by the governing elite. Interestingly enough, the same paranoia vis-à-vis "communism" would cause the city, over and over again, to reject federal offers of aid for subsidized public housing.

THE WARTIME RECOVERY

The second phase, one of recovery, began toward the end of the 1930s, and most analysts credit the outbreak of hostilities in Europe with providing just the boost to demand needed to get the production lines rolling again. But here, too, the effects were experienced somewhat differently in the three urban centers. Reindustrialization was not evenly distributed. Each of the three metropolitan regions played a different role in the armament-led recovery because of what it produced.

New York received a decided boost to its shipping and related industries, as the port became the chief location from which war matériel was sent to European allies (even before the official entry of the United States in the war). Its aircraft production also boomed as plants on Long Island expanded to meet the burgeoning demand. Cities of the Midwest such as Chicago and Detroit also received much-needed infusions, as orders for trucks, tanks, and other "machines of war" caused a reopening of retooled plants and a backward-linkage demand for the steel from which machines were to be built. But Los Angeles, which had already begun to expand its industrial base by the mid-1930s, was best positioned for the changes that lay ahead.

Los Angeles's tire, aircraft, and motor vehicle plants were already up and running when the United States entered the war, and there were optimistic predictions about the region's future as a major steel producer. But it was not until after the United States entered the war officially, triggered by the Japanese attack on Pearl Harbor on December 7, 1941, that the West Coast in general, and Los Angeles in particular, became the leader in what Ann Markusen and her coauthors have termed the "gunbelt" economy—that is, industrial development fueled by war industries.[14] This "favoring" of the West Coast by the Department of Defense would later be solidified during the Korean War of the early 1950s and then by the 1960s war in Vietnam—both of which seemed to dwarf concerns with the Cold War, despite the rhetoric.

The "edge" gained by the gunbelt was intensified by the space wars. The headquartering on the West Coast of the newly important Pacific fleet, along with a virtual explosion of its shipbuilding capacity, was supplemented by its aircraft and, later, missile industries. It would not be until after the collapse of the Soviet Union that such preferential treatment of the West Coast would be inhibited, precipitating the region into a recession all the deeper because it was unexpected and late (but more of this in Part IV).

The prosperity induced by gearing up for a wartime economy ushered in an expansive phase for the entire country, one in which the major cities and industrial regions were highly privileged. World War II also stimulated one of the highest geographic mobility rates the United States had known since the "closing of the frontier." Mobilization into the armed forces, coupled with mounting labor shortages in defense plants, induced a massive movement of blacks from the rural South to northern and western industrial centers and enticed women into nontraditional jobs, from which they would not be dislodged until demobilization occurred.[15]

With civilian construction at a virtual halt, however, there was not only a mismatch between needs and facilities in various parts of the country, but the creation of pent-up consumer demands that would be unleashed after the war. In New York, Los Angeles, and especially Chicago, existing black ghettos became more densely populated and hypersegregated, laying up tensions over turf that would manifest themselves in the postwar period. In Los Angeles, this was compounded by the import of laborers from Mexico, a reversal of their deportation in the 1930s.

Racial and ethnic tensions had already begun to surface during wartime, and 1943 marks three events that foreshadowed the postwar situation in industrial cities that had experienced rapid growth and black in-migration: the Detroit race riot, the so-called zoot suit riots in Los Angeles, and New York's Harlem riot of that year.[16] Chicago was spared widespread violence, although it continued to have minor skirmishes in its "border wars" on the fringes of its Black Belt, and at least one major confrontation occurred when African American war workers were moved into the Frances Cabrini public housing project, which had been constructed in an old Italian quarter on the north side.[17]

THE POSTWAR EXPLOSION OF METROPOLITAN REGIONS

Given the pent-up demands for housing, marriages, and families, all of which had been delayed by the war, and assisted by new federal programs that expanded the funds available for veterans to invest in education and homes, the postwar housing boom led to remarkable growth within metropolitan regions between 1945 and 1965. Rather than repeating the anticipated economic retraction that had occurred in 1919, the American economy prospered, fueled by the rebuilding of destroyed European economies through the Marshall Plan; by eased credit, which unleashed massive spending on consumer durables; and by a period of new "Fordism," as stronger labor unions reached attractive accords with large corporations to share in the prosperity. The period was particularly notable in generating greater income equality and expanding mass consumption, although minorities benefited less than whites from these trends.

Among the most important consequences was the creation of new residential communities, mostly beyond the limits of center cities, and the beginnings of a decentralization of retail establishments, light industry, and, eventually, offices. The construction of improved highways and, at least in New York and Chicago, expanded commuter rail lines assisted this process physically,[18] whereas federally subsidized loans to "community builders" and individual buyers propelled it financially. Trends toward geographic expansion, already evident in the 1920s but aborted by the war, resumed in the late 1940s.

The New York World's Fair of 1939 had predicted a glorious future for urban America, replete with clover-leafed freeways and decentralized planned suburban communities that would transform the American landscape. By 1960 this utopian dream seemed well on its way to achievement, although reality revealed flaws that had not been anticipated and not all classes and races entered its coveted domains. What the fair utopia had not predicted was the civil rights movement, which essentially demanded that those still excluded from the "gates of paradise" be admitted on an equal footing.

Ironically, but not illogically connected, the 1950s marked both the acme of American prosperity/hegemony in the world and the first stirrings of the civil rights movement. Although the movement was initially focused on the South and oriented toward issues of voting rights and the desegregation of public facilities, such dramatic manifestations of racism were paralleled in northern and western cities by bread-and-butter job and housing segregation grievances that were of long standing. In the area of jobs, the Fair Employment Practices Act proscribed job discrimination, but enforcement was haphazard and often ineffectual. In the area of housing, however, major changes were taking place.

The Public Housing Authority reversed its original ruling that public housing occupancy should mirror the racial composition of its neighborhood, opening the way for black occupancy of units in "white" neighborhoods. New York complied, continuing to construct public housing throughout the five boroughs until decades later, when cuts in federal funding forced a downscaling of these programs. In Chicago, the construction of public housing was actually aborted for a time when the effort to find "acceptable" vacant sites on which to build relocation housing was blocked by members of the City Council representing white districts that feared a "black invasion" of their turf. Only after the conflict was resolved—through the approval of sites immediately adjacent to neighborhoods already predominantly black—was construction resumed. In Los Angeles, which built almost no public housing, opposition was framed not so much on racial as on ideological grounds; the city's elite viewed the program as "socialist" and therefore rejected it.

Two crucial U.S. Supreme Court rulings, however, were undermining the status quo of race relations in cities outside the South. In the 1948 Los Angeles case of *Shelley v. Kraemer,* the Supreme Court declared that racially restrictive covenants could not be enforced in the courts. Such covenants were primarily to be found in owner-occupied areas of single-family houses or small apartment buildings, more typical of Los Angeles and Chicago than of New York. In the latter city, more informal means (rental "steering" and "cooperative" ownership) were the common mechanisms for racial exclusion, and these continued. With the invalidation of racial covenants, however, a first "wave" of white flight ensued, especially from the South Side of Chicago, but also from the expanding zone of traditional black occupancy in Los Angeles, south of downtown. Within New York City, there was considerable open land available in the outer boroughs, so that racial redistributions did not necessarily drive fleeing whites beyond the city limits.

The second change came in 1954, when the Supreme Court ruled (in *Brown v. Board of Education of Topeka*) that "separate" schools were inherently unequal. This decision led each city to a different response to school desegregation. In Chicago, where most lands within the city's boundaries had already been built up, the decision triggered a second wave of "white flight" into suburbs beyond the city limits and a hardening of exclusionary zoning in those communities, because the court decision called for desegregation *only* within each city's limit. The result was excessive abandonment within the city, rapid movement of blacks into the vacated zones, and hardly any suburbanization of the black population, except into a few suburbs that had been "traditionally" black.

White flight was more modest in New York, in part because vacancies remained low, rent controls inhibited residential mobility, and there were already black settlements scattered throughout Manhattan, the Bronx, and Brooklyn. Some neighborhoods, such as the South Bronx, experienced "blowout," and parts of Brooklyn and the northern Bronx underwent significant racial succession, but the existence of vacant land and newer housing developments in these boroughs meant that the proportion of minority residents could rise without any significant overall decline in the number of whites in those same boroughs. Racial animosities were perhaps more muted in New York than in Chicago, possibly because residents had greater tolerance for diversity, and perhaps because there were so many "intermediate groups" (especially

Latinos and, later, Asians) that simple racial polarization was impossible.[19] In New York, greater latitude in public school choice (and a strong tradition of both Catholic and elite private schools) also muted some of the struggles over busing.

In Los Angeles there was a unified school system that included not only the city of Los Angeles but parts of the county as well. But as I have already noted, the county also contained a large number of independent communities that were immune to the mandates of *Brown v. Board of Education.* Furthermore, and increasingly, developments were taking place in suburbs and towns in the outlying counties around Los Angeles, where demographic compositions were quite specialized. Court challenges to de facto school segregation were yet to come, as was the court-ordered mandate to achieve greater integration in the schools of the unified school district. Because this mandate for integration was not issued until late in the 1970s, I reserve this discussion to Chapter 12.

TRAVAIL IN THE 1960S

In the 1960s, the economic health of the three urbanized regions had already diverged significantly. By the late 1950s, Chicago's postwar flush of prosperity had begun to pale, especially within the city limits. Growth in the region's jobs and population was leveling off, and within the city limits the total population had actually begun to decline. New York City had not yet reached the limits of growth within the five boroughs, even though most of the region's new industrial, commercial, and residential growth was taking place in areas well beyond the city's taxing jurisdiction.[20] But it was in the Los Angeles–Orange County region that the most explosive growth occurred. By the 1970s, that region was on a growth trajectory that outstripped the other two, so it should come as no surprise that in 1990 Los Angeles displaced Chicago as the second largest city in the country. By then, its CMSA population was even closing the gap between it and New York.

The "Riots" and Local Responses

As local economies began to contract in the second half of the 1960s, paralleling the wind-down of the Vietnam War and foreshadowing the "restructuring" that would occur in the 1970s, the optimism that blacks had experienced in all three cities as law after law was passed (for open housing, an end to job discrimination, and a widening of welfare supports under "Great Society" programs) began to dissipate. Minorities were the first to feel the brunt of "globalization" and "restructuring," even before such troubling conditions spread to the rest of society and were noticed by scholars.

The theory of "rising expectations," very popular among political scientists studying revolutions at that time, gives the impression that the causes of black dissatisfaction were all in blacks' heads. Reanalysis of economic data, however, suggests that there were also material bases for the disappointments being experienced in various ghettos of the nation. Indeed, it is just as probable that the programs of the "Great Society" came after rather than before the fact, because by the time they were institutionalized, the opening battles of ghetto revolts in the cities were already under way.

Regardless of the underlying causes, however, the trigger in each case was the one that had traditionally touched off revolts in American cities, namely, the use of arbitrary or excessive force by the police against a member of a minority group. Just as the 1935 and 1943 Harlem riots had been precipitated by such events, so the 1964 Harlem/Bedford-Stuyvesant riot in New York was triggered by an altercation between a black youth and a policeman, yielding one of the very first events in a widespread series of outbursts that wracked American cities later in the decade. It was followed in 1965 by the Los Angeles Watts riot, again triggered by a nasty encounter between a black driver and the L.A. police. However, it is important to point out that both of these events had been preceded by Chicago's ongoing "border wars" over the expansion of the South Side Black Belt; indeed, Chicago was one of several northern cities in which civil unrest first exploded in 1963.[21] Note that these events occurred *before* rather than after revisions in national policies.

In the summer of 1967, President Johnson appointed the so-called Kerner Commission on Civil Disorders, whose findings were announced amid great fanfare less than one year later.[22] The panel addressed the underlying causes of racial unrest and warned (in one of its most widely quoted statements) that "the nation [was] moving toward two societies, one black, one white—separate and unequal."[23] On April 4, 1968, less than a month after the report was released, Martin Luther King Jr. was assassinated, triggering explosions in some 215 cities throughout the country. Among these was a major one on the West Side of Chicago, where King had led marches for open housing in 1966. Ironically, the open housing and civil rights legislation finally passed in 1968, coupled with white fears that had been intensified by the civil unrest, resulted in even greater white flight to the suburbs—intensifying the predicted trend to a separation of the races.

HOW CITIES RESPONDED TO THE TROUBLES THROUGH FISCAL POLICIES

Given the turmoil of the late 1960s and the more generous allocations that were forthcoming from Washington to deal with poverty and racism, one might have expected cities in the United States to have responded rather uniformly to the challenges by stepping up their efforts to construct social supports for minorities and the poor (not necessarily coterminous). In actual fact, however, the political regimes in the three cities followed quite different policies that were attributable more to their different political cultures and their local power structures than to the relative needs of their populations.

Despite its collapsing economy and its massive white flight, Chicago, evidently prizing "fiscal solvency" above compassion, remained largely indifferent to the increasing poverty of its growing proportion of minority residents. Its white-dominated Democratic political machine held such a lock on power that perhaps it felt it could afford to ignore constituents who had so little capacity to influence primary election outcomes.[24] In contrast, New York, which had always maintained a more charitable approach toward its underprivileged, managed to forestall further racial unrest by incorporating dissident groups into the power structure and by expanding its allocations to housing, health, and welfare so rapidly, with or without federal assistance, that by 1975 it was "going broke."[25] And Los Angeles, despite its post-Watts pious promises to ameliorate conditions, soon returned to the status quo ante of benign neglect (and sometimes not-so-benign neglect, with stepped-up police harassment in Mexican American and black neighborhoods), offering only the window dressing of electing a black mayor (former football hero and police chief) in 1973, who, in the two decades of his reign, did little to upset the balance of power favoring Anglo downtown and Westside interests.[26] I discuss some of these issues in the three chapters that constitute Part III, but I reserve to Part IV many of the post-1970 developments.

CHAPTER 7

A New York: A New Deal

NEW YORK "INCUBATES" THE NEW DEAL

A special census of the unemployed taken in January 1931 estimated that there were almost 610,000 persons in New York City's five boroughs "able to work, willing to work, . . . looking for a job . . . [or] laid off"; another large segment was working only part-time at seriously reduced wages. Factory employment had dropped to three-fourths of its level in the prosperous 1920s.[1] Because there were as yet no public institutions to cope with an emergency of this magnitude, two of New York's oldest philanthropies stepped immediately into the breach. The Association for Improving the Condition of the Poor and the Charity Organization Society joined forces to raise more than eight million dollars for the Emergency Work Bureau, which, between December 1930 and April 1931, actually engaged some 37,500 workers in "paving roads, surfacing playgrounds, repairing fences, fixing water fountains, cleaning hospitals, renovating city properties, and clearing vacant lots."[2] But the needs were far vaster than private charities could ameliorate.

Pressures for government action came, inter alia, from the Welfare Council of New York City. Between October 1930 and May 1931, the council surveyed some nine hundred social workers and public health nurses to find out how the Depression was affecting their clients. Among the findings were that a significant "downgrading" of housing standards had occurred, as families moved to smaller, cheaper quarters or doubled up with relatives (especially in Harlem, where housing was already overcrowded); that diet and health were already deteriorating; and that families were suffering from severe psychological distress and strife.[3]

When the Welfare Council's urgent appeals to Mayor Jimmy Walker[4] were met with a feeble appropriation and the excuse that the City Charter did not permit more, Council Director William Hodson appealed directly to Franklin Delano Roosevelt, then New York's governor. "In August of 1931, Roosevelt summoned the state legislature to a special session on relief," proposing the twenty-million-dollar Temporary Emergency Relief Administration (TERA) "to underwrite municipal aid to the distressed."[5] Roosevelt appointed Harry Hopkins director of TERA, and Hopkins promptly exceeded his mandate—until his program was covering one out of every ten families in the state.[6] This initiative was hailed enthusiastically by Fiorello La Guardia, then a New York congressman representing East Harlem, who had been proposing similar relief measures at the federal level but with no success. A basic coalition was forming that would lead eventually to a close working relationship between Washington and New York in the New Deal, once FDR assumed the presidency in 1932 (taking Harry Hopkins to Washington with him) and La Guardia was elected mayor of New York in 1933.[7]

When he took office in 1934, however, La Guardia inherited a city in great distress: city aid had lagged behind the state, and its relief programs were riddled with graft and corruption; a fiscal crisis had been imminent by the end of 1933, when the city had to be rescued from receivership.[8] There was much to be done, and the city turned to Washington. It received help, thanks to the political coalition of FDR, Hopkins, and La Guardia that had already been established, even before FDR put together his New Deal, which built, in part, upon experiments begun in New York State. This close relationship between New York City and Washington greased the wheels for numerous programs that often were begun in New York City, even before they became national policies.[9]

NEW YORK "INVENTS" PUBLIC HOUSING

Subsidized housing was, of course, one of those areas in which New York City led the way, well before the Housing Act of 1937 extended federal assistance to other cities. Because New York was basically a city of renters rather than home owners, the effects of depressions were always felt more quickly there, as evictions for rent arrears take place much faster than banks are able to foreclose on delinquent owners. The city's poor, therefore, had a long history of resisting forced dispossessions, with well-honed neighborhood techniques to block marshals and reinstall furniture that had been dumped at the curb.[10]

But this time the scale was beyond the capacity of such local actions. In the eight-month period that ended in June 1932, some 186,000 families had already been served with dispossession notices. "Small neighborhood bands often stopped marshals from putting furniture in the street; other times, crowds of up to 1000 neighbors blocked evictions. One estimate is that such grass-roots resistance succeeded in restoring 77,000 evicted families to their homes in New York City."[11] However, this left more than a hundred thousand families unassisted. In addition, a large population of homeless men, after having abandoned the families they could no longer support, were building "Hoovervilles" in interstices throughout the city, even raising one in Central Park on the future site of the "great lawn."

First Houses

The initial response to the "housing crisis" was extremely modest: a tiny rehabilitation project on the Lower East Side, appropriately named First Houses. However, it marked the beginning of a long-term and massive program of public housing construction that by 1990 was providing homes to at least half a million low-income New Yorkers.[12] First Houses, even though it contained only some 122 subsidized units intended for employed working-class tenants, illustrates the informal way the special coalition between Washington and New York worked.[13]

One month after he took office, Mayor La Guardia appointed Langdon Post, former head of the city's Tenement House Department, to direct the newly established New York Public Housing Authority (NYPHA).[14] Taking Vincent Astor up on his offer to unload a row of decrepit (and unprofitable) tenement buildings on the Lower East Side, and having "wangled $300,000 and free Public Works Administration labor" from Washington,[15] Post gutted, reorganized, and rehabilitated the units around an interior court, an arrangement that had been recommended at the turn of the century by architect reformers. This proved so successful (in terms of livability, if not economics) that not only is the project still occupied, but in 1974 it was designated a New York City "landmark."

By the time the U.S. Housing Act (sponsored by New York Senator Robert Wagner Sr.) passed Congress in 1937, New York already had 2,330 public housing units under construction or completed, and between 1937 and the U.S. entry into World War II in 1941, another 10,648 were begun.[16] Although this is hardly an impressive total, it did constitute a substantial proportion of all new housing built in the city during the Depression. As Peter Marcuse notes:

> In nearly eight years . . . the NYPHA built 12,978 units of housing in a city with over two million households. . . . [Thus it built] housing for less than one percent of the city's people. . . . [But between 1934 and the end of 1938] a total of only 6,641 new units were built in the city, of which the public units started before the 1937 act constituted 35 percent; for the whole period 1934–1941, 55,465 units were completed, of which public housing provided 23 percent. Public housing, therefore, was important because of its relative, not absolute, numbers.[17]

But from the start the city administration had more ambitious schemes. Two larger-scale projects, to be built on vacant land, were successively planned: the Williamsburg Houses in Brooklyn, intended for white occupancy and designed by a famous Swiss architect, and, somewhat belatedly, Harlem Houses, intended for black occupants.[18]

The Harlem Riot of 1935

The building of Harlem Houses was undertaken in rapid response to racial unrest. According to Marcuse, the Harlem riot of March 1935 precipitated Mayor La Guardia's announcement that "the very next housing project to be built would be in Harlem."[19] Although this may appear "manipulative," most scholars credit La Guardia and the growing political power of Harlem blacks with more positive motives. Dominic J. Capeci Jr. notes that although between 1933 and 1943 race relations in New York City were not ideal, "they were more harmonious than in other urban centers. *This was partly due to the combined efforts of black leaders* [such as Adam Clayton Powell] *and white public officials* [such as La Guardia]."[20]

La Guardia certainly was quick to recognize the dangers of racial conflict. After "a minor incident involving a young black shoplifter and a white store manager ignited a riot that swept through Harlem, [La Guardia] appointed a biracial Mayor's Commission on Conditions in Harlem . . . [that] conducted twenty-five hearings, and listened to the testimony of 160 witnesses."[21] Howard University sociologist E. Franklin Frazier was given a staff of thirty to conduct a study of the appalling socioeconomic conditions in Harlem, which was hardest hit by the Depression.[22] Not surprisingly, the investigating commission found that the problems of blacks were due chiefly to inadequate incomes.

> Discriminatory hiring practices deprived AfroAmericans of adequate employment and . . . [therefore] of nourishing foods, decent lodging, necessary medical care, and a healthy family relationship. Hence many became wards of the state, depending upon others, often the discriminators, for charitable assistance. . . . During the first week of September 1935, 43 percent of Harlem's black families were on relief. Throughout the state that year, two-and-a-half times as many blacks as whites were on relief because of unemployment. . . . blacks registering as unemployed in 1937 constituted 40 percent of all gainful AfroAmerican workers, while the corresponding percentage for all other groups was 15.[23]

All the earlier negative findings of the Welfare Council were found in extreme form within the black population: they lived doubled up in overcrowded slum housing; they suffered from high rates of illness (especially tuberculosis and malnutrition) and were inadequately treated in Jim Crow hospitals; their schools were segregated through district gerrymandering and were overcrowded, old, and dilapidated and lacked adequate teaching materials; furthermore, students often had unsympathetic white teachers and read textbooks filled with demeaning images of blacks.[24]

It was no wonder that crime rates were high, especially given that the police were overzealous in arresting black youth and that blacks tended to view the police as "the boldest examples of northern racism. . . . Critics of the police compared large concentrations of patrolmen in black ghettos to 'an army of occupation' and complained of constant brutality."[25] Given these conditions, it was not surprising that the Harlem riot of 1935 "brought to the surface aggressive, resentful feelings. Unlike earlier disorders in which whites attacked blacks, Harlem's was a hostile outburst 'against racial discrimination and poverty in the midst of [comparative] plenty.'"[26]

Although La Guardia rejected the commission's report and its recommendations,[27] several actions to improve Harlem conditions were immediately undertaken. "By 1940, the Harlem River Houses, the Central Harlem Center building, the Women's Pavilion at Harlem Hospital, and two Harlem schools were completed. Also, the number of black nurses and attendants of the Hospital Department doubled and that of black physicians and medical board members tripled."[28]

Harlem Houses

The 574 units of the Harlem River Houses were constructed on vacant land that John D. Rockefeller owned, between built-up Harlem and the Harlem River and adjacent to the Dunbar Co-ops, which Rockefeller had earlier constructed for middle-class blacks (a project then in foreclosure). The federal Public Works Administration contracted with the New York City Housing Authority to plan and design the project, but the PWA actually built the project before leasing it back to the NYPHA to operate.[29] Some fifteen thousand families applied, so admission could be highly selective.

However, because the unemployed and persons in "atypical" households were disqualified from admission (it was not until the late 1950s, for example, that single mothers were admitted), even if much more public housing had been built, it could never have solved the problems of unemployment generated by the Depression, although it could, and did, give work to construction workers. Nor could it solve the endemic competition between the city and its suburbs for resources.

THE NEW DEAL FOSTERS DECENTRALIZATION

La Guardia's arch rival for power over the city's form during the Depression was Robert Moses, whom Robert Caro calls "the power broker" and Jerome Charyn refers to simply as "the pharaoh."[30] More than any single other figure in the city's history, Moses, who never held any elective office, shaped the spatial pattern of the New York region—before, during, and after the Depression—by utilizing powers he accumulated in the independent empire he had amassed through his appointed sinecures as state and city parks commissioner and through his freedom to reinvest the lucrative tolls from the Triborough Bridge and Tunnel Authority, which he headed. Thus, despite the close relationship between La Guardia and Roosevelt and their mutual distaste for Moses, the latter had an independent edge vis-à-vis Washington.

To understand this, one must refer back to the 1920s. Peter Hall reminds us that Roosevelt was heavily committed in principle to a "mass return to the land," a position Hall attributes to the influence of Roosevelt's uncle, Frederic Delano, who had guided the New York Regional Plan and whom he later appointed to the National Resources Planning Board.[31] Given this predilection, no conflict was recognized between the New Deal's commitment to cities and its commitment to suburban development. Robert Moses, as parks commissioner, availed himself of subsidized PWA labor to rebuild and expand his park empire in both the city and its suburbs, and the highways and bridges he constructed eventually midwifed the predictions of the 1920s New York Regional Plan into the reality of 1950s suburban sprawl.

NEW YORK AS A KEY PLAYER IN LABOR ORGANIZING

While the WPA absorbed a fraction of the unemployed, the cutting of wages and the job insecurities of the employed nurtured long-standing radical labor movements in New York, movements that were strengthened in the early 1930s by federal legislation protecting workers' rights. In 1932 Congress passed the Norris–La Guardia Act, blocking federal injunctions against strikers and outlawing yellow-dog contracts, and in 1935, stimulated by a rash of strikes the previous year, the Wagner-sponsored National Industrial Recovery Act guaranteed labor's rights to organize and to bargain collectively. (At Wagner's initiative, the Social Security Act was also passed in the same year.)

Indeed, whereas the post–World War I labor movement had been severely weakened in the 1920s, the crisis of the 1930s revitalized it. Despite the poor bargaining position of labor (how do you strike when you don't have a job?), the AFL/CIO, working largely out of New York, took advantage of the new legislation to mobilize greater union strength and to build a national network of unions in the late 1930s that was sufficient to pressure for the Fair Labor Standards Act, passed by Congress in 1938.[32] (This act established the long-sought forty-hour week, set a minimum wage, and banned child labor.)

The opportunity for labor to flex its growing muscles, however, was interrupted by World War II, when the emergency led to a temporary moratorium on strikes. Strikes would resume immediately after the war. The most spectacular actions were in the prospering fields of transportation: railroads, mass transit, and the ports. In the late 1950s, municipal workers—of whom New York City had an inordinate number, especially after the quasi-independent subway companies were unified and placed within the public sector, thus absorbing the previously unionized transit workers—also gained the right to bargain collectively. Encouraged by this precedent, New York's police officers, firefighters, social workers, and teachers rapidly transformed their professional organizations into bargaining unions. Thus the principles of the NLRB devised by Robert Wagner Sr. a generation earlier, which originally applied only to private firms, were later extended to public employees by his son, Robert Wagner Jr., when he was mayor of New York City.[33]

NEW YORK AS CULTURE INCUBATOR

New York Introduces "Modern" Architecture

I have already noted that two exemplary "skyscrapers" (the Empire State Building and the Chrysler Building) were already under construction when the Depression struck. Despite the ensuing hard times, interest continued and, perhaps surprisingly, new developments were added—not only in Manhattan but in the outer boroughs as well. Leonard Wallock credits the Museum of Modern Art's International Exhibition of Modern Architecture in 1932 with introducing European modern architects to the United States. The exhibit displayed the works of Le Corbusier, Walter Gropius, Mies van der Rohe, and other European avant garde architects, thus helping to popularize the international style. It was followed by a 1934 exhibit of "machine art" and, in 1938–39, by an exhibit titled "Bauhaus, 1919–1928."[34]

Many of these influences would be manifested in the 1939 World's Fair.[35] But even before that, one could see similar simplifications in the buildings of Rockefeller Center, such as the Time & Life, Eastern Air Lines, and Associated Press buildings, and other commercial structures used themes from European modernism and art deco.[36] Krinsky suggests that a desire to save money through simplification "may have been the real catalyst to the widespread acceptance of a sparer aesthetic during the Depression years"[37]—a most interesting hypothesis.

Novels and Noir Films

Cheaper still than simplified buildings were words and images. Although it is difficult to separate individual writers' angst from the somber realities of the 1930s, noir views of New York became even darker when outside circumstances piled on internal tensions. Shaun O'Connell's chapter on literary New York City in the 1930s suggests that negative literary images of New York, previously tempered by fascination and exaltation in the city's freedoms, turned to unrelieved disillusionment once prosperity disappeared.[38] The vitality of the iconoclastic and creative Greenwich Village/Harlem Renaissance scenes nurtured by the 1920s Jazz Age gave way to new forms of creativity in the dismal thirties. Nathanael West (né Nathan Weinstein), born in New York, gained early fame for his *Miss Lonelyhearts* (a book begun in 1929 but not published until 1933), which presents a sordid view of New York's callous soul.[39] And Clifford Odets's play *Waiting for Lefty* was so inflammatory when first performed in 1935 that the audience greeted its rhetorical ending not with applause but with rhythmic shoutings of "strike, strike."[40] Perhaps these two exemplars capture the range of responses to the depression.[41]

On the other hand, the 1930s were not a time when films could afford to depress; rather, Hollywood catered to the desire to escape from harsh reality, if only momentarily, through voyeurism on the lives of the pampered rich. A profusion of true "noir" films on New York had to await recovery. If *Blade Runner,* set in the "future," is *the* quintessential noir film about Los Angeles, and "backward-looking" gangster films of the Prohibition 1920s are the chief noir images of Chicago, New York continues to inspire an enormous output of dystopic films set in the "present."

In 1994, a two-month retrospective showing of sixty-four New York noir films made between 1941 and 1976 ran at New York's Film Forum. The deep connection in these films between plot and setting is highlighted in William Grimes's review:

> If ever a city was made for black and white, it's New York. The city is a place of harsh light, dark shadows, strong angles and violent extremes. . . . Manhattan, it's all black clothes and pale skin. The skyline itself, the city's most durable, destructive image, achieves full power, Lucifer-like, as darkness descends and a million cold white diamonds begin to glitter. *New York is a noir city.* . . . "The city's uncompromising landscape and the endless surge of its anonymous crowds make an ideal setting for pitiless moral dramas in which doomed characters move inexorably toward a violent end. *In the classic New York noirs, the city's skyscrapers and streets play the role of the gods and the chorus in Greek tragedy.* They are the impassive observers, the iron enforcers, of a bleak moral code."[42]

A cursory survey of film titles highlights recurring themes: death, terror, stranger, phantom, wrong man, wrong number, lost, no way out, screaming, crying, alone, dark corner, victim, strangers, killer, double life, silence, shadows, crime, jungle, middle of the night, naked city, force of evil. Such themes were nurtured by the Depression, even though the films that incorporated them would not appear until later (but recall that Fritz Lang's dystopic view of New York dates back to the mid-1920s). In art as well, grim and sordid images of the city replaced the glowing impressionist palette of Childe Hassam.

1939: ON THE CUSP OF THE FUTURE

Although New York's economy in the Depression had neither plunged as deeply as Chicago's nor recovered as rapidly as Los Angeles's, by the late 1930s a dim light had appeared at the end of the tunnel. As elsewhere, full recovery would not be achieved until the involvement of the United States in World War II. We might, therefore, take stock of the city just before 1940, when its population, troubled as it was, was approaching 7.5 million, a total somewhat higher, it should be noted, than in 1990, when it stood at 7.3 million (the population of the five boroughs actually peaked in 1970). This seems an appropriate moment: before the United States entered the war and less than a decade before the region began its total transformation through fissive explosion. The year 1939 offers a Janus-like opportunity to look both backward and forward.

Looking Backward

In 1939, perhaps the best "guide" to the "real" New York City ever written was published. This seven-hundred-page book was one of the finer achievements of the Depression or, rather, of the Federal Writers' Project, which marshaled a crew of talented unemployed scholars and writers as well as skilled photographers, artists, and mapmakers, drawn from the Federal Art Project, to create the *WPA Guide to New York City.*[43] Each of the boroughs and its neighborhoods is mapped and described in loving detail, with attention to its historical development, its economy, its landmarks, and its relation to the rest of the city.

The "mental map" of the city projected by the *Guide* is, of course, grossly distorted, an error that persists to this day. Reflective of its economic power and its symbolic centrality, Manhattan, which by then housed less than a quarter of the city's population, consumed almost four hundred pages of text. Brooklyn warranted only seventy-five pages, even though it was home to some 37 percent of the population. The Bronx and Queens, accounting respectively for some 20 and 18 percent of the population, were each covered in about forty pages, and Staten Island, with only 2 percent of the city's residents, was accorded some twenty-five pages.[44] And yet it would be in these "outer boroughs" and their suburban extensions that the city of the future would be constructed, and where, with time, the most dramatic transformations would take place.

The image of the city projected in the *Guide* was also distorted by nostalgia and affection, which caused a certain blurring of harsh realities. Although New York was still deep in the Depression when the book was written, the volume repeatedly boasts of New York's financial power, industrial might, and active ports, as well as the creativity of its art, theater, and music. A more dispassionate look would have revealed that deep deindustrialization was already taking place, even though the coming war would temporarily mask this decline in manufacture.

Looking Forward

The year 1939, however, was one of enormous optimism and hope, which perhaps accounts for the upbeat tone of the *Guide.* Chicago had the misfortune to open its "Century of Progress" Exhibition (commemorating one hundred years of the city's existence) in 1933, during the darkest days of the Depression, an eerie parallel to its 1893 fair, which had coincided with an earlier crash. In contrast, the United States seemed finally to be emerging from its ten-year slump when New York's greatest world's fair opened on April 30, 1939, amid great fanfare heralding the "dawning" of a new utopia.[45] Its theme was "Building the World of Tomorrow." That world was to be "urban," but in a different mold.

Today, cities, even "good" ones, have a bad reputation. It is therefore amazing to recognize how central "the city" was to the 1939 vision of tomorrow. Although many of the exhibits of the fair focused on science's contribution to new technologies and blatantly "pushed" new consumer products (both television and fax machines vied with pure foods and domestic equipment for attention), three of the most noteworthy and best-attended exhibits were Democracity, Futurama, and the panorama of Manhattan produced by Consolidated Edison.

Democracity, sponsored by the fair theme committee under architect Robert Kohn and designed by Henry Dreyfuss with the advice of Lewis Mumford and Clarence Stein, was a vast model built inside the Perisphere itself, depicting an ideal metropolitan region of a million people.[46] For twenty-five cents, visitors were treated to a six-minute show in which they circulated through Utopia, as light changed from day to night and as music swelled from a "thousand-voiced chorus." The transition between cycles was marked by the dawning of a great day.[47] The *Guide* describes the show as follows:

> Two enclosed escalators carry visitors . . . to Perisphere entrances. . . . Around the interior—twice as large as Radio City Music Hall—two "magic carpets" or revolving platforms bear passengers "two miles" above [ground for a bird's-eye view of the model]. . . .
>
> Democracity, with a working population of 250,000, is represented as the business, administrative, and cultural core of a community of more than a million people. It lies on the banks of a river and has no residents. The population is housed in a rim of garden apartments, suburban areas, and in neighboring, semi-industrial towns. Green-belt areas circle the city and the towns, with intervening tracts of land devoted to intensive farming.[48]

Figure 7.1. Uneasy bedfellows: (left to right) Robert Moses, Grover Whelan, and Fiorello La Guardia at the opening of the 1939 New York World's Fair. Courtesy of the La Guardia and Wagner Archives, La Guardia Community College/The City University of New York; used with permission.

It is a fantasy Ebenezer Howard and Patrick Geddes might have instantly recognized, but its neat arrangement failed to predict the form of suburbanization that would splinter metropolitan areas in the postwar period.

Democracity was second only to the most popular exhibit of the fair, Futurama, designed by Norman Bel Geddes and sponsored, not surprisingly, by General Motors.[49] This model offered the "technofix" for achieving Democracity's utopian goal (albeit not as extreme) of an ultimate disengagement between places of residence and work. Futurama, which promised to "transport you into 1960," was an automobile manufacturer's wish-dream. Wide highways equipped with overpasses and cloverleafs crisscrossed the continent, linking the cities and towns of America into a vast network capable of absorbing an infinite number of cars, preferably made by GM.

After visitors to the Futurama exhibit had completed their conveyor-belt moving-chair passage over an enormous model of the United States, alternating between wide angles and zoomed close-ups, each was given a blue-and-white button that read "I Have Seen the Future." Indeed, they had. If Democracity was the reincarnation of Ebenezer Howard, Futurama was the model behind Robert Moses's plans for New

York, which may be why it was a better predictor: highways and bridges were his "thing."[50] More wide-scale (outside the New York region) construction of elevated "superhighways" that would slice through the centers of existing cities or bypass them entirely would, however, have to await federal involvement in heavily subsidized highway construction in the 1950s.

Both Democracity and Futurama depicted "dead" landscapes bearing little resemblance to existing "living" cities. Devoid of slums, of older historic structures, and even of churches (which were added belatedly, when their absence was noticed), they lacked humanity, movement, and excitement. To my mind, the really exciting exhibit was the one mounted by Consolidated Edison, even though it was designed to "push" electricity:

> The fairgoer who ever dreamed of seeing the whole New York panorama, from Coney Island to Westchester, could see it in the Con Ed Building. "The City of Light," a diorama long as a city block and high as a three-story building . . . was complete with Manhattan's towers and subways in action, and it was dramatized with sound effects . . . to simulate a twenty-four hour cycle in the city's life.[51]

Frankly, I still find that "real" city more interesting. And on the grounds that the best "predictor" is often the present, it was as accurate (and as inaccurate) as the more imaginative ones in the Perisphere and the General Motors exhibit.

THE FUTURE "ON HOLD FOR THE DURATION"

But what appeared to be a light at the end of the tunnel actually turned out to be a brief clear moment poised between one crisis and the next. Five months after the fair opened, Germany invaded Poland, and in June 1940 Paris fell. The fairgrounds closed briefly in early October to allow (male) workers to register for the draft, and on October 27 its doors closed in bankruptcy. If the future was not dead, it was at least postponed "for the duration." The brave new world of plenty and technology in the service of the consumer envisaged at the fair was put on a cold back burner; technology in the service of death took its place. At first, the United States only provided war matériel to Europe under Roosevelt's "lend-lease" program (not unrelated to recovery), but finally entered World War II at the end of 1941 as an active belligerent.

Although the economy of the New York metropolitan region never benefited from war-related demand as much as that of Chicago, which specialized in heavy armaments and ordnance, or that of Los Angeles, whose Pacific ports and burgeoning air industry were stimulated by hostilities in the Pacific, it, too, experienced an infusion—albeit only temporarily and more in transport than in heavy manufacturing.

The Port

Especially during the brief interim period of lend-lease, the combined ports of New York/New Jersey regained some of their former dominance over American shipping. Throughout the 1920s, an average of about twenty-five million long tons of bulk

Figure 7.2. Consolidated Edison's City of Light. Courtesy of the Photo Archive Collection of Consolidated Edison; used with permission.

and general foreign trade goods per year had passed through those ports, which accounted for more than a quarter of all such tonnage through American ports. The worldwide depression caused a precipitous decline in the flow of absolute tons, but New York's share remained fairly constant. Thanks to the war, however, tonnage increased dramatically in the 1940s, cresting in 1943 and 1944 to about thirty million tons each year, when New York's share represented more than 40 percent of all American long tons. Although imports and exports rose steadily after the war, peaking in 1965, when the foreign tonnage handled by ports of the New York region reached fifty million, the region's share of the country's waterborne trade had already dropped back to only 15 percent. Pacific and Caribbean ports were becoming the real growth centers.

Fluctuations in the "competitive share" of general cargo were even more marked. The year 1941 was noteworthy because New York ports were then handling almost half of all U.S. general cargo, thus temporarily interrupting a gradual but steady decline from 40 percent in 1923 to only 17.5 percent by 1965. (What New York ports lost in oceangoing activity in later years, however, they would make up in air cargo; in the 1960s New York's airports accounted for half of all U.S. long tons of foreign air cargo.)[52]

Physical Fragmentation in Port Facilities

The complexity of the region's harbor and its fragmentation among multiple government jurisdictions, however, meant that New York City itself would never reap the full financial benefits or multiplier effects of the region's ports. Indeed, as time went by, the center of the region's shipping activity was continually displaced, until it eventually abandoned the city proper altogether. But up through World War II, port activity was still concentrated in Manhattan and Brooklyn, which together accounted for about four-fifths of all traffic. Across the state line in New Jersey, Hoboken and Jersey City accounted for another 12 percent of traffic, whereas Port Newark handled only 2 percent. During the war, Brooklyn's facilities became more important, especially in the vicinity of its shipbuilding naval yards. By 1960, Brooklyn was handling some two-fifths of all traffic. It was not until containerization of cargo in the early 1960s that New York's assorted piers and terminals began to be abandoned in favor of the new modern facilities at Port Newark.[53]

Governmental Integration

The physical and jurisdictional fragmentation of the region's ports called for administrative innovations in governmental structure, ones that would later serve as models for other multistate conurbations. Although the quasi-independent Port Authority of New York and New Jersey had been established by an interstate compact as early as 1921, its scale and functions expanded tremendously in the ensuing years. (Today, the Port Authority also has jurisdiction over the region's multiple airports.)

Robert Wood's remarkable contribution to the New York Regional Plan Association's studies in the late 1950s divided the more than fourteen hundred governmental units within the New York tristate metropolitan region into two major types: strictly "local" governments of cities and towns as well as special-purpose districts for schools, fire or water; and a newer system of "metropolitan giants"—at the center of which were the "Port of New York Authority" and the Triborough Bridge and Tunnel Authority.[54] Wood emphasizes how distinct the latter were from ordinary concepts of government, despite their incredible power to shape the metropolitan region:

> In place of more or less fixed governmental boundaries, of formally developed public institutions, of long-established rules of procedure, of more or less clear-cut allocations of responsibilities, is a much more elusive political system. The public functions which seem most critical to the course of Regional development . . . are carried out . . . by unique organizational devices and *ad hoc* understandings, developed in a maze of divided responsibility and authority. The statutory basis for action is more complex; so is the involvement of different levels of government; so are the provisions with respect to financial support and the participation of local constituencies. And the pattern of activity . . . emerges without clear reference to the characteristics of the Region's population and economic activity. *The definitions of needs, of resources, and of appropriate action take on increasingly the coloration of the institutions involved.*[55]

All of this is a polite way of saying that necessary as these quasi-independent empires are, given the obdurate reality of political fragmentation, each has tended over time to develop vested interests of its own, unaccountable to the people the authorities are intended to serve. Furthermore, their very insulation from ordinary politics offers unprecedented opportunities for unchecked, and possibly arbitrary, power. Much of the animosity many New Yorkers harbored toward Robert Moses was due to his unrivaled power to shape the transportation pattern of the region through control over the tolls from the Triborough Bridge and Tunnel Authority.

Furthermore, the conspiratorial "theory" that appears in Robert Fitch's muckraker *The Assassination of New York* arises from his recognition of the power of the Port of New York Authority (and specific individuals in the power structure of city and state), which Fitch blames for the *intentional* destruction of the city's economic base.[56] Conspiratorial or not, the changing policies of the Port Authority and the alterations in the technology of waterborne transport had as much to do with the "migration" of port activities as did the geographic complexity of the harbors that made it possible. For example, as early as 1947 the Port Authority began to invest more heavily in Port Newark and in 1962 opened its first prototype container facilities there. After that, New York City harbors, including the extensive waterfront land in Brooklyn, essentially ceased their active roles as ports. By the end of the 1970s, New Jersey piers were handling seven times the amount of seaborne commerce as those on the New York side, and long-derelict lands along New York's waterfronts were being planned for "recycling."[57] But we return now to our chronological account.

Decentralization of Manufacturing

Although the maximum "benefits" from World War II were felt at New York's ports, manufacturing was not neglected. However, the newer industrial plants, including defense-related ones such as aircraft, were much more likely to be located on the peripheries of the built-up urban areas, not only because their larger scale required more space than was available closer in, but also because it was the systematic policy of the War Production Board to *decentralize* factories to protect them from wholesale bombing.[58] Thus the major airplane manufacturing plants were placed far out on Long Island, which put them beyond the taxing jurisdiction (and easy mass-transit access) of the city. This decentralization did not initiate a new trend, but rather intensified one that had been observed as early as Pratt's 1911 survey and was certainly becoming more evident in the 1930s.

The New York Metropolitan Region Study reprised some of these observations when it found that whereas New York City's share of manufacturing employment in older "declining" industries had remained relatively constant at about half of all manufacturing employment in the twelve-county New York industrial area between 1929 and 1939, its share of employment in the new and growing industries of the region declined from 73 to only 65 percent of manufacturing employment in the industrial area over the same period.[59] During the war, manufacturing employment

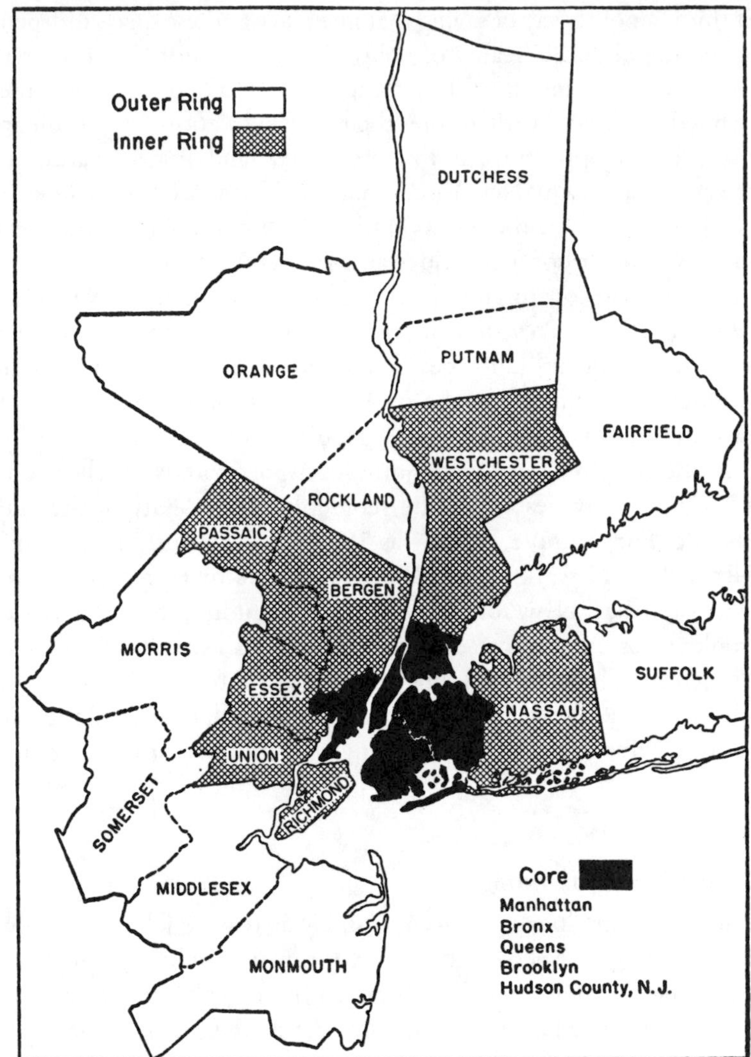

Map 7.1. The New York region in 1958, according to the New York Regional Plan Report. Source: Raymond Vernon, *Metropolis 1985: An Interpretation of the Findings of the New York Metropolitan Region Study.* Courtesy of the Regional Plan Association.

grew in all parts of the region, but by the mid-1950s New York City's share of old and new industrial employment in the region had dropped to about half of the total.[60] This relative decline was compounded by a drop in the New York region's share of all manufacturing jobs in the country. Deindustrialization in New York was already well under way before the recent "restructuring."

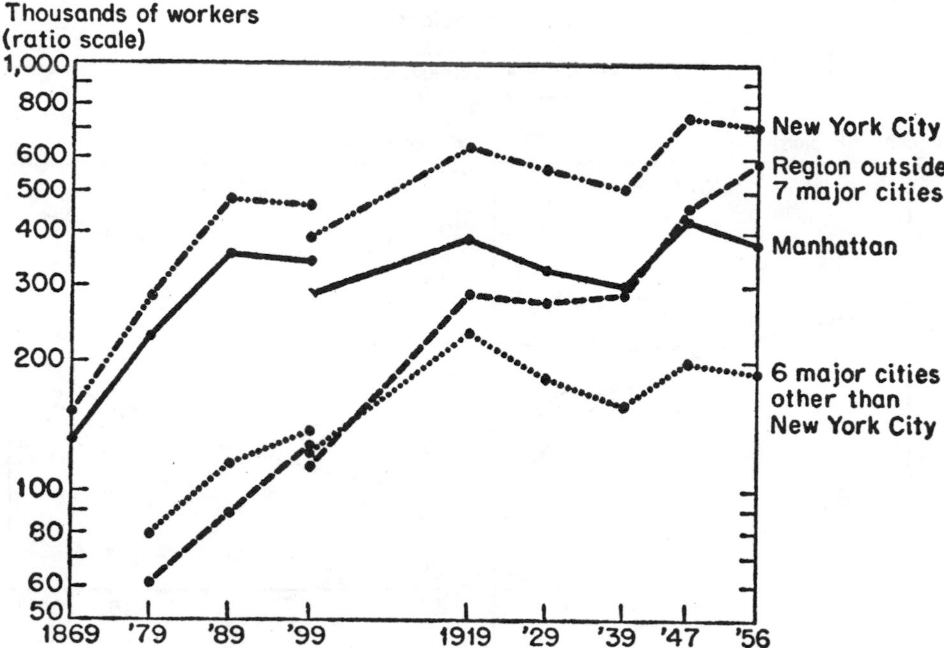

Figure 7.3. Manufacturing production workers by parts of the New York metropolitan region, 1869 to 1956. Raymond Vernon, *Metropolis 1985*. Courtesy of the New York Regional Plan Association.

RACE AND NEW YORK'S CHANGING DEMOGRAPHIC STRUCTURE

Despite the facts that (1) a sizable migration of African Americans to New York City dated only back to World War I, (2) blacks suffered disproportionally during the Depression in comparison with whites, and (3) in comparison to Chicago or Los Angeles, New York's employment opportunities did not expand as markedly during World War II, steady migration to the city persisted, perhaps because of Harlem's reputation as America's largest and most vital "black city," and perhaps because of the city's reputation as the most politically liberal of all destinations.[61] New York was the "promised land" to which another 145,000 blacks came between 1930 and 1940. By the latter year, some 6 percent of New York City's population of almost 7.5 million were African American, up from 3 percent a scant decade earlier. By then, some 90 percent of the state's black population lived inside the city limits. Although the close to four hundred city blocks that by then constituted Harlem (roughly between 110th and 155th Streets and stretching between Third and Amsterdam Avenues) held most of this population, there were secondary settlements in Brooklyn and, by wartime, in the Bronx as well.[62]

Despite its small proportion, but perhaps because it was so concentrated, the black population had built up considerable political strength within the city government, which had a long history of sensitivity to new "ethnic" voting blocks. Even during the Depression, blacks in New York sought, and sometimes gained, more power through economic as well as political actions. Capeci notes:

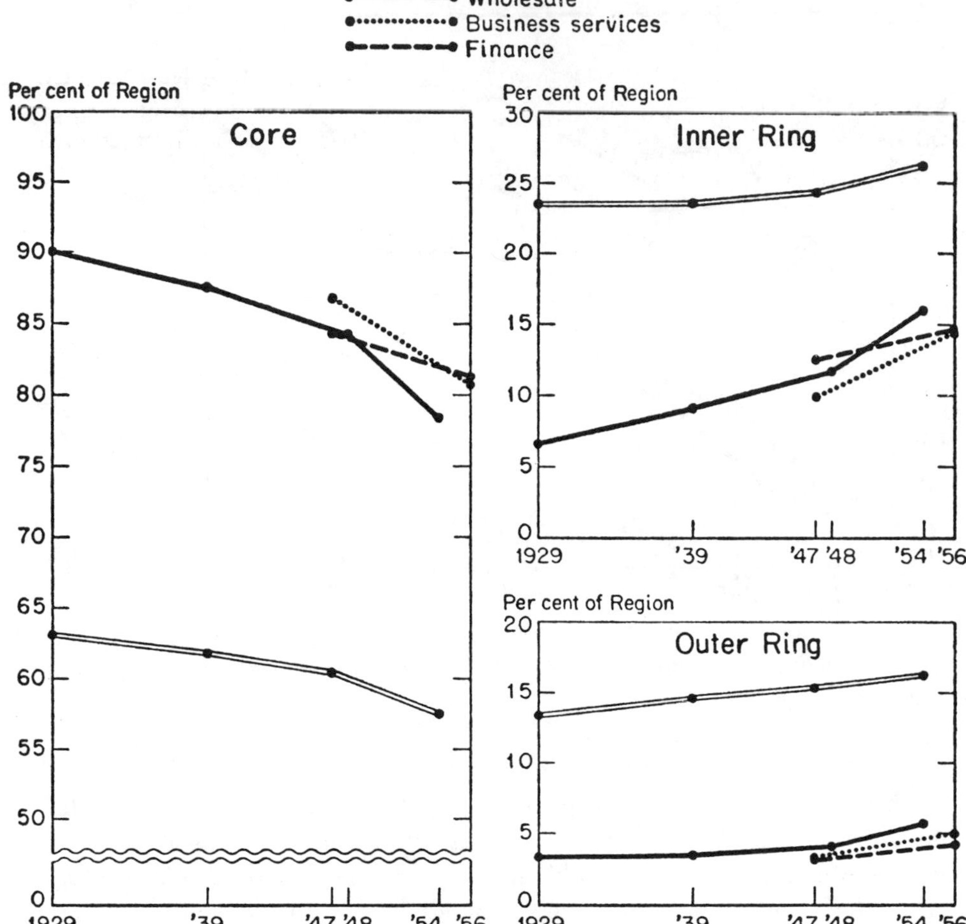

Figure 7.4. Employment distribution in manufacturing, wholesale trade, business services, and finance for the three main zones of the New York metropolitan region, 1929 to 1956. Raymond Vernon, *Metropolis 1985*. Courtesy of the New York Regional Plan Association.

> Economic boycotts, for example, were organized against businesses that refused to hire black personnel. Relief programs enacted after 1933 indicated concern. . . . Roosevelt included black Americans in his New Deal programs . . . and in New York, . . . Lehman and . . . La Guardia . . . [committed] state and municipal governments to the economic and civil rights of black residents.[63]

And even though New York's war-induced labor shortage was modest in comparison to those of Chicago and Los Angeles, new opportunities for employment opened up for blacks and women, due partly to conscription and partly to a decline in foreign immigration.[64] But expectations rose faster than performance.

Racial Unrest in 1943

By the summer of 1943, racial tensions were boiling over in several American cities: in Mobile, in Los Angeles, and especially in Detroit, which in June experienced one of the bloodiest race riots ever. Because Detroit had heavy concentrations of war industries, it had attracted many black workers; a false rumor that whites were being assigned to a new public housing project intended for black war workers triggered an attack by whites (reinforced by police) on the black applicants who had preempted occupancy. But tensions were more general. They finally exploded over the weekend at Belle Isle recreational area and quickly spread throughout the city. For two days, whites attacked blacks caught outside their neighborhoods, and blacks retaliated by assaulting invading whites and destroying white-owned businesses in the ghetto.

> [The] police exchanged continuous gunfire with black snipers on the ghetto fringes. . . . More than a hundred fires burned out of control as riot activity covered three-fourths of the city. Finally, federal troops entered the fray and restored order. . . . In the riot's wake, thirty-four lay dead—including twenty-five blacks, most of whom were killed by policemen—more than seven hundred were injured, and more than two million dollars' worth of property was destroyed.[65]

Repercussions in New York

Some observers expected that New York, given its more "liberal" attitudes and laws, would be immune to the racial tensions developing elsewhere, but most of the precipitating grievances were not location specific. Even in wartime, unemployment rates remained high for New York blacks, who held only 1.3 percent of all defense jobs in the state.[66] And the irony that blacks, even as they were called upon to risk their lives for their country, were subjected to segregation and discrimination in the armed services was not lost on them. Thus, although the city took precautions to avoid a Detroit-type riot, setting up its by-then routine interracial committees, it failed.[67]

A large-scale riot erupted in Harlem the night of August 1 and lasted twelve hours, but New York's response during the outburst was quite different from the responses in other cities. The immediate casus belli was an altercation between a white policeman and a (female) client at a local hotel. An uninvolved black soldier intervened; he allegedly shoved the policeman, who then fired at him as he escaped. False rumors spread that a white policeman had killed a black soldier, and within hours fires were set, windows were broken, and stores looted in an area that, although it centered on commercial 125th Street (the "main drag"), extended all the way from 110th to 145th Streets along Seventh, Eighth, and Lenox Avenues.[68] When the curfew the city imposed on the quarter was finally lifted some two weeks later, the toll was six African Americans dead, hundreds injured, more than 550 blacks arrested (mostly for looting or receiving "stolen goods"), and property damage estimated at two million dollars.[69]

Space Matters

Social scientists engaged in the growth industry of analyzing American racial tensions single out the 1943 Harlem riot as the paradigmatic event presaging the series of racial outbreaks that would wrack American cities in the second half of the 1960s. They talk about a "transition from the communal to the commodity type of riot," suggesting that "it was the Harlem upheavals of 1935 . . . and [even more so] 1943 that ushered in Watts, Newark, and the second Detroit."[70] Later, in the 1960s, naive observers were to question why *they* were destroying *their own communities.* Leaving aside the symptomatic "they" and an implied "us," this question ignores the spatial elements that allowed police to follow a control strategy of cordoning off "riot" areas, keeping whites out and making it impossible for blacks to choose alternative targets.[71]

By 1943, Harlem was so large, racially homogeneous, and densely settled that during the hostilities only armed police, among the white population, dared to enter. Soon after the first incidents, La Guardia ordered all police on full duty and by 1:30 a.m. had deployed five thousand of them to Harlem. (He simultaneously ordered the closing of all bars and liquor stores in the area.) In time, the riot zone was sealed off. (As had happened during the 1935 riot, even the exits to relevant subway stops were closed.)

> Traffic was diverted around the entire area of West Harlem. . . . As rioters burned themselves out on the morning of August 2, the Mayor moved to prevent a recurrence. . . . [His radio broadcast] carefully [avoided] any condemnation of the ghetto's citizenry as a whole [and described] measures taken to restore full order. Traffic would be limited and nonresidents denied entrance to Harlem. Liquor stores would be closed indefinitely.[72]

Volunteers, mostly black, helped the city and military police to restore order, and the eight thousand New York State guardsmen who were on standby at city armories never had to be deployed. Emergency medical services operated and food was distributed. Only one day after the riot, 90 percent of Harlem's milk deliveries had been restored, pushcarts and emergency shops were operating, and vendors were allowed to enter. Gradually, the curfew and traffic bans were lifted, stores began to reopen (even the liquor stores), and by August 14, the police force in Harlem "returned to normal size."[73]

New Yorkers tended to blame the uprising on "hoodlums" and congratulated themselves on how well the city had weathered the crisis.[74] But as Capeci notes, although this may have "eased their consciences," it also caused them to *"disregard the reasons for ghetto resentment and the need for measures to improve the living conditions of black residents."*[75] There was a growing discrepancy between what blacks were expected to contribute to the war effort and how little they benefited from it. Segregation in the military, exclusion from defense jobs, and an inflationary spiral in rents and prices (which blacks blamed on white landlords and shopkeepers) were a few of the more obvious underlying grievances. A survey conducted in Harlem by Kenneth Clark just after the riot found that at least a third of those queried thought the riot might trigger some positive results; perhaps they were right.

Up to that time, New York had not imposed rent controls or enforced price regulations, even though other cities had already done so.

> Within one week of the riot, the Office of Price Administration announced plans to open an office in Harlem. . . . In addition, the OPA announced in mid-September "that a special study was being made of the possibility of establishing rent control in New York City." . . . *Federal rent control was . . . implemented before the year ended, making New York the last major city to be regulated.*[76]

And as had happened after the 1935 riot, additional public housing was promised on a nondiscriminatory basis. Delivery had to await the end of the war, however. So, too, did the delivery of the World's Fair's (white) "suburban dream," although the achievement of both simply widened the fissure between the races.

VISIONS OF THE FAIR MATERIALIZE IN THE POSTWAR PERIOD

It was not until after the war that the visions of the suburban utopia projected at the fair materialized, but whether utopia represented "hope" or "disaster" remained untested. In any case, the decade and a half after the war's end was a period of population churning and very high mobility.

White Flight: An Only Incomplete Diagnosis of New York's Postwar Suburbanization

Suburbanization, as a general phenomenon, was almost as old as urbanization in the United States, as Kenneth Jackson has stressed in his history of early suburban developments.[77] And the massive expansion of urban areas into the suburbs during the immediate postwar era was too general a phenomenon to be attributed simply to white flight. For one thing, it occurred in places that had few or no "minority" populations, as well as in cities with growing numbers of "people of color"; indeed, it was so pervasive that no single cause can be expected to account for it.

Among the multiple causes were the cessation of housing construction during wartime, which created a pent-up demand for additional units once demobilization occurred; resumption of marriages and births that had been delayed by military service, which generated a pent-up demand not only for wedding gowns and bassinets but also for "starter" housing units to accommodate the new families; and federal housing policies that facilitated the purchase of single-family homes by returning veterans who sought to achieve the ideals of suburban life (formerly restricted to the upper middle class) that had been portrayed in the media and partially popularized in the world's fairs of Depression days. And all this was facilitated by the "revolution" in transportation foreseen in Futurama—not only commuter rails stretching out into the countryside, but government-subsidized freeways and limited-access highways that opened large parts of formerly peripheral lands to urban development.

Robert Moses's Highways

Even before the Depression, New York had innovated in the construction of limited-access highways to facilitate suburban growth: the Long Island Motor Parkway (1906–11, the world's first), the sixteen-mile Bronx River Parkway (1906–23); the Hutchinson River Parkway (1928), and thc Saw Mill Parkway (1929). Using state legislation that Moses had drafted in 1924, his parkways made it possible for commuters to reach their Manhattan offices from twenty to thirty miles away. "There was an immediate effect: the population of Westchester and Nassau Counties, served by the new roads, increased by 350,000 during the 1920s. But the full implications would emerge only in the suburban building boom after World War Two."[78]

Filling the Land with Single-Family Houses

In the postwar period the country as a whole experienced a remarkable building boom. Annual single-family home starts, beginning from a level of about 114,000 in 1944, approached a million in 1946, climbed to almost 1.2 million by 1948, and peaked in 1950 at an all-time high of 1.7 million.[79] Enterprising "community builders" emerged from humble beginnings to take advantage of these pent-up needs and a chance to reap enormous profits, leveraging small (or totally risk-free) investments into fortunes by the clever manipulation of government and banking incentives designed to encourage mass construction.[80] In all fairness, however, they also innovated in building techniques, cutting costs by applying "factory" methods to the assembly of uniform parts on extensive sites that had been bulldozed of all obstructions.

Aesthetes may have been appalled by these "cookie-cutter" developments, and social snobs may have dismissed them derisively, assuming that mass-produced houses would mass-produce homogeneous inhabitants, but in actual fact, it was a remarkable quantitative if not qualitative achievement—to build so much housing so quickly. The sheer magnitude of these operations created their own ancillary needs for community facilities of all kinds—public and private. The multiplier effects were impressively large.

Levittown, New York: Everyone's Quintessential Case

Levittown, the community whose name came to symbolize this entire genre, was referred to in an emergency survey made by the School of Education of New York University in 1954 as a "Community without Precedent."[81] This is not an inaccurate description, for when six thousand "basic" single-family houses are suddenly constructed on more than six square miles of farmland that formerly "housed" potatoes, *everything* else that goes with life—schools, shops, community facilities, health services, not to mention jobs—also has to be provided in a hurry.

The model established by the Levitts was replicated at the suburban fringes of every large city. Suburbia had begun to be "the American Way of Life" (more than half of the U.S. population now lives in suburbs). The repercussions on the central cities were equally significant, although they certainly did not attract the encomiums reserved for the new areas at their edges.

THE DARKENING OF THE OUTER BOROUGHS

If young middle- and working-class whites "decentralized" from the Manhattan and outer-borough neighborhoods where they had grown up to raw suburbia and eventually to "exurbia," a similar decentralization, but within the city limits, was also occurring among minorities who had previously been concentrated so heavily in the northern part of Manhattan. But because the net growth rates for minorities within the city limits exceeded those for whites, there was a gradual shift in their proportions between 1940 and 1960.

As late as 1940, 94 percent of the city's total population was classified as "white." Thanks to Harlem's size and, to a lesser extent, such enclaves as Chinatown and other small "minority" pockets, Manhattan was the only borough with a significant proportion of "nonwhites" (17 percent). In contrast, the outer boroughs, while containing large numbers of "ethnics" (mostly Jews, Italians, and Irish),[82] were overwhelmingly white: 95 percent in Brooklyn, 98 percent in the Bronx and on Staten Island, and 97 percent in Queens. And yet it was from those boroughs that the majority of suburban settlers were recruited. The vacancies thus created opened up housing opportunities in the outer boroughs and allowed for partial (and very spotty) decentralization of Manhattan's overcrowded black population.

But because of additional migration to the city by nonwhites and Puerto Ricans, the proportion of non-Hispanic whites decreased throughout the city. By 1960, 85 percent of New Yorkers were still classified as "white." The highest proportion of nonwhites was found in Manhattan (with 26 percent), followed by Brooklyn (with 15 percent). Staten Island, Queens, and the Bronx still remained overwhelmingly white (with 95, 91, and 88 percent, respectively).[83]

Decentralization of minorities, however, was not a random affair. Rather, certain subareas within Brooklyn and the Bronx changed "complexion" in radical fashion, while leaving other parts of the boroughs almost untouched. The role that public housing played in "opening up" the boroughs increased the "spottiness" of this distribution (see below). Brooklyn's Bedford-Stuyvesant provides a relevant example, in part because it was one of the first outer-borough zones to contain a significant proportion of blacks, and in part because it became the setting for one of the first "new round" urban uprisings that exploded in hundreds of American cities in the later years of the 1960s. Although the 1965 Los Angeles Watts riot is sometimes considered the opening round in this later sequence, events in Harlem and "Bed-Stuy" (as well as in New Jersey) actually preceded it by a year.[84]

Bedford-Stuyvesant

Bedford-Stuyvesant lies at dead center of the borough of Brooklyn and also at the geographic center of the five boroughs.[85] Although its historic transformation into a

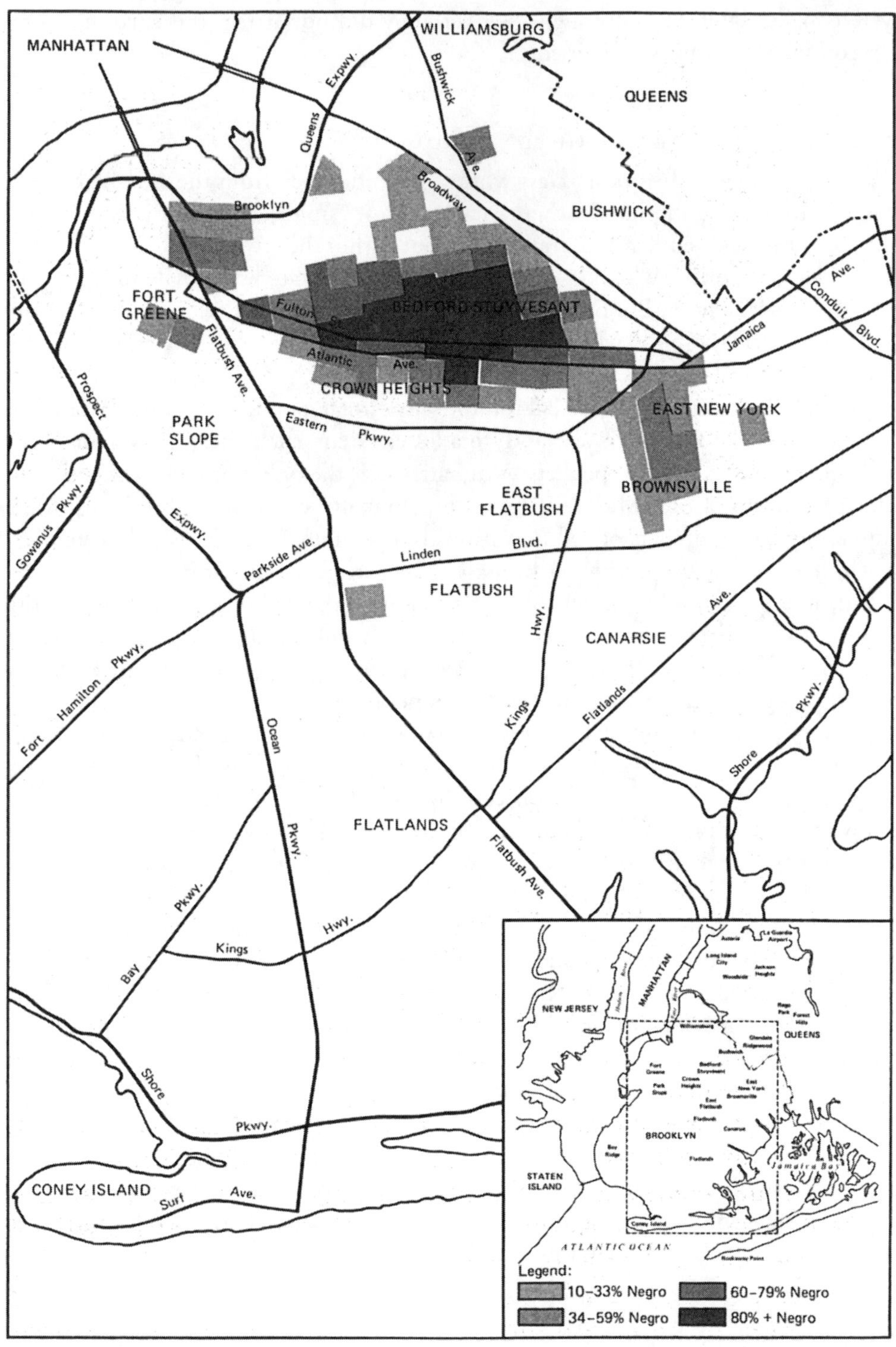

Maps 7.2 and 7.3. The thickening of the Bedford-Stuyvesant ghetto, 1950 to 1970. Source for both maps is Harold X. Connolly, *A Ghetto Grows in Brooklyn;* used with permission of New York University Press.

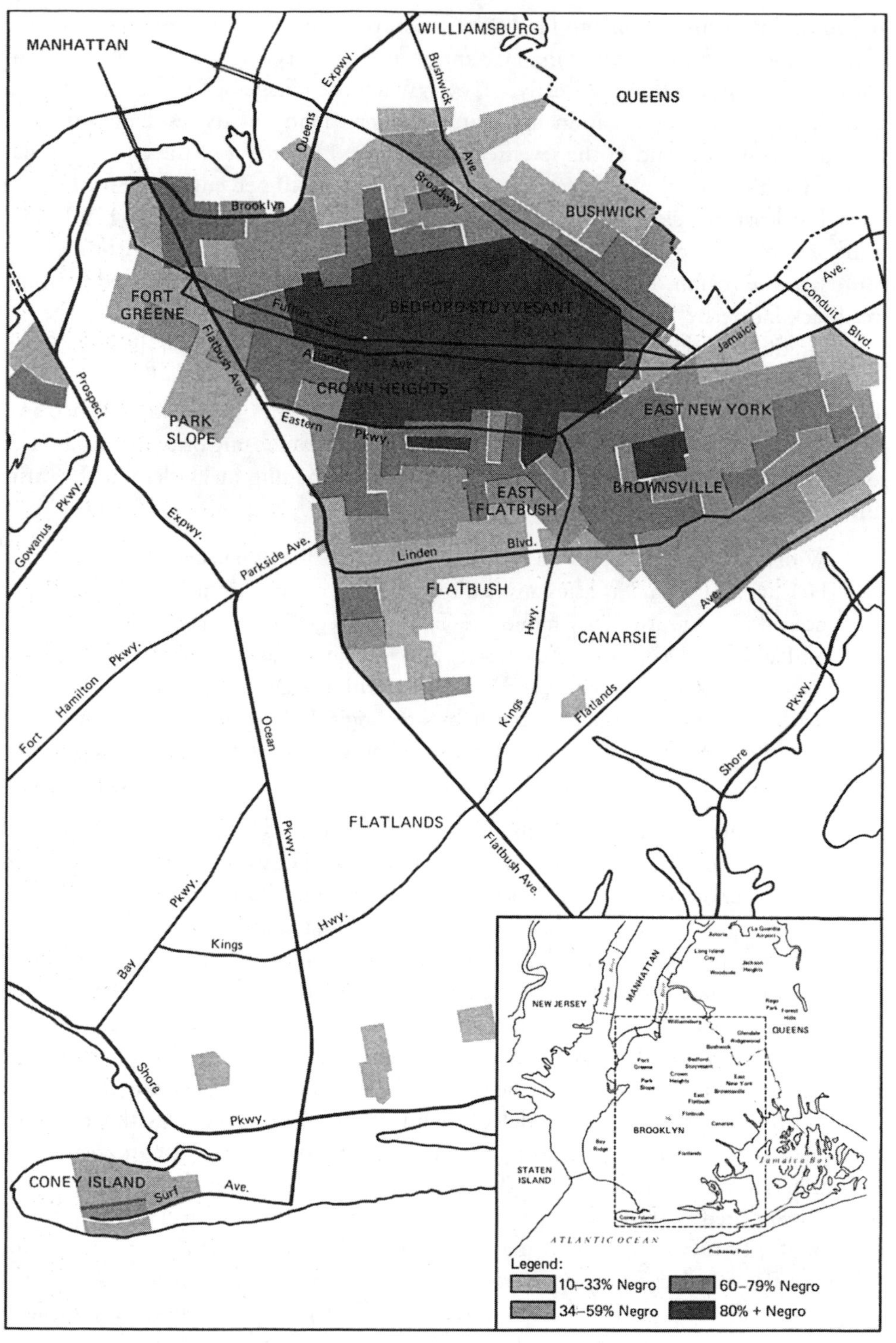

MANHATTAN
WILLIAMSBURG
QUEENS
Queens Expwy.
Bushwick Ave.
Broadway
Brooklyn
BUSHWICK
FORT GREENE
Fulton St.
BEDFORD-STUYVESANT
Conduit Blvd.
Ave.
Jamaica
Flatbush Ave.
Atlantic Ave.
CROWN HEIGHTS
Prospect
EAST NEW YORK
PARK SLOPE
Eastern Pkwy.
BROWNSVILLE
EAST FLATBUSH
Gowanus Pkwy.
Expwy.
Parkside Ave.
Linden Blvd.
FLATBUSH
Hwy.
CANARSIE
Ave.
Fort Hamilton Pkwy.
Ocean
Kings
Flatlands
Shore Pkwy.
FLATLANDS
Pkwy.
Flatbush Ave.
Hwy.
Bay Pkwy.
Kings
Shore
Pkwy.
CONEY ISLAND
Surf Ave.
NEW JERSEY
MANHATTAN
QUEENS
BROOKLYN
STATEN ISLAND
ATLANTIC OCEAN
Legend:
10–33% Negro
34–59% Negro
60–79% Negro
80% + Negro

ghetto is remarkably parallel to Harlem's, it is important to recognize that blacks had been a presence in Brooklyn (King's County) from the very beginning, albeit as a minority and mostly as slaves. As early as 1663, when the village of Bedford was still an agricultural/trading way station for Dutch farmers, many of its residents owned a slave or two. By the end of the seventeenth century, 15 percent of the entire population of King's County were black slaves, and more than 40 percent of the freeholders owned at least one slave. From the middle of the eighteenth century to 1790, one-third of Brooklyn's population consisted of black slaves, the highest proportion of any county in the region. Early in the nineteenth century, they had been joined by some free black farmers.[86]

Gradually, however, as farms began to be replaced by residential developments, the number of whites in Bedford-Stuyvesant began to increase rapidly. By the last decades of the nineteenth century, once transportation lines to Manhattan had improved, the area began to be transformed into a fashionable zone of two-story houses for middle- and upper-class white buyers. As was happening in Harlem at the same time, real estate speculation was rampant.

> With the influx of the upper-class, and the formation of the fashionable "Stuyvesant Heights" section and its mansions of the wealthy, came servants. And the servants needed places to live. They formed the first [*sic*] Negro community in the Bedford area. . . . The [cycle of] collapse of Stuyvesant Heights society came during the early 1920's when prices soared, and then, with the Depression, many of the lovely brownstones became too much for their original owners to maintain. They moved out and the prices dropped until the houses were within reach of Negro families.[87]

Houses were subdivided, and blockbusting "developed into a fine art." As happened elsewhere (e.g., on Prairie Avenue, south of Chicago's Loop), panic selling preceded the major black influx into this "in-town" leafy suburb. Gradually, the first nucleus along Fulton and Atlantic Avenues expanded. By 1940, the area around Pratt Institute was becoming predominantly black, and ten years later nonwhites constituted more than half the population of an expanded Bed-Stuy. By 1970, most whites had left the surrounding area for points farther out in Brooklyn, in Queens, or on Long Island. By then, more than four-fifths of the population in a greatly enlarged "ghetto" were either African American (many of them of Caribbean origin) or Puerto Rican.[88]

Confounding a simple model of "white flight," however, was the role that slum clearance and public housing played in changing the racial composition of Brooklyn. Even though, unlike in Chicago, early public housing in the borough was not concentrated within the ghetto itself, some of the earliest projects were in or near Bedford-Stuyvesant, which may have speeded up the racial transition. In the 1940s and 1950s, large projects were built in Brownsville, Fort Greene, and Crown Heights, all districts into which the ghetto would expand. By 1964, nine projects with almost fifty thousand (mostly black) residents were located in the Bedford-Stuyvesant ghetto, where the total population by then had climbed to an estimated four hundred thousand.[89] (See Maps 7.2 and 7.3.)

The Thickening of the Sparsely-Settled Outer Boroughs

Although the stereotypical narrative speaks in such metaphorical terms as "white flight," "racial succession," and "neighborhood burnout/blowout" (especially with reference to the South Bronx and Bedford-Stuyvesant, where this sequence is not totally inaccurate), its major flaws are its failure to acknowledge that New York City's "suburban" expansion in the immediate post–World War II period took place not just in outlying villages or newly constructed subdivisions or even whole towns such as Levittown, beyond the city limits, but in the outer boroughs themselves, where vacant land was still available. The white population leaving Brooklyn may have left more space for the expanding number of blacks and Puerto Ricans, but whites were as likely to move to newer developments within the city limits as to the suburbs. This was particularly true in Queens and the Bronx, where white, black, and Puerto Rican populations all increased between 1950 and 1960.

But by the 1960s this began to change. Toward the end of that decade it was evident that the demographic trajectories of the three groups had split apart. Manhattan, the Bronx, and Brooklyn had begun to experience sharp declines in their white populations, compensated for by substantial increases in the number of their black, Hispanic, and Asian populations. The transition in Queens took another decade, but eventually it also joined this trend. In 1930, only a million persons lived in Queens, most of them white. The population in that borough rose steadily to peak at almost two million by 1970, of whom only some 15 percent were classified as "nonwhite." In the decade of the 1970s, however, the total population of Queens declined by about 5 percent, the net effect of a loss of some 344,000 white residents (a decline of about 20 percent) and an increase of 38 percent of its nonwhite population.[90] Between 1930 and 1990, the number of black residents increased from few than 19,000 to almost 421,000, and "others" increased from 877 to approach 400,000, but white flight accounted for less of the change than one might have imagined. Although Queens is perhaps the most extreme case, many of these observations apply also to Brooklyn and the Bronx. Outlying portions of those two boroughs also experienced not so much population succession as additional growth, as blacks and others inherited older zones and whites relocated in newer developments within the borough.

The Characteristics of "Invading" Minorities

Not only is "white flight" an inaccurate and partial description, but racial succession in New York in the 1960s also deviated somewhat from the usual stereotype of an invading underclass spearheaded by public housing. One of the only studies to examine racial changes in New York City during the 1960s found a far more complex pattern. Ronald Denowitz studied the socioeconomic status of blacks who moved into previously white neighborhoods in New York City and found a number of fairly distinctive patterns, depending upon the *location* of the neighborhoods with respect to existing zones of minority concentration, the *density* of settlement (which varied by borough), and the *newness* of the housing stock. In high-density areas there were at least three different patterns of racial succession.

> One was found in tracts near areas of black concentration . . . led by younger adult renters with above average educational attainments but low incomes. . . . A second pattern characterized white residential sections . . . distant from black ghettos—in which one-third of all housing was in single and two-family structures. Invasion was led by middle-age adult home buyers with high incomes and education. Although immigrant blacks were higher in SES than most white residents, their entry tended to precipitate substantial out-movements by white renters. . . . A third pattern occurred in white residential sections with rather large numbers of recently constructed housing units. Initial black populations [were predominantly] . . . middle-age adults with above average incomes and education. [At least during the ten-year period studied, there was] relative stability in racial composition and above average increases in black income levels.[91]

Denowitz identifies a "tipping point" at about 25 percent, but questions "whether the specific patterns of succession found in New York are generalizable to other cities."[92] I will argue that they are not—especially with reference to Chicago.

AMBIGUITIES OF RACE AND ETHNICITY

In the above discussion, I have used the distinction between "black" and "white" *as if* it had a transparent and firm meaning. Race, however, is a highly ambiguous category, telling us more about the values of the society that defines and uses the concept than about any abstract characteristic possessed by individuals. My previous generalizations are confounded in New York by two additional factors: first, the wide range of variation within New York's black community itself, and second, the existence of racial "infill" groups—constituted chiefly by Puerto Ricans, who, before the "new immigration" that began in the mid-1960s, constituted New York's dominant "Hispanic" group.[93] (Later variations in the Hispanic category are explored in Part IV.)

Freed Slaves and the Caribbean Influx

Given New York's demographic diversity, race is an especially inaccurate concept having very limited statistical and analytic value. Just as "whites" are crisscrossed by dimensions of national ancestry, religion, time of arrival, class, and political power, not to mention linguistic and phenotypical characteristics,[94] so New York's "black" population challenges the boundaries of simple dichotomies. Contrary to the situation in Chicago, for example, where poverty, rural southern origin, and dark-skinned appearance are characteristics that have tended to go together, this congruence between phenotype and nativity has broken down in New York.

A sizable minority of New York's "blacks" are of "foreign" origin (largely from Jamaica, but also from other Caribbean islands);[95] indeed, many of the political leaders and entrepreneurial elite of New York's black community have been drawn from this subgroup. Second, native "blacks" have varied widely by superficial appearance. Especially after the Civil War, the freedom of the city drew ambitious newcomers of mixed parentage, some of whom "passed" while others, of equally indeterminate appearance, remained identified with the black community.[96] New York "blacks," like "whites," have varied by class, ethnicity, accent, ancestry, and, increasingly, by language (the largest group of recent immigrants to New York is made up of Spanish speakers from the Dominican Republic).

Puerto Ricans Arrive: The Formation of East Harlem

The second-largest "minority" in New York from the 1950s onward consisted of persons of Puerto Rican birth or descent. In this highly mixed population, "race" (i.e., skin shade) was an even less relevant marker, and "immigration status" was not a desideratum. The island had first become a U.S. "colony" as a result of the Spanish-American War of 1898, and in 1917 the Jones Act conferred the rights of "partial" citizenship upon its residents. Migration between the island and the mainland was freed of legal routines and restrictions, and Puerto Ricans' eligibility for welfare, public housing, and other social services was the same as that enjoyed by "full" citizens.

Nevertheless, the number of Puerto Ricans in the city remained tiny until mass migration began in the 1950s, spurred by economic involution on the island and facilitated by the introduction of inexpensive direct air travel, which, although it actually began in 1945, became much cheaper in the 1950s. The mechanisms of labor placement that were put into operation during World War II further assisted in "steering" Puerto Ricans into the city and into industrial jobs. As late as 1940, Puerto Ricans in New York City numbered only some sixty thousand, less than 1 percent of the total. The 1950s, in contrast, were the years of peak migration to New York. By 1960, Puerto Ricans' numbers exceeded eight hundred thousand, or about one-tenth of the city's population.[97] The main concentration of Puerto Ricans at that time was in East Harlem (La Guardia's old congressional district), which by then was being referred to as "El Barrio," although it was not exclusively Puerto Rican, nor did all Puerto Ricans live there by any means.

To what extent did the categories "black" and "white" overlap with this growing "Hispanic" group? Nowhere is the issue of "race" so ambiguous as among migrants from the island, whose "racial" stock has long been mixed. Glazer and Moynihan capture the changing "social definitions" of racial identity within this group:

> While in their own minds a man's color meant something very different from what it meant to white Americans, [Puerto Rican migrants] knew very well its meaning for Americans. About one-fifth of the Puerto Rican group in New York in the thirties was listed in census returns as Negro (a slightly smaller proportion than were then listed as colored in the Puerto Rican census). . . .
>
> . . . [By 1940, this had dropped in East Harlem] to about 11 per cent. . . . By 1960 the proportion of colored among the New York Puerto Ricans was only 4 per cent.[98]

This is stunning information. Given that there is no reason to believe that suddenly there was a highly selective out-migration of light-skinned "Spaniards" from the island, one can only surmise that the progressive "whitening" of New York's Puerto Ricans was a social act.

Given this, one must question all figures that "divide" borough populations into dichotomies of white and black.[99] Such figures both overestimate and underestimate the amount of integration that was occurring in various parts of the city. This is particularly true within New York's public housing projects, where Puerto Ricans (who may report themselves as "white" or, increasingly, as "other") and African Americans now make up the largest proportion of tenants.

The "Disembourgeoisement" of the Puerto Rican Community

Distancing themselves from the presumed low status of blacks, however, did not protect most Puerto Ricans from eventually sinking to a socioeconomic status even below that of African Americans. They were to be trapped between the "rock" of deindustrialization and the "hard place" of newer (Asian) immigrants willing to work for even lower wages. In the early 1950s, Puerto Rican migrants "increasingly found jobs in the labor market niche of center-city blue-collar positions left behind by the exodus of workers to new industries in the suburbs or by the occupational advancement [or aging] of existing workers. Puerto Rican migration was viewed as crucial to salvaging New York industries that depended on inexpensive labor, such as the garment industry."[100] Labor force participation rates for Puerto Rican men and women, mostly in the category of "operatives," were higher than those of other groups, and dual- (or triple-)income families seemed on their way to economic security.

However, the situation began to unravel soon afterward, as such jobs increasingly disappeared from the New York economy and as circular migration stirred the pot of tenuous family arrangements, often breaking them apart. Female-headed households multiplied, becoming increasingly dependent upon public housing and Aid to Families with Dependent Children, two programs for which, because of their citizenship status, they enjoyed immediate eligibility. By the mid-1960s, the sex ratios within the Puerto Rican community were tipped heavily toward women, and the rates of dependency for the Puerto Rican community as a whole exceeded those of any other subgroup in the city.[101]

The plight of Puerto Ricans was further intensified by programs that were intended to enhance living conditions for inner-city residents. At the peak of urban renewal and urban redevelopment activities, the city engaged in large-scale slum clearance concentrated in zones where the most deteriorated tenements were to be found. Because these were also zones in which Puerto Rican communities had formed, this entailed considerable shifting from one slum to another. If in Chicago urban renewal became known sarcastically as "Negro removal" and in Los Angeles "Chicano removal," in New York the common phrase for it was "Puerto Rican removal."

East Harlem became a prime target for slum clearance, which was not an illogical choice, given that, along with the Lower East Side (which also housed a sizable

Puerto Rican community), it contained an enormous concentration of badly deteriorated tenements. Kessner called it perhaps the worst slum in the city:

> Here [in East Harlem] stood the ugly offscourings of American industrialism, grimy factories amidst junkyards, warehouses, used-car lots, and repair shops. Coal yards and oil storage depots belching gaseous pollutants tinted the sky an ashen gray and raw sewage fouled the river. A transient population filled East Harlem's bars and whorehouses, while its residents occupied seedy tenements and deteriorating housing.[102]

Once the Jews and Italians, who had previously predominated in the area when La Guardia had represented it, died or deserted, the Puerto Ricans inherited it. And once their quarters were razed and public housing projects were put up, many eventually moved back in.[103] And although the original inhabitants were mostly non-Hispanic, by 1980 some 80 percent of project residents were Spanish-speaking, largely Puerto Rican. A similar transformation occurred in Red Hook Houses in Brooklyn, which changed from reputedly Jewish white occupancy when it was built to Puerto Rican preponderance today.

Public Housing Changes Its Functions

As earlier noted, unemployed persons and single mothers were originally disqualified from obtaining entry to public housing, admission was highly selective, and during the war priority was given to war workers. Over time, however, these rules were changed, and despite efforts by the NYPHA to retain non-Hispanic whites and to "integrate" housing on a stable basis, gradually many of the projects became almost entirely black and/or Hispanic, as working-class whites moved out. Because public housing projects had been constructed in all boroughs, and sometimes on open land rather than slum-cleared sites, minority populations were introduced into many formerly white parts of the outer boroughs, albeit in isolated pockets. It *may* be this that prompted the erroneous quip in Meyerson and Banfield's otherwise superb analysis of race and public housing in Chicago that it is possible for public housing "to ruin" a city, which they imply happened in New York.[104]

NEW YORK TAKES FULL ADVANTAGE OF URBAN RENEWAL/PUBLIC HOUSING IN THE 1950S

In marked contrast to Los Angeles or even Chicago, New York City took full advantage of all federal assistance programs designed to clear slums and build subsidized housing. Whereas in the 1930s and 1940s, these programs were government initiated, built, and managed, the 1949 urban renewal law brought private entrepreneurs into the act, and later the programs shifted to rehabilitation and rent subsidies. Whatever the program, New York participated with alacrity. The results have been impressive.

According to a report issued by the New York City Housing Authority, by 1989 the Authority was supervising 316 operating projects containing a total of 179,045 dwelling units serving a population of 472,088 in 2,787 buildings, not including FHA-recovered and -resold houses.[105] The overwhelming majority of these projects had been federally funded (291 out of 316, containing 157,040 out of the 179,045 dwelling units and serving 412,702 out of the total resident population of 472,088). In contrast, the city had sponsored only seven projects serving some 20,000 occupants, and the state had sponsored eighteen projects serving fewer than 39,000 occupants.[106] Clearly, federal funding was absolutely essential to New York.

An examination of the dates of completion of the 316 projects reveals that New York City has been providing public housing since 1936, that projects have been scattered throughout all the boroughs, but that the pace of construction has closely paralleled expansions and then contractions in federal funding. By counting the number of units added in each decade and calculating the "average" size of projects by decade, one can learn much. Before 1940, New York had built only four projects—First Houses, with only 123 apartments; Harlem Houses, with 577 units; Red Hook, with 2,545 units; and Williamsburg Houses, with 1,630 apartments—yielding a total of 4,875 units. During the 1940s, close to 25,000 dwelling units were added to the city's public housing supply. Almost all of the more than twenty projects completed in that decade contained between 1,000 and 2,000 units each. Only four had fewer than 1,000 apartments, and one, in Queens, had more than 3,000.

This pattern of building large high-rise projects (usually Le Corbusier-type towers that left large common green space) persisted into the 1950s. In that decade, when Los Angeles discontinued its modest public housing program and Chicago's program ground to a temporary halt when it ran aground on the rock of racial integration, New York City added the largest number of public housing units ever—more than 75,000 subsidized apartments in some seventy new projects scattered throughout the five boroughs. As had been the case in the preceding decade, these projects were large in scale (the average number of dwelling units per project was more than a thousand) and high-rise. Many were on the sites of cleared tenement areas and were located on "prime" land.[107]

Given the growing opposition of planners and sociologists to large-scale projects, the 1960s witnessed a general decrease in the average size of the projects. In that decade, only 42,500 dwelling units were added, scattered among some seventy-eight projects. By then it was already becoming more difficult to obtain federal funds for public housing. In any case, the 1950s and 1960s represented the heyday of public housing: some 43 percent of all NYCHA units were built in the 1950s and another 24 percent in the 1960s. Retrenchments at the federal level subsequently and drastically curtailed New York's capacity to provide subsidized housing. During the decade of the 1970s, fewer than 18,500 units were added (accounting for about 10.5 percent of the supply), but these tended to be in much smaller units (some infill, some rehabilitated buildings, some new state-supported construction), distributed among close to eighty separate projects. And in the 1980s (up to January 1989 only, the date of the report's publication), some sixty additional projects were completed, but these yielded fewer than 10,000 total units—mostly in small turnkey or rehab projects, and deriving an increasing share of funds from New York State. The public housing cycle in New York was coming to an end. Thus the recent decline in public housing construction has been due not to local opposition, but to the disappearance of sources of funds.

But the very act of massing so much public housing, albeit in various boroughs, had two unanticipated consequences: first, it triggered heightened white flight, and second, like Marx's thesis about how the aggregation of workers in large factories inadvertently contributed to the growth of class consciousness, the massing of large numbers of impoverished families in housing projects created potentially explosive conditions for rebellion.

NEW YORK TOUCHES OFF THE RACIAL CONFLICTS OF THE MID-1960S

Despite the construction of massive amounts of subsidized housing on a nondiscriminatory basis, the existence of a long-standing and vigorous set of institutions in the mayor's office intended to defuse racial tensions and to "empower" minority leaders, and a tradition of appointing blacks to higher offices and to civil service positions, New York City was not immune to the rising national racial tensions of the 1960s. But the manifestation that did occur, beginning on July 15, 1964, tells us much about the changes that had taken place in the racial distribution of population in the city between 1943 and then.[108]

The trigger was "typical," in this instance the shooting in Manhattan of a fifteen-year-old black boy by a white off-duty policeman. The incident had escalated from an altercation between some kids "on break" and the janitor of one of the nearby buildings into a pitched battle—between hundreds of other students who saw the dead boy and the seventy-five police reinforcements who had been called in to quell the riot.[109] The spark

> fell into Harlem and, with fire-tending, intentional or unintentional, flamed into the Harlem and Bedford-Stuyvesant [Brooklyn] riots of 1964. . . . For six nights, mobs roamed the streets of the two boroughs. As many as 4,000 New Yorkers dedicated themselves to attacks on police, vandalism, and looting of stores. When it was all over, police counted 1 rioter dead, 118 injured, and 465 men and women arrested. . . . [The 1964 New York riots] can be said to have caused the riots that plagued other cities in succeeding weeks, because those riots were patterned on the ones touched off in New York.[110]

The well-organized civil rights movement distinguished this riot from that of 1943, when black leadership had joined the city "establishment" to cool things out. This time the Congress of Racial Equality (CORE) organized picketing of the school the next day to protest the violence and demonstrate for the establishment of a civilian review board to discipline the police, and at the end of the march, "teen-agers gathered around television cameras and told the reporters how angry they were."[111] This anger was manifest in Harlem during the next few days, peaking on Saturday, July 18, a particularly hot day.[112] It was certainly bloody. "Louis Smith, a CORE field secretary who said he was just back from Mississippi, was at Harlem Hospital that night and was upset by what he saw. 'This is worse than anything I ever saw in Mississippi,' he said."[113] The scene the next morning was sobering. There were

> broken windows, ransacked stores; streets littered with broken glass, rubbish, and empty cartridges; crowds of sullen Negroes; and tired policemen, semimilitary in their helmets. Most startling were the gates which merchants had put across their windows the night before and which now snaked crazily across the sidewalks amid the litter on Lenox, 125th, Seventh, and Eighth. . . . Police Commissioner Murphy [gave a press conference in which he reported] the statistics for the night: 1 dead; 12 policemen and 19 civilians injured, 30 persons arrested, 22 business places looted.[114]

Cleanup began the next day, but the deeper problems defied "cleaning."[115] That night hostilities recurred, and by early Monday morning, twenty-seven police officers and ninety-three civilians were officially listed as injured (although hospitals reported treating more than two hundred), forty-five stores had been damaged or looted, and 108 arrests had been made.[116] On the third night, despite the appointment of a commission of inquiry and attempts by Harlem clergy to deflect anger, rioting began again, even though all of Harlem had been cordoned off to traffic and special units of "technical" police were sent in—to break up crowds and to take over the rooftops, from which residents were throwing loose bricks and even Molotov cocktails.

But just as things seemed to be "under control" in Harlem,[117] the police got a call for reinforcements in Bedford-Stuyvesant, to which looting had spread by Tuesday night.[118]

> With the approach of dusk [on Wednesday night], loungers had already begun to gather on Fulton, and if the mayor's speech had little effect in getting them off the street, neither did it seem to bring anyone onto the street. . . . the crowds increased, and, as on the previous night, at least nine out of ten came not to riot or loot, but "for a look-see around." . . . Wednesday evening they had something new to gawk at. . . . The cavalry had arrived. A troop of mounted police had taken over the four corners of Nostrand and Fulton. . . . Police had been afraid to use horses in Harlem because of their vulnerability to the Molotov cocktail, *but the lower buildings and wider streets in Bedford-Stuyvesant reduced the danger from the rooftops.*[119]

From then on, the battle escalated and spread, with wide-scale looting and property destruction, until rain ended Wednesday night's rioting.[120] By the next day, Bed-Stuy had calmed, although in Harlem it took a few more days before the riot ran its course.[121]

THE "COLLAPSE" OF NEW YORK'S INDUSTRIAL BASE AND THE BEGINNINGS OF RESTRUCTURING

The rioting in Harlem and Bedford-Stuyvesant, however, needs to be placed in a wider context. The late 1960s were troubled times, not only in the United States but in the world. Perhaps nowhere were the symptoms of America's economic decline more evident than in New York. The 1964 "riot" may not have been a trigger to more widespread racial conflict, but rather an early warning that despite the progress made in the civil rights movement and the apparent health of the American economy, troubles lay ahead.

It must be recalled that the so-called restructuring of the global economy in 1973–74, the date analysts have used as a "marker" between eras, was actually preceded by considerable industrial contraction and unrest. In the 1960s, anti–Vietnam War protests, student uprisings, civil rights struggles that seemed to be reaching a limit, and the rash of riots in minority areas where populations were most affected by marginalization had become common occurrences in major American cities. Defense investments connected to the Vietnam War were partially masking this decline, but such investments had little impact in the ghettos of the country. Just as canaries are the first to perceive and suffer from gases in mining shafts, so the black ghettos in the United States may have been the first to experience signs of more pervasive distress. I address the full impact of such restructuring on New York in Chapter 10.

CHAPTER 8

Fordist Chicago: Down but Not Quite Out

> And there is that great iron city, that impersonal, mechanical city, amid the steam, the smoke, the snowy winds, the blistering suns. . . . that self-conscious city . . . so deadly dramatic and stimulating. . . . Many migrants like us were driven and pursued, in the manner of characters in a Greek play, down the paths of defeat; but luck must have been with us, for we somehow survived. . . . Chicago is the city from which the most incisive and radical Negro thought has come; there is an open and raw beauty about that city that seems either to kill or endow one with the spirit of life.
>
> Richard Wright, introduction to Drake and Cayton's *Black Metropolis*[1]

THE CRISIS OF INDUSTRIAL CONTRACTION

The collapse of industry in the Great Depression affected Chicago more harshly than it affected either New York or Los Angeles, as might have been expected in a city organized along classical Fordist lines of large-scale and capital-intensive industrialization. As early as 1919,

> more than 70 percent of the 400,000 wage earners working in Chicago manufactures labored in the company of at least one hundred employees and almost a third of them in establishments employing over a thousand workers. . . . The typical Chicago mass production company was big not only in scale but in capital as well. Ninety percent of wage earners worked for corporations, not individuals, and almost 60 percent for employers with annual products worth at least $1 million. A job seeker in Chicago looked toward giant employers. . . . Despite their diverse jobs, Chicago's semiskilled and unskilled workers shared the experience of working in an enormous plant for a corporate employer.[2]

By 1923, the 4,776 manufacturing plants in Chicago that employed at least 4,000 workers apiece constituted more than half of all manufacturing establishments and accounted for 60 percent of all industrial workers.[3]

The closing of a single major plant, therefore, could, and did, throw hundreds of workers out of their jobs at one fell swoop. And the closing of even a few of the major plants could reduce thousands of workers to unemployment. It would be hard to find a more dramatic contrast to New York, with its typically small size of establishment, which gave it perhaps less power but, in compensation, greater flexibility to adapt to changing circumstances.

Some estimate of what happened to industrial production in Chicago during the Depression appears in Table 8.1, which shows the cycle of decline and recovery in manufacturing firms and industrial employment that Chicago experienced between 1929 and 1945. This cycle contrasts both with New York, where the decline was less steep, and with Los Angeles, where recovery occurred earlier and more robustly. Indeed, one could say that in some ways Chicago never fully recovered from the Depression's blows, even though the war infused its economy with a temporary vitality.

CLASS STRUCTURE AND THE UGLY HEAD OF RACE/ISM

As demonstrated in Chapter 5, the multiple cleavages within Chicago's industrial working class along ethnic and racial lines inhibited the kind of class solidarity required to resist the strength that single large employers could marshal. In a downturn, instead of building solidarity and mutual support, this same fragmentation caused a scramble for the remaining jobs. The Depression, therefore, did not affect all workers equally; as elsewhere, it struck various occupational groups with different vigor. Despite the occasional if spectacular suicides of formerly wealthy investors and the displacement of some middle-class professionals into the ranks of apple sellers, unemployment rates among managerial and white-collar workers were significantly lower than those among industrial workers. And within the latter group, there was often a stepwise downgrading.

Given the ethnic/racial pecking order of working-class Chicago, as white "ethnics" were ratcheted downward in the occupational hierarchy, they bumped blacks and other minorities out of even the meanest jobs. By the end of 1932, when the general unemployment rate in the city stood at about one-third, between 40 and 50 percent of black workers were unemployed, and Mexicans had lost their newly won footholds in the packinghouses and steel mills.[4]

Coping through Private Charities

In Chicago, the hardships engendered by the Depression were less ameliorated by private charities than in New York. With the notable exception of Julius Rosenthal, the callousness of most of Chicago's local philanthropists, who were oriented more toward subsidizing ostentatious palaces of culture than toward succoring poor immigrants and blacks, left large masses uncared for. After all, Chicago's elites had, in the

Table 8.1. Number of manufacturing establishments and wage workers employed in manufacturing, Chicago, 1929–47

Year	Chicago manufacturing establishments (in thousands)	Chicago wage workers in manufacturing (in thousands)
1929	10.2	405.4
The Crash		
1930	9.8	390.8
1931	9.5	376.1
1932	9.1	361.5
1933	8.8	346.8
1934	8.4	332.2
1935	8.1	317.5
1936	7.9	354.3
1937	7.7	391.1
1938	8.1	369.5
1939	8.5	347.8
1940	8.6	387.8
World War II		
1941	8.9	427.7
1942	9.1	467.7
1943	9.4	507.6
1944	9.5	547.6
1945	9.8	587.5
1946	10.0	627.5

Source: Wesley Skogan, "Chicago since 1840: A Time-Series Data Handbook" (unpublished manuscript, University of Illinois Institute of Government and Public Affairs, 1976), 24–26, Table 2.

Burnham plan, already demonstrated their capacity to ignore the plight of the city's industrial workers and its African American minority, except when riots and strikes forced them to take occasional notice and episodic (and usually repressive) action. And after the outburst of union activities in the aftermath of World War I, such efforts by the working class foundered, both vis-à-vis actions against major corporations and via the route of electoral politics.

Before the New Deal programs reached Chicago, therefore, the city's hard-pressed workers were chiefly dependent not on the kindness of strangers but on their own churches (ethnicity and race specific) and their fellow countrymen.[5] And such kindness could stretch only so far when times made everyone poor. True, the Catholic Church made heroic efforts to rise to the challenge of relief, offering assistance to many of its parishioners. Blacks, however, were largely excluded from these funds, in part because they were more likely to be Protestants. Lacking a central hierarchy, each Protestant sect or congregation was really left to its own devices in providing aid.

Coping through Political Channels

What elite charities, ethnic mutual aid, and religious relief could not ameliorate, the political system attempted to. As Cohen rightly notes, it was only in the 1930s that working-class Chicagoans began to look to "electoral politics to achieve a class agenda, and this time their numbers, the party, and the circumstances [were] completely different."[6] After fifteen years of Republican rule, Chicago turned Democratic in the Depression, building with worker support one of the most powerful party machines in the country. In the early 1930s the monolithic Chicago Democratic machine finally consolidated into the one-party rule that would subsequently control Chicago and Cook County for decades to come. And it was the welfare functions that precinct captains and ward heelers performed—distributing material gifts in times of need and intervening on behalf of their "clients" to gain them access to city jobs and the resources of social service agencies—that insinuated party politics more deeply into everyday life.[7]

But it would be a mistake to see this solidification of Democratic Party power as an ideological shift to the left. In New York, La Guardia's election had signaled such a turn; in Chicago, as Harold Gosnell argued at the time, it did not. Gosnell asked: "Did [Chicago] voters show a disposition to support reform movements, as in New York City? Was there a drift away from the spoils tradition?" His answer was an unequivocal no. Although there was some "shuffling of the political cards" as "Democrats were substituted for Republicans in practically all of the local offices," the basic spoils system did not change, because "these Democrats were not New Deal Democrats at heart." Indeed, the problematic Gosnell set for himself was "to consider why there [were] so few fundamental changes in the outlook of Chicago politicians during this period of economic crisis."[8]

One reason may have been that in this first iteration of Democratic machine politics in Chicago, it was the "white ethnics," rather than the African American minority, who monopolized the benefits.[9] The former had been quick to mobilize behind the Democratic Party by 1931, helping Anton Cermak defeat Thompson as mayor.[10] Blacks, on the other hand, initially remained solidly behind Mayor Thompson, through whom they had achieved some modicum of power and influence. Although they certainly had the most pressing needs for assistance, because they had been so slow to change party affiliation they forfeited what bargaining power (and patronage) they had formerly enjoyed. But as the various New Deal measures went into effect, the "Republican grip upon the Negro vote was [gradually] broken as people began to 'vote for bread and butter instead of for the memory of Abraham Lincoln,' . . . [and by] 1936 Black Metropolis was a 'New Deal town.'"[11] The federal government was to perform services for them that the local machine had to support, albeit without enthusiasm.

SYMBOLIC CHICAGO

I might digress here to acknowledge that by the early 1930s, two less complimentary symbols of Chicago had already supplanted the mythical phoenix of the Great Fire—

by then exhausted by its futile attempts to rise yet again. These characterizations of Chicago still dominate the stereotypes outsiders hold of the city: Chicago, the violent city ruled by gangsters; and Chicago, the city of unrelenting racial segregation.[12] Both images became central once the opposite metaphor of industrial might (Carl Sandburg's city of broad shoulders) crashed in the Depression.

Noir Films

If New York's noir films have usually focused on individual "disorganization," random crime, fear of the streets, callous indifference to victims, and the impersonality of menacing skyscrapers,[13] and those about Los Angeles, at least until recently, have focused on environmental disasters, one searches in vain for dystopic film *fantasies* about Chicago. After I had puzzled over this for some time, it occurred to me that Chicago's "nightmares" have tended, instead, to be about "real" figures in "real" organized crime.[14] It is as if the city did not need to invoke fictionalized projections of anxiety; its noir images already existed, set in the recent past.[15]

Three "classic" gangster films based loosely on the career of Al Capone were made in the 1930s, within a decade of his climb to power in the Chicago underworld: *Little Caesar* (1930), *The Public Enemy* (1931), and *Scarface* (1932). All of them depict Chicago as the home "of an immigrant [who had made] good at his business of crime."[16] Prohibition in the "Roaring Twenties" created a window of opportunity for organized crime in major U.S. cities—an opportunity "niche" that recent immigrants seized.[17] Whereas organized crime was certainly not confined to Chicago, only for that city did "mobsters" become an almost exclusive icon.

In sin, as in business and aesthetics, however, one notes the close connections between New York and Chicago. Capone actually grew up in New York's Five Points slum. It was not until 1920 that he moved to Chicago, where he joined a local Italian mob. By 1928, Capone was running

> a $60 million business that bought police, politicians, and judges and boasted its own army of enforcers, an empire carved out of meeting the desires and demands of Americans for things that their government had declared illegal: alcohol, drugs, prostitution, gambling. And it was Prohibition that provided 60 percent of the syndicate's income during the twenties. Prohibition financed the take-off stage for large-scale organized crime in America.[18]

By the 1930s, with the end of Prohibition, however, competing "mobs" were struggling to retain their shares of a declining pot, and the myth of the mob was being romanticized, at least in Chicago.[19]

Race: The Other Noir Reality of Chicago

Ignored by filmmakers, but of growing importance to the future of Chicago, was its expanding concentration of African American residents, as black/white cleavages gradually began to supplant those that had separated "foreigners" from "natives." As Drake and Cayton point out:

> On the eve of the Depression there were still over 800,000 persons of foreign birth in Midwest Metropolis, but the city was in the process of becoming an "American" city, peopled primarily by Negroes and native-whites. . . . The foreign-born whites were dying out (and leaving the city) faster than they were being replaced. During the Depression years there was a 20 per cent decrease in the foreign-born population . . . balanced by a 20 per cent increase in the Negro population.[20]

Although Chicago novels, and the films about the city based on them, continued to play on the themes of "growing up Irish" in the city, it was the black migrant's "journey to Chicago" that remained, until recently, the untold story.[21]

THE GROWTH OF THE GHETTO

It is hard to explain why Chicago remained a magnet for black migrants, given its harsh economic conditions in the Depression and its long history of violently enforced segregation. Nevertheless, more than forty thousand additional southern blacks settled in the city during the 1930s.[22] The only explanation is that the newcomers were escaping from even more depressed conditions at home and were following a chain pattern typical of other migrations.[23] And although the New Deal did little to revive Chicago's flagging smokestack economy, it did make available relief and work programs. What the New Deal could not provide were jobs with a future and more and better housing in the overcrowded Black Belt.

The deplorable housing conditions within the ghetto had already been graphically depicted in the report of the Commission of Inquiry made after the Chicago race riot of 1919. The commission found that more than 40 percent of the city's blacks lived in grossly deteriorated housing and that fully 90 percent lived in the least desirable areas of the South Side, wedged between narrowly spaced rail lines at the fringe of the city's segregated vice districts.[24] Even though these conditions deteriorated significantly during the Depression years, migrants continued to pour into a zone that was surrounded by hostile whites who "held the line" against spatial expansion, thus intensifying the physical deterioration of the ghetto. The question for "white Chicago" was: Could anything be done to eliminate the worst housing *without* expanding the borders of the ghetto, which they feared even more than slums per se? Replacing slums with sanitized public housing seemed a logical answer, especially if the replacement of slums could be achieved without "spreading" their minority populations into white residential areas.[25]

The Belated Birth of Public Housing

Although Chicago did not initiate its public housing program before passage of the 1937 Housing Act, it did eventually take modest advantage of the new program, building some five thousand units throughout the city by the end of World War II.[26]

Given the lower densities in the city, most of these early projects were designed as low-rise walk-up flats. The first and largest of these developments was the Ida B. Wells project, initially constructed on forty-seven acres of cleared slum land in the heart of the ghetto and designed to rehouse 1,662 black families.[27] At first, the prospect of this new housing was greeted enthusiastically in the Black Belt. Black leaders, hncluding the influential publishers of the *Chicago Defender,* not only did not object at that time to the PHA's policy of "maintaining the neighborhood's racial balance," but hailed the Chicago Housing Authority for employing black professionals and skilled and unskilled workers in the construction, even though slum clearance removed almost as many housing units from the ghetto as the new project provided.[28] Furthermore, progress was so slow that by the time the project was ready for occupancy in 1941, many years after the original occupants of the site had been displaced, the United States was on the brink of war and priorities would shift to housing war workers.

For the most part, therefore, public housing did little to expand the supply of housing for the growing numbers of African Americans, and the newcomers who poured into Chicago during the war in response to heightened labor demand had to be accommodated within the constricted borders of the existing ghetto. Room was made for them primarily through division and subdivision of the area's meager supply of housing, heightening densities and speeding up further deterioration of the housing stock.

THE WAR EFFORT RESCUES CHICAGO—BUT ONLY TEMPORARILY

Chicago was the last of our three cities to pull itself out of the Depression. New York's revival began even before the United States entered the war, largely because of the stepped-up activity in its ports generated by lend-lease shipments. Los Angeles, as we shall see, had already begun its ascent by the mid-1930s, as surviving industrial firms opened modernized plants in California at the same time they shut down obsolete ones in the "rust belt." Chicago's rescue, however, had to await orders from the military, which came only when the United States was actively engaged as a belligerent. It was only after army and air force orders poured into the Midwest—for ordnance and munitions, and for trucks, aircraft, and airplane engines,[29] as well as for the steel and machine tools to make them—that Chicago's closed plants reopened and even expanded. At the peak of the war effort, the steel mills and many other plants were operating on three shifts.

In contrast to the glut of labor during the Depression, the war economy created new shortages. Mobilization into the armed forces drew manpower away from the factories at the very time these plants needed more hands. As had happened during World War I, African Americans were again vigorously recruited from the South. But the same pecking order that had governed the devolution of Chicago's industry guided its remobilization. Black Metropolis, according to Drake and Cayton, was the last Chicago area to benefit from the "recovery." During the early phases of the war effort, blacks had to wait until white labor had been reemployed, but after Pearl Harbor, demand for workers exploded and "Negroes were reintegrated into the main stream of industrial life at an accelerated pace," assisted by the FEPC and the War Manpower Commission. "Between Pearl Harbor and D Day some 60,000 more Negroes came to Chicago. . . . In 1944, there were 337,000 Negroes—almost one person in every ten—living in [Chicago]."[30] Of these, 300,000 (or 90 percent) continued to live in "the city within the city," the Black Belt, then still only seven miles long and one-half mile wide.[31]

In 1943, after the Detroit and New York riots, Chicagoans feared a similar large-scale outburst, but this did not materialize. The newly established Chicago Commission on Human Relations worked furiously to defuse racial tensions.[32] Instead, the city experienced what would become its most typical pattern of expressing racial tensions: what can be called "border wars." While these were waged consistently at the edges of the Black Belt, they also erupted wherever blacks had made inroads into existing slum pockets away from the South Side ghetto—both just west and northwest of the Loop. The case of the near northwest side was perhaps emblematic.

Cabrini Homes

Some African Americans had already found housing in a decrepit Sicilian immigrant district, known both as "Little Sicily" and "Little Hell," when slum clearance began there in the late 1930s to make room for a modest-sized public housing project—the Frances Cabrini Homes (later expanded by high rises to become the infamous Cabrini-Green project).[33] In conformity with PHA policies, the Chicago Housing Authority had promised that four-fifths of the 586 new units would be assigned to Italians and the rest earmarked for others. However, construction had not even begun when Pearl Harbor was attacked, and once the United States had entered the war, priority was given instead to war workers, many of them African Americans. When the latter were moved into the project in 1942, however, they were met by violence, which recurred in the aftermath of the Detroit riot of 1943.[34] This was only a minor skirmish, however, compared to the battles, both literal and figurative, that would erupt in the postwar period.[35]

THE POSTWAR PERIOD

When the war ended, many in Chicago expected a replay of the 1919 economic downturn, but this did not occur. In fact, the war-induced recovery lasted in reflected glow for another decade before it petered out. Between 1946 and 1956, the number of industrial firms within the city stabilized at just over 10,000, and the number of workers employed in manufacturing fluctuated between 575,000 and 660,000. By 1957, however, both figures had begun to drop again, until in 1972 only 7,318 firms were left, employing some 430,000 wage earners.[36] It is true that by then the suburbanization of Chicago's large industries was well under way, but even taking this into account, one must conclude that the great Fordist powerhouse of the Midwest was in decline, along with the rest of the "rust belt."

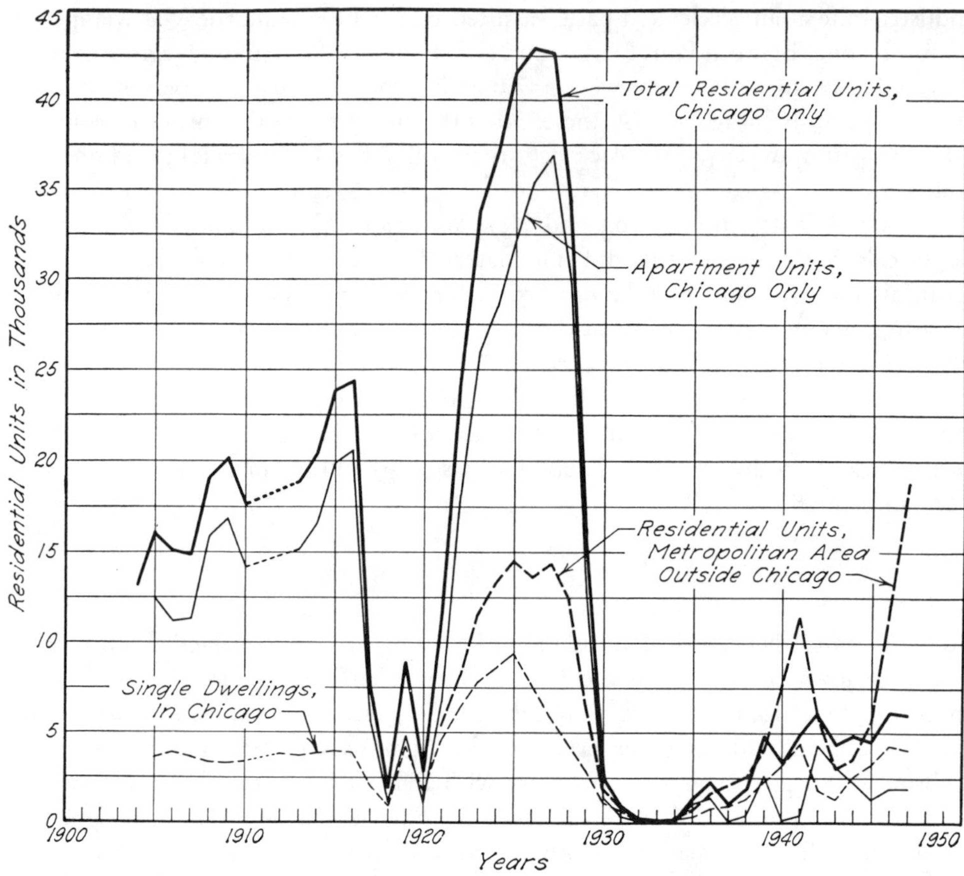

Figure 8.1. New construction within and outside city limits of Chicago. Reproduced from Frank A. Randall, *The Development of Chicago Building Construction* (Urbana: University of Illinois, 1949), 297. Courtesy of the Chicago Historical Society.

White "Collar Counties"

During the first decade of the postwar period, the most obvious trend was a revival of a development that was already modestly evident in the 1920s, an expansion in the construction of housing in the metropolitan area outside the Chicago city limits. As Figure 8.1 shows, most residential construction in the Chicago region in the 1920s was in the form of apartment houses within the city—some thirty-seven thousand units built in the peak year of 1928.[37] A small number of single-family bungalows were also built on the little remaining open land toward the city's edge. However, by the mid-1920s almost fifteen thousand residential units were being built annually in the metropolitan area beyond the city's borders. These were primarily single-family houses.

The absolute cessation of residential construction during the Depression is clear from this figure, as is the radical change favoring suburban location by the end of the

1930s. It is evident that the trend toward eschewing the city actually began in earnest just prior to the war and was only temporarily aborted when construction halted in wartime. As soon as the hostilities ceased, however, suburban construction "took off" on an exponential path, leaving in-city construction far behind.

When one compares Chicago with New York, the contrast is striking. Although neither city had the option of extending its borders through annexation, after World War II New York still had significant amounts of vacant land within its outer boroughs. Therefore, residential construction of two-flats and apartment buildings (including monstrous projects such as LeFrak "city" and Co-op City in Queens, to which local whites "fled") continued well into the 1960s at the outer reaches of that city, although those developments were also copiously supplemented by single-family house construction in the suburban and even exurban reaches.

The case was quite different in Chicago, which by the war was already reaching the "limits" of its growth. The urban area continued to expand in the same concentric/sectoral pattern that had been so graphically analyzed in the 1920s and 1930s by sociologist Ernest Burgess and economist Homer Hoyt, but it now did so into territories increasingly beyond the jurisdiction of the city.[38] If this were all that happened, one could simply attribute the changes in Chicago's city/suburban distribution to "natural" forces. However, the suburban growth was an overreaction, not just to the demand for new housing, but to the city's long-standing racial animosities. It was, indeed, a classic case of white flight, uninhibited as New York's was by rent control and possibly by that city's more tolerant attitudes toward minorities.

The clearest evidence of this overreaction is that Chicago's total population actually declined precipitously as whites escaped to the suburbs, leaving African Americans (and eventually Latinos as well) behind in an increasingly impoverished and deindustrializing city. Within a twenty-year period, the proportion of whites in the metropolitan area who lived within the Chicago city limits dropped from 68 percent in 1950 to 51 percent in 1960 and down again to 39 percent by 1970. During this same period, African Americans experienced hardly any "suburbanization" at all. Fully 90 percent had lived within the city limits in 1950, and the same percentage still remained within the center city at the end of those two decades.[39] The net result was, by 1970, an almost complete bifurcation of the social and demographic structure of the urbanized region: an emptying-out center city, increasingly inherited by minorities who fell heir to a decimated industrial base, and a largely white and wealthier set of "collar counties" around the semicircular city, which attracted not only residences but, eventually, new higher-tech factories, office headquarters, and white-collar service sector jobs.

POSTWAR BORDER WARS: FIGHT *AND* FLIGHT

It is impossible to explain this shift without reference to the border wars that white Chicagoans had fought almost from the time the Black Belt began to form and that they lost decisively, as one after another barricade crumbled *within the city* during the postwar period. As Boskin notes with reference to Chicago:

> From the end of World War II until 1964, there were several large-scale urban disturbances which reflected the underlying potential of social violence. None of these conflicts expanded into major urban conflagrations. . . . The most intense violence occurred when minority groups attempted to change the residential patterns. . . . Several urban racial clashes were instigated by Caucasians who resented attempts by Negroes to move into all-White neighborhoods. . . . *Between 1945 and 1948 there were more than a hundred attacks on the persons and property of Negroes who moved, or attempted to move, out of the Black ghettos into other areas.*[40]

The number of racially motivated housing-related events escalated and shifted from isolated attacks to larger-scale confrontations and "preemptive strikes" during the 1940s.[41] The Chicago Commission on Human Relations reported 485 racial "incidents" between 1945 and 1950, of which almost three-quarters concerned housing or property. More than 85 percent of these incidents took place on the fringes of predominantly black areas. "The pattern of terrorism [was] easily discernible. . . . It [was] at the seams of the black ghetto in all directions."[42]

There were important legal as well as demographic reasons for the escalation of the border wars in the late 1940s. Not only had the black population piled up within the ghettos' existing boundaries and therefore intensified demands for more space, but the "legal" means (deed restrictions) that had previously been deployed to exclude blacks from adjacent areas were collapsing. As Drake and Cayton point out in their analysis of the relationship between racial restrictive covenants and contested areas, it was largely "in middle-class white neighborhoods adjacent to Negro communities, when a mass invasion is feared, that antagonisms become most highly organized. Such spots become 'contested areas.'"[43]

On the eve of World War II, one such contested area already existed just east and south of the Black Belt. In 1937, more than 95 percent of the property frontage in the "white island" around the University of Chicago (including Washington Park and Woodlawn) was reported to be "protected" by restrictive covenants on the deeds of ownership, which proscribed owners from renting or selling to African Americans. Despite this, a few "well-to-do Negroes managed to persuade one or two white property owners to sell." However, the local property owners' association obtained an injunction to prevent one of the new owners from moving into the home he had bought, and the "Chicago Title and Trust refused to give him a clear title."[44] The case was eventually heard by the Illinois State Supreme Court, which found in favor not of the black buyer, but of the property owners.[45] In the years that followed, other court cases were instigated, but it was not until 1948 that the U.S. Supreme Court ruled that racially restrictive covenants could not be enforced by law.[46]

This denial of court redress intensified white feelings of "vulnerability." The substantial portion of Chicago's white population that dreaded residential integration felt it was left with only limited options. Renters could flee to other areas of the city or leave for suburbs that remained all-white, or they could escalate the "hidden battle" through continued harassment of "invading" blacks.[47] Owner-occupants could move out, either subdividing and renting their homes and small apartment buildings to incoming blacks at higher rates or selling their properties at distressed prices, often at the urging of unscrupulous real estate agents who helped foment panic sales. Many of these agents then resold the same buildings to eager black buyers willing to pay premium prices.[48] In white neighborhoods distant from the expanding Black Belt, residents fought isolated "invasions" with firebombs. And in all-white areas, public housing projects were suspect because they could introduce "undesirables."

Not that public housing constituted a large-scale threat. After the war, the Chicago Housing Authority was operating only 7,644 permanent low-income housing units, including the nearly 4,000 that segregated blacks in the Ida B. Wells, Robert H. Brooks, and Altgeld Gardens projects. In those early days black projects were all located inside the ghetto. The Lathrop and Trumbull Park Homes, located in white areas, excluded black residents, and the Jane Addams Homes, the only integrated project, had racial quotas.[49] This was to change after 1949, when there was a sudden interest in using "Negro removal" to free prime land near the Loop for profitable redevelopment.

Thus the shortage of low-income housing available to minorities was exacerbated by the federal Urban Redevelopment Act of 1949, which subsidized private redevelopment by offering cities financial incentives to condemn "blighted areas," clear the land (of buildings *and* people) at public cost, and then sell the vacant land, at a substantial "write down" in price, to private builders who agreed to construct rental housing for moderate-income tenants.[50] Written into the law was an obligation for cities to find relocation housing for residents who lost their homes in slum clearance sites. If they otherwise qualified, displaced persons were supposed to be given priority placement in public housing. Needless to say, in Chicago many of the sites slated for "slum clearance" were in areas predominantly occupied by blacks, and if new projects were to serve relocation purposes, they would logically have to be built earlier and on vacant sites—which were chiefly available toward the city's periphery. Furthermore, the Chicago Housing Authority was no longer permitted to segregate its clients by race. What happened next was, at least in hindsight, fairly predictable. The border wars expanded to public housing site wars.

CHICAGO'S PUBLIC HOUSING: ENCOUNTERS IN BLACK AND WHITE

In 1949 the Chicago Housing Authority proposed to construct some forty thousand additional units in the next six years, favoring open sites so as to minimize displacement and achieve a net gain in the housing supply. This plan would have "involved putting large numbers of blacks into white areas."[51] Meyerson and Banfield describe the political fiasco that ensued in excruciating day-by-day detail in their book *Politics, Planning and the Public Interest,* which is an absolutely essential source for understanding how the "strengths" of Chicago's political system—namely, its ardent neighborhood attachments and their expression through a powerful city council—mortally wounded the public housing movement in Chicago.[52]

Once the older policy of the federal PHA, which had been to fund projects on sites that reproduced the racial composition of an area, was reversed and public housing could no longer be used to reinforce racial segregation—and, indeed, was

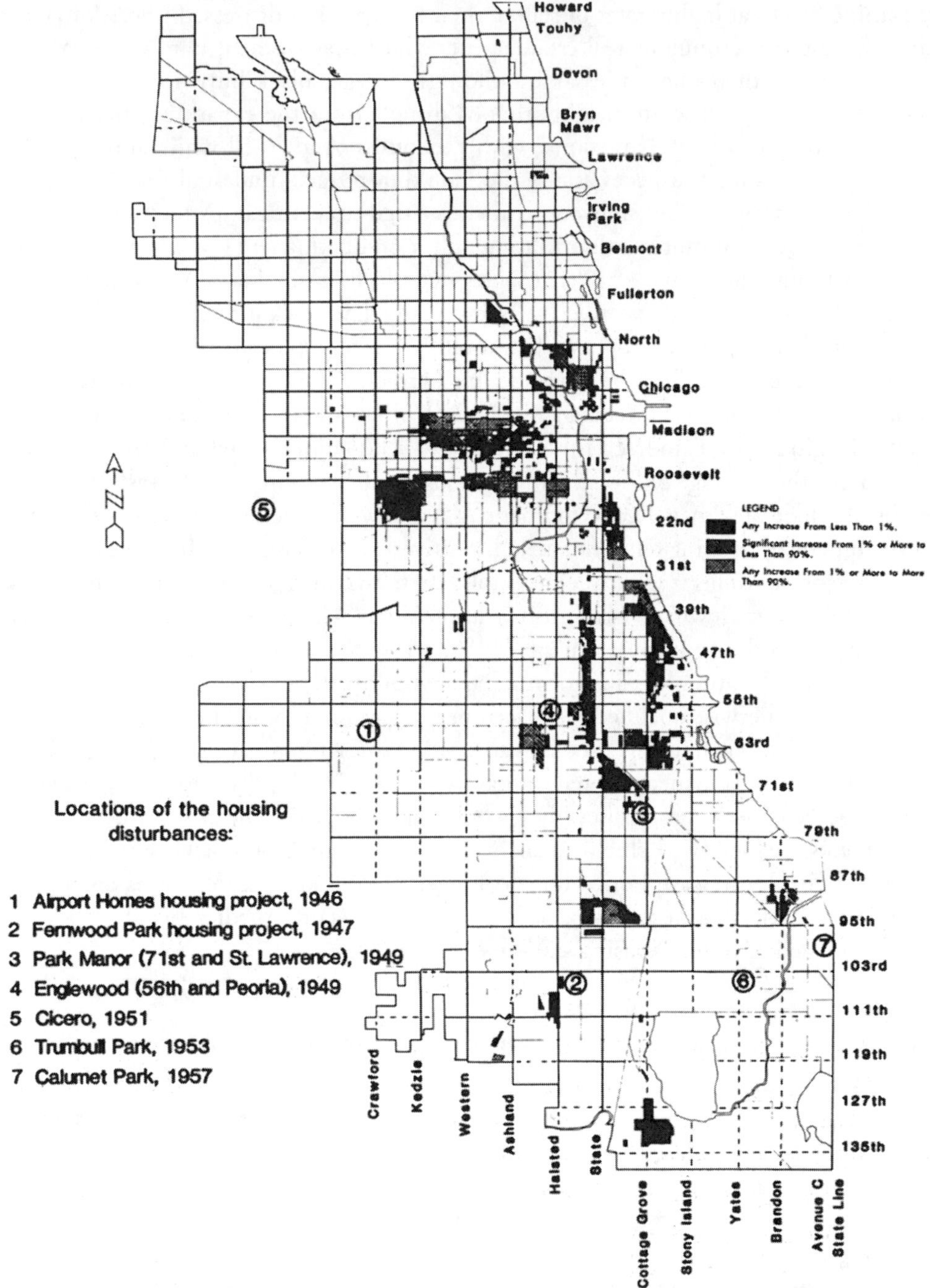

Map 8.1. Locations of racial conflicts over housing in Chicago between 1946 and 1957. Source: Arnold Hirsch, *Making the Second Ghetto;* used with permission from Oxford University Press.

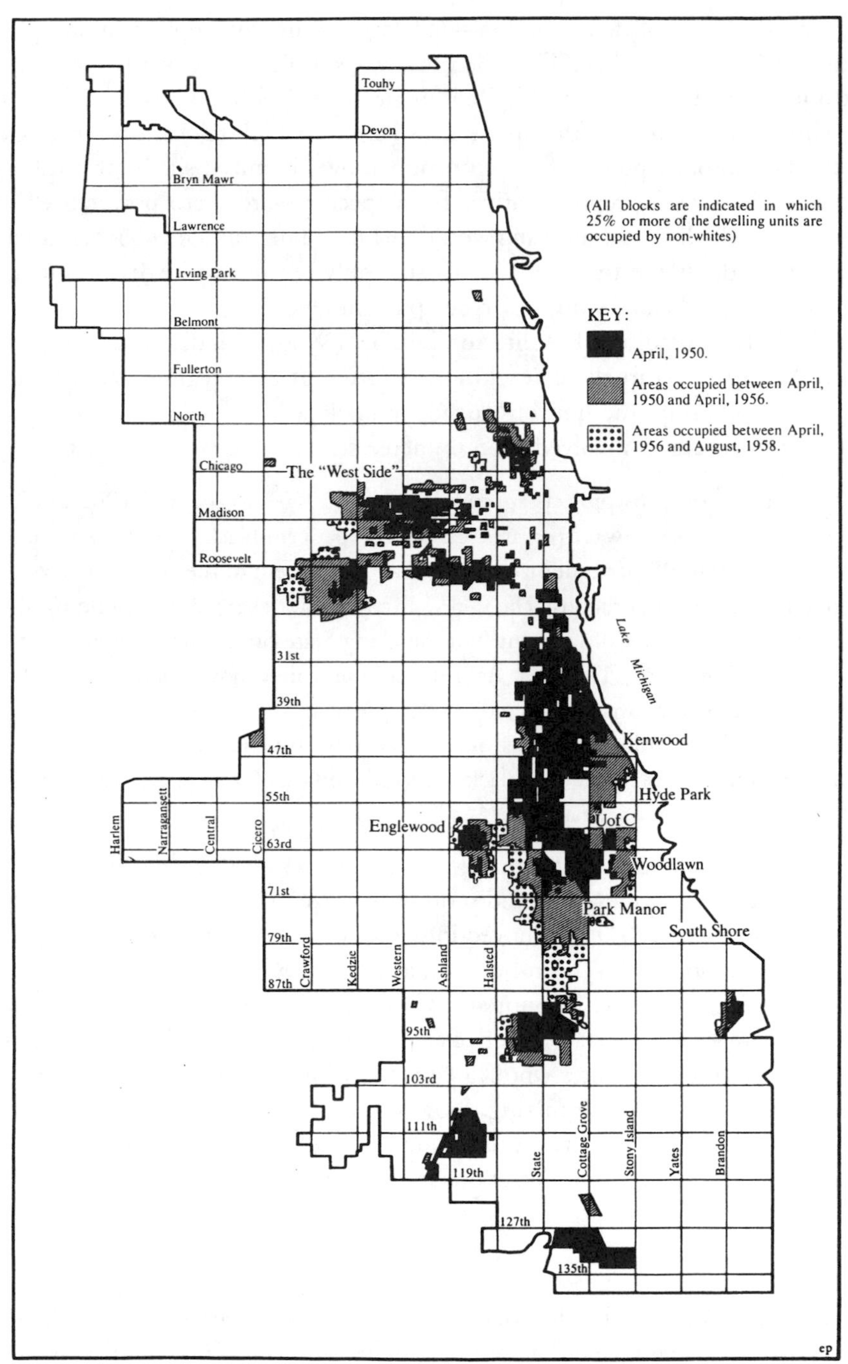

Map 8.2. Chicago ghetto expansion between 1950 and 1958. Source: Drake and Cayton, *Black Metropolis.*

now seen as a "tool" of desegregation—Chicago essentially stopped building public housing, at least for a while. The dilemma was simple: black wards contained the worst housing and a population eligible for subsidized public housing, whereas outlying white wards contained the only vacant land on which relocation housing could be built. The absolute power of the city council over itemized site approval for projects essentially gave the representatives from specific wards veto power over where, and therefore whether, such housing would be built. The council aldermen used their veto powers with little restraint, approving sites only in a few white districts represented by "breakaway liberals" who "deserved" punishment.[53]

Finally, the crusading CHA director, Elizabeth Wood, was dismissed and planning director Meyerson returned to teaching; the attempt to integrate was abandoned. Under new leadership, the housing authority made a "deal" with the city's political leaders and thus became involved in an immense scheme of de jure segregation.

> Of thirty-three CHA projects approved between 1950 and the mid-1960s, only one when completed was in an area less than 84 per cent black; all but seven were in tracts at least 95-per-cent black; more than 98 per cent of the apartments were in all-black neighbourhoods. The CHA, as critics later charged, was building almost a solid corridor of low-rent housing along State Street and near-by streets from 22nd Street to 51st Street. As it did so, the whites moved out: of 688,000 new homes built between 1945 and 1960, more than 77 per cent were built in the suburbs, where hardly any blacks were found. By 1969 a judge found that CHA family housing was 99 per cent black-occupied, and that 99.5 per cent of its units were in black or transitional areas.[54]

With the "racial issue" of public housing presumably resolved within the city, the next events involved more widespread and serious organized violence beyond the city limits (the Cicero riot of 1951) and moved into a third phase of racial strife, with "battles over the use of schools, playgrounds, parks, and beaches."[55]

The ruling of the U.S. Supreme Court in the case of *Brown v. Board of Education of Topeka* in 1954, which declared "separate but equal" schools inherently unequal, represented to whites who feared integration the fall of one of their last defensive bastions against racial mixing. However, because the new policy required desegregation only within the city's jurisdiction and did not extend to the metropolitan region, a second wave of white defections from the city to the suburbs ensued.[56]

FROM BORDER WARS TO GHETTO REVOLTS

By 1960, therefore, the border wars were ending, not because race relations in Chicago had become more cordial, but because most of the barricades that whites had erected around the Black Belt were being dismantled, and whites were rapidly retreating to zones beyond the city limits. The city neighborhoods they vacated along the southern borders of the South Side Black Belt (Hyde Park and, even more so, the South Shore, formerly an elite zone)[57] were even more extensive than the stabilizing black population of the city needed.

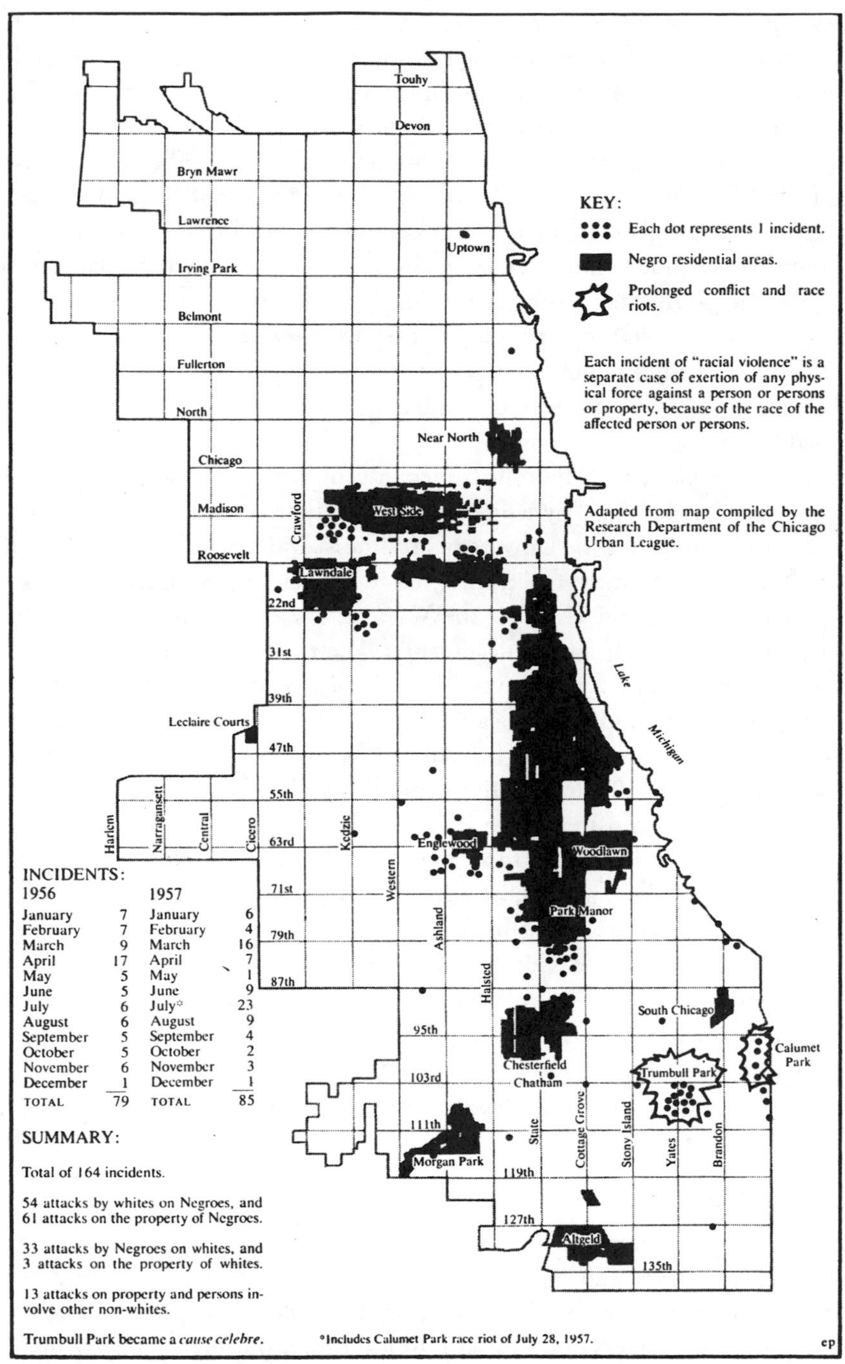
Touhy
Devon
Bryn Mawr
Lawrence
Irving Park
Belmont
Fullerton
North
Chicago
Madison
Roosevelt
22nd
31st
39th
47th
55th
63rd
71st
79th
87th
95th
103rd
111th
119th
127th
135th
Uptown
Near North
West Side
Lawndale
Crawford
Leclaire Courts
Harlem
Narragansett
Central
Cicero
Kedzie
Western
Ashland
Halsted
State
Cottage Grove
Stony Island
Yates
Brandon
Englewood
Woodlawn
Park Manor
Chesterfield
Chatham
South Chicago
Trumbull Park
Calumet Park
Morgan Park
Altgeld
Lake Michigan
KEY:
Each dot represents 1 incident.
Negro residential areas.
Prolonged conflict and race riots.
Each incident of "racial violence" is a separate case of exertion of any physical force against a person or persons or property, because of the race of the affected person or persons.
Adapted from map compiled by the Research Department of the Chicago Urban League.
INCIDENTS:
1956
January 7
February 7
March 9
April 17
May 5
June 5
July 6
August 6
September 5
October 5
November 6
December 1
TOTAL 79
1957
January 6
February 4
March 16
April 7
May 1
June 9
July* 23
August 9
September 4
October 2
November 3
December 1
TOTAL 85
SUMMARY:
Total of 164 incidents.
54 attacks by whites on Negroes, and 61 attacks on the property of Negroes.
33 attacks by Negroes on whites, and 3 attacks on the property of whites.
13 attacks on property and persons involve other non-whites.
Trumbull Park became a *cause celebre*.
*Includes Calumet Park race riot of July 28, 1957.
ep

Map 8.3. Location of border wars (164 incidents) between 1956 and 1957. Source: Drake and Cayton, *Black Metropolis.*

As supply began to outstrip demand, at least at rates that owners considered a proper return, arson and abandonment spread, in some areas yielding scenes that resembled Dresden after carpet bombing. In the vicinity of the University of Chicago, new town houses were constructed north of the Midway, often on land already owned by the largest slum landlord of the zone, the university itself. The area immediately south of the Midway, except for the institutional buildings that abutted it, was abandoned to its increasingly marginalized black residents. With its customers decimated, the thriving South Side commercial strip along 63rd Street collapsed. Farther south, on the so-called South Shore, the racial transition was smoother. As the middle-class (mostly Jewish) departed for greener fields, they were replaced by their black counterparts, who were assisted in buying property in the area, in no small measure because of the progressive efforts of citizens' groups and the lending policies of the South Shore Bank.[58]

The smaller black and Hispanic settlements on the near West Side continued to expand into areas abandoned by whites, although urban renewal, the construction of a new Chicago campus for the University of Illinois, and a major highway preempted the zone nearest to downtown, creating a *cordon sanitaire* near the Loop and the Chicago River.[59] It was therefore on the West Side, rather than in the South Side's much expanded Black Belt, that Chicago's first "ghetto revolts" of the 1960s occurred. And interestingly enough, they involved both blacks and Latinos (mostly Puerto Rican but also including some Mexicans).[60]

In August 1965, just after the Los Angeles Watts "riot," there was an uprising in West Garfield Park, set off when a fire truck killed a black pedestrian. More than two thousand National Guardsmen were called in to occupy the area.[61] In June 1966, Puerto Ricans set fires and threw rocks, bricks, bottles, and Molotov cocktails when the police intervened in a nationalist rally.[62] In July 1966, a second West Side outburst, triggered when police ostensibly interfered with teenagers opening fire hydrants to cool off in Lawndale, led to wide-scale looting.[63] Some forty-two hundred National Guardsmen were deployed. With tensions so high, it should come as no surprise that the Chicago riot that erupted in 1968 in the aftermath of Martin Luther King's assassination raged out of control not on the South Side, but on the West Side. By then, Chicago was becoming a minority-majority city, ringed by white suburbs.

Blacks in the Political Structure

Given their growing demographic strength within the city limits—the joint result of their numerical increase and the even greater desertion of the city proper by white residents—it is remarkable that African Americans failed to translate their new proportionally higher numbers into greater political power during the 1960s and 1970s. It was not until 1983 that a coalition of black voters and "lakefront liberals" finally managed to elect Chicago's first (and to 1999, the city's only elected) black mayor, Harold Washington. But this "capture" of city hall was fated to be brief. Washington died soon after being reelected to a second term; he was succeeded by an African American council-appointed interim mayor, but power soon reverted to the "white" machine with the election of Boss Daley's son, Richard M. Daley.[64] However, as we shall see in Chapter 11, even the brief regime under Washington made a difference.[65]

The high degree of racial segregation in Chicago from its start, coupled with the system of strong ward organization in city government, had made a few representative "bosses" of the smaller black population in Chicago quite pivotal in local government during the early decades of the twentieth century.[66] Indeed, they "became a powerful political force . . . during the first administration of William Hale Thompson" beginning in 1915, when he needed a solid, unchanging Republican base.[67] But as we have noted above, this early gain was lost with the shift to Democratic rule during the New Deal, and "from the 1950s to the election of Harold Washington in 1983, Chicago [had become] a glaring example of African-American subordination and powerlessness."[68] This seems to have gone unrecognized by the overly optimistic authors of the 1961 postscript to *Black Metropolis,* who expressed pride in the social progress of Bronzeville and the growing economic and political power of Chicago's black community.[69] At the same time, however, they sounded a cautionary note: if "*the masses* are driven too far they are likely to fight back, despite their sometimes seemingly indifferent reactions to discrimination and segregation. *A potential for future violence within Black Metropolis* exists that should not and cannot be ignored."[70]

However, due to caution, this "potential" would not be realized until 1968. When "the masses" in Harlem, Rochester, and Philadelphia (in 1964) and in Watts (in 1965) had begun to fight back, Chicago's black leaders tried to head off violence by inviting Martin Luther King Jr. in 1966 to lead peaceful marches for open occupancy into white neighborhoods on the West Side. Nor did the city explode in 1967, although dozens of other, possibly less likely, cities did.[71] But the limits had been tested. In April 1968, following King's assassination, the cauldron boiled over; "burn, baby, burn" consumed vast portions of the West Side, following the path of the still-festering border wars on the way to the suburb of Cicero.[72]

By 1969 few were sanguine about "race relations" in Chicago. Although an appendix to *Black Metropolis,* titled "Postscript 1969," proudly noted that the eight hundred thousand blacks in Chicago in 1960 had increased to almost a million by 1969, it complained that the community's earlier gains seemed to have reached a dead end. "Open occupancy was no closer to realization in 1969 than it had been in 1961, when the City Council passed the buck for fair housing legislation to the State Legislature." And the concerted efforts to reduce housing discrimination in rentals and sales had not "increased residential integration . . . but rather [resulted] in enlargement of the existing ghettos and genesis of some new ones. *Middle-class Chicagoans still have a tendency to flee to the suburbs to avoid Negro neighbors.*"[73]

Politics as Usual

Neither the "riot" (insurrection) nor the changing demographic "balance" within the city altered the basic political structure of governance. The white-dominated Democratic Party, through its traditional bosses (Mayor Richard J. Daley in the city and Jake Arvey as head of the Cook County machine),[74] still exercised virtually complete control over an increasingly minority city population. True, as African Americans increased their votes, more blacks benefited from patronage or became city councillors, but they served chiefly at the forbearance of the machine and only so long as they remained in discipline.[75]

A number of political scientists have puzzled over the "strange" fact that the Chicago regime remained so fiscally conservative during the 1960s and 1970s—the same decades during which New York's expenditures on social welfare, health, housing, education, and city services skyrocketed. Ester Fuchs has suggested that the explanation for this difference is that the unbeatable Chicago machine needed to "pay off" supporters only *after* elections, whereas in New York City payoffs were required *before* the more contested elections in order to attract voters.[76]

There may, however, be a simpler answer to the question of why Chicago's politicians could economize on municipal social services. Until the death of "the Boss" (Richard J. Daley Sr.) in 1976 and the subsequent weakening of the Democratic machine, those in power could afford to ignore the needs of the city's large, growing, and increasingly poor minority population, just *because* the latter were relatively powerless to affect outcomes. Furthermore, the demands of the wealthier white population—except for low taxes, improved parking facilities and expressways, and better city services in the northern Loop, which was still almost exclusively "white" (i.e., items that served the interests of the Loop's business "growth machine")—could also be relatively ignored, because so many white voters had already deserted the city for the mostly Republican suburbs. And finally, as we shall see in Chapter 10, Chicago was able to off-load many of its health, welfare, and transit functions to other levels of government, whereas New York could not.

BLACK CITY/WHITE SUBURBAN RING

If ever there has been a classic case of white flight, it happened in Chicago. Whites moved beyond the city limits, following the relatively simple geography of Chicago's concentric circles arranged in sectors, leaving behind center-city areas that experienced net population losses. Arson and "riots" helped this "natural" process along. In 1950 the city of Chicago was home to some 3.6 million residents, of whom only 492,000 (about 14 percent) were "nonwhite," in comparison to 3,112,000 whites.[77] Ten years later, the nonwhite population (primarily native-born blacks) within the city limits had increased to some 813,000, whereas the number of white residents had declined to 2,713,000. By 1960 almost one in four Chicagoans was nonwhite.

The defection of whites had been quick and dramatic, prodded by "a series of riots between 1947 and 1957, in which the retreating whites . . . had defended their turf" but had essentially lost ground, as each successive barrier fell.[78] These border wars and Chicago's intractable public housing controversies during the postwar period are indicative of the deep racial animosities that drove Chicago's transformation in the booming postwar decade.

By the early 1960s, the ecological structure of the Chicago region had been transformed: there had been a massive transfer of the white population out of Chicago and

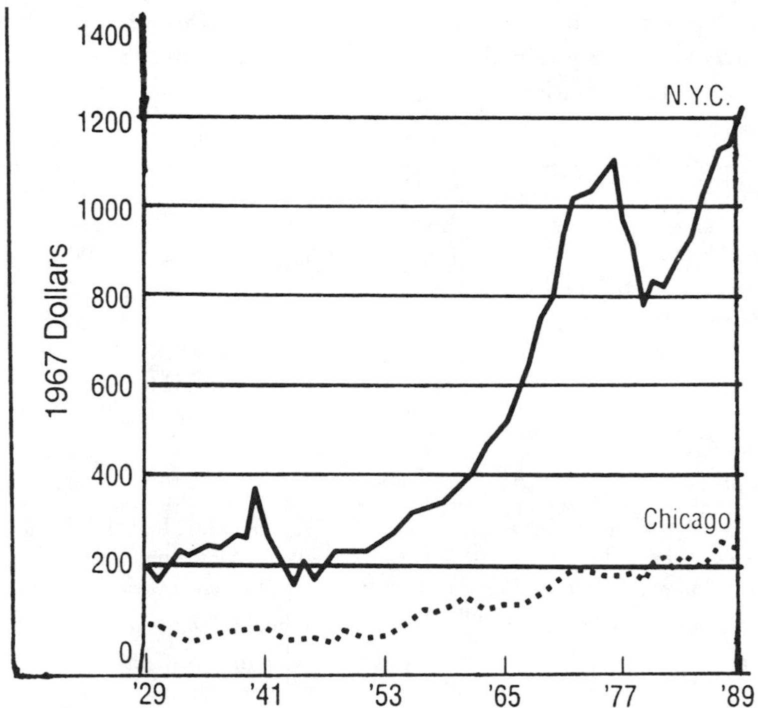

Figure 8.2. Comparing trends in per capita municipal expenditures, Chicago and New York City, 1929 to 1989. Used by permission of the University of Chicago Press.

into the outer rings of suburban Cook County and, increasingly, into the so-called collar counties that stretched beyond Cook County (DuPage, Kane, Lake, McHenry, and Will). This trend still shows no signs of tapering off. Table 8.2, generated from successive U.S. Census reports, shows the postwar developments through 1990. By 1960, only 62 percent of Cook County's population lived *inside* the city of Chicago, down from its peak in 1950. This slippage continued in the ensuing decades. Therefore, the increase in the percentage of blacks (and other minorities, chiefly Latinos) within the city was the outcome of a combination of two major factors: an absolute decline in the city's total population and the selective out-migration of whites to the suburban rings along with the almost exclusive settlement there of white newcomers.[79] By 1966, African Americans constituted almost a third of the city of Chicago's population and the "ghetto" itself had expanded enormously—but largely because whites took disproportionate advantage of the supports offered by other federal agencies to "flee" to suburban areas. By 1970, of the Chicago-area SMSA population of close to 7 million, almost 2 million (or about 30 percent) lived in suburban Cook County and another 1.5 million (more than 20 percent) lived in the so-called collar counties just beyond. Most of these suburbanites were "white."

If residential mobility had been partially inhibited or delayed in New York City by the large proportion of the housing stock for which monthly costs were kept in

Table 8.2. Population (in thousands) of the Chicago SMSA 1950 to 1990, by political jurisdiction: city of Chicago, suburban Cook County outside Chicago, and the five "collar" counties.

	1950	1960	1970	1980	1990
Chicago SMSA	5,178	6,220	6,978	7,103	7,261[a]
Chicago city	3,621	3,550	3,367	3,005	2,784[a]
Rest of SMSA	1,557	2,671	3,612	4,099	4,477
Cook County outside of Chicago	—[b]	—[b]	1,974	2,252	2,321
Collar Counties	—[b]	—[b]	1,485	1,850	2,156
DuPage County[c]			492	659	782
Kane County			251	278	318
Lake County[c]			383	440	516
McHenry County			112	148	183
Will County			248	325	357

[a] City officials claim that there was an undercount in 1990 amounting to 236,274, but the Bureau of the Census has refused to correct for urban undercounts. Many cities brought suit to request revisions for 1990, but the courts did not require the Census Bureau to correct for these.

[b] These figures are not readily available but are lower than those in later years.

[c] Note that these are north and northwest of Cook County, in the traditionally favored (whiter and richer) suburban sector. Figures do not add exactly because of rounding.

Sources: Northeastern Illinois Planning Commission, *Population Trends* (Chicago: Northeastern Illinois Planning Commission [1992?]), Table 1; Chicago Fact Book Consortium, ed., *Local Community Fact Book: Chicago Metropolitan Area* (Chicago: Review Press, 1984), Table A. It should be noted that in order to keep roughly comparable boundaries, the table does not include figures for the larger region now identified as the consolidated metropolitan statistical area, which runs over into Indiana and Wisconsin. But even in this instance, there are minor differences between the numbers in the two listed sources; because these are relatively small, I have not bothered to adjudicate between them.

check by rent control and rent stabilization laws (which made them great bargains, but only for those who stayed in place), no such inducements counteracted desertions in Chicago. This classic example of white flight dispersed them into the newer developments mushrooming beyond the city limits.

The city limits, however, were to prove no impermeable "defense" border for white Chicagoans. Just as the Supreme Court decisions in 1948 and 1954 had theoretically removed the "legal" barricades erected by restrictive covenants and segregated schools, so the Chicago-originated case of *Hills v. Gautreaux* was finally resolved by the U.S. Supreme Court in April 1976 by a unanimous ruling "that federal judges could order the U.S. Department of Housing and Urban Development to administer federally subsidized housing programs throughout the six county Chicago metropolitan area to help remedy the effects of past racial bias in Chicago's public housing."[80]

But by then there were few federal funds available to build new public housing units, and large-scale projects were, in any case, in disrepute. Section 8 funds were used either to build housing for the aged (who were mostly white) or to subsidize rents for larger families (mostly "minority") in existing buildings at scattered sites.

True, some of these subsidized units were located in the "more vulnerable" suburbs, but not enough to achieve any substantial integration. The degree to which "suburban" African Americans, whether poor or middle-class, were confined to only a few suburbs south and west of the city was striking; Chicago's segregated housing pattern was simply being writ large beyond the city limits, as we shall see in Chapter 11.

THE CONTINUED DECLINE IN INDUSTRIAL PROWESS

The decline in the economic base of Chicago, however, was proving an even more recalcitrant problem than dilapidated housing, the growing population of poor minority residents, and the low investments in public services (so-called fiscal conservatism). Only better jobs, conveniently located within the city along mass-transit lines, could have turned conditions around. But employment improvements were slow in coming, and the newer high-tech industries and elegant managerial/office complexes, like the white population, were locating almost exclusively in the collar counties, especially once these were better served by additional federally sponsored spoke-and-ring expressways that provided rapid access from the Loop to outlying suburbs and facilitated movement between suburbs along routes that avoided the center city.[81]

One reason for the very poor economic showing of Chicago during the Cold War period was, of course, the virtual absence of so-called high-tech defense-related government spending in the region, which contrasted strongly with Los Angeles (especially in its industrial "fringes" of Burbank, Santa Monica, and Orange County), or even with the New York–Connecticut region. Markusen and McCurdy's analysis demonstrates how little money the Department of Defense spent on research and development, innovative weaponry, or even production in the Illinois/Chicago region. Their Table 1 shows the "per capita prime [defense] contracts relative to U.S. average" for selected states in the years between 1951 and 1984. Whereas in 1951 Illinois was still near the middle rank of the eighteen states Markusen and McCurdy studied, by 1984 it had dropped to the very lowest.[82] Illinois was even more neglected in defense contracts than the remaining midwestern states on their list, such as Wisconsin, Michigan, Ohio, and Indiana. Only with respect to army, navy and air force defense installations did Illinois and Chicago fare well, but that could not compensate for their lack of high-tech contracts. After 1984, the Chicago region and, indeed, the entire Midwest would continue to slip, even as the East and South recovered.

I explore this slippage more fully in Part IV, but it should be noted here that Markusen, who is one of the originators of the term *gunbelt* (which calls attention to the close relationship between military spending and high-tech industrialization)[83] has also used the term *defense perimeter,* which refers to the peripheral ring around the nation that extends from New England through Long Island, Florida, Texas, the southwestern states, California, Washington, and Alaska."[84] The important point for Chicago is that it is neither in the gunbelt nor on the defense perimeter. Some suggest that because Illinois had only a weak voice in Washington, it was systematically bypassed while contracts went to more populous states with greater political clout in Washington,[85] but there is another important reason defense production debouched to the coasts. Because arms production is heavily geared to the *international* market, armaments are exported largely from coastal cities, such as New York, San Francisco, Los Angeles, and Miami.[86]

THE LOSS OF ARCHITECTURAL DISTINCTIVENESS

Just as Chicago lost the powerful industrial lead it had enjoyed from the late nineteenth century through World War II, so it also lost the distinctive architectural style that had led the nation in steel-frame construction methods and skyscraper design before World War I. Its strong tradition may ironically have intensified its resistance to trends so noticeable in New York and, even more so, in Los Angeles, as art deco, art moderne, and art nouvelle swept the field in the 1920s and 1930s. Even the transplanted Bauhaus touched Chicago only lightly, and might not have at all without the buildings designed by Mies van der Rohe. Neutra and Schindler stayed in Chicago only briefly before moving on to Los Angeles to create their masterpieces. From the 1950s on, stripped-down commercial high-rise buildings came to dominate the downtowns of cities all over the United States; Chicago was to be no exception.

By 1989, Manhattan had become the undisputed champion of high-profile buildings, with 117 structures at least 500 feet in height (the tallest of which was 1,350 feet). Chicago ranked a distant second, with only 39 buildings of that height, even though by then it boasted (but only briefly) the tallest building in the world, the Sears Tower, measuring 1,455 feet. Los Angeles had the third-tallest building in the country (at 1,017 feet) but ranked sixth (after Dallas, San Francisco, and Houston) in the number of 500-foot-plus buildings, with only 13 of them.[87]

But it was not height so much as distinctiveness that Chicago architecture lost. Chicago had been the putative birthplace of the skyscraper, and yet by 1930 its tall structures had been almost eclipsed by the towering profile of Manhattan. Why had the two cities diverged in the three-dimensional "shape" of their business cores? It was certainly not because the demand for office space in the Loop was proportionately lower, or that capitalism and the profit motive were weaker there than in New York. But if "skyscrapers are the ultimate architecture of capitalism," as Willis puts it,[88] then why did Chicago not build towers? It was certainly "capitalist" enough.

Here the answer Willis offers has compelling logic. One key was to be found in the larger block lengths (eight blocks to the mile in comparison with up to twenty blocks to the mile in Manhattan) and larger original lot sizes in the subdivision of Chicago's Loop. The tiny lot sizes of Manhattan forced builders to go higher. In contrast, large plots were easily assembled in Chicago, and such plots were sufficient, without extensive accumulation, to accommodate large office buildings. However, given the need for natural lighting, such massive structures required different design solutions. In Manhattan, narrow structures spiraled upward to grasp for their light and air; in Chicago, it was often necessary to design interior courts or hollow cores in order to maximize the surfaces exposed to light. Thus the typical "skyscraper" in Chicago presented a massive exterior cube to the outside, but hidden within it was often a glassed atrium. The most famous of such structures, of course, was the Rookery.

Figure 8.3. The skyline of Chicago. Note boxed appearance and flat roofs. Source: private collection of Carol Willis, reproduced courtesy of Carol Willis.

Another good example was the Diana Court building (no longer extant), which was one of the few art deco buildings in the city.

Massive exteriors, however, did not in themselves explain the squat profiles of their roofs. The second key Willis offers, already hinted at earlier, was the municipality's conscious decision, as early as 1893, to cap the permitted height of structures—a cap that, although it rose and fell in response to real estate pressures, was not removed until 1923.[89] In that year, the cap was removed entirely, and the new zoning law permitted tower constructions. "By 1930, more than twenty spires punctured the old 260-foot limit. The tallest was the 612-foot Board of Trade, but there were also eight buildings higher than 500 feet and eleven exceeding 400 feet."[90] The reasons for this change were also to be found in real estate interests, as a severe shortage of office space had developed in the expansionary period following World War I and rents had risen precipitously.[91] The Depression put an end to this building boom, and the postwar recovery period, unlike elsewhere, failed to jump-start it. The last Chicago skyscraper of the boom of the 1920s was the Field Building, finished in 1934,

> which was in a way, poetic [justice], since to construct it, the Home Insurance Building, the putative first skyscraper, was torn down. No new office space was undertaken in Chicago until 1952, when work began on the Prudential Building. In New York, however, recovery began almost immediately after World War II, and by 1959, 54 million square feet of new office space was completed or in development. In Chicago, during the same period, only 2.6 million square feet of office space was constructed. . . .
>
> . . . the most significant fact about the Chicago skyscraper in the post-war decade was its absence.[92]

Nor did the situation change much in the 1960s. By the latter part of that decade, the major area of upscale commercial life within the city had become the "North Loop"—a clear misnomer, given that it was well outside the defining mass-transit loop, being above the North Branch of the Chicago River on Upper Michigan Avenue. By

Figure 8.4. The interior atrium of the Rookery. Courtesy of the Chicago Historical Society; used with permission.

then, the central business district was essentially undergoing mitosis, which can again be traced to Chicago's intractable "race problem." The South Loop, except for the area around Orchestra Hall and the Art Institute, both unmovable institutions (the new Opera House was built beyond the declining downtown), was increasingly ceded to minorities as *its* CBD, while the North Loop became the exclusive domain of wealthier whites from the "Gold Coast." The redevelopment area that supplanted the near West Side slums around Maxwell Street would eventually blossom into high-rise tinted-glass office buildings that overlooked the river, but most of their workers commuted from the suburbs. Middle- and working-class whites, continuing their successive moves outward to more distant suburban rings, mostly avoided the shopping and recreational areas of either the south or the north downtowns, preferring the massive outlying malls of Edge City that the ring highways made more easily accessible.

Thus Chicago's persistent racial split continued to shape not only the relationship of suburban and city residences, but the locations of retail trade and offices. In the next few decades, the industries of the "city of broad shoulders" died; and when and if they were replaced, their plants, too, had departed from the increasingly "minority" city for the rings. The contrast that had begun with the enforced formation of the Black Belt was now writ large on a landscape that had been ambitiously delimited by the Burnham plan of 1909, but the "new order" was no more egalitarian and inclusive than its original concept. It had simply been turned inside out.

CHAPTER 9

Los Angeles Becomes Industrial

An international crisis in agriculture was already evident by the early 1920s. Perhaps because Los Angeles's economy was so heavily weighted to crops, it may have been one of the first American urban regions to experience a foreshadowing of the impending crisis. It is possible, if only in retrospect, to read some early warning signs there between 1925 and the October 1929 crash of the New York stock market. By the mid-1920s, property sales in Los Angeles had slowed and applications for building permits had taken a downward turn; new construction leveled off and then actually decreased in 1926. And early in the summer of 1928, prices on the Pacific Coast Stock Exchange dropped precipitously, more than a year in advance of the New York crash.[1]

Difficulties were also spreading to industry. Even though Los Angeles's urban economy in the late 1920s (and even into the early 1930s) depended chiefly on commerce and services, manufacturing had been increasing; in fact, industrial activity had tripled between 1921 and 1929.[2] Ironically, this advance made the city more vulnerable to international fluctuations, especially because oil, so dependent upon external demand, was, after agricultural products, its major export. Mullins has disputed the view of local boosters "that the depression struck California with less strength than other parts of the nation." He claims, on the contrary, that not only was Los Angeles "affected to the same degree as eastern cities but [it was] also affected at about the same time." Oil prices collapsed in 1929 and factory employment in the city dropped by almost a quarter between October 1929 and October 1930.[3]

Nevertheless, there is good evidence that California's economy did begin to recover somewhat earlier than the rest of the country. Although the opening years of the Depression aborted some of the industrial expansion that had occurred in the 1920s, by the mid-1930s there was renewed industrial growth, and by 1939 the industrial sector had recovered almost to its pre-Depression level. By then, rubber, tire, car, steel, and aircraft production were supplementing the older industries of oil (of declining significance) and filmmaking, which, indeed, had experienced a dramatic expansion to meet the demands of escapism engendered by despair. The city was fully prepared for the phenomenal takeoff that would occur in wartime (see Table 9.1).

Cheap energy and a more "docile" labor force were among the attractions Los Angeles offered to cautious industrialists. By the mid-1930s the municipality had taken over the management of its own power supply, setting one of the lowest electric rates in the country. A further inducement was the city's improved water situation; toward the end of the decade vast new quantities of water were being supplied, thanks to the federally financed Hoover Dam over the Colorado and the supplementary Parker Dam, which served the urban region.[4] But the city also employed the stick, using its police powers and its ruthless "Red Squad" to discipline labor. Both carrot and stick proved attractive to business.

These developments led to another countercyclical trend. Whereas other major urban areas actually lost population during the 1930s, Los Angeles continued to gain, albeit at a slower rate than before. The "footlooseness" of populations fleeing from even worse disaster areas, and the fact that industry began to revive earlier in California than elsewhere, made it a magnet for internal migration throughout the Depression. But some of the urban improvement projects had to be put on hold, among them Union Station, which, although proposed as early as 1911, was not completed until 1939, in time for the national recovery.[5]

RESPONSES OF LOS ANGELES TO THE DEPRESSION

Although the timing of the onset of the Depression in Los Angeles may have been the same as elsewhere, local responses to it had some unique features, of which the most noteworthy were the city's particularly vindictive treatment of its resident Mexican and Mexican American populations, its attempt to "blockade" its borders against internal migration, and the ruthless suppression by its long-time antiunion and anticommunist oligarchy of any "radical" worker response to the crisis.[6]

Anti-immigrant Sentiment

American society has long been tortured by a deep ambivalence toward "foreigners." On the one hand, virtually every American is descended from a "foreigner." (Only Native Americans and, to some extent, descendants of African slaves, who stress the involuntary character of their entry into the New World, are exempted.)[7] But on the other hand, antiforeign sentiment has been endemic, flaring up especially during times of economic retrenchment. Although all three regions experienced the same vicissitudes of national policy that sometimes embraced and at other times rejected foreign immigration, contingent largely on cycles of economic prosperity and depression, differences are also obvious. New Yorkers today, perhaps more aware of their own recent immigration histories than Anglo-Angelenos, seem to be the most accept-

Table 9.1. Employment, total wages, and value added in the industrial sector, Los Angeles Region, 1929 to 1939

Year	Number of average wage earners	Total wages (dollars)	Value added (dollars)
1929	114,480	175,812,298	609,048,374
1931	79,034	79,336,470[a]	312,323,288
1933	70,531	70,847,105	220,556,392
1935	96,499	109,048,970	324,684,501
1937	128,555	164,763,028	466,080,362
1939	126,391[b]	166,630,467	512,526,749

[a]The figure that appears in the original table (10,399,428) is obviously a misprint. I have recalculated this and substituted my suggested correction.

[b]Wage earner data for 1939 were not strictly comparable.

Source: Compiled from data in Frank L. Kidner and Philip Neff, *An Economic Survey of the Los Angeles Area: Statistical Appendix* (Los Angeles: Haynes Foundation, 1945), 1–12, Appendix I.

ing of diverse origins; white Chicagoans, albeit mindful of their fierce racial cleavages, seem similarly aware that their city is the product of immigrants. But Anglo Los Angeles is tortured, when it permits itself to notice, by its Mexican-origin minority, perhaps because there is subliminal and symbolic acknowledgment of Mexico's prior claims.[8] Its ambivalence can be traced to the conquest and seems to play itself out through simultaneous romanticism and denial.[9]

This ambivalence is compounded by the ongoing centrality to the Southwest's economy of the institution of "temporary guest worker." From its origin as a state, California has benefited from a "circulation" of temporary workers without citizen rights. At first there were the Chinese "coolies" who had been imported to build the western railroad lines. Later they were replaced by Mexican workers who, in addition, were recruited to work as migrant farm laborers to help bring in crops during peak harvest seasons. The coexistence in Los Angeles of (an admittedly small number of) descendants of the original Mexican population, of "guest workers," and of Mexican immigrants (naturalized as well as legally admitted and undocumented aliens) and their American-born descendants—and the overlapping among these categories even within the same families—has created a situation quite different from that in New York and Chicago.[10]

As we have seen, the first national-level legal restrictions placed on immigrants were the series of Chinese Exclusion Acts, initiated in 1882 with reference to "coolies" but by 1884 extended to all Chinese. Less stringent laws regulated the admission of Japanese immigrants, who were originally fishermen and farmers. These restrictions chiefly affected the West Coast. It was not until the depression of the 1890s that support began to build to restrict European immigration as well, and to enforce greater "quality control," especially because by then immigrants were being drawn from the "less developed" regions of eastern and southern Europe. A massive study commissioned by the federal government resulted in forty-two volumes by Dillingham in

1911. This, in turn, served to guide the first quota law imposed in 1917.[11] The new law not only required literacy (for males over sixteen years old) but insisted on good health and "morality." The law also established an Asiatic "barred zone" that included China, Southeast Asia, India, most of Polynesia, parts of Russia, Afghanistan, and Arabia, although it did not overturn the gentlemen's agreement with Japan.[12]

At the end of World War I, general fears of an influx of "unwashed masses" were compounded by a somewhat hysterical "Red Scare" reaction to the Russian Revolution. Quotas were sharply reduced by the acts of 1921 and 1924,[13] and politically motivated deportations were stepped up. Because of this reduction in European immigrants, the proportion of all immigrants who came from Mexico, which had been relatively small before World War I, began to increase. Between 1921 and 1930, 11 percent of all "legal" immigrants were coming from south of the border. The Depression of the 1930s had a paradoxical effect: it both greatly reduced the amount of voluntary immigration and heightened the animus toward existing resident aliens and potential immigrants.[14] With at least one-fourth of the U.S. labor force unemployed when the Depression peaked in 1933, there was a resurgence in nativist sentiments. It was at this time that a proviso in the immigration laws denied entry to anyone who was "*likely* to become a public charge."

In California this clause was applied with particular vigor to would-be immigrants from Mexico, although employers seeking cheap labor often managed to circumvent the restrictions. Furthermore, with only limited relief funds available, "rationing" of aid took the form of discrimination against aliens already in the country (and even against citizens who were "foreign" in accent or appearance). While not legally barred from federal relief, aliens received very little assistance because in practice such relief was administered locally in highly discriminatory ways.[15]

Given the high rates of unemployment in the opening years of the 1930s, many in Los Angeles's Mexican community left voluntarily, hoping to find less destitute conditions at "home," but agitation also grew among Anglo workers to repatriate them as aliens. Repatriation was difficult to accomplish for aliens who had come from Europe; Mexicans, who could just be sent across the border, thus bore the brunt of this policy. It was in Southern California that the worst abuses were experienced. Not only were the borders sealed against further illegal immigrants, but over the objections of Southern California employers, who, as usual, benefited from cheap Mexican labor, the federal government began deporting "indigent aliens" in the 1930s.[16] This policy was adopted with alacrity by the Los Angeles County Board of Supervisors, which arranged to pay the Mexican National Railroad a fare of $14.70 per adult and half that for each child to "remove" the offending residents. Mullins reports that more than thirteen thousand were repatriated in this manner between 1931 and 1934 (most in 1931 and 1932), but this figure takes into account only those actually placed on trains by the government.[17] Mullins's figures are undoubtedly an underestimate, and his interpretation much too benign.

Armando Morales prefers the term *deportation,* and places it within the larger framework of long-standing hostilities toward Mexicans/Mexican Americans:

> A little over 80,000 Mexicans were rounded up with their household effects, domestic animals, and personal belongings, loaded into railroad cars, and shipped back to Mexico, taking with them their children, many of whom were born in the United States and were therefore U.S. citizens. . . . Only a few years earlier many of those now rejected had been actively recruited by American enterprises. [The grounds for deportation were on the new American law that permitted excluding those] "likely to become a public charge." . . .
>
> . . . The magnitude of the exodus (voluntary and involuntary) is illustrated by the decline in the Mexican born population in the United States from 639,000 persons in 1930 to little over 377,000 in 1940. The Mexicans were literally railroaded out of the mainstream of American life.[18]

The best study of Los Angeles's expulsion of Mexicans and Mexican Americans is Abraham Hoffman's *Unwanted Mexican Americans.* Hoffman estimates that some half a million persons of Mexican origin or descent left the United States in the decade between 1929 and 1939, some voluntarily but many victims of systematic if not official expulsions.[19] While this was a national phenomenon, also found in such industrial centers as Chicago and Detroit, "no other locality matched the county of Los Angeles in its . . . efforts to rid itself of the Mexican immigrant during the depression years. . . . On the federal level, no other region in the country received as much attention from immigration officials as Southern California."[20]

Negative press campaigns, designed to foment fears among the victims and to exacerbate the animosities toward them (tactics originally honed in the "Red Scare" at the end of World War I), were systematically employed to supplement by "voluntary flight" the trainloads of expellees organized by the county.[21] The federal government even assisted Los Angeles in "rounding up" suspects.[22] It is generally agreed that about one-third of Los Angeles's Mexican/Mexican-descended population left during the Depression.

The "Bum Blockade"

The hysteria about surplus indigents was not directed exclusively against Mexicans. Californians, recognizing the fact that the state offered somewhat better conditions than other parts of the country but still lacked sufficient relief funds to go around, also feared an "invasion" of their state by fellow Americans. They sought ways to stem internal migration, especially of "Okies" driven from the Dust Bowl. In 1931 "the Los Angeles Chamber of Commerce . . . moved toward what later became known as the 'Bum Blockade.' A committee of the Chamber wanted National Guard troops stationed at the state's border to keep undesirables out."[23] This same fear would be exploited mercilessly when the mass media waged its vicious campaign against Upton Sinclair's 1934 bid for the governorship of California. Images of hordes of "invaders" riding the rails into the state, as well as the very real squatter settlements that were springing up not only on peripheral lands but at the very edges of elegant residential quarters, intensified feelings of threat.

Figure 9.1. A squatter shack in Los Angeles during the Depression. From a series of photographs taken under the auspices of the Works Progress Administration in the 1930s. Reproduced by permission of The Huntington Library.

Suppression of Protests

Despite Los Angeles's reputation as a refuge for retired "gothic" midwesterners being served by an army of real estate agents, by the late 1920s the county also had a sizable working class of industrial workers who were largely concentrated in suburbs south and east of downtown near the industrial districts. Viehe suggests that the success of the elite's campaign for the open shop had long been aided by the dispersal of Los Angeles's industrial districts and by the suburban residences of its workers, which made labor organizing more difficult. These factors "kept both the working class and organized labor divided," thus prolonging the city's "reputation as a conservative bulwark and an open shop town."[24] True as that may be, this did not prevent the unemployed from demonstrating. In March 1930, when the unemployed were holding protest marches all around the country, Los Angeles's unemployed participated.

It was not the passivity of the city's destitute but the city's responses to their actions that distinguished Los Angeles. In many other communities, the authorities reacted to demonstrations with conciliation or co-optation. But in Los Angeles, from the very first, "some one thousand police stood ready to repel the marchers with blackjacks and clubs." Despite this response, protest marches by the unemployed continued into 1931. Indeed, "the jobless took to the streets in Los Angeles more than in

[Seattle, San Francisco and Portland]. . . . Each time, as often as once or twice every month . . . , the police met the marchers and violence was the outcome."[25] The "Red Squad" (Los Angeles's Intelligence Bureau of the Metropolitan Police Division), which had been organized in the 1920s to break unions under the guise of fighting communism, "was active throughout the Hoover years, and . . . became a part of Los Angeles's response to the depression."[26]

By then, some 20 to 30 percent of Los Angeles's workforce was unemployed, and although crops continued to be harvested, prices dropped so low that it hardly paid to market them. As elsewhere, self-help and barter began increasingly to substitute for the market.

> The Angeleno self-helpers gleaned unwanted crops, engaged in clothing manufacture and assorted handicrafts, and helped run the organization. The groups used a barter system that was facilitated by payments in scrip, which happened to be illegal in California and caused problems as some challenged its worth. . . . Some onlookers raised the valid concern that the groups might establish themselves outside the economic framework or become politicized. The latter worry almost materialized when Upton Sinclair successfully sought the self-help groups as part of his End Poverty in California constituency in 1934.[27]

UPTON SINCLAIR AND EPIC

It was into these circumstances that the muckraking author and former socialist Upton Sinclair (1878–1968) charged, proposing a utopian scheme that was quintessentially "California." Sinclair was not a native Californian, having been born in Baltimore and raised in poverty in New York. He attended City College and studied law for a time at Columbia University before switching to literature, all the while supporting himself by publishing jokes and stories in New York newspapers. He became a socialist in his teens, although he resigned from the Socialist Party during World War I because the party opposed U.S. entry into the war. Saved from destitution by the unexpected success of *The Jungle,* he used his profits to found a utopian community in New Jersey (called Helicon Hall) in 1906, but the settlement burned down in early 1907 under suspicious circumstances. By 1914 he had settled in Pasadena, California, with his wealthy second wife; there he started a newsletter and a press to publish his own books.[28]

The Depression set Sinclair on a more activist path, and much to everyone's surprise, he won the nomination of the Democratic Party for governor of California in 1934[29] on the platform of EPIC (End Poverty in California), which proposed putting unemployed workers to work in bankrupt factories, settling unemployed landless farmers on unused farms and prematurely subdivided land, and instituting a barter system to exchange food and manufactured products. This plan drew much from the existing self-help movement and gained its members' enthusiastic support. The EPIC plan was outlined in a book Sinclair prepared for the campaign, modestly titled *I, Governor, and How I Ended Poverty in California* (1933):

> What Sinclair outlined . . . [in this book] was a plan to end poverty by putting the unemployed to work in state-owned industrial colonies supported by bonds of small denomination and by confiscatory taxation of banks, stock shares, high incomes, and inheritances. After Sinclair won the Democratic Primary in August 1934, he changed his formula somewhat to "Immediate EPIC," dropping the idea of confiscatory taxes and obviously trying to appeal to middle and even upper-class voters.[30]

Despite his efforts to tone down his program to placate more conservative voters, his bid for the governorship failed, albeit by a narrow margin.[31] Not only was he unable to gain an endorsement from Roosevelt, he was the victim of one of the first "dirty tricks" media campaigns in American politics—a type that would unfortunately later become all too common.[32] The sordid details are recounted in a very detailed and fascinating book by Greg Mitchell, who claims that Sinclair's defeat was carefully engineered by a coalition of newspaper magnates (especially the publishers of the *Los Angeles Times*), evangelists (including Aimee Semple McPherson), and the heads of Hollywood studios. Newspapers, using themes familiar from the old Red Scare days, pounded away at his "communist" leanings; the evangelists warned followers of his antireligious views; and moviemakers produced faked newsreels (using paid extras) that showed masses of "bums" riding the rails into California to take advantage of Sinclair's promised assistance. It was the "bum blockade" with a vengeance. From the other side, he was also opposed by socialists and communists for "selling out."

Withdrawing from politics, Sinclair licked his wounds, fantasizing success in his 1936 novel *Co-op*.

> The plot of the novel revolves around the growth of the fictional San Sebastian (probably Long Beach) Self-Help Exchange . . . a cooperative organization of the unemployed for the purpose of production and barter. It is begun by several men who at the beginning of the novel live in a "Hooverville." . . . Over eighty characters appear . . . ranging from the poorest unemployed . . . to the richest capitalists. . . . As the story progresses the San Sebastian Self-Help Exchange carefully avoids politics, wins the favor of a number of rich capitalists because of its goal of avoiding the "dole" by making the unemployed productive and self-sustaining, and grows in membership and effectiveness. . . . [The leader of the co-op] travels to Washington where he is finally able to present the co-op's case to Roosevelt, who agrees to consider it.[33]

What he could not achieve in real life he thus fantasized in fiction.

THE GROWTH OF POPULATION AND INDUSTRY DURING THE 1930S

Bad as conditions in California were, they were less disastrous than in the rest of the country. During the Depression, California was the only state that attracted significant numbers of migrants, despite its deportations and "blockades." Between 1930 and 1940, Los Angeles's population rose by almost 600,000 (from 2,318,526 to

2,904,596), with more than 87 percent of that increase due to net migration.[34] The sources of migration were changing, however. Although before the mid-1930s most American migrants had come from the Midwest or, to a lesser extent, the East Coast, after that, three-fourths of the in-migrants were drawn from states west of the Mississippi River; and contrary to stereotype, such newcomers were much more likely to be urbanites than Dust Bowlers. Despite repatriations, the largest proportion of foreign-born residents in 1940 continued to be of Mexican origin, although almost half of the 400,000 foreign-born in the city had actually come from northern European countries.[35]

Also contrary to the national pattern, industrial employment rose sharply in the second half of the 1930s as existing plants expanded and new ones opened.[36] By the mid-1930s, Los Angeles had added a burgeoning aircraft industry to its older mix of oil extraction and movies, positioning it to assume its future role as a "military-scientific-industrial complex."[37]

By the end of the decade,

> Los Angeles County . . . ranked eleventh in wage earners employed and ninth in "value of products" and "value added by manufacture" among the 33 industrial areas of the Nation. There were 5,594 establishments, apart from motion picture production, employing 126,391 average wage earners earning $166,630,467 and turning out products valued at $1,219,433,652. . . . In 1939, Los Angeles City was the third largest in the Nation in volume of retail sales.[38]

This progress, coupled with the decline in older places, meant that by 1939 Los Angeles County not only remained the first-ranking county in the country in agricultural wealth and income, but stood first in the production of airplanes and motion pictures, second in auto assembling and rubber tires and tubes, third in furniture production and retail trade, fourth in women's apparel, and fifth in overall value of industrial production.[39] And of course because it remained first in motion picture production, it had enticed a number of New York writers into Hollywood, where several promptly succumbed to malaise at the Garden of Allah apartments.

THE TRUE URBAN GROWTH MACHINE: WARTIME IS L.A.'S TIME

Such progress, however, would be dwarfed in comparison to the boom unleashed by U.S. involvement in war production, even before the nation's official entry as a belligerent. Ann Markusen and her coauthors use the term *gunbelt* (a marvelous play on *sun belt* and *rust belt*) with good reason. Whereas the Midwest benefited somewhat from orders for tanks, trucks, and ordnance, and the East Coast ports received orders for ships and some aircraft, most of the contracts for planes, ships, and, later, even military bases were awarded to West Coast sites,[40] a preference that continued even after Japan's defeat, given that subsequent "hot" wars (the Korean and then the Vietnam conflicts) were fought exclusively in the Pacific arena. As a result, whereas the centers of New York, Chicago, Charleston, and Boston all lost population between 1940 and 1960, Los Angeles's population nearly doubled.[41]

Figure 9.2. The earliest industry of Los Angeles: oil wells in residential front yards. Reproduced by permission of The Huntington Library.

> With its giant aircraft industry, its harbor facilities, its petroleum industry, and its great resources of relatively cheap water and power, the Los Angeles area was equipped to produce a staggering amount of war material. . . . The war brought great expansion of manufacturing, chiefly in industries producing ships and planes, rubber products, nonferrous metals and their products, machinery, chemical and allied products. *More than 1,000 plants expanded, while 479 new plants were built in the years 1942, 1943, and 1944.*[42]

Noteworthy among the newer industries were those producing iron and steel, especially the Bethlehem Steel plant and the Kaiser Works at Fontana, where large-scale production began in 1942. A report on the iron and steel industry in Los Angeles County estimated that the county's steel consumption was more than two million tons by 1942, more and more of which could be locally produced.[43] The report therefore predicted a glowing future for the industry in Southern California.[44]

Table 9.2 shows the value of war supplies and facilities contracts awarded to the Los Angeles industrial area between 1942 and 1945. It is no wonder that the city's economy boomed and that its demand for labor was answered with alacrity by persons from less prosperous parts of the country.[45] Sometimes there was a chain migration that led to the transposing of whole communities, as this anecdote illustrates:

Figure 9.3. The movies: "Girlies" as Los Angeles's leading industry? Reproduced by permission of The Huntington Library.

> Back in 1936, two brothers . . . left Malvern, Arkansas, to work in a West Coast lumber mill. . . . When the defense program got underway, the . . . [brothers] got jobs in a Southern California shipyard. . . . they wrote letters back home to Malvern. . . . Soon a great exodus of Malvernites to Southern California was under way. By midsummer 1944 almost the entire town of Malvern had moved to Long Beach, San Pedro, and Wilmington to work in the shipyards.[46]

WARFARE AT HOME: RISING ETHNIC TENSIONS

African Americans

Economic demand also drew minorities to the city. In 1930, fewer than 39,000 African Americans lived in the city of Los Angeles, where they accounted for only about 3 percent of the total population; they were then outnumbered by Mexicans, Japanese, and other "races," who, combined, totaled some 125,500, or more than 10 percent of the total.[47] By 1940, the city's African American population had risen gradually to about 65,000, but after that, the rise was sudden and clearly related to wartime inducements. By 1944, there were close to 119,000 blacks residing in the city; by 1945–1946, more than 133,000; and the 1950 census reported some 171,200 black residents in the city.[48]

Figure 9.4. Mixing architecture and industry: the art deco headquarters of a tire manufacturer. Reproduced by permission of The Huntington Library.

The proportion of all blacks who lived in Los Angeles County outside the city limits rose from 16 to 21 percent between 1930 and 1950, but this was probably due more to specific concentrations in nearby independent towns than to either dispersal or desegregation.[49] It was during the 1940s that Watts changed from a largely white area to predominantly black, accepting the overflow of population from the adjacent, and by then severely overcrowded, ghetto on Central Avenue.

> For a vast majority of Blacks, settling in the Los Angeles area was tantamount to residing in Watts. Blacks who came to Watts during the 1940's did so in search of more permanent and better paying employment opportunities. Yet the newly arrived immigrants [*sic*] were unable in most cases to break the poverty cycle. . . . The war . . . influenced nearly 95% of the decision to move into the Watts area. Yet the employment offered by the defense plants was seasonal, low paying, and during the war costly because it was located some distance from Watts.[50]

And when the war ended, many black workers were let go. Social conditions in the now expanding ghettos of South-Central and Watts deteriorated, as racially restrictive covenants continued to hem in and isolate these burgeoning slums, even as their populations continued to rise. Trouble was brewing.

Table 9.2. Value of war contracts for Los Angeles area, 1942–45

Date	War production and facilities	War supply contracts	War facilities
June 1942	3,183,446,000	2,906,053,000	277,393,000
September/October 1943	8,502,479,000	8,110,876,000	391,603,000
October/November 1943	8,472,707,000	8,077,782,000	394,925,000
January 1944	8,581,003,000	8,167,122,000	328,753,000
March/April 1944	10,072,565,000	9,511,527,000	452,111,000
November 1944	10,407,146,000	9,984,434,000	422,712,000
January 1945	10,558,878,000	10,076,844,000	482,034,000

Source: Compiled from data in Frank L. Kidner and Philip Neff, *An Economic Survey of the Los Angeles Area: Statistical Appendix* (Los Angeles: Haynes Foundation, 1945), 586, Appendix XIII.

The "Mexican" Minority

To some extent, the newer unskilled African American migrants from the rural South were in competition for jobs with Mexican immigrants (who had begun to enter Los Angeles for the same war-related reasons) and with more established Mexican Americans, whose chief bases were in the enlarging "barrios" east of the Los Angeles River.[51] A solid base of this community had survived the deportations of the 1930s, and in the 1940s the survivors were joined not only by newcomers seeking war-industry jobs (many working in the shipyards of Long Beach), but by agricultural laborers actively recruited by growers who were short of hands to harvest their crops.[52]

It is remarkably difficult to obtain accurate figures on the growth of Los Angeles's population of Mexican origin or descent. Even Sanchez, in his definitive *Becoming Mexican American,* despairs of presenting a systematic time series, not only because of the changing categories employed by the Bureau of the Census, but because, of all immigrant groups, Mexicans were the most likely to be undercounted. I have thus far been unable to find any reliable estimate of the size of the Mexican American community during or immediately after the war. Nevertheless, by 1950 persons of Mexican descent in the County of Los Angeles were estimated at close to three hundred thousand (less than 7 percent of the total), and the 1960 estimates show about twice that number. Growth therefore took place, despite the mounting prejudice the members of this community experienced.

Regardless of the exact numbers, the presence of visually distinctive Mexican Americans in Los Angeles did trigger some bizarre reactions from sailors stationed in the city or enjoying shore leaves there—reactions that did little to decrease tensions or to mollify what both Skerry and Sanchez call "ambivalence."[53] In ten days of June 1943, after a series of preliminary scuffles, some two hundred rampaging sailors

> from the Los Angeles Ravine Armory set out in taxis to "punish" Mexican zoot suiters. According to Time Magazine, "The LAPD practice was to accompany the caravans [of taxis carrying the sailors] in police cars, watch the beatings, and jail the victims. Their orders were to let the Shore Patrol and Military Police handle

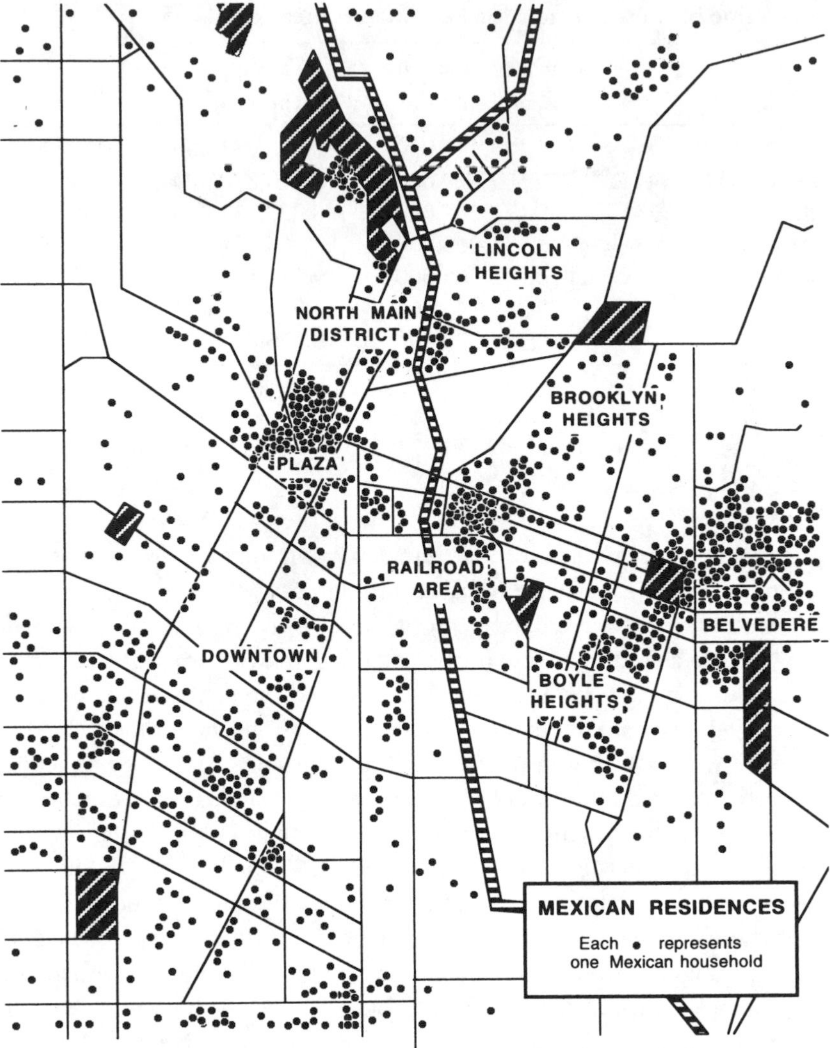

Map 9.1. Map of major areas of Mexican settlement in Los Angeles, 1920–40. Source: George Sanchez, *Becoming Mexican American;* used with permission from Oxford University Press.

> the rioting sailors." During the weekend riots, Mexican American boys were dragged from theaters, stripped of their clothing, beaten and left naked on the streets. . . . A protest from the Mexican government to the United States government finally resulted in the establishment of military control and the end of the riots.[54]

All this further widened the gap between Mexican Americans and the system of local law enforcement, which they had long viewed as discriminatory.[55] These resentments would resurface in later years.

The Japanese Minority

Difficult as conditions may have been for blacks and Chicanos during the war, they were easy in comparison to the fate of the Japanese minority. On February 19, 1942, less than three months after Pearl Harbor, an executive order was signed by President Roosevelt authorizing "the Secretary of War . . . to prescribe . . . military areas . . . from which any or all persons may be excluded."[56] Who would have thought that *all* of Los Angeles County would be included among those "military areas" and that some 40,000 residents of Japanese origin or descent would be unceremoniously "removed" from that extensive area?

But by spring whole colonies of first-, second-, and even third-generation Japanese were being rounded up and "evacuated" under the suspicious eyes and fixed bayonets of the army. By fall, more than 110,000 persons had been placed in ten concentration camps, where they were kept until 1945.[57] When internees were finally allowed to "return home," they found that their homes had been occupied by others and their farms, businesses, and private possessions had been stripped bare.[58] It is ironic that fifty years later, Japanese Americans have been redefined as members of the Asian "model minority" and that Los Angeles's economy is now heavily dependent upon Japanese trade and investments, even though Japanese immigration to the area has virtually stopped.

COPING WITH GROWTH: THE POSTWAR DOMINANCE OF LOS ANGELES

As early as 1939, two economists had predicted that opportunities for foreign commerce would increasingly integrate the five-county region's economy with the Pacific Rim, and that greater regional self-sufficiency would make it the powerhouse of the Southwest.[59] Carey McWilliams, writing a decade later, noted that California, with ten million residents "today" and possibly twenty million "tomorrow," was not just another state, but was "a revolution within the states . . . tipping the scales of the nation's interest and wealth and population to the West, toward the Pacific," and with that tipping, "California's influence in the electoral college and in the national political conventions . . . will be substantially increased."[60] We return to these points in Part IV when we examine how this shift commensurately reduced the power of New York and Chicago.

Economic Expansion and Dispersal

A perceptive remark by Mel Scott sums up the changing nature of Los Angeles's functions in the national and international economy in the postwar era: "Before the war the Los Angeles area produced largely for local and western consumption. By the time peacetime conditions prevailed it was a large producer of durable goods and heavy machinery, the market for which is national and international."[61] Indeed, when production was gearing down in other centers, Los Angeles's industrial growth boomed, especially in the county zones beyond the city limits.[62]

> In fast-growing cities like Los Angeles, fingers of manufacturing crept out for thirty and forty miles from the old central core. . . . As the metropolis became a major national manufacturing region, freeways paralleled the old rail network, and industry stretched farther and farther. . . .
>
> The benefits accruing from the changing patterns of work locations were obvious and substantial. With the improvement of metropolitan highways, immense tracts of industrial and residential land opened for use and the cost of urban sites fell. . . .
>
> this freedom from spatial restrictions offered an unprecedented array of urban arrangements for all degrees of population density. . . .
>
> The principal drawback . . . lay in its entrance fee: private ownership of a car.[63]

A comparison between the locations of industrial plants in metropolitan Los Angeles in 1924 and in 1960 demonstrates more dramatically than words the extent of this industrial decentralization (see Maps 9.2a and 9.2b).

Aerospace and Decentralization

Leading the way to such dispersal were the air and missile industries, which benefited from continued government investments, for the "hot war" was soon supplanted by the "Cold War," and then the air-power-based Korean and Vietnam conflicts. It is perhaps a misnomer, then, to call the 1950s and 1960s in Southern California a "postwar" era. Markusen et al. divide the development of the aircraft and related industries in the Los Angeles area into four or five overlapping histories: the "age of the founding fathers" between 1905 and 1935; the age of the "rocket scientists and the generals" (1925–46), which included assembly-line production during the war (1941–45); "from aircraft to aerospace, 1946–1960"; and the high-tech present, beginning in the Cold War of the mid-1950s, "which marked the real birth of the military-industrial complex."[64]

Each of these phases had a particular "spatial fix" that not only reflected but sometimes led the dispersal of industry in the metropolitan region. In the first phase, Los Angeles was only one of several areas in the country that pioneered the new field, and plants were still located near the city (albeit in somewhat distant suburbs such as Santa Monica and Burbank). By the time of the Second World War, Southern California, with four out of the top five aircraft producers (three of them in Los Angeles County), had become the leader in the industry.[65]

It was in the 1950s, however, when war-related production in planes and then missiles intensified, that shortages of space near the L.A. International Airport led to expansion in the southeast periphery. By the 1960s, "Orange County [which had previously housed only a few plants] developed through spin-offs and subcontracting into an industrial complex of small firms, characterized by dependence on a common labor pool and infrastructural services," to become one of the country's most important high-tech manufacturing centers.[66]

PREREQUISITES OF GROWTH AND DECENTRALIZATION

As before, transportation and housing played essential and interlinked roles in shaping the postwar metropolitan region. We have already seen how, even before the war, Los Angeles was a far more decentralized city than New York or even Chicago. Its low density was attributable to its dependence upon the single-family home. "Unlike any other major city at the time, more than half of its residents lived in single-family dwellings. Its nearest rival among the three other largest American metropolises was Chicago with 15.9 percent of its population residing in detached houses."[67]

Despite this low density and the expansion of its suburbs, commercial and governmental uses in Los Angeles remained distinctly centralized, with most commuting still taking place between the suburbs and the center city. Getting to the center, however, was taking longer and longer. Before 1930, one could travel by mass transit to downtown from Santa Monica in half an hour; ten years later, "the same trip required an hour by rail and forty minutes by car."[68] After the war, the mass-transit system was cut back considerably, and downtown underwent a significant decline as commercial facilities followed housing to more outlying centers.[69] Factories had been even less well served by mass transit than downtown, and by the late 1930s most factory workers were already driving to reach their more decentralized places of employment.[70] An accommodation to the burgeoning number of automobiles was urgent.

The Freeways

As might have been anticipated, it was the Automobile Club of Southern California that again led the campaign for improved highways.[71] As early as 1937, that organization's planning team proposed an ambitious network of limited-access routes. The layout the team devised would later serve as the armature for Los Angeles's current freeway system. Somewhat ironically, these proposals were supported by downtown business interests, who hoped that the new roads would facilitate travel *to* the center; they apparently failed to recognize that roads run in two directions, and what could bring people to the center could also encourage them to move farther away.

Planning and executing the scheme were complicated, however, by the diffuse political structure of the region. Not only did the city planning commission and the city council have to approve the plan (which they finally did by 1941), but coordination required agreement from all other governing bodies of the metropolitan region as well. The plan received the immediate imprimatur of the Los Angeles Regional Planning Commission and the County Board of Supervisors, but by the time everyone else had reviewed the proposal, the plans had to be shelved because World War II had broken out. By the time of the war, only a short stretch of Arroyo Seco had been built. And even when peace came, despite wide official support, construction was delayed because no one had yet figured out how to finance this costly venture.[72]

After hostilities ended, the private automobile reigned supreme. Mass transit via rail gave way completely to highway building. The Pacific Electric was delighted in 1953 to unload its passenger service to a bus company, Metropolitan Coach Lines,

Maps 9.2a and 9.2b. Locations of industrial plants in metropolitan Los Angeles in 1924 and in 1960. Sources: Scott Bottles, *Los Angeles and the Automobile;* used with permission of the University of California Press. Original source of maps is Dudley Pegrum, *Urban Transport and the Location of Industry in Metropolitan Los Angeles* (Los Angeles: Bureau of Business and Economic Research, University of California, Los Angeles, 1963).

which ran the rail service at a loss for the next five years, until it managed to sell out to the state-owned Metropolitan Transit Authority. The latter terminated all rail service in 1961.[73] Only recently has the old transportation plan of 1924 resurfaced—this time with a subway scheme whose construction has suffered disaster after disaster and may never be completed.

The construction of the freeways served more than transportation functions. Freeways not only benefit car owners at the expense of the poor, who still depended on the disappearing mass transit, but their construction frequently required the clearance of poor people's housing.[74] Furthermore, the location of the freeways often gave spatial definition, in massive *concrete* form, to the social barriers of class and race that had, up to 1948, been maintained largely through "legal" instruments. Thus Watts and South-Central, which had formerly been well served by street railways, became more isolated from downtown and industrial districts by a disappearance of that system, and these increasingly black districts were both surrounded by and separated from one another by the construction of the wide and forbidding Harbor Freeway. What had once been corridors of connection were thus transformed into walls of separation.

Building the Residences

Just as the highway system that was put into place in the postwar period had been conceived and planned before the war, so the mechanisms and institutions for large-scale community developments were in the works before construction was interrupted by the war. One of the ways that the federal government became more involved in housing finance was through legislation passed by Congress in 1934, which established the Federal Housing Administration (FHA). To stimulate growth in the moribund housing market, the FHA was authorized to insure certain highly attractive low-cost mortgage loans extended by private banks.[75] But in return, borrowers and builders were required to follow detailed guidelines specified in the FHA's *Underwriting Manual.*

Although rental housing in inner cities was theoretically eligible for FHA-insured loans, in fact the guidelines favored single-family housing in the suburbs and even proscribed offering loan insurance in minority or racially-mixed inner-city neighborhoods.[76] Los Angeles offered a most attractive setting for such preferences. In 1940, for example, a not untypical year, California garnered more than "twice the volume of insured mortgages than any other state: 83 percent of these mortgages were on newly-constructed single-family houses."[77]

The system not only gave preference to houses in new neighborhoods, but actually assumed the risks for builders of new large-scale residential subdivisions by making available "conditional commitments" for loans based not on the costs of construction, but on the "projected appraised value of the completed houses and lots."[78] These mechanisms, which had been strongly supported and, indeed, even designed by the

Map 9.3. The freeway plan of the Automobile Club of Southern California. Source: Automobile Club of Southern California, *Traffic Survey, Los Angeles Metropolitan Area, 1937,* as reprinted in Scott Bottles, *Los Angeles and the Automobile;* used with permission of the University of California Press.

real estate lobby, were already in place when construction (except for federally funded housing for defense workers in isolated places) shut down during the war. They were thus available in the postwar period when pent-up demand unleashed a period of frenzied suburban construction.

Park Forest, south of Chicago (1947), and Levittown, on Long Island (1949), are perhaps the best-known examples, but these efforts paled in comparison to developments in and around Los Angeles. In that area, the

> biggest operator by far was Louis H. Boyer, who had started as a developer in 1939 with $700 in borrowed capital. Through FHA guarantees he secured huge loans covering most of the development costs, and then built enormous tracts with comparatively little personal investment. His greatest promotion was Lakewood Park, which he launched by purchasing 3,375 acres of farm land . . . in 1950.

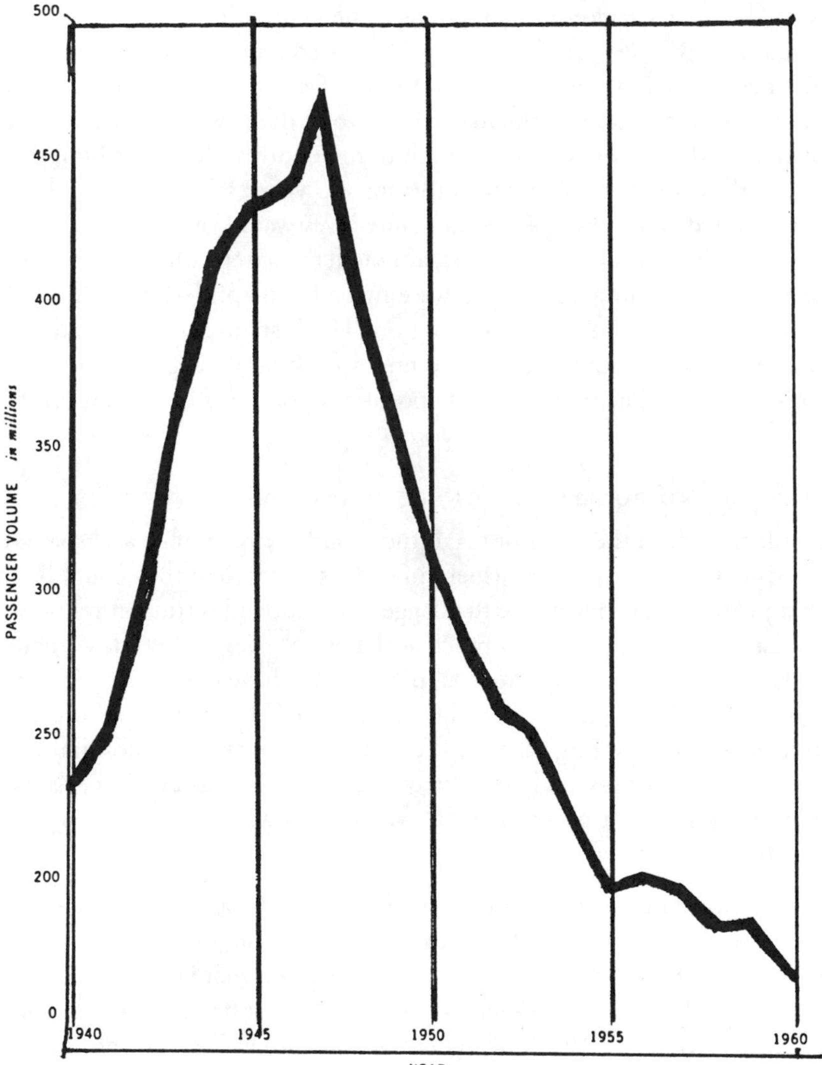

Figure 9.5. The decline in mass-transit public transportation between 1940 and 1960. Source: Los Angeles Metropolitan Transit Authority.

> Here, with the help of professional city planners, he laid out a community of 17,000 homes for a population of 70,000—the biggest single-ownership development in the nation and twice as big as the famed Levittown of Long Island, New York.[79]

It was chiefly in the vast space of the San Fernando Valley, which as late as 1944 was mostly agricultural (containing a population of only 170,000 in an expanse as big as Chicago), that the new crop of housing mushroomed. Construction began in earnest by 1946, and in the next decade and a half the valley's population grew to some 850,000. But the open spaces between earlier settlements also filled in, until much of the county became a region of contiguous settlement, with spillovers into adjacent counties as well. By 1960, the city of Los Angeles contained a population of close to 2.5 million.[80] The county had grown at an even faster rate, with some 3.56 million living in the towns and unincorporated areas beyond the city limits by that year.

Such growth was the composite result of three forces: the "baby boom" that was experienced throughout the country in the postwar years; selective internal migration within the United States as population decanted westward;[81] and renewed foreign immigration, chiefly from Mexico and Asia, although the latter would not soar until drastic changes in U.S. immigration laws were made in the mid-1960s. But something beyond mere "decentralization" was going on. The instant cities that had previously bloomed mostly within the county were now sprouting throughout the five-county metropolitan region. The sixty-mile city (postmetropolis) was becoming a reality.

THE SPATIAL AND POLITICAL CONSEQUENCES OF GROWTH

Such a sudden shift in the order of magnitude (both demographic and spatial) of the region had serious consequences, generating needs faster than they could be met, requiring adjustments in governance that lagged behind, and setting in motion a chain reaction that affected the centers as much as the peripheries. Carey McWilliams, writing in 1949, noted that "thirty times as many people have come to California in the past eight years as came during the gold-rush decade,"[82] and that, perforce, many of them settled in zones lacking schools, fire and police protection, hospitals, libraries, adequate water and sewers, and even direct telephone lines to Los Angeles. Not only did amenities lag, but a governmental structure capable of coping did not exist. McWilliams complained:

> The state constitution is a monstrous patchwork of 340 pages. . . . And the present charter of the city of Los Angeles, adopted only twenty years ago, is today almost as obsolete as the state constitution. . . . The county of Los Angeles . . . is a governmental monstrosity. Within the county are forty-five independent municipal governments. . . . Within the county 500,000 people live in unincorporated areas. . . . Within the city of Los Angeles are dozens of "conscious provinces," such as Hollywood and Eagle Rock, which continue to think of themselves as separate municipalities. . . . for the past fifteen years the city has shown the incompetence of an idiot giant . . . bungling . . . such problems as traffic, transportation, spoiling of its beaches, the sewage, smog, and related items.[83]

Inadequacies in newly constructed areas were more than matched by deterioration in already built-up zones near the center. As had happened elsewhere, whole inner neighborhoods underwent population succession, as better-off whites left for the periphery, where, aided and abetted by deed restrictions, minimum lot size zoning, and racially restrictive covenants (and more informal mechanisms, once the latter were deemed unenforceable), they threw up barriers to "undesirables." Blacks (and some poorer whites with few options) remained largely in South-Central and Watts, and the growing Hispanic population inherited much of the inlying territory east of downtown, as Jews and Italians who had previously predominated there left for greener pastures.

Segregation by race and ethnicity intensified between 1960 and 1970, as the careful analysis of Massey and Mullan demonstrates.[84] But by the latter year, Hispanics had begun to move into zones such as Watts and South-Central, which had hitherto been almost exclusively black. Segregation by race and class increased the probabilities that amenities, when they were expanded, would be invidiously distributed. Even Sam Bass Warner, an otherwise uncritical admirer of the city, reluctantly acknowledges, in a mild understatement, that

> like all American cities, the Los Angeles automobile metropolis does not extend its amenities equally to all its residents but reinforces sharp differences governed by class and race. . . .
>
> Los Angeles is no better than most cities when it comes to racial discrimination, segregation, and disadvantages for its poor. The county population is 10.8 percent black, 13.5 percent of Spanish surname. *The isolation of blacks is almost as extreme as in Chicago. The Mexican Americans are less rigidly segregated . . . than the blacks, but nonetheless they are highly segregated.*[85]

Despite the growth of the black population during the war, by 1950 African Americans still constituted only 5.5 percent of the city's population and less than that of the county's (a proportion only half of what their representation would reach in 1970 at its peak), but they were then the poorest community in the city.[86] As suburban construction opened new areas for whites, the defense line along Slauson Avenue collapsed,[87] and by 1960 the three largest black neighborhoods—Central Avenue–Furlong Tract, Watts, and West Jefferson—had coalesced. Writing in 1976, Nelson and Clark described Los Angeles's "black belt" as

> a massive segregated area, stretching from the southern part of downtown Los Angeles southward more than a dozen miles, and reaching from three to seven miles westward. . . .
>
> As is to be expected in an area of *nearly forty square miles,* much variety is present in the main ghetto of south central Los Angeles, and even its older and meaner areas do not have the appearance of slums in the usual sense. . . . there are no tenements, two-thirds of the dwellings are single family houses . . . , and even the public housing development consists of one or two story stucco buildings. West of the [Harbor] freeway much of the area is distinctly middle class, and on its northwestern edge in the Baldwin Hills takes in some fine homes, often with swimming pools.[88]

Prescription for Rebellions

Single-family houses and swimming pools notwithstanding, conditions in parts of this forty-square-mile tract were appalling. The fact is that poverty does not always show the same face in different settings, but, as housing critic Charles Abrams (a New

Yorker) put it in 1950, there were already "rats among the palm trees" in Los Angeles. The rats had literally made their nests in stately palms in fine neighborhoods, but after steel plates were installed to block them, they took refuge in slum areas. With characteristic sarcasm, Abrams continues:

> Did I say slums? Los Angeles has no slums—to speak of. . . . Every year tons of copy go out from this county seat of make-believe—never a word about slums. . . . But behind the palm trees are grim four-story wooden structures affording a miserable shelter to tens of thousands of families. One in every six of Los Angeles' city buildings is substandard, according to the last census. . . . In one wooden tenement I saw a single hot-water faucet servicing some seventy-two families, a condition outlawed in New York City fifty years ago.

Abrams notes that slums were not only confined to these central areas, however. They could also be found "hidden on the hills, along side roads, or behind store fronts. Shacks made out of old crates and little garages on back alleys house thousands of recent immigrants."[89]

Furthermore, land clearance for urban redevelopment and the freeways was cutting into the zones available for minority residence and, unlike New York or even Chicago, both of which had made efforts to replace some slum housing with subsidized public housing projects, Los Angeles had done virtually nothing to avail itself of federal aid in this area. Although the city housing authority did construct some public housing for minorities (exclusively in black areas), at the time Abrams was writing the Los Angeles County Board of Supervisors had just turned down an offer of $300,000 from the federal government for public housing. Abrams attributed this to pressure from California's powerful real estate lobby, which had also just engineered the defeat of state-aided housing in a statewide referendum. In short, Abrams concluded that not only did Los Angeles not admit that it had slums, but real estate interests blocked public housing because it feared racial integration.

The best account of the political controversies over public housing and urban redevelopment in Los Angeles is given by Donald Parson, who quickly disabuses us of the notion that the city had no "slum problem."[90] In Los Angeles during the Depression "there were tracts of housing either underoccupied or vacant (due to unaffordable rents), severe overcrowding in other districts, such as Watts, and cardboard shantytowns or 'Hoovervilles' in the dry bed of the Los Angeles River." And in "Los Angeles County, 30% of all dwellings had no inside toilet, 50% had no bathtub, while 20% were considered unfit for human habitation."[91] As in New York and Chicago, poor tenants organized to resist evictions, and "home guards" and "huskies" from the self-help movement moved evicted families back in and reconnected utilities.[92]

Despite such poor conditions, Los Angeles took no initiative to provide subsidized housing until several years after the 1937 Wagner Act was passed. Although enabling legislation was passed quickly in other states, California's Republican governor vetoed such legislation three times before it passed. When the newly established Housing Authority of the City of Los Angeles (HALA) published the results of its housing survey in 1940, the study revealed that almost one-fourth of the more than

250,000 dwellings examined were substandard, establishing a clear need. "The first public housing project in Los Angeles, Ramona Gardens, was under construction by March, 1939, followed by nine more projects, 3468 units, within a two year period."[93] But then the war started and housing for war workers, under the Lanham Act, took priority. "By the end of 1943, 27,000 people were living in both Wagner Act and Lanham Act projects managed by the HALA."[94] But these projects did little to relieve the housing shortages in minority areas or to further racial integration. Following accepted federal practice, the projects were either all white or all black, and black demand far outstripped white.[95]

After the war ended, California, in contrast to its reluctant participation in public housing, led the way in using public powers to assist private redevelopers, thus anticipating the federal Housing Act of 1949. In 1945, the state legislature passed the California Community Redevelopment Act, which allowed local governments to set up redevelopment agencies to clear slums for private investors. In response,

> the city of Los Angeles formed the Community Redevelopment Agency (CRA) in 1947 and, under the auspices of the CRA, the City Planning Commission undertook a survey of 70 square miles of the inner city, discovering that a great deal of Los Angeles was indeed "blighted" and (therefore) ripe for redevelopment. The survey . . . reported that slums or blighted areas comprised 20% of the metropolitan area, embraced 33% of the population, and accounted for 45% of the city's service costs while contributing only 6% of the tax revenues.[96]

One would have thought that improved housing would therefore have received special attention, but it did not. Instead, the act marked the start of an assault on "inner-city" areas with minority occupancy. Not only did the city cease to build public housing by 1952 and 1953, but it accelerated the bulldozing of existing poor neighborhoods. While similar reorientations occurred in other cities, the Los Angeles case was both more extreme and more transparent in its internal politics—politics in which minorities and labor were significantly underrepresented in a progrowth coalition that appealed to Cold War anticommunist sentiments. Indeed, Parson had selected Los Angeles as his case study

> because it was the site of a large and intense McCarthyistic "red scare" that was employed against the public housing program during 1952 and 1953. This red scare not only destroyed the national and the local public housing program but was also a very important point in the negation of party politics and the subsequent rise of movement politics for the working class. Los Angeles' large-scale urban renewal program helped consolidate the Democratic pro-growth coalition in the city in the late-1950s and early-1960s and, in so doing, accelerated the ghettoization of minorities and provided one basis for the "commodity riots" in Watts and on the Chicano Eastside.[97]

In Parson's dissertation he describes these developments in detail, concluding that in Los Angeles, anticommunism and antiblack sentiments combined to undermine support for public housing—as both dangerously "socialist" and "integrationist."[98] In any event, Los Angeles built its last "pure" public housing project in 1955,[99] although relocation housing was reinstituted in the 1960s—albeit only in the context of urban renewal, with very different goals. According to Parson:

> By the early-1960s, urban renewal plans for Los Angeles were extensive, visionary, and blatantly racist. Watts, Little Tokyo, Temple-Beaufry, Lincoln Heights, Thomas Jefferson (the ghetto surrounding the private University of Southern California), Pacoima, etc. either had redevelopment work underway or were designated as study areas by the Community Redevelopment Agency (CRA). All were primarily residential minority ghettos or *barrios.* Eastside activists dubbed the CRA the "Chicano Removal Agency."[100]

Two urban renewal projects were especially controversial: the clearing of Bunker Hill for a massive government/cultural center zone and the clearing of a poor Chicano neighborhood in Chavez Ravine to create the new stadium for the Los Angeles Dodgers.[101] Before 1954, cities had been required to replace with housing slums cleared through subsidized land write-downs, but after that, other uses were permitted. In Los Angeles, once public housing had been defeated, urban renewal was used "to replace low-income housing with corporate offices, cultural complexes, luxury housing, and shopping centers."[102]

Bunker Hill, once the most fashionable part of downtown, stood in the way of the CBD's expansion. Despite a neighborhood coalition against the project, by 1961 the CRA was acquiring the site. A suit filed with the Supreme Court of California (*CRA v. Henry Goldman*) was rejected as not within its jurisdiction, and "corporate headquarters, luxury condominiums, fashionable shops, and prestigious office space began to appear on the Hill."[103] The "reuse" of Chavez Ravine was an even more egregious violation of public purpose. Originally, this relatively open and semirural Chicano area north of downtown was slated for public housing, but after this program effectively ended, the CHA sold the site to the city "with the provision that the land be put to 'public use.' Between 1953 and 1959 Chavez Ravine residents remained in their houses, uncertain as to their future."[104] But to entice the Dodgers to relocate to Los Angeles, urban renewal laws were used to offer the land free for the construction of a stadium to house the new team. "After losing their final lawsuit, the residents of Chavez Ravine were, on March 9, 1959, given notices to vacate within 30 days." Those who resisted the bulldozers that demolished their homes after that were arrested, which triggered a militancy that foreshadowed later forms of resistance.[105]

Even though urban renewal had harmed Chicanos more than blacks, the latter were the first to respond to the widening gap between aspirations nurtured in the civil rights movement and the declining position of minorities in the economic and political power structure of the city. And while the Watts riot of 1965 was not the very first in the series of urban rebellions that would wrack the country in the second half of the 1960s, it was both one of the worst and, given the somewhat more favorable conditions of the black community in Los Angeles, at least in comparison to those in Chicago or even New York, one of the least expected.

The 1965 Watts Riot

On December 2, 1965, the Governor's Commission on the Los Angeles Riots issued a final report on the six days of civil disorder that had occurred in Watts and surrounding areas between August 11 and August 17 of that year. The title of the commission's brief summary volume (sometimes referred to as the McCone Report) was *Violence in the City: An End or a Beginning?* which proved more prophetic than its authors intended.[106] While neither the beginning of black protests (Harlem/Bedford-Stuyvesant had initiated that series in the previous summer) nor the last (since protests would break out in hundreds of cities before reaching temporary exhaustion in 1970), for Los Angeles it was both a beginning and an end—at least until history repeated itself a generation later in April 1992.

White Angelenos were "stunned" by the "explosion," and even after the events, the distinguished authors of the report seemed at a real loss to account for the rage that had resulted in close to four thousand arrests and forty million dollars' worth of damage.[107] Giving evidence for Charles Abrams's earlier accusation, they denied that "Negro districts of Los Angeles" were slums. And although they acknowledged high unemployment rates and poor schools, they essentially blamed the riot on federal poverty programs that had failed to "live up to their press notices"; "almost daily exhortations, here and elsewhere, to take the most extreme and even illegal remedies to right *a variety of wrongs, real and supposed*"; and in a moment of rare insight, acknowledged that "many Negroes here *felt and were encouraged to feel that they were affronted by the passage of Proposition 14*—an initiative measure passed by two-thirds of the voters in November 1964 *which repealed the Rumford Fair Housing Act* . . . [and thus] will bar any attempt by state or local governments to enact similar laws."[108] Dismissing these "real and supposed" grievances, the authors blamed the riot on the backwardness of southern migrants and their poor education and training, despite the fact that detailed scholarly investigations carried out by a team of UCLA researchers later revealed that participants in the riot were *more likely* to have been born in Los Angeles and to have had *more education* than the docile southern migrants who had tended not to join in.[109]

But the riot itself and the reactions of official Los Angeles tell us a great deal about "race relations" in the city and the role that "space" played in permitting and even encouraging the development of two societies—a concept the Kerner Report would later take as its theme. First, there was the trigger itself, the usual altercation between a white police officer and a black motorist in the "ghetto," which then escalated. Second, there was an attempt by the city police, later supplemented by 13,900 members of the National Guard, to reestablish order by placing 46.5 square miles of territory under curfew, an area larger than the city of San Francisco and one and a half times as large as Manhattan Island.[110] Within this vast zone were assembled more than 80 percent of Los Angeles's black population of 650,000. I cannot go into the details of the riot here, but must point out that it took place within the context of a national civil rights movement and that many in the black community, whether they participated in the riots or not, hoped that the violence would force white Americans to acknowledge long-standing grievances that had been callously ignored.

One of the most fascinating studies made during the post-Watts period, when riot studies became a cottage industry among social scientists in Los Angeles, was a survey of "Negro Attitudes toward the Riot."[111] Refuting the myths that only a tiny segment of the Negro community viewed the riot "favorably," or that most Negroes saw "the riots as purposeless, meaningless, senseless outbursts of criminality" from which no good could come, this survey of a random sample of curfew-zone residents found that only half held somewhat or very unfavorable attitudes toward the riot and only 42 percent expressed strong or moderate disapproval of the participants. Furthermore, many respondents viewed the riot in revolutionary or insurrectional terms, believing that it had a purpose and that it would have favorable effects."[112] These findings were distinctly at odds with the views of white Angelenos,[113] and, unhappily, after a brief flurry of attention, the chief outcome of which was the construction of a modern hospital in the zone,[114] rebuilding efforts ceased and the destroyed zone remained significantly deserted. The black community may have spoken, but its remarks had fallen largely on deaf ears. Not surprisingly, many of the grievances expressed in 1965 would resurface in 1992.[115]

Reverberations in the Mexican Community

At the time of the Watts uprising, Los Angeles contained another minority group with even greater numbers and less economic and political power. By the 1970s metropolitan Los Angeles was home to some 1.7 million persons of "Spanish" heritage, chiefly of Mexican origin; in fact, it was reputed to contain the largest urban concentration of Mexicans in the world outside of Mexico City.[116] And yet this population constituted an anomaly, individually "invisible" but an indispensable "part of a dual lifestyle, in an unseeing city." As Nelson and Clark put it, in this city that thought of itself as "Anglo,"

> the presence of the Mexican-American is ubiquitous . . . "seen" whenever laborers are present. . . . Mexican restaurants are widespread; Mexican food is present in every supermarket; . . . and [these foods] are standard items in every school cafeteria, factory vending machine, or institutional food stand. Twist the dial of a television set or radio and Spanish voices are heard on several stations. A dozen or more theaters show Mexican films, the daily Spanish-language newspaper *La Opinión* circulates widely, and Dodger baseball games are broadcast in Spanish as well as English. . . . Spanish is . . . taught as the second language in schools.[117]

What is remarkable is that this "minority," easily as oppressed as blacks, remained relatively unnoticed, possibly because despite some political organizing, it was, in comparison to Watts, more quiescent in the turbulent 1960s.[118]

But events in 1970, often overlooked when the 1960–70 "riot cycle" is chronicled, reveal that not only did the Mexican American community share in disaffection and complaints against police harassment, but it was sufficiently "Americanized" to be roiled by the same anti–Vietnam War involvement that was triggering widespread white protests.[119] Indeed, in 1970 there were three outbreaks of what Morales has called the "Los Angeles Chicano-Police Riots": on January 1, August 29, and September 16.[120] Morales points out that there were

> more similarities than differences in the prime, explosive mixture components that led to riots in 150 cities . . . in 1967. Comparing the U.S. Riot Commission Report findings and basic causes of the riots with the East Los Angeles situation proved to be a frightening experience. *All that had to be substituted was the word "Mexican American" for "Negro" and "barrio" for "ghetto" in order for the conditions to be identical.*[121]

The direct impact of the Watts riots had been to heighten police precautions against similar "outbursts" in East Los Angeles. In fact, in the wake of the ghetto and antiwar riots of 1968, and "anticipating civil disorders in East Los Angeles, various city, county government and business leaders decided to build a $567,386 riot control center *in* East Los Angeles." A Special Enforcement Bureau was set up, and there "were angry rumors in the Mexican American community that the Special Enforcement Bureau was designed to be used against them."[122]

The first signs of conflict came as part of the 1970 New Year's celebration on Whittier Boulevard, when some hundred persons out of a crowd of five thousand participants smashed windows and looted stores, primarily those owned by "non-Spanish surnamed whites who [did] not live in the Mexican American community."[123] The second event occurred on August 29, when some fifteen to twenty thousand persons joined an East Los Angeles National Chicano Moratorium march "to protest America's involvement in the war in southeast Asia and, simultaneously, to decry the high percentage of Mexican American battle casualties, both wounded and killed in action."[124] Even before the march started, an altercation broke out between the police and the demonstrators, causing many of the marchers to flee.

But the largest battle occurred on September 16. Although Los Angeles's Mexican American community had for almost thirty years celebrated the anniversary of Mexican independence with a parade, because of the August experience the event was almost canceled. But

> a week before the 16th, it was decided, after consultation with the Sheriff's Department, the Mexican consul general and the sponsors to hold the parade with the help of monitors. The sponsors wanted to take the crowd to East Los Angeles College Stadium. . . . But the conservative majority of the [college] board voted 4 to 3 against allowing the Mexican American groups to use the college stadium. . . . [Nevertheless at] 5:15 p.m., the parade began. . . .[The parade headed to Belvedere Park but then bypassed it to head to the college where the crowd gathered in the stadium parking lot.]
>
> By that time, several hundred of the unofficially estimated 150,000 persons who had lined the parade route began to join the more militant elements among the marchers. The first sign of violence came at 7:10 p.m., a few minutes before the parade ended officially. The last marching group, predominantly teen-agers and militant youths, reportedly began throwing rocks and eggs at reserve deputies

> who were riding motorcycles, policing the end of the event. [Additional skirmishes broke out in Monterey Park, at Floral Ave. near the college campus, in Belvedere Park, and the Atlantic Square Shopping Center.]. . . The sound of smashing glass and shots continued for several hours. More than 100 persons were injured and three persons—one a sheriff's deputy—were shot. At least 68 persons were arrested.[125]

Although this event in no way compares to the Watts riot in scale or destruction, two of the underlying motivations were quite parallel: a widespread mistrust of the police and a pessimistic belief that reform could not be achieved through normal political means.[126] To those who knew about the earlier unrest in the barrio, it came as no surprise that in the 1992 riots in South-Central (a district that was by then shared equally by blacks and Hispanics—Chicanos supplemented by Salvadorans and others), Latinos also participated; in fact, more than half of the arrestees were classified as Hispanic.

SPATIAL POLITICS

Up to now I have hinted at the peculiar ways in which Los Angeles's "boundary situation" affected its spatial pattern of expansion, the distribution of its ethnic and racial minorities, the location of industrial establishments, and the mechanisms available for regional planning and governance. It is in this area that parallels between Chicago and New York, on the one hand, and Los Angeles, on the other, break down completely. Whereas New York's consolidation *absorbed* five counties, reducing each county to a mere member of a confederation, and Chicago *expanded* through annexations to absorb almost the entire area of its containing county (Cook), Los Angeles County, even after its boundaries progressively contracted (see Maps 6.1 and 6.2 in Chapter 6) remained much larger than the city, whose boundaries had expanded so haphazardly through annexation. What are the implications of this special situation?

In Chapter 6 I described how resistance to annexation grew in the late 1920s, a resistance that further solidified in the 1930s and 1940s.[127] Finally, with the Lakewood option opened in 1954, making it possible for towns and unincorporated areas outside the city to contract with the county of Los Angeles for municipal services without having to join the city juridically, the last shred of enticement was gone. In addition, the county took over a number of functions previously the responsibility of the city. A rash of petty "deannexations" even occurred, as parts of the city exercised the option to secede.[128]

This underlined what had always been true, namely, that the *county's* government was potentially as important as, if not more important than, the city's. In the United States in general, county governments, which are representative agents of state governments, tend to be strong in rural areas but weak in urban. California has been a conspicuous exception to that rule. In 1912, only one year after the administrative reorganization of the city was achieved, Los Angeles County took advantage of a state option to receive a county home-rule charter.[129] Both units of government vied for taxing powers and decision-making primacy. In fact, however, they were not only somewhat in competition with one another over similar functions, but as suburban developments filled more and more of the territory beyond the city limits, the county had a decided advantage: it became the sole agent for regional planning and development, albeit supplemented by the ubiquitous "special districts" that were proliferating in large metropolitan regions all over the country.[130]

Given the impossibility of separating "city" from "suburb" according to simple spatial criteria (i.e., in terms of inner core and outer periphery), the division of labor between county and city government levels remained ambiguous, and localities could often play one against the other. Nor did the "division of labor" between city and county remain constant over time. This also had its positive side, because as the independent towns and cities proliferated, the county eventually became the only unit capable of rational planning.[131]

Whereas the county (and special districts) therefore played an extraordinary role in managing regionwide services—schools, libraries, recreational facilities—as well as supervising unincorporated (and usually sparsely settled) areas, the multiple local governments with home rule (forty-five in the late 1940s, more than eighty-two today) were free to pass their own zoning ordinances and to use other mechanisms to control entry;[132] hence the "spottiness" of ethnic and class segregation so conspicuous in the Los Angeles region.

But perhaps the most important political feature of both the city and the county of Los Angeles is the very small number of elected representatives at these levels of government: fifteen city council members, each elected from a district as large as a "big city" (with a current average population of 600,000 persons), and only five members of the county board of supervisors (making each member presumably "responsible to" an average of 1.8 million persons).[133] Three other features further undermine the ability of any interest group or locality to negotiate or gain concessions through the political process. The approval of the entire electorate, or at least a goodly proportion of voters, is required to recall an elected official, to initiate consideration of a new law, or to pass a referendum. Because these activities are undertaken "at large," a considerable plurality of active citizens can overrule "special interests," even when those interests raise options that would be valuable to pursue.[134]

To easterners, or even midwesterners, this is indeed a striking phenomenon, and one with significant implications for the degree to which minorities in the city have been able to have a "voice" in determining policy.[135] There is a certain irony here. The Progressive Era reforms, which peaked in Los Angeles in about 1910, were designed to overthrow the despotic control over the city by the Southern Pacific Railroad (run by a local "machine") by substituting members from a more locally based elite. This reform worked fairly well when the ethnic, cultural, and racial composition of the city was primarily Anglo-midwestern and a certain degree of consensual politics was possible and expected. But the result has been to retain this same elite in power, even after consensus had broken down.[136]

THE END? OF AFFLUENCE

In the 1950s and even the opening years of the 1960s, it appeared that Los Angeles's prosperity was sufficient to raise all boats, so government by a technocratic corps executing the wishes of Anglo business interests and home owners seemed a reasonable way to run the city and county. In the immediate postwar period, the U.S. economy still held a virtual monopoly over industrial production, and Los Angeles had gained a disproportionate share of the "good" (high-paying) industries. Even as late as 1960, after Europe had recovered, "Western Europe and North America [still] produced over 70 per cent of gross world output and almost 80 per cent of the world's 'value added in manufacturing.'"[137]

But the world economy was already undergoing changes, due to several basic causes. First, the age of imperialism was coming to an end. Only a handful of "colonies" were still under the control of imperial powers. Second, the resurgence first of Japan and then the Pacific Rim's newly industrializing countries was well under way, thus breaking the West's monopoly in the exchange of expensive industrial goods for cheap raw materials. It was then that American hegemony began to falter. The Bretton Woods Agreement, which had pegged international currencies to the dollar, was abandoned, and books began to appear that ominously discussed the "deindustrialization" of the United States and a "new international division of labor."[138] Something new was clearly going on—a "restructuring of capitalism and the advance in economic internationalisation."[139] Changes in the very processes of production were taking place, variously called "post-Fordism," "flexible production," and even "bringing the Third World back home" or the "empire strikes back."

These are the themes to be explored in Part IV. However, it is important to note that the effects of these changes were felt by poorer people long before they attracted the notice of academicians.[140] The crises that would be felt by city governments in 1973 were already being experienced by the cities' poor and minority populations in the 1960s (hence the "uprisings"). And although "global restructuring" has been dated by many as beginning in about 1973, few macroanalysts seem to notice that this was the year in which the Vietnam War ended (possibly because many of the theorists are European). And despite the continuing demands from the Pentagon, there was at least a partial return to a peacetime economy. The seeds of both internationalization and deindustrialization were nurtured by that defeat,[141] and although it took some time for the trends to catch up with Los Angeles, because its economy was tied so closely to its role as part of the "gunbelt," it, too, was fated to experience difficulties in the years ahead.

PART IV

Restructuring the Global Economy: The Three Cities Today

Restructuring the Global Economy: The Three Cities Today

Analysts are in general agreement that somewhere between the late 1960s and the middle 1970s something dramatic began to happen within the economies of the developed world. These changes had been foreshadowed in the United Kingdom, were mirrored to some extent in other northwestern European countries, and would be reflected somewhat later in Japan and Germany, suggesting that what was occurring in the United States was far from unique.[1]

Although economists have itemized a variety of "causes"—operating at levels from the local to the global—they are far from agreement on how to *weigh* the separate contributions of various factors to the general changes that were showing up at that period, and how to interpret variations from country to country. And almost no one has tried to trace the specific effects of these changes on particular urbanized regions within the United States.[2] One can sympathize with these disagreements and avoidances, given the lack of clarity with which the changes were slowly being revealed.

TECHNODETERMINISM: THE INFORMATION REVOLUTION

Some explanations have emphasized the appearance of a "third industrial revolution," as powerful as the ones that transformed economies in the Western world from the eighteenth century onward, when inanimate energy was harnessed through machinery to totally transform manufacturing processes and to unleash apparently limitless increases in the productivity of labor. These explanations tend to overemphasize the "technological determinism" of the recent change,[3] alleging that computers and the associated information revolution are (or should now be) generating similar spurts in the productivity of labor within the service sector, while at the same time virtually eliminating spatial constraints.[4]

Thus far, however, both the productivity gains and the despatializing effects of what has been inaccurately termed the *postindustrial age* have been less than anticipated. Computers are indeed proving to be powerful record-keeping, management, and even production-guiding devices (the automation predicted a half century earlier), but the fruits of these gains have thus far gone quite narrowly to the top of the American class structure, while at the same time corporations have used the power of computers to "downsize," by displacing some of their white-collar clerical and middle-management workers.[5] There has been considerable despatialization, especially in financial transactions, where volume and velocity have soared,[6] but paradoxically, rather than diffusing power, the control centers for such transactions are becoming even more concentrated in national nodal cities serving international or global functions: the Chicago Mercantile Exchange, the Chicago Board of Trade, and the New York stock markets continue to expand their operations in monetary exchange futures.[7]

On the other hand, thus far there has been only modest disengagement between centralized offices and home workplaces. It is true that by 1993 about twenty-five million persons were already working at home, twice as many as ten years earlier, but most were home workers by choice, that is, independent contractors, freelancers, and entrepreneurs.[8] Theoretically, "virtual" offices linked by computer networks are clearly feasible and have an added attractiveness to companies, which can use them to eliminate or reduce overhead costs (lower rents and even, in some cases, the removal of "employees" from health insurance and other fringe benefits). However, personal and virtual interactions are not perfectly substitutable, and many businesses still require face-to-face meetings to achieve speedy responses and synergistic vitality. In addition, many workers enjoy the structure and sociability they gain by being anchored spatially to the workplace. For many workers at the professional level, home computers have not substituted for but primarily have supplemented (and often expanded) "office time."

TECHNODETERMINISM: TRANSPORTATION

A second set of explanations focuses on faster and cheaper means of transportation (as well as lower transactional costs due to containerization), which, together with enhanced informational controls, have permitted manufacturing (and now even information processing) to be radically decentralized to countries outside the United States that enjoy markedly lower labor costs. This offshoring of production has widened the gap between returns to U.S. capital and wages paid to U.S. labor, paradoxically causing both a glut of industrial and now service labor at home and higher profits for owners and managers of the exported capital. Some of these same mechanisms are of course routinely used *within* the country, especially through the employment of nonunionized labor outside the major metropolitan areas and/or (often illegal) immigrant workers.[9]

There remain many unanswered questions. For example, to what degree are these changes due to underlying technological changes (the so-called third industrial revolution) pandemic throughout the international system, and to what extent have their manifestations been specific to the United States? And given the special circumstances within the United States, how have government policies encouraged or militated against these presumed effects of international changes? Additionally, to what extent, and why, have their repercussions been felt so differentially within various regions and urbanized areas in the country?

GENERAL ECONOMIC CHANGES IN THE UNITED STATES

Productivity

A number of explanations have been advanced for the downward cycle of the American economy between 1973 and the early-1990s. Some come from conventional economists, who have argued that the U.S. economy is just not growing as fast as it did in the century before 1973; for them, the decline in productivity signals an end to American affluence.[10] According to Angus Maddison, who compiled long-term growth rates for world nations, in the century between 1870 and 1972 the American economy grew at an astounding average rate of 3.4 percent per year (real growth after the effects of inflation have been removed), thanks primarily to the spread of Fordist methods of mass production. In contrast, in the twenty years from 1973 through 1993, real growth averaged less than 2.4 percent each year. Although this 1 percent drop in growth rates may seem small, Madrick estimates that, because it compounds over time, the loss to the U.S. economy in those two decades was as much as $12 trillion (in 1987 dollars).[11]

Economists also disagree on the causes of this decline in productivity. At first, some tended to blame the slowdown on the rising price of oil in the aftermath of the 1973 Middle East war, but subsequent drastic declines in energy costs did not restore "productivity." Others have blamed federal deficits for the slowdown, without recognizing that the deficits began later and may, indeed, have in part been the result of slower growth.[12] Instead, Madrick has suggested that more intense competition from other developed economies and the trend toward more flexible production and distribution may actually be responsible.[13] Surprisingly, the effects of the shift to services (which may never generate the same productivity boosts available from manufacturing) and of the reduced purchasing power that has followed from deunionization, lower wages, and changes in the tax structure to favor the rich are seldom mentioned by conventional economists, nor do they discuss the effects of the uncontrolled pricing of Department of Defense investments in war industries. These could also be contributing to the slowdown in real productivity.[14]

Immigration and Surplus Labor

Some economists and social policy analysts suggest that it has been the substantial increase in the volume of immigration to the United States since the liberalization of immigration laws began in 1965 that has swelled the ranks of available labor and has thus, through heightened internal competition, driven wages down in the United States. It should be noted, however, that the number of new immigrants to the United States had been rising fairly steadily since its lowest point in the 1930s, and even when illegal immigrants are included, the numbers remain below those prevailing during the early twentieth century, when the total population was much smaller. For the country as a whole, immigrants today still constitute an extremely small percentage of the total population, only slightly more than they did in the 1930s. Their selective distribution within the country and their concentration within only a few major metropolitan areas in a limited number of states make immigrants far more "visible" as a category, but the total numbers are insufficient to explain a sudden drop in real wages.

In any case, there is also considerable disagreement about whether such immigrants constitute a net gain or loss to the economy. Supporters of immigration stress the net contributions that energetic and ambitious immigrants make to the economy's growth, whereas opponents argue that new immigrants, especially those from the less developed world, have lowered the quality of the workforce and swelled the demand for government expenditures on welfare, health care, and educational systems.[15]

CHANGES IN U.S. INCOME DISTRIBUTION: RISING INEQUALITY

Regardless of the causes, analysts agree that the U.S. income distribution has been growing more unequal in recent decades. Certainly, the evidence for such increased inequality has been mounting and can no longer be questioned. Most analysts agree that the gap became greatest in the 1980s and first half of the 1990s, but opinions vary as to when (and why) the bifurcation of incomes/wealth first began. Lester Thurow traces the roots to the late 1960s, an interpretation that is convincing to me.

Thurow reminds us that even though 1968, with its assassinations and riots (racial, political, and campus), was among the worst years of this century in the United States, "an event that attracted little or no attention at the time may ultimately prove to have the most lasting and destabilizing effects of all. *Suddenly that year, like a surge in a long immobile glacier, economic inequality started to rise.* Among men working full time—the group most sharply affected—inequalities in earning between the top 10 percent of wage earners and the bottom 20 percent doubled in the next two and a half decades." Between 1973 and 1993, the real earnings of working men dropped by 11 percent, "even though the earnings of the top 20 percent grew steadily and the real, per-capita gross domestic produce (G.D.P.) rose 29 percent." Disaster was averted only by the entry of wives into the labor force and by men's overtime or moonlighting, which "kept median household incomes slowly rising until 1989." But since 1989, correcting for inflation and family size, "median household incomes have fallen more than 7 percent." Inequalities in the distribution of assets/wealth also increased in the 1980s. *"By the early 1990's the share of wealth (more than 40 percent) held by the top 1 percent of the population was essentially double what it had been in the mid-1970's and back to where it was in the late 1920's, before the introduction of progressive taxation."*[16]

Findings from the U.S. Census of 1990 (see Figures IV.1 and IV.2a–b) and sub-

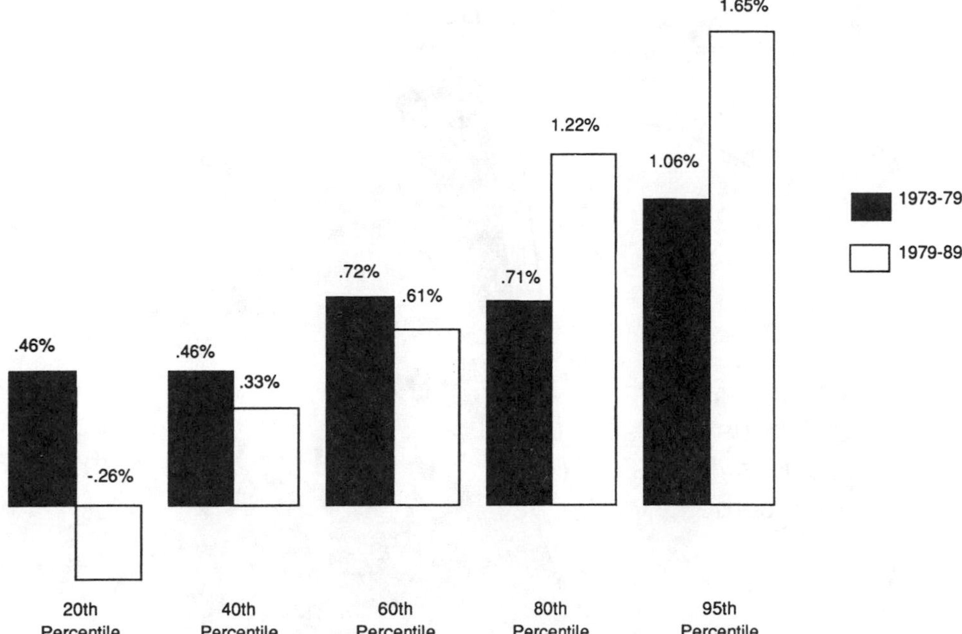

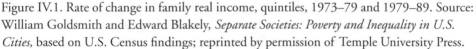

Figure IV.1. Rate of change in family real income, quintiles, 1973–79 and 1979–89. Source: William Goldsmith and Edward Blakely, *Separate Societies: Poverty and Inequality in U.S. Cities,* based on U.S. Census findings; reprinted by permission of Temple University Press.

sequent sample studies by the Census Bureau confirm these trends toward greater income inequality.[17] Between 1989 (the prior calendar year for which annual incomes were recorded in the 1990 decennial census) and 1993, "the typical American household lost $2,344 in annual income, a fall of 7 percent," while during the same interval the percentage of Americans whose incomes fell below the poverty line increased from 13.1 to 15.1. Even though average per capita income rose slightly, the distribution became more skewed, since by 1993 *"the top fifth of American households [was] earning 48.2 percent of the nation's income, while the bottom fifth earned just 3.6 percent."*[18] Figures released by the Census Bureau in June 1996 indicated no reversal.[19]

Among the causes of this growing inequality that have been suggested are increased international competition, the shift from manufacturing to service jobs, the decline in unionization, and the erosion of the minimum wage through inflation, but such an enumeration of impersonal forces conceals the private business and public policy/political decisions that have generated them.

NATIONAL ECONOMIC POLICIES

The argument that declines in productivity, greater international competition, and relatively unrestricted immigration from "less developed countries" since 1965 account for the growing income and wealth gap in the United States ignores the role played by public policies specific to this country. In some ways, the global cities

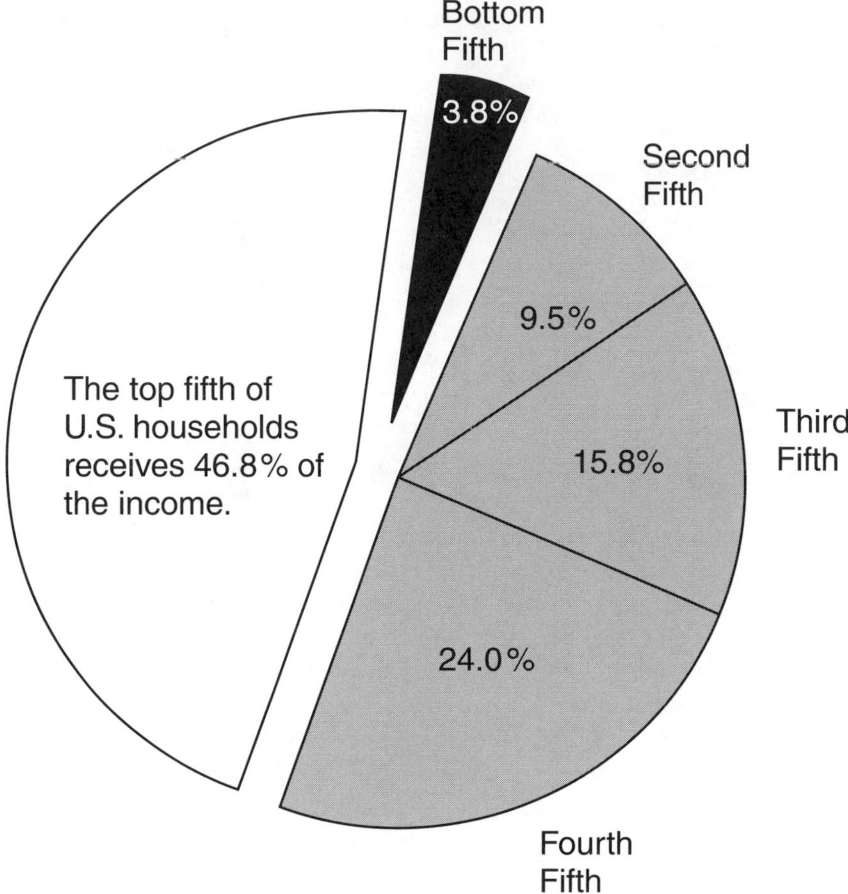

Figure IV.2a. Income shares by quintile, 1989. Source: William Goldsmith and Edward Blakely, *Separate Societies: Poverty and Inequality in U.S. Cities;* reprinted by permission of Temple University Press.

argument, which has tended to attribute these inequalities primarily to the international system, has basically ignored the effects of national taxation, labor, and welfare policies in radically altering income distribution. In contrast, Goldsmith and Blakely have taken a much broader view of the rapid expansion of poverty in the United States, arguing that

> national industry, the domestic economy, and politics are entangled in a new and debilitating international web. Global-scale social and technical transitions *are combining with new domestic politics* to reverse long-term national trends. For nearly 50 years the nation committed itself to reduce poverty, equalize resource distribution, and augment the middle class. These improvements, incomplete though they were, have been reversed. Economic and political forces no longer combat poverty—they generate poverty![20]

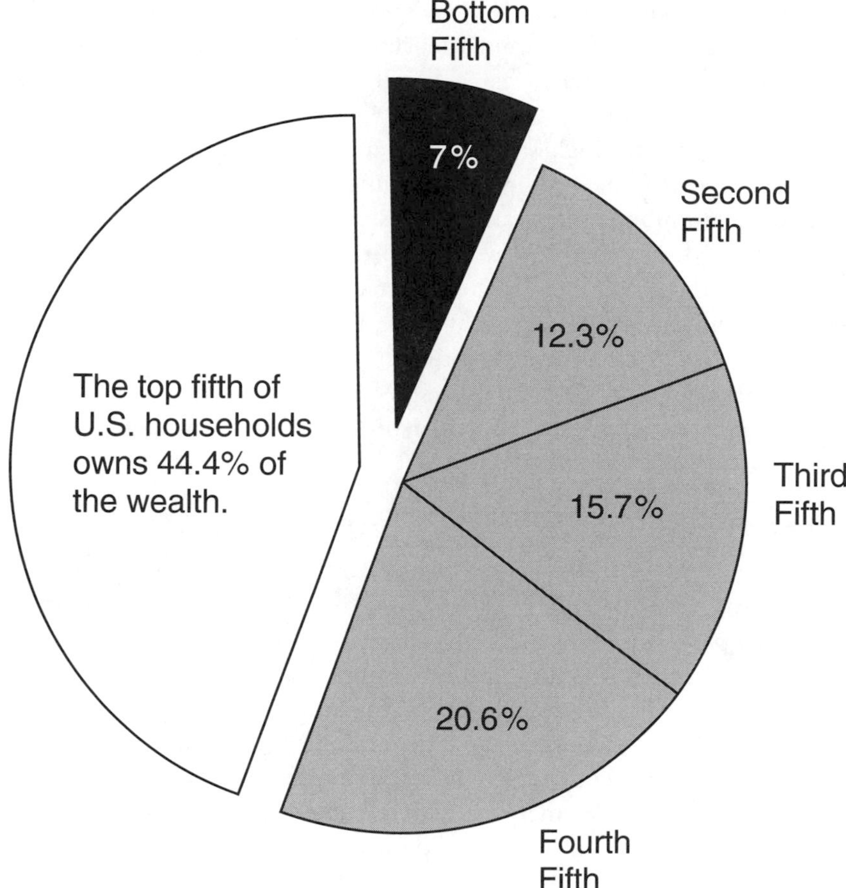

Figure IV.2b. Household wealth distribution, 1988. Source: William Goldsmith and Edward Blakely, *Separate Societies: Poverty and Inequality in U.S. Cities;* reprinted by permission of Temple University Press.

These authors remind us that between 1973 and 1989, despite some economic growth, about four out of every five American families experienced declines in their relative incomes, whereas only one in five saw its relative income rise, with the top 1 percent experiencing the greatest gains. And between 1977 and 1990, inequalities in real disposable income (i.e., after taxes and transfer payments) actually grew more extreme.[21]

This regressive shift in income distribution cannot be blamed exclusively on changes in technology or on the international system. It has also resulted from politically engendered policies, a fact that becomes clearer when we compare the United States with other industrialized countries that presumably are subject to similar technological and international forces. Already by the 1980s, the gap between rich and poor Americans was greater than in the fifteen other industrialized countries examined in the most comprehensive international study of income distribution.[22]

The study, commissioned in 1991 by the Organization for Economic Cooperation and Development (OECD), used reliable data from the Luxembourg Income Study.[23] The researchers found that although income inequalities generally grew greater in the 1980s in sixteen countries of the developed world, the U.S. inequality ratio (5.9 in 1987) was the highest of all.[24] Finland (with a ratio of 2.59) evidenced the least inequality by the same measure. Another measure of distribution confirmed that the United States exhibited the greatest dispersion, as the after-tax per capita incomes of the richest tenth of Americans were more than 200 percent above the median, whereas those of the poorest tenth were 35 percent below the median.[25] (The respective figures for Finland were 150 percent above and 60 percent below.) Thus Finland, Sweden, Belgium, the Netherlands, Norway, West Germany, Luxembourg, Switzerland, New Zealand, France, Britain, Australia, Canada, Italy, and Ireland, in descending order, all had less income inequality than did the United States.

The Unwelfare State

These measures, however, ignore government transfer payments that, if included, further increase the gap between the United States and other developed countries. One study that compared six advanced industrial nations (the United States, Sweden, the United Kingdom, Australia, Canada, and Germany) in terms of their social wages did include transfer payments, distinguishing between the net returns to labor and those to capital.[26] This better account of the differences among "welfare states" found that the United States lagged considerably behind the other developed nations. Whereas government transfers in the other countries tended to *reduce* inequality, those of the U.S. government not only failed to redistribute wealth to assist workers but over time actually tended to transfer wealth in the opposite direction.[27]

Regressive Taxation

Not only declining welfare supports but differential tax burdens have been responsible for the deteriorating position of middle-class and poor Americans. As Mishel and Frankel note, "Changes in federal, state, and local taxes since 1977 have worsened the distribution of after-tax income by taxing the middle class and poor more heavily and giving large tax cuts to the richest 1%. A less progressive personal income tax, higher payroll taxes, and lower corporate taxes resulted in an average federal tax break of $45,565 in 1990 for the richest families."[28]

Even more significant had been rising unemployment and the downgrading of jobs in the face of superprofits to capital. The unemployment rate inaccurately reflects the true situation because it omits the fluctuating numbers of potential wage earners who have been thrust out of the wage economy entirely—that is, who have been so marginalized that they are too discouraged even to seek work within the legal economy.

A rise in the number of families in poverty has occurred at the very time that executive salaries in large U.S.-based corporations have gone through the roof. Richard Barnet reports that "while millions in the workforce dropped out or dropped down,"

CEOs in large U.S. corporations were experiencing dramatic increases in pay. "Between 1960 and 1992, the average salary of a CEO jumped [by] $3.6 million while the average worker's pay rose from $4,465 to $24,411."[29] More recent figures reveal that the increase in executive incomes has escalated to what can only be considered obscene levels. Preliminary findings from a survey of compensations received by the CEOs of 76 of the 150 largest corporations in the United States indicate that the median CEO in these companies received more than $2 million in salary and bonuses in 1995, which represented a 15 percent increase over 1994. And if one adds in other forms of compensation, such as options to purchase company stock at insider prices, "the median increase in total compensation rose 31 percent . . . to nearly $5 million."[30] These increases contrast sharply with the relative stagnation in wages. In the 1960s the ratio between compensation to the chief executive and to the typical worker in a company was on the order of thirty to one; it now stands at one hundred to one.[31]

Several factors seem to underlie these developments. First, CEO compensations have been shifted from salaries per se, which are subject to taxation, to other forms of payment that evade or reduce taxation. Second, compensations for CEOs are increasingly linked to the value of their company stocks, which, because of the booming stock market, have greatly inflated CEO incomes (although it should be noted that compensation *decreases* do not necessarily follow from a loss of stock value). Such linking of profits/stock values to compensation may indeed further motivate executives to cut labor costs by intensifying the workday, outsourcing partial production needs to "independent" contractors (who are not unionized, receive no fringe benefits, and so on), even at the expense of productivity. In the face of these management strategies, labor has lost much of its bargaining position.[32]

The Weakened Position of Labor

The loss of labor's political power since the immediate postwar period partially accounts for this state of affairs, but this, in turn, has been linked to labor's weakened bargaining position in the marketplace. Among the symptoms are underemployment, falling real wages, and the increasingly skewed income distribution.[33] Here again, analysts point the finger at the global economy but disagree about *how much* of the declining status of American labor is directly attributable to international changes.[34] It is certainly undeniable that American businesses have taken advantage of wage differentials to drive labor costs down while keeping profits up, and that the "globalization" of the economy has facilitated this strategy. As Goldsmith and Blakely point out:

> In essence, U.S. policy has moved to include the domestic labor pool inside the world workforce. This change not only weakens domestic labor, but prevents it from finding a new perch in the American economy, given labor's isolation from those who control American politics. . . . in the game of industrial restructuring, the bad cards have been dealt to labor. U.S. industry has responded to reorganized global markets by reducing wages as a short-term measure to meet competition. They have worsened working conditions, increased unemployment, and raised

> poverty. Minorities and others trying to get on the bottom rung of this economic ladder have discovered that the rung has been sawed off and shipped overseas.[35]

As we have seen, however, only some of the precipitating factors have their origins in the international system, and in any case the strategies selected to meet these challenges have been facilitated by government policies.

In the early period of restructuring, relocation of production plants overseas was the preferred strategy of transnational corporations (facilitated by the opportunities to repatriate profits with minimal taxation), but more recently an additional strategy has been "internal corporate restructuring, designed to enhance flexibility, increase profits, cut costs, reduce risks, and gain markets."[36] The consequences of this strategy have been lower wages, job losses, and an increased bifurcation of the labor force, both in manufacturing and in services. The power of unions has been undercut by plant relocations to open-shop regions of the country and by the "deals" unions have been forced to make to keep plants operating.[37] "Capital-intensive oligopolies . . . have created relatively small cores of full-time workers and a larger set of part-time employees and subcontractors," a trend that has been exacerbated by "government's reluctance—even refusal—to enforce social legislation designed to protect workers."[38]

To some extent, outsourcing to "independent" subcontractors, through the mechanism of flexible production, and the growing dependence upon temporary workers are merely ways to undermine union strength and cut costs by eliminating the hard-won fringe benefits that have been the focus of union bargaining. Organized labor has only recently begun to counter this loss of power. John Sweeney, in his 1995 acceptance speech after being elected president of the AFL-CIO, emphasized his commitment to reversing a forty-year trend during which union membership plunged from 34.7 percent of the workforce in 1954 to only 15.5 percent in 1994. He noted that as "long as we speak for scarcely one-sixth of the work-force, we will never be able to win what we deserve at the bargaining table or in the legislative process."[39] Reversing the trend will not be easy. The traditional bastions for organizing, the heavy Fordist industries, have been decimated in recent years. By 1995 the number of United Automobile Workers was down to 800,000 from 1.5 million in 1979, and United Steel Workers membership had dropped from 380,000 to 140,000 in the same period. The organization of dispersed service and municipal workers will have to take up the slack in the face of recent downsizing in these sectors as well.

Unemployment and "Bad" or No Jobs

Thus the conclusions reached earlier by "radical" economists, who pointed out that the fraying of the welfare net, the deregulation of finance and industries, and regressive government taxation policies would lead to a dangerous polarization by class (and, by implication, race) in the United States, are now being confirmed by more mainstream studies. According to a 1994 report by the Dunlop Commission, the country has shifted from high-paying industrial jobs to low-paying service jobs that do not provide a living wage, despite long hours.[40] The report includes statements that "stagnation of real earnings and increased inequality of earnings is bifurcating the U.S. labor market, with an upper tier of high-wage skilled workers and an increased 'underclass' of low-paid labor."[41] The graphic material accompanying the article by Noble that summarizes the commission's report shows the following trends:

1. Between 1960 and 1990, the shift away from manufacturing as a share of total employment was gradual but steady, from 30 percent of all employment in 1960 to about 17 percent by 1990.
2. The share of employment in services increased from about 61 percent in 1960 to about 78 percent by 1990.
3. The positive change in average family income, adjusted for inflation, between 1977 and 1992 was greatest for families in the top 1 percent of family income distribution and most negative for families with incomes in the bottom 20 percent of family income.[42]

Families in the highest 1 percent of income experienced more than a 100 percent rise in average family income between 1977 and 1992. The next 4 percent saw their average incomes increase by more than 20 percent. The incomes of the next 5 percent increased by about 10 percent, the next 10 percent of families by about 8 percent, and the next 20 percent by perhaps 2 percent. This accounts for 40 percent of all families. The remaining 60 percent of all families experienced net percentage declines in real (adjusted for inflation) terms; those in the middle range of incomes (from the fortieth to sixtieth percentiles) experienced a corrected-for-inflation loss of about 7 percent between 1977 and 1992. The next lower 20 percent of families had a net loss of about 10 percent in average family income corrected for inflation between 1977 and 1992, and the 20 percent of families with the lowest incomes experienced a percentage drop in family wages (corrected for inflation) of about 11.5 percent. A significant amount of the losses at the lower percentiles is traceable to job losses. (The erosion of purchasing power for persons earning the minimum wage also contributed to losses at the bottom.)

Job Losses in the United States since 1979

In March 1996 the *New York Times* ran a series of articles on "the downsizing of America" that reported the newspaper's analysis of U.S. Bureau of Labor Statistics data on job losses in the country. The series notes that between 1979 and the early 1990s, more than forty-three million jobs (roughly a third of all jobs in the United States today) were eliminated, and "all signs indicate [that] the trend continues unabated [in 1994 and 1995]. The rate of job loss hit a peak of 3.4 million a year in 1992 and has remained nearly that high ever since, even while the economy grew and the stock market boomed."[43] Although blue-collar jobs in manufacturing experienced the greatest declines, there were also layoffs among service workers, administrators and professionals.[44] Maps in the March 3, 1996, installment of the series showed that although between 1981 and 1983 it was mostly factory workers in the heartland who

Table IV.1. Number of lost jobs (in millions) in the United States by blue- and white-collar and by gender, 1979–95 (est.)

Year	Total (in millions)	Blue-collar		White-collar	
		Males	Females	Males	Females
1979	12.3	5.5	3.0	2.0	2.0
1980	14.2	6.2	3.2	2.2	2.8
1981	19.4	8.7	3.9	3.2	3.8
1982	26.2	12.0	4.2	4.6	5.0
1983	30.4	14.0	5.1	5.2	6.0
1984	25.7	11.2	4.8	4.9	5.0
1985	25.1	10.4	4.5	5.0	4.9
1986	25.4	10.3	4.0	5.0	5.8
1987	23.4	9.2	3.2	4.8	6.0
1988	20.9	8.0	3.0	4.1	5.3
1989	20.3	8.0	3.0	4.0	5.4
1990	24.8	10.0	3.9	4.3	6.7
1991	33.0	14.0	4.4	6.3	8.2
1992	34.3	13.6	4.6	7.2	8.8
1993	33.8	12.4	4.3	7.2	9.7
1994 (est.)	33.4	12.6	4.9	6.5	9.7
1995 (est.)	33.6	12.1	5.0	6.2	9.2

Source: I have constructed this table from pictographs that appeared as part of the *New York Times* series titled "The Downsizing of America." See *New York Times,* March 3, 1996, 27. The pictographs were based upon data gathered by the U.S. Bureau of Labor Statistics.

experienced the largest number of layoffs, by the 1991–93 period, the greatest percentage of layoffs affected white-collar workers on both coasts. The same installment included a chart showing this trend over time; I have constructed Table IV.1 from the data shown in this chart.

This is not a complete disaster. It should be pointed out that "most workers who lose a job find another before very long [and even] in years when layoffs are at a peak, more jobs are usually created than destroyed," so that despite the forty-three million jobs that disappeared, the total number of nonagricultural jobs grew from 90 million in 1979 to 117 million in 1995.[45] However, many of those who have lost jobs have been forced to take pay cuts or have subsequently been able to find only part-time work. And many have been forced to move to find work.

The Implications for Economic Growth

One of the key points of Fordism, coupled with Keynesian theory, is that fewer jobs and lower wages would make it impossible for consumers to purchase the goods produced by an economy and, therefore, would in the end shrink demand and cause contractions in production in an intensifying downward spiral. Barnet emphasizes this point, invoking Henry Ford, whom Barnet quotes as having once said that "if you cut wages, you just cut the number of your customers."[46]

> Now, however, the social system based on high-volume assembly-line production employing well-paid workers who can afford to purchase what they make is fast disappearing. Since 1989, the United States has lost 1.6 million manufacturing jobs, and such losses will continue to mount. . . .
>
> Thanks to automation, the increasing use of subcontractors, suppliers, and temporary workers (many of whom cut, sew, and punch data at home), and the reorganization of the workplace . . . , steady jobs for good pay are becoming poignant memories. . . . This is true not only in factories but in banks, stores, insurance companies, brokerage houses, law firms, hospitals, and all sorts of other places where services are rendered. Between 1979 and 1992, the Fortune 500 companies presented 4.4 million of their employees with pink slips.[47]

In the 1970s and 1980s it was factories that were being moved abroad, and optimists were saying how the United States was exporting its dirty work, which would be done in poor countries, while specializing in high-paid producers' services and the like; these wealthier consumers would, in turn, generate many low-paying service jobs through a multiplier effect. But the same trends have now spread to the services. By 1991, producer services companies had begun to downsize, and managers discovered that they too were "swimming in a global labor pool."[48]

These trends are being intensified by two additional developments: reductions in the budget for the military, which the Bureau of Labor Statistics estimated would result in the loss of close to two million more jobs by 1997; and gains in "productivity," which can have a perverse effect because "workers who raise their hourly output eliminate jobs for other workers and in the long run may endanger their own jobs."[49] Education and training alone, therefore, will not solve the problems created by an inadequate number of good jobs.

THE IMPACT OF GROWING INEQUALITY ON U.S. REGIONS AND MAJOR URBAN AREAS

Persistently high poverty rates within the United States have generally been concentrated in rural and urban areas of the South, as well as in the central areas of "rust belt" cities. However, it is important to recognize that the *largest numbers of poor persons* live in the largest cities of the United States—that is, in New York, Chicago, and Los Angeles.[50] Despite this tendency for poverty to be concentrated in the largest cities (i.e., making them areas of special needs), impending insolvencies, exacerbated by taxpayer revolts in a number of places, have eroded local capacities to cope with the growing needs.

In 1975, the New York City financiers who directed the emergency Municipal Assistance Corporation temporarily averted city bankruptcy by issuing special MAC bonds and installing an austerity program similar to those imposed on Third World countries by the International Monetary Fund. In 1977, California voters passed

Proposition 13, which drastically limited property tax rates and therefore undermined Los Angeles's financial capacity to fund education, public services, and a multitude of locally supported public programs.[51] Only Chicago seems to have avoided fiscal crisis, but that city's solvency has been achieved through the maintenance of a consistently low level of services within the poorer zones of the city. In contrast, suburban residents enjoy the much higher standards that their wealth and autonomy have made possible, which further contributes to racial and income disparities and encourages desertion of the city by middle- and upper-income whites. Furthermore, the role that federal policies have played in bringing large central cities to the brink of insolvency and the role that racial animosities and antagonism toward immigrants have played in encouraging voters to snip larger and larger holes in the security net cannot be ignored in any analysis of conditions in the New York, Chicago, and Los Angeles urbanized regions. The new "workfare" programs may, indeed, tear the net more.

The general trends in the economy over the past two decades, however, have not affected the three regions equally or simultaneously, nor have they been translated on the ground into the same spatial patterns. In the case of New York, the spatial inequalities are most visible within Manhattan, but they are also evident between the wealthier zones of Manhattan and the increasingly minority-occupied outer boroughs (except for tiny and relatively insulated Staten Island). In Chicago, the class/race bifurcation has largely occurred at the boundary between the city proper and its ring of collar suburbs (including parts of suburban Cook County), although the outlying counties also include isolated pockets of poverty and/or racially segregated enclaves. In Los Angeles, the spatial divisions in the "fragmented metropolis" are more complexly patterned, although the bifurcation along the social dimensions of class/race/ethnicity may be no less extreme.

The chapters that follow explore the ways that international, national, and local circumstances play themselves out within the three regions, demonstrating both the general and particular effects on the lives of residents and on the built environments within which these lives occur. Among the more important variables are ones that have been traced in earlier portions of this book, namely, demographic composition (especially by race and immigrant status) and their spatial distribution, the economic bases both within and outside the cities (looking at growing and declining sectors and occupations), the financial and investment patterns that underlie differential growth and spatial transformations, and, finally, the political institutions and civic cultures that determine how each region copes with the radical changes now under way.

CHAPTER 10

The New York Region: Expanding, Contracting, and Restructuring

WHAT IS THE REGION?

For quite some time now it has been misleading to consider economic changes in New York City without reference to the larger urbanized region of which it is a part. As early as the 1920s, the New York Regional Plan Association had already delineated a metropolitan zone that included some twelve counties in three states (New York, New Jersey, and Connecticut). When the association commissioned its ten-volume restudy in the late 1950s, it identified twenty-two counties as constituting integral parts of the metropolitan region. By 1995, the Regional Plan Association had expanded its purview to thirty-one counties, encompassing numerous cities, large and small, and countless suburbs that spread over an area extending, at its farthest point, to some 125 miles from the center in Manhattan (see Maps 10.1a and 10.1b for RPA data for 1960 and 1990).[1] By then, the total population of the expanded region was approaching twenty million.

Even this larger zone, however, fell short of the conurbated region that Jean Gottmann, writing on the basis of the censuses of 1950 and 1960, had named Boswash—the megalopolis between Bos(ton) and Wash(ington, D.C.)—which, even a generation ago, already contained thirty-eight million residents (see Maps 10.2a and 10.2b).[2] And it is considerably smaller than the area included in the newly unified telephone service zone established by the merger between Nynex and Bell Atlantic, which now extends from Maine through Virginia. The area designated by the Bureau of the Census in 1990 as the consolidated metropolitan statistical area (CMSA) of New York-New Jersey-Connecticut was, of course, much smaller than these more

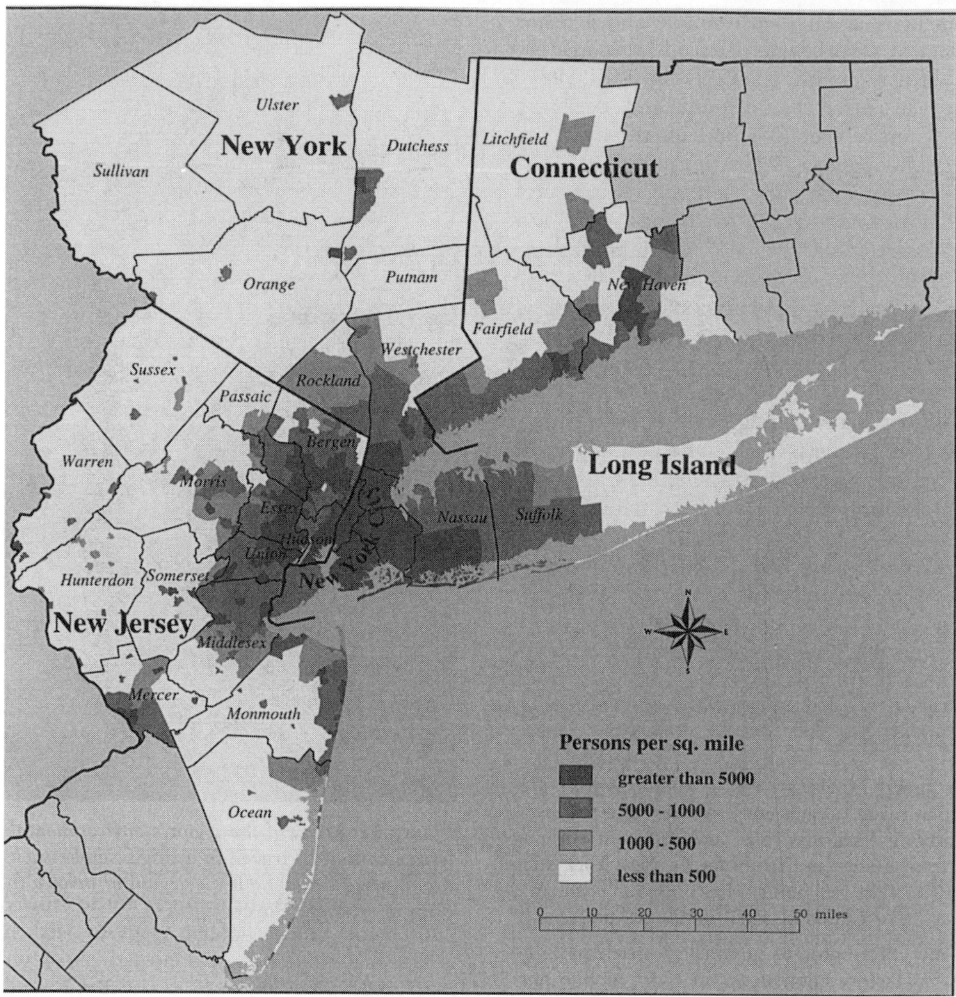

Map 10.1a. Population densities in 1960 for the thirty-one counties of the New York RPA area. Source: Robert D. Yaro and Tony Hiss, *A Region at Risk: The Third Regional Plan for the New York-New Jersey-Connecticut Metropolitan Area* (Washington, D.C.: Island Press, for the Regional Plan Association, 1996); used with permission from the Regional Plan Association.

ambitiously defined regions.[3] Nevertheless, it encompassed an area of some 7,796 square miles in which more than eighteen million people lived in 1990.

From this it is readily apparent that there are no "natural" boundaries to so long and wide a band of continuous, albeit still spotty, urbanization. There are only multiple, semiarbitrary limits that analysts select for specific purposes. This is because, over the course of the twentieth century and at ever-increasing rates, urbanization in the developed world has broken through the spatial bounds of the nineteenth-century city, yielding what Sudjic has termed the "hundred mile city."[4] This deconcentration

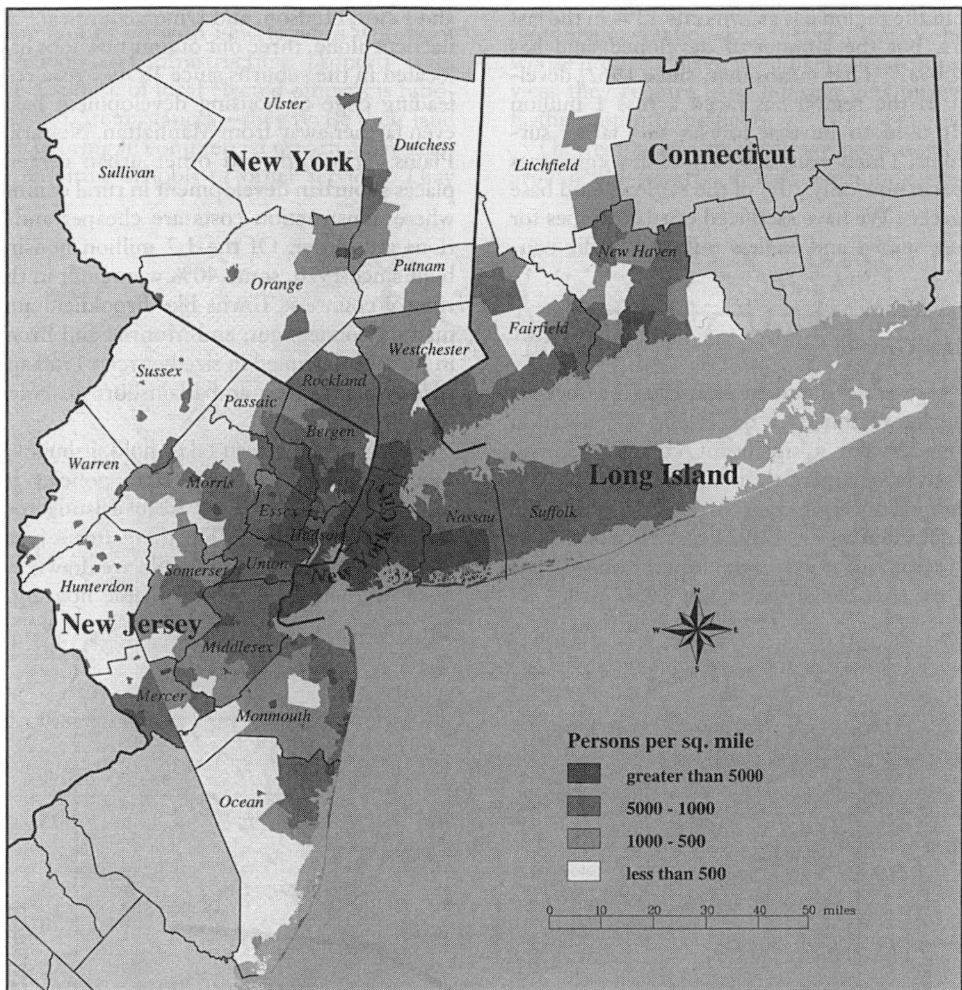

Map 10.1b. Population densities in the mid-1990s for the thirty-one counties of the New York RPA area. Source: Robert D. Yaro and Tony Hiss, *A Region at Risk: The Third Regional Plan for the New York-New Jersey-Connecticut Metropolitan Area* (Washington, D.C.: Island Press for the Regional Plan Association, 1996); used with permission from the Regional Plan Association.

of the built environment mirrors the wide-ranging and complex social networks of human connections and the even more complex networks of economic transactions known as the globalized (or world) system.

In this chapter I shall, therefore, weave back and forth, sometimes specifying the five boroughs when only municipal services and politics are the focus, and at other times referring to larger regions when economic and social developments are considered. But the reader should always try to bear in mind the global context within which these changes occur.

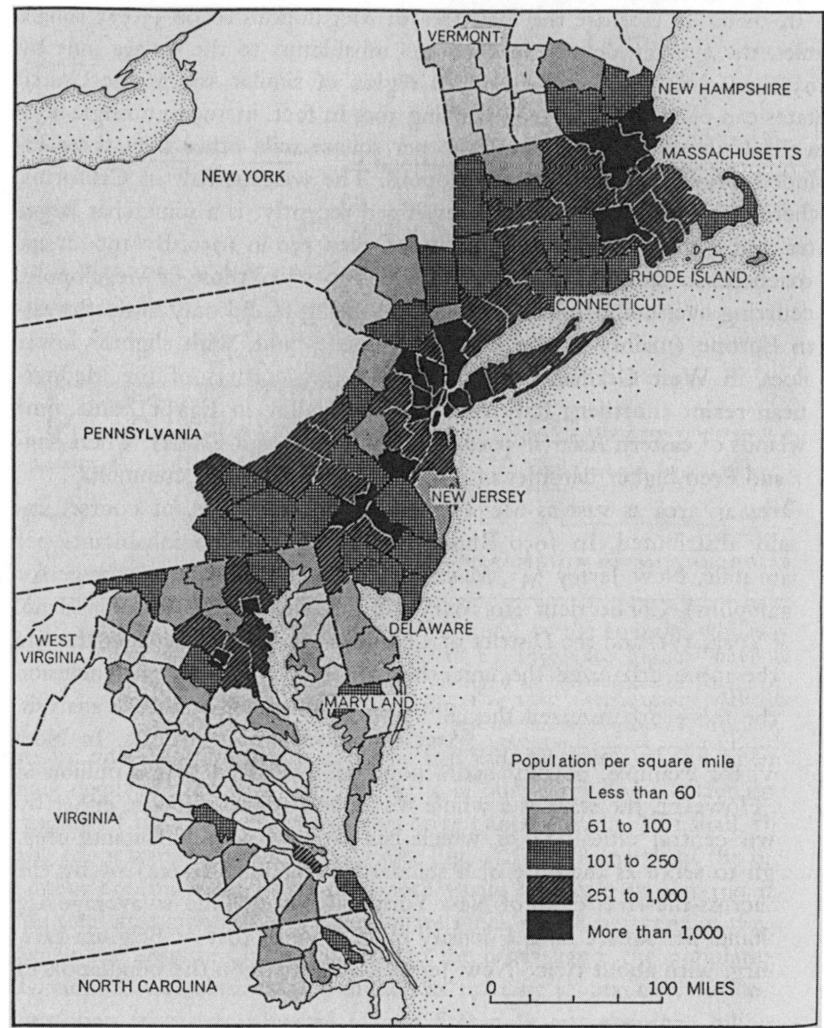

Map 10.2a. The conurbation of Boswash and density of population of Boswash counties, 1950, according to Jean Gottmann. Source: Jean Gottmann, *Megalopolis: The Urbanized Northeastern Seaboard of the United States*; used with permission from MIT Press.

NEW YORK IN THE INTERNATIONAL ECONOMY: A NEW(?) GLOBAL CONDITION

As I have already argued, the increasing "globalization" of the world's economy that has been occurring during the last quarter of the twentieth century should not be expected to have exactly the same effects on the limited number of vast urbanized regions that serve as world cities and control centers for the upper circuit of international exchange. New York, which from its origins always served global functions and which, except for a fleeting moment early in the country's history, never served

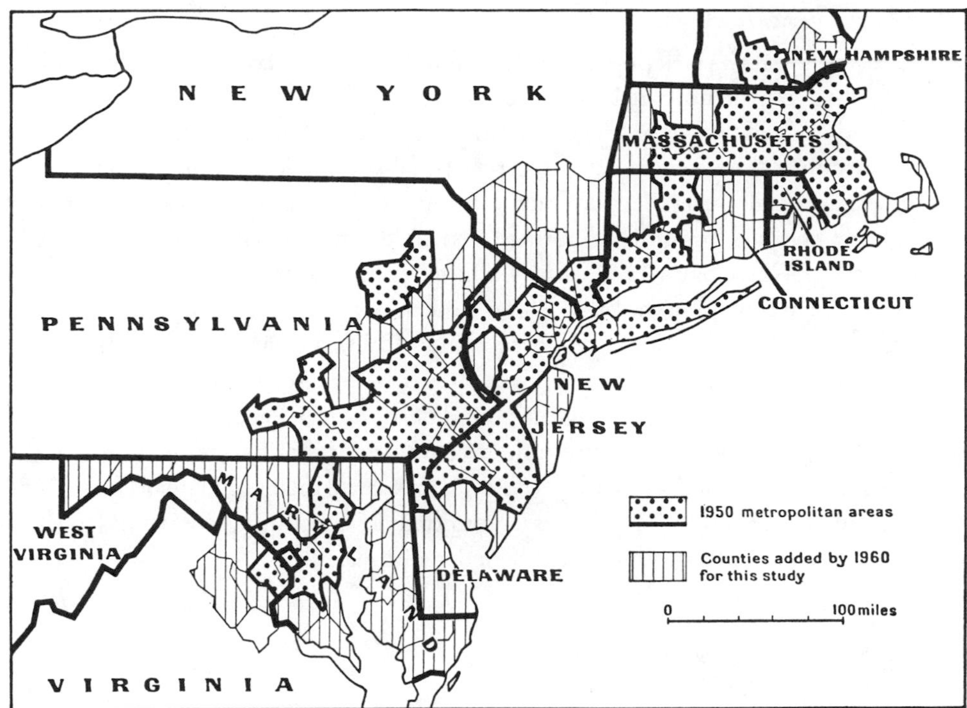

Map 10.2b. The expansion of the conurbation of Boswash between 1950 and 1960. Source: Jean Gottmann, *Megalopolis: The Urbanized Northeastern Seaboard of the United States*; used with permission from MIT Press.

as the political capital of the country, is perhaps an especially deviant case among world cities.

Ann Markusen and Vicky Gwiasda, in a subtle critique of Saskia Sassen's path-breaking *The Global City*, stress that New York, in particular, "is distinctly dissimilar from London and Tokyo, both because it operates in a much more decentralized and multi-polar national urban system, a trait not shared with the other two, and because the long term deterioration of the national industrial base weakens its transnational portfolio, a trait shared with London but not with Tokyo." In comparison with the other global cities, then, New York works under some important disadvantages. Situated within a nation far vaster than England or Japan, it must compete with other major American cities for primacy in "postindustrial" producers' services, while internationally it must compete with other world cities for financial and business-service supremacy. Markusen and Gwiasda's thesis is that New York increasingly "lacks the layering of urban functions—political, industrial, financial, educational—that is the essence of primate cities" and on which such cities depend to retain their positions as "seedbeds of innovation and generators of new types of employment."[5] In the United States, such functions are distributed among many centers. However, it needs to be emphasized that, despite these disabilities, New York did manage earlier to retain its vitality. Has something now changed? Apparently, but not in all areas.

The Decline in Political Clout

In the past, New York's lack of political centrality (because, in contrast to almost every other "global" city of note, it is not also a political capital)[6] did not hinder it from growth and, indeed, as I have suggested earlier, may actually have "freed" its residents to concentrate on pure commercial entrepreneurialism. Its political power within the nation was generally exercised indirectly, through its populous voter strength and through the personal linkages that formed a triangle running from the city to Albany, from Albany to Washington, and from Washington back to the city.

Only in recent years has that clout eroded, as California's fifty-four electoral votes outstripped New York's thirty-three, and as California succeeded to the role of Republican "kingmaker," beginning in 1968 with the ascent of Richard Nixon.[7] Washington's policies, which during the period of the New Deal and Democratic "liberalism" served to support and sustain the welfare "state" that had been crafted in the city since the days of the La Guardia-Roosevelt axis, have increasingly worked to New York's fiscal disadvantage. The city is committed to continuing social and welfare functions that are no longer supported by federal funds.

Cultural and Educational Leadership

Despite its loss of political clout, New York remains the leader as a cultural and media innovator and as an educational center. True, Los Angeles continues to be its chief competing media center, and the proliferation of colleges and universities has naturally diffused higher educational functions to many other parts of the country. But in terms of book and magazine publishing, New York remains the prime point. Furthermore, no other city has as many institutions of higher learning or as large a system of public colleges and universities. The City University of New York—the nucleus of which was founded in 1926 and which, until the state took it over during the fiscal crisis of 1975, was funded primarily by the municipality[8]—remains the largest urban higher educational system in the country, with twenty colleges and professional schools, an enrollment of almost 190,000 students, a faculty of some 7,500 unionized teachers, and an operating budget of $1,000 million.[9] To this must be added at least four dozen other private institutions scattered throughout the five boroughs.[10]

THE ECONOMY: A MIXED SITUATION

The Growth in Producer Services and Capital Investment

As we shall see, a serious erosion of the New York economy was already apparent in the 1960s, even before the international "oil crises" of 1973–74 and the city's fiscal crisis of 1975. Nevertheless, despite this relatively dim picture, New York retained, and indeed strengthened, its financial and producers' services sector, even after other American cities had begun to grow in these areas. As the booster authors of *A Region at Risk* noted with pride in 1996:

> In capital market functions, [the New York] region accounts for half of all securities traded on a global basis, leading London and Tokyo by a wide margin. In 1994, turnover exceeded $3 trillion in equities traded on our stock exchanges, compared to under $1 trillion in Tokyo, the second most active market. Today, more foreign companies are listed on New York's exchanges than in London or in Frankfurt, Paris, and Tokyo combined. In international law and accountancy, where Anglo-American structures are the acknowledged standard, London is our only competition, and . . . [New York] dominates the market with 12 of the 20 largest international law firms. We are also the headquarters to five out of the six largest accounting firms in the world.[11]

The New York region's financial institutions are so crucial to centralized trade that, by spring 1998, even the computerized NASDAQ exchange, headquartered in Washington, D.C., was considering relocation to New York. But at the same time, New Jersey continued to court the New York Stock Exchange.

A Decline in Manufacturing and Shipping

It appears, then, that Markusen and Gwiasda must be referring primarily to the reduction in New York City's productive economic base in manufacturing and shipping. And in these areas it must be acknowledged that slippage has definitely occurred. In part, the decline in manufacturing has simply paralleled the general decline within the larger region and, indeed, in the nation. But the drop has been even more profound in the New York region than in the country as a whole. This may be connected causally to the state's loss of political power, which has been translated at the national level into lower defense investments in the region. (California still receives the lion's portion of this admittedly reduced total, although it must now share this investment with nearby states.)

As late as 1960, the New York metropolitan region's share of manufacturing jobs exactly matched the national average of 31 percent. However, between 1969 and 1990, the region lost more than 800,000 manufacturing jobs, a shrinkage of 44 percent in only two decades. By 1990, less than 15 percent of the metropolitan region's workforce and less than 10 percent of the city's workers had jobs in manufacturing, considerably below the national average.[12] In the tristate region delimited by the New York Regional Plan Association in its most recent iteration, the erosion of manufacturing since 1970 was drastic and seemingly inexorable, with the proportion of the region's workers engaged in manufacturing dropping from more than 25 percent in the early year to only 12 percent by 1994.[13]

Recent trends have been even more discouraging. Manufacturing jobs declined by 6.5 percent in the brief period between 1992 and 1995 and construction jobs were down by 2.4 percent. Trade and governmental employment remained relatively constant over those years, and only two relatively small sectors showed modest increases: FIRE (finance, insurance, and real estate), up by a negligible 2.4 percent, and transportation and utilities, up by 4.5 percent. The only employment category to show a significant rise (of 9.3 percent) was "undifferentiated services"—heavily weighted to jobs that pay close to the minimum wage. Polarization between "good" and "bad" jobs has therefore continued unabated. For every high-paying job added in the region, there have been a dozen added at the lowest service ranks. If anything, such shifts have made New York even more dependent upon its "new" world-city functions in trade, finance, and tourism, and, we might add, as a reception center for immigrants.[14]

The tendency for jobs and people to continue decentralizing within the larger region intensifies New York City's declining position. Maps 10.1a and 10.1b demonstrate clearly that demographic growth has been strongest at the peripheries of the region. Map 10.3 shows that job gains and losses have paralleled population changes. Within the urban core of the region (including New York City and older cities on the New Jersey side), the number of jobs has declined, whereas net job additions have taken place almost exclusively in the peripheral counties of all three states.

In the area of air and sea transport, as well, there has been a decline in New York's proportional share of U.S. international traffic, even though the actual volume continues to rise. This loss of share, however, was inevitable, given that the Atlantic is no longer *the* monopoly route for international trade; Los Angeles dominates shipping on the Pacific Rim, which is now the trade route experiencing the fastest growth. Furthermore, New York is no longer even the indispensable "break-in-bulk" point for air and water transport from the Atlantic, especially since containerization has delinked landfall and inventory taking. Even so, as late as 1989, New York's ports (including Albany but not New Jersey) still led those of Chicago and Los Angeles in raw tonnage imported, although they fell behind the ports of Los Angeles as measured by raw tonnage exported.[15]

New York City's share of the region's shipping, however, has been slipping as the New York harbor itself silts up and as the Port Authority of New York–New Jersey favors further investments in New Jersey.[16] For some time now, New York City's maritime installations have required government subsidies to make up operating losses at major terminals along the Brooklyn shore, western Manhattan, and Staten Island. A set of new plans to recycle the city's waterfronts for more "profitable" uses is already under discussion, suggesting that shipping terminals on the New Jersey side have already won the competition.[17]

The differences among New York, Chicago, and Los Angeles are much smaller with respect to revenues from air freight.[18] Not only has increased airplane capacity for weight bearing and distance made it possible for direct shipments to be sent from and received at other eastern international airports (notably Miami and Atlanta), but the removal to or supplementing of local air and sea port facilities on the New Jersey side have naturally reduced the city's share of jobs connected to air travel and transport. Passenger service has followed air freight, with new installations at Newark Airport aiming to surpass John F. Kennedy International Airport as the busiest regional hub for air travelers.[19]

Bimodal Expansions in Services

Countering these downward trends in manufacture and transport, of course, has been the increase in the proportion of the region's labor force engaged in services. As late as 1978, manufacturing and services each provided some 22 percent of the region's jobs, but after that date, manufacturing employment declined whereas the proportion in services rose steadily; by 1994, almost one-third of all workers had jobs in "undifferentiated" services.[20] This was by far the largest employment sector, providing some 2.8 million jobs in 1995 and dwarfing, in descending order, the 1.4 million workers employed by governments, the 1.2 million employed in retail trade, and the somewhat more than 800,000 employed in the much-touted FIRE sector, which many analysts claim to be the real growth engine of globalization.[21]

The FIRE sector, however, is especially unstable. After the economic downturn of 1987 associated with the Wall Street disaster, job creation plummeted to reach a nadir in 1991; since then, recovery on Wall Street has been sharp, although it has not succeeded in spreading its benefits to the rest of the region.[22] If anything, job growth within the city seemed by 1996 to be outpacing job growth in suburban areas.[23] It is true that much of this gain was registered in the low-paid services demanded by the wealthy or in immigrant-related jobs serving ethnic needs. However, high-tech and computer services, so closely associated with California, are not absent from the New York scene. Recently, Manhattan has been innovating in these fields—in a zone of lower Manhattan punned as "Silicon Alley."[24] In this zone are located thousands of minifirms in the so-called new media industry (developers of "internet sites, multimedia software, online entertainment and other digital offerings"). Altogether, "they now employ more workers in the city than traditional media industries like television, book publishing or newspapers."[25]

POLARIZATION OF INCOMES AND SPACE

Many of the general economic trends affecting the country as a whole have had particularly strong impacts on New York City and its region. In the most recent period, there has been a polarization in the location of economic activities and in the class and racial distribution of the city's and region's population. These patterns, however, cannot all be attributed to the single factor of "globalization." Furthermore, the patterns are far more complex than any simple model of a bifurcation between city and suburb would suggest. Given the geographic and jurisdictional fragmentations that have characterized the unbounded New York region almost from its inception, it is necessary to decompose the parts to explore the types of polarizations that are manifest. I propose, therefore, to look first at Manhattan, then at Manhattan in comparison to the other four boroughs, and finally at the city as a whole in relation to other parts of the larger CMSA and the Regional Plan Association's thirty-one-county region. In this way, it should be possible to unpack the nature, degree, and patterns of differential "polarization" taking place.

We have already seen from the earlier map series the degree to which spatial polarization has occurred between the region's central counties (in New York and New Jersey), with their stagnant or declining populations, and the more peripheral counties that have been growing faster, in terms of both population and jobs. This is the context within which more particular trends must be placed.

Income Polarization in Manhattan

Throughout history the rich and the poor have shared Manhattan Island, and it is impossible to determine whether the gap between the fabulously wealthy Astor family and Jacob Riis's "other half," so evident at the turn of the century, is now more or less extreme than it was then. Hard evidence for the relative "degree" of polarization today is inconclusive. It depends upon how the gap is measured, which units are selected for comparison, and over what time span change is examined. But because of the dense settlement of Manhattan Island and its patchwork quilt of neighborhoods, the contrasts appear particularly stark there.[26]

One attempt to trace changes in income distribution in the New York region is reported in a pair of graphs that appear in Mollenkopf and Castells's edited volume *The Dual City: Restructuring New York.*[27] These graphs, reproduced here in Figure 10.1, show the estimated distribution of households by income class in the New York metropolitan area in 1949 and again in 1979.

The graphs reveal that as early as 1949 (and I would suggest much earlier as well, although Vernon's data do not go back before that), Manhattan already exhibited a marked bimodal class pattern, indicating that it was the residence of both the region's very rich and its very poorest. Middle-class residents were significantly underrepresented. In contrast, the core region just outside Manhattan (then consisting mostly of the outer boroughs of Brooklyn, the Bronx, Queens, and Staten Island) was the preferred home of working- and middle-class New Yorkers in 1949. In this zone the distribution of households by income class followed an almost normal bell-shaped curve, with most household incomes concentrated within the middle range. At that time, the "inner ring" of suburbs surrounding the city itself contained households whose incomes were skewed neatly toward the upper ranges, identifying early "suburbia" with middle- and upper-class residents. (In contrast, the zone that then constituted the "outer ring" of the region showed a relatively flat income distribution, suggesting that its range and diversity were still relatively independent of the trends in the city and its immediate suburbs; that zone included fishing and agricultural settlements as well as industrial communities and "normal" small towns.)

By 1979, these distributions had altered dramatically. Manhattan remained the only borough with more low- and high-income than middle-income families, but the extremes evident in 1949 had become considerably muted; the U-shaped curve was much flatter. The outer boroughs, in the meantime, had become much more "proletarianized," with a monotonic descent from the lowest to the highest income classes. This reflected the radical changes initiated in the postwar period, when many of the predominantly white middle- and working-class residents of the outer boroughs moved

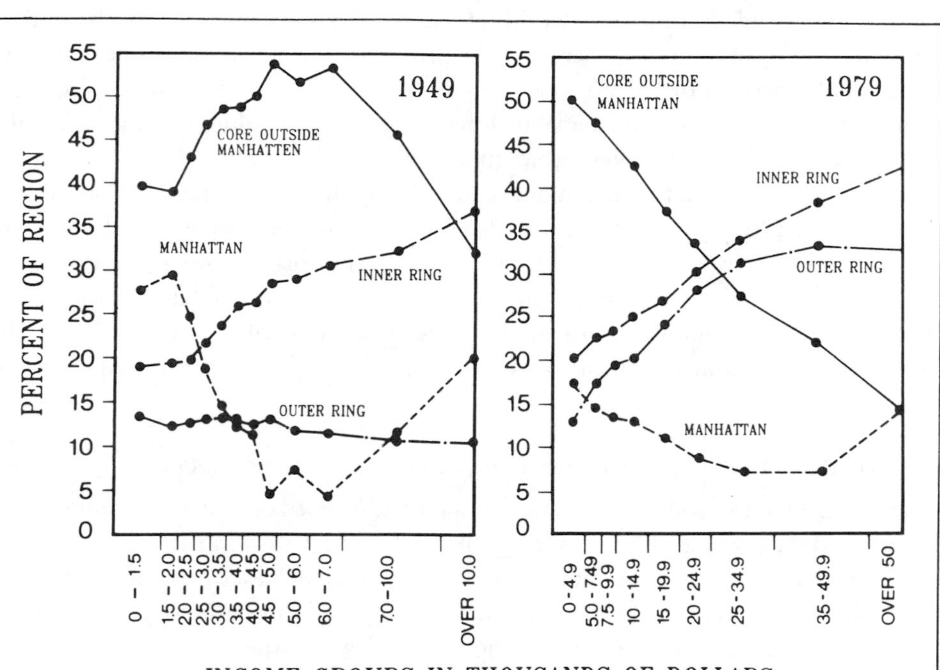

Figure 10.1. Pair of graphs showing estimated distribution of households by income class in the New York metropolitan area in 1949 and 1979. Source: Richard Harris, "The Geography of Employment and Residence in New York since 1950," in *The Dual City: Restructuring New York,* ed. John Mollenkopf and Manuel Castells (New York: Russell Sage Foundation, 1991). The 1949 graph appeared originally in Raymond Vernon, *Metropolis 1985* (Cambridge: Harvard University Press for the Regional Plan of New York, 1960), 148.

farther out into the new mass suburbs that were mushrooming. Their places were taken by "minorities" (mostly Puerto Ricans and African Americans), supplemented later by the "new immigrants" from the Caribbean and Asia, who have used these districts to gain a foothold in the metropolis.

During the 1980s, income inequalities within Manhattan may have again widened. This is certainly the point that Andrew Beveridge's computer maps of census tract data from the 1990 U.S. Census bring out clearly.[28] Summarizing these findings, Sam Roberts notes that "while the income disparity has historically been large in Manhattan, it widened to a greater degree in the 1980's than in any other county with 50,000 or more people." By 1989, the richest 20 percent of households in Manhattan had incomes more than thirty times as large as the poorest fifth. (This discrepancy was even greater than the increase in inequality for all U.S. households.) And the contrast between the average family income in Manhattan's poorest census tract (West Harlem, where it was only about $6,000) and its richest one (Carnegie Hill on the Upper East

Side, where average family income exceeded $300,000) was unbelievably large. As might be expected, Manhattan's wealthiest heads of households tend to be native-born and employed in management and the professions, whereas many of the poorest are African American or Latino (both native Puerto Ricans and Caribbean foreign-born), unemployed or out of the labor force, and include children living in female-headed households—the poorest group in the city.[29]

Roberts concludes that the middle class is being squeezed out of Manhattan, but as we have seen from Figure 10.1, at midcentury the middle class usually did not live in Manhattan anyway. Although the largest proportion of jobs in the New York region are still located in Manhattan, the best-paying ones are often held by commuters from the inner and outer rings of suburbia, whereas many of the poor living in the city are aged, unemployed, or underemployed members of "minority" groups.

NEW YORK CITY'S OUTER BOROUGHS: INCREASING POVERTY

Despite Manhattan's ability to selectively retain and/or attract well-paid younger professionals, demographic changes during the 1970s and 1980s in the rest of the city, most particularly in Brooklyn and the Bronx, meant that New York City as a whole has become more polarized by ethnicity, race, and class. Whereas New York City's five boroughs had ranked only eleventh among those cities with the largest income disparities in 1980, its growing class polarization had moved it "up" to fifth among such cities by 1990. And within the larger New York metropolitan area, poor people were "more concentrated in the city itself than in any other major metropolitan area except San Antonio."[30] Furthermore, between 1980 and 1990, the city's poor had gotten poorer,[31] and in Manhattan, Brooklyn, and the Bronx (and in Newark across the state line in New Jersey), the proportion of middle-class residents had declined precipitously. These changes were, in part, traceable to racial and ethnic factors.

Racial and Ethnic Polarization by Boroughs

Transfers of population account for most of the radical shift in the racial composition of the outer boroughs, as shown in Table 10.1. This ethnic/racial transition was accompanied by an absolute net decline in the total population in just those boroughs where the demographic composition changed most in the years between 1960 and 1990. Thus Manhattan's population declined from close to 1.7 million in 1960 to only 1.4 million by 1980, before rising slightly to almost 1.5 in 1990. The population of Brooklyn dropped from 2.63 million in 1960 to 2.23 million in 1980, before rising slightly to 2.3 by 1990. The Bronx's population decreased steadily for two decades—from 1.4 million in 1960 to 1.17 million in 1980, recovering only slightly to 1.2 million by 1990.

The "whiter" outer borough of Queens, after increasing from 1.8 million in 1960 to almost 2 million by 1970, actually experienced a slight dip in the total by 1980 (to about 1.9 million by 1980), before rising slightly to more than 1.95 million in 1990. But its moderate change in total conceals a fairly radical shift in the bor-

Table 10.1. Population (in thousands) of New York City by borough, 1940–90, showing the estimated declining percentages of "whites"

	1940	1950	1960	1970	1980	1990
New York City	7,455	7,892	7,782	7,895	7,072	7,323
Percentage "white"	94	90	85	NA	61	52
Manhattan	1,890	1,960	1,698	1,539	1,428	1,456
Percentage "white"	83	79	74	NA	59	59
Brooklyn	2,698	2,738	2,627	2,602	2,231	2,301
Percentage "white"	95	92	85	NA	56	47
The Bronx	1,395	1,451	1,425	1,472	1,169	1,173
Percentage "white"	98	93	88	NA	47	36
Queens	1,298	1,551	1,810	1,986	1,891	1,911
Percentage "white"	97	96	91	NA	71	58
Staten Island	174	192	222	295	352	371
Percentage "white"	98	96	95	NA	89	85

Note: The 1990 figures have not been corrected for undercount. Hispanics have been apportioned to "white" and "nonwhite/other," depending upon their self-identification. The figures for 1970 have been omitted because Hispanics were not allocated by race in that census. In 1980, 21 percent of the city's residents were of Hispanic origin, a figure that had increased to 25 percent by 1990. See the discussion in Chapter 7 of the "ambiguities" of the terms *white, black,* and *other* among Puerto Ricans in New York. If the Puerto Ricans (who have increasingly tended to report themselves as "white") are omitted, the proportion of "non-Hispanic whites" had declined to 43 percent of the total by 1990 (see City of New York Department of City Planning, *New York City Population Trends* [July 1995]) and the degree of segregation between "whites" and "minorities" would increase. In the analysis that follows, I calculate the borough-by-borough redistribution of blacks and Puerto Ricans over the past few decades.

Source: Susan S. Fainstein, Ian Gordon, and Michael Harloe, eds., *Divided Cities: New York and London in the Contemporary World* (Oxford: Basil Blackwell, 1992), 27, Table 1.2. They compiled their data from various tables in Ira Rosenwaike, *Population History of New York City* (Syracuse, N.Y.: Syracuse University Press, 1972), U.S. Census returns, and E. B. Fiske, "New York Growth Is Linked to Immigration," *New York Times,* February 22, 1991, Table A.

ough's composition: from the 1980s on, Queens became the prime destination for a variety of new immigrants. Staten Island, in contrast, experienced overall population increases during the entire thirty-year period, even as its modest minority population also grew.

But here again, the situation in New York City is far more complex than can be captured by the simple model of invasion-succession and white flight. Table 10.2 conveys a part of the story, although because the boroughs, except for Staten Island, are so large, the overall figures conceal the degree of *resegregation* that has taken place *within* certain boroughs that, at the aggregate level, may give the impression of being more racially integrated. Rather than scattered at random in those boroughs, minorities tend to be concentrated within specific subsections. Confounding the story also is the presence of Puerto Ricans, still the single largest subgroup of Hispanics in the city, who, as I have pointed out earlier, have tended to report themselves as "white" in

Table 10.2. Estimated distribution of African American "blacks" and persons of "Puerto Rican birth or descent" by borough, New York City, 1960–90

	1960	1970	1980	1990
Total New York City[a]	7,781,984	7,599,419	7,071,639	7,322,564
Manhattan	1,698,281	1,539,233	1,428,285	1,487,536
The Bronx	1,424,815	1,471,701	1,170,344	1,203,789
Brooklyn	2,627,319	2,602,012	2,230,936	2,300,664
Queens	1,809,578	1,986,473	1,891,325	1,951,598
Staten Island	221,991	295,443	352,121	378,977
"Black" population[b]				
Total New York City	1,087,931	1,670,115	1,784,337	2,102,514
Manhattan	397,101	380,442	309,854	326,969
The Bronx	163,896	357,681	371,926	449,399
Brooklyn	371,405	656,194	722,812	872,305
Queens	145,855	258,006	354,129	423,211
Staten Island	9,674	17,792	25,616	30,630
Estimated Puerto Rican origin/descent				
Total New York City	612,874	811,839	862,372	896,763
Manhattan	225,639	185,323	166,328	154,978
The Bronx	186,885	316,772	322,098	349,115
Brooklyn	180,114	271,769	279,646	274,530
Queens	17,432	33,141	83,245	100,410
Staten Island	2,804	4,834	11,055	17,730

Note: The common designations of the boroughs appear in this table instead of their formal county names, which appear in census volumes. For the uninitiated, Manhattan is New York County, Brooklyn is Kings County, and Staten Island is Richmond County. The Bronx and Queens are those boroughs' official names, which are also used in common parlance.

[a]The subtotals for blacks and Puerto Ricans should not be added because of some overlap. The number of whites cannot be estimated by subtracting the number of blacks and Puerto Ricans from the total, because persons of Asian and "other" races are not included in this table.

[b]"Black" population includes not only native-born African Americans but some immigrants from the Caribbean and Africa, as well as an unknown number of Puerto Ricans and other Hispanics who reported their race as "black."

Source: My own calculations based on successive U.S. Census returns.

sufficiently large numbers to lead analysts to overestimate the degree of racial integration in boroughs that now have "minority majorities."

In Table 10.2, I have estimated the changing size of the two largest "minority" (mostly) nonimmigrant groups[32] in the city—African Americans and Puerto Ricans—in the individual boroughs, even though it is impossible to differentiate the two completely. I have employed an ingenious method of tracking Puerto Rican identity through the changing definitions used over the last four census returns. While my figures are only approximate and contain some overlap, I believe that they shed new

Table 10.3. Estimated percentage distribution of African American and Puerto Rican populations in the five boroughs of New York City, 1960–90

	1960	1970	1980	1990
New York City				
All boroughs	100.0	100.0	100.0	100.0
Manhattan	21.8	20.3	20.2	20.3
The Bronx	18.3	19.4	16.5	16.4
Brooklyn	33.8	34.0	31.5	31.4
Queens	23.3	26.1	26.7	26.7
Staten Island	2.9	3.9	5.0	5.2
"Black" population[a]				
All boroughs	100.0	100.0	100.0	100.0
Manhattan	36.5	22.8	17.4	15.5
The Bronx	15.1	21.4	20.8	21.4
Brooklyn	34.1	39.3	40.5	41.5
Queens	13.4	15.4	19.8	20.1
Staten Island	0.9	1.1	1.4	1.5
"Puerto Rican" population				
All boroughs	100.0	100.0	100.0	100.0
Manhattan	36.8	22.8	19.3	17.3
The Bronx	30.5	39.0	37.4	38.9
Brooklyn	29.4	33.5	32.4	30.6
Queens	2.8	4.1	9.7	11.2
Staten Island	0.5	0.6	1.3	2.0

Note: Figures do not add to 100 because of rounding. I have calculated percentages only to show *relative* decentralization. Given the manner in which the figures have been "reconstructed," it would be illegitimate to derive percentage distributions by race and origin/descent for the city and boroughs as a whole over time. The situation in 1990 is best reconstructed from Table 10.4.

[a]The "black" population includes immigrants from the Caribbean basin, of which the largest groups came from Jamaica and the Dominican Republic. Haiti and other Caribbean islands, as well as Africa, have also contributed to the growing black population of New York.

Source: My own calculations based on successive U.S. Census returns.

light on the locations of New York's poorest minority groups: African Americans and Puerto Ricans (whose current socioeconomic status is even more precarious than that of New York blacks).[33] As is readily apparent from the table, not only have the numbers of blacks and Puerto Ricans increased over the past three decades, but there has been a progressive "decentralization" of these two "minorities" from Manhattan to the outer boroughs. Table 10.3 presents estimates, over that period, of the percentages of all "blacks" and all "Puerto Ricans" who lived in the various boroughs.[34]

It should also be noted that ever since the late 1960s, after the immigration laws were changed in 1965, "Hispanics" other than those of Puerto Rican origin and descent have become more numerous in the city. By 1990, persons of Puerto Rican origin/descent constituted only half of all Hispanics in the city. At present, the largest number

Table 10.4. Percentage distribution by race/Hispanic origin of the population of the NY/NJ/CT CMSA, the NY PMSA, Manhattan only, and the outer boroughs of New York City, 1990 Census

	% in geographic unit or subdivision reporting			
Race/ethnicity	CMSA	PMSA	Manhattan	Outer boroughs
White non-Hispanic	63.2	47.9	48.9	41.8
Black non-Hispanic	16.4	23.2	17.6	27.2
Amerind non-Hispanic	0.2	0.2	0.2	0.3
Asian non-Hispanic	4.6	6.2	7.1	6.6
Other non-Hispanic	0.2	0.3	0.3	0.3
Hispanic (any race)	15.4	22.1	26.0	23.9

Note: Hispanic refers to persons identifying themselves as of Hispanic origin, regardless of the races they reported. This is particularly important in New York because of the ambiguities of Puerto Rican responses and because a large proportion of Hispanics actually reported themselves as "other race."

Source: My own calculations based on U.S. Census returns.

of foreign-born Hispanics hails from the Dominican Republic. They totaled some 333,000 by 1990, and their numbers may have risen by the mid-1990s to half a million.

Immigration has also increased the number of non-Hispanic blacks in the city, as immigration from English-speaking and Francophone islands in the Caribbean has increased. Although the native-born population of African Americans continues to grow from natural increase, in recent decades there has actually been a net outflow from migration, both to selected other parts of the metropolitan region and to southern cities. A recent projection made by the New York City Department of Planning suggests that by the year 2000, the proportion of the city's population that is of Hispanic origin will, for the first time, exceed the proportion of black non-Hispanic residents (29 versus 26 percent).

RACIAL AND ETHNIC POLARIZATION BY CENTRAL COUNTIES AND SUBURBAN RINGS

By 1990, the ethnic and racial distributions in space over the entire New York-New Jersey-Connecticut CMSA reflected the further dispersal of the "white non-Hispanic" population to areas outside the city of New York, as the population within the city proper became increasingly "minority." Table 10.4 shows my calculations from the 1990 census returns. The reverse pattern was true for both the inner and outer suburban rings, which demonstrated a roughly monotonic increase in incomes and, as can be inferred from Table 10.4, contained populations that were more likely to be classified as "white non-Hispanic." The percentage of "whites" in the "really suburban" areas would, of course, be much higher if the CMSA did not also include such "majority-minority" large cities as Newark and some of its surrounding areas.

Table 10.5 shows my reconstruction of the racial/ethnic composition of the four "truly suburban counties" adjacent to New York City that fall within New York State

Table 10.5. Estimated number of "whites," "blacks," and "Puerto Ricans" (in thousands) living in four New York State suburban counties adjacent to New York City, 1960–90

Year	Nassau County	Suffolk County	Rockland County	Westchester County
"Whites"				
1960	1,258	632	130	746
1970	1,356	1,066	216	803
1980	1,204	1,185	232	730
1990	1,115	1,190	223	694
"Blacks"				
1960	39	33	7	61
1970	66	53	13	85
1980	91	71	18	105
1990	111	83	27	120
"Puerto Ricans"				
1960	4	7	2	3
1970	7	17	4	6
1980	14	36	6	18
1990	18	44	8	27

Note: Figures do not add to the county totals because of rounding and because Asians and "others" have been left out of the "racial" categories.

Source: My own calculations based on successive U.S. Census returns.

(Nassau and Suffolk on Long Island to the east, and Rockland and Westchester to the north).[35] As is readily apparent, even though these counties represent "overflow spaces" from Brooklyn-Queens and the Bronx that, in the immediate postwar period (1950s and 1960s), absorbed many new suburbanites,[36] there was little initial movement of African Americans and Puerto Ricans into them. The number of Puerto Ricans and "blacks" increased only in the 1970s and 1980s, after the heaviest influx of population to these counties had already ceased. Some minority succession or dispersion can thus be inferred. During the two decades between 1970 and 1990, however, the "peripheral" areas that absorbed most of the decentralizing minority residents were the cities and their immediate suburbs in northern New Jersey.

Given these findings, it is hard to claim that globalization and economic restructuring have been the sole causes of class bifurcation in New York City or its region, although they may certainly have contributed. A second factor, however, and one more directly linked to globalization, is immigration, which has brought a large recently arrived population to New York—many of them just starting out in their new setting.

IMMIGRANTS ENTER NEW YORK CITY

Between 1980 and 1990, New York City added close to a million and a half residents through immigration, which more than compensated for the loss of native-born "whites" in that decade.[37] Although this total was smaller than the more than two million immigrants received by Los Angeles in the same decade, the sources from which New York's newcomers have been drawn are far more diversified than those of Los Angeles. The five top "sending countries" to New York City in the 1980s were the Dominican Republic (more than 145,000),[38] followed by China and Jamaica (each with about 74–75,000), Colombia (some 67,000), and Korea (about 58,500). Thus the largest source (the Dominican Republic) accounted for only about a tenth of all immigrants, and each of the next four countries for one-twentieth or less of the total. Altogether, the top five countries contributed only 28 percent of all immigrants. The remainder came from virtually every other country in the world. In contrast, more than 40 percent of Los Angeles's immigrants in the same period hailed from a single country, Mexico.[39]

As has traditionally been the case, recent immigrants have favored the center cities of the region. In 1990, one out of every five residents in the tristate consolidated metropolitan statistical area had been born abroad. In the somewhat smaller New York primary metropolitan statistical area, the proportion was closer to 27 percent. And by that year, the proportion of foreign-born in New York City approached 29 percent. Indeed, without this immigration, the city would actually have lost population in the intercensal period, instead of gaining. The diversification of immigrant streams, coupled with the contribution to population growth that immigrants have made in New York, may account at least in part for the somewhat more favorable attitude toward immigrants that New York, as contrasted with Los Angeles, has shown.[40]

The foreign-born population is not distributed at random within the five boroughs. As the data presented in Table 10.6 show, although the proportion of foreign-born residents increased everywhere in the city between 1980 and 1990, certain boroughs absorbed disproportionate shares. During the 1980s, Queens became the major recipient of immigrants, and by 1990 well over a third (36 percent) of its population had been born abroad. Brooklyn came next, with more than 29 percent foreign-born. The proportion of foreign-born in Manhattan was 25.8 percent. The Bronx absorbed an even smaller percentage of immigrants, with only 23 percent of its population born outside the United States, many of them "people of color." On Staten Island, the "whitest" of the boroughs, the proportion of the population born abroad was still less than 12 percent.[41]

The category "foreign-born," however, is too broad to unpack the ethnic diversity of New York City, because various nationality groups have tended to concentrate within specific boroughs and neighborhoods. Dominicans have settled largely in Washington Heights on the northwest side of Manhattan, whereas Chinese immigrants have favored Chinatown in lower Manhattan or its satellite settlements in Brooklyn and Queens. Jamaicans and other English-speaking West Indians have been inserted largely into African American areas in Brooklyn, such as Bedford-Stuyvesant and its extensions, where English predominates. Francophone black immigrants have formed their own subareas. Brooklyn and, even more so, Queens have received most of the immigrants who speak languages that are not included in the schools' usual bilingual programs (which concentrate on Spanish and English).

Table 10.6. Percentage of residents born outside the United States by borough, 1980 and 1990

Year	New York City Total	Manhattan	The Bronx	Brooklyn	Queens	Staten Island
1980	23.6	24.4	18.4	23.8	28.6	9.8
1990	28.4	25.8	22.8	29.2	36.2	11.8

One response to this linguistic diversity is found in the public school system, where immigrant children now account for about a third of the city's 150,000 new students. In 1995 the New York Board of Education proposed a new school to be located in Queens and designed for speakers of languages other than English or Spanish. Initially, the students would be taught in eighteen different languages.[42] The executive director of the New York Immigration Coalition hailed this, calling it "an example of New York being a lot more courageous than other parts of the country in remaining level-headed in the dialogue about immigrants."[43] To attract students, the establishment of the school was advertised in the many foreign-language newspapers published in the city, but its projected enrollment of only a thousand students will fall far short of the magnitude of need.

The inflow of immigrants to the city has shown no signs of letting up. In fact, from 1990 to 1994, well over half a million new (legal) immigrants entered the city,[44] and one can presume a minimum of perhaps another 50,000 to 100,000 are illegal entrants. During this interval, the Dominicans remained the largest contributors (more than 110,000), but the "new" item was that the second-largest group came from the former Soviet Union (66,301). China, including Hong Kong and Taiwan, ranked third with 59,798. The remaining groups slipped in numbers: Jamaica was fourth with 32,918, then came Guyana with 30,764, Poland with 19,537, the Philippines with 17,378, Trinidad and Tobago with 15,878, Haiti with 14,957, India with 14,486, Ecuador with 143,980, Ireland with 12,403, Colombia with 11,309, Bangladesh with 9,556, Korea (North and South) with 8,626, Pakistan with 7,465, and down to Ghana (fortieth rank, the last shown in the table) with 1,696.[45]

Rearranging the top forty sending countries by world regions, we find that almost half (212,000) came from various parts of the Caribbean (mostly black, including English, Spanish, or French Creole speaking). Asia contributed almost 125,000 legal immigrants (mostly from the various "Chinas" but also from assorted countries such as the Philippines, India, Bangladesh, Korea, Pakistan, Vietnam, and Japan, in descending order). European countries also accounted for a considerable number (close to 100,000), most but not all of whom came from behind the former Iron Curtain, including more than 66,000 from the former Soviet Union, by then the second-highest sending source. In marked contrast to Los Angeles, for example, the nine Central American and South American sending countries in the top forty contributed only 46,139 Spanish speakers.[46] Immigrants from the Middle East and Africa were toward the bottom of the list.

Because of this linguistic and ethnic diversity, it is difficult to claim that immigration per se has been responsible for the class bifurcation in the city, although it undoubtedly has contributed to changing the racial composition of the city's population, with Dominican and Jamaican immigration increasing the proportion of "blacks" and Chinese and Koreans the proportion of "Asians." It would be illegitimate, however, to translate these changes into direct economic effects. Far more important have been the general changes in the economy, as well as in the opportunity structure for immigrants that these changes have wrought. For example, it is unlikely that the New York garment trade (sweatshops and all) would have revived as it has without the presence of a large available labor pool of new immigrants.[47]

Economic Niches for Immigrants and "Natives"

The most sophisticated attempt that has been undertaken to date to decompose the new immigration into its component parts and to trace how immigrants and indigenous "minorities" are differentially inserted into the complex mosaic of New York City's class/job structure is Roger Waldinger's *Still the Promised City?*[48] Waldinger attempts to refute the popular thesis that the growth of an African American underclass in large city "ghettos" is due simply to deindustrialization and the spatial mismatch between center-city residence and peripheral job locations.[49] Instead, Waldinger argues that, in New York City at least, African Americans have not been adversely affected by the decline in industries, largely because they had never been part of the industrial workforce. Furthermore, he notes that some African Americans in New York have undoubtedly experienced some occupational mobility, moving into economic niches, primarily in the public sector, that are quite distinct from those for which the new immigrants are eligible. Aside from pointing out that such civil or social service jobs cannot generate the same mobility ladder that immigrant entrepreneurship can offer, he tends to rest his case there.

However, there are some problems with Waldinger's argument. His data are about jobs (i.e., employed persons), not persons or families. Indeed, his analysis is confined to *job holders between the ages of twenty and sixty-five.* It therefore excludes black and Puerto Rican teenagers and very young adults, many of whom are unemployed or underemployed or have become discouraged in a fruitless search for jobs. And even within the targeted prime working-age group, his analysis omits persons without jobs (the imprisoned, the unemployed, and individuals no longer "in the labor market"). Thus Waldinger actually ignores the putative "underclass"—the half million New York City residents on welfare, the half million residents of public housing, the teenagers and adults who are not working (these groups are not mutually exclusive). If he had included these, his conclusions would be quite different.

Despite the mobility of educated African Americans into the civil service and into the growth sector of public and private health care, a sizable proportion of the community has been left behind. Between 1970 and 1990, employment rates for native-born black and Hispanic men between the ages of twenty-five and sixty-five dropped from 80 percent to less than 70 percent, whereas those for native-born whites and the foreign-born (including blacks, Hispanics, and Asians) remained over 80 percent. Among women in those age categories, labor force participation rates generally increased during those two decades, but the discrepancies were much greater. In 1970, some 70 percent of foreign-born black women were working, a rate that had increased to three-quarters by 1990. White native-born women also increased their employment—from 50 percent working in 1970 to more than two-thirds by 1990. Native-born black and Asian-born women had lower rates of employment, with both groups more likely to have been employed in 1980 than in 1990. By 1990, Hispanic women (both native- and foreign-born) had the lowest rates of employment, with the foreign-born only slightly higher than the native-born (chiefly Puerto Rican).[50]

The native-born black and Puerto Rican men least likely to have jobs were those with the least education. The mismatch thesis essentially assumes that, had there not been deindustrialization (and/or new immigration), such men *could have* started on the job ladder at unskilled levels and gradually moved up. Regardless of whether or not that might have happened, the fact is that a substantial proportion of New York's African American and Puerto Rican populations are poor and are trapped at the bottom, in part because they are not working. Thus Waldinger's findings on the niches of immigrants versus minority native-born persons are not necessarily inconsistent with the "underclass" argument. To the contrary, there is evidence that the number of poor families in the city has increased (or at least not declined) in recent decades, a phenomenon linked both to family structure and to differential labor force participation.

THE GROWING NUMBER OF POOR IN NEW YORK CITY

Changes in the composition of the city's population by race, ethnicity, and place of origin (Puerto Rican or immigrant) have contributed to the recent increase in the number of poor New Yorkers. However, it is impossible to determine exactly how much of this additional poverty has been caused by the globally generated economic decline in the city, region, and nation and how much is attributable to the city's changing compositional "mix" of population. There is a strong interaction effect that, when coupled with the diversity concealed *within* categories of race, ethnicity, and national origin, makes the situation extremely complex.

Certainly, poverty increased throughout the United States in the 1980s and early 1990s. The number of poor people in the nation increased from 26 million to 37 million between 1979 and 1992, and the poverty rate rose from 11.7 to 14.5 percent of the total during that interval.[51] It would be strange if New York had escaped this trend, and, indeed, increases in poverty in New York City neatly tracked it. In 1979, the number of poor New Yorkers was close to 1.4 million, and the "poor" constituted about 20 percent of the total population; in the 1980s the total number of poor persons in the city fluctuated between 1.5 and 1.8 million, and by 1992 it stood at 1.65 million. Since 1984, at least, about 24 percent of all city residents have been classified as poor.[52]

Table 10.7. Number of poor (in millions) and poverty rates by race/ethnicity, New York City, selected years between 1984 and 1992

	Total		Non-Hispanic white		Non-Hispanic black		Hispanic	
Year	Number	Percentage	Number	Percentage	Number	Percentage	Number	Percentage
1984	1.735	24	.306	9	.587	32	.781	43
1985	1.757	24	.326	10	.534	32	.931	44
1986[a]	1.483	21	.294	9	.408	27	.677	36
1987	1.680	23	.282	8	.549	34	.753	42
1990	1.839	25	.359	12[b]	.583	33	.826	43
1991	1.712	24	.380	12	.512	29	.767	44
1992	1.651	24	.372	12	.593	33	.650	40

Note: Race/ethnicity categories are mutually exclusive.

[a]The figures for 1986 diverge so drastically from the "norm" that I find them suspicious.

[b]This sudden increase to a new and higher level may be related to immigration from Russia and other parts of Eastern Europe after "the fall."

Source: Data are from Terry J. Rosenberg, *Poverty in New York City, 1993: An Update* (New York: Community Service Society, 1994), 8, Table 1B. Figures have been processed from successive March Current Population Survey tape files, available in the following year.

Although the overall poverty rate in 1992 was higher than in 1979 for all racial/ethnic subcategories, the differences between the race/ethnicity-specific poverty rates have remained remarkably stable, suggesting that the rise in overall local poverty has been due, at least in part, to a change in the racial/ethnic "mix" of city residents. Rosenberg's study for the Community Service Society of New York carefully disaggregated the poor into three mutually exclusive categories (non-Hispanic whites, non-Hispanic blacks, and Hispanics of any race) and traced changes in their poverty rates in the 1980s and early 1990s.[53] According to Rosenberg's analysis, the number of poor people in New York City and the proportion of the city's residents who were poor increased between 1979 and 1992, even though the poverty rates *within* each racial/ethnic category remained quite stable. This suggests that some portion of the overall change came from a recomposition of the population, rather than from an overall decline in the average (see Table 10.7).

Among non-Hispanic whites, the proportion of poor remained quite low throughout the period—hovering under 10 percent up to 1989 but afterward rising to and then stabilizing at about 12 percent by the early 1990s, a rise possibly attributable to an influx of new immigrants from Eastern Europe. Throughout the period, the proportion of non-Hispanic blacks who were poor fluctuated between 27 and 34 percent, but no clear trend line can be identified. Most of the annual variance in the poverty rate was contributed by Hispanics (a category that includes not only new immigrants from Central and South America, but also Puerto Ricans). Hispanics consistently evidenced poverty rates of 40 percent or higher, and their numbers in the population have been rising. (Hispanics now constitute more than one-fourth of the population of New York City.)

Poverty among Puerto Ricans and Other Hispanics

As noted earlier, the economic condition of the Puerto Rican population of the city has become increasingly precarious over time, with poverty rates well above not only those of African Americans but those of immigrant Hispanics as well. In 1978, some 43 percent of Puerto Ricans (who then constituted about 12.3 percent of the city's total population) were classified as poor. At that time, "other Hispanics" exhibited a much lower poverty rate, with less than 6.6 percent having incomes below the poverty line. (This may be an underestimate because illegal immigrants may have been uncounted as well as poor.)

These discrepancies have subsequently narrowed. Gradually, the Puerto Ricans were joined by newer Hispanic immigrants, so that by 1987 the number of Puerto Ricans (by birth or by descent) was just about equal to that of "other Hispanics," a situation that has continued to prevail through the 1990s. By then the Puerto Rican poverty rate of 43 percent was only marginally higher than the 37 percent reported by "other Hispanics," many of whom were recent immigrants from the Dominican Republic.[54]

The Contribution to Poverty of Family Type

As in other places, however, the association between poverty and single-female headed households is very strong, so that family poverty differentials are partially due to differences in the prevalence in each group of families with children headed by women. In each year for which data are available, the number of black and Hispanic families in poor female-headed households containing children under eighteen years of age was twice the number of comparably situated non-Hispanic white families, with blacks and Hispanics roughly similar in magnitude. Table 10.8 shows the interaction between race/ethnicity and poverty in female-headed families with children. It is clear, then, that the rise in poverty rates in New York is partially due to changes in the composition of the population, with Hispanics demonstrating the highest poverty rates, which in part is a function of the large number of "broken" families, especially among Puerto Ricans.[55]

The somewhat more favorable condition of blacks in New York, in comparison to Hispanics, warrants comment. There has been some social mobility for black New Yorkers now that this population is no longer heavily weighted toward recent migrants from the South and has been infused by ambitious Jamaicans. Blacks are generally better educated than Hispanics (Puerto Rican as well as others) and are better positioned for jobs in the public sector because of citizenship and English proficiency. Despite this, a major gap remains between white non-Hispanics and black non-Hispanics. I will return to this theme when I discuss the pattern of New York's public expenditures and its large municipal labor force. Without the redistributive effects of the former and the job opportunities provided by the latter, the plight of minorities in New York would be even worse than it currently is. In conclusion, one cannot dismiss either the "job mismatch" or the declines in family stability and labor force participation as factors contributing to the growth of "need" in center cities of the New York region, especially among minorities.

Table 10.8. Percentage of female-headed households containing children under eighteen years of age with incomes below the poverty line, by race and ethnicity, New York City in selected recent years

	1984	1985	1986	1987	1990	1991	1992
Total	64.2	66.5	62.0	62.9	65.3	63.5	56.5
Non-Hispanic “white”	42.9	41.3	39.6	16.9	30.4	42.4	38.4
Non-Hispanic “black”	52.3	55.0	56.7	58.1	62.1	56.1	50.6
Hispanic	80.2	81.8	71.6	77.3	76.8	74.9	70.9

Note: In this table, the three racial/ethnic categories are mutually exclusive. Rosenberg has calculated the race/ethnicity-specific poverty rates using March Current Population tape files for each of the subsequent years.

Source: Terry J. Rosenberg, *Poverty in New York City, 1993: An Update* (New York: Community Service Society, 1994), 18, Table 4B.

THE REGIONAL ECONOMY AND JOBS

Ever since the problem was first identified in the 1960s, analysts have been concerned with the erosion of jobs in the New York region. This problem has intensified over the past decade. Although this erosion has certainly not been as extreme as in the Chicago region, it is equally unlikely to be “turned around” through reindustrialization.

The issue of employment occupies a central position in the 1996 report *A Region at Risk,* which devotes a very strong chapter to concerns over employment. According to data presented by the report’s authors, of the 19,747,964 people who lived in the thirty-one-county region in 1975, there were 6,214,900 employed workers (or 31.5 percent of the population).[56] Most of these workers (3.2 million) were concentrated in the urban centers of the region, which contained 9,239,468 of the total population;[57] of these 6.2 million jobs, 2.7 million were located in New York City, more than half of them in the central business district of Manhattan.

By 1985, despite the much-touted “globalization” of New York’s economy, the population of the thirty-one-county region had declined to 19,190,960, even though jobs in the private sector rose dramatically to 7,568,800. Much of the gain in jobs was experienced by Manhattan’s central business district, where employment rose from 1.5 to almost 1.7 million in the ten-year period. On the other hand, there was a steady erosion of jobs from other more local business zones, such as downtown Brooklyn, Jamaica, and Long Island City. Outer-ring suburban cities, such as White Plains, Poughkeepsie, and Stamford, Connecticut (favored as sites for corporate headquarters), did gain jobs, whereas jobs hemorrhaged from such formerly industrial cities as Newark and Trenton.

By 1993, despite an overall increase in the region’s population to 19,843,157, the number of jobs in private employment had dropped to about 7.3 million, and the losses were pervasive in every center city. Employment in New York City dropped from 2,931,400 in 1985 to only 2,698,500 eight years later, with most of that decline absorbed by the Manhattan central business district. By then, employment was growing *only* in the outermost reaches of the thirty-one-county region.

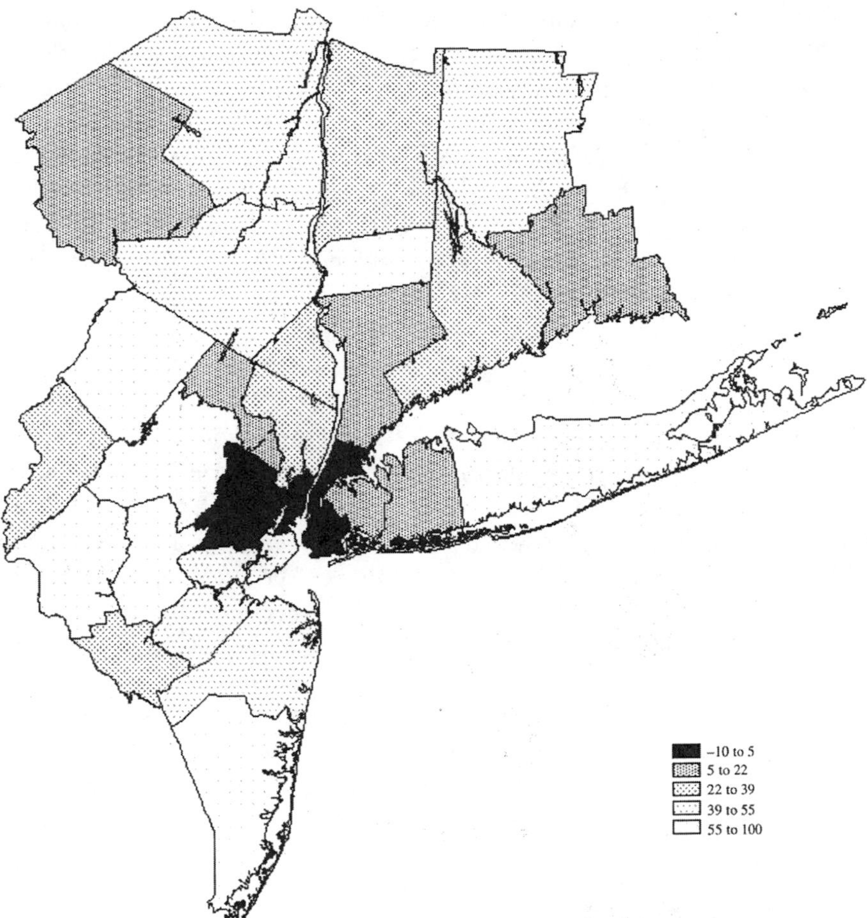

Map 10.3. Jobs decline at the center, grow on the periphery. Percentage change in regional employment in the thirty-one counties of the region deliminated by the RPA, 1975 to 1992. Source: I am indebted to Dr. Steven Weber of the New York Regional Plan Association for generating this map from computerized data from the U.S. Bureau of the Census.

Government Employment in New York City

The one area in which the city has *not* lagged behind in employment is the public sector, which accounts to some extent for the higher levels of municipal expenditures in the city in comparison to other major urban areas. For example, in 1977, even after the retrenchment required by the 1975 fiscal crisis, the city employed about 350,000 workers, and this number increased to 393,290 by 1985, at a time when other cities were still downsizing.[58] By 1989, according to a very careful analysis by political scientist Ester Fuchs, New York City was employing about fifty-five workers per one thousand residents, as contrasted with only fifteen per thousand in Chicago.[59]

Conservative politicians and economists often attribute New York's recurrent budget crises to the power of its municipal labor unions,[60] but this seems not to be true. As Fuchs's careful comparisons show, the "average expenditure per municipal employee was quite similar in New York and Chicago during the pre-fiscal crisis period."[61] It was only because New York City was performing so many more functions than Chicago, and therefore required a commensurately larger labor force, that expenditures for labor were so high in New York. (See Table 10.9 for a controlled comparison.) On a more optimistic note, however, it is clear that without such public employment, the job situation in New York would be even dimmer than it is, and without the redistributive health, educational, social, and welfare functions these employees serve, the situation of poorer New Yorkers would be more desperate.

Unionization

Nevertheless, the fact that, in general, New York has led the country in unionization has undoubtedly caused *some* of the outmigration of jobs from the region. A recent report by the U.S. Bureau of the Census noted that "New York [State] has reclaimed its position as the most heavily unionized state, surpassing Hawaii, with a union membership . . . nearly double the level nationwide."[62] Almost 29 percent of New York State's labor force belonged to a union in 1994, whereas in the country as a whole less than 16 percent of workers belonged to unions, only half the rate that obtained in the 1960s. But because much of New York's increasing union strength has come from the organization of public employees,[63] and, indeed, the rate of unionization among nongovernment employees has dropped precipitously—by 1994, down to only 18 percent—unionization alone cannot be blamed for the relocation of jobs from the area.[64] Rather, the unionization of public employees has tended to stabilize the local economy, even though such stabilization may have contributed to the city's fiscal crisis in 1975.

THE FISCAL CRISIS

The year 1975 will go down in New York City's history as the time when the city almost "went broke" and had to be rescued by bankers, the State of New York, and, eventually, the federal government. But for a brief time it appeared that the worst might happen.[65]

> On October 29, 1975, residents of New York City awoke to a banner headline on the front page of the *New York Daily News*: "FORD TO CITY: DROP DEAD.". . . The harsh realities . . . were that the nation's largest and most prosperous city was seriously threatened with the prospect of bankruptcy, its debt obligations were unpaid, and its banks were refusing to extend its credit line without federal loan guarantees.[66]

The explanations for this distressing event are disputed. It would be easy simply to blame the fiscal disaster on the "global economy" and "restructuring," as some analysts have done. Such an explanation is not entirely without merit. As we have seen, weaknesses in the American economy had already begun to appear in the second half of the 1960s, although it was largely the poor who first experienced them. In the opening years of the 1970s, the winding down of the Vietnam War led to a decline in short-term military production (although not in weapons development). And then the sudden rise in energy prices in 1973, as Arab oil exporters cut back production in reaction to renewed Arab-Israeli fighting, had a further dampening effect on industrial production, not only in the United States but in other developed countries as well. Such economic contractions naturally had exaggerated effects in "global" cities, especially in New York. Furthermore, currency destabilization on world markets was also occurring, as the Bretton Woods Agreement, which had up to then pegged exchange rates to the dollar, was ended.[67]

In the larger picture, the simultaneous transfer of industrial production to overseas sites was becoming more common, so that although the profits of transnational corporations were holding up and even increasing, a rash of plant closings within the United States was beginning.[68] The demand for unskilled and semiskilled workers declined, as cheaper labor overseas was substituted for domestic. Eventually, some of that "cheap" labor found its way into large U.S. cities, thanks to major changes in immigration regulations that were instituted beginning in 1965.

All of these trends had adverse effects on the incomes of many workers in the New York region, thus increasing the number of persons eligible for income supplements, subsidized housing, free higher education, and governmentally supported health services, which the city had long accepted as part of its responsibilities to its citizens.[69] Indeed, the optimism of the postwar period had earlier led the city to expand its responsibilities toward its poorer residents, especially in the 1960s, when funds were forthcoming from Washington, either directly or indirectly through much-touted programs such as the "War on Poverty" and the "Great Society."[70]

The proximate cause of the "fiscal crisis" of 1975, of course, was a gap between expenditures and income that had grown so large that it could be bridged, year after year, only by short-term borrowing, artfully concealed through overestimates of projected income, delays in payments, and some fanciful accounting procedures. In 1975, lenders finally balked at guaranteeing the city's fiscal capacity to meet its debt obligations.[71] To understand the fiscal crisis, then, we must examine two variables: "excessive" spending and "inadequate" income.

Spending Patterns

Although Ester Fuchs, in an otherwise impeccable study, suggests that elected officials in New York City consistently "overspent" because they had to compete to "buy" voter support by expanding (presumably unnecessary?) services to the poor,[72] a different and less cynical interpretation is also possible. The political culture of New York has traditionally been committed to social welfare goals in a manner that distinguishes it quite dramatically from most other major cities, even though voter turnout among the poor and minorities tends to be quite low, and few black politicians have exercised much power in the city, except in Harlem and sometimes, by extension, aided by "West Side liberals" in Manhattan.[73]

Certainly, La Guardia had no need to "buy" votes when he instituted relief in the city in the depths of the Depression, nor was Robert Wagner Sr. simply trying to "buy" votes when he sponsored the first federal public housing law and the laws that instituted social security and gave unions protection against unfair employer practices. I think it is highly probable that Robert Wagner Jr. (Democratic mayor from 1954 to 1965) saw himself primarily as following in his father's footsteps when he expanded welfare and opened the way for collective bargaining with municipal unions, and that John Lindsay (Fusion mayor 1965–73) may have seen himself as inheriting La Guardia's mantle of compassion when he joined with alacrity the "War on Poverty."[74] It was during the terms of these two mayors that spending increased dramatically to weave a wider net of social supports for poor New Yorkers.

Nor were these two "spenders" mavericks on the political scene of New York. In many ways, New York had always taken pride in being rich enough to assist its less-privileged residents: by providing subsidized (originally free) institutions of higher learning; by replacing tenements with better housing; by making available access to a large system of health care facilities in clinics and hospitals; by offering nourishment, home care, and recreational facilities, as well as direct financial assistance, to its dependent children and the aged;[75] and by supplying all residents who wished to avail themselves of it with an extensive (and unzoned) mass-transit system that needed permanent subventions to keep it running.[76] Once such services have been institutionalized, it is very difficult to cut back on them or to raise their prices,[77] and in times of optimism, it is highly tempting to expand them as additional needs are perceived, especially when federal policies support such expansions. It is therefore not hard to understand how New York's operating budget could have increased fivefold between 1960 and 1975, primarily in those functions Fuchs designates as "non-common."[78]

Following the dual categories conventionally employed in fiscal data reporting, both Shefter and Fuchs distinguish between functions ordinarily performed by municipal governments in the United States and those that are not (see the discussion in Chapter 8, above). This distinction is crucial for understanding the differences in "political climate" between New York on the one hand and Chicago and Los Angeles on the other. Common functions include municipal administration and government buildings, as well as police and fire protection, sanitation, sewerage, highways, and recreation; these are ordinarily performed by all municipalities or their special districts. Noncommon functions involve more discretionary services—those designed to provide (some) city residents with, inter alia, health and hospital services, welfare, libraries, utilities, mass transit, corrections, education, and so on. As Fuchs points out, "Common function services have been classified as 'middle class,' 'allocational,' or 'essential' services," whereas "non-common functions are usually considered 'poor people's services' or 'redistributive services,'" most of which are strictly for the use of the city's low-income population.[79]

It is clear that New York City, more than any other large city in the country, has been committed to giving greater assistance to the needy. By 1975, close to three-fourths of all municipal expenditures in New York City were directed toward non-common, (i.e., redistributive) functions. In contrast, in that same year only one-fifth of Chicago's much lower budget was allocated to such purposes, even though, as a percentage of total city residents, Chicago's poor easily made up as large a proportion of the population as in New York.[80] Los Angeles, also, has devoted very little of its city budget to "redistributive" services.

But differing internal power systems and even ideologies are not the sole explanation. Part of the reason both Chicago and Los Angeles appear to be spending so little on welfare functions is that both cities have been able to "off-load" onto their respective counties (and even states) expenses for many functions that appear in the New York City budget because it has no "containing" larger county that could tap into the resource base of its suburbs. The legitimate comparison, then, is not between center cities, but between the five counties that make up New York City and the counties that include Chicago (i.e., Cook County), and Los Angeles (i.e., Los Angeles County).[81] Although New York's costs still appear slightly higher, the differences are substantially reduced and can be accounted for largely by New York's higher transit and welfare costs.

It is extremely difficult to compare costs directly, especially when one wishes to include county as well as city expenditures. Therefore, in the discussion that follows I use the number of local government employees per function as a surrogate measure, especially because costs per worker are roughly similar in New York and Chicago (and can be presumed to be similar in Los Angeles).[82] If costs per worker are so similar, then the difference in expenditures (and thus the "excessive costs" of municipal services in New York) can be explained largely by the fact that the New York City government performs a much greater number of functions and therefore requires a substantially larger staff of municipal employees.

Table 10.9 compares the number of employees by function for New York City and for the cities and their respective counties of Chicago and Los Angeles in 1974, the year just prior to the fiscal crisis. The table has been constructed using data that appear in the Twentieth Century Fund report of 1980, which estimated the number of government employees (in all local governments within their central county[ies] per ten thousand inhabitants) by function.[83]

From this table it is clear that the residual differences among the cities in *common* functions can be explained largely by New York City's more complex and extensive transit system, compared with Chicago's smaller (and regionally supported) and Los Angeles's (until now) insignificant systems. In terms of *noncommon* functions, most of the difference can be attributed to New York's greater responsibility for welfare (because by 1974 the state of Illinois was responsible for Chicago-Cook County's welfare system, and many of Los Angeles County's poor were ineligible for welfare),[84] health, including hospitals, and public housing, in which New York City leads the nation. My conclusion is that there is some evidence of New York's greater commitment to the welfare of its residents, but when one includes all functions by taking into account the role of county and state government responsibilities in Chicago and Los Angeles, what initially appears as New York's extravagance tends to decrease, although not to disappear entirely. More than due to "local political strategies," then, the differences are attributable to political-institutional arrangements in which New York,

Table 10.9. Employees per ten thousand residents in October 1974 (all local governments in central county/ies) for New York City, Cook County (including Chicago), and Los Angeles County (including the city of Los Angeles) by function

Function	New York City	Cook County	Los Angeles County
Estimated full-time employees	596.4	392.1	473.5
Estimated full-time and part-time employees	642.5	455.4	481.3
Common functions:			
Employees			
Fire protection	18.3	11.6	12.0
Local utilities	61.0	29.2	29.7
Police protection	47.4	37.4	29.9
Sanitation	15.9	7.1	3.2
Sewerage	2.8	6.7	2.7
Corrections	8.1	2.6	9.5
Financial administration	5.6	4.1	7.7
General control	13.5	13.4	17.0
Water supply	3.8	6.2	8.1
Parks and recreation	8.2	12.3	11.6
Highways	10.4	9.6	8.3
Libraries	4.8	4.3	4.6
Other miscellaneous	53.1	57.2	64.0
Transit	57.2	22.9[a]	7.9
All common functions	313.9	230.8	224.3
Common functions minus transit	256.7	207.9	216.4
Noncommon functions:			
Employees			
Public welfare	36.7	0.1[b]	19.8
Hospitals	62.5	18.1	29.2
Health	10.7	5.0	5.2
Housing/urban renewal	18.7	4.7	2.1
All other unidentified	27.0	16.4	11.8
Education	176.7	170.1	180.5
All noncommon functions	305.3	198.0	234.7
Noncommon functions minus education	128.6	27.9	54.2

Note: The totals given on the first line do not add up to the totals derived if one adds the individual functions listed in the table. My attempt to locate the source of this discrepancy failed, so I assume the error may be in the original table.

[a]Chicago provides most of its mass transit through a regional authority that has its own revenue-raising powers.

[b]The state of Illinois absorbs all the costs of welfare for Chicago, whereas in New York, the state requires matching funds.

Source: Reorganized and reprinted with permission from Twentieth Century Fund/Century Foundation, *New York—World City* (New York: Priority Press, 1980), 91, Table 4.5.

because of its boundaries and its relation to state government, has assumed budgetary responsibility for many functions that elsewhere are funded by county and/or state governments. Nevertheless, these arrangements, which perhaps had few consequences when the city's finances were being supplemented by federal contributions, led to the disaster of 1975, when federal funds began to disappear.

Since that time there is some evidence that the city's commitment to redistributive goals has been undermined both by the harsher "discipline" imposed by the bankers in the Municipal Assistance Corporation (MAC), which backed the bond offer to rescue the city from receivership in 1975 in return for retrenchment, and by the state government, which, in return for absorbing certain expenses for the City University and a modest proportion of welfare costs, now supervises the city budget with even greater stringency.[85]

The defection from the "welfare state" noticeable in recent years in the city, however, has come not only from intractable institutional arrangements, but from a falling away of middle-class support for services that seem more and more to be used by the city's minorities. Conflicts over public schools and over subway fares reflect some of these new alignments of power in the city. In the former, at least, New York is not that different from either Chicago or Los Angeles, as I show in Chapters 11 and 12.

Education

One of the major expenditures in city government in New York is for the public school system, which increasingly serves a nonwhite population, substantially greater than its representation in the general population, and, what has been a bone of contention for many years in the school system, employs a teaching and supervisory staff racially and ethnically distinct from its student body. As the city's white population has aged or has moved, and has been only partially replaced by childless professionals, the enrollment of white students in the public school system has declined, a trend that has been intensified by a growing dependence of working- and middle-class residents upon religious schools and by the continued reliance by the wealthiest residents upon expensive "private" schools (a functional "substitute" for a move to the suburbs).

The net result of these changes is that, by 1990, some 80 percent of all students in the New York City public school system were classified as "nonwhite." This has sharpened the racial contrast between students and public school employees and fed the movement for community control of local school boards. Despite efforts to recruit minority teachers, by 1990 only 29 percent of the teachers and 28 percent of the school principals were nonwhite. The tensions between the (white/Jewish-dominated) teachers' unions and the (mostly "minority") local groups seeking decentralized empowerment over the schools must be read in this context. (The Ocean Hill battle was the opening shot in this conflict.)

Given the overwhelming preponderance of nonwhite students in city schools, the question of using "busing" to foster racial integration has become somewhat irrelevant, especially given that free transportation by bus or subway is made available to all students. Nor have recent attempts to offer "choices," or to set up magnet schools or "schools within schools," stanched the flow of "white" students from the public school system. In Manhattan, for example, with the exception of one oddly shaped school district (encompassing, inter alia, Battery Park City, Tribeca, Greenwich Village, Chelsea, and the wealthy Upper East Side) where enrollment of nonwhites was just under three-quarters in 1990, nonwhite students constituted 90 to 99.8 percent of all enrollees in that borough's remaining public schools. Of the twelve school districts in Brooklyn, there were only two in which whites constituted at least half of the students; many of the borough's other school districts (especially in the "midsection" of Bedford-Stuyvesant and neighboring zones) had enrollments that exceeded 90 percent nonwhite. In the seven school districts of Queens, only the two most outlying districts adjacent to suburban Nassau County had less than 60 percent nonwhite enrollment. The student body of East New York, in contrast, was 93 percent nonwhite. Staten Island was the only borough where nonwhites constituted a lower proportion, and even there, the 27 percent nonwhite enrollment exceeded the representation of nonwhites in the borough total. At the public college and university level, the proportion of nonwhites admitted has climbed dramatically, particularly after City College switched to an open enrollment policy. Since education is one of the major outlets for noncommon expenditures in New York City (and one that does not even appear in the city budgets of Chicago or Los Angeles), one can readily see why New York City's budget should be so high, even after retrenchments.

Privatized "Subsidies" for Common and Uncommon Functions

As the city has been forced to cut back on street-cleaning expenses and to redeploy its police force to areas of high crime and the narcotics trade, neglected commercial areas in the city have moved increasingly to set up paragovernmental service zones (business improvement districts, called BIDs), in which adjacent property owners contribute to a fund that substitutes for or enhances services no longer provided by the municipality. This privatization, which amounts to a "user tax" on adjacent businesses (and, in some cases, even residences), conceals the level of financing of "common" expenditures, but at the cost of redistributing benefits in an unequal manner. In addition, the city has attempted to "extract" from private commercial builders subsidies, or even the direct provision of general amenities, through a complex bargaining system whereby the city planning office grants exceptions to zoning and height restrictions in return for builder-financed quasi-public open space at the street level. Because such amenities are located exclusively in thriving business zones and are often privately policed to exclude "undesirables," these, too, increase inequities.

Public Buildings, Housing, and Redevelopment

On the other hand, New York has not been able to unload onto other levels of government or onto private developers the costs of improvements in the built environment. As noted in Chapter 7, New York City provides subsidized housing for about half a million of its residents, a far greater proportion than in Chicago and astronomically greater than the number the city of Los Angeles provides. Construction of these subsidized units has continued with state and local funds, albeit at a lower level, after the federal subsidies virtually vanished. In contrast, Chicago stopped building public housing projects when federal funds dried up, and has now turned over its public housing entirely to the U.S. Department of Housing and Urban Development.[86] And Los Angeles had always lagged well behind the other two, even when funds from Washington were still available.

In addition, both Chicago and Los Angeles have been allowed to establish quasi-independent "nonprofit" organizations for reconstruction—in the case of Chicago, its Public Building Commission, and in Los Angeles, its Community Redevelopment Authority, both of which have independent revenue-creating powers and have access to restricted self-sustaining financing to carry out activities that in New York City remain part of the capital budget.[87]

Resources

The year 1975 was a critical turning point for New York City's ability to garner the resources needed to pay for its generous redistributions. The resources at the city's command were shrinking,[88] not only because of economic contractions, defections from the city of job-providing enterprises, and the movement of higher-income (i.e., taxable) residents to suburbs in other states, but also because, increasingly, the city had become dependent upon other tax-collecting levels of government, both federal and state, to return at least a portion of the taxes city residents paid in order to support local needs. It was this increased dependence upon intergovernmental transfer payments that made New York City so vulnerable in that year.

In 1929, just before the Depression, some 80 percent of New York City's revenues came from property taxes and the rest from license fees and other locally generated revenues. Very little came from intergovernmental transfers. This began to change during the Depression, but even so, up to 1965 intergovernmental transfers accounted for only about a quarter of the city's revenue, still less than the steadily declining proportion derived from the property tax.[89] Beginning in the mid-1960s, while the proportion of revenues coming from property taxes continued to decline, there was a real increase in the amount (and proportion) coming from the state and, especially, from the federal government, an amount that, under President Johnson, rose dramatically. By the early 1970s, such transfers were accounting for about half of the entire revenue at the disposal of the city, although to receive them, the city often had to put up matching funds. As the Twentieth Century Fund's task force reports in its analysis of the causes of the 1975 fiscal crisis:

> Between 1960 and the end of fiscal 1975 . . . , New York became adept at tapping both local and intergovernmental sources of revenue. It taxed what seemed like every conceivable revenue base, and it took advantage of every applicable federal and state program. The largest part of this financing effort was in the form of intergovernmental aid. From 1960 to 1975, local revenues increased by 306 percent,

> state aid by 696 percent, and federal aid by 2,282 percent. . . . Although all localities began to make more use of federal and state financing during this period, New York received close to three times as much money per capita as the average for local governments in the seventy-four Standard Metropolitan Statistical Areas.[90]

By the mid-1970s, however, there was a sudden reversal, as commitments made earlier began to lapse. The administration in Washington under Nixon had little interest in continuing Johnson's "war" on poverty. Although federal aid to cities was not cut off, it was scaled down and directed toward more specific capital projects. Money coming to the city from the state government, although it increased somewhat, was insufficient to make up the shortfall when federal moneys were cut back. This was the immediate precipitating factor in the fiscal crisis that hit the city in 1975, a crisis intensified by the global *and* local economic contractions that reduced locally raised taxes at the same time that the number of poor residents needing assistance increased. The latter's political power was insufficient to pressure for continued levels of support in the face of financial retrenchments and racial and ethnic differences.

Fiscal Subsidies in the Wrong Direction

The fiscal situation, however, is even more inequitable when one takes into account the structures of federal taxation and redistribution. New York State contributes far more, proportionately, to the federal budget than it receives back, resulting in something described recently as an "imbalance sheet." New York, New Jersey, and Connecticut are among the top ten states that contribute far more per capita to the federal government than they receive back in payments. (Significantly, the midwestern states of Michigan, Minnesota, Illinois, and Wisconsin are also among the top ten.) In contrast, "net surplus" states are all in the South or the Rockies.[91] The possibility that such discrepancies will increase when welfare program subsidies are decentralized through block grants is worrisome to political officials of the city and state, because New York State is among those with the highest payments and the lowest ceiling (below the poverty line) for eligibility.[92] It is also the only state where welfare responsibilities are mandated by the state constitution.

Although fiscal imbalances and welfare expenditures are not issues that affect only minority residents, given the associations among poverty, needs, and ethnic and racial groups, one would imagine that there might be a disproportionate political interest that ought to be reflected in struggles for local political power. Although the political system in New York City is more open to such representation than are the systems in Chicago or Los Angeles, there remain significant problems.

THE POLITICS OF MINORITY EMPOWERMENT

New York City elected its first (and as of 1999 only) black mayor, David Dinkins, in 1989. His election, however, did not signal any significant shift in the power system. First, Dinkins had risen to become the president of the borough of Manhattan through normal channels of the Democratic Party. Second, his margin was very slim in a three-way contest with Democratic incumbent Ed Koch (who ran as an independent) and Republican candidate Rudolph Giuliani. And third, Dinkins, after serving only one undistinguished term, was defeated for reelection in 1993 by Giuliani. This belated and brief capture of the mayoralty was long overdue. In 1983 Chicago had elected its first black mayor, Harold Washington, and reelected him four years later. Only after his untimely death in 1987 did the "white" democratic establishment in Chicago begin to recapture the office of mayor through the son of its longtime machine boss, Richard Daley (who was elected with only 10 percent of the "black vote"). The mayor of Los Angeles from 1973 to 1993 was Tom Bradley, a black former football star and police chief, whose elevation to power had been supported by a coalition of "Westside (heavily Jewish) liberals" and minorities.[93] Only the white backlash from the South-Central riots propelled the political novice Republican businessman Richard Riordan to the office of mayor in that city.

It is logical to ask why, given the more liberal stance of New Yorkers, black politicians have been so underrepresented in city government.[94] Shefter, in trying to account for the fact that in 1985 the black candidate running against Koch in the Democratic primary had garnered only 13 percent of the vote, suggests that low voter turnout among minorities and a fragmentation of interests among them, split largely along black versus Hispanic lines, were largely responsible for the poor showing of the black candidate,[95] to which might be added the often tense alliance between New York's native blacks and its black immigrants from Jamaica, who have provided a disproportionate share of successful elected officials.[96] But an alternative explanation is also possible. The urgency to achieve formal power may have been moderated to some extent by the fact that white mayors of either party were not necessarily viewed as antiblack or antipoor (although, in his later years in office, Koch appeared to be). Indeed, it had been during the administrations of Wagner and Lindsay that the most visible expansions in New York's "welfare state" occurred, and when black neighborhoods in other cities were exploding in the aftermath of the assassination of Martin Luther King Jr., Mayor Lindsay walked unguarded into black areas of New York to reassure his constituents of his sympathy.

Here again the contrast with Chicago needs to be reinterpreted. Up to his death in 1976, Mayor Richard Daley ruled a strong white-dominated Democratic machine in both city (Chicago) and county (Cook). The alliance he put together—between "white ethnics" interested in preserving their own neighborhoods and downtown businessmen who supported a strong "growth machine" to preserve the Loop's vitality—could perhaps afford to ignore the demands of the black community. This began to unravel only after Daley's death. A brief interregnum ensued when a coalition of blacks and Hispanics succeeded in electing former congressman Harold Washington as mayor.[97] But as we shall see, after his untimely death, control eventually returned to the Daley family. Instead of asking why African Americans failed to achieve power in New York, we must really ask why Chicago's far larger black population has been unable to wrest control from the "white establishment," and why Chicago's poor have been so neglected. We turn to these questions in Chapter 11. The different political constellation in Los Angeles will be taken up in Chapter 12.

REEVALUATING THE EXTENT TO WHICH GLOBALIZATION "EXPLAINS" NEW YORK

It is clear that changes in the global economy have been partially responsible for the deindustrialization of the New York region. It is also true that the recent increase in economic "globalization" (especially in the areas of media, finance, producer services, and international tourism) and foreign immigration has served to shore up the city's vitality. However, it must be remembered that trends in manufacturing decline long preceded the current pattern of restructuring, and that New York's dependence upon global functions (and immigrants as a source of demographic growth) had similarly preceded recent expansions in the scale and scope of the international economy. Globalization has enhanced New York's role as "the capital of capitalism," but it must also be recognized that it has made the city more vulnerable to forces originating in the world economy.

However, global forces interact in New York, as elsewhere, with many far more national and local conditions. In the last analysis, both its political handicap of a fragmented region and its political culture of adaptability to change will determine what responses the region can make to powerful tectonic shifts in the world beyond.

CHAPTER 11

Postapocalypse Chicago

A SIMPLER BUT MORE TROUBLED REGION

In contrast to the cases of New York or even Los Angeles, locating the regional "boundary" of the Chicago metropolitan region is simple. One can easily delineate the rough dimensions of the symmetrically expanded semicircular urbanized region that still contains Chicago as its undisputed, if increasingly troubled, core. Not only is Chicago's regional structure more visible and coherent, but, because virtually all of the region (except for a small overflow into industrial Indiana) is contained within the state of Illinois, many of the jurisdictional and fiscal complications that have increasingly hindered solutions to New York's thorny problems are solvable, at least on a theoretical level, in the Chicago metropolitan region.

Given these "advantages," one might anticipate fewer disjunctures and conflicts and hence perhaps a stronger coherence in Chicago's adaptations to restructuring and the new global order. That, however, has been far from the case. From its origins Chicago has been a city divided within itself; today large parts of the city proper are essentially sealed off from the "periphery," isolated by widening racial and class rifts.

TIMES OF TROUBLE, TIMES OF CLEAVAGE

By the late 1960s, those rifts had made Chicago a very troubled city. Despite its glorious lakefront facade (extending almost to the city's northern edge, albeit truncated abruptly south of the Loop), the backstage city was restless. The West Side, a second-settlement multiracial/ethnic ghetto, had just exploded in violent protest. The fires, as elsewhere, had been ignited by the assassination of Martin Luther King Jr., but they were fed by the frustrations of the neighborhood's impoverished black residents. Undampened by civil rights "progress" and several years of "Wars on Poverty" followed by the "Great Society," the explosion destroyed a wide swath of territory along West Madison Street and Roosevelt Road, suggesting a modest replay of the Great Chicago Fire a century earlier.

This was perhaps a rehearsal for what was to come. The troops that had suppressed the ghetto rebellion in April 1968 were seasoned when, six months later, Chicago police, backed by the National Guard, were called upon to control thousands of antiwar protesters who had gathered in Grant Park to demonstrate against the Vietnam War and President Johnson, and to make their views evident to delegates at the Democratic National Convention, which was meeting across Michigan Avenue.[1] The resulting violence suggested a replay of National Guard beatings of strikers, also a recurrent theme of Chicago's labor "relations." According to Chicago folklore, the officers had taken to heart Mayor Daley's orders, issued during the previous riot, to "shoot to kill," although there were no fatalities.

These tensions were perhaps symptoms of the fact that, although the old power structure had been superficially maintained in Chicago, deep economic and demographic transformations were threatening the status quo. For decades, the local Democratic machine had kept a lid on tensions and had defused any attempts to challenge it, except from *inside* the party. Patronage and a complex hierarchy of precinct captains and ward committeemen had perpetuated the power of a coalition between "white ethnic" neighborhoods and downtown business interests to exercise their will over the city; their hold, however, was weakening.

The antiwar demonstration signaled a shift in national politics as well, one that would undermine Daley's (and thus Chicago's) voice in the country. The election in that year of Republican Richard M. Nixon as president inaugurated a period of more than two decades that, except for the single-term interregnum of President Carter, left the White House firmly in the hands of a party beholden to neither the city nor its mayor. It was, perhaps, no accident that during this period Chicago experienced an accelerated decline in its economic base and the final desertion of perhaps half its white electorate to the suburbs.

When Boss Richard J. Daley died in 1976, with him died much of Chicago's clout, both at home and in Washington.[2] Although by 1987 his son had recaptured the office of mayor, Richard M. Daley presided over a shakier empire. Both economic and political power were slipping away from the place that had for so long proudly borne the title of America's "Second City." It was stripped of even this last distinction, as Los Angeles's population surged ahead and Chicago was demoted to "Third City."

ECONOMIC DIFFICULTIES

Decline in Manufacturing

Deindustrialization continued to hit the Fordist economy of Chicago very hard between the late 1960s and the mid-1990s. However, it would be difficult to attribute the collapse solely to changes wrought by globalization. The rout of the economy had been particularly marked in the 1960s and early 1970s, even before international restructuring had made very much headway: "The City of Chicago had been losing manufacturing jobs steadily since its peak of 668,056 in 1947 and after 1967 the Chicago region as a whole declined in manufacturing employment. The decline was particularly devastating between 1967 and 1982, when a quarter of a million, or 46 percent of the city's manufacturing jobs, were lost."[3]

In 1971 the Chicago stockyards closed, bringing to a close a century during which the city had remained prime hog butcher to the world. Big steel held on only a little longer.[4] Although the bear stock market of 1973–74 struck Chicago hard, as late as 1973 the great South Works still had steel orders that "outpaced supply and its parent, U.S. Steel made record profits." The wars in the Pacific, however, were winding down, and the mills would not survive the next local recession, which recurred between 1979 and 1983. By the latter year, the rust belt, of which Chicago was a part, was crumbling in earnest. After having dominated the southern shore of Lake Michigan and given employment to many big shoulders—both immigrant and black—for almost a century, the "vast mill complex [of U.S. Steel] became as silent as a tomb."[5] Nearby plants dependent upon ready steel supplies also began to close in a domino effect.

Initially, it appeared that manufacturing plants might merely be relocating beyond the city limits, and that "restructuring" to a postindustrial service economy would take up some of the employment slack within the region, if not the city. Between 1972 and 1981, although the city of Chicago lost one-tenth of its private sector jobs, employment in the entire metropolitan area was up by 25 percent. Such expansion, however, was racially selective: "On both sides of the city limits, black and racially mixed neighborhoods lost jobs while predominantly white communities experienced net gains."[6]

Contraction was also selective by economic sector. Although jobs in manufacturing were actually increasing (numerically and proportionately) in many newer suburban areas during the 1970s, within the city of Chicago one-quarter of all factories closed during that decade. Furthermore, deindustrialization had not spared the southern industrial suburbs (including Gary, Indiana), especially the heavy industries of steel and associated products around the closed mills. Even though suburban Cook County and other suburban parts of the Chicago standard metropolitan statistical area (SMSA) gained about as many factory jobs as Chicago lost in that interval, this still did not prevent an overall loss of jobs in the region, once the Indiana (mostly steel mill) losses were factored in.

Thus the postwar boom that had buoyed the Chicago region's economy in the 1950s and even into the early 1960s had ended. Between 1947 and 1981 the entire region experienced a net loss of 14 percent of all manufacturing jobs, which represented "a loss of 1.9 jobs through closings, relocations, and contractions for every new job created due to startups, in-migration, and expansion."[7] As Squires et al. conclude, "The smokestacks have certainly not disappeared, but the loss to the city of 25 percent

Table 11.1. Manufacturing employment in the Chicago region, 1947, 1982, and 1992: number of jobs and percentage share in city of Chicago, suburban Cook County, and the five collar counties

	1947		1982		1992	
Area	Number	Percentage	Number	Percentage	Number	Percentage
Chicago	668,000	78	277,000	37	187,000	31
Suburban Cook County	121,000	14	279,000	37	235,400	39
Collar counties	64,000	8	189,000	25	185,200	30
Total	853,000	100	745,000	100	607,600	100

Source: The 1947 figures are from John F. McDonald, *Employment Location and Industrial Land Use in Metropolitan Chicago* (Champaign, Ill.: Stipes, 1984), 10, Table 1.4. The figures for 1982 are from U.S. Bureau of the Census, *1982 Census of Manufactures,* Geographic Area Series, Illinois (MC82-A-14) and Indiana (MC82-A-15) (Washington, D.C.: U.S. Government Printing Office, 1985), as reproduced in Gregory Squires, Larry Bennett, Kathleen McCourt, and Philip Nyden, *Chicago: Race, Class, and the Response to Urban Decline* (Philadelphia: Temple University Press, 1987), 26, Table 2.1. I have recomputed the figures in Squires et al. to omit Lake County, Indiana. The figures for 1992 are my calculations from Illinois Department of Employment Security, "Supplementary Statistical Tables: Industry Breakouts, 1992," in *Where Workers Work in the Chicago Metropolitan Area,* Tables 1 and 2. The situation for Chicago in 1992 was even worse than the figures reveal, because by then the booming area around O'Hare Airport was being reported with Chicago, thus shoring up the latter's employment figures. (In 1947 and 1982 the O'Hare area of "Edge City" had been included with Suburban Cook County.)

of its factories during the 1970s represents a trend that is not likely to be reversed in the near future."[8]

In the period subsequent to 1982, these dire predictions have proven all too correct, not only with respect to the city, but more recently with respect to the entire metropolitan area. Manufacturing jobs began to disappear from the suburbs as well. In the decade between 1982 and 1992, manufacturing employment in the metropolitan area dropped 18 percent, and in the single year 1991–92, some twenty-five thousand manufacturing jobs disappeared from Chicago, suburban Cook County, and the five surrounding "collar" counties. Even though most of these "lost jobs" (nineteen thousand) were in the city, it is significant that the remaining six thousand jobs that disappeared were in the rest of the SMSA.[9]

Can the industrial economy be revived? Can substitutes for Chicago's traditional Fordist base be found in other sectors of the economy? Opinions differ. Perhaps the most optimistic answer was offered by contributors to a 1989 conference on "restructuring" in the rust belt, even though the picture they actually painted was a somber one. The editors of the conference's published proceedings acknowledge that restructuring (by which they actually mean deindustrialization) was occurring in the Midwest—with jobs moving away from the "goods-producing sector of the economy," which in 1959 had accounted for 40 percent of all employment, to the services, broadly defined, which by 1989 accounted for 75 percent. They acknowledge also that more than a simple dip in the business cycle had caused these changes, and that the Midwest, which had been particularly adversely affected by retrenchment, did not appear to be recovering.[10]

The conference proceedings comprise a set of case studies of major urban centers in the Midwest. Of these, the chapter on Chicago is the most "upbeat," arguing that the size and diversity of Chicago's economic base would allow it to reorient, using old industries as seedbeds for new ones. Whistling in the dark, the authors opine that this development *could* (might?) prevent the kinds of collapse that other more specialized cities had experienced.[11] However, their optimistic scenario is belied by the information they present in their Table 4-2, which compares the rate of employment growth for Chicago between 1979 and 1986 with that of the country.[12] During this seven-year period, when total U.S. employment grew by 12 percent, Chicago's dropped by 1 percent. Similarly, whereas U.S. manufacturing employment was down by 11 percent in the same period, Chicago's manufacturing employment dropped precipitously by 23 percent. And although U.S. employment in transportation and wholesale and retail trade grew modestly, Chicago's remained essentially stable (only in air transportation did Chicago's employment picture look healthy). Even in the much-touted (but very small in actual numbers) "new service" sector, Chicago's rate of growth was much lower than that of the country's. For example, national employment in finance increased by 23 percent, whereas Chicago's grew by only 13 percent; in the country's economy, other types of service jobs grew by 36 percent, while the growth in Chicago's other service employment was only 21 percent. All of this undermined the rosy picture the authors try to paint. In the end, they are forced to conclude that *"Chicago appears to have suffered the disadvantages of a concentration in manufacturing on the downside of the business cycle, but did not reap the benefits of it on the upswing."*[13] Thus it is hard to blame Chicago's difficulties over the past thirty years exclusively on international restructuring, given that these trends were well under way before the 1970s.

Diversity versus Defense

Why, one must ask, did Chicago suffer such problems? I agree with Ann Markusen and Karen McCurdy's conclusion that the lack of federal defense contracts, particularly in research and development, was largely to blame for manufacturing losses.[14] In Chapter 8 I presented findings from the study by Markusen and McCurdy that analyzed prime defense contracts per capita between 1951 and 1984. It will be recalled that whereas Illinois had been the recipient of a moderate amount of such contracts in 1951, the state's per capita share of these contracts had already begun to decline in 1958 and by 1967 was dropping dramatically. By 1984, Illinois had slipped to the bottom of the eighteen ranked states, falling below even such other shortchanged midwestern states as Wisconsin, Michigan, and Ohio.[15]

Markusen, Hall, Dietrich, and Campbell's earlier book on the "gunbelt" prepared the ground for such a development. As these authors note, up through the Second World War, "and to a lesser extent during the Korean and Vietnam [War] periods, the industrial heartland hummed with factories devoted to the production of tanks, airplanes, ordnance, and other war materiel. . . . the early lead in defense production was only logical, for these industrial cities were the nation's most innovative centers in metals, heavy machinery, autos, appliances, and consumer electronics." Despite this lead and the existence of top engineering schools and a skilled workforce, the Midwest lost out. "Decade by decade, *especially after 1950,* midwestern industrial cities lost ground to the emerging 'gunbelt.'"[16]

Certainly one must acknowledge that Illinois's loss of "political clout" in Washington was partially responsible for the state's unattractiveness, because, as Markusen rightly points out, what Chicago (and, therefore, Illinois) lost in both the political and economic arenas, other states, such as Massachusetts (under Kennedy and Tip O'Neill), Texas (under Johnson), and California (under Nixon and Reagan) gained. But the fact that the arms industry is largely an *export* business also helps to explain the Department of Defense's preference for coastal locations.

More Than Manufacture Was Involved in the Decline

The theories of postindustrial society and global cities, however, suggest that deindustrialization and internationalization merely create a shifting demand for labor—away from manufacturing and toward the services, especially those involved in finance, control, and producers' services geared to the new forms of the economy. While expanding services have indeed taken up some of the slack in employment, in the Chicago economy this has been insufficient to replace all lost jobs. Between 1991 and 1992 alone, the Chicago metropolitan area also lost 12,000 *nonmanufacturing* jobs. The gain of 19,000 nonmanufacturing jobs in the region took place exclusively in the suburban counties, but this failed to compensate for the 31,000 service jobs lost in the city of Chicago.[17] Even in the "new" service areas of FIRE, business services, engineering, and management and related services, the early 1990s proved disappointing. In the single year of 1991 to 1992, Chicago experienced a net loss of 13,782 jobs in these "Loop"-type occupations. Although suburban Cook County gained 2,943 and the five collar counties gained 9,087 jobs in these sectors, their combined gain still fell 1,752 jobs short of compensating for Chicago's losses.[18]

By now even the most enthusiastic Chicago boosters are finding it hard to ignore the metropolitan region's decline. A study of the financial industry in the region, prepared by the Chamber of Commerce, euphemistically singles out the years between 1990 and 1993 as a "period of adjustment."[19] It notes that employment in financial services "has leveled off at about 266,000," that office vacancy rates had risen from 17 percent in 1991 to 18.5 percent in 1992 and stood at 19.1 percent in 1993, and that nonresidential building permits were substantially off in those three years.

Given these depressing facts, it is no wonder that Chicago has begun to intensify its efforts to publicize its competitive advantages. A very glossy publication produced by the city in 1990 advertises Chicago's good "business climate," but the advantages singled out are those more appropriate to a backward southern community than to the formerly great Fordist powerhouse. Comparing the city to its "rivals" (especially

New York and Los Angeles), the publication stresses that Chicago has *lower wages, less road congestion, lower rents for office space, lower utility rates, lower corporate and individual taxes,* and a *more "cooperative" administration.* Although the slick brochure does not spell out the implications of these advantages, it is evident that lower wages and lower taxes can only mean more poor people and fewer funds to assist them.[20] And, as we shall see, the poor are disproportionately black and Latino residents of the center city. The overall figures conceal a growing gap between the city and its suburban ring and, concomitantly, a growing gap between the city's minorities and the overwhelmingly white populations that monopolize all but a handful of suburban communities.

Before exploring the spatial and social gaps that now bifurcate the metropolitan region, however, it may be necessary for me to defend the inclusion of Chicago among the global cities of the world—a defense that no one would require for New York or even Los Angeles.

CHICAGO'S ROLE AS A COMMAND CENTER OF THE INTERNATIONAL ECONOMY

When I began this study, I noticed that Chicago had frequently been overlooked in various enumerations of world/global cities.[21] Several knowledgeable colleagues questioned why I was including a landlocked metropolis that so clearly had lost its traditional economic base. Initially I defended my choice on two grounds. First, Chicago was still the third-ranking metropolitan region in the country, demographically far ahead of the next contender, San Francisco, and numerically ahead of Los Angeles in terms of the number of headquarters for America's largest firms (although both lagged well behind New York).[22] And second, I argued that Chicago could provide a significant contrast to New York and Los Angeles *because* the newer international developments were not reinfusing the region's economy, as they arguably were New York and Los Angeles.

Chicago also offers a theoretically interesting counterfactual. If, indeed, globalization is restoring vitality to major control centers because they are involved in the upper circuits of trade and finance, then Chicago should also be benefiting from these trends. Certain of its institutions, indeed, now constitute central nodes of the higher circuit of arbitrage and currency trading that Sassen, among others, has identified as the chief desideratum of the new global economy. These Chicago-based financial institutions undoubtedly play a crucial role in the operation of the international system. However, because they have an extremely low employment multiplier, they have only a minor impact on the region. The most impressive of these international financial institutions is the Chicago Mercantile Exchange.

Chicago Mercantile Exchange, Center of Capitalist Finance

One of the points stressed in the literature on global cities is that what makes them "world cities" is not their productive might per se, but their control over upper-circuit financial transactions. Such functions, however, are heavily dependent upon the communications revolution and thus exist, for the most part, in cyberspace. There is no necessary relationship, then, between the relatively tiny portion of the labor force required to perform these functions within a given node and the enormous scale of the financial transactions that flow through it.[23] Indeed, the degradation of much of Chicago's economic base is not incompatible with the fact that the city hosts a financial institution the value of whose transactions far outdistances those taking place in any other world city—including New York.

That institution is the Mercantile Exchange of Chicago (the MERC) which, since the early 1970s, has been home to the International Monetary Market (IMM), inter alia. Its story is a fascinating one, too complex to be recounted here; interested readers can find details in a lengthy book by Bob Tamarkin.[24] In brief, Tamarkin traces how a simple commodities exchange—which began its first operations just after the Chicago Fire, specializing in futures and "hedges" on butter and eggs and, later, on pork bellies (precured bacon)—"invented" a postmodern role for itself, one that placed Chicago at the very core of the futures market in international exchange rates. The wild success of this innovation can be conveyed by a "simple" statistic. By 1991, the Chicago Mercantile Exchange, thanks to its International Monetary Market, "supported trading with an underlying value of approximately $50 trillion—almost forty times as much as the value of all equities traded on the New York Stock Exchange."[25] Just how this preeminence was achieved illustrates vividly the interactions among global, national, and local events.

In the early 1960s, the Chicago Mercantile Exchange was going through difficulties, reeling from stock market declines and the failure to find an expanding role for itself beyond the proverbial pork bellies, Idaho potatoes, lumber, and, newly added, shrimp; investor interest in commodity futures had declined. Revival came in 1969 in the wake of the Vietnam War, as investors liquidated holdings in the securities market and began to speculate in processed commodities. As Tamarkin explains, in 1969 "the 50-year-old Merc surpassed the 122-year-old Chicago Board of Trade in dollar volume for the first time. . . . Commodity trading had experienced its greatest activity in United States history. Trading in government-regulated futures markets rose to a record $81.5 billion in 1969, up 36 percent from the previous year."[26] The MERC was improving its communications technology to more than keep pace with this expanded demand and was thus prepared for the starting gun of the internationalization of currency futures when deregulation occurred.

We must back up here to the period just after World War II, when the U.S. dollar became the dominant currency for international trade and when other major currencies in the industrialized world were "pegged" to it through the so-called Bretton Woods Agreement, signed by ten advanced nations in the summer of 1945. The International Monetary Fund and the International Bank for Reconstruction and Development were also set up at the same time. The Bretton Woods Agreement remained unchanged until the last day of 1971, after which exchange currencies were delinked from both the dollar and gold, allowing them to fluctuate more freely. Just before the latter change had been ratified and the papers signed, University of Chicago economist Milton Friedman had written that "changes in the international financial structure will create a great expansion in the demand for foreign cover" and proposed that the market for these be located in the United States. At the MERC his former students moved ahead with alacrity to develop this market in Chicago, setting up a futures trade in currencies to capture an enormous share of the potential arbitrage. Although other competitors now exist, the IMM of the MERC remains the giant in the field.[27]

The irony is that enormous quantities of "fictitious" funds and futures gambles now move around the globe at lightning speed, twenty-four-hours per day, at the behest of Chicago's computerized "market," but few of the benefits from such transactions are reaped by the city itself. Far-flung investors may profit handsomely, and small numbers of local brokers may become wealthy indeed, but most Chicagoans have not benefited. Becoming a "global" city via the MERC has not contributed general prosperity to the region's population; indeed, if anything, it has widened the gap between the "haves" and "have-nots."

UNEVEN DEVELOPMENT: THE INTERACTIONS OF RACE, CLASS, AND SPACE

Squires and his coauthors put the problem succinctly. They acknowledge that although "diversity is one of the pluses of Chicago's regional economy, the picture of a thriving economy with happily employed workers obscures the increasingly apparent inequality within the work force, the overall uneven development of the region's economy, and many of the social costs of that development."[28]

Just as in the early days of Chicago's development, when glaring inequalities along class and ethnic fault lines were increasingly inscribed on the spatial structure of the city, so in the present era of stagnation or decline, the racial, ethnic, and class cleavages of the region are being writ large on the more extensive canvas of metropolitan space. In many ways, the prognosis for unity and peace is even dimmer now than in the late nineteenth and early twentieth centuries, when industrial conflict was tearing Chicago's social structure apart, even as the city's ruling elite figuratively painted the aquatints of the Burnham plan while ignoring the needs of most of its citizens, whom they dismissed as "strangers." As Squires et al. point out:

> The 1980 census revealed that Chicago ha[d] 10 of the 16 poorest neighborhoods in the country. At the same time, its corporate bedroom suburbs [were] thriving. Unemployment rates in the city have soared above the national average, while many of the newer and more affluent suburbs have kept their unemployment rates well below the average. . . .
>
> *In many ways there are two communities moving in divergent directions in this urban area.* On the one hand are the city's central business district, the gentrified city neighborhoods such as Lincoln Park, old affluent neighborhoods such as the Gold Coast, and the more prosperous suburbs such as those on the North Shore. On the other hand are the low-income black and Hispanic communities like the West Side and Logan Square, struggling white ethnic neighborhoods like Chicago Lawn, and the older suburban industrial communities like East Chicago and Hammond, Indiana. Propelled by the Chicago growth machine, one group is accelerating while the other is running on empty.[29]

THE CITY VERSUS THE SUBURBS: THE NIGHTMARE PREDICTED BY THE KERNER REPORT

Deindustrialization and the decentralization of business firms and the remaining (higher-tech) industries have thus operated in tandem to widen the gap between whites and "minorities" in the Chicago region. According to a 1991 report issued by the Chicago Urban League, in recent years the Midwest experienced the greatest increase in black poverty of any region in the country, and because of a rapidly widening gap between white and black family incomes, the Chicago metropolitan region now outranks all others in the level of economic disparity between racial groups.[30] The report "explores spatial patterns of economic growth and juxtaposes them with patterns of segregation and economic decline. The analysis reveals that the geography of opportunity is a key factor in explaining the extraordinary racial disparities in economic well-being in the Chicago area economy."[31]

As background to the findings of the Urban League researchers, some basic trends need to be understood. Tables 11.2, 11.3, and 11.4 confirm three crucial and connected demographic developments in the Chicago region between 1970 and 1990: (1) the relative *and* absolute decline of population within the city limits of Chicago, contrasted with the overall growth of the suburban counties; (2) the gap in per capita income evident by 1989 between the city and its suburban areas; and (3) the current bifurcation of the region into "minority" city and "majority(?)" periphery. As can easily be seen, the city, together with the western portion of suburban Cook County, experienced significant population declines between 1970 and 1990; southern suburban Cook County remained almost stagnant; and the five collar counties, along with the northwestern and southwestern sectors of suburban Cook County, absorbed virtually all of the population increase.

Income disparities follow these same vectors, indicating that the class gap between the declining city and its growing suburbs widened in the years between 1979 and 1989, a trend that shows up clearly in Table 11.3. Note that the northwestern and southwestern suburban sectors, which grew fastest between 1970 and 1990, also experienced the most radical increases in per capita income, whereas those directly north and south of the city experienced below-average increases.

At the same time, Chicago's population grew relatively poorer. Although Table 11.3 includes dollar amounts, because of inflation it is better to concentrate on the percentage changes during the preceding decade. These are expressed as deviations above or below the Illinois percentage change (i.e., the income changes have been indexed against Illinois as one hundred). It is evident that the gaps have widened and reflect a center city that has "failed to thrive," demographically and economically. Even in the larger context of the Midwest, which has not done as well as either the West or East Coast, the city's situation has been disastrous and the decline has spread beyond the city limits into the western and southern sectors of suburban Cook County.

To complete the picture we must now add information on racial and ethnic changes and on immigration in the larger region. Table 11.4 shows that by 1990 a very large proportion of white non-Hispanics had essentially removed themselves from the city of Chicago, moving to the more outlying suburban counties, or actually entering them directly when they migrated to the region, where they constituted an overwhelming majority. Between 1970 and 1990, the absolute number of "white" non-Hispanic residents within the city of Chicago dropped from 2.2 million to 1.26 million, which represented a net decline of some 942,000, or 43 percent.

The most important portions of Table 11.4 are the last two columns, which highlight the contrast between the city and its suburban areas. By 1990 less than 38 percent of the city's residents reported themselves "white non-Hispanic," and this category included many of the most recent immigrants from the Middle East, the Indian subcontinent, and less-developed parts of Europe. The percentage foreign-born was much lower than in either New York or Los Angeles; only 17 percent of the city's population had been born abroad. Indeed, between 1980 and 1990 both New York City and the city of Los Angeles *would actually have lost population,* as Chicago did, had it not been for the influx of large numbers of immigrants. By 1990, African Americans slightly outnumbered white non-Hispanics, accounting for almost 39 percent of the city's total population.[32] The Hispanic population (originally primarily Puerto Rican, but now increasingly Mexican or from varied sources) had risen to almost 20 percent of the total by 1990. Since that time there has been some out-migration of black non-Hispanics (some to the suburbs but most to other regions of the country) and also a continuing in-migration of Hispanics, so that by the late 1990s as much as one-fourth of the population may be Hispanic, whereas only about 35 percent are African Americans. In contrast with New York and especially Los Angeles, Asians still constitute only a negligible, albeit growing, proportion of the population in the city and its suburbs.

I want to call attention in particular to the final column of Table 11.4, which shows the racial and ethnic (non-Hispanic) "whiteness" of the suburban ring (suburban Cook County and the five collar counties). If suburban Cook County and its municipalities were shown separately, this table would also reveal that Cook County outside the city limits now houses almost all of the minority population living in suburban areas, and that African American and other minority residents (except for fair-skinned Hispanics and some Asians) are essentially isolated in only a small number of suburban municipalities.

The City Divided into Largely Segregated Racial and Ethnic Turfs

The degree of segregation between center city and suburbs is reproduced even more graphically within the city itself. As Maps 11.1a and 11.1b illustrate, most of the non-Hispanic whites who still live within the city limits are concentrated within almost exclusively "white" residential zones: in either Area 7 (Lake Shore, that narrow strip along the lake north of downtown, parts of which are still referred to as the "Gold Coast") or Areas 1 or 2 (located at the outer fringes of the northwestern and southwestern sectors, respectively, near the city limits and adjacent to the prosperous white suburbs that extend outward from them, especially on the northwest side). In marked contrast, African Americans are heavily segregated in either Area 5 (the extensive

Table 11.2. Absolute population change between 1970 and 1990 and two-decade percentage change in population for Illinois, the Chicago CMSA, the suburban counties, and the city of Chicago

	1970 population	1990 population	Percentage change 1970–90
Illinois	11,110,000	11,430,602	+3.0
Chicago SMSA	6,977,573	7,261,176	+4.1
City of Chicago	3,366,957	2,783,726[a]	-17.3
Suburban Cook County[b]	1,974,294	2,120,516	+10.9
North Cook	439,678	412,370	-6.2
West Cook	500,020	448,543	-10.3
South Cook	402,314	419,665	+4.3
Northwest Cook	294,101	491,174	+67.0
Southwest Cook	338,181	417,051	+23.3
Collar counties[c]	1,485,204	2,156,109	+45.2
McHenry	111,555	183,241	+64.3
DuPage	492,181	781,666	+58.8
Will	247,825	357,313	+44.2
Lake (Ill.)	382,638	517,418	+35.0
Kane	251,005	317,471	+26.5

[a]The city of Chicago maintains that the population was undercounted by 236,274 in 1990. But even if the total is adjusted upward by this amount, the city would still have lost population in the most recent decade.

[b]Suburban Cook County virtually surrounds the city of Chicago, so this figure represents Cook County minus the city of Chicago.

[c]Lake County (Illinois) is located just north of Cook County limits, and McHenry County lies just west of Lake. DuPage County is due west of Chicago, wedged between the city and Kane County, which lies farther west. Will County is located directly south of the city and contains the town (and prison) of Joliet.

Source: U.S. Bureau of the Census reports on population. I have found many of the publications of the Northeastern Illinois Planning Commission helpful for assembling relevant data, which I have rearranged.

South Side "Black Belt") or Area 6 (the West Side "second ghetto"). Hispanics occupy "buffer zones" (Areas 3 and 4) between these black and white sectors. The few suburban zones that contain minorities are for the most part mere extensions of the West or South Side districts, which are almost exclusively black.

Over time, then, racial segregation has persisted and, with the flight of whites either beyond the city limits or into explicitly identified city "bunker" zones, areas of minority residence have expanded without leading to greater integration. Thus, despite open housing laws that have been on the books for the past two decades and much talk about the growing middle class among blacks, racial segregation remains almost complete in Chicago, underscoring Massey and Denton's contention that residential segregation and the increased *physical* isolation of blacks in American cities are the underlying causes of class formation, especially of the "underclass."[33] They point

Table 11.3. 1979 and 1989 per capita incomes for Illinois, the Chicago CMSA, the suburban counties, and the city of Chicago, with percentage change between 1979 and 1989 indexed to Illinois change

	Per capita income (in $)		Percentage change in decade (index)
	1979	1989	
Illinois	8,071	15,201	100
Chicago SMSA	8,568	16,739	108
City of Chicago	6,939	12,899	97
Suburban Cook County[a]	9,976	19,381	107
North	12,914	27,058	130
Northwest	10,285	20,807	116
Southwest	9,118	17,149	100
West	9,034	15,945	87
South	8,535	14,724	82
Collar counties	9,505	19,207	115
McHenry	8,646	17,271	113
DuPage	10,475	21,155	115
Will	7,999	15,186	102
Lake (Ill.)	10,106	21,765	131
Kane	8,469	15,890	99

Note: The over-the-decade increase in per capita income in Illinois was 88.4 percent. An index number above 100 indicates that per capita income in a given area grew more than the Illinois average in the decade; a number under 100 indicates a negative relative growth in per capita income compared to the state.

[a]The subregional figures for suburban Cook County sectors are unweighted averages of the per capita incomes of municipalities in each sector and therefore are not quite comparable.

Source: Compiled by the Northeastern Illinois Planning Commission from successive U.S. Census returns.

out that either scholars have benignly assumed that open housing laws have changed involuntary segregation to voluntary congregation or they have misused Wilson's argument (that class is more important than race) to assert that middle-class blacks *can* move out of the ghetto, often ignoring the fact that the suburbs to which they move tend to resegregate. They remind us that

> black segregation is not comparable to the limited and transient segregation experienced by other racial and ethnic groups, now or in the past. No group in the history of the United States has ever experienced the sustained high level of residential segregation that has been imposed on blacks in large American cities for the past fifty years. *This extreme racial isolation did not just happen; it was manufactured by whites through a series of self-conscious actions and purposeful institutional arrangements that continue today.* Not only is the depth of black segregation unprecedented and utterly unique . . . but it shows little sign of change with the passage of time or improvements in socioeconomic status. . . . [Such segregation] concentrates poverty to build a set of mutually reinforcing and self-feeding spirals

Table 11.4. Race/Hispanic origin (in percentages), population of the Chicago, Illinois-Indiana and Wisconsin CMSA, the Chicago PMSA, the city of Chicago, and the surrounding Illinois counties (Cook County minus city of Chicago and DuPage, Kane, Lake, and Will Counties), 1990 census

Race/Ethnicity	CMSA	PMSA	City of Chicago	Surrounding counties
White non-Hispanic	66.7	62.3	37.9	82.1
Black non-Hispanic	18.9	21.7	38.6	7.7
Amerind non-Hispanic	0.2	0.1	0.2	0.1
Asian non-Hispanic	3.0	3.6	3.5	3.3
Other non-Hispanic	0.1	0.1	0.1	0.1
Hispanic	11.1	12.1	19.6	6.6

Note: Non-Hispanic here refers only to the non-Hispanic population reporting a given race. As in other tables, such figures must be used with caution. When the residential patterns of Hispanics are cross-tabulated with their race, it is found that darker Hispanics (and Caribbean-origin populations) are almost as residentially segregated as African Americans. However, they are not necessarily likely to report themselves as "black," which leads to an overestimate of exactly how much desegregation has actually taken place. "Mixed areas" are often constituted by a mixture of "blacks" and "Hispanics," rather than "blacks" and "non-Hispanic whites."

Source: My own calculations based on 1990 U.S. Census returns. I have recalculated to separate that portion of Cook County that falls within the city limits of Chicago from that portion outside the city. The suburban Cook County residual has been added to Will, Kane, DuPage, McHenry, and Lake (Illinois) Counties, and the composite of these suburban regions immediately surrounding the city has been summed and then calculated.

> of decline into black neighborhoods . . . [constraining] black life chances irrespective of personal traits, individual motivations, or private achievements. For the past twenty years this fundamental fact has been swept under the rug by policymakers, scholars and theorists of the urban underclass. Segregation is the missing link.[34]

Massey and Denton conclude that "racial segregation—and its characteristic institutional form, the black ghetto—are the key structural factors responsible for the perpetuation of black poverty in the United States." Such segregation has persisted in Chicago even though the number of black residents actually declined slightly between 1970 and 1990. (In the former year the city of Chicago had 1,102,620 black residents; by 1990 it housed 1,086,389.)

Other minority groups, however, have been growing in size. The greatest gainers in representation were Asian American, American Indian, and "other" residents, whose combined numbers increased from 56,570 in 1970 to 431,384 by 1990. Also increasing their representation in the two decades were Hispanics (of any race), who in 1970 had constituted only 7 percent of the city's population; by 1990 they represented 20 percent of the city's residents.[35]

Changes in the racial and ethnic composition of Chicago's population, however,

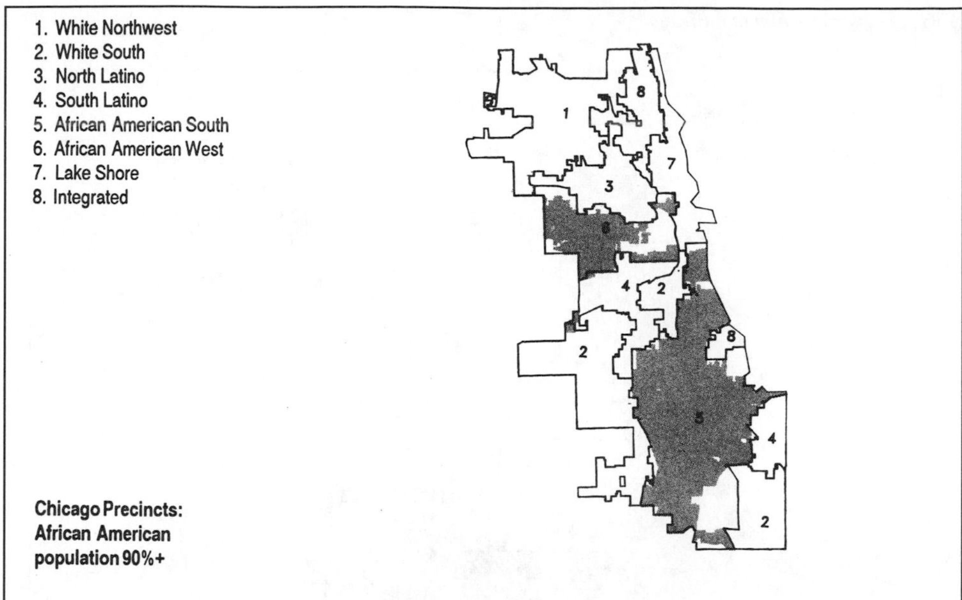

Map 11.1a. Distribution of minority residents by contiguous precincts, city of Chicago, 1990: precincts with 90 percent or more African American residents. Source: *Metro Chicago: Political Atlas, 1992,* prepared by the Chicago Urban League, Metro Chicago Information Center, Northern Illinois University. Courtesy of D. Garth Taylor and the Urban League.

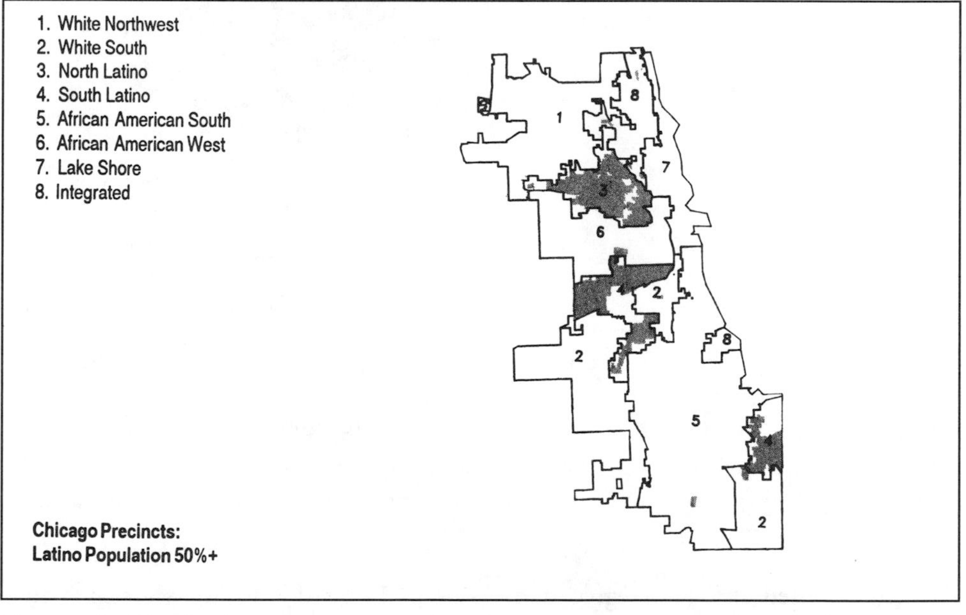

Map 11.1b. Distribution of minority residents by contiguous precincts, city of Chicago, 1990: precincts with 50 percent or more Latino residents. Source: *Metro Chicago: Political Atlas, 1992,* prepared by the Chicago Urban League, Metro Chicago Information Center, Northern Illinois University. Courtesy of D. Garth Taylor and the Urban League.

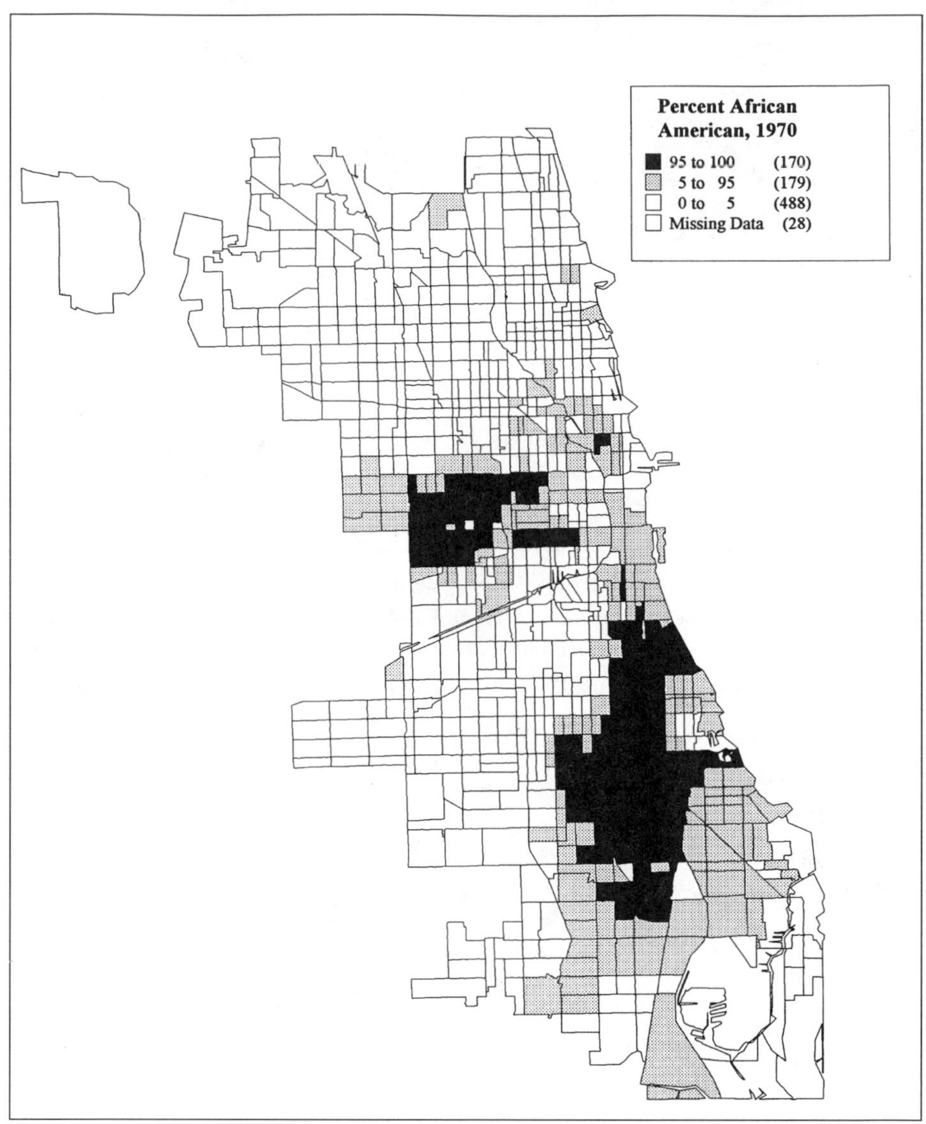

Map 11.2a. Expansion of zones occupied by blacks between 1970 and 1990: distribution of mostly black census tracts in 1970. Source: Jeffrey D. Morenoff, "Neighborhood Change and the Social Transformation of Chicago, 1960–1990" (master's thesis, University of Chicago, Center for the Study of Urban Inequality, 1994). I am grateful to Dr. Morenoff for making available to me special computer printouts from his data files.

have contributed little to desegregation. As Maps 11.2a–d illustrate, segregated areas of both black and Hispanic residence within the city not only grew larger and became even more clearly defined in the period between 1970 and 1990 but have also taken on distinctive patterns whereby blacks and Hispanics are increasingly separated from one another, albeit in adjacent zones.

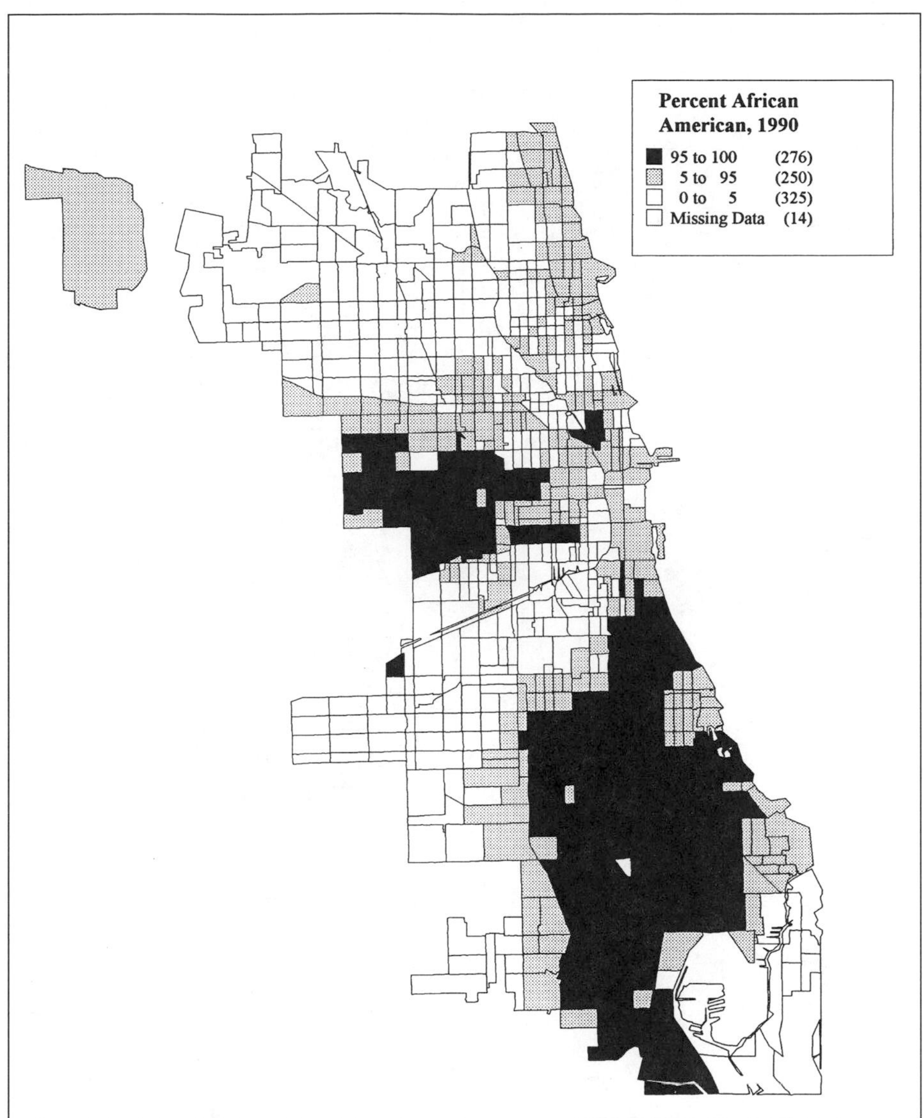

Map 11.2b. Expansion of zones occupied by blacks between 1970 and 1990: distribution of mostly black census tracts in 1990. Source: Jeffrey D. Morenoff, "Neighborhood Change and the Social Transformation of Chicago, 1960–1990" (master's thesis, University of Chicago, Center for the Study of Urban Inequality, 1994). I am grateful to Dr. Morenoff for making available to me special computer printouts from his data files.

THE GEOGRAPHY OF OPPORTUNITY

Although it may be theoretically conceivable that racial and ethnic segregation could exist without economic consequences, in actuality, given the considerably lower incomes of minorities, the degree of their segregation within the city, and the persistence of discrimination in the job market, places of employment tend to disappear

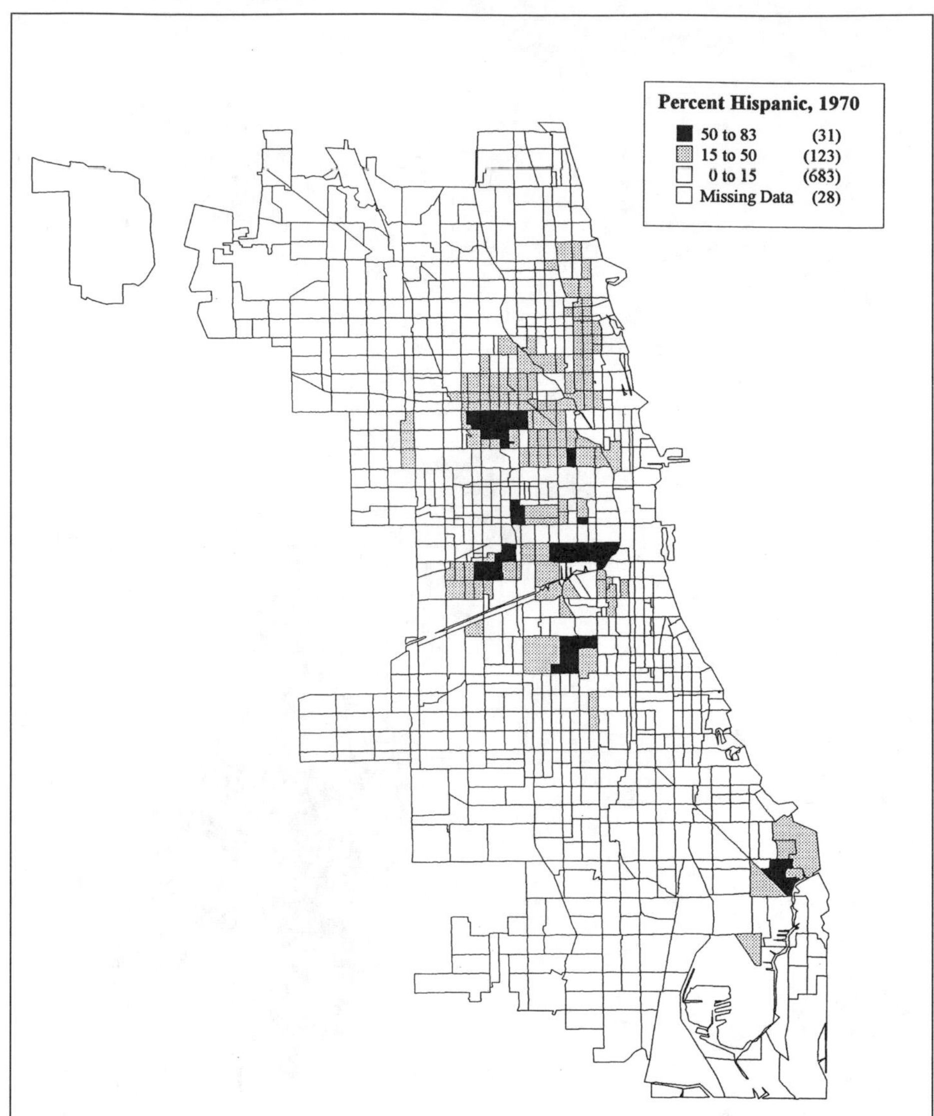

Map 11.2c. Expansion of zones occupied by Latinos between 1970 and 1990: location of census tracts with high representation of Hispanics in 1970. Source: Jeffrey D. Morenoff, "Neighborhood Change and the Social Transformation of Chicago, 1960–1990" (master's thesis, University of Chicago, Center for the Study of Urban Inequality, 1994). I am grateful to Dr. Morenoff for making available to me special computer printouts from his data files.

from areas that contain minorities. This means that the poor become isolated in locations that are especially vulnerable to economic fluctuations and are subject to "the wholesale withdrawal of commercial institutions and the deterioration or elimination of goods and services distributed by the market."[36] Extending Massey and Denton's argument somewhat, we can examine the case of the Chicago region (the country's

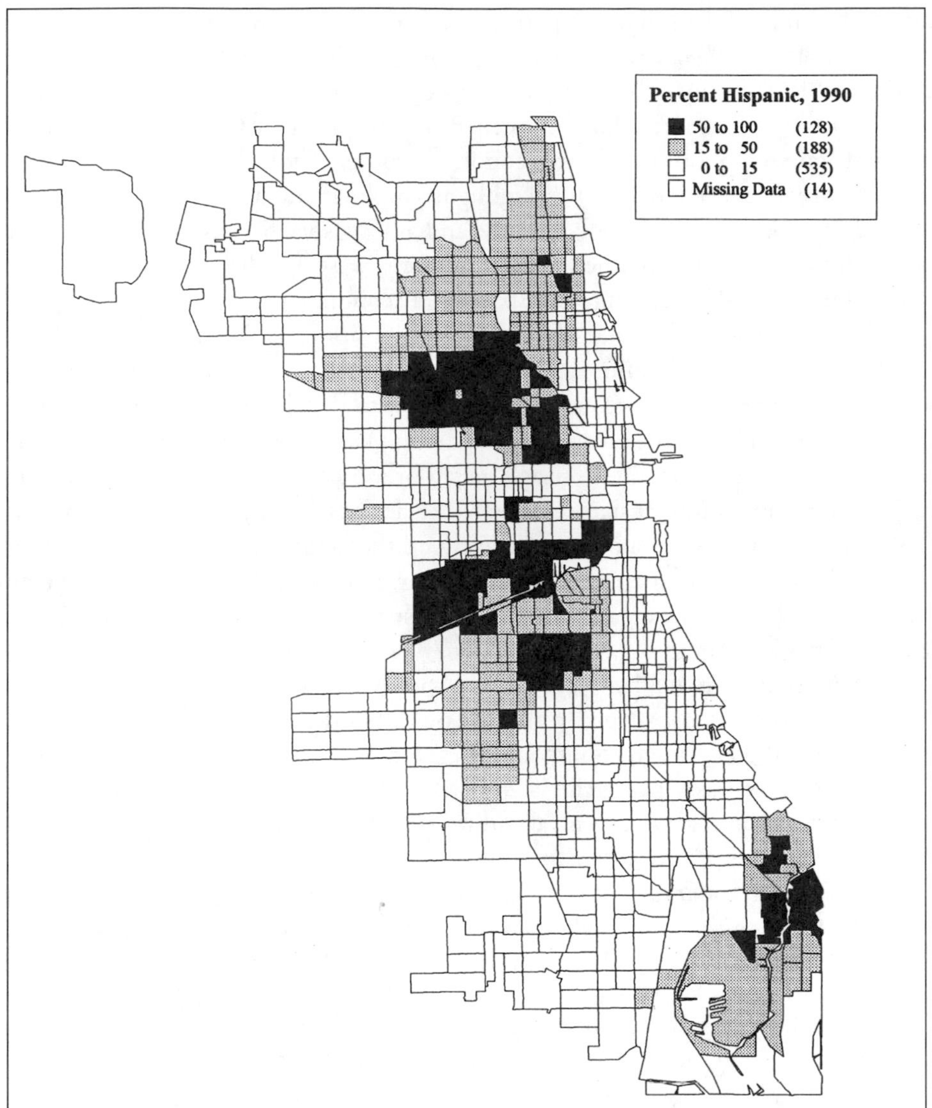

Map 11.2d. Expansion of zones occupied by Latinos between 1970 and 1990: location of census tracts with high representation of Hispanics in 1990. Source: Jeffrey D. Morenoff, "Neighborhood Change and the Social Transformation of Chicago, 1960–1990" (master's thesis, University of Chicago, Center for the Study of Urban Inequality, 1994). I am grateful to Dr. Morenoff for making available to me special computer printouts from his data files.

most segregated setting)[37] to explain just *how* deindustrialization, global restructuring, and racial segregation *work together* to transform "ghettos" into zones that are increasingly marginal to the larger economy.

A recent report from the Chicago Urban League allows us to do exactly this.[38] Analyzing detailed data on Chicago and suburban Cook County employment from the 1987 edition of the Illinois Department of Employment Security (IDES) publication *Where Workers Work in the Chicago Metropolitan Area,* Theodore and Taylor evaluate the employment histories and job prospects in forty-seven "neighborhood areas" in Chicago as well as sixty-three municipalities in suburban Cook County, making reasoned "guesses" about the future economic prospects of these areas on the basis of past performance.[39] Their findings highlight employment differentials between the city and its suburbs within Cook County, and among specific sectors of Chicago and suburban Cook County that lie north, northwest, west, southwest, and south of the Loop. The relationships among race, space, and economic prospects are striking.

Theodore and Taylor's stark findings can be simplified. The major sectoral zones within the city in which minorities are heavily concentrated—namely, west of the Loop and, with few exceptions, southward from it to the city limits[40]—are exactly the zones that have suffered the greatest past losses in places of employment and are likely to continue to do so. The nine Chicago neighborhood areas expected to continue losing jobs, and the additional sixteen expected to decrease their jobs although not quite so disastrously, are located almost exclusively on the West and South Sides (although some job losses are also expected along the northwest corridor). Significantly, "the nine [Chicago neighborhood] areas with the greatest projected loss in employment . . . have a population that is, on average, nearly 70 percent African American."[41]

These trends are neither new nor unexpected. Squires et al. note that the districts that had been most adversely affected by earlier deindustrialization were almost all concentrated on Chicago's South and West Sides: "Between 1963 and 1977, while the city as a whole was experiencing a 29 percent decline in jobs, available factory jobs in predominantly black West Central and near South Side neighborhoods dropped by 45 to 47 percent respectively."[42]

On the other hand, of the ten Chicago neighborhood areas that the Urban League report projected as likely to gain employment, eight were predominantly white areas located at the northern or northwestern perimeters of the city, adjacent to booming white suburbs. The other two were the Loop and the small middle-class enclave of South Shore.[43] (Only the latter had an African American population greater than 15 percent.) As the Urban League authors remind us, "Chicago is well known for having the most segregated housing market and one of the most segregated school systems in the country."[44] This segregation, coupled with the disproportionate disappearance of manufacturing jobs and businesses in minority areas, yields disastrous consequences.

The same spatial/racial split is found beyond the city limits and extends to commercial opportunities as well. Although the Urban League authors expect total employment to grow in most parts of suburban Cook County, the fourteen suburban areas with the greatest projected job growth were almost all located in the wealthy northern and northwest parts of Cook County, where black residents constitute 2 percent or less of the population. In contrast to the generally optimistic projections for suburban Cook County as a whole, however, there are a few peripheral municipalities where further job losses are expected. Significantly, these are the handful of "suburban" communities that were formerly industrial and/or have traditionally

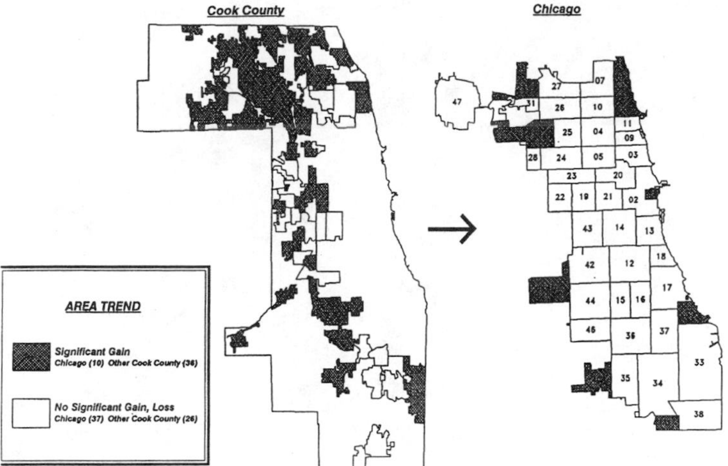

Map 11.3a. Zip code areas of suburban Cook County and city of Chicago predicted to experience a significant gain in employment. Source: Nikolas C. Theodore and D. Garth Taylor, *The Geography of Opportunity: The Status of African Americans in the Chicago Area Economy,* Report of the Department of Research and Planning, Chicago Urban League, March 1991. Courtesy of the Urban League and D. Garth Taylor; used with the permission of the Chicago Urban League and the generous help of D. Garth Taylor, director, Metro Chicago Information Center.

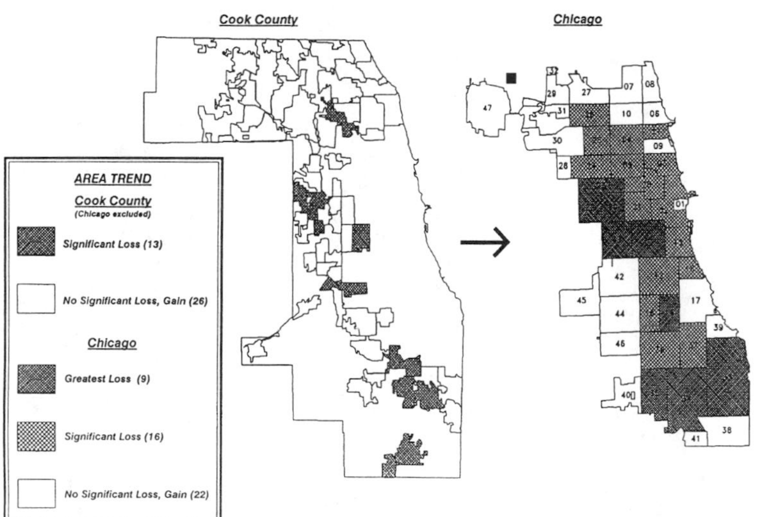

Map 11.3b. Zip code areas of suburban Cook County and city of Chicago predicted to lose more employment. Source: Nikolas C. Theodore and D. Garth Taylor, *The Geography of Opportunity: The Status of African Americans in the Chicago Area Economy,* Report of the Department of Research and Planning, Chicago Urban League, March 1991. Courtesy of the Urban League and D. Garth Taylor; used with the permission of the Chicago Urban League and the generous help of D. Garth Taylor, director, Metro Chicago Information Center.

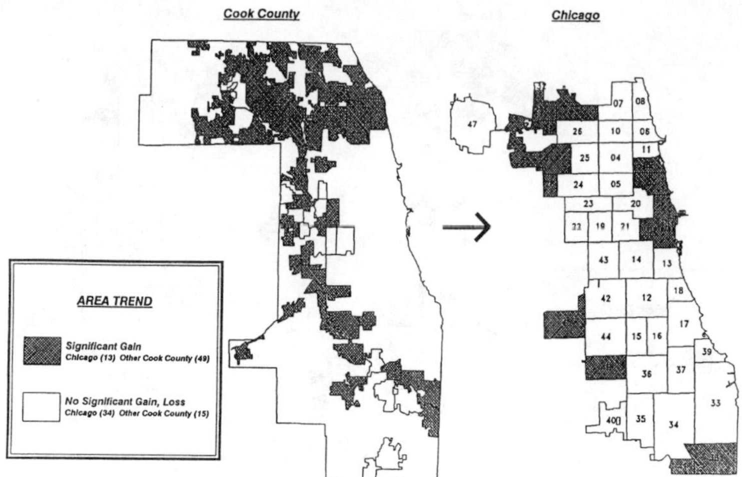

Map 11.3c. Zip code areas of suburban Cook County and city of Chicago predicted to gain business establishments. Source: Nikolas C. Theodore and D. Garth Taylor, *The Geography of Opportunity: The Status of African Americans in the Chicago Area Economy,* Report of the Department of Research and Planning, Chicago Urban League, March 1991. Courtesy of the Urban League and D. Garth Taylor; used with the permission of the Chicago Urban League and the generous help of D. Garth Taylor, director, Metro Chicago Information Center.

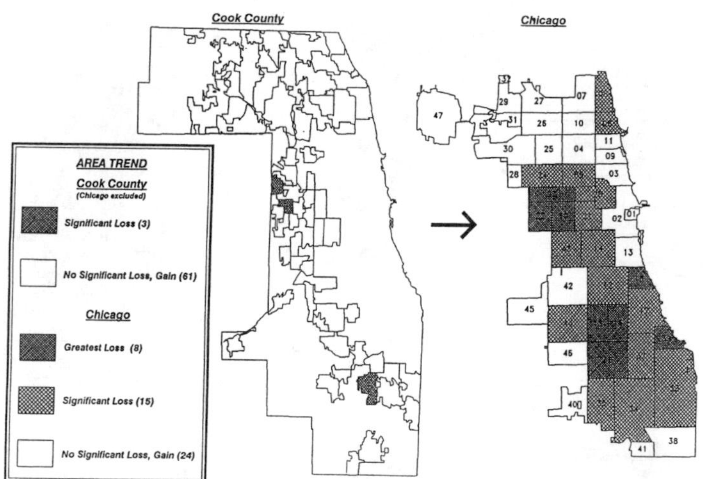

Map 11.3d. Zip code areas of suburban Cook County and city of Chicago predicted to lose more business establishments. Source: Nikolas C. Theodore and D. Garth Taylor, *The Geography of Opportunity: The Status of African Americans in the Chicago Area Economy,* Report of the Department of Research and Planning, Chicago Urban League, March 1991. Courtesy of the Urban League and D. Garth Taylor; used with the permission of the Chicago Urban League and the generous help of D. Garth Taylor, director, Metro Chicago Information Center.

housed minority residents. Thus employment losses in suburban Cook County have been confined to municipalities (with the exception of Evanston) in the southern and western quadrants, including the five suburban Cook County towns that in 1980 housed almost 80 percent of the approximately one hundred thousand African Americans who lived in suburban Cook County: Harvey and Chicago Heights[45] to the south along Route 94 and a southern rail line; Maywood and Bellwood along the western rail line; and Evanston, the northern terminus of an old slave railroad. These towns had already lost and will continue to lose jobs.[46] The rest of the municipalities where continued job losses were expected lie mostly along the western path of black expansion.

The patterns for service and business jobs parallel those for industry. In all parts of the metropolitan area, the highest employment growth sectors are service industries and businesses. In the city of Chicago, however, only the Loop, the area near O'Hare Airport, and the Near North along North Michigan Avenue were expected to gain businesses. In contrast, between 1972 and 1986, "nearly half of Chicago neighborhood areas experienced a significant decline in the number of business establishments and are projected to continue to do so." Most of the declining areas were in the west, southwest, and south sectors. In suburban Cook County, gains were expected mostly in the northwest and, to a lesser extent, the northern parts of the county. In the rest of suburban Cook County, jobs in business were expected to remain stable or to gain only modestly.[47] Thus, for Cook County as a whole (including Chicago), the city-suburban mismatch thesis accounts for a significant amount of the deterioration of minority areas in the city.

However, the mechanisms by which these changes occur are neither as "automatic" nor as "technologically driven" as "mismatch" theoreticians believe. Jobs evidently disappear from minority areas *just because they are minority areas.*[48] As the Urban League report points out in a section titled "Racial Disparity in the Labor Market," blacks are underrepresented not only in good jobs in the city, but also in suburban jobs, even when these workers live outside the city. As was the case in New York, the only two "niches" where blacks did better were in government employment and health services. So it is not just good jobs that are missing in minority areas, it is bad ones as well, and in the suburbs as well as the city. In suburban Cook County, minority residents suffer from considerably higher rates of unemployment than do whites. Table 11.5 shows 1988 unemployment rates by age, gender, and race in the city/suburbs.

Theodore and Taylor conclude the Urban League report on a sad note:

> African Americans in Chicago's poor neighborhoods are particularly isolated from employment and business opportunities. . . . If we examine the maps in this report showing areas of employment and business decline and overlay them with maps showing housing deterioration/abandonment, bank loan availability, home foreclosure, housing construction, or population decline, it is apparent that multiple factors operate . . . to brand communities and geographical areas as problematic for employment and business growth.[49]

Table 11.5. Percentages unemployed by age, gender, race, and location, city of Chicago and suburban Cook County, 1988

	Chicago	Suburban Cook County
All ages (16+)		
White males	7.1	3.4
White females	6.5	3.4
Black males	20.9	18.6
Black females	18.1	16.9
Teenagers (16–19)[a]		
White males	27.4	9.5
White females	12.7	11.2
Black males	44.8	47.2
Black females	39.4	43.7

[a]Very similar rates apply for young adults (ages 20–24).

Source: Data from Nikolas C. Theodore and D. Garth Taylor, *The Geography of Opportunity: The Status of African Americans in the Chicago Area Economy* (Chicago Urban League Department of Research and Planning, March 1991), 36–37, Figures 5, 6.

They stress that, at least with reference to Chicago's "ghetto" population, affirmative action has thus far been an empty myth, with respect to both employment and pay. Even if the "spatial mismatch" could be eliminated by a massive decentralization of the city's black population to the suburbs, differences would still remain. Furthermore, even if the problems of the third of Chicago's black population who are poor could be solved, this would still not yield equality, because income differentials by race exist at all levels of occupation and skills. Thus racial discrimination continues to be a significant factor in the social inequalities that exist in Chicago, independent of any additional effects from international restructuring and globalization.

This is also the conclusion reached in a comparative urban analysis conducted by Massey, Gross, and Shibuya, who argue that it is racial segregation and discrimination, rather than selective out-migration of successful African Americans from urban ghettos, that account for the concentrated poverty found in many center-city ghettos.[50] Using very sophisticated methods that linked individual income records to the movement of "poor and nonpoor people into and out of five types of neighborhoods," they found "very little support for the view that the geographic concentration of black poverty is caused by the out-migration of nonpoor blacks or that it stems from the net movement of blacks into poverty." Rather, "concentrated poverty among African-Americans follows ultimately from the racial segregation of urban housing markets, which interacts with high and rising rates of black poverty to concentrate poverty geographically."[51]

This is easily confirmed in the Chicago metropolitan region by the close correlation between the poverty rate and the proportion of county residents who are African American.[52] African Americans made up 39 percent of Chicago's population, and the poverty rate was almost 22 percent. Will County, with 11 percent African Americans, had a poverty rate of 6 percent. The remaining collar counties all had relatively small proportions of African American residents and extremely low poverty rates. Although a correlation says nothing about a causal connection, it does suggest that location, race, and poverty are closely related.

This situation has not been caused by globalization, although the precipitous economic decline of Chicago has exacerbated conditions for African American city residents and accounts in part for the growing income gaps between center-city and suburban residents and between blacks/Puerto Ricans and non-Hispanic whites. One cannot deny that the disappearance of Fordist-style industry and the collapse of industrial-union power, which had helped to sustain high wages not only for white but for a small number of minority workers as well, has increased black unemployment rates and lowered wages for employed blacks.[53] It is therefore no accident that Chicago constituted the primary case studied by Wilson and his students and reported in Wilson's book *The Truly Disadvantaged*.[54]

The "White" White-Collar Counties versus the City

Our earlier discussion about jobs focused on the economic and racial differences between the city of Chicago and suburban Cook County. But this contrast has become less and less crucial as the critical racial and economic borders have been pushed even farther out geographically. They now stand between a gradually declining Cook County (Chicago *and* suburban) and the five collar counties beyond.

The growing gap between the city and the five collar counties, both in racial composition and income, was already apparent as early as 1960, but it has grown wider with time. Between 1960 and 1980, the number of middle- and upper-income families living in Chicago decreased by almost a third, whereas in the five collar counties beyond suburban Cook County, the number of middle-income families increased by 67 percent and upper-income families by 124 percent over that twenty-year interval.[55] The trend for suburban Cook County fell between these two extremes. Since 1980 the income differentials between Chicago/Cook County on the one hand and the five collar counties on the other have continued to widen. In the decade between 1979 and 1989, incomes failed to grow as fast in the city and suburban Cook County as they did in the nation, whereas in the collar counties they grew faster than the country average, as is clearly evident in Table 11.6.

To some extent, these differences can be attributed to differential rates of unemployment in the city itself. Between 1981 and 1991, Chicago's average annual unemployment rate was (except in 1987 and 1988) consistently higher than the U.S. rate. And because unemployment rates were so high, the proportion of the population living below the poverty line skyrocketed from 14.4 percent in 1970 to 21 percent by 1990. Chicago's median family income (in 1990 dollars) dropped from $34,500 in 1970 to $30,707 by 1990, with median household income in that year even lower ($26,301).

The correlation between race and income in the city was marked. In 1990, whites had the highest average household income ($41,663), followed by Asian Americans

Table 11.6. Per capita income of residents in the Chicago SMSA and its constituent parts, 1979 and 1989, and percentage change above or below the change in the U.S. average in the same ten-year period

Area	Per capita income (in $)		Percentage change	Change relative to U.S. change (as index)
	1979	1989		
City of Chicago	6,939	12,899	85.9	-11.7
Suburban Cook County	9,976	19,381	94.3	-3.3[a]
Collar counties	9,505	19,207	102.1	+4.5
Chicago SMSA	8,568	16,739	95.4	-2.3
United States	7,298	14,420	97.6	100.0

[a]As might be expected, average incomes in the declining southern and western sectors of Cook County experienced "below-average" increases, whereas northern and northwestern sectors of Cook County continued to experience "above average" increases.

Source: My own calculations based on data from the 1980 and 1990 U.S. Censuses.

($35,419), and Native Americans ($33,897). In contrast with New York, Chicago's Latinos were doing slightly better than African Americans. (The mean household income for Hispanics was $28,831, compared with only $25,532 for African Americans, the lowest group.)[56] This was the case even though African Americans were generally better educated than Latinos. Unemployment undoubtedly accounted for many of these income differences. Differential job losses in suburban areas created parallel income discrepancies by race. Of the twenty suburbs with the highest percentage gains in jobs between 1986 and 1990, most were located in the fast-growing and higher-income white sectors around the city; of the nineteen suburbs that had the highest percentage of job loss between 1986 and 1990, almost all were west or south of the city, where minorities were more likely to live.[57]

The congruence between race and location is particularly evident in Table 11.7. As is clear, there has been very little "decentralization" of blacks in the region, except into limited portions of suburban Cook County, and between 1980 and 1990 the "whiteness" of the collar counties was reduced only slightly, from 89 to 85 percent, due primarily to an increase in Hispanics and Asians, rather than African Americans.[58] Furthermore, it was only municipalities that already had some black residents that gained more in the interval.

The same was true within Chicago, where the proportion of black residents tended to increase primarily in areas marked by increases in the 1970s and by large concentrations in neighboring areas. On the north side, there were some modest increases, especially in the area adjacent to the already black zone of southern and western Evanston. In contrast, there was little change in the northwest quadrant of the city, except for Logan Square, adjacent to Humboldt Park, which experienced significant racial change between 1980 and 1987. The "Near West Side, adjacent to the Loop, and Austin and Humboldt Park farther west, all showed marked increases in

Table 11.7. Percentage of residents in Chicago, suburban Cook County, the collar counties, and the Chicago metropolitan area by race/ethnicity, 1980 and 1990

	White non-Hispanic		Black non-Hispanic		Hispanic		Other	
	1980	1990	1980	1990	1980	1990	1980	1990
Chicago	43	38	40	39	14	20	3	4
Suburban Cook County	88	76	7	10	3	6	2	4
Collar counties	89	85	4	5	4	7	2	3
Total	69	66	20	19	8	12	3	4

Source: My own calculations based on data from the 1980 and 1990 U.S. Censuses, rounded.

the estimated percent black," which was a continuation of the western expansion of the West Side ghetto in the aftermath of the 1968 riot. "The southern expansion of blacks in Chicago was well established immediately south of the Loop even in the 1960 census. This expansion has continued all the way to Chicago's southern border."[59]

Hartman observes that any suburbanization of the black population was resulting in *resegregation* along a corridor running south, parallel to the Illinois Central line and extending all the way to University Park in Will County, as well as extending westward from the West Side ghetto. He concludes that the overall picture is one of continued black concentration, even within the five collar counties. In short, some decentralization of minorities has occurred, but at a disappointingly low rate.

Given the racial polarization between the center city (and now parts of suburban Cook County as well) and the outer collar counties, one might have predicted that, as in Gary and Detroit, which were similarly deserted by white residents and economic activity, political power in Chicago might have been bequeathed to its minorities. That has not been the case, even though there was a brief period (1983–87) in its political history when a three-way split of votes among mayoral candidates and (what turned out to be) a short-lived coalition between Hispanics and blacks propelled Harold Washington into office as the first (and so far only) elected black mayor of the city.

His regime did have fairly significant effects on city policy, but the reforms instituted during Washington's mayoralty were too easily reversed after he died unexpectedly in the first year of his second term. As noted earlier, the son of old Mayor Daley was then swept into office, after the smoke of the council wars had cleared and the brief tenure ended of the black council person who replaced Washington until elections could be held.

Nor has there been any move, as has been suggested for Miami vis-à-vis Dade County, toward absorbing the city government into the county as a way of retaining white political control, much less any effort to establish a metropoliswide government with jurisdiction over the six Illinois counties. There *is* an officially designated metropolitan region, the Northeastern Illinois Metropolitan Area, defined in 1957 by the Illinois legislature to include the six counties of northeastern Illinois: Cook, DuPage,

Kane, Lake, McHenry, and Will. At the same time, the Illinois legislature created the Northeastern Illinois Planning Commission (NIPC), charging it with devising "a comprehensive general plan that would guide and coordinate development in the six counties, . . . [but] its powers are advisory only and are not binding upon units of local government or state or federal agencies." It collects data, prepares and recommends zoning and building ordinances to local communities, prepares comprehensive plans, and recommends policies to guide development in the region.[60]

Given these limitations, NIPC has proven to be a fine research information source but hardly an effective planning body. If it has any policy function, it is simply to bring together agents or representatives of the *real* planning bodies of the region, the numerous "special-purpose districts" that operate regionally. By 1982 there were some 184 special districts in Cook County alone, including 90 park and recreation districts, 41 fire protection districts, 31 sewerage districts, 8 water supply districts, 6 drainage districts, 4 health districts, 1 irrigation and water conservation district, and 1 soil conservation district—each created under state legislation defining its powers and structure. It is in those special districts that regional plans take on substance, and all of them lie *outside* the power of the city's electorate to influence. With so much going on outside city government, one must ask: What remains for the city and how can citizens affect outcomes through the electoral process?

CITY-SPECIFIC FUNCTIONS

In addition to the distribution among neighborhoods of various local services, housing and education are the chief functions that are performed *within* the city, albeit by special agencies. Theoretically, these might be venues through which black and Hispanic electoral "power" could be expressed. However, given what we know about the "political culture" of the city, it should not surprise us to note that racially based conflicts in Chicago have infected successive attempts to decentralize (and equalize the distribution of) city services and to adjust Chicago's public housing and schools in conformity with national desegregation mandates.

Public Housing

Organized under state law in 1937, the Chicago Housing Authority was set up as an independent municipal corporation, headed by a board appointed by the mayor with city council approval. By 1985 there were about 145,000 residents in public housing projects built under its auspices, or some 4.8 percent of the city's residents, in six programs. The largest of these programs (and the oldest) were apartments for low-income families with children (111,000 persons in 153 high-rise and 1,030 low-rise buildings).[61] As we have seen in Chapter 8, these projects were concentrated in predominantly black wards or just adjacent to them. According to Gerald Suttles:

> Throughout the 1950s and early 1960s, large-slab high rises were placed in all black neighborhoods, and tenant selection progressively seemed to favor the more

> destructive. After the heights of the Civil Rights movement, rents were not raised, maintenance lapsed, and city officials made regular pilgrimages to Washington for emergency operating funds. In 1966, the [first] *Gautreaux* decision prohibited further construction in all black areas and mandated new construction, much of it in all white areas.[62]

But the CHA had already anticipated this development. As early as 1959, it began to concentrate its access to federal funds by building housing for senior citizens, largely to avoid the issue of racial segregation, which was coming to a head at that time. By 1985, about 10,500 seniors (most of them white) had received subsidized housing, primarily in new smaller apartment complexes located on the North Side of the city, where whites predominated.

In 1975, a third program began that emphasized small projects on scattered sites. Designed to provide new and/or rehabilitated housing for low-income tenants, "it was placed in receivership in 1987, following a class action suit which charged racial discrimination in the location of public housing and CHA's inability to meet a court order concerning acquisition, building and rehabilitation of scattered sites. As of the end of 1987, 3,900 units had been completed, and HUD had authorized and funded 292 additional units."[63] Another program, begun in 1976 under Section 8, was intended to provide rent subsidies to almost 4,000 low-income families and more than 2,800 seniors living in privately owned structures.[64] These were supplemented by a very small number of Section 8 units that had been moderately rehabbed and close to 2,000 more that had been substantially rehabbed, largely using city and state funding.[65] Desegregation, however, was not high on the priority list and, in any case, the widening racial divide between the city and its surrounding counties was making desegregation increasingly difficult to achieve *within* the city limits.

Once again, fear of racial integration led to the cessation of housing programs. By 1976 the long-simmering case of *Hills v. Gautreaux* had reached the U.S. Supreme Court, which finally ruled unanimously "that federal judges could order the U.S. Department of Housing and Urban Development to administer federally subsidized housing programs throughout the six county Chicago metropolitan area to help remedy the effects of past racial bias in Chicago's public housing."[66] But the ruling came too late, because by then the federal programs had contracted, the Chicago programs were revealed to be scandalously mismanaged, and when emergency rescue funds were released by HUD, it was later discovered that the new mayor, Jane Byrne, had diverted at least a quarter of the moneys to pay off the snow removal bills Chicago had incurred during the previous winter.[67]

The new program of scattered sites was supposed to "empower neighborhoods" by giving them a voice in the plans,[68] but Suttles has sarcastically referred to these developments as community "theaters of the unreal":

> If the city-wide drama of public housing was played out as irresistible comedy, the scatter-site program in the neighborhoods took on the appearance of a theater of the unreal. . . .

> [In the battles that ensued in neighborhoods over the scattered sites program] a ready-made vocabulary of reduced images found increasing use. People no longer spoke to one another, they "dialogued." . . . Community groups clothed themselves in exalted names. . . .
>
> There were heartrending displays on either side. An old, arthritic white woman was trotted out as the typical resident of subsidized housing. One youth opposed to subsidized housing threw himself in front of a bulldozer. These morally charged displays and vocabulary of reduced terms did not so much polarize people as they led to a growing sense of unreality.[69]

The "reality" remained the same. From beginning to end, the Chicago public housing program revealed a continuation of the obsessive fear of racial desegregation on which earlier attempts had foundered.

School Desegregation and Decentralized Control

Plans to desegregate Chicago's schools in the context of federally mandated desegregation orders, and later to decentralize control over schools to more local units, paralleled the fiascoes of public housing. According to a report issued in 1965 by the Chicago Urban League, public controversy over Chicago's school segregation had reached crisis proportions in 1961, when, instead of integration, racial segregation was found to be increasing dramatically. "In 1963, the Illinois Legislature passed the Armstrong Law that amended the State's school code . . . [directing] Illinois School Boards to draw attendance areas so as to prevent public school segregation." A Panel of experts studied the de facto segregation situation and made recommendations to the Board of Education on March 31, 1964. It concluded that "not only [were] the schools segregated, but . . . the quality of education in Negro-segregated schools [was] inferior to that offered in white-segregated schools."[70]

Recommendations were made for ways to ameliorate the situation. Nevertheless, a series of racial "head counts" made in 1963 and again in 1964 revealed that "a year and a half after the Chicago Board of Education sought expert advice on school segregation, and a year after its Advisory Panel on Integration [the so-called Havighurst panel] reported, public school segregation ha[d] increased rather than diminished."[71] Only the enrollment of "others" (i.e., Hispanics and Asians) in segregated black or white schools gave rise to any change.[72] It is worth quoting at length from the Urban League's analysis of 1964–65 enrollments:

> Schools which were white-segregated in the 1963–64 school term are still overwhelmingly white-segregated this school term. The same is true of Negro-segregated schools. All of the *absolutely segregated* (100 percent) white schools that changed either to *effectively segregated* (90–99.9 percent) or integrated schools did so due to the entry of "others." Two-thirds of the *effectively segregated* white schools which changed to *integrated* schools did so due to the entry of "others." Eight (8%) percent of the *effectively segregated* white schools which changed became *absolutely segregated* white schools. No type of white-segregated school

> changed to Negro-segregated status. All of the *absolutely segregated* Negro schools which changed to *effectively segregated* Negro schools did so due to the entry of "others." Ninety-four (94%) percent of the effectively segregated Negro schools which changed became *absolutely segregated* Negro schools. None became white-segregated and only one became integrated. . . . *It is painfully apparent that the Chicago Board of Education has not only failed to supervise implementation of its own policy of school integration; it has failed to obey State law.*[73]

By the 1970s, the opportunity to achieve any degree of racial integration had passed; the white pupils with whom minorities *could have integrated had largely disappeared* from the city's public schools. In an unpublished report, Marcia Turner Jones notes that between 1970 and 1980, "the school population in the Chicago area [Chicago and suburban Cook County] experienced rather dramatic shifts." During that period, both the city and suburban Cook County experienced sizable reductions in their school-aged populations. The losses were greatest at the elementary school level, but there was also a modest drop in high school enrollments in the city and a slight increase in the Cook County suburbs. Interestingly enough, the drop in enrollment was proportionately greater in private than in public schools, and it was Catholic schools that lost out most, both in the city and in suburban Cook County.[74] Table 11.8 is taken from Table 4 of the report's appendix.

Combining both types of schools and comparing 1970 to 1980 (as shown in Table 5 of Jones's appendix), we find the following racial differences: in the city of Chicago, black enrollment dropped by 6.5 percent while white enrollment dropped by almost 48 percent, resulting in an overall loss of 21 percent. In suburban Cook County, black enrollment rose by 60 percent while white enrollment dropped by 25 percent. The overall loss was 18 percent. Only modest evidence of any decentralization of black students was found. In 1970, 93 percent of all black students within Cook County were enrolled in Chicago schools, as contrasted with only 7 percent in suburban Cook County schools; by 1980, almost 89 percent of black students were in Chicago, as contrasted with 11 percent in suburban Cook County. White students had deserted Chicago schools as well, but at much greater rates. In 1970, about 45 percent of white students in the area were enrolled in city schools, compared with 55 percent in suburban Cook County schools; by 1980, only a little more than a third of all white students were attending Chicago schools, while more than two-thirds were enrolled in suburban Cook County schools. It is clear, therefore, that by the 1980s, only by combining the school districts of Chicago and suburban Cook County could any measure of desegregation have been achieved, but the separate jurisdictions were never joined. And of course, by 1990, the white school-aged population had already effectively removed itself to the five collar counties to avoid integration, as indicated by the very strong drop in white enrollment in both the city and suburban Cook County.

With integration hopes thus stymied, attention turned to school reform and to a decentralized plan for greater local empowerment within city school districts. In this process, Chicago lagged behind New York by some twenty years (New York began in

Table 11.8. Total student enrollments in public and Catholic private schools in Chicago and suburban Cook County, 1971–81

	Chicago		Suburban Cook County	
Years	Public schools	Catholic schools	Public schools	Catholic schools
1971–72	573,480	164,552	475,623	93,266
1976–77	524,221	131,299	433,430	69,424
1981–82	442,889	117,071	347,590	64,327

Source: Marcia Turner Jones, "Chicago Area School Enrollment Trends 1970–1982" (mimeo, n.d.), 27, Appendix Table 4.

1969, Chicago not until 1989).[75] In both cases, it was hoped that bringing supervision and policies closer to the "users" would make schooling better and more relevant. This goal was not achieved in either city. In New York, the decentralization plan sparked the eruption of a battle royal in Ocean-Hill between black parents and (mostly) Jewish schoolteachers, setting back the cause of Jewish-black relations in the city in ways that have resisted recovery and initiating a prolonged period of power struggles between city hall and local school boards. In Chicago, the reforms unraveled in 1996, when Mayor Richard M. Daley effectively dismantled the only recently instituted decentralization plan by appointing a new "czar" over the Chicago school system, who was charged with control over failing schools.[76] Who the mayor is has proven to be a more important variable than "political culture" per se, although not unrelated.

The pressures for local control over Chicago public schools had been building during the four years of Harold Washington's regime and finally succeeded in 1988, when

> the Illinois State Legislature and the governor responded to a strong coalition of city interests' demands . . . for school decentralization which shifted decision making from the central-city school bureaucracy to local school councils . . . in each school. . . . Given the radical character of the plan, it was surprising how little opposition arose to challenge the legislative action.[77]

Gittel attributes the differences between the New York and Chicago experiences to the political cultures in the two cities, but there were significant demographic differences as well.[78] She is certainly right, however, in seeing a connection between support for the plan and Mayor Washington's commitment to school reform and the MacArthur Foundation's support of his efforts.[79]

However, Gittel's prediction that Chicago's decentralization plan would work better than New York's (which she brands a "failed reform"), has not proven correct. She correctly notes that

> the New York City school-decentralization plan adopted in 1969 by the New York State legislature reflected an already defeated community agenda for political decentralization. . . . Limited coalition politics, the activist school groups backed by the city's political leadership, the governor, the mayor, and a newly appointed

> foundation leader with strong commitments to social change were unable to sustain the battle to achieve a shift in power.[80]

But her reasons for predicting better results in Chicago are perhaps overly romantic. She notes that "in the last analysis, New York lacked what Chicago had, that is, a long tradition of building grassroots organizations." Thus she claims that New York's plan failed because it was top-down, and expected that Chicago would succeed because of its broad coalition of grassroots and strong neighborhood organizing.[81] But she failed to recognize how ephemeral Chicago's neighborhood organizations and black empowerment would prove to be.

EPHEMERAL BLACK EMPOWERMENT

I have earlier noted that Chicago's strong city council and the Democratic machine's ability to mobilize local politics through its ward organization gave Chicago's neighborhoods a potentially more powerful voice in public policy, but interestingly enough, it was not until the machine was contested that the ideology of "local empowerment" became a central trope for reform.[82]

For thirty years (from 1946 to the death of Richard J. Daley in 1976) the fabled Chicago machine retained uncontested power through its system of discipline over its fifty committeemen, elected every four years in the party primary, who in turn appointed precinct captains charged with "delivering the vote." As Squires et al. note, "It [was] commonplace for Democratic committeepersons in Chicago also to hold public office, some as elected alderpersons on the city council, others as administrators in departments such as Streets and Sanitation, and a few as legislators in Springfield or Washington, D.C."[83] In turn, the route from committee chairperson to mayor was a natural one. A year and a half after Daley had been elected Democratic Party chair in 1953, the central committee nominated Daley as its 1955 mayoral candidate, which assured his election.

> During most of Daley's tenure as mayor and party boss, the mechanics of electioneering in Chicago were highly labor intensive. . . . Daley, . . . as chief executive of a municipality with above 40,000 employees—and one who authorized the filling of even the most trivial positions—had at his disposal a huge army of patronage workers . . . [who were] not just willing to work precincts but had been favored in the first place due to skills of this sort.[84]

The administration also paid city-contract workers very well, which forestalled efforts at unionization. Daley also courted Chicago's business elite, co-opting them through urban renewal projects, expressway plans, extension of mass transit, and development of O'Hare—that is, he made common cause with Chicago's "growth machine" while still maintaining control over the wards through patronage and the machine.

> Given the intermunicipal hostilities that divide Chicago and its suburbs, the main avenue for metropolitan cooperation has run from Chicago to Springfield, specifically from the mayor's office through the governor's mansion. Mayor Daley

> for the most part maintained good relations with Illinois governors and, with Republican Richard Ogilvie, resolved the early 1970s transit crisis by the creation of the RTA.[85]

There was always tension between neighborhoods and the "downtown growth" forces, which was exacerbated by the issue of race, but until the middle 1960s, Chicago's black electorate remained loyal to the machine. "From that time onward the diminished allegiance of Chicago's blacks to the machine, in conjunction with their expanding portion of the electorate, foreshadowed problems for the regular Democrats."[86]

The split became evident after Daley's death in December 1976. Although according to the City Charter, the black president pro tem of the City Council should have replaced the deceased mayor until elections could be held, white party loyalist Michael Bilandic became acting mayor and in the next primary defeated both Alderman Roman Pucinski and South Side state legislator Harold Washington. The deficiencies in the democratic machine, however, were becoming more visible, especially when Democratic "reform candidate" Jane Byrne defeated Mayor Bilandic in the 1979 primary. Despite her attempts to court neighborhoods by distributing power and resources to them, she herself succumbed to defeat for reelection in 1983 in a three-way contest in which the machine attempted to regain control through the candidacy of the former mayor's son, thus splitting the "white vote." Democratic defector Harold Washington benefited from this split, assisted by a concerted effort on the part of Chicago's black activists to register large numbers of formerly alienated potential voters and to forge a political alliance with Chicago's growing Latino population. Wealthier white voters who were disgusted with "the machine" (which in turn disdainfully labeled them "lakefront liberals") added to Washington's small margin of victory.[87]

Harold Washington Did Make a (Temporary?) Difference

Doug Gills, one of the contributors to a book evaluating how the election of Chicago's first black mayor in April 1983 was brought about and with what effects, contends that "a loosely unified coalition of reform-minded institutional elites (dubbed 'insiders' herein) and progressive community activists and political insurgents ('outsiders')" should be credited with Washington's successful bid, although I think he underestimates the role played by mobilization of black and Latino voters.[88] Gills is correct, however, that the economic decline of the city had undermined the machine's patronage system, which *"had become increasingly inappropriate to address the needs of large numbers of African-Americans . . . as well as the needs of Latinos and Asians."*[89] This economic crisis "manifested itself in the political arena as the heightened contradiction between declining sources of public revenues and the growing level of legitimate demands for public services and assistance."

> In 1983 there was the widespread perception that interests of importance to blacks as a whole were being threatened. Unity was possible. For a magical moment, there was the occurrence of all-class unity among blacks. . . . This unity, initially

defensive in nature, was transformed into an offensive to capture city hall . . . fueled by an unprecedented political solidarity among blacks and supported by most Latinos and significant numbers of whites.[90]

The question is how successful was the Washington administration in resisting the power of the machine and its alliance with the "downtown growth machine" and in diffusing power to minorities, both as individuals and as residents of a large number of previously neglected neighborhoods. Several observers contend that it was very successful.

Larry Bennett, for example, credits Washington with building "a political coalition and [leading] a big-city administration whose programmatic agenda explicitly sought to advance social and racial justice," despite the Reagan retrenchments, but he acknowledges that blacks benefited far more than other members of the coalition, which undermines the idea that Washington's progressive policies were designed simply to "serve the needs of Chicago's most disadvantaged residents and neglected neighborhoods."[91] Bennett points out that "whites and Latinos were often treated as unloyal outsiders by African-American supporters," and that an analysis of Washington hires found that of the city's new employees in 1985, 64 percent were African-American whereas only 11 percent were Latino.[92] Latinos felt they were not getting their "fair share" and complained that Washington was not listening to the ideas of Latino leaders because a black clique denied them access to the mayor.

> The black/Latino cleavage within the Washington administration was thus a specific instance of the coalition's unwieldiness. . . . There was a second, more subtle, consequence of the "black/brown" cleavage. [In order to cool out some of the Latinos, rewards were distributed to Latino elites, so that] . . . as Harold Washington managed black/brown disputes in his administration [through these payoffs] he also reduced his reach to Chicago's grass roots.[93]

Despite this fraying of the coalition, the payoffs to the neighborhoods and Washington's support for community control over schools were sufficient to keep his constituency united enough to return him to office for a second term.

The Washington administration also tried to address the underlying economic weaknesses of the city and its minority labor force through imaginative policies designed to stem the deleterious effects of restructuring. Giloth and Mier claim that "these local experiments . . . [nurtured] principles of social justice, fairness, openness, and participation as seeds for a national strategy." They looked at Chicago between 1983 and 1987, when

> several elements came together . . . that created a climate for experimentation in progressive economic development. The first was the maturation of an extensive network of neighborhood organizations interested in economic development. . . . The second was the evolution of an alternative set of development ideas. . . . Finally, these ideas and networks expanded dramatically beginning in 1983 . . . [as these] gained new legitimacy as part of Washington's development program.[94]

In retrospect, however, we can see that many of the programs so enthusiastically embraced failed, either because they were insufficient or because their momentum was not sustained after the regime change.[95] Giloth and Mier are forced to acknowledge that a "major impediment to . . . networking [across neighborhood groups] . . . [has been] the challenge of social integration across racial boundaries," a most familiar story in Chicago.[96]

Post-Washington

So the questions remain. Could these new configurations of politics outlive the personal popularity of the charismatic Washington? Had he built a solid replacement for the old Chicago machine? Bennett expressed confidence that, even after Washington's death, the old Democratic Party organization would not return, and that the philosophy of cooperation between city agencies and grassroots organizations introduced under Washington would be sustained. In this, he was certainly wrong.

The regime transition that occurred upon the death of Richard J. Daley in 1976 replayed, in reverse, when Washington died of a sudden heart attack only seven months after he won reelection in 1987. The City Council, after a bitter struggle that replayed the ongoing "Council Wars" that had plagued Washington's tenure, selected an ineffectual black councilman, Eugene Sawyer, to serve as interim mayor. But in 1989, Richard M. Daley was elected mayor—and as of 1999, he still is. "The king is dead; long live the king."[97]

In 1989, when the younger Daley took office, despite the growing deficit he acknowledged and said he wanted to reduce, he lowered taxes (but not by very much, so it was largely a symbolic gesture aimed at middle-class property owners). He privatized some city services but was unable to withstand pressure from municipal unions to prevent austerity. And the shortfall, not as large as predicted, was taken up by the state of Illinois, reproducing the older arrangement his father had used to bypass both the suburbs and his urban constituents.[98] In Chicago, once again, whites are resisting paying for services and schools that will differentially benefit other racial groups—a continuation of an old pattern in the city's political culture.

PROGNOSIS FOR THE FUTURE

So many predictions for Chicago's future have erred on the side of either boosterism or despair over the 160 years of its existence that I must confess my inability to peer with confidence into what will happen during even the next few decades. In the short run, the picture looks dim indeed, as deindustrialization and international restructuring remove more and more of the city's traditional economic underpinnings. In terms of race, there seems to be only halting "progress" in the direction of less overt animosity between whites and blacks, but that defusion of confrontational hostility has been achieved largely through the separation of the combatants into different spaces and political jurisdictions.

On the positive side, however, it would be premature to demote the Chicago urbanized region from the ranks of world cities, since by sheer weight of numbers and by the presence of markets that are indeed global, there is little chance that the city will cease to be a major player in the U.S. system. Indeed, should the NAFTA treaty yield enhanced trade between Mexico and Canada, the positioning of Chicago in midcontinent may yet prove not a defect but an asset. Concerning the racial and ethnic composition of the region's population and the intergroup relations among blacks, Latinos, and whites, much depends upon two things: whether the apparently irreversible trend toward marginalization of poorer African Americans within the city can be reversed through a reduction in racism and the achievement of enhanced educational and social equality; and whether a more stable coalition between blacks and Latinos can be constructed that might break the stranglehold of the white city-state axis that reestablished itself in the wake of Washington's death.

Such desired changes, however, are not likely to occur under conditions of persisting scarcity. The reconstruction of the region's economic base is a sine qua non of such solutions, and the interrelationship between racial change and the local devolution of the economy requires simultaneous attention to both problems. If revival is confined to Edge City, as it has been thus far, the fragmentation will at best undermine recovery, and at worst lead to revolt. The unknown factor lies, therefore, in whether the social fabric of the Chicago region can be mended sufficiently to yield synergism rather than continued counterproductive fission. Many of the same conclusions, as we shall see, are relevant to the case of Los Angeles, fragmented not along a single dominant fault line of black/white but, from the beginning, along a multidimensional (prismatic) fission of space, race, ethnicity, and class.

CHAPTER 12

The Los Angeles Region Transformed

THE HUNDRED MILE CITY

Because the "Americanized" city of Los Angeles was founded more recently and under such different technological conditions than either New York or Chicago, its current regional geography now illustrates quite purely the "new-style" megalopolis poetically described by Sudjic:

> Imagine a force field around a high-tension power line, crackling with energy and ready to flash over and discharge 20 000 volts at any point along its length, and you have some idea of the nature of the modern city as it enters the last decade of the century. The city's force field is not a linear one, however. Rather, it stretches for a hundred miles in each direction, over towns and villages and across vast tracts of what appears to be open country. . . . Without any warning, a flash of energy short-circuits the field, and precipitates a shopping centre so big that it needs three or five million people within reach to make it pay. Just as the dust has settled, there is another discharge of energy, and an office park erupts out of nothing, its thirty- and forty-storey towers rising sheer out of what had previously been farmland. The two have no visible connection, yet they are part of the same city, linked only by the energy field, just like the housing compounds that crop up here and there, and the airport, and the cloverleaf on the freeway, and the corporate headquarters with its own lake in the middle of a park.[1]

Although the description may be accurate for at least some portions of the Los Angeles urbanized region today—and, indeed, Sudjic considers that region his quintessential exemplar[2]—the simile cannot serve in lieu of a causal theory. It is unnecessarily mystical and, therefore, in the last analysis merely obfuscatory, concealing the real driving forces that have yielded such apparently irrational "sudden eruptions" and "sheer risings." There is no abstract energy force that simply discharges itself capriciously (unless the calculated profit motives of investors are demeaned in this manner), nor is the landscape upon which such "energy" is discharged featureless, independent of political jurisdictions, proprietary rights, and the game of politics. The "fields" are already inscribed, as in Italo Calvino's mythical Zaira, with the "relationships between the measurements of its space and the events of its past."[3]

The pattern of "fission" in the Los Angeles urbanized region that now sprawls over five counties covering a combined area of more than thirty-three thousand square miles was potentially there from the start. Although it was made manifest in part by the interaction between culture and the natural and human-made terrains that Banham captures in his four "ecologies" (Surfurbia, the Foothills, the Plains of Id, and Autopia),[4] it was shaped even more, as we have already seen in earlier chapters, by the economic and political actions of real people "creating" real usable space through the capital resources and technologies available to them.

Their actions had already given rise to Fogelson's fragmented city as early as 1930 (when his narrative ends).[5] Since then, terrain, water supplies, public policies, and investment decisions, as well as private property interests and speculation, have continued to operate together to yield today's even more extreme scatterdom of "confetti city"—a mosaic of urban, rural, suburban, and exurban uses interspersed over a vast terrain that now houses more than fourteen million persons in more than 140 incorporated cities and numerous unincorporated areas.[6] In the process, the rich agricultural land of Southern California is gradually being cannibalized by urban uses.[7]

Of the five counties included in this region (Los Angeles, Ventura, San Bernardino, Riverside, and Orange), it is Orange County that has had the most dramatic modern history, one that clearly illustrates causal patterns that, to a lesser degree, were previewed and are being recapitulated throughout the region.

Orange County and the Irvine Ranch

Orange County was once part of an overbounded Los Angeles County. In 1889, "after long and persistent agitation," it was detached and "the portion lying south and east of a line drawn approximately along the course of Coyote Creek" became a separate jurisdiction.[8] The Irvine Ranch occupied approximately a third of the new county, right in its midsection. It thus generated discontinuity. Why this zone remained unavailable for urban development so long, even after dramatic changes had "erupted" around it, had nothing to do with electrical fields. It had to do with a particularistic history.

Writing in 1950, Cleland captured this anomaly, noting that:

> The Irvine Ranch of Orange County is one of the few large landholdings of southern California that has survived the vicissitudes and revolutionary changes of the passing generations. The ranch owed its origin to the old land-grant system of

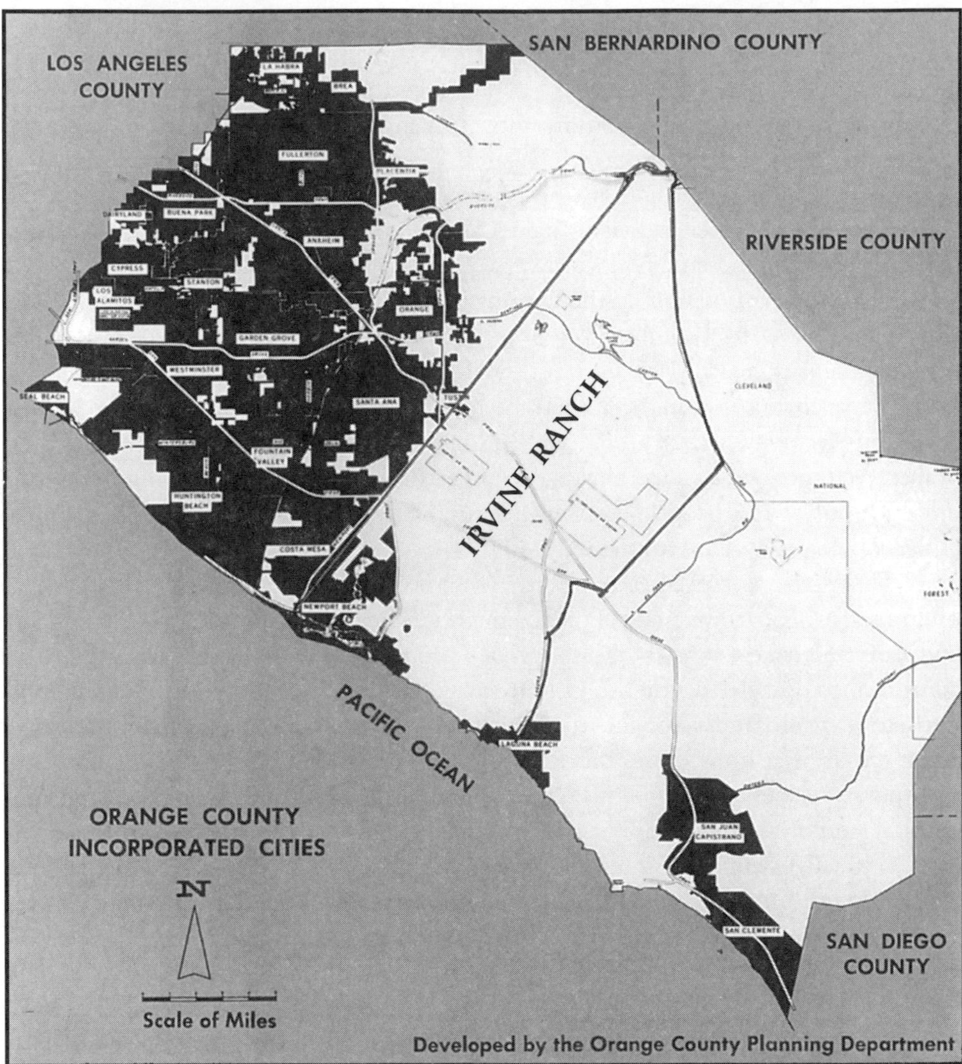

Map 12.1. Truncated urban developments in Orange County circa 1960. Boundary of the Irvine Ranch added in midsection. Reproduced by permission of The Huntington Library.

> the Spanish-Mexican regime. It has now been in the possession of a single family for over eighty years and thus enjoys a continuity of ownership rare indeed. . . . It still retains substantially the area and boundaries established by its founder.[9]

The origins of the Irvine Ranch, located on valley land between the Santa Ana Mountains and the sea that, by 1950, had become one of the richest agricultural regions in California,[10] can be traced back to before the American conquest, when "large grants or ranchos were the dominant feature of the province's economic and social life. They remained the controlling factor in much of the state's settlement and agricultural development for many years . . . [and] thus constituted one of the few enduring legacies that California inherited from Mexico and Spain."[11]

Just after the Civil War, the Irvine Ranch was assembled from two such grants and part of a third by several Yankee (a misnomer) entrepreneurs from San Francisco who had originally met on their way to take part in the gold rush.[12] When Irish-born James Irvine, the dominant member of the group, died in 1886, just as the real estate boom in Southern California was touched off by the arrival of direct rail lines, he left an estate that included the ranch—twenty-two miles long and nine miles wide, covering more than one hundred thousand acres.[13] For the next eighty years, the ranch remained in family ownership. At first the agricultural uses of the ranch remained marginal, and several attempts to sell it fell through, but eventually an irrigation project permitted its conversion to citrus crops, which extended its profitable agricultural life.[14]

Change, albeit delayed, was perhaps inevitable, given the urban developments in the rest of the county, and especially the demand for beachfront properties. During World War II, the U.S. government requisitioned some of the underutilized land for military installations, and after the war, the Irvine Company began to subdivide its most valuable coastal land for suburban developments along Newport Bay and in Laguna Beach.[15] By 1950, when Cleland was completing his book, James Irvine's grandson, Myford Irvine, was initiating ambitious plans for new residential developments to be carved out of the ranch.[16] The way was opened not only for Orange County's explosive growth, but for a planned development on a massive scale seldom if ever achieved in the history of American urbanization.[17]

By the late 1980s, Orange County as a whole was already hosting a "powerful subregional economy, which exceeded $60 billion in 1989 (compared with $13.5 billion in 1975), making it the nation's tenth largest county economy . . . [and one that would have ranked] among the top thirty in the world, along with the economies of Argentina, Austria, Denmark, and Egypt." During the postwar period it had

> evolved from a rural county into an industrial region and bedroom adjunct to Los Angeles and finally into a complex metropolitan region, consisting of twenty-eight separate municipalities, with its own economy and cultural life. In 1940 Orange County's population [had been] less than one-tenth that of Los Angeles. . . . Starting in the 1950s, as Los Angeles grew and its open space became scarce and expensive, some residents and major aircraft firms sought cheaper land to the south in Orange County [where the] postwar population . . . multiplied ten times, from two hundred thousand in 1950 to more than two million by 1987. Commercial firms that owned massive parcels of land developed whole planned communities in Irvine, Laguna Niguel, and Mission Viejo. . . . [In the 1970s and 1980s, Orange County's regional economy became] increasingly integrated into a worldwide capitalist market system.[18]

According to Kling et al., the area no longer fits the "suburban" pattern of white middle-class bedroom communities, nor do the terms *urban* and *rural* capture its character. The authors call the new pattern "postsuburban," because it is not simply decentralized but organized around many distinct specialized centers which differ markedly from one another in terms of land uses, social classes, and ethnic composition, in a complex and decentralized mixture of urban, suburban, and rural spaces.[19]

Edward Soja, in his inimitable prose, refers to Orange County as "exopolis," and quotes a California tourism promotional brochure that represents it as "a theme park," "Tomorrowland" and "Frontierland" combined—a truly "postmodern experience."[20] Kling and associates use less charged language to the same effect:

> This multicentered region can appear as a hodgepodge of specialized centers built miles apart and separated by large suburban-style housing tracts. But this postsuburban spatial formation differs from the traditional suburb by having lively commercial and cultural centers for residents. It differs markedly from more distinctly suburban regions . . . which are more demographically homogeneous and where the major nearby cities are the primary sources of high culture, lively street life, and ethnic diversity. . . . [Postsuburban regions] are not sleepy provincial regions. . . . Their most important aspects . . . are their origins in the suburban periphery of another urban core . . . *from which they have broken away,* and the emergence within them of a new decentralized environment possessing the economic vitality and cultural diversity formerly associated with the traditional central city. . . .
>
> . . . *One Orange County regional center—the Costa Mesa-Newport Beach-Irvine complex—is California's third largest "downtown," as measured by office and business space.*[21]

The emergence of this "third largest downtown" was made possible by the virtual tabula rasa provided by the Irvine Ranch, now also home to the University of California's Irvine campus and its associated planned town. The Irvine Company donated a thousand acres for the campus, but in turn has seen the land values of its remaining holdings skyrocket from the magnet thus created. The plan of 1960 "mapped ten thousand acres of undeveloped land and presented a master plan for a university-oriented community to be organized along the lines of the venerable garden-city model."[22] Although the usual political battles between developers and antigrowth factions occurred in the Irvine area, "the development firms have won most of their major battles."[23]

But What Kind of Development?

Authors who have examined recent changes in Orange County do not agree, however, on how to characterize its economy, although all recognize quintessential elements of "the global city." In their introductory chapter, Kling, Olin, and Poster contend that it is a perfect product of "information capitalism," which they distinguish from both the "service" economy and from "high tech."[24] They argue that their concept of information capitalism is

> especially useful in analyzing the economic changes that led from an industrial economy to an information economy because it anchors new strategies of managing information in the practical activities of businesses and governments. *Information capitalism refers to forms of organization in which data-intensive techniques and computerization are key strategic resources;* these forms of organization occur in all sectors of the economy—agriculture, manufacturing, and services.[25]

There is some merit to their approach, but because these sectors include workers at the highest levels of skill as well as the more numerous, largely immigrant and/or minority residents who are concentrated in specific centers of Orange County (notably Santa Ana), the concept fails to capture the class, race, and ethnic "division of labor" within sectors.[26]

An alternate definition by Allen Scott may help us to understand better the actual structure of the "new economy." If Kling et al. prefer the terms *postsuburban* and *information society* to the older references to *suburbs* and the *service society,* Scott questions whether the term *postindustrial* is appropriate to capture Los Angeles's or even Orange County's economy. In lieu of Sudjic's mysterious electrical forces, Scott posits that the landscape derives "from the basic production apparatus of capitalist society," whereby the urban process emerges—via complex patterns and dynamics of the division of labor.[27] His view, which I share, is that "the modern metropolis is both the creation of the social and property relations of capitalism and a specific condensation of them."[28]

Although restructuring has deeply affected advanced capitalist societies, industry still remains the most significant generator of national income, especially in California and other parts of the sun belt. This is particularly true of Los Angeles and Orange Counties, which can hardly be considered postindustrial.[29] Indeed, as in the Depression, when manufacturing jobs were disappearing in other parts of the country but increasing in Los Angeles, so in the 1970s, when deindustrialization continued in Chicago and New York, the five-county Los Angeles region added more than 225,000 manufacturing jobs.[30]

In a prescient report on economic changes in the Los Angeles region issued in 1985, at the peak of Los Angeles's prosperity, Soja, Heskin, and Cenzatti also express their discontent with all conventional terminology, concluding:

> In the kaleidoscope of contemporary restructuring . . . the global and the local have converged and condensed to create [a] more complex landscape of contradictions tensely combining "Sunbelt" and "Snowbelt," "Core" and "Periphery," "North" and "South," "East" and "West," city and non-city, high technology factories and nineteenth century sweatshops, some of the most expensive luxury-housing in the world and the cardboard hovels of the homeless. Opposites unite and the extremes become more visibly interdependent.[31]

It would be difficult to put the contradictions more succinctly.

But Orange County is only one example of these new developments, albeit perhaps the most extreme. Similar transformations have now spread to other "collar counties" of the region that Edward Soja has called "exopolis."[32] Indeed, in addition to Orange County, Soja identifies three other outlying economic regions: the "Greater Valley," a zone that extends from the San Fernando Valley eastward to encompass Burbank and Glendale (and, we might add, Pasadena), as well as northward from the city at Chatsworth-Canoga Park into Ventura County and even into the canyon and desert zones of northern Los Angeles County;[33] another industrialized belt that stretches all along Los Angeles County's Pacific shore from Malibu to the powerful port of San Pedro, a zone sometimes referred to as "Aerospace Alley"; and a third area located in the "Inland Empire," which

> extends from the eastern edge of Los Angeles to the most developed parts of San Bernardino and Riverside counties. . . . [Although] this subregion of exopolis is the least developed of the four in terms of industrial employment and office growth, . . . [l]ured by the success stories of other Outer Cities, hundreds of thousands of people have moved to planned new communities in anticipation of soon finding . . . jobs [that] do not arrive, leaving huge populations stranded up to sixty miles from their places of employment.[34]

HIGH-CLASS TECH, LOW-CLASS GRIND

However, although juxtapositions of urban forms and class and ethnic differences appear throughout the region (and Orange County has not been immune to them),[35] it is in Los Angeles County that they are most glaringly evident. As late as 1985, the aircraft industry in Southern California remained concentrated in Los Angeles County, although firms had begun to relocate to Orange County.[36] The same was true for industries involved in missiles and space, although their overflow to Orange County was significantly greater.[37] Firms and employees in the advanced electronics industries were more evenly distributed between Los Angeles and Orange Counties, although the lion's share remained in the former.[38]

But even within these so-called high-tech industries, a quite rigid gender and ethnic division of labor exists, with white males chiefly in the high-paid "clean" activities and minorities (especially minority women) concentrated in the lower-paid and "dirtier" jobs. In the research reported by Allen Scott in his very important book *Technopolis,* a factor analysis of the actual types of jobs in Southern California electronics assembly plants reveals three status tiers of work in this "high-tech" (and informational) industry, each with its own ethnic and gender specificities. Jobs at the top of the hierarchy are divided into two types: managerial and quality-control jobs, dominated by white males; and inspection and testing, largely performed by Asian males with advanced education and special training in electronics assembly. The middle (and numerically largest) level consists of jobs that involve tedious unskilled work calling for patience and cooperativeness; the occupants of these jobs are largely Hispanic women, followed by Hispanic men, but they also include a disproportionate representation of Asian females.[39] Finally, "at the very bottom of the hierarchy . . . is . . . a small group of Hispanic males engaged in cleaning electronics assemblies, and constituting the most marginal and lowest-paid workers in the industry," doing tasks that are dirty, strenuous, and dangerous because of their toxicity.[40] The same pattern exists in many other so-called high-tech industries, as studies conducted in Silicon Valley reveal.[41]

Therefore, although high-tech industrial regions may be remarkable for the sophisticated human resources they assemble, the latter constitute only a small percentage of those who work in "advanced" industries. And in the Los Angeles region, rivaling aerospace and electronics as growth industries have been menial services and garment manufacture, definitely "low tech." Up to 1985, "nearly 15% of new manufacturing jobs have been in the garment and apparel industry, while low paying service jobs have grown by at least 500,000 since the 1960's." Most of the growth in low-paying service work and especially in garment making has been facilitated by the large-scale immigration of Hispanics and, to a lesser extent, Asians.[42] The location of sweatshops is decidedly centralized in Los Angeles and tied to major areas of Hispanic settlement.

THE ECONOMY: UP AND DOWN AND SIDEWAYS

In the 1960s and even the 1970s and early 1980s, Los Angeles's economy continued its remarkable expansionary tendencies, which fueled industrial, service, and population growth in the surrounding counties in all directions, but particularly southward into Orange County. These trends were in marked contrast to the precipitous collapse of Chicago's Fordist structure and the more gentle easing off, if not attrition, of job and population growth in the New York region. Table 12.1 compares employment changes in selected sectors within the economic regions of New York, Chicago, and Los Angeles between 1974 and 1985. The contrast is dramatic.

As the table shows, although the expansions predicted by the theories of the global city are largely illustrated by the consistent enlargement of producer-related service sectors, in all cases the percentage changes in the decade were greatest for the Los Angeles economic region. And what is even more spectacular, even though manufacturing employment went down in the New York region and collapsed in the Chicago region, it continued to climb in Los Angeles. This latter trend was not reversed until the late 1980s, when the Cold War ended, reductions began in defense-related spending, and some of the remaining government-funded defense/aerospace contracts went to lower-cost and "more stable" states in the Southwest. Only then did industrial growth level off in Los Angeles.

Detailed figures are lacking for defense spending in the city and its region. However, because the Los Angeles CMSA is the major industrial region of California, Los Angeles's cycle of defense-linked activities in the 1980s can be roughly gauged from statewide figures indicating the value of defense prime contracts awarded within the state of California. From 1980 on, the numbers increased steadily, with 1985 marking the peak year. In 1981 these contracts had been worth only $16.7 billion, but by 1985 they reached more than $29 billion. After 1985, however, the numbers declined steadily to reach a low value of $22.3 billion in 1990.[43] The drop in high-technology employment was most marked in missiles/space and in communications equipment, but in fact, it was pervasive, excluding only the production of "soft goods" such as garments.[44] Reflecting these cutbacks, by 1991 there was a sharp drop in the growth of California personal incomes and a sudden rise in the state's unemployment rate (higher than the national average).[45]

Table 12.1. Absolute employment in selected economic sectors, Bureau of Economic Analysis economic regions of New York, Chicago, and Los Angeles, 1985, showing percentage change from 1974 to 1985

Employment by industry	New York in 1985	Chicago in 1985	Los Angeles in 1985
Manufacturing			
Number of jobs	1,319,083	778,713	3,230,785
Percentage change 1974–85	-15.4	-27.7	+15.0
Wholesale trade			
Number	579,536	245,255	350,107
Percentage change	+20	+9.8	+47.7
FIRE			
Number	803,102	277,295	375,392
Percentage change	+21.4	+6.8	+63.2
Business services			
Number	567,131	213,222	331,292
Percentage change	+76.4	+67.0	+106.7
Administrative Services			
Number	431,071	182,031	184,881
Percentage change	+13.3	+9.9	+51.6
Health services			
Number	573,148	242,035	348,222
Percentage change	+57.5	+57.6	+65.6
Education services			
Number	172,891	69,841	87,087
Percentage change	+32.1	+25.8	+106.4
Legal services			
Number	94,995	31,021	48,595
Percentage change	+83.9	+106.5	+142.0
Professional services			
Number	135,637	49,990	94,102
Percentage change	+62.9	+76.6	+125.0
Miscellaneous services			
Number	67,144	31,455	72,509
Percentage change	+44.4	+55.2	+120.5

Note: The Bureau of Economic Analysis has its own definitions of economic regions, which are not identical either to PMSAs or CMSAs.

Source: This table is constructed from data assembled originally in William B. Beyers, "The Producer Services and Economic Development in the United States: The Last Decade," a report prepared for the U.S. Department of Commerce in April 1989. A truncated version appears in Ann R. Markusen and Vicky Gwiasda, "Multipolarity and the Layering of Functions in World Cities," *International Journal of Urban and Regional Research* (June 1994).

Polarization by Class, Race, and Ethnicity

There was also increased polarization of class. In the city of Los Angeles the proportion of individuals with incomes below the poverty line had increased considerably by 1989 and was continuing to rise in the early 1990s. The gap between the poor, concentrated chiefly in the southern portion of the city[46] and in the easternmost "barrios," and the rich, who live largely in "self-governing" communities in Los Angeles County and in selected "suburbs" and "exurbs" in the surrounding counties, widened drastically in the 1980s and continued to do so in the early 1990s.

In 1989, a group of graduate students in Urban Planning at UCLA investigated what they called "the widening divide." Many of their findings were later incorporated into Paul Ong and Evelyn Blumenfeld's chapter in *The City*.[47] Ong and Blumenfeld begin their chapter by stressing that, in contrast to industrial declines in the Northeast and in North Central major cities, "by the late 1960s, Los Angeles had emerged as a major industrial center, with 30 percent of its workforce employed in manufacturing," not only in the protected defense industries but in the standard smokestack industrial sectors. This growth in manufacturing, when coupled with the burgeoning Pacific Rim trade and an influx of Asian capital, "enabled Los Angeles to plot a course unlike that of any other major urban area in the United States. *Los Angeles did not deindustrialize during the 1970s and 1980s but rather continued to generate new manufacturing jobs.*"[48]

Despite this healthy growth, however, the poverty rate rose from 10.9 percent to 15.1 percent between 1969 and 1989.[49] Futhermore, during that interval of growth, the gini index (which measures the degree of income inquality) rose from .368 in 1969, only slightly higher than the .349 in the country, to .444 by 1989, substantially higher than the .396 for the country as a whole. Much of this growing inequality was attributable to deeply entrenched racial divisions, which, although not new, were being intensified during restructuring and the changing composition of the population. As Ong and Blumenfeld point out, "Asian, Latino, and African-American migrants to Los Angeles had long experienced low wages, poverty, and racism," and, indeed, the evolution of the city into a multiethnic "world city was built on ethnic and racial inequality. . . . The occupational positions of racial and ethnic minorities translated into enduring earning disparities," which resulted in much higher rates of poverty for blacks and Hispanics than for whites.[50]

In short, a strong industrial economy has not protected Los Angeles's minority workers. To some extent, this has been due to a substantial substitution in both the types of manufacturing and the locations of plants under restructuring. Gone are the unionized Fordist-type plants producing cars, tires, and so on, that were centrally located and within easy commuting reach of areas inhabited by blacks and Hispanics. In their place, garment production, often under sweatshop conditions, has expanded, not only in central areas but in peripheral ones as well.

Post-1990 Retrenchments

The Center for Continuing Study of the California Economy (CCSCE) monitors changes in the "economic health" of California counties.[51] By the middle of 1990, the

CCSCE was finding evidence that a significant retrenchment in California's economy was under way, especially in the defense-related aerospace manufacturing sector.

> California has lost more than 200,000 jobs in the manufacturing sector since the recession began. The largest share—over 80,000 jobs or 40% of the total decline—is in the aerospace sector. The major job losses have been in aircraft, missiles, and defense electronics. Aerospace jobs in California have fallen by over 20% since mid 1990. Construction related jobs also fell by over 20%.[52]

The rate of decline in manufacturing employment in California during that period exceeded that for the United States as a whole. California's aerospace jobs dropped by 22.3 percent, compared with the country as a whole, which dropped by 16.4 percent; high-tech employment in California dropped by 7.4 percent, somewhat more than the U.S. loss rate. Jobs in construction dropped by 20 percent in California, compared with only 8 percent in the country. Between May 1990 and September 1992, total manufacturing jobs were down by 9.5 percent in California in comparison with a drop of only 6.3 percent in the country.[53]

The most recent declines in manufacturing (other than garment making) are thus attributable to the end of the Cold War, signaled by the transformations in the Soviet Union and Eastern Europe that began in 1989. If investments in the "gunbelt" during the post-World War II period fueled earlier hyperactivity in the Los Angeles region, the recent reductions had the opposite effect.[54]

POPULATION CHANGES IN THE 1980S AND 1990S

To some extent, the gross population changes in the Los Angeles urbanized region have simply paralleled the movement of the economy, albeit with a lag, but that economy has, in turn, been reshaped by the compositional shifts in the population, encouraging selective expansion in "cheap wage" sectors dependent upon immigrant growth. The paradox is that at the very time the region was experiencing a relative decline in its high-wage economic base, its total population continued to increase, largely due to immigration. In the process, both the ethnic and racial composition of the population and their distribution in space underwent significant transformation.

Between 1980 and 1988, the population of Los Angeles County was estimated to have increased by 15 percent to become the most populous county in the country, with 8.5 million residents.[55] In addition, two of its adjacent counties were capturing a remarkable overflow. Orange County was up by close to 18 percent, and in 1988 San Bernardino County was the fastest-growing large county in the United States, having increased 44.4 percent between 1980 and 1988, rising from below 900,000 in 1980 to 1.3 million by 1988. By the mid-1990s, despite the economic retrenchments, the trend of demographic increase seemed not to have ended, and projections suggest that growth will continue, albeit at a slower rate.[56]

Table 12.2 shows the intercensal growth for the Los Angeles CMSA and its components between 1970 and 1990; the more detailed Table 12.3 updates these figures to 1992 and projects them to the year 2000. The enormous demographic

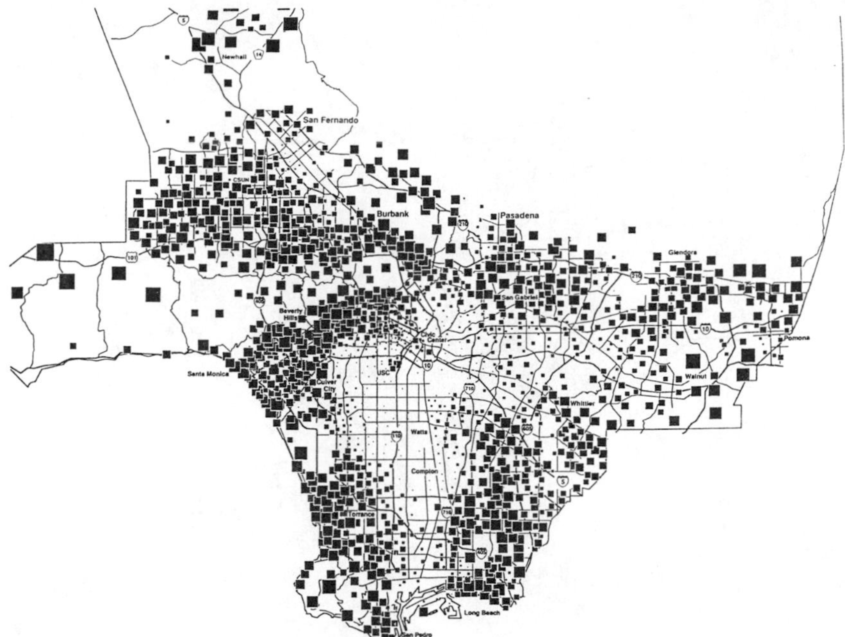

Map 12.2a. Distribution of non-Hispanic white population, Los Angeles County, 1990. Source: U.S. Census data as mapped by Professor William Bowen, Department of Geography, California State University, Northridge; reproduced with the generous permission of Professor Bowen.

Map 12.2b. Distribution of Asian population, Los Angeles County, 1990. Source: U.S. Census data as mapped by Professor William Bowen, Department of Geography, California State University, Northridge; reproduced with the generous permission of Professor Bowen.

Map 12.2c. Distribution of black population, Los Angeles County, 1990. Source: U.S. Census data as mapped by Professor William Bowen, Department of Geography, California State University, Northridge; reproduced with the generous permission of Professor Bowen.

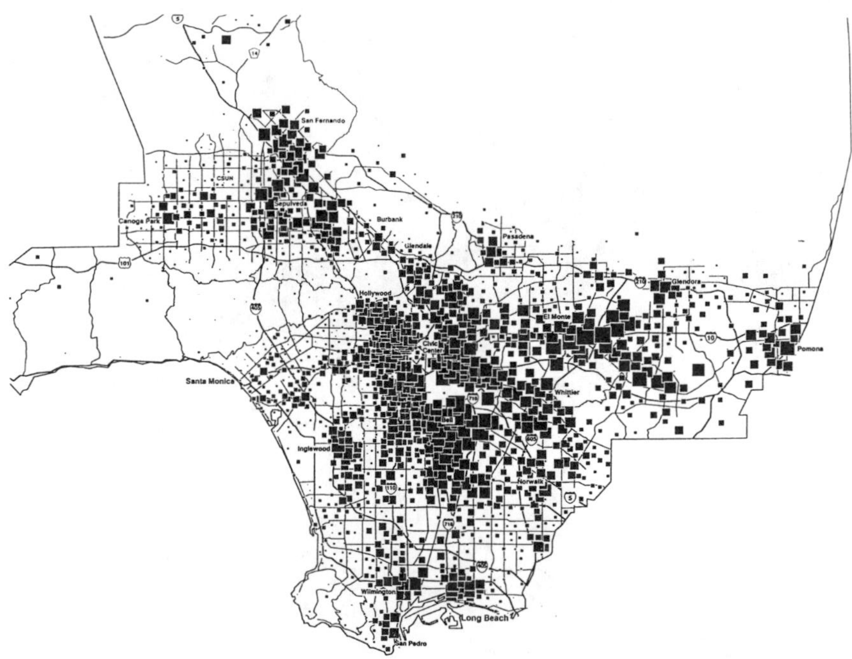

Map 12.2d. Distribution of Hispanic population, Los Angeles County, 1990. Source: U.S. Census data as mapped by Professor William Bowen, Department of Geography, California State University, Northridge; reproduced with the generous permission of Professor Bowen.

increase in the 1970s and 1980s was largely due to foreign immigration. Indeed, Sabagh and Bozorgmehr point out that in the 1970s, "had it not been for international migration, Los Angeles County would have lost about 1 million people through net migration instead of the 123,000 it did lose."[57]

Between 1975 and 1980 alone, Los Angeles County gained some 177,000 Hispanics (mostly Mexican) while losing more than 200,000 non-Hispanic whites.[58] In the 1980s, net migration increased to nearly half a million people within Los Angeles County alone, while the entire Los Angeles region increased by 1.8 million, again due primarily to international immigration. "Between 1970 and 1990, the dramatic increases from 11 to 32 percent foreign-born in Los Angeles County and from 10 to 27 percent in Greater Los Angeles make clear the demographic contribution of immigrants."[59]

Absent better "controls" on the number of immigrants, these trends show no signs of abating. As Sabagh and Bozorgmehr stress:

> Recent information on immigrants' intended metropolitan area of residence suggests that Los Angeles continues to be a magnet for immigrants in the 1990s. . . . [attracting] a large number of undocumented immigrants, probably more than any other place in the United States [mostly from Mexico]. . . . Of the 1.8 million who applied for permanent residence status under the Immigration Reform and Control Act (IRCA) in 1990, 35 percent resided in Los Angeles County, as compared with only 6 percent in New York. In the Los Angeles region as a whole, there were over three-quarters of a million applicants for legalization. As of January 1, 1992, it is estimated that there were as many as 1.5 million people who either received amnesty or were still unauthorized residents in Los Angeles.[60]

Sabagh and Bozorgmehr have "decomposed" the racial and ethnic groups in the Los Angeles region and have tracked changes between 1970 and 1990.[61] Table 12.4 selects out crucial details from their lengthier and more detailed entries. What is

Table 12.2 Population of Los Angeles CMSA, county of Los Angeles (including the city of Los Angeles), and the remainder of the census-delimited CMSA, and percentage intercensal growth, 1970–90

	Total population in thousands			Percentage 10-year change	
Unit	1970	1980	1990	1970–80	1980–90
L.A. CMSA	9,981	11,498	14,531	15.2	26.4
L.A. County (PMSA)	7,042	7,478	8,863	6.2	18.5
Other four counties of the CMSA	2,939	4,020	5,668	36.8	41.0

Source: Georges Sabagh and Mehdi Bozorgmehr, "Population Change: Immigration and Ethnic Transformation," in *Ethnic Los Angeles,* ed. Roger Waldinger and Mehdi Bozorgmehr (New York: Russell Sage Foundation, 1996), 82, Table 3.1, which cites as its source U.S. Bureau of the Census, *State and Metropolitan Areas Data Book 1991* (Washington, D.C.: U.S. Government Printing Office).

Table 12.3. Population growth in the Los Angeles Basin by county between 1980 and 1992, projected to the year 2000

	Population (in thousands)			Average annual growth rate/100	
				1980–92	1992–2000
County	1980	1992	2000	estimated	projected
L.A. Basin	11,589.7	15,224.2	17,323.3	2.3%	1.6%
Imperial County[a]	92.1	117.4	140.9	2.1	2.2
Los Angeles County	7,477.5	9,087.4	9,879.8	1.7	1.0
Orange County	1,932.7	2,512.2	2,811.5	2.3	1.4
Riverside County	663.2	1,289.7	1,730.4	5.8	3.6
San Bernardino County	895.0	1,530.6	1,990.4	.7	3.2
Ventura County	529.2	686.9	770.5	2.2	1.4

[a]Imperial County is not part of the Los Angeles CMSA. Its small population does not cause much distortion to the total.

Source: Center for Continuing Study of the California Economy, *California County Projections—1992* (Palo Alto, Calif.: CCSCE, n.d.), 46, Table 1.

rather striking about these figures is how stable the *absolute numbers* of native-born whites and blacks have remained over time. Marginal net gains in population have come almost exclusively from immigration, supplemented by higher rates of natural increase among the immigrants themselves. Immigrants continue to come chiefly from Mexico, although there has also been a much smaller but increasing contribution from other Central and South American countries, as well as from several Asian countries. This makes the situation very different from that in Chicago and New York, both of which have been magnets for immigrants (the latter much more so than the former) but of very different kinds.

It is the resulting change in the ethnic composition of Los Angeles's population that has generated "anxiety" on the part of the "Anglos" who formerly dominated the region both numerically and politically. Such white anxiety is projected in the Anglo-centered title of Ashley Dunn's article "In California, the Numbers Add Up to Anxiety," and in a series of articles that ran in the *New York Times* in 1993 titled "Reinventing California," in which it is noted that the "welcome" whites had formerly extended to immigrants has been replaced by "resentment."[62]

The changes to which dominant whites are reacting are quite real and are clearly visible to them "on the ground." In the ten years between the censuses of 1980 and 1990, the Hispanic community increased by almost two million, largely because of immigration from Mexico.[63] Asian countries contributed the next three largest groups: 114,000 from the Philippines and a little more than 91,000 each from Vietnam and Korea. Therefore, although Los Angeles had more immigrants than New York, the places from which they came were far less diversified. In terms of sheer numbers, the overwhelming bulk of all immigrants (42 percent) came from Mexico, which, when Salvadorans were added, accounted for slightly more than half of all immigrants. No

Table 12.4. Major ethnic groups[a] by nativity, Los Angeles region,[b] 1970–90

Ethnic/nativity	1970	1980	1990
All Hispanics	1,399,600	2,862,120	4,697,509
Native-born	1,001,400	1,665,980	2,338,369
Percentage native-born	72	58	50
Foreign-born	398,200	1,196,140	2,359,140
Percentage foreign-born	28	42	50
of foreign-born Hispanics			
Percentage Non-Mexican	29	22	27
Percentage Mexican	71	78	73
All Asians	256,200	596,080	1,326,559
Native-born	147,00	222,640	414,427
Percentage native-born	58	37	31
Foreign-born[c]	108,600	373,440	912,132
Percentage foreign-born	42	63	69
Non-Hispanic whites[d]	7,135,900	7,020,640	7,193,802
Native-born	6,602,600	6,476,860	6,584,994
Percentage native-born	93	92	92
Foreign-born	533,300	543,780	608,808
Percentage foreign-born	7	8	8
African Americans	781,000	1,043,800	1,145,684
Native-born	778,700	1,026,800	1,114,269
Percentage native-born	100	98	97
Foreign-born	2,300	17,000	31,415
Percentage foreign-born	0	2	3

[a]Note that "racial" categories have disappeared from this label.

[b]In 1990 this region was the CMSA and included the counties of Los Angeles, San Bernardino, Orange, Ventura, and Riverside. I assume that the 1970 and 1980 figures refer to the same area.

[c]The foreign-born Asians were, by 1990, coming from China, the Philippines, and Korea, in that order.

[d]These figures include an increasing number of Middle Easterners, whom Sabagh and Bozorgmehr treat separately in their table. However, because Middle Easterners in 1990 totaled only a little more than three hundred thousand, less than one-third of whom were native-born, and because most live in "white" zones, I have included them with the white non-Hispanic population.

Source: Extracted from Georges Sabagh and Mehdi Bozorgmehr, "Population Change: Immigration and Ethnic Transformation," in *Ethnic Los Angeles,* ed. Roger Waldinger and Mehdi Bozorgmehr (New York: Russell Sage Foundation, 1996), 95–96, Table 3.2. Rearrangement and percentage calculations ours. Numbers will not add exactly to the total population because of omissions of native Americans and "others."

other country contributed more than six percent of all immigrants. (Contrast these figures with those for New York, as presented in Chapter 10.)[64]

In the process, entire sections of the urbanized area have undergone highly visible transformations within the past few decades. For example, in 1970 only 2 percent of the population of Westminster (a town to the south of Los Angeles city that is now called "Little Saigon") was Asian; this had increased to 8 percent by 1980, and almost 25 percent by 1990. In 1970 the number of Chinese residents in Monterey Park and Alhambra had been negligible; by 1980 some 34 percent of Monterey Park's population and 13 percent of Alhambra's were Asian. By 1990, Asians constituted 58 percent of Monterey Park's population and 38 percent of nearby Alhambra's.[65] South-Central Los Angeles, which in the 1960s had been predominantly black, is now at least half Hispanic. Hispanics constituted 10 percent of its population in 1970, 21 percent by 1980, and 45 percent by 1990. Furthermore, what some authors are calling "mega-barrios" have been "thickening" outside the city limits in East Los Angeles, yielding vast territories that Anglos view as alien and that they scrupulously avoid by hugging the freeways, just as New York whites tend to avoid predominantly black areas such as Bedford-Stuyvesant and the South Bronx (the latter is the setting for the events that initiate the protagonist's troubles in Tom Wolfe's novel *The Bonfire of the Vanities*).

These changes have intensified the ambivalence Anglo residents feel toward "their" minorities. Although much of the special culture of Los Angeles is acknowledged to have been deeply influenced by its Mexican origins and the continued presence of Mexican Americans, the romanticism enshrined in the Ramona myth has now given way to fears of a *reconquista.* Nelson and Clark remind us that even by the 1970s, metropolitan Los Angeles was already home to some 1.7 million persons of Spanish heritage and that the Mexican American population was "the largest urban concentration of Mexicans in the world outside of Mexico City." Although the authors claim that "Mexican-Americans have not influenced Los Angeles in the same way the Irish affected Boston, or the Italians San Francisco, or the Jews New York,"[66] as we shall see, they are beginning to have an impact on Los Angeles's political balance of power. This may be one reason resentments are now surfacing.

Los Angeles's middle- and upper-class "Anglos" have long benefited from the "invisible hands" that make possible their luxurious gardens and their clean houses (much as in the fairy tale, where guests of the giant are catered to by unseen servants), and investors in agribusiness, hotels and restaurants, and manufacturing firms (especially garments) have long profited from the depressed wages of docile Mexican workers.[67] And much of the new entrepreneurial energy in the region is now coming from certain Asian immigrant groups, who have also stimulated the demand for housing and consumer goods.[68] The resentments seem to be fomented by three recent changes in degree, if not in kind: (1) the economic recession in the early 1990s, which has generated fears for job security, even in those sectors where immigrants are hardly relevant competitors; (2) the dramatic recent decline in the *ratio* of Anglos and blacks to "others,"[69] along with a concern that the newcomers (both legal and undocumented) are draining the public coffers by their expanded needs for educational, welfare, and health services, as well as requiring an increase in police protection/repression; and (3) a fear, whether grounded or not, that these new demographic realities may be translated into a redistribution of political power, thus breaking the long-term Anglo monopoly over government policies and the distribution of public resources.

In the 1970s, at the time Nelson and Clark were writing, it was clear that despite the ubiquity of "Spanish" culture, Hispanics had failed to translate their numbers into meaningful representation in the political system.[70] This has now begun to change, but not without a noticeable backlash made evident in a series of defensive referenda in the state—on taxation, on eligibility rules for publicly provided services, and, most recently, on affirmative action programs.

The Changing Composition of Mexican Angelenos

Not only have the numbers of residents of Mexican origin/descent in the Los Angeles region changed, but their composition and status have changed as well. As late as 1960, most of those identified in the census as "Mexican" were either native-born or long-term residents living within Los Angeles County or "temporary" migrant farm laborers, largely scattered in the other more outlying and still agricultural counties. The 1965 Hart-Celler Act set in motion dramatic changes,[71] as the population identified as "Mexican American" or of Mexican origin/descent increased spectacularly within the next twenty-five years to reach some 3.7 million by 1990.

But the overall figures conceal two trends with important implications for the future composition of the population and its increased spatial and jurisdictional segregation. First, there is a built-in demographic dynamic that, even in the absence of further immigration, will continue to "tilt" the ratio between Anglos and Hispanics, namely, the very different age structures and fertility rates in the two communities. The existing Hispanic population is quite young and will grow rapidly through natural increase; in contrast, in the absence of considerable in-migration from other states, the Anglo population will continue to decline because, on average, it is much older, and even those in the childbearing years have low fertility rates. Indeed, the population distribution in Los Angeles is tending toward bimodality, with youth being "minority" and the old being "Anglo."[72]

These intrinsic factors are amplified rather than counteracted by two opposing migration trends: a net in-migration of Hispanics and Asians and a net out-migration of "Anglos," especially in the 1990s as the economic belt tightened in the higher-paying job market and after the region was struck by an accumulating sequence of catastrophic floods, fires, riots, and earthquakes. However, these desertions merely continued trends that were already evident from the 1960s onward, as can be seen in Tables 12.5 and 12.6.

It is worth emphasizing a few points illustrated in these tables. The first has to do with the continuing isolation of blacks within the city of Los Angeles and Los Angeles County and their virtual absence from the remaining four counties of the region, where they constitute only 4 percent. The second is that, although the data suggest a lesser degree of segregation for Hispanics, this is somewhat deceptive, because the outer counties still include significant agricultural areas where many Hispanic migrant farmworkers can be found, as well as a few cities and towns in which urbanized Hispanics still tend to be concentrated.

Table 12.5. Race/Ethnicity, Los Angeles region, 1960–1990

Region	1960	1970	1980	1990
Los Angeles PMSA population[a]	6,038,771	7,032,075	7,477,503	8,863,164
Percentage white non-Hispanic	80.5	67.1	52.9	40.8
Percentage Hispanic[b]	9.6	18.3	27.4	36.4
Percentage black non-Hispanic	7.6	10.8	12.6	11.2
Balance of Los Angeles CMSA	1,513,707	2,939,962	4,020,046	5,668.365
Percentage white non-Hispanic	86.1	81.3	75.5	63.7
Percentage Hispanic	10.7	14.4	17.1	24.4
Percentage Black non-Hispanic	2.1	2.3	2.9	4.2
Total Los Angeles CMSA	7,551,616	9,972,037	11,497,568	14,530,529
Percentage white non-Hispanic	81.7	71.3	60.8	49.7
Percentage Hispanic	9.8	17.2	23.8	31.8
Percentage black non-Hispanic	6.4	8.3	9.2	8.5
Percentage Asian	1.9	2.9	5.5	9.4
Percentage "minority"	18.3	28.7	39.2	50.3

[a]The PMSA is actually the county of Los Angeles.

[b]Figures for Hispanics should be used with caution, especially in 1970, when a racial breakdown of Hispanics was not available. Census definitions have been changing over the years. Excluded are a small proportion of Hispanics classified as black in earlier years.

Source: Figures are derived from an unpublished paper by Georges Sabagh and others.

POPULATION IN FLUX: OUT WITH ANGLOS, IN WITH MINORITIES

The Flight of Whites: Catastrophes and Pocketbooks

In the absence of updated census figures, one indirect and crude way to estimate the post-1990 net out-migration of white Angelenos is by analyzing transfers of driver's licenses into and out of the state.[73] As can be seen in Table 12.7, up through the first half of 1991 transfers to the state were positive, but then, in the aftermath of the 1992 riot and the 1994 earthquake, there was a marked reversal of this trend, suggesting that the post-1985 defense-related drop in industrial activity was not the only cause of out-migration.[74] The California Department of Motor Vehicles reported that, of those drivers who moved out, the largest number went to other western states, such as Nevada, Washington, Oregon, Arizona, and Colorado, whereas newcomers were drawn primarily from Texas, New York, Florida, and Illinois.[75]

There are recent signs that this trend may have begun to taper off by the mid-1990s, although out-migrants continue to outnumber in-migrants from other parts of the United States. As Lee notes:

> For the first time since 1990, the number of Californians exchanging their driver's licenses for ones in other states has dropped. . . . During the twelve months ended in November [1994], the number of people who turned in their California driver's licenses in other states fell to 387,022, down from 405,000 in the comparable

Table 12.6. Race/Hispanic origin (in percentages), population of the Los Angeles CMSA, the Los Angeles PMSA (same as Los Angeles County), the city of Los Angeles, and the sum of four adjacent counties (Orange, Riverside, San Bernardino, and Ventura), according to the 1990 census

Race/ethnicity	CMSA	PMSA (Los Angeles County)	City of Los Angeles	Four adjacent counties
White non-Hispanic	49.8	40.8	37.3	63.7
Black non-Hispanic	8.0	10.5	13.0	3.9
Amerind non-Hispanic	0.4	0.3	0.3	0.5
Asian non-Hispanic	8.8	10.2	9.2	6.5
Other non-Hispanic	0.2	0.2	0.3	0.1
Hispanic	32.9	37.8	39.9	25.2

Note: The PMSA of Los Angeles is the same as Los Angeles County. The city of Los Angeles, because of historic accidents and the deannexation option that has been available to subareas within the city since the Lakewood case in the 1950s, is peculiarly shaped. Not only are there "holes in the Swiss cheese" created by successive deannexations, but the city of Los Angeles incorporates its port area much to the south, via a thin thread that passes through independent local jurisdictions. Given this, the county/PMSA may be the best unit to use. However, it should be noted that county areas that deannexed or resisted annexation, with the exception of East Los Angeles, tend to be somewhat better-off than the city proper.

Source: My own calculations based on U.S. Census of 1990, volume for the Los Angeles CMSA. I have recalculated the combined populations by race and ethnicity for the four counties adjacent to Los Angeles County.

> period a year earlier, the state Department of Finance reported. Since 1988, more than 2 million people have exchanged their California driver's licenses for those in other states.[76]

Lee mentions the difficulties these emigrants have faced in selling their homes at depressed prices (down as much as 50 percent); in dealing with hostility toward them in the states to which they have moved; in finding work in other labor markets, to which they have contributed overcrowding; and in finding housing in markets to which their influx has contributed rising house prices.

Acts of God and of humans are both blamed for the defections of Angelenos in the early 1990s. But floods, fires, and even earthquakes were no strangers to the Los Angeles area, nor were riots or economic contractions, as we have seen in earlier chapters. And given the multiracial origins of Los Angeles's first "white" settlers, a concern with the tipping of the racial and ethnic "balance" should not have been so salient. Certainly, these factors had not deterred immigration of Anglos in the past.[77] Why, then, did they generate an exodus in the 1990s?

If economic factors alone were involved, one would not find the political backlash so evident even among residents who remained. For some time now, the Anglos of the Los Angeles region have been participating enthusiastically in referenda involving tax revolts, denying admission to schools and health and welfare benefits to

Table 12.7. Transfer of drivers' licenses into and out of the state of California between 1988 and first half of 1994

	Licensed drivers who were		
	Moving to California	Leaving California	Net change[a]
1988–89	437,000	306,000	131,000
1989–90	430,000	346,000	84,000
1990–91	376,000	340,000	36,000
1991–92	342,000	355,000	-13,000
1992–93	289,000	389,000	-100,000
1993–94	274,000	400,000	-126,000

Note: Of course, not all former holders of California drivers' licenses were "Anglo," nor were Californians leaving the state exclusively drawn from the Los Angeles area. However, there is independent evidence that the out-migration from California has been primarily non-Hispanic white and has been preponderantly drawn from Southern California.

[a] How many people left is not known; however, the California Department of Motor Vehicles estimates, on the basis of license transfers, that more than six hundred thousand people moved to other parts of the country in the fiscal year that ended June 30, 1994.

Source: Paul Jacobs, "Hitting the Road: Record Number of Drivers Join Exodus, DMV Says," *Los Angeles Times,* August 18, 1994, A26.

(undocumented) "foreigners," and, early on, stalling integration of the local school system until it was beyond feasibility. These actions, albeit many of them were or may be found unconstitutional, reveal not only job and economic insecurities but a deep-seated fear of the conversion of their "land of dreams" into a nightmare, perhaps similar to that projected in the classic dystopic film of Los Angeles's polyethnic future, *Blade Runner.*

Clouds in the Crystal Ball

When I first mentioned to colleagues that I was studying Los Angeles, a number of them responded, "You must see *Blade Runner.*" The film is a lurid and violent "projection" of a variety of anxieties—over environmental pollution, robotic alienation, and "ethnic contamination." But what is most interesting to me about this nightmare is that anxieties about the future Hispanicization of Los Angeles are distinctly muted, if not entirely absent.

Made in 1982 and based only loosely on a futuristic novel written several decades earlier, the film is set in the year 2019 in Los Angeles and depicts a totally bifurcated physical city: a "Third World" street-level city, replete with vaguely menacing and exotic "foreigners" (mostly "Oriental" in appearance and speaking a gibberish of Asian-sounding languages with only a few words of Spanish mixed in); and the other, an above-surface Anglo city containing a population phenotypically Anglo. Control over the entire city via ubiquitous circling helicopters (which have since become one of the major mechanisms of control used by the LAPD) is exercised from a massive fortified pyramidal structure that houses the head of the Tyrell Corporation as well as its employees. These bureaucrats supervise "law and order" on the ground and interrogate Anglo-looking subjects to determine whether they are really "human" or merely "androids"—that is, robots called replicants. Although these replicants have been designed in the elites' "own image" and are manufactured by the corporation to do much of the modern work of society, the ruling class now fears that their mechanically produced (high-tech) servants have aspirations to cross caste lines by developing human emotions.

While the topography thus parallels the split between the subterranean city of workers and the surface city of capitalists in Fritz Lang's 1926 film *Metropolis,* the differences are striking. Whereas Lang's film was clearly based on class conflict between dehumanized "proles" and their "masters" of the same race, the film set in Los Angeles places the Anglo "masters" squarely between two threats: the first concerned with "ethnic pollution" (Anglo versus "foreigner"), the second preoccupied with alienation (Anglo humans versus look-alike androids). It thus speaks simultaneously to the anxieties of scientific dehumanization and racial dilution.

It is worth thinking about both themes, because they suggest a profound reluctance to grant humanity and inclusion—both to robotic "hands" who might entertain ambitions to become "real people," and to unassimilable and marginalized "exotics," whose existence is noted but then cordoned off in deteriorated zones of urban abandonment. Were the film to be made today, one wonders what group would occupy both roles. I suspect it might be Mexicans/Mexican Americans. The film may, indeed, be more accurate than it appears on the surface. It may inadvertently capture a form of local schizophrenia, in which docile Mexicans are seen as not-quite-human robots appreciated for their services, while their unassimilated or potentially rebellious "others" are increasingly hidden from view in "Third World" quarters.

In with Minorities

Despite the defections of Anglos, the CCSCE expects continued population growth for the five Los Angeles counties and predicts that by the year 2005, the five-county region should host a resident population of about 18.3 million. Significantly, however, the CCSCE also expects that by that year the proportion of "minorities" in the population will rise from the 55 percent estimated in 1995 to about 62 percent.[78]

Because the number of African Americans in the region has stabilized and may now even be declining, the overwhelming majority of these "minorities" will be Hispanic, and of these, most will be of Mexican origin or ancestry. It must be acknowledged that this "rising tide" of Mexican irredentism may be contributing to the further exodus of Anglos and the withdrawal of many of the remaining into defensive "gated communities" in outlying suburban and exurban areas. Certainly, a sizable backlash, even in Orange County, with its polarized class/ethnic system, has been building steam in recent decades.[79] It is within the context of this changing composition that the political battles over schools, taxes, welfare eligibility rules, and political redistricting in California must be understood.

THE BACKLASH IN THE EDUCATIONAL SYSTEM

At first the school desegregation mandated in the 1954 U.S. Supreme Court case of *Brown v. Board of Education of Topeka* seemed to be of only minor relevance in Los Angeles because the region was fragmented into so many separate communities (most with their own independent school districts), because in comparison to other major U.S. cities only a relatively small proportion of the Los Angeles population (10 percent) was black, and because it was then unclear whether Mexican American (and Asian) children were also to be included in any plans for "integration." Furthermore, school financing through locally raised real estate taxes—a tense political issue that plagued other localities forced to integrate—was also not salient in California. Ever since an early 1960s ruling of the Supreme Court of California (in *Serrano v. Priest*), school districts received most of their funding from the state, rather than from local governments. (These payments, however, are then redistributed to localities according to an allocation formula that does not take into consideration special requirements.)

However, school desegregation did become a burning issue in one important location: the Los Angeles Unified School District (LAUSD), which is by far the largest system in the state, covering 710 square miles of territory and including, in addition to the city of Los Angeles, ten independent cities—Carson, Cudahy, Bell, Gardena, Huntington Park, Lomita, Maywood, San Fernando, South Gate, and Vernon, as well as some unincorporated parts of the county, such as East Los Angeles.[80] After New York City, it is the second most populous school district in the entire country. And given its boundaries, it is evident that it now enrolls the overwhelming proportion of the metropolitan region's "students of color": African American, Asian, and Hispanic. It was therefore a logical target for integration.

As early as 1970, a Los Angeles Superior Court judge (in *Crawford v. Board of Education of the City of Los Angeles*) ruled that "the city's schools were illegally segregated on the basis of race."[81] But it was not until the late 1970s that, after long delaying tactics and appeals, the California Supreme Court eventually got around to mandating desegregation. In the interim, California voters sought to subvert mandated desegregation through a series of tactics.[82] In 1970, the State Assembly (via the "Wakeville" law) tried to rule out busing as a solution. But although the California Supreme Court eventually held that parental consent for busing was needed, it set aside the original aim, which was to undermine desegregation by requiring parental consent for all school assignments. In 1971, a bill was passed by the California State Legislature that required school boards to collect racial statistics and to consider plans to correct racial imbalances.[83] An attempt was then made to circumvent this ruling. In a November 1972 referendum, voters approved Proposition 21, saying that no California child could be assigned to a school solely on the basis of race or creed. This reversed the 1971 state law, but again the state Supreme Court declared the proposition unconstitutional. Then the Los Angeles Board of Education took a position against busing and the state again tried to get a petition going to pass a constitutional amendment limiting busing of public school pupils for the purpose of desegregation. Finally, in 1976, the California Supreme Court handed down a decision that ordered the Los Angeles Unified School District "to bring about 'reasonably feasible' desegregation in its schools." Although the state's highest court thus ordered the district to desegregate and required the LAUSD to submit its plan for approval by the court, "the interpretation of the order was left up to the local policy makers."[84]

It was not until the fall of 1978 that the court finally accepted the LAUSD's plan for desegregation. The plan had both voluntary and mandatory "options." It began with voluntary choices in the 1977-78 school year, offering "parents and pupils of the District an opportunity to pair or cluster their respective (segregated) schools, or to choose a magnet school program."[85] The following academic year, the magnet school program was created, establishing ten magnet centers at the secondary school level, ten "mini-magnet" elementary schools for the "gifted," four mini-magnet junior high school programs, and eight mini-magnet elementary schools. This mechanism permitted and, indeed, as we shall see, encouraged racial/ethnic *resegregation,* even *within the same physically integrated school buildings.* Furthermore, the mandatory part applied only to pupils in fourth to eighth grades in "segregated" schools (defined as those in which enrollment was "less than 30 per cent combined minority, not exceeding 70 per cent combined minority, or at least 30 per cent other white, but not exceeding 70 per cent white").[86]

But by then the opportunity for true integration had passed. The courts had earlier ordered the LAUSD to monitor the racial and ethnic composition of students in each of its more than seven hundred schools and to "show its progress" by publishing these data annually in an *Ethnic Survey Report.*[87] The "progress" revealed by these successive reports shows that Los Angeles was rapidly moving backward, not forward. A graph inside the cover of the *Fall 1992 Ethnic Survey Report* demonstrates how the racial and ethnic composition of LAUSD students had already altered between 1966 and 1976, when the final desegregation order was rendered. Integration *might* have been feasible as late as 1966, when students of "Caucasian white non-Hispanic origin" (the category used in the reports) still constituted about 56 percent of the total and "combined minorities" were about 44 percent. After that, however, there was a monotonic decline in the percentage of Anglo students and a reciprocal straight-line increase in the proportion classified as "combined minorities." (The two trend lines intersected in 1970, when both stood at 50 percent.)

By the time the court order was issued in 1976, however, minorities already constituted almost two-thirds of all students (24 percent black, 32 percent Hispanic, and 6 percent Asian), and in subsequent years the imbalance became so great that no amount of busing or school pairing could have repaired the damage. By 1992, the LAUSD reported that 65.1 percent of its pupils were Hispanic, 14.6 percent were black non-Hispanic, and 7 percent were Asian or Filipino. This left only 12.7 percent who were classified as "white non-Hispanic."[88] Examining enrollment data for individual schools in that year, it becomes evident that the "mini-magnet schools," set up in conjunction with the desegregation plan, were absorbing most of these declining numbers of Anglo students.

Table 12.8. Changing proportion of students enrolled in the Los Angeles Unified School District by race/ethnicity for key selected years, 1966–76

	Percentage distribution by year			
Race/ethnicity[a]	1966	1970	1973	1976
Caucasian non-Hispanic	56	50	44	37
All others (called "minorities")[b]	44	50	56	63
"Minority" breakdown by race/ethnicity				
African American	21	24	25	24
Hispanic	19	22	25	32
Asian and "others"[c]	4	4	6	7

[a]The categories are those used in the source report.

[b]This is clearly a misnomer.

[c]I have grouped together the categories of Asian, Filipino, Pacific Islander, and Native American, because these were not consistently reported separately in various time periods.

Source: Figures derived from Los Angeles Unified School District, Information Technology Division, *Fall 1992 Ethnic Survey Report* (Publication 119) (Los Angeles: LAUSD, 1992), graph on inside front cover.

In short, the Los Angeles school system has become the repository for minority and/or immigrant children. Actually, enrollment in the Los Angeles Unified School District would have declined by 23 percent between 1980 and 1990,[89] instead of increasing by 12 percent in those ten years, had it not been for immigration. Students with limited English proficiency (LEP) now constitute a very large proportion of the enrollment. (Most of the LEP students are Latino or Asian/Pacific Islanders.)[90] The challenge and additional expense of teaching LEP students places a heavy burden on the system, which may be why minority dropout rates are so high.

Because it is the State of California that is responsible for funding education, support for public schools ran into the same backlash that has fueled other anti-immigrant initiatives and the state's tax revolt. Even though the needs were becoming greater, education bonds were consistently rejected by voters, which eventually led to the state's being ranked twenty-third in the country on per capita spending for education.[91] By 1994, the state ranked forty-second of the fifty states in spending per pupil, and its fourth graders tied with Louisiana for last place on a national standardized reading test. Only in 1996 did a windfall in state tax revenues give the state a surplus, which for the first time in years could be directed to education.[92]

Whether funds alone will solve the LAUSD's problems remains to be seen, especially given that they will be granted on a uniform per student basis, regardless of LAUSD's greater need for compensatory training. But as we shall see below in the discussion of recent changes in local politics, Latino voters went to the polls in groundbreaking numbers in the Los Angeles mayoral election of April 1997, mobilized in a campaign to support Proposition BB, the school bond measure.[93]

THE POLITICAL BACKLASH AGAINST FOREIGNERS AND MINORITIES

The political backlash resulting from recent demographic transformations has been perhaps more extreme in California than elsewhere, a backlash that, because of the "over-representation" of remaining Anglos on the voter rolls, has up to now been relatively unrestrained by counterforces.[94] The forms of backlash have been financial and legal.

A Tax Revolt: Proposition 13

In 1978, the voters of California passed Proposition 13 in a referendum that set the maximum real estate tax that could be imposed by any locality at 1.25 percent of the market value of a property.[95] This "tax-cutting initiative reduced the property tax rate in Los Angeles by 80 percent, and collections fell 50 percent between 1978 and 1979."[96] Although attractive to many home owners, it was differentially embraced by whites and minorities. Sonenshein compares the vote in four key council districts in the city, each with a different racial/ethnic constituency. Fully 80 percent of the voters in a conservative white district voted in favor of Proposition 13, and even in the white "liberal Jewish" and "moderate Latino/white" districts, small majorities approved the measure. Only voters in the predominantly black district opposed, by a margin of 78 to 22 percent, the draconian measure that would force reductions in city and county services, especially when compounded by cutbacks in federal aid.[97]

Antiforeigner Sentiment: Proposition 187

Whereas opposition to school desegregation, the rejection of school-funding bonds, and the passage of Proposition 13 were only *indirectly* aimed at minorities and Hispanic newcomers, Proposition 187 directly expressed the demographic "resentment" of California voters, especially Anglo voters living in urbanized parts of Southern California where Mexican immigrants were most numerous. This proposition, approved overwhelmingly by California voters in November 1994 but still unenforced in 1999 as court appeals continue, denied "illegal" immigrants the right to place their children in public schools, to use government hospitals and health services, and to otherwise benefit from most public services (except transportation). Employees of these public institutions were directed not only to deny service but to report the offending students/clients/patients to the U.S. Immigration and Naturalization Service (INS), presumably to facilitate their deportation.[98] Thus California voters previewed the backlash, equally contested, that would come several years later on the national level when welfare rules were changed to deny public assistance even to legal aliens (a throwback to the Depression period).

Even though the constitutionality of Proposition 187 continues to be appealed in the courts, its passage had an immediate chilling effect on immigrants (whether "legal" or "undocumented") and even citizens, especially within the sizable Mexican American community. First, legal immigrants were quick to pick up the message that although the proposal seemed to be directed only at "illegal" immigrants (those most vulnerable to bashing), the application of the law would inevitably affect legal immigrants (and even native-born persons of "foreign" appearance), who might be subject to detailed scrutiny and be considered guilty until proven innocent.[99] They have correctly sensed that the emotions behind the referendum vote were directed against all Mexicans, regardless of immigration status. Second, legal Mexican immigrants, especially those whose status was regularized through IRCA, have now accumulated enough "residence time" to be eligible for citizenship. Even those who for years may have settled for legal immigration status or permanent residency have been rushing to be naturalized.[100] If they do so in large numbers and translate their new citizenship rights into voter demands, they could potentially shift the balance of power in the area.

Although these anxieties run particularly high in California, anti-immigrant sentiments in other parts of the United States have similarly been pressuring legal immigrants to apply for citizenship. By the end of the fiscal year on September 30, 1997, it was estimated that "nearly 1.1 million immigrants will have become citizens . . . , shattering the record, set just last year, of 455,853 naturalizations, according to the Immigration and Naturalization Service. . . . More than 75 percent of the new citizens are concentrated in and around six cities, all in states with large electoral votes: New York, Los Angeles, Chicago, San Francisco, Miami and Houston."[101] The INS estimated that another 1.1 million persons would become citizens by the fall of 1998.[102] This new surge to naturalization can be traced directly to anxieties generated not only by forerunner Proposition 187 but by the latest national welfare "reform" law, which threatens to substantially reduce benefits even for legal immigrants. Nor is the end to naturalization in sight. In 1997 there were some 10 million *legal noncitizens* in the United States, of whom about 7 million were eligible to apply for citizenship.[103] If they do so, and then exercise their power at the ballot box, they could tip support toward the Democrats. And in California and especially in Los Angeles, their new voting power might just undermine current political coalitions, a theme to which I return below.

It is especially interesting to contrast the position of California's politicians toward immigrants with that of political leaders in New York. Not only has New York State resisted discriminatory actions against immigrants, documented or not, but Rudolph Giuliani, the city's Republican mayor, has been an active force in opposing anti-immigrant legislation. In October 1996, he "sued the Federal Government to block a provision in the laws that allows city employees to turn in illegal immigrants who seek services like police protection, hospital care and public education." And in spring of 1997 he joined the battle against the new welfare law, "charging that the law's cutoff of Federal benefits to legal immigrants is unconstitutional."[104]

Clearly, the two cities that have absorbed the largest number of immigrants in recent years are responding quite differently to the social, economic, and political implications of high immigration. Only part of that difference is attributable to economic factors or to shortsighted predictions about Democratic or Republican votes. What I have been calling *political culture* throughout this book accounts for much of the difference. The differences are also evident in California's recent reversals of affirmative action.

Affirmative Action in the California University System

On July 21, 1995, despite vocal opposition and demonstrations on all campuses and speeches by "outside agitators" such as Jesse Jackson, the twenty-six-member Board of Regents that supervises the University of California system voted, after only a dozen hours of deliberation, to do away with affirmative action in awarding university contracts and in selecting students. This seems symptomatic of further "displacement" panic on the part of white Angelenos, a panic to which the political establishment is responding with alacrity.

The *Los Angeles Times* ran a lead article in 1995 that repeated California scuttlebutt that Governor Pete Wilson, an earlier advocate of affirmative action, had changed his position, hoping thereby to advance his bid for the presidential nomination, and that he had applied pressure to get the vote.[105] He was able to do so because the California state constitution, with the goal of insulating the public universities from politics, had made the board independent of the legislature but, significantly, not independent of the governor. (Eighteen of the members of the Board of Regents are actually appointed by the governor, whereas the rest serve ex officio.)

But Wilson was also reflecting the growing popularity of rejecting affirmative action throughout the state. In November 1997, California voters approved Proposition 209, calling for an end to all race- and sex-based preferences in state government hiring, contracting, and educational programs. The constitutionality of this proposition was litigated, but in April 1997, a U.S. Court of Appeals in California upheld its legality, although opponents still hope to appeal the decision to the U.S. Supreme Court.[106] However, the effects of Proposition 209 were already being felt in spring of 1998, when the number of black and Latino applicants to California colleges and universities dropped drastically, as did admissions of such students.[107] Some state institutions are now scrambling to undo some of the damage.

The supports to end affirmative action, then, must be seen as another part of the backlash against minorities and fear of their further empowerment in what Anglo Californians seem to view as a zero-sum game. It is a game that in the past has triggered periodic outbursts of revolt from the disempowered, that has occasionally led to attempts at co-optation (but only after an uprising), but that now requires far deeper surgical changes. It is the interaction between political empowerment (for some) and protest movements (by others), within the context of Los Angeles's peculiar governmental institutions, that has thus far kept the region from responding to its changing circumstances.

FAILED(?) ATTEMPTS TO CONTAIN AND CO-OPT "MINORITIES"

If the dominant characteristic of "race relations" in Chicago is the sharp white-versus-black divide, the subterranean problem in Los Angeles lies along the Anglo-versus-Latino (largely Mexican) fault line.[108] Although these tensions were temporarily submerged in the 1960s, when the 1965 Watts riot called attention to the struggle of marginalized African Americans in the context of the wider civil rights movement, it should be remembered that African Americans never constituted more than a relatively small proportion of the city's and region's population, and that, in the period subsequent to the riot, some attempts were made to ameliorate the condition of their exclusion, although they have clearly been insufficient to dislodge Anglo rule.

As in Chicago and New York, educated blacks in the Los Angeles region have recently gained some limited upward job mobility, primarily in the media and the public sector. As in other cities, this has largely resulted in a growing gap between a small middle class and the majority of native-born blacks, who have increasingly been marginalized from the economy and confined to deteriorated and segregated quarters.[109] In Los Angeles, these gaps have increasingly appeared within the Latino population as well.

Until fairly recently, however, the conventional approach to the "race question" in urban analysis has been to focus almost exclusively on the rift between "white" and "nonwhite" groups, on the assumption that almost all "nonwhites" are "black." In earlier chapters I have explored some of the inaccuracies in this racial dichotomization. Although it has until fairly recently been a powerful analytic tool in Chicago, even there, where the "black" population is twice as large as the combined Hispanic groups, it fails to capture new spatial and political realities. In New York City, the dichotomy has always had far less validity. Although the numbers of "blacks" and "Hispanics" in that city will soon reach equality, as we have already seen, each of the categories is crosscut by other factors, such as place of birth and juridical status. In Los Angeles, where Hispanics now outnumber blacks three to one in the city, the dichotomy is even less accurate, because it misses many of the complexities of inter- and intraminority relations.

In actuality, the racio-ethnic situation in all three cities needs, at the minimum, to be reanalyzed as three-way "contests" among African Americans, "whites," and Hispanics. The outcomes of such contests are far from foreordained. As Simmel astutely noted long ago, the social dynamics of the dyad (a set of two) are fundamentally different from those of the triad, where *tertius gaudens* reigns, yielding potentially shifting alignments and coalitions.[110] Although in all three cities "blacks" have had to contend not only with "whites" but with "Hispanics" (and/or foreigners) in their search for physical space and for a politically empowered voice at the local bargaining table, the variations from city to city are certainly as significant as the similarities.

In the city of Chicago, the overwhelming proportion of "people of color" are African American, with Hispanics (consisting mostly of Puerto Ricans and Mexicans in equal numbers) occupying a decidedly secondary position. Although the latter often live in neighborhoods adjacent to black ghettos (see the distribution maps in Chapter 11), proximity has not necessarily led to amity or unity. In large measure, relations between the two "ethnicities" have been competitive and often conflictual. Only in the brief period that preceded the first election of Mayor Harold Washington was a sufficiently effective coalition built between the two groups that, with the help of so-called (anti-machine) lakefront liberals, gained the office for him. And as we have seen, the coalition later unraveled, as Hispanic leaders (mostly Puerto Rican) complained that they were being ignored by city hall. Once the coalition was broken, and aided by Washington's untimely death, the old "machine," thanks to its support from downtown business interests, was able to reentrench itself despite the exodus to suburbia of a considerable number of its former supporters.

In New York, the complexities of race, ethnicity, and immigrant status have yielded a situation that resists neat polarization, despite the important break between Jews and blacks that occurred in 1968 in the context of the struggle in Ocean-Hill/ Brownsville and the teachers' strike.[111] To some extent, the multiple routes to political influence (given the hierarchical structure of mayor, borough presidents, and a functioning ward system), the relative openness provided by the possibilities for building ethnically balanced (and multiparty) Fusion tickets, and the declining power of the traditional Democratic machine after Carmen DeSapio was deposed in the 1960s made it possible for at least the major ethnic, religious, and racial groups to be represented in city government. What Ester Fuchs asserts is a structural "weakness" in New York—that is, the need to renegotiate power continually (or, as she says, to "pay off" interest groups) in a potentially fragile or at least unstable system[112]—might be viewed from another perspective as providing opportunities for new groups to break into the coalition game and be heard.

In Los Angeles, changing demographics, coupled with and thus restricted by a political structure designed to "professionalize" government according to the ideals of the turn-of-the-century Progressive movement, have served to calcify an entrenched power structure that has thus far been extremely successful in excluding or co-opting dissident voices. It is ironic that because the system managed for so long to silence minority demands, the only recourse has been periodic explosions in the streets.

The Watts riot of 1965 was just such an explosion. It set in motion an apparent change of regime in the city that lasted from 1973 to 1993. When it was again contested, this time by the blacks and Hispanics of South-Central, the old coalition ended. One way to understand the racio-ethnic dynamics in Los Angeles better, then, is to look more closely at city and county politics in the period bracketed by the riots of 1965 and 1992. The most scholarly attempt to do so has been undertaken by Raphael J. Sonenshein. His book *Politics in Black and White* focuses on the twenty-year reign of Tom Bradley as the first and so far only black mayor of Los Angeles. What is perplexing about this otherwise well-researched book is that it couches the inquiry almost exclusively within a dyadic framework of black and white[113]—a frame that might have been appropriate for Chicago, but that is particularly inapposite for Los Angeles. In the following, I therefore offer a reinterpretation of much of the excellent information in Sonenshein's book (and other sources)[114] to build a somewhat different narrative about how minority voices—both of poorer blacks and Hispanics—have consistently been excluded in the city and county of Los Angeles.[115]

The "Progressive" Structure of Government

One of the most important facts to remember about California politics is that it is the legacy of Progressive reformers who sought to "remove" local administrations from politics by emphasizing technical administrative powers and by making elections for municipal and county officials "nonpartisan."[116] The goal was to keep the number of elected officials to a minimum. Today, the entire county of Los Angeles is "represented" by only five members of the County Board of Supervisors, and the entire city of Los Angeles elects only fifteen representatives to the city council.[117] The latter are selected on a ward basis, but ward boundaries are continually gerrymandered at the will of the incumbent council members. Similarly, the LAUSD's school board has only seven elected members, originally selected at large but now representing different but spatially enormous districts.

This approach to local government has had two serious consequences. First, as Skerry notes, "government agencies in Los Angeles are notoriously well insulated from elected officials, and local government has alternately been praised for its professionalism and denounced for inattention to the will of the people."[118] This is especially true of the police department, whose chief cannot easily be removed even for dereliction of duty (as occurred in both the Watts riot of 1965 and the South-Central riot of 1992), and whose "hold" over politically elected representatives is alleged to have been exercised through "blackmail."[119] And second, each of the so-called elected representatives now stands for a constituency so enormous that the costs of running for office are prodigious, and it is almost impossible for small groups to influence outcomes. The five-person Board of Supervisors for Los Angeles County "presides over a land area nearly four times larger than the State of Rhode Island" and represents a population that as of 1990 included 8.9 million persons—or one representative for every 1.8 million residents.[120] The average population in each of the seven LAUSD districts is now more than six hundred thousand, and each of the fifteen members of the Los Angeles City Council represents nearly a quarter of a million persons.[121] Given this structure of governance, it has been remarkably easy for entrenched powers to exclude growing minorities and for well-funded business interests to continue to dominate local decision making.[122]

Urban Gerrymandering

One important mechanism whereby minority representation has been kept to a minimum, thus causing blacks and Mexican Americans to be cast into a zero-sum game within a limited number of potentially dissident wards, is the authority of incumbent city council members to *redraw district boundaries,* a power that has served to divide the city up into "multicultural" electoral zones so as to dilute any concentration of racial/ethnic power. Although the complex details of this system cannot be explored here, the results are patently obvious. Until 1985, only one Mexican American (Edward Roybal) had ever been elected to the Los Angeles City Council; he served from the Ninth District between 1949 and 1962.[123] When he resigned to run for Congress, the city council had the authority to appoint a temporary replacement until the next election could be held in 1963. Up to that time, no black had ever served on the council, but under pressure from the black community (and also as part of the dual processes of divide-and-conquer and containment), the council selected a black over an alternate Latino. As Sonenshein remarks, "A Black-Latino struggle was shaping up, as ascendant Blacks sought to hold on to their one seat—itself the only seat Latinos had ever won."[124]

In the 1963 election, black candidates carried not only the Ninth District, but also the Eighth (which contained the largest proportion of blacks in the city) and the Tenth, in which former UCLA athlete, retired police officer, and then lawyer Tom Bradley emerged through a vigorous campaign that tapped the middle-class black areas of the district (Baldwin Hills, the most exclusive) as well as Jewish voters of the Westside who had long resented exclusion from the Protestant power structure. For the next thirty years, African Americans held on to all three seats (but could not enlarge their grasp), and Bradley, after several failed attempts, parlayed his coalition to win the mayoralty ten years later. During that period, the Latino voice was essentially silenced, in part because of a growing animosity between Chicanos and African Americans that had been fomented by the blatant strategy of pitting them against one another, in part because of a growing split between more assimilated and conservative factions within the Chicano community and the poorer and/or more progressive elements in it. These gaps would not become fully evident until the 1997 local elections.

One other significant change—perhaps the last attempt to divide and conquer—had been a 1971 decision on the part of the council to redistribute (gerrymander) the fifteen districts on the basis of population rather than citizenship. This allowed the boundaries of "mixed" districts to be redrawn to include many Latinos who, because they were not citizens, could not threaten Anglo dominance at the ballot box. The city council continued to gerrymander districts in 1972 and 1986, in part to contain the growing strength of the Chicano minority but also to block blacks from gaining more than "their" three seats. (See Maps 12.3a, 12.3b, and 12.3c.)

The Election of Bradley as Mayor

In 1965, Los Angeles's disenfranchised poor African American population in Watts was totally without voice. Watts was politically isolated from the other zones with significant numbers of black residents by being placed within the Fifteenth District, which was attached to the port zones of Wilmington and San Pedro by the umbilical cord created by the "shoestring addition." Although Watts's voice was thus silenced in the political process, its voice in the streets did have effects, both by calling attention to the threat of violence and by generating a heightened backlash against "the dangerous classes."[125]

In the short run, the Watts riot seems to have strengthened the hand of Mayor Sam Yorty and his police chief by convincing Anglo and many better-established Chicano voters that law and order should take precedence over other goals.[126] But the riot may also have suggested that unless growing black "power" could be co-opted, it might bring down the house. In the long run, the latter proved even more significant in Los Angeles's political future because it led to an elite alliance between whites and blacks that opened the way to Tom Bradley's successful bid for the mayor's office in 1973.

Although Bradley had lost his 1969 challenge to Yorty because at that time he attracted only black voters, poor Latinos, and some of his liberal Jewish supporters from the Tenth District, by 1973 he had broadened his base and carried the city by a narrow margin. Assured of the "black vote" but correctly reading the signs that he also

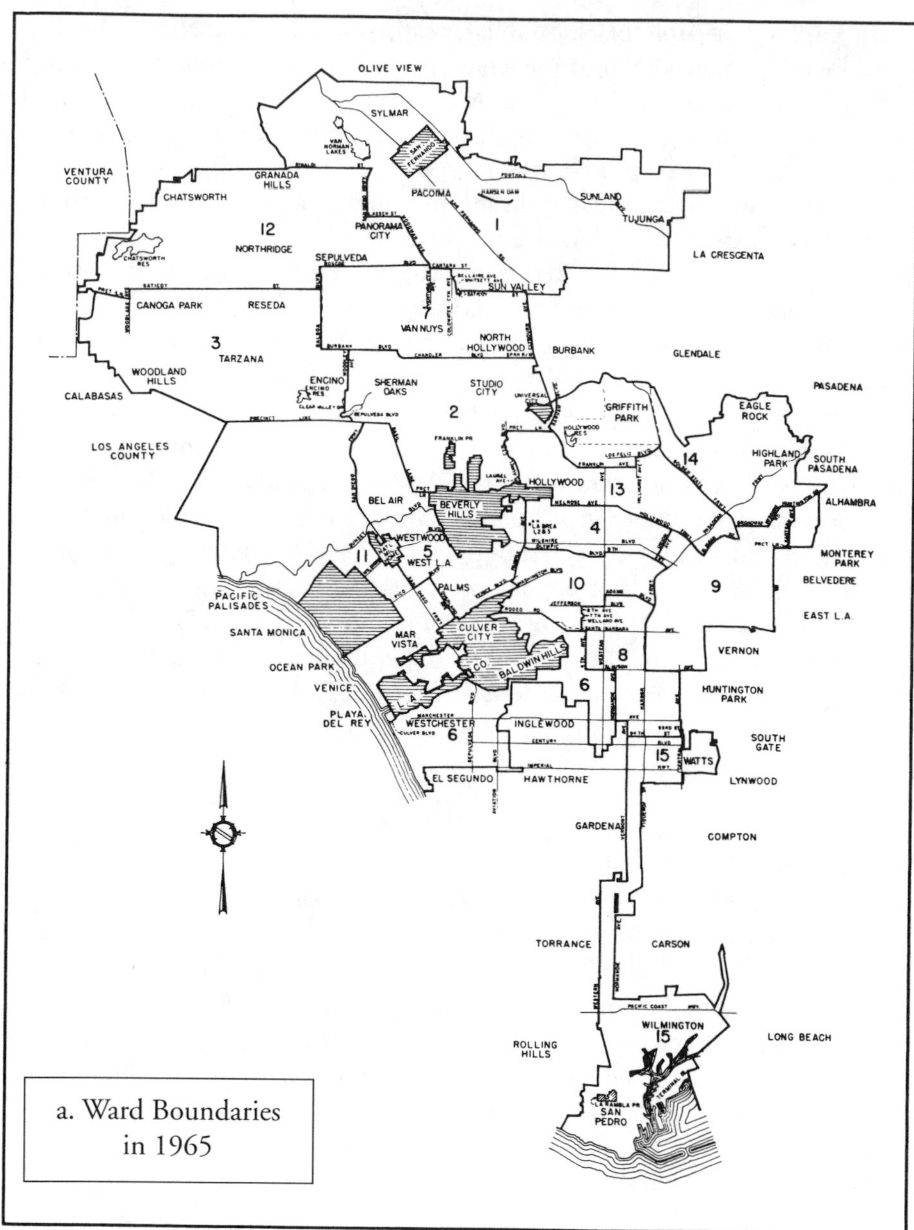

Maps 12.3a, 12.3b, and 12.3c. The continual gerrymandering in 1965, 1972, and 1986 of city council electoral districts to manipulate council representation by whites, blacks, and Latinos. Source: Raphael J. Sonenshein, *Politics in Black and White: Race and Power in Los Angeles*; copyright 1993 Princeton University Press, reprinted with permission of Princeton University Press.

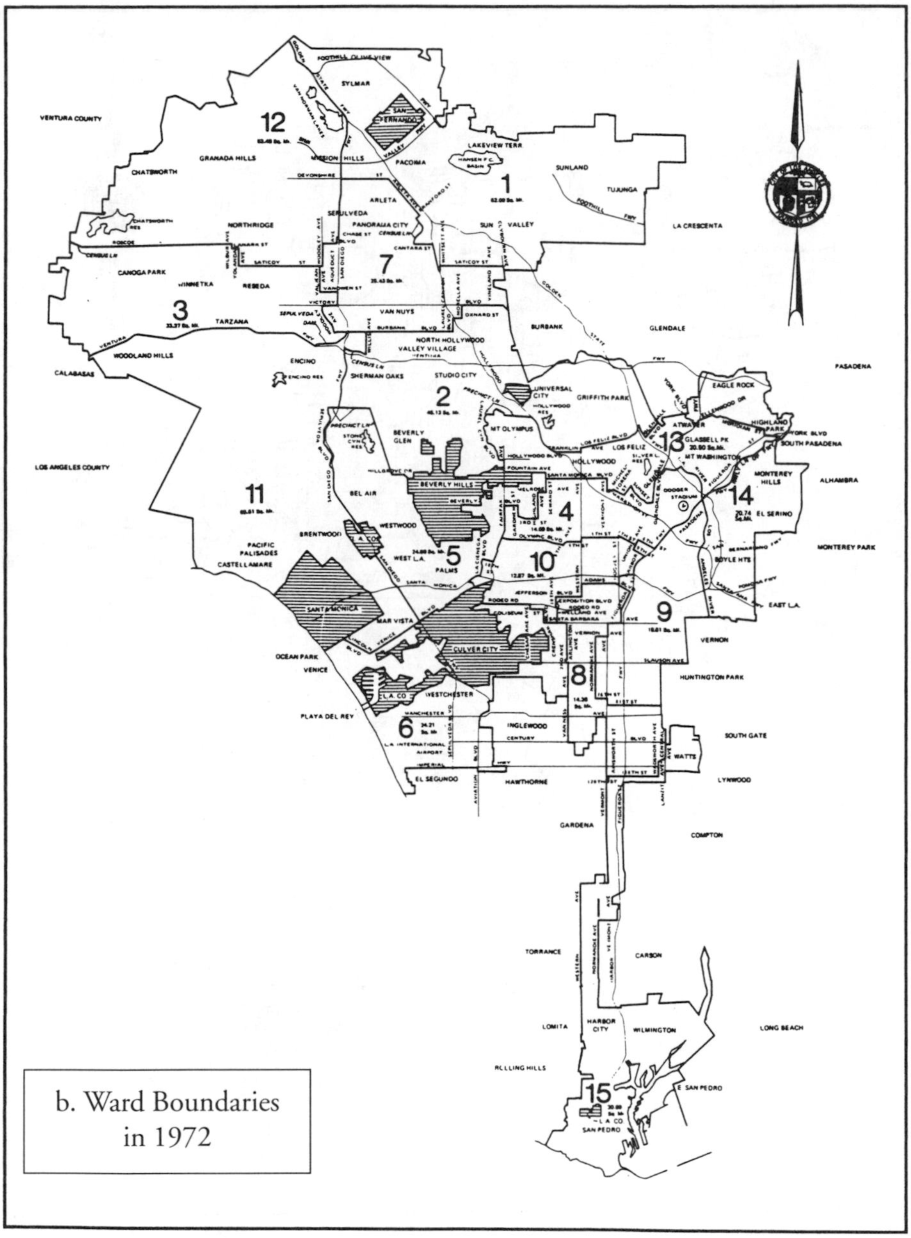

b. Ward Boundaries in 1972

needed the backing of Anglo business forces and moderate Chicanos, he intensified his linkages to elites in these communities.[127] It may also be that many Anglo voters thought they could "buy off" further rebellions by putting a personable African American in office, one who would not rock the business boat, whom anxious whites and middle-class Hispanics viewed as a defender of law and order (a former policeman), and in whom both lower- and middle-class blacks could take pride as the symbol of their arrival.

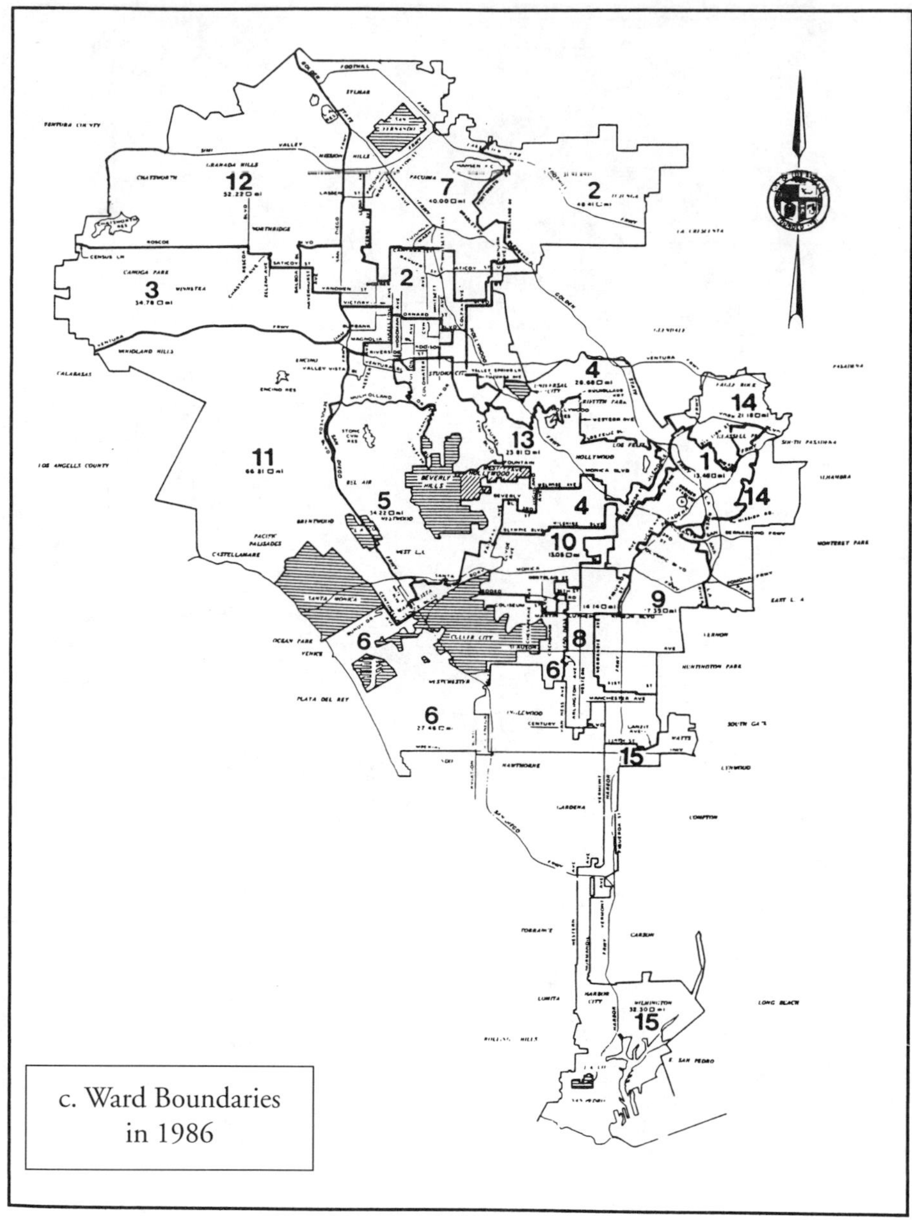

c. Ward Boundaries in 1986

But increasingly, Bradley fell into the same patterns to which Yorty, who had entered office as a "reformer" determined to take the wind out of the sails of an oppressive police chief and to help the poor, had succumbed. Not only did Bradley not displace the police chief who was to fail so abysmally in the 1992 riot, but he also failed to gain federal aid for the poor. Furthermore, he gave free hand to the downtown business interests, who were operating in a structure *outside* city funding, the CRA. The Community Redevelopment Agency offers the best example of how downtown interests were able to insulate their power and finances from the normal political channels.

> The Community Redevelopment Agency's function is to conduct comprehensive studies of social, physical and economic conditions in a target area, to formulate a plan to correct blighted conditions and to carry out the plan in the project area. . . . The Agency is authorized under state law to issue tax allocation bonds. Tax increment revenues, which reflect the increase in assessed value in the project areas as a result of redevelopment, may be used only to reinvest in the project or to clear debts, such as on bonds, incurred in development. The bonds are an obligation not of the city but of the Agency.[128]

As is evident, especially after local revenue-raising powers were curtailed via Proposition 13, this real estate "empire," controlled by Anglo businessmen and oriented heavily toward the profit motive, became a source of considerable extragovernmental power beyond the reach of the electorate. The projects it engaged in—the clearing of "slums" near the city center and their rebuilding with global-function offices and banks, and its earlier project to build the new stadium for the Dodgers on the site of a poor hilly area from which Mexicans were dislodged—further contributed to the exclusion of poor and minority residents from decisions affecting their fate.[129]

It would be unfair to "blame" Bradley for all these failings. Indeed, given the persisting power structure, the "Progressive" governmental institutional framework, as well as the never-displaced financial "rulers" of the city,[130] he had little leeway if he wished to remain in office. Although he did enlarge middle-class black participation in his administration, he did little to reform the police department (uniformly the trigger for recurrent riots), and he did nothing to ameliorate the worsening conditions in the poorest minority zone of the city—South-Central.

In any case, in 1992, both of these deficiencies came together in a major rebellion, after which Bradley declined to run for reelection in 1993. His political career was thus bracketed by the two most violent events in recent Los Angeles history. His departure left the way open for the election of a wealthy Anglo/Catholic businessman with no prior governmental experience. The Anglo power structure, this time with the help of formerly excluded Latinos, reappeared from behind the mask of its black figurehead.

The Police Out of Control

In almost every instance of interracial, interethnic, and interclass conflict that has erupted over the past hundred years in American cities, police actions have been the tinder spark that ignited preexisting tensions.[131] "Reforms" to diversify the racial composition of the police, to train officers in techniques for defusing tensions, to make police more accountable (via greater mayoral control over the police department and/or establishment of civilian review boards to fight corruption) have all been in evidence in Chicago and New York, albeit not necessarily successful. Their absence in Los Angeles is conspicuous. I have already noted the inordinate independence of the LAPD vis-à-vis elected officials. We now turn to an examination of some of the consequences.

One author who has compared police brutality in New York and Los Angeles, inter alia, is Paul Chevigny, in his *Edge of the Knife: Police Violence in the Americas.* According to Chevigny:

> The governments of New York City and Los Angeles . . . have taken almost opposite approaches to policing. The Los Angeles police, both in the city and the county, have had a reputation as the quintessential anticrime force, with a semimilitary attitude both to the job and the public. There have been no major corruption scandals for decades, and morale has been good among the police, at least up to the Rodney King scandal. In contrast, the New York City Police Department (NYPD), which is more than three times the size of the Los Angeles Police Department (LAPD), has been concerned with controlling the discretion of its officers and maintaining good relations with the public and political forces. . . . The relation between superior officers and the rank-and-file in the NYPD is often wary, at best, and there are periodic corruption scandals, both large and small. *The reasons for the divergence in the styles of policing in the two urban areas lie in the differences in municipal government and the history of the cities and their police.* [Therefore, although] each of the cities has had endemic problems with the abuse of non-deadly force—police brutality—as have many other American cities, Los Angeles made no serious effort to control such violence before 1991 [the year the Rodney King case began], while New York yielded much earlier to pressure to set up at least some systems of accountability. New York long ago took the lead in the nation in trying to make officers accountable for and reduce the use of deadly force through stringent internal regulations, while the police in Los Angeles have continued to shoot more people than any other police department in the largest U.S. cities.[132]

Chevigny's contention is borne out by data from the 1993 U.S. Justice Department's *Uniform Crime Report,* presented as a boxed item in the *Los Angeles Times* in the spring of 1995. These figures, showing comparative police-caused fatalities in 1993 for selected cities, suggest that it is very dangerous to live in Los Angeles. Washington, D.C., with 13 fatalities caused by 4,424 officers, had the highest police-caused fatality rate: 2.9 officer-caused deaths per 1,000 officers. Los Angeles came a close second, with 21 deaths caused by 7,800 officers, or a rate of 2.7 persons shot to death per 1,000 officers. In contrast, Chicago and New York each had only one officer-caused fatality per 1,000 policemen, hardly a commendable record, but possibly reflecting ongoing programs in each city to "integrate" the police and to train officers in "human relations." These were attempts not made in Los Angeles.

Although the actions of a largely white police force against Los Angeles blacks are most publicized, it must be recalled that there is also a long history of police oppression against the city's Mexican minority. The Watts riot of 1965, widely covered in the media, gave the false impression that in contrast to African Americans, the Mexican American community was either not discriminated against or had docilely accepted its second-class status. Neither of these is true.

In his account of three large and violent confrontations between the police and Chicano activists in East Los Angeles in 1970, Armando Morales reviews the history of police-Mexican relations over the centuries and contends that discriminatory treatment of Mexicans is older than and at least as great as that vis-à-vis blacks. Pointing out that "in 1969, Mexican Americans in Los Angeles had by far the highest percent of arrests (Mexican American community 58%; Black community 24%; Anglo community 18%) for 'interfering with police' in episodes involving police malpractice," he asks, "Can this behavior be explained historically?" He suggests that "because of the long standing experience of living in an environment of alienation, [Mexican American] feelings of disrespect and distrust toward American law enforcement-legal institutions have intensified." He suggests that Mexican Americans "have been 'conditioned' to respond in this manner for survival purposes."[133]

He attributes the distrust to a double standard of justice that has always been applied by law enforcement agencies. According to Morales, the Western Center on Law and Poverty studied the sentencing of Mexican Americans and found that "the average judicial sentence *was harsher* for convicted felony defendants who were of Spanish surname or Blacks than for Anglos."[134] When this is compounded by the constant threats of arbitrary arrests by the INS and immigration officials' hounding of persons of Mexican appearance, whether legal or undocumented, one can understand why fear and resentment should be the dominant emotion toward enforcers. It is not surprising, then, that periodic clashes have occurred.

Social activism and protests in East Los Angeles have been chronicled by several Chicano scholars.[135] Chapter 8 in Morales's pamphlet is titled "The 1970–71 Los Angeles Chicano-Police Riots," which says it all. It recounts the battles that took place in East Los Angeles on January 1, August 29, and September 16, 1970.[136] Morales places these confrontations directly within the context of the black riots of the 1960s, claiming that "comparing the U.S. Riot Commission Report findings and basic causes of the riots with the East Los Angeles situation proved to be a frightening experience. *All that had to be substituted was the word 'Mexican American' for 'Negro' and 'barrio' for 'ghetto' in order for the conditions to be identical.*"[137]

In fact, Morales claims that the situation of Mexican Americans in Los Angeles was worse than that of blacks.[138] Reinterpreting the so-called commodity/antipolice riots between 1964 and 1970, he suggests that these were really attacks by minorities on the white police force that represented the agent of their domination by white society. He suggests that although "the 'race riots' of the 1940s primarily involved white *citizen* aggression toward ethnic minorities that were making economic progress in the war years . . . the white citizen attitude of the 1940s is now being expressed *through* and *by* the white police and, more important, *with the sanction of the dominant white society.*"[139]

Even though the causes of unrest in Chicano and black communities were similar and were intensified by a common resentment of police oppression, that does not imply a "natural" alliance between the two. True, in the 1992 South-Central riot blacks and Latinos seem to have participated together (and, indeed, Latinos suffered even higher rates of arrest than blacks), but that was inevitable, given their equal proportions in the district, their common class position, and their common negative experiences with the forces of "law and order." Such collaboration, however, could hardly be expected in the political arena. As Alistair Rogers has suggested, the relationship between the two "minority" groups in Los Angeles "is not fixed but ambiguous."[140] How ambiguous it is, and how the political game of city power now turns on the relationship between these groups, was revealed in the April 1997 elections.

LATINO/BLACK DIVISIONS? A NEW ANGLO-LATINO COALITION

The reelection in April 1997 of Richard Riordan as mayor of Los Angeles was not unexpected, given that, in addition to his advantage as incumbent, his opponent was Tom Hayden, a progressive (if no longer "sixties" radical) probably as well-known today for being the ex-husband of Jane Fonda as for his latter-day entry into state politics. According to an exit poll, Riordan garnered 62 percent of male votes and 59 percent of female votes, so gender was not a variable, nor was general education level (he was favored by 60 percent of high school graduates or below, 63 percent of those voters with some college, and 60 percent with a college degree or higher).[141]

Race and ethnicity, on the other hand, were the most important variables. Some 65 percent of all voters were white and, of these, 71 percent favored Riordan. Fifteen percent of the voters were Latino, of whom 60 percent favored Riordan.[142] Riordan also captured 62 percent of the voters who were of Asian origin or descent. Only African Americans, who made up 13 percent of those voting, deviated—and by a wide margin—from this support. Fully three-quarters of black voters supported Hayden; Riordan received support from less than one in five black voters. The "old game" of divide and conquer was being played again, but this time through a coalition of white and Latino voters against blacks and, to some extent, "liberals."[143]

The explanation for why blacks and Latinos participated equally in the 1992 South-Central riot and yet divided so dramatically in the 1997 mayoral election lies in the many complexities of race, ethnicity, class, and juridical status elaborated in earlier sections of this chapter. And these complexities suggest a potential transformation in the power structure and political culture of Los Angeles.

Let us first examine the intersection of class, race, and juridical status in the relations between blacks and Latinos.[144] In a very careful study that examined the impact of Latino immigration on the position of "lower-class" blacks (those with low educational achievement) in the Los Angeles economy, Ong and Valenzuela found that heightened immigration, especially of unskilled and (even more vulnerable) undocumented Latinos, was directly associated with growing unemployment within the poorest sectors of the African American community, although racial discrimination and labor market segmentation both intensified the impact.[145] They conclude that, in Los Angeles at least,

> both Latino immigration and racism play significant roles in disadvantaging African Americans in terms of joblessness and earnings. . . . [Although] the addi-

> tional joblessness associated with racial disparity is three to four times greater than that associated with immigration . . . the impacts of racism and immigration [however] are not unrelated. . . . The higher concentration of blacks in the secondary labor market, where the bulk of low-skilled Latino immigrants have been incorporated, exposes blacks to greater job competition and perhaps contributes to their increased joblessness rates and their lower earnings relative to non-Hispanic whites.[146]

Neither class solidarity nor ethnic competition at the lower levels of the economy translates immediately into local politics, because so many of the Latino unskilled and service workers are not citizens. According to Sonenshein, in past elections, poorer Latinos who were citizens tended to support Bradley, whereas better-off Chicanos did not; in the most recent election this difference seems to have disappeared. At the more advanced educational levels of government and white-collar employment, where until recently African Americans had been better situated than professional immigrants to compete because they were more likely to be citizens with a good command of English, there is evidence that ethnic competition *within* that class has increased. And among Hispanic-origin citizens, whether immigrant or native-born, gains in the political arena have largely been at the expense of black empowerment. Part of the key to understanding the recent transformation of politics in the city and county of Los Angeles lies with the ambivalence and differentiation within the Latino community itself.

Intra-Latino Cleavages

Within the Latino community, juridical and class differences are central. The assumption that "race" and/or "ethnic solidarity" within the Latino community should result in a common attitude toward immigration restrictions was never correct and has become even less likely under conditions of economic retrenchment. High legal and undocumented migration from Mexico and Central America poses a potential threat to the social mobility of some of the more established Latinos and even newly sworn-in citizens, while not adding, in the short run, to their expanding power in the electorate. Many well-established Chicanos are alarmed by the white backlash and may therefore place pacification above confrontation. Against this, however, is a conflict over the status of their own relatives, who may be seeking to immigrate and whom they would not wish excluded. In short, the situation is very complex and needs to be watched carefully. The only conclusion that can be reached at this moment is that the political structure in Los Angeles is undergoing a significant transformation. Whether this will result in a deep redistribution of power or represents merely another ploy of divide and rule and co-optation remains to be seen. And how poorer Latinos and blacks will react to the new coalition cannot be predicted exactly. Changes in policy may lead to improvements, but if they do not, the poor may again take to the streets, in the ever-repeating responses of 1965 and 1992.

LOS ANGELES AS A DIFFERENT GLOBAL CITY

It is clear, even if there had been any prior doubt, that Los Angeles's claim to be a global city—in terms of both economy and demography—has been fully established. But the nature of "globalism" in the Los Angeles region is quite different from that in Chicago and New York. I explore the similarities and differences in Chapter 13, where I sum up the cities' comparative histories to explore the question of *how much of the variance* is due to globalism, how much to context, and how much to the unique qualities of the three.

CHAPTER 13

Conclusions and a Look to the Future

GLOBALIZATION REVISITED

In its most literal sense, globalization is simply an ongoing process whereby larger and larger portions of the world become increasingly linked to one another[1]—via material exchanges of resources, commodities, and currencies, as well as through a widening of the geographic range over which populations move, whether temporarily or permanently. Inevitably, this process not only entails more "integration" on the economic and political levels, but also permits more contact on the symbolic and cultural levels.[2] Contacts may be direct or indirect. In the latter case, globalization can also include an increased "range" and "depth" of awareness, as larger numbers of people in many regions of the globe know about one another and can be influenced, at least potentially, by ideas, values, and practices that originate far beyond the localities in which they live. This process of growing global awareness, while it by no means creates the ideological unity of the "one world" foretold by Wendell Willkie in the intermath of World War II, does result in an intermingling and even "hybridization" of cultural patterns.[3] The range and depth of all such interconnections define the *shape* of the world system at any given time.[4]

It is important to recognize, however, that just because the contemporary international system involves greater entailment of the fates of each of its parts, the roles assigned to various regions and nation states in this loosely integrated system are not necessarily either similar or equal. Rather, in general, effects are disproportionately caused by forces emanating from hegemonic powers (whether imperial, neocolonial, or class based) and hegemonic cultures (whether consumerist, religious, or politically ideological), and different subunits are affected, both inside nations and between nations, in ways that vary in depth and significance.

This variability is also evident in what analysts have referred to as *global* or *world cities,* that is, those urban concentrations or nodes through which a disproportionate fraction of national and international interactions flow. Such flows, although almost always two-way, are also neither symmetrical nor of equal import. Degrees of economic, political, and cultural dominance help to distinguish hegemonic from subordinate cities, even when they may be equally integrated into the global system. Although dominant and subordinate major cities of the world have all, on occasion, been loosely referred to as global cities, a crucial distinction needs to be made between those major urban areas that contain the control or "command" centers of the international system and those that merely help to mediate between the highest circuits of that system and lower regional ones. With this in mind, it should be clear that the effects of globalization vary, not only between global cities but within them.

Because of this, the insights and generalizations that have been advanced as "new theories" about global cities, while appearing persuasive on the surface, are of only limited value in explaining variations between and within specific urban places. The purpose of this chapter is to move beyond these generalizations to demonstrate how the effects of globalization have changed over time and space, not only because the world system itself has been reconfigured, but because forces generated at that higher level always interact with preexisting conditions on the ground to yield consequences that are quite place and class specific. In the process of this inquiry, I want to raise, although not fully answer, some fundamental questions:

1. Is the process of globalization as it is now occurring at the turn of the twenty-first century merely different in degree from earlier increases in the scale of world system integration, or is it so different in character from previous instances that a sharp discontinuity has occurred?
2. How has globalization evolved over time? And to what degree can recent changes in the major megacities of the world be attributed directly to alterations in the contemporary phase of world system transformation?
3. What *partial* generalizations can be made concerning the effects of globalization on world cities within the Western core of dominance? How do these differ from effects on subordinate regions of the world?[5]
4. What common effects of globalization are now being felt in America's largest global cities: New York, Los Angeles, and, with reservations, Chicago?[6]
5. On the basis of this comparative history of these three cities, to what extent and in what ways have the variables identified in Chapter 1 worked together to generate the specific spatial, social, and political structures of New York, Chicago, and Los Angeles, thus accounting not only for their unique character, but for the way each now responds to current patterns of globalization?[7]

These are, of course, ambitious questions that go far beyond the analysis presented in this book. Here we begin to search for answers, but only in the three American mega-urban regions that have been our focus. However, this approach might be applied to more than the specific cases examined. A replication of this study in other non-American global cities could yield even more precise answers to the questions posed here.

THE GEOHISTORICAL CONFIGURATION OF THE WORLD

Throughout this book I have argued that the topics of globalization and global cities require a much closer attention to history than they have thus far received. Such a historical approach needs to take into consideration the changing shape of the world system that constitutes the largest context for developments within today's major cities; the history of the expansion of the United States over the course of the nineteenth and twentieth centuries, within which the national urban hierarchy developed; and more specifically for New York, Chicago, and Los Angeles, the more detailed histories of these individual urbanized regions that, over time, have generated the physical and social "terrain" onto which the newer global forces are now being inscribed and with which they interact.

In scattered parts of this book I have noted changes in the world system context within which the three cities were developing. It may be appropriate here to review these changing contexts briefly but more systematically.

The Historical Context of Globalization and Global Cities

Cities as nodes in networks are not a new phenomenon. Indeed, the fact that cities lie at the center of complex networks constitutes their *essential* feature. Throughout world history, certain cities—some of them imperial capitals remarkably large for their times, but a few relatively tiny "city-states"—have served as key nodes through which wider circuits of production, exchange, and culture have been coordinated, at least minimally. But in these earlier manifestations of integration, the territorial reach of even the most extensive "transnational/transimperial" systems was limited to only small fractions of the globe. Entire continents were excluded or were in touch at their peripheries only with the outer fringes of core regions. Nevertheless, urbanization per se was, in fact, both a symptom and a consequence of the construction of such regional systems, whose cores exerted dominance over their agricultural hinterlands and/or, via rivers or even the edges of the sea, increased the surplus available to the cities through conquest and/or tribute or through favorable terms of trade with distant points.[8]

The first of these mini-world-systems climaxed toward the beginning of the second millennium B.C.E. when the three river-valley cradles of urbanism—along the Nile, the Tigris-Euphrates, and the Indus Rivers—came in more intimate contact with one another by multiple networks of trade that threaded through deserts, skirted the shores of the eastern Mediterranean and the Arabian Sea, transited the Red Sea and Arabo-Persian gulfs, and sent out probes to more distant areas in Anatolia, the Iranian plateau, and the zones beyond the Indus River Valley. (Almost contemporaneously, another minisystem was developing in the Yellow River region of China, one that would eventually form linkages with regions south and west of it.)

A second surge in integration began during the Hellenic Age, when Alexander's conquests briefly unified the eastern Mediterranean and reached beyond it—as far as India.[9] This system climaxed during Roman imperial hegemony, when the entire littoral of the Mediterranean Sea became part of a central core that eventually stretched into western Europe as far north as England and reached, via trading circuits, not only the eastern coast of the Indian subcontinent but, indirectly, even China.

After a hiatus marked by the fragmentation of western Europe (glossed somewhat inaccurately as the "fall of Rome" but more accurately described as the devolution of the so-called Western Roman Empire), a third partial world system emerged, extending over an even larger area. This system climaxed in the thirteenth century when very large portions of Europe, Eurasia, the Middle East and North Africa, coastal zones of east Africa, India, Malaysia, and Indonesia, and even China were becoming more interactive—in both commercial and cultural contacts and through military conflicts. Needless to say, northwestern Europe was then still at the periphery of this system and the New World was not yet connected to it.[10]

Perhaps shaken by a series of pandemics that culminated in the Black Death, whose highest mortalities occurred in zones most tightly integrated into the ongoing world system, there was another hiatus.[11] Within this breathing space, a fourth world system was reorganized, admittedly on the basis of the old but expanding rapidly through the so-called Age of Discovery to encompass parts of the New World and eventually other "terra incognita" in the South Pacific and southern Africa. This was the early phase of what Immanuel Wallerstein has called "the modern world-system,"[12] and it constituted the context within which New York first developed, albeit as a subordinate node.

During this period of early modern restructuring, the "balance of power" began to shift away from the Mediterranean and Asia to the increasingly powerful Atlantic sea powers, first Portugal and Spain and then England and the Low Countries (including Holland and Spain, which were then in a common "nation"). In the process, the formerly forbidding Atlantic was added as the third central sea (albeit more treacherous) of the evolving system, joining the Mediterranean and the Indian Ocean-South China Sea, which continued to serve as major pathways of trade, commerce, conquest, and the movement of peoples.[13] But minor European incursions were also being made into the Pacific as well. By the end of the nineteenth century, this system climaxed in classical European colonialism, achieved through the conquest of Africa and portions of Asia. By then, most countries in the Americas had been liberated.

Because throughout these earlier eras transport by water was considerably cheaper than transport over land, the key points of exchange were, almost without exception, river or sea ports (the exceptions, of course, were oases along desert routes). It is in the context of the modern world-system, then, that the ports along the northeastern seaboard of North America became linked to a European core, and that, eventually, New York solidified its lead in the U.S. subsystem, a lead that, although later challenged by inland and Pacific coast cities, has never really been superseded.

The Geohistorical Context for American Development

For much of the first centuries of its existence, then, New York remained a key American link into a world system that focused increasingly on the Atlantic. Throughout the nineteenth century and into the early years of the twentieth, American history reads as the integration and eventual consolidation of a transcontinental subsystem, spreading from east to west. Even when the midcontinent was settled up to the Mississippi, and St. Louis (soon to be overtaken by Chicago) became the hinge for the drive to Manifest Destiny, New York retained and indeed strengthened its dominance as a core in its own right. As I have argued, it was, almost from its start, a "global city." Chicago could never have achieved the eminence it did without its prime outlet to the sea, New York.

It is important to recall that the integration of Chicago with the nascent U.S. system to its east and south was initially by water, the historically preferred transportation pathway. In the first quarter of the nineteenth century, decades before the railroad terminals consolidated Chicago's lead as midcontinental nexus, the outlets to the Atlantic coast via the Erie Canal-Great Lakes system and to the Caribbean Sea via the internal thoroughfare of the Mississippi River were already in place.[14] What the rails did that waterways could not do, however, was link the zones west of the Mississippi to Chicago and from there on to New York. Without these linkages, Los Angeles's later growth (at least in the form it took) would have been inconceivable.

As we have seen, it was not until the tiny Mexican settlement of Los Angeles, conquered a bare quarter of a century before, was finally connected to the U.S. network via railroads—at first indirectly through San Francisco in 1875 and then via a direct route a decade later—that its modern growth spurt began. And it was not until the twentieth century, after the formation of America's first "overseas empire" (thanks to territories ceded in the 1898 Spanish-American War), that the Pacific became a true, albeit still a secondary, focus of American geopolitics. Heightened by these strategic interests, the sea circuit from the Pacific to the Caribbean was significantly shortened a dozen or so years later by the construction of the Panama Canal. Thus New York was the point of departure for Manifest Destiny, Chicago was its midwestern switching yard, and Los Angeles ultimately became its terminus.

Institutional and Technological Factors

It would be an error, however, to think in such geographically determined ways. Although an advantageously located site is a sine qua non for urban development, the agency of "men" (and they *were* mostly men in those days), acting politically and economically, has always intervened to favor certain of several otherwise equiprobable locations and to mobilize private and public financing to exaggerate the potential of such favored sites. And changes in technological capacity often have served to reduce or increase the viability of any natural setting.

Thus New York's port, so favorably endowed by nature, did not expand dramatically until the commercial invention of direct port auctions gave the city's brokers a monopoly over foreign trade, and until the engineering achievement of a through waterway to the Great Lakes made New York the dominant break-in-bulk point in internationally linked trade. And it was the capital accumulation facilitated by sophisticated institutions of insurance, banking, and credit that consolidated New York's lucrative role as broker for the slave-produced cotton crop, in preference to any southern port.

Similarly, both drainage of Chicago's waterlogged site and the clever machinations of land-speculating politicians in attracting rail termini and "hub" functions were essential in consolidating that city's lead over potential competitors, just as the later engineered reversal of the flow of Chicago's river reduced the need for portage to the Mississippi. "Nature's metropolis" may have drawn upon a rich agrarian and mineral hinterland, but it was, in the last analysis, the city's skill at centralizing the processing of these raw riches by means of machines and accounting inventions that made it "the metropolis of midcontinent."

The case of Los Angeles is even clearer, because initially the region had neither a water supply sufficient to support a major city nor a natural harbor able to compete with the better-endowed ports at San Francisco to the north or San Diego to the south. Only the political clout of local businessmen, exploiting access to both local and national public funds, enticed a continental rail terminus to the area, secured distant water for the municipality's monopoly (assisted by the engineering skills of the compulsively driven genius immigrant Mulholland), and gained the enormous federal subsidies necessary to construct an expensive, artificially enhanced massive port complex.

Differential Urban Growth as Affected by Military Conflicts

Unhappily, wars also play their part in creating locational advantages out of potentials. Just as Los Angeles's modern history was born in the 1847 conquest, expanded in the 1898 Spanish-American war, and further consolidated with the construction of the Panama Canal just before World War I, so the city was not decisively catapulted into the first ranks of the American urban system until World War II, when the Pacific arena drew the United States into an irreversible involvement with the "East" (to its west). The Second World War also boosted the economies of New York and Chicago: the former primarily through its ports, from which lend-lease shipments were funneled to Europe, and its expanding shipbuilding and airplane manufacture directed to the European theater; the latter through the burgeoning demand for war matériel produced by its heavy Fordist industries.[15]

By then, the world system was moving into the culminating phase of late-modern globalization. The evidence is obvious. One has only to contrast the First World War with the Second. The first had really encompassed only a portion of the European-Atlantic "world." The second signaled that the world system had incorporated the countries of Asia and the Pacific Rim as well. To this day, the postwar period has seen the "reach" of this system extend to virtually all parts of the globe, including most of Central and South America. Only a few mountainous redoubts, some interior deserts in Africa, Asia, and Australia, and a handful of off-course islands lie temporarily beyond global reach, and their days are numbered.

Weapons of war, produced first in the United States for its own defense, have fueled the remarkable economic prosperity of the Southwest, including Los Angeles; have partially infused the economies of the Northeast and Mid-Atlantic states, including New York's extended region; and have, by their absence, further undermined the economies of the Midwest, including Chicago's. But weapons produced for export have also enhanced the hegemonic position of the United States in the world economy and, through sales to Third World countries and the deployment of forces in subregional conflicts, have reconfigured the shape of the entire world system.

CONTEMPORARY INTERACTIONS BETWEEN CONTEXT AND THE THREE CITIES

History, however, does not end with globalization. The present fates of the urbanized regions of New York, Chicago, and Los Angeles are linked to a changing geography of power, and thus, ultimately, to the shape of the larger system. Reflecting the Janus-like position of the contemporary United States as both an Atlantic and a Pacific power, and the increased integration of North America with the Caribbean and the Latin American continent, the three seacoasts of the United States have become even more important magnets for people, both through internal migration and external immigration. In recent decades the population of the United States has continued to decant toward those coasts, not only in the conventional directions of east and west but southward as well. The rapid rise of gateway Miami almost to world-class status is certainly linked to the growing importance of the Caribbean and "our neighbors to the south," as that zone of influence is increasingly integrated with the American core, if only, it sometimes seems, by illegal traffic in drugs. Chicago's tragedy is that it is not in these growth zones.

The Global and the Local within New Technological Parameters

Technological advances have continued the age-old process of disengaging decisions from actions on the ground, with the ironic effect of facilitating the dispersal of production and people while increasingly centralizing what many analysts now refer to as "command functions." We saw this at earlier moments: the substitution of the commerce in "chits" in New York for the "real" midwestern wheat that remained in place in Chicago's silos; the removal of factories to the outskirts of cities at the same time company headquarters expanded in city centers, where telephones and later computers could monitor production farther afield and even abroad; the diffusion of stock ownership at the same time professional managers concentrated their hold over important decision making.

To some extent, these processes continue, but the scales at which they now operate often disengage or camouflage any clear lines between causes and effects, between those who command and those who labor, as capital and labor move with increasing freedom beyond not only the metropolitan boundaries but national borders as well. This disengagement means that healthy growth in command functions is not incompatible with dire destitution in those parts of the system (whether highly localized, at the national level, or at the global level) that are "out of the loop." Such marginalized zones can now be found in Manchester and Sheffield, England, in downtown Detroit, in the South and West Side ghettos of Chicago, in South-Central Los Angeles, in Bangladesh, and in many parts of the African continent.

Thus the effects of globalization now seldom fall *directly* on the physical ground that lies beneath their electronically flashing nodes and circuits; rather, they flow through the increasingly disembodied cyberspace of information and high finance. In evaluating the impacts of global changes, then, it is important to distinguish between those functions or transactions that remain tied to space and those more globalized functions that have been freed from spatial (and often regulatory) constraints. From this vantage point, there is no contradiction between the evisceration of localized functions and the proliferation of transactions in cyberspace, such as those, for example, that flow through the computers of the Chicago Mercantile Exchange.

Nor, given the fact that these exchanges *are* truly free of spatial constraints, is there any guarantee that any early spatial monopoly can be sustained. As we have already seen, by the bold stroke of anticipating a global market for financial futures and currency options, the then-foundering Chicago Mercantile Exchange was the first to grasp this opportunity, which, by 1995, came to account for some 90 percent of its contracts. However, because the market is truly international, the MERC has seen some of its base erode through competition from private deals and unregulated non-U.S. exchanges.[16]

SPACE STILL MATTERS IN THE DIRECT ECONOMICS OF GLOBALIZATION

Common to all three cities have been general forces generated at the global level, even though their consequences have not been uniform because they have fallen upon different preexisting terrains. As we have seen, in Chicago the major effects have come from the global restructuring of production methods and the redistribution of places of production, with less coming from the concentration of foreign investments or foreign immigrants. In contrast, although both New York and Los Angeles have been the recipients of major "restructurings" in their economic bases, some of these shifts have made them more unlike (Los Angeles continues Fordist industrial production, whereas New York's minor Fordist base has virtually disappeared), whereas other changes, such as their enhanced attractiveness to foreign investments and company (sub)headquarters, indicate their common greater reliance on the international system. New York and Los Angeles are also capitalizing on their touristic appeal, especially to international visitors (more Asians to Los Angeles, more Europeans to New York), and the media centers of both cities are having disproportionate effects on the transmission of American popular culture to the rest of the world.

Such changes are directly attributable to the increased internationalization of trade, investments, cultural production and consumption, and the communications revolution itself. As before, however, social and technological innovations in space-based transportation and more fungible communications systems have reshaped the roles of all three.

Foreign Trade, Shipping, and Air Freight

Although theoretically one would expect that the tonnage and value of commodities involved in international trade would be important measures of globalization, the actual figures reveal so many anomalies that this crude measure must be used cautiously.[17] True, geographic position still determines the flow of imports and exports through specific ports. Thus Chicago's Custom House, with direct access to only one water-adjacent foreign country (Canada),[18] cannot be expected to process as much international shipping as the major coastal seaport regions. Because of the city's location, many of the bulk commodities originating at Chicago terminals that are destined for overseas will be transshipped through other coastal ports.

Nor, more surprisingly, are the ports of the New York and Los Angeles regions hegemonic. For example, raw figures for 1988–90 indicate that with respect to foreign tonnage, the ports of both Houston and New Orleans outranked those of the New York region, and that Los Angeles ranked only tenth. Chicago's rank among American ports was even lower (fifty-eighth in 1988, forty-fourth in 1989, and fifty-ninth in 1990). Comparing only New York, Chicago, and Los Angeles on raw tonnage of imports and exports, the range is narrowed somewhat, as Table 13.1 shows, but the discrepancies are even more interesting than the raw numbers. New York ports receive far more tonnage than they ship out; in contrast, imports and exports are more nearly balanced through the ports of the Los Angeles region.[19]

As might be anticipated, however, given the increasing importance of airborne shipping, the gaps are much reduced when commodity transfers via air freight are compared. In recent years, the airports in the three urbanized regions have accounted for about one-third of all revenue tons enplaned in the United States, confirming their hegemonic position as global cities.

Table 13.1. Raw tonnage of shipborne freight imported and exported from the ports of New York, Los Angeles, and Chicago, 1989

Region	Raw tons imported	Raw tons exported
New York region	47,121,436	7,179,929
Los Angeles region	13,492,146	11,261,409
Chicago region	3,162,718	1,078,530

Note: The ports of Chicago includes Chicago, Peoria, East Chicago, Gary, Davenport, and Rock Island; New York ports include Albany but not New Jersey ports; Los Angeles ports include Los Angeles, Port San Luis, Long Beach, El Segundo, Ventura, and Port Hueneme. Including New Jersey ports would significantly raise the New York region's share.

Source: U. S. Army Corps of Engineers, Navigation Data Center, Waterborne Commerce Statistics Center, *Annuals of 1991 and 1992.*

Table 13.2. Enplaned revenue tons of freight passing through airports of New York, Chicago, and Los Angeles, 1990–91

Regional airports	1990	1991
New York/Newark	462,297	419,361
Los Angeles[a]	368,240	364,644
Chicago	304,959	292,179
Total, large hubs	3,001,217	2,960,604

[a]Includes the Hollywood/Burbank, Long Beach, Los Angeles International (almost all), and Orange County airports.

Source: U.S. Department of Transportation, Federal Aviation Administration, Research and Special Programs, *Airport Activity Statistics of Certified Route Air Carriers,* annuals, 1990 and 1991. Unfortunately, the data do not distinguish between domestic and foreign destinations.

Investments Flow

Another measure of "globalization" has to do with the "permeability" of local economies to external investments. But an important caveat should be introduced concerning changes in the role of foreign investments in so-called global cities. As we have seen throughout this book, foreign investment is no new element in the growth of American megacities. Much of the early infrastructure of the United States was indeed put into place through funds from abroad. However, in the 1980s, the scale of such investments took on a new dimension. During that decade direct foreign investments in the United States more than doubled, and these headed disproportionately toward the three urbanized regions.

Ideally, it would be desirable to know just how much of this expanded international activity ends up in specific urbanized regions. Unfortunately, I have been able to locate such data only at the level of states, so these figures must serve as indirect measures. In the 1980s, when such investments were expanding rapidly, a significant and increasing share was directed toward the very states that contain our urbanized regions. As Table 13.3 illustrates, between 1981 and 1988, when the amount of foreign investment in the United States more than doubled, the combined investments in New York/New Jersey, Illinois, and California increased even more, by 174 percent. By 1988, almost 29 percent of all foreign investment in the United States was concentrated in the states containing the three megaregions, up from less than 23 percent at the beginning of the decade. Certainly, "globalization" was having a disproportionate impact on the three regions, although California received even more investment than the New York/New Jersey region and both far outranked Illinois as outlets for overseas capital. California's proximity to the burgeoning Asian market undoubtedly accounts for this prominence, suggesting that globalization has had a far greater impact on the landscape of Los Angeles than on the other two cities. (See below for a discussion of real estate.)

Some of the foreign investment actually went to foreign-owned corporations that provided employment to American workers. Again, although data on U.S. residents

Table 13.3. Foreign direct investment (in millions of gross book value dollars) in the United States and in the states of New York/New Jersey, Illinois, and California, 1981 and 1988

Place	1981	1988	Percentage increase 1981–88
New York/New Jersey	14,444	43,092	198
Illinois	5,646	19,491	245
California	20,404	48,270	136
Three-state total	40,494	110,853	174
U.S. total	178,003	385,734	117
Three-state share (percentage)	22.8	28.8	

Source: My own calculations from data in U.S. Department of Commerce, *Statistical Abstract of the United States, 1991* (Washington, D.C.: U.S. Government Printing Office, 1992), 795, Table 1392, which is based on U.S. Bureau of Economic Analysis, *Survey of Current Business* (July 1990) and *Foreign Direct Investment in the United States, Operations of U.S. Affiliates of Foreign Companies* (preliminary 1988 estimates).

employed in foreign-owned firms are available only for states rather than individual urbanized regions, here too they suggest disproportionate locations and increases in our megaregions, with New York outranking the other two. Although the percentage increases between 1981 and 1988 are not as dramatic as those noted in overall foreign direct investment, it is clear that local employment by foreign-owned firms has also disproportionately infused the three largest urbanized regions, with New York/New Jersey consolidating its lead over the other two. This is due largely to New York's continued importance as the world's leader in international business and the services connected to it. In contrast, despite its recent doubling, Illinois remains a very secondary player in international business.

Real Estate and Control Exercised through Corporate Headquarters

Globalization is also apparent in the landscapes of the three cities, because one important area in which foreign investment has had a visible impact has been in prime urban real estate, especially commercial and office structures in downtown areas. Foreign investors (Dutch, Middle Eastern, and Japanese in New York; Japanese, Taiwanese, and Hong Kong Chinese in Los Angeles) have purchased or built impressive banks, spending surplus funds on "trophy" properties with famous names,[20] and have opened headquarters for their transnational firms in all three cities. They are seeking immediate access to the headquarters of major American firms and to the business and legal services that cater to them, and have naturally flocked to New York, Los Angeles, and Chicago, where these "command" functions remain concentrated.

Again, although exact totals are missing, the latter can be inferred from the concentration of headquarters of the largest U.S. businesses in New York, Chicago, and Los Angeles. Over the years, several measures have consistently been employed as

Table 13.4. Employment (in thousands) by foreign firms in the United States and in New York/New Jersey, Illinois, and California, 1981 and 1988

Place	1981	1988	Percentage increase 1981–88
New York/New Jersey	345.2	571.2	65.5
Illinois	113.6	224.2	97.4
California	248.4	388.3	56.3
Three-state total	707.2	1,183.7	67.4
U.S. total	2,402.3	3,662.6	52.5
Three-state share (percentage)	29.4	32.3	

Source: My own calculations from data in U.S. Department of Commerce, *Statistical Abstract of the United States, 1991* (Washington, D.C.: U.S. Government Printing Office, 1992), 795, Table 1392, which is based on U.S. Bureau of Economic Analysis, *Survey of Current Business* (July 1990) and *Foreign Direct Investment in the United States, Operations of U.S. Affiliates of Foreign Companies* (preliminary 1988 estimates).

indicators; all use some variant based upon the location of *headquarters* for large corporations of various kinds. According to these criteria, the three top-ranking "world cities" in the United States are clearly New York (with a long, albeit decreasing, lead), followed by Chicago, and then Los Angeles.

By the end of the 1980s, of the 500 largest corporations in the United States (most of them with transnational connections), the New York metropolitan region was home headquarters for 138; Chicago occupied second place with 42, and Los Angeles ranked third with only 25. New York's dominance among *transnational* corporations was even more pronounced. Of the 100 firms receiving the most foreign revenues, 40 were headquartered in New York City or its suburbs, and in 1986 some 55 percent of the $137 billion foreign revenues received by these top 100 transnational corporations went to the 40 firms headquartered in the New York region.[21]

The degree of centralized dominance, however, varied with the type of business. Large firms engaged in retail trade, commercial banking, insurance, utilities, and transportation were least concentrated, whereas headquarters of manufacturing, advertising, and diversified financial companies (all singled out by theory as exercising "control" functions) were most likely to be concentrated in the three world cities and their extended suburban regions. Table 13.5 shows the number of headquarters of the two hundred largest manufacturing companies and of the largest fifty of the other types of companies that in 1990 and 1992 were located in the New York, Chicago, and Los Angeles metropolitan areas. Most corporate offices remain in the central business districts, despite suburban growth.

Concentration of Producer and Corporate Services in City Centers

Economic restructuring is hypothesized to concentrate producer and corporate services within world cities, thus enhancing their hegemony. Counteracting this trend

Table 13.5. Number of firm headquarters in cities and suburbs of New York, Chicago, and Los Angeles by type of firm, 1990–91, for the largest in the United States

Type of firm	Percentage in the three cities	New York	Chicago	Los Angeles
Manufacturing (*n*=200)	37	42	17	14
Advertising (*n*=50)	82	34	5	2
Finance (*n*=50)	54	20	6	1
Diversified services (*n*=50)	34	8	3	6

Source: My own calculations from data in Rand McNally, *1992 Commercial Atlas and Marketing Guide* (Chicago: Rand McNally, 1992), 48–49; data appeared originally in *Fortune,* April 22, 1991, and June 3, 1991; and in *Advertising Age,* March 25, 1991. The totals are only approximate.

has been the recent decentralization of such services in office complexes around metropolitan cores. Suburbanization per se, however, has not undermined the dominance of metropolitan centers in these all important sectors, despite the excitement over "Edge City." Alex Schwartz has compared New York, Chicago, and Los Angeles in this regard.[22] Analyzing data from the *Corporate Finance Bluebook,* he tabulated entries for the 1,452 companies in the CMSAs of New York, Chicago, and Los Angeles that provide actuarial, auditing, banking, investment banking, and legal services to corporations. Of these, 54 percent were located in the New York region, 26 percent in the Chicago area, and 20 percent in the Los Angeles area. Although more than half of these corporate service firms were physically sited outside the city limits, the firms located in the central cities were nearly twice the size of those located in the suburbs.[23] Chicago proved to be the most centralized, and that city has continued to outstrip Los Angeles in the volume and control over at least these five types of producer's services.

Presence of International "Markets"

Another economic criterion that, if Sassen is correct, has become increasingly important in distinguishing "world cities" from other megacities is the presence of international investment, commodity, and financial markets.[24] Significantly, Los Angeles is the only one of the three that does not host an important international exchange. New York is, of course, home to the major stock market exchanges of the United States and to a limited number of pricing markets for world commodities (notably sugar, oil, gold, and the like). And Chicago still contains the all-important agricultural commodities/futures markets, which have hitherto been overlooked in discussions of world cities. Whereas normally one thinks of exchange markets in terms of industrial/service firms and of monetary instruments, it is important to remember that agricultural commodities still constitute the chief "civilian" export of the United States, earning the largest trade surplus and thus helping to reduce the imbalance in the nation's international accounts. And we have already seen the role that the Chicago Mercantile Exchange, which used to specialize in pork bellies, now plays in the International

Monetary Market, which sets futures on all international currencies. This is a quintessentially world-city function.

Thus, despite the argument that the transportation and communications revolutions have virtually eliminated the frictions of space and that cyberspace has made transaction spaces increasingly substitutable (fungible), still, location matters. But space is now written on a larger continental canvas, even though many of the effects of phantom global transactions have become harder to trace and more indirect in their impacts.[25]

REGIONAL POPULATION MATTERS AND IS SPATIALLY GROUNDED

Large size, high density, and demographic diversity have always been defining qualities of cities because, as impressive as the international comings and goings may be, most economic and transcultural activities are still manifested locally. Some of the differences among our three cities can be attributed to overall growth rates in their regions, not all of which are traceable to international causes. This is particularly evident with respect to Chicago. Even though O'Hare's boast that it is the busiest air terminal in the country is not to be dismissed, it must be acknowledged that the vast midwestern and plains hinterlands of that city have not been growing as before, and indeed, the population in many parts of it has actually been in decline, relatively if not in absolute numbers. The demographic "failure to thrive" of the Midwest, Chicago's service-area cachement zone, has had serious repercussions on the city's economic health that compound, as well as in turn are caused by, the loss of its Fordist base. Thus only a portion of these consequences flow from specifically local causes, such as post-Fordism or even Chicago's contentious race relations, although the negative effects have been experienced most severely by poor people of color.

In contrast, the easternmost and westernmost "gateway cities" to the United States, while to some extent subject to the same evisceration of their old-style production bases as Chicago (New York far more so than Los Angeles), have continued to hold their own demographically because, especially in the past three decades, they have served as major magnets for the expanded numbers of immigrants now being admitted to the United States. When the unbounded conurbations around them, rather than the zones within their legal city limits, are the units of analysis, both conurbations have continued to grow.

Thus the "hollowing out" of the continent has been achieved not only through low rates of natural increase and internal migration out of the Great Plains[26] but, increasingly, through the recently enlarged streams of immigrants from abroad whose "ports of entry" remain the coastal cities—even though the movers now travel by air (or foot) rather than ship. The recent demographic recovery of the New York urbanized region and, even more so, the growth of the Los Angeles megalopolis (despite the recent defection of "Anglos") is clearly attributable to the heightened immigration from abroad that resulted from changes in national policy. Whereas this is clearly an indirect result of the new globalization, it can also be seen as a revival of earlier patterns of recruitment, albeit from very different sources.

INTERNATIONAL IMMIGRANTS FOSTER URBAN POPULATION GROWTH AND DIVERSITY

The Scale of Immigration

How significant has the impact of recent immigration been? Using the larger CMSA as our unit, we find that the Los Angeles region, with 27 percent of its 1990 (enumerated) population born abroad, and the New York region, with 20 percent foreign-born, are among the large American urban regions that have been most radically affected by transnational movements of people.[27] In contrast, immigration to the Chicago region has been insufficient to stem incipient demographic decline. Clearly, with only 11 percent of the Chicago CMSA region's population classified as foreign-born, the region is far less dependent upon immigration than it has been in the past. Both the interior location of that city and the precipitous decline in its demand for brute labor may account for its lack of attractiveness, although a garment industry there has, as in the other cities, generated a parallel symbiosis between Asian capital and Latino hand operators.

The CMSA is not the most sensitive unit to capture the impact of foreign immigration, however. In all three regions, foreign immigrants have settled disproportionately within the city limits, although this selective settlement has varied by class and ethnic origin. Wealthier and better-educated South Asian, Pacific Rim, and Middle Eastern immigrants have often favored peripheral and/or suburban locations, whereas their more proletarian compatriots, as well as most Latinos in all three cities, have gravitated toward center cities (or, in the case of Los Angeles, to its containing county), where they live in close proximity to other "persons of color." Thus in 1990 almost 29 percent of the population in the five boroughs of New York had been born abroad, 38 percent of the population of the city of Los Angeles were of foreign birth, and 14 percent of the population in Cook County (including the city of Chicago) were immigrants.

The Origin of Recent Immigrants

Even where the numbers of immigrants may be roughly similar (as is true for New York and Los Angeles), however, the cities differ drastically in terms of the places from which their immigrants come, a factor that yields a variation in their degrees of "cosmopolitanism" and contributes to or inhibits social polarization along ethnic and racial lines. As we have seen, the predominance in Los Angeles of Latino and especially Mexican immigrants facilitates polarization (as well as makes possible coordinated political action), whereas the sheer diversity of groups in New York militates, for better or worse, against such strategies of identity politics. The city of Chicago lies somewhere between these two extremes, in part because its native-born African American population, although no longer growing, still constitutes a much higher percentage of the city's population vis-à-vis the foreign-born.

Selective attractiveness is partially affected by the space of "least effort." However, although geographic proximity to sending countries has shaped the composition

Table 13.6. Percentage of CMSA population in 1990 that was black, Asian, or Hispanic in New York, Chicago, and Los Angeles

Race/ethnicity	New York	Chicago	Los Angeles
Black (non-Hispanic)	18.2	19.2	8.5
Hispanic	15.4	11.1	32.9
Asian	4.8	3.2	9.2
American Indian	0.3	0.2	0.3
Total minority	38.7	33.7	50.9

Note: The category of Hispanic still presents difficulties, because in some 1990 census data I have examined, small percentages of Hispanics report themselves as black or Asian, a larger percentage report white, but an overwhelming majority classify themselves as "other," thus confounding American racial categories.

of immigrant streams to the three cities, the entailments of the world system and the role of the United States in that system have also drawn selectively from the potential universe of migrants. Transnational movements of people are hardly random, nor are they independent of the politics and economics of the larger system and, more particularly, the place of the United States within it. Both the size and selectivity of immigration work through the highly politicized filters of national law and local policies, even though the consequences may not always be those that were intended.

Some simple examples may illustrate this. Asian immigration in particular has been highly selective, drawing largely from countries linked to the United States through prior wars (the Philippines, Taiwan, Korea, Vietnam, Cambodia) or from anticipated changes in alliances (China, Hong Kong). Much of that population and capital has congregated on the West Coast for obvious geographic reasons.

The same is true of Latino growth. Relations between Mexico and the United States provide the context for periodic and massive inflows to California and the Southwest, and political involvements in Central American and Caribbean affairs have set in motion the movement not only of Cubans to Miami, but of Nicaraguans, Guatemalans, and Salvadorans to Los Angeles and of Dominicans to New York. Although not strictly to be considered "immigrants," the population of Puerto Rican origin, as well as true immigrants drawn from other Caribbean islands (Spanish, French Creole, and English speaking), have concentrated chiefly in New York, because it is more accessible to them. Given its more centralized location, Chicago's Hispanic minority has been drawn almost equally from Puerto Rico and from Mexico, the former community established earlier, the latter of more recent origin. Their areas of settlement, however, are often quite geographically separated and their political unity far less assured.

The sheer diversity of New York's immigrant streams reflects that city's more global role, especially vis-à-vis Europe. The recent spurt in the number of Russians and Poles settling in New York is clearly linked to changes in the former Soviet Union and its former dependencies, although Eastern Europeans are still cumulatively outnumbered by Dominicans and other Caribbean-origin immigrants.[28]

The Insertion of Immigrants into the Existing Class and Racial Structures of the Three Cities

Given the diversity of the new immigrants by race and national origin, and given variations in the human and economic capital they bring with them, it is to be expected that their insertion into the unique racial, class, and occupational structures already existing in their cities of destination would take quite different forms and have radically different effects on their political cultures and on their native-born minority populations. Not only do different sending countries provide immigrants with widely varying human capital characteristics, but once within the country, developments at the more local level help to determine how immigrants will be absorbed, what economic niches will be open to them, and how they will interact with native-born citizens, both white/Anglo and African American.[29]

Structures of opportunity intersect with the skills that immigrants bring with them, but not in the same ways in all places. Thus Korean immigrants in Los Angeles and in New York found their way into small-business niches (often vacated by Jews) in minority areas, which has led to their inheriting many of the interethnic hostilities of past eras. But outside of these parallels, diversity is evident. In all three cities, Koreans have capitalized small garment factories (often employing labor from immigrant groups farther down the pecking order), but the widely distributed Korean groceries that now service New Yorkers in most neighborhoods have no parallels in either Chicago or Los Angeles, where Korean shops may cluster in specific ethnic areas or dominate minority areas, but where Koreans occupy a far wider range of occupations.[30] Mexican immigrants have entered blue-collar occupations as well as restaurant services in the New York and Chicago regions, whereas agricultural work, including its extension to urban gardening, has continued to absorb more of them in Los Angeles.

Attitudes toward Immigrants

Numbers and composition of the immigrant stream have, of course, been crucial in shaping responses. The fact that California received more "legal" immigrants than any other state in the fiscal years between 1983 and 1992 (peaking in 1991, when close to three-quarters of a million, or some 40 percent of all immigrants, entered by way of California), at the very time when the local economy was contracting, explains in part, but only in part, why the backlash there has been so much more extreme than in New York or even in Chicago. The fact that the largest percentage of California's immigrants were drawn from Mexico and that these "legal" numbers were supplemented by another 750,000 (or 75 percent of all undocumented immigrants) suggests that responses to this form of "globalization" are deeply affected by the scale and composition of the immigrant population.[31]

The attitudes of New Yorkers may be more "liberal," as some have claimed, but it must also be acknowledged that the fears of "invasion" and "cultural dilution" that are so pervasive in California are not exclusively attributable to "racism." Despite the joint participation of poor Latinos and African Americans in the "riot" of 1992, the latter have good cause for concern, because it appears that vulnerable immigrants are tending to replace unskilled African Americans in the job market, exacerbating the latter's already high unemployment rates. Although similar substitutions appear to be occurring in Chicago and New York, they are less extreme in their effects. New York's immigration, while rivaling Los Angeles's in terms of numbers, has been far more diversified in terms of countries of origin and levels of human capital. Although there has been some tendency for Jamaican immigrants to displace native-born blacks and for Dominicans and other Hispanics to displace Puerto Ricans, the compensation for both "displaced" groups, at least those with education, has been public employment, where the citizenship requirement places them in an advantaged position.

In Chicago, immigration has been proportionately lower than in either Los Angeles or New York, and has been only moderately diverse. The backlash against immigrants has thus not been extreme, and the older Chicago pattern of ethnic enclaves (which tends to "separate the combatants") seems to be persisting. African American and Latino tensions, however, continue. And although both groups are disproportionately disadvantaged and are largely concentrated in the inner city, they are more likely to live adjacent to one another but not to intermingle, as poor Latinos and blacks have done in South-Central Los Angeles.

Incorporation of Immigrants into the Political Structure

Experience in the three cities has also varied drastically in the incorporation of immigrants, depending not only upon their numbers and composition but upon their relationship to native-born citizens (both white and black) and upon the institutional structures that characterize their zones of incorporation. "Latino power," for example, has very different meanings in the three cities.

In Los Angeles, because of the large size of wards and the incumbents' power to redraw boundaries drastically at will,[32] ethno-racial minority groups must develop city- and countywide coalitions if they are to influence political outcomes. Only recently has the Anglo power structure begun to court the growing numbers of Latino voters (still mostly of Mexican origin), whose widespread distribution (admittedly in semisegregated zones) has made them more attractive to the power structure than the more highly segregated African Americans, who are now increasingly cut off from legitimate avenues of expression. The divide-and-conquer strategy in Los Angeles continues, albeit with somewhat different players, as was illustrated in the most recent mayoral election.

In Chicago, the split between Puerto Ricans and Mexicans and the inability of Latinos and African Americans to forge a lasting alliance eventually allowed downtown business interests and white property owners to reverse the temporary capture of power by Harold Washington's regime. Although minorities (now a majority when their numbers are combined) are well represented in the city council because of their plurality in many wards, the gates to office holding are still controlled by a white-dominated Democratic machine in a city where only a single party really matters. The bipolar racial animosities that run deep in Chicago history continue, forcing newer "people of color" to choose one camp or another. (Asians have chosen "white"; Latinos are split between identifying with whites or blacks or, increasingly, neither.)

In New York, a city long accustomed to an ethnic "poker game" in which no single group commands most of the chips and where the politically federated system provides numerous entry points, albeit not equally advantageous, the sheer diversity of subgroups—both old-timers and new immigrants, and the crisscrossing of pigmentation, immigrant/citizen status, and religious identities by class and residence—has tended to mute the polarities found along language-descent lines in Los Angeles and along the color line in Chicago. Over time, there have been "ethnic successions" in the borough and city halls, as Irish shared power with Jews and both stepped aside to make room for Catholic Italians, as African Americans absorbed and ceded roles to Jamaicans, and as the new Latino immigrants (especially Dominicans) have challenged or allied with the Puerto Ricans. These successions have also been evident in residential areas, where multiple segregated pockets have been more widely distributed throughout the boroughs and where, to some extent, rent regulations have inhibited radical and complete displacements of former groups. This means that although the city has certainly not been tension-free, the lines of battle are more indistinct and complicated than those between north and south in Chicago and between east and west in Los Angeles.

CONSEQUENCES OF GLOBALIZATION

In the foregoing I have perhaps belabored the proof that the three cities whose evolution I have traced in this book are, despite their differences, quintessential global cities. That, however, does not mean that everything or even most things that take place within these urbanized regions are attributable, either directly or even indirectly, to the current processes of world system restructuring or the role of the United States as the dominant, if no longer the completely hegemonic, player. If international forces were so overwhelmingly powerful, one would anticipate that their effects in the three cities would differ only in degree. That is patently untrue, as I have tried to illustrate through the comparisons presented here.[33]

This, then, returns us to the larger question posed at the beginning of this book: Given the large changes in the world's restructuring, why are the effects on the three cities so different—not only in economic but in social and spatial terms? My argument throughout has been that common forces originating at the level of the global economy operate always through local political structures and interact with inherited spatial forms. They are therefore always manifested in particular ways that differentiate cities from one another and that militate against the facile generalizations that have hitherto been made about a class of cities called *global.*

Clearly, then, I believe that there are no absolutely inevitable consequences of globalization, even in places that clearly warrant inclusion in that category. To conclude, I focus on three fundamental sources of differentiation that have shaped the developments in New York, Chicago, and Los Angeles: (1) the problem of political boundaries; (2) the problem of income distribution, presumed to be bifurcating; and (3) the problem of social relations as these occur within the *spatial* terrains and inherited *cultural* patterns of the three urbanized regions. Although these differences may perhaps appear obvious, some of their consequences, and especially the interrelationships among them, need to be teased out.

The Problem of Political Boundaries

Many American urbanized regions are particularly difficult to plan for and coordinate for several reasons, including the peculiar history of unmovable state boundaries; the special characteristics of the American federal system, which theoretically operates only in those zones of power not reserved to the states;[34] and the dependent juridical character of municipalities, which are legally the "creatures" of state-enabling legislation and are therefore never completely independent of the governmental level that created them.[35] Some of the variable degrees of freedom that our three cities can exercise to respond to the challenges of globalization are linked to inherited boundaries, because of the impossibility of making adjustments across state borders and the increasing resistance to annexation on the part of their suburbs. The recent solution in many metropolitan areas has been to try to move urban functions up to the surrounding county unit, but this solution is not open to all.

Ironically, of the three cities covered in this book, Los Angeles, with its strangely fragmented city jurisdictions (albeit all within a single county in a single state), seems in the strongest position to overcome some of the problems generated by irrational boundary conditions. As we have seen, functions such as water and education have already been moved up to the county level, thus placing subareas and municipalities that contain highly differentiated ethnicity-, race-, and class-specific populations within a single governmental jurisdiction. The downside of this arrangement, of course, is the lack of an adequately representative governmental institution that could serve as a truly democratic arena for the resolution of controversies and the expression of dissent. On the positive side, the county itself is a level of government that makes coordination with surrounding counties somewhat easier. This asset is enhanced by the fact that the urbanized region falls within a single state, a second boundary issue of the greatest import.

The Chicago urbanized region also benefits from its virtual containment within a single state, although admittedly there is some overflow into western Indiana and southern Wisconsin. Furthermore, the region has a certain neat symmetry, in that the city lies nested within (and occupies most of the territory of) a single county, which, in turn, is neatly surrounded by its collar counties. Theoretically, this should facilitate common governance. However, this potential is never realized; indeed, the potential for coordination founders on the same "race question" that has plagued much of Chicago's history throughout the twentieth century. Fearful that minorities will "invade" suburban communities or that they will make claims on the tax bases of the more affluent wider region, the Maginot Line of the persisting border wars has now been reset at the city limits, and where that line of defense fails, at the outer limits of Cook County (which on the west is identical to the city border).

It is hard to avoid the conclusion that the maintenance of racial-ethnic segregation has been the overarching goal of regional strategies. Within the sectorally segmented region, whites have essentially ceded the southern quadrant to minorities (with the exception of the University of Chicago's enclave, whose planned *cordon sanitaire* is now firmly in place, thanks to destruction around it).[36] A certain amount of white "reconquest" of the central business district is also taking place. Although Michigan Avenue north of the river and the residential Gold Coast that fans out from it along the lakefront remain the zones of highest prestige (and the whitest), the south Loop, now anchored at the new Harold Washington Library at Congress Street and stretching into the Printer's Row/Dearborn Station renewal area, has succeeded, to some extent, in continuing "Negro removal."[37] And to the west of the Loop, redevelopment zones have deposited elegant commercial and residential high-rises on land formerly claimed by the poor. Minorities, both black and Latino, have been pushed farther west until they reached the city limits at the final defense line of Austin/Cicero. As we have seen, the largest fraction of Chicago's economic vitality is funneled into the north and northwest quadrants, both inside and beyond the city and county limits. This portion of the urbanized region is largely white and becoming more so. Decaying "in-fill" zones in the northwest quadrant that were temporarily preempted by minorities are now beginning to undergo gentrification and "bleaching." The current (white) ruling elite of Chicago has managed to manipulate borders and to gain needed regional coordination through the long preexisting system of special districts that bypass conventional governmental boundaries, and has equally controlled its fiscal problems by passing on to the state government responsibility for covering many costs that would otherwise have had to be borne by urban and suburban residents. This has been achieved despite the traditional tensions between Chicago and "downstate" in the state legislature. Thus, although borders may hinder or facilitate, they do not predetermine goals or prevent political maneuvering around them to achieve solutions.

In the New York region, however, none of these regional solutions has proven very adequate, and the relations with adjacent states, not to mention those between "city" and "upstate," remain contentious. The latter is evidenced annually in the battles over the budget that are waged long beyond the end of each fiscal year and, most recently, have been highlighted—in the almost quintessentially western drama of a standoff at the old corral—when proponents favoring retention of state rent regulations (of vital concern mostly to renters in New York City) squared off against those who preferred to let the law lapse (mostly owners throughout the state). The antagonists argued well beyond the midnight deadline for renewal of the regulations, before a compromise extension was worked out.

Underlying the perennial budget controversy vis-à-vis the state government is the issue of how much New York City's tax revenues subsidize state expenses and what proportion of locally raised taxes ought to be returned to the city to cover its fairly liberal but costly social benefits. City politicians complain that New York's wealth is siphoned off not only to the federal government, as I have shown, but to "upstate" as well.[38] In return, the state attempts to micromanage and impose limits on the city's expenditures and its welfare programs. As Ester Fuchs has astutely noted more than once, New York, in comparison to other large cities, has the largest fiscal burden and the least control over its policy.[39]

All of these problems are compounded by the intractable issue of state borders, especially now that the urbanized region sprawls not only over New York and New Jersey (as before), but into adjacent areas of Connecticut and, most recently, even parts of Pennsylvania. This leads to what can only be described as the New York region's unsolvable problem of governance.[40]

One idea that recurrently surfaces in New York is the (unrealistic) suggestion that the region *could* become manageable if only its parts were "detached" from their containing states and the zone unified politically as a "city-state." This would presumably make the city solvent—by retaining the funds that now go to Albany,[41] by freeing it from incompatible legal restraints (although more effective home rule might be a less draconian solution), and by muting the fierce zero-sum competition between New York and New Jersey with respect to industrial and commercial location, taxation, and especially investments and revenues from its ports and airports. A lesser, but no less facetious, suggestion is for the city simply to secede from the state of New York. Periodically, the suggestion is floated, as it was during the 1969 mayoral campaign by Norman Mailer and Jimmy Breslin, that New York City should become the fifty-first state. More recently, Breslin has recommended "declaring New York an 'international city' instead."[42]

Regardless of how seductive these suggestions may appear, they remain a pipe dream. The New York region will have to continue to temporize, not only because of intractable boundaries but because entrenched interests are not likely to be dislodged. Nonetheless, the patchwork of jurisdictions does militate against the simple class bifurcations that some have argued are a direct effect of globalization. It is to this argument that we now turn.

Is Class Bifurcation in Global Cities Really Just a Function of Globalization?

First set forth in 1982 as a tentative hypothesis in Friedmann and Wolff's article on world cities,[43] the proposition that changes at the international level are leading, via a clear causal line, to growing inequality in global cities has now become an article of faith in the growing literature. It is easy to slip into the obverse, namely, that because class inequalities on the local level are largely attributable to causes originating "elsewhere," they therefore lie beyond the capacities of states and cities to rectify.

I have already argued (especially in my introduction to Part IV of this volume) that whereas since the time period coinciding with post-1973 restructuring, the United States has indeed experienced a widening class gap between the richest and poorest segments of its population, this has largely been a *reversal* of a trend that, since the empowering of labor unions under New Deal legislation and the prosperity of the war and postwar periods, had succeeded in narrowing a gap that had formerly been easily as wide. In the preceding era, the labor shortages entailed by reduced immigration and by the booming postwar economy had raised the floor for all but dirt farmers and inner-city blacks. The creation of an admittedly modest welfare state for dependent children and the elderly also contributed to the process of leveling upward.

Toward the end of the 1960s, however, this process began to unravel. The inflationary stagnation of the 1970s and regressive government policies thereafter rapidly culminated in the present moment, undermining many of the labor empowerment programs initiated in the 1930s and 1940s and curtailing entitlements that had expanded in the decades thereafter. We seem now to have returned to a status quo ante, albeit one in which the new international options (more footloose overseas investments and more liberal immigration policies) provide the leverage by making people at the bottom seem more expendable.

It may be true that in today's global cities there is a return to the old pattern of "the citadel" and "the ghetto," as Friedmann and Goetz have suggested, but the causes run deeper than the overarching process of globalization.[44] If bifurcation were a mechanical and inexorable consequence of globalization, one would expect to find few variations from country to country and from global city to global city. This is clearly not the case. I do not question the general finding of growing inequality, but the story of its causes and its spatial consequences is far more complex and is being played out somewhat differently region by region and in rural and urban places both large and small. The evidence from the three cities suggests important variations that call into question a single monolithic set of causes.

In the New York region, for example, economic restructuring and the wild fluctuations on Wall Street pull in opposite directions, which may be a fairly new phenomenon. Kirk Johnson reports that in 1996, "New York City's unemployment rate . . . climbed even as Wall Street was cheering repeated record highs. Brokers earning seven-figure bonuses shopped for summer homes while about one in 11 people looked for jobs." In contrast,

> through most of the 1980's . . . securities industry profits acted like a lever on the economy; in most years when profits were up, the rate of growth of personal income in New York State surpassed the national average, and in years when profits declined, New York was dragged down and trailed the nation. . . . Since the 1987 market crash, and particularly in the last few years, however, the lever has simply not worked. . . . In short, Wall Street's health is no longer enough to compensate for erosion in other areas.[45]

This has led to greater disparities in income and unemployment rates.

However, if in New York one can partially blame the problem of rising inequality on the new failure of Wall Street to serve as an economic multiplier (hardly a sufficient cause), in Chicago the inequities appear chiefly to be due to the end of Fordism, as refracted differentially through the prism of that city's racial tensions. In Los Angeles, the in-migration of poorly educated Mexicans seems to be the most significant factor in growing inequality.

Thus, even if the global system itself does generate greater inequities by removing some of the privileges formerly enjoyed in a fortress United States with less permeable borders, the chains of causation are highly complex and the results are felt in local areas well beyond those of mere global cities, and even differently in the global cities themselves. And, as I have already noted, the whole matter is complicated by intentional political policies adopted at the state and federal levels. In the last analysis, these variations are needed to account for the fact that other "developed" countries seem to have followed more redistributive policies and, therefore, now exhibit less inequality than the United States. Untangling such knotty problems lies far beyond the task of this book.

Bifurcations in the Spatial Patterns of Global Cities

Friedmann and Wolff's metaphor of the citadel and the ghetto, however, was intended to have meaning not only in socioeconomic space, but in physical space and in power relations as well. The metaphor tries to capture class-based spatial segregation as well as the antagonistic relationship between two "camps"—one that requires walls and fortifications to keep some in and others out. Although walls are certainly rising—around gated communities and heavily guarded commercial and residential high-rises of the wealthy, as well as along the racial *cordons sanitaires* of white Chicago—the contrasts among the three cities are as illuminating as the common elements and are not manifested in exactly the same patterns.

As I have indicated, such disparities are only indistinctly reflected on the urbanscape in New York. In Manhattan, the classes are probably more mixed spatially than they were in earlier times and, at least in public space, assorted racial and ethnic groups now mix more freely than in Chicago or Los Angeles. Whether this should be attributed solely to cultural differences, however, cannot be determined. Certainly, rent regulations in that borough have inhibited gross siftings and sortings by income and race/ethnicity—more so than in the outer boroughs, where, given higher rates of home ownership and a narrower discrepancy between regulated and open-market rents, demographic successions have been more volatile and extreme. In short, much more than global forces are at work.

The Social Consequences of Spatial Patterns

Throughout this book I have paid special attention to the evolution of spatial patterns in New York, Chicago, and Los Angeles, not only as indicators of the sites on which they were constructed and the technological, economic, and political forces that shaped their forms, but because their contrasting physical appearances constitute the most visible "signatures" of their individual characters.

If you were to ask anyone familiar with all three urban places (or even someone who has only seen photographs) whether they could ever confuse one city with the others, the answer would probably be a laugh. True, they are all "global cities," and thus manifest, admittedly in different ways, some of the attributes of this contemporary genre of cities. True, they are all gigantic primates of their regions, and thus, regardless of their problems, exercise the controls and dominance to which their size and resources entitle them. True, they are cosmopolitan in their demographic compositions, bringing diverse types of people together in concentrated space (the bedrock of any definition of *urban*), even though the exact components of their diversity vary in significant ways.

But it is also true that they are places of strong physical/symbolic representation, containing icons so internationally recognizable that one does not need to append a city name to locate the Statue of Liberty, Sears Tower, Hollywood, Times Square, the Loop, the Outer Drive. Their skylines and streets, and often their heroes and villains, are engraved on the retinal memories of most moviegoers. And stereotypes of popular culture, accents, and behavior patterns also abound. There are shared preconceptualizations about "typical New Yorkers," "broad-shouldered Chicagoans," and laid-back occupants of "LaLaLand."

In short, these cities are more than the sums of their parts, just as they are much more than the products of globalization. Throughout my analysis I have so often picked apart the pieces that I seem somehow to have lost their essences—what I have always referred to as the unique "personalities" of individual cities. I cannot end, then, before reassembling the parts to demonstrate how different are the cityscapes, the mannerisms, and indeed the social relations that people form with one another in these three "typical" American global cities.

I begin with urbanscape, because in many ways cities provide the stage settings that channel the movements of their actors and choreograph their steps. But from such obvious physical differences we are led to more abstract elements such as persisting plots and mannerisms, because these stage plays have had a long run. Actors, even new ones joining the cast, must learn their parts from those already on the scene; they must learn how to fit into the patterns already etched on the urbanscape, learn to adapt to what is expected of them. It is in this sense that stereotypes are not totally false, although there is always more variation than the superficial ones allow. Furthermore, like open-ended improvisations in hyperspace, the plots do keep being modified, as scenery is rearranged and fixtures added or removed, and as the stage is periodically crowded with large groups of strangers who arrive with their own props and pursue subplots that do not exactly match or mesh. Furthermore, stage designers (planners?), investors, and directors leave one city stage to alight in another, cross-pollinating designs for living that will influence, but not determine, the effects.

Space, in its grossest sense, is one such shaper of behavior, and impressionistic journalists are sometimes better able to capture essential differences than are more cautious social scientists. One attempt I like very much is by Joseph Giovannini, who explores his reactions to moving from Los Angeles to Manhattan and the alterations this required in his own behavior. He argues that "there is no such thing as a genetic New Yorker or Angeleno" and that "if you drop any New Yorker other than Woody Allen in Los Angeles, he will eventually become acquisitive about cars. . . . if you drop any Angeleno other than a Beach Boy in New York, he will eventually choose his neckties for their coded social meanings."[46]

Although this may be too extreme a comment, Giovannini does capture the fact that the two cities are based on "fundamentally different spatial premises": "Space in New York collects people; in Los Angeles it separates them. New Yorkers occupy a community; Angelenos occupy their own privacy."[47] He contrasts his privatized driving commute to work in Los Angeles with his highly sociable walk to work in Manhattan, where he has

> anywhere from three to seven short conversations . . . and . . . sees hundreds of persons. Even when I am not speaking, I am conversing with the city—looking at faces, buying something incidental, thinking about the lives of people I don't know. There are split second juxtapositions of people from vastly different walks of life; there are quick remarks, sometimes sharp. It is a city of conversation. . . . You are . . . always physically close enough to have a conversation or to overhear a wonderful tidbit.[48]

This makes New York quite different from Los Angeles which is "a private rather than a public city." In Los Angeles, commuting by car "extends the privacy of the single-family house . . . keeps you circulating among people you know . . . [which] limits your exposure to other age groups, social classes, even races." Furthermore, in Los Angeles, "the street is often without sidewalks . . . whereas the street in New York is often a place . . . that collects all the other people who have left their incomplete apartments." Because of this, public spaces have very different ambience in the two cities. In New York, "many public spaces are slightly small for the traffic they bear, and the sense of overflow that pervades them . . . gives New York a feeling of enormous energy. . . . New Yorkers pick up the tensions of the city. . . . But if Los Angeles has few surface tensions to make it taut, it can be appreciated for its tranquillity."[49]

I, too, have lived in both places, as well as spent much more time in Chicago than in either, and like a chameleon I have learned to adapt to the different settings, savoring what they have to offer but also missing elements only possible in the others. As did Giovannini, I live in the collective hive of Manhattan, which spews crowds onto the streets at all times of day and night, especially when the weather is beautiful. Who can remain in a crowded apartment when the spectacle of the streets beckons?

Last evening I returned from the movies (on foot, of course, because some ten movie houses lie within walking distance of my apartment). Passing through Union Square Park, on the paved, relatively small open rectangle that several days a week hosts a movable farmers' market, I stopped with my companion to marvel at a juxtaposition one would be extremely unlikely to find at a single location in Los Angeles or Chicago. Despite the hot night, a group of medieval jousters in full coats of armor (and Reeboks) wielded heavy cudgels against each others' shields. Just adjacent to this show, but respectfully careful not to infringe on its space, young men seriously practiced their skateboard skills, oblivious of their interracial mixing and blind to the equally diverse passersby. On a raised wooden platform, recently constructed by the labor intensity that makes blue-collar workers so visible in the city, two black musicians were grooving in percussion (plastic pails and drumsticks), while at nearby tables people read by the poor streetlight or conversed quietly in small groups. We stopped to decipher a small stone marker usually obscured by the makeshift stands of the farmers' market; it commemorated the massacre of Armenians so long ago and far away. We nodded. We had experienced quintessential New York.

A few weeks earlier in Chicago, I caught a more formally planned collective event—the Blues Festival set up in Grant Park at the lakefront, in which most of the "audience" sat in rows of folding chairs set up in front of provisional stages. Beer and bratwurst were in the air. The music and almost all of the musicians were "black," and Chicago could have been in the Deep South, except that because this event was being staged at the lake, almost all of the informally dressed attenders and appreciators were white. Authentic, and perhaps even better, blues are available in the Black Belt, but this would have been considered off-limits by most listeners. I thought this was quintessentially Chicago.

And in the ten months I lived and worked in Los Angeles, I had to relearn (with great trepidation) how to drive, a skill I had lost in the ten years I had been living in New York. I trained myself to stare down adjacent drivers and to exercise extreme caution when a tight-lipped blonde girl was behind the wheel of the next car. And I experienced, like Reyner Banham, the exhilaration—and freedom—of executing skillful and swift maneuvers on highways that seemed to lack true lanes and rules. As Giovaninni notes, however, "in LA you can see the sky" and the "car moves at just the right speed to appreciate the landscape; on foot it is rather boring."[50] But most of the time I lived in Los Angeles I did without rented wheels. On buses I admired the courtliness of the Mexican American drivers and the cordial Spanish banter when the bus picked up (again, mostly) Mexican passengers at corners near the sweatshops at the fringe of "downtown," only to discharge them all at the single intersection along Wilshire Boulevard where the city changes abruptly from Latino to Anglo. I also did a lot of walking, despite the distances that result from low density. Except along the promenades of Santa Monica or the "ethnic" shopping streets, I was often the sole walker, although sweating joggers often veered around me; occasionally, I overtook homeless men with shopping carts, and one of my self-appointed "jobs" was to help them negotiate their carts over humps in the seldom-used sidewalks. Along the half mile of elegant houses but empty streets (except for Latino gardeners and repairmen) between my apartment and the UCLA campus, I once counted 176 small signs that threatened "armed response" from three different private protection agencies. Chicagoans are subtler in their exclusions and New Yorkers, although used to more mixing on the streets and in the subways, have an "en garde" personal alertness to potential incursions by others.

But even these poetic fancies fail to capture the cities. For every crowded street in Manhattan there are more relaxed places where kids still play stoop-ball and neighbors chat over shared driveways and rose gardens. My graduate students and I have even invented the phrase "Brooklyn is another country," to acknowledge how little Manhattan can stand for the city or region. But so also are Jackson Heights and Chinatown and Boerum Hill and Washington Heights. The same is true for Chicago and Los Angeles, for all three places are now microcosms of an American world that includes the "rest of the world."

If the three cities can be said to have special personalities, we must acknowledge that these personalities are by now split into multiple personae. In this book I have tried to trace some of the roots of these differences, both those internal to the cities and those that distinguish among them. At the end, however, I must admit to inevitable failure, because cities must be directly experienced. Writing about them is only the weakest substitute for being in them.

Notes

1. AN OVERVIEW

1. In 1990, the census-delimited consolidated metropolitan statistical area (CMSA) of New York encompassed almost 8,000 square miles of territory; the comparable figure for the Chicago CMSA was some 5,600 square miles, and the Los Angeles CMSA extended over a zone some 34,000 square miles in extent. One must not think of these areas as saturated with buildings and continuous urban developments, however. Rather, as Jean Gottmann notes in his pathbreaking study of the Boston to Washington conurbation along the eastern seaboard, which by 1960 already contained a population of some thirty-seven million people, urbanized regions contain forests, truck farming lands, and other open spaces interspersed among multiple densely populated centers. See Jean Gottmann, *Megalopolis: The Urbanized Northeastern Seaboard of the United States* (Cambridge: MIT Press, 1961), 5.

2. See John Friedmann and Goetz Wolff, "World City Formation: An Agenda for Research and Action," *International Journal of Urban and Regional Research* 6 (1982): 309–44, for the earliest statement of what became "global city" literature. See also Saskia Sassen, *The Global City: New York, London, Tokyo* (Princeton, N.J.: Princeton University Press, 1991); Susan Fainstein, Ian Gordon and Michael Harloe, eds., *Divided Cities: New York and London in the Contemporary World* (Cambridge, Mass.: Blackwell, 1992); Paul L. Knox and Peter J. Taylor, eds., *World Cities in a World-System* (Cambridge: Cambridge University Press, 1995). See Ernest Mandel, *Late Capitalism* (London: New Left Books, 1975). *Postindustrialism* is a term coined by Daniel Bell in his *The Coming of Post-industrial Society: A Venture in Social Forecasting* (New York: Basic Books, 1973) that is now in wide use. The term *informational age* has been applied to urban studies most conspicuously by Manuel Castells in his *The Informational City: Informational Technology, Economic Restructuring and the Urban-Regional Process* (New York: Blackwell, 1989).

3. Thus Indian trails—such as Broadway, which deviates diagonally from the later orthogonal plan of Manhattan Island; El Camino Real, which links Los Angeles with Monterey;

the route through the Sepulveda Pass that underlies the San Diego Freeway of Southern California; and even the Indian Green Bay trail, which traces the path from Chicago's Loop to its northern suburbs—form armatures of passage that long predate any fixed settlements.

4. Thus German cities, after having been carpet bombed in World War II, regenerated within the confines of their ghostly armatures of passages and borders, due in part to the survival of underground utility lines and in part to the survival of proprietary boundary lines.

5. One of the most sensitive treatments of this theme is Dolores Hayden's *The Power of Place: Urban Landscape as Public History* (Cambridge: MIT Press, 1995). Hayden argues for the preservation in Los Angeles of signs and symbols of its working-class and ethnic past, as well as the less controversial symbols of elite occupancy.

6. So-called race riots are the most dramatic breaches of these borders, but there are also subtler forms of noncompliance. Earlier laws against loitering were differentially enforced in rich and poor urban quarters. A sensitive study of the hobo's or tramp's search for inconspicuous shelter space is found in James S. Duncan, "Men without Property," *Antipode* 10 (March 1978): 24–34. The current concern over growing levels of visible homelessness on the streets of our major metropolitan centers, and the frequency with which schemes are proposed to remove such "offenders" to less conspicuous quarters on the peripheries of cities, illustrates the common and long-standing local governmental response to the breaching of spatial borders and the types of sanctions imposed.

7. My periodicity adheres closely to conventional usage, although my characterization of the cycles deviates considerably. To the conventional three periods of 1820–1870, 1870–1920, and 1920–the present, originally set forth by Patrick Geddes and then adopted by Lewis Mumford in his *The Culture of Cities* (New York: Harcourt, Brace, 1938), I add a crucial pre-1820 formative stage and close the third cycle around 1965. I posit a subsequent phase, initiated sometime between 1965 and 1973 and still unfolding, that I contend marks a significantly new stage in world history. My analysis depends in part on material presented in greater detail in Janet L. Abu-Lughod, *Changing Cities: Urban Sociology* (New York: HarperCollins, 1991), 79–182. However, I have expanded it using material in Eric H. Monkkonen's *America Becomes Urban: The Development of U.S. Cities and Towns 1780–1980* (Berkeley: University of California Press, 1988), which became available too late to be integrated into my textbook. Monkkonen's periodicity, however, is too gross: pre-1830, 1830–1930, and beyond 1930. This may serve his purposes, as he focuses chiefly on the political role of cities; for purposes of my discussion, I need a more complexly segmented system.

8. A number of superficial studies of the demographic increases in the three cities have erred by ignoring the all-important issue of boundary expansions. Although for certain purposes it may be useful to accept population totals as a measure of "real" demographic growth within a metropolitan region, regardless of changes in legal boundaries, this approach can be quite deceptive when time series for New York and Chicago straddle the crucial decade of the 1890s, because New York's consolidation was achieved in 1898 and, as we shall see, Chicago did not annex any appreciable area after 1893.

9. See James E. Vance Jr., *The Continuing City: Urban Morphology in Western Civilization* (Baltimore: Johns Hopkins University Press, 1990), 361, Table 7.4. But here again, one must be cautious, because as we shall see in Chapter 6, it was the annexation of more than 176 square miles in the San Fernando Valley in 1915 that interrupted Los Angeles's time series, although admittedly, the population in that enormous zone before irrigation was sparse.

10. New York was least affected by this trend, because agriculture was only a weak function in its hinterland to begin with; Chicago would feel the effects most strongly as "nature's metropolis" supplemented its preoccupation with processing food products by heavier depen-

dence upon iron and steel and their processing. Los Angeles would lag behind, remaining largely agricultural until this base was later supplemented by industry in the 1930s and 1940s.

11. It never reached more than 27 percent, even before trends of "deindustrialization" set in by 1970.

12. This was to be most typical in places like Philadelphia and Chicago. We will soon see that New York never really experienced this transformation, and by the 1920s this pattern had still not reached Los Angeles.

13. Theoretical reasons are buttressed by empirical realities. Because I selected the primate cities of the East Coast, the Midwest, and the West Coast, and have argued that their sequential appearance is a crucial part of the story, it is useful to examine the "dates of founding" of major U.S. cities (those that had populations of more than one hundred thousand by 1870) by region. Of the forty-nine such cities in the eastern United States, thirty-three had been founded before 1850, and of these, a dozen trace their origins back to the seventeenth century. The median decades for their founding were the 1830s and 1840s. In contrast, only one of the fifty-four major cities in the Midwest was founded before 1800, and thirty-six began between 1830 and 1870. The median decades of founding were the 1840s and 1850s. The story is quite different for the western zone: of the fifty-five major cities in that region, none, according to Monkkonen, had been founded before the middle of the nineteenth century; the modal decade for city founding was the 1890s, and the median decades were the 1880s and 1890s. Monkkonen, *America Becomes Urban,* 80, Table 3, compiled retrospectively from the U.S. Census of 1970. (In fact, Monkkonen is not entirely correct; San Francisco and Los Angeles were both founded in the eighteenth century.)

14. I have conceptualized the first "restructuring" as taking place during the so-called Age of Discovery.

15. Note that there was no necessary congruence between economic cycles in the European core of the world system and those of the Americas, especially in the earlier periods when the United States was not only a periphery but an arena to which economic overaccumulation at the core was often diverted. Thus the downswing of the Kondratiev cycle that Western Europe experienced between about 1825 and 1845, and the ensuing debt crisis that persisted until about 1856, constituted an expansionary era in the United States. Not until the next downswing initiated in the 1870s did Europe's crisis hit the United States simultaneously. By then, the U.S. economy had become more closely integrated with that of the world. See Christian Suter, *Debt Cycles in the World Economy: Foreign Loans, Financial Crises, and Debt Settlements, 1820–1990* (Boulder, Colo.: Westview, 1992), esp. 66 and 70–71, Table 5.3.

16. The classic work on the role immigration played in American urbanization remains David Ward's *Cities and Immigrants: A Geography of Change in Nineteenth Century America* (New York: Oxford University Press, 1971).

17. The best work on this theme is Kenneth Jackson's *Crabgrass Frontier: The Suburbanization of the United States* (New York: Oxford University Press, 1985), especially chaps. 1–3, which describe how the "transportation revolution" transformed peripheral slums and/or farmland into spotty zones of elite residence.

18. Eric Hobsbawm, *The Age of Empire, 1875–1914* (New York: Pantheon, 1986).

19. Ironically, in Lenin's 1916 essay "The Highest Form of Capitalism," he described some features of globalized capitalism that would reach fullest flower only in the fourth and fifth cycles, which began after he wrote his essay.

20. See, inter alia, Alfred D. Chandler Jr., *The Visible Hand: The Managerial Revolution in American Business* (Cambridge, Mass.: Belknap, 1977).

21. For a remarkably detailed exploration of this transformation in one American city,

see the work of the Philadelphia History Group, especially Theodore Hershberg, ed., *Philadelphia: Work, Space, Family, and Group Experience in the 19th Century* (New York: Oxford University Press, 1981).

22. *Fordism* is of course a rather controversial term. In this context I refer really to the original Gramscian meaning, that is, mass production and scientific management. The term later came to be applied to a negotiated "peace" between unionized labor (the labor "aristocracy") and large corporations; such peace never extended to most industrial sectors, and no agricultural sectors ever achieved it. The reader is referred to the introductions to Parts III and IV for more nuanced and critical discussions of Fordism and post-Fordism as applied to the three urban regions.

23. Sam Bass Warner Jr., *The Urban Wilderness* (New York: Harper & Row, 1972), 62.

24. Perspective controls the evaluation. Whereas some analysts focusing exclusively on New York have interpreted this loss of dominance as a "setback" for New York, when one takes a national perspective, one sees this development as a natural and inevitable consequence of the expanding continental system. It is important not to confuse objective growth with relative "share."

25. Frederic Cople Jaher traces the origin of the "important" figures in Chicago's development during the nineteenth century in *The Urban Establishment: Upper Strata in Boston, New York, Charleston, Chicago and Los Angeles* (Urbana: University of Illinois Press, 1982), 453–575. Of the more than two hundred "millionaires" in Chicago in 1892, only 6 percent had been born in that city; 30 percent hailed from the Middle Atlantic states and another 30 percent from New England (496, Table 6).

26. New York was the chief competitor to host the so-called Columbian Exposition and was deeply disappointed when Chicago was able to outbid it. Regardless of location, however, personnel moved freely between the two cities. New York architects participated in designing the fair buildings, and Charles Dyer Norton joined New York planners after the fair and subsequent Chicago Plan had been completed. Norton had been the chair of the Commercial Club of Chicago when that organization sponsored the 1909 Burnham plan for Chicago. He later moved to New York to become the treasurer of the Russell Sage Foundation, where he conceived the idea for a Regional Plan for New York—one that culminated only in 1927, after his death.

27. The Spanish-American War of 1898 produced the first U.S. "colonial empire" in the Caribbean and the Pacific, a world system factor often overlooked in studies of urban growth in Los Angeles. The old Spanish "galleon trade" now plied under an American flag between Los Angeles and the Philippines (and from there to the Chinese coast), which accounts for the fact that the federal government invested so heavily in constructing a deep harbor at San Pedro in 1899 and fortifying it in 1916, and that the port of Los Angeles became the base for the U.S. Pacific fleet in 1922. Boosts to harbor activity, however, came from oil, which was the chief commercial export by the early 1920s. The completion of the Panama Canal allowed tankers to deliver California oil to New Orleans and East Coast ports at much lower costs.

28. It is important to note the importance of New Orleans as a port linking the entire Mississippi Valley to world trade.

29. The best book on this period is Robert M. Fogelson's aptly titled study, *The Fragmented Metropolis: Los Angeles, 1850–1930* (Berkeley: University of California Press, 1993 [1967]).

30. The first flights took thirty-six hours, including an overnight stop, to bridge the continent.

31. From about 1935 onward, Southern California, and especially the Los Angeles region, attracted industries that had failed elsewhere. This demonstrates that the national level is

too gross a unit for analysis in the American "slash and burn" system of urbanization. Los Angeles attracted industry not only because of the city's weak unionization but because, as is generally true in capitalist development, the greatest profits are achievable only from new enterprises in low-cost locations. The "frontier" of investment would shift to the Third World in the next cycle.

32. As early as the Depression years, automobile, tire, and airplane manufacture had begun healthy growth in Southern California. At first, the new installations were branch plants of midwestern firms, but particularly in aeronautics, the companies were new and innovative ventures.

33. The internment of West Coast residents of Japanese origin is the ugliest chapter in a long history of exclusion and discrimination against Asians.

34. Not only had an enormous backlog of demand for housing been built up during the war, when domestic construction had to be postponed, but in the postwar period, new family formation, equally delayed by the war, reached astronomical proportions, unleashing a "baby boom" that temporarily interrupted the long-term decline in American birthrates. Both trends stimulated the expansion of urban regions.

35. The transformation between the 1960s and the 1970s is well documented in Thierry J. Noyelle and Thomas Stanback Jr., *The Economic Transformation of American Cities* (Totowa, N.J.: Rowman & Allanheld, 1984).

36. By 1964, Southern California boasted some 1,321 "high-tech" firms (employing more than 315,000 workers), of which between two-thirds and three-quarters were defense related. See Allen J. Scott, *Technopolis: High-Technology Industry and Regional Development in Southern California* (Berkeley: University of California Press, 1993), 38, Table 3.1, based on data from the U.S. Department of Commerce, Bureau of the Census, *County Business Patterns.*

2. THE FIRST GROWTH CYCLE TO 1820

1. Kenneth Jackson, "The Capital of Capitalism: The New York Metropolitan Region, 1890–1940," in *Metropolis 1890–1940,* ed. Anthony Sutcliffe (Chicago: University of Chicago Press, 1984), 319, emphasis added.

2. "According to legend, Gotham was a town in England that became known as the place of 'wise fools' when its inhabitants tricked King John out of setting up house there. When the king's men came riding through the town to scout the location, the residents simply behaved like madmen. The royal retainers rode off and a saying was born: 'More fools pass through Gotham than remain in it.' Washington Irving is believed to be the first to call New York Gotham; in his periodical Salmagundi, which he published between 1807 and 1808, he deployed the name as a comment on his sophisticated, if pretentious, contemporaries." *New York Times,* February 5, 1994. Perhaps no writer combined so deep an affection for the city with the level of sarcasm that Washington Irving directed toward his hometown. His whimsical but acerbic biography of the city and its Dutch founders/inhabitants is *Knickerbocker's History of New York,* originally published in 1809 (New York: Frederick Unger, 1928).

In a series of short stories, O. Henry played off the Arabian Nights tales but set them in a more cynical New York. In these stories Caliph Haroun Al-Rachid, disguised as a poor man, attempts to bestow special favors on the needy he meets in New York, but all are rejected by suspicious urbanites, on their guard against ubiquitous con artists.

"Our Babylon" is urbanophile Morley's affectionate sobriquet. He says lovingly: "She is the only city whose lovers live always in a mood of wonder and expectancy." See Christopher Morley, *Christopher Morley's New York* (New York: Fordham University Press, 1988), 11.

According to the entry on p. 107 of Kenneth Jackson, ed., *The Encyclopedia of New York City* (New Haven, Conn.: Yale University Press, 1995), the affectionate term "Big Apple" was introduced in the 1920s by a racetrack journalist who heard it from black stable hands in New Orleans, and was adopted by jazz musicians in the 1930s. After falling out of use, it was revived in a 1971 publicity campaign conducted by the New York Convention and Visitors Bureau.

3. The Austrian filmmaker Fritz Lang visited the United States in 1924 to observe motion picture production in New York and Hollywood. He got the idea for his next film, *Metropolis* (released in 1926), when he was detained in New York harbor. The film took two years to produce and almost bankrupted his company. *Metropolis* portrays the "Dual City" with unmitigated horror.

4. E. B. White, whose affection for the city was transparent, wrote in *Here Is New York* (New York: Harper & Brothers, 1949) this perceptive description of New York's gift to her residents: "On any person who desires such queer prizes, New York will bestow the gift of loneliness and the gift of privacy. . . . The capacity to make such dubious gifts is a mysterious quality of New York. It can destroy an individual, or it can fulfill him, depending a good deal on luck. No one should come to New York to live unless he is willing to be lucky" (9–10). He goes on, "New York blends the gift of privacy with the excitement of participation; and better than most dense communities . . . succeeds in insulating the individual . . . against all enormous and violent and wonderful events that are taking place every minute" (13).

5. Because it served as headquarters for the British forces during the Revolution, it was isolated from the independence struggle, and thus its patriotism remained suspect. Lord Bryce, writing in the second half of the nineteenth century in his *The American Commonwealth* (opening sentence of chap. 2), called New York a "European city of no particular provenance." Diverse immigrants continually fueled this alien character. The *New York Times* on May 16, 1994, reported, "Since 1986, immigrants to the New York metropolitan area have jumped from under 120,000 per year between 1986 and 1988, to about 130,000 in 1989, way up to almost 200,000 in 1990 and 1991, before dropping again to about 150,000 in 1992 . . . [although t]he "net" number planning to stay in New York rose only from about 90,000 in the early year to about 115,000 by the later year." Even today, many Americans insist that New York is not America! And instead of a European city, it is now sometimes called a Third World city.

6. Jan Morris, *The Great Port: A Passage through New York* (New York: Oxford University Press, 1969). This quotation is found on the overleaf of the unpaginated "Reservations" that precede the text.

7. For a deeper discussion of this poem, see Peter Conrad, *The Art of the City: Views and Versions of New York* (New York: Oxford University Press, 1984), 16–17.

8. Manuel Castells, *The Informational City: Information Technology, Economic Restructuring and the Urban-Regional Process* (New York: Blackwell, 1989).

9. The early history of the region's growth is best viewed as a process whereby somewhat isolated settlements that had developed *prior* to the connections among them were gradually knitted together by bridges (from the Brooklyn Bridge, 1883, on down), rail lines (most western lines terminated at the Jersey shore until about 1910, when Penn Station finally brought them onto the Island), and mass-transit elevated and subway lines (elevated lines toward the end of the nineteenth century, and then subways developed in the opening decades of the twentieth). The boroughs were not unified politically until 1898, after which virtually no annexations, except for an extension of the Bronx into Westchester County, took place. And the New Jersey and Connecticut shores always remained jurisdictionally "independent" although tightly entailed economically. Despite the numerous and inventive techniques and institutional arrangements devised to rectify these blunders from the colonial legacy, none has been fully satisfactory.

10. George W. Carey, *A Vignette of the New York–New Jersey Metropolitan Region* (Cambridge, Mass.: Ballinger, 1976), 1, emphasis added.

11. Edge city is no phenomenon new to Chicago: suburban, then exurban, rings have successively appeared at intervals of ten to twenty miles beyond the core, the most recent of which is the edge city of the Fox River Valley, which now contains the fastest-growing suburbs of the urbanized region. Ring roads and diagonal highways divide this outer region into sectors, thus replicating the basic ecological structure of Chicago.

12. Of course, political boundaries deflected Chicago's outward flow somewhat. After the great wave of annexations toward the end of the nineteenth century, which added almost all of Cook County to the city of Chicago, the city ceased to absorb its growing suburban fringe. Thus today the metropolitan core region consists of the city, a small fringe of independent townships mostly to the north and west within Cook County, and the so-called collar counties juridically independent of the city. One "regional" planning agency (the Northern Illinois Planning Commission) tries to coordinate the suburbanized region of northern Illinois, but it has no official linkage with Chicago.

13. Topography rules Los Angeles, as will be shown in Chapter 3, Map 3.5.

14. Conditions of drought are far more typical than the torrential rains and flooding Southern California saw in January 1995. The region, given its only occasional storms, is ill prepared for heavy rains, and policies have actively exacerbated the consequences. The paving over of the bed of the Los Angeles River prevents soil absorption, and the mud slides of the canyons have been intensified by construction of housing on land that would better have remained forested. See John McPhee, "Los Angeles against the Mountain," in *Control of Nature* (New York: Farrar, Straus & Giroux, 1989), 183–272, for a scathing indictment of hillside developments.

15. Workers of the Writers Program of the Works Projects Administration of New York, comp., *A Maritime History of New York* (New York: Haskell House, 1973), 5–6. This is a reprint of something that came out in the 1930s; it contains a forward by Fiorello La Guardia.

16. Ibid., 9.

17. At the same time that the Dutch East Indies Company was implanting itself in Indonesia, the Dutch West Indies Company made New Amsterdam the center of its North American operations. See Immanuel Wallerstein, *The Modern World-System II: Mercantilism and the Consolidation of the European World-Economy, 1600–1750* (New York: Academic Press, 1980), for the details of the bitter contest between the Netherlands and England.

18. Workers of the Writers Program, *A Maritime History of New York,* 15.

19. Elizabeth Blackmar, in her wonderful history of the development of the real estate market in New York, *Manhattan for Rent, 1785–1850* (Ithaca, N.Y.: Cornell University Press, 1989), notes: "All cultures have their creation myths. . . . The persistence of . . . [the story of the purchase of Manhattan] tells us more about the justifying strategies of our own times than about the past" (1). She continues: "The myth that celebrates a real estate deal as New York's primal historical act lends an aura of inevitability to the real estate market's power to shape the city landscape and determine the physical conditions of everyday life" (12). Her book, in contrast, explores how that market was itself created out of social relations during the first half of the nineteenth century. However, as I shall suggest later and Blackmar's own evidence shows, the template for the orthogonal plan of 1811 was to be found on Manhattan even before the Revolutionary War.

20. The street market for stolen goods is ubiquitous in New York to this very day.

21. Eric Lampard, "The New York Metropolis in Transformation: History and Prospect. A Study in Historical Particularity," in *The Future of the Metropolis: Berlin–London–Paris–New York,* ed. H. J. Ewers, J. B. Goddard, and H. Matzerath (Berlin: Walter de Gruyter, 1986), 29–31.

22. Ira Rosenwaike, *Population History of New York City* (Syracuse, N.Y.: Syracuse University Press, 1972), 2–3. Rosenwaike has compiled the earliest published statements on the demography of Manhattan Island. His book constitutes a basic source, integrating data from archives, documents, all existing censuses, and more. He tells us that when the municipality fell into English hands, it contained some fifteen hundred inhabitants drawn from very diverse backgrounds.

23. Workers of the Writers Program, *A Maritime History of New York,* 21–22.

24. As cited in Robert Greenhalgh Albion, *The Rise of New York Port, 1815–1860* (New York: Scribner, 1970 [1939]), 235. This is the definitive work on the role that the sea played in the life of New York up to the time of the Civil War. My account owes a considerable debt to this fine work.

25. It is perhaps not at all a strange coincidence that in 1995, when New York City established a new multilingual school designed to provide a transitional environment for new immigrants, instruction was to be given in eighteen languages, although not the same ones spoken by Manhattan's early settlers.

26. Frederic Cople Jaher, *The Urban Establishment: Upper Strata in Boston, New York, Charleston, Chicago and Los Angeles* (Urbana: University of Illinois Press, 1982), 160. Jaher's Chapter 3 deals with New York City.

27. Ibid., 160. Jaher is very explicit about this. He claims that it therefore resembled the southern gentry more than it did the Puritan merchants, magistrates, and ministers who ruled seventeenth-century Massachusetts Bay Colony. However, others have read the evidence quite differently. For a different account, see Blackmar, *Manhattan for Rent.* Blackmar claims that the "Dutch" system of inheritance gave equal shares to the heirs. I am not certain how to resolve this discrepancy in the accounts.

28. Jaher, *The Urban Establishment,* 164.

29. Ibid., 165, emphasis added.

30. Ibid., 161.

31. Ibid., 163.

32. Ibid., 171–72.

33. Workers of the Writers Program, *A Maritime History of New York,* 75.

34. Jackson, "The Capital of Capitalism," 319.

35. Brooklyn was incorporated as a village in 1816, and a few years later, in 1819, Brooklyn Heights was being promoted by developers as a commuters' suburb. Commuting between the two shores of the East River was still by ferry, as it would remain until the construction of the Brooklyn Bridge in 1883 provided an alternative.

36. Unless otherwise cited, all population figures come from Rosenwaike, *Population History of New York City.*

37. Charles N. Glaab and A. Theodore Brown, *A History of Urban America* (New York: Macmillan, 1967), 37. A fuller source on this development is Albion's impressive study *The Rise of New York Port.* Albion argues quite persuasively that although New York's magnificent natural harbor, more ice-free than Boston's, gave the city an undeniable edge over its northeast coast rivals, it was the entrepreneurial talents and sheer aggressiveness of her merchants that translated potential capacity into a firm monopoly over foreign trade in the post-1812 years through the auction system.

38. See the discussion in Albion's *The Rise of New York Port,* 12–13, which claims that the advantage New York gained by having been selected as the preferred port for British dumping would not have lasted without a legislated innovation concerning auctions. The new law was "designed to secure final sales for all goods put up for auction (b)y discouraging

the withdrawal of goods in case the bidding ran low" (13). An "information revolution" also played a role in consolidating New York's monopoly over international shipping. The New York Shipping and Commercial List was started in 1815, and up to the era of the telegraph it "provided the most detailed reports on non-local shipping arrivals and clearances available anywhere in the United States." Allan R. Pred, *Urban Growth and the Circulation of Information: The United States System of Cities, 1790–1840* (Cambridge: Harvard University Press, 1973), 24–25.

39. Jaher, *The Urban Establishment,* 176. As Pred writes: "Until 1838 and the coming of transatlantic steamship service, the New York packets—carrying 'general news for the press; special information affecting the price of cotton or flour; regular mails; and official dispatches'—were able to provide the city with a near monopoly of first information encounters." *Urban Growth,* 29. Pred's source is Robert Greenhalgh Albion, *Square-Riggers on Schedule: The New York Sailing Packets to England, France and the Cotton Ports* (Princeton, N.J.: Princeton University Press, 1938).

40. See Albion, *The Rise of New York Port,* 51–53.

41. Edward K. Spann, "The Greatest Grid: The New York Plan of 1811," in *Two Centuries of American Planning,* ed. Daniel Schaffer (Baltimore: Johns Hopkins University Press, 1988), 11–39.

42. Blackmar, *Manhattan for Rent,* 24–25.

43. Ibid., 31. Blackmar cites her own archival research for this fascinating information. Indeed, New Yorkers complained of the especially congested road conditions on May 1, the traditional "moving day" in the city.

44. Spann, "The Greatest Grid," 14.

45. The exceptions were only fifteen cross streets that were sixty feet wide and placed at infrequent intervals.

46. "Even before their estates disappeared, the gentry withdrew from trade . . . [forsaking] the sea for urban real estate." Jaher, *The Urban Establishment,* 173.

47. Just before he died, Astor is reported to have said that he regretted not having bought up all the land of Manhattan. Jackson, *The Encyclopedia of New York City,* 63.

48. Is that because what counts is what England, France, and the Netherlands did, rather than what the Spanish did? Or is it an unwillingness to admit that the present Latinization of Los Angeles is not a new phase to be deplored, but rather what I call Mexican irredentism?

49. Howard Nelson, *The Los Angeles Metropolis* (Dubuque, Iowa: Kendall/Hunt, 1983), 126.

50. The Spanish feared Russian and perhaps English activity in the northern Pacific, and the expedition to southern California that was ordered in 1768, rather than being motivated by the intrinsic attractions of the region, was designed to head off such moves. See ibid., 126–27.

51. Ibid., 127.

52. Ibid., 131.

53. Nelson, *The Los Angeles Metropolis,* 132–33. For additional information, see the primary documents in John Caughey and LaRee Caughey, *Los Angeles: Biography of a City* (Berkeley: University of California Press, 1977).

54. This was typical of almost all Spanish implantations. Unlike the colonies of other European nations, those founded by Spain were planned according to centralized directives.

55. Nelson, *The Los Angeles Metropolis,* 133, emphasis added.

56. Ibid., 134, 135.

57. The fort was ordered evacuated during the War of 1812, at which time Indians ambushed the fleeing settlers and soldiers and burned the fort down. It was not rebuilt until

1816. Irving Cutler, *Chicago: Metropolis of the Mid-Continent* (Dubuque, Iowa: Kendall/Hunt, 1976), 16.

58. In violation, the British actually stayed on until the 1794 Jay Treaty, in which they finally promised to leave.

59. I have not tried to regularize the transliterations of either tribal names or places, which appear in different sources in wildly varying forms.

60. These were the north and south branches of the Chicago River, which diverged from the future "Loop" of downtown Chicago, and the Desplaines River, which the southern branch joined.

61. See Christopher R. Reed, "'In the Shadow of Fort Dearborn': Honoring De Saible at the Chicago World's Fair of 1933–34." *Journal of Black Studies* 21 (June 1991): 398–413.

62. Ibid., 401. In actual fact, du Sable was reputed to have been the child of a French Canadian fur trader and an African American slave mother. African American claims have a certain irony, of course, because the Indians were there before, and du Sable left "Chicago" to marry a Potawatami Indian woman whose tribe he joined. Reed acknowledges this: "De Saible's activities were extensive and went beyond his involvement in the lucrative Great Lakes fur trade to include European-indigenous politics. De Saible was an influential outsider among the Pottawamie, Ojobwa (Chippewa), Winnebago, and other indigenous peoples of the lake and portage area. . . . It is believed that he later sought a position of power among the Pottawamie before he decided to sell his homestead in 1800. His relationship with the Pottawamie was, no doubt, strengthened when he married within their group and began a family. To the indigenous people of the area, he was a 'white man' but one to whom they could relate on an amicable basis. References to his activities and stature are found in the three major works on Chicago by Andreas (1884), Quaife (1933), and Pierce (1937)" (412, n. 1). However, in order to sustain their claim, the black advocates for du Sable referred to him "as *the first civilized man* in the area" (402–3, emphasis added).

63. Harold Mayer and Richard Wade, *Chicago: Growth of a Metropolis* (Chicago: University of Chicago Press, 1969), 10. This volume remains the definitive source on the geographic expansion of the city.

64. Jaher, *The Urban Establishment,* 454.

65. This story is told in beautiful detail by William Cronon in *Nature's Metropolis: Chicago and the Great West* (New York: W. W. Norton, 1991). Cronon's narrative essentially ends with the Chicago World's Fair of 1893. The Chicago Board of Trade was organized by grain merchants in 1848, but by 1852 had only fifty-two members. Only after the Civil War did it begin to play a significant role in policing futures on grain. See Bob Tamarkin, *The MERC: The Emergence of a Global Financial Powerhouse* (New York: HarperCollins,1993), which focuses on the historical development of the Board of Trade's rival, the Mercantile Exchange of Chicago.

3. DEVELOPMENTS BETWEEN THE 1820S AND THE 1870S

1. Sam Bass Warner Jr., *The Urban Wilderness: A History of the American City* (New York: Harper & Row, 1972), 84. Significantly, this is the only historical source I have found that attempts to compare the three American giants, but even Warner eschews true comparison, selecting instead to describe the cities sequentially: treating New York in the period 1820–1870, Chicago between 1870 and 1920, and Los Angeles from 1920 on. This strategy forfeits the opportunity to trace their convergence in the current period, or even to explore over time the important interrelationships among them.

2. Ibid., 79.

3. Eric H. Monkkonen, in *America Becomes Urban: The Development of U.S. Cities and Towns 1780–1980* (Berkeley: University of California Press, 1988), argues that the tendency of urban historians to focus so exclusively on technological changes distracts them from recognizing equally important social and political factors. I agree, but I believe that it would be equally foolhardy to underestimate the prime significance of such aspects. In my account I try to give due weight to environmental and demographic characteristics, as well as to mechanical (technology) and social (organizational and political) inventions. See Janet L. Abu-Lughod, *Changing Cities* (New York: HarperCollins, 1991).

4. Warner, *The Urban Wilderness,* 68.

5. Ibid., 68–69.

6. Frederic Cople Jaher, *The Urban Establishment: Upper Strata in Boston, New York, Charleston, Chicago and Los Angeles* (Urbana: University of Illinois Press, 1982), 198–99, emphasis added.

7. The depot was at the current site, but was initially a very modest structure. See Christine Boyer, *Manhattan Manners: Architecture and Style, 1850–1900* (New York: Rizzoli, 1985), 135.

8. I borrow the apt spider metaphor from Sven Beckert, "The Formation of New York City's Bourgeoisie, 1850–1896" (unpublished manuscript, New School for Social Research, 1993), 1. The quoted sentence can be found in Beckert's completed doctoral dissertation, "The Making of New York City's Bourgeoisie, 1850–1886" (Columbia University, 1995), 30.

9. In the words of Jaher: "By every measure of economic growth, rising population, expansion of capital resources, and assessed property values, New York forged ahead of her rivals. . . . the city had become the economic capital of the United States." *The Urban Establishment,* 177–78.

10. Kenneth Jackson, "The Capital of Capitalism: The New York Metropolitan Region, 1890–1940," in *Metropolis 1890–1940,* ed. Anthony Sutcliffe (Chicago: University of Chicago Press, 1984), 321. Jaher tells us that "in 1860 two-thirds of the nation's imports and one-third of its exports passed through New York." *The Urban Establishment,* 177.

11. Jean Heffer, *Le Port de New York et le commerce extérieur américain, 1860–1900* (Paris: Publications de la Sorbonne, 1986), 22. It is hard to reconcile the figures presented in these various secondary accounts with the primary sources assembled by Eric Lampard in his careful scholarly chapter, "The New York Metropolis in Transformation: History and Prospect. A Study in Historical Particularity," in *The Future of the Metropolis: Berlin–London–Paris–New York,* ed. H.-J. Ewers, J.B. Goddard, and H. Matzerath (Berlin: Walter de Gruyter, 1986). According to Lampard's Table 3, p. 45, which compiles data on international commerce in U.S. ports between 1821 and 1860 from various issues of the *Annual U.S. Report on Commerce and Navigation,* New York's dominance was not overwhelmingly established until midcentury. I have computed the following percentages of values of import and export trade handled by major U.S. ports from 1821 to 1860, based on Lampard's data:

Port	% value of exports					% value of imports				
	1821	1831	1841	1851	1860	1821	1831	1841	1851	1860
New York	20	31	27	39	36	37	55	59	50	69
Boston	19	9	9	6	4	23	14	16	15	11
New Orleans	11	20	28	25	27	0	1	1	1	1

12. Warner, *The Urban Wilderness,* 71, emphasis added.

13. See Jaher, *The Urban Establishment,* 178, 184–91. In the words of Beckert: "Finance had been one of the principal lines of business of early general merchants—extending credit was a means of securing trade flows—and with the growing specialization of traders some merchants found this business so profitable that they eventually dropped merchandising and concentrated on banking." "The Making of New York City's Bourgeoisie," 43. He cites Glenn Porter and Harold C. Livesay, *Merchants and Manufacturers: Studies in the Changing Structure of Nineteenth Century Marketing* (Baltimore: Johns Hopkins University Press, 1971).

14. Lampard, "The New York Metropolis," 50.

15. Jaher, *The Urban Establishment,* 191.

16. A Jacksonian policy requiring specie for the purchase of western lands caused the collapsing panic in investment circles. See the fascinating maps of these banking connections in Allan R. Pred, *Urban Growth and the Circulation of Information: The United States System of Cities, 1790–1840* (Cambridge: Harvard University Press, 1973), 250–52, Maps 7.1, 7.2, 7.3.

17. See Henry W. Lanier, *A Century of Banking in New York, 1822–1922* (New York: Gilliss, 1922). Beckert notes: "In the 1850s . . . New York's banks largely directed British and continental capital into American agriculture and trade. . . . Thus the two most important bankers of the city were the chief agents for European capital: George Cabot Ward represented the London banking house of Baring Brothers, and August Belmont . . . the house of Rothschild." "The Making of New York City's Bourgeoisie," 44.

18. Jaher, *The Urban Establishment,* 179.

19. Inter alia, see Beckert, "The Making of New York City's Bourgeoisie," 44. But see also Lanier, *A Century of Banking,* as well as Edward K. Spann, *The New Metropolis: New York City, 1840–1857* (New York: Columbia University Press, 1981), 412–17. Expansion came to an abrupt end in the Panic of 1857, precipitated by a crisis in railroad financing, when New York lenders had trouble collecting on loans extended to the Midwest, but the crisis was brief.

20. Jaher, *The Urban Establishment,* 190–92.

21. Beckert, "The Making of New York City's Bourgeoisie," 46, citing R. C. Mitchie, *The London and New York Stock Exchanges, 1850–1914* (London: Allen & Unwin, 1987), 181. The original Exchange had been destroyed in the 1835 fire.

22. Lampard, "The New York Metropolis," 56.

23. Jaher, *The Urban Establishment,* 193–94.

24. Other insurance ventures grew out of the earliest prototype, the more ancient marine insurance. For a fuller discussion, see Robert Greenhalgh Albion, *The Rise of New York Port, 1815–1860* (New York: Scribner's, 1970 [1939]), as well as Beckert, "The Making of New York City's Bourgeoisie," 47–48.

25. Jaher, *The Urban Establishment,* 200–201. But see also Elizabeth Blackmar, *Manhattan for Rent, 1785–1850* (Ithaca, N.Y.: Cornell University Press, 1989); and Tom Shachtman, *Skyscraper Dreams: The Great Real Estate Dynasties of New York* (Boston: Little, Brown, 1991), 9–44, for some information on early real estate fortunes.

26. As early as 1842, John Jacob Astor was listed as the richest man in New York (and therefore the entire country). He was also the largest landowner, even before his heirs enlarged their real estate holdings by buying up properties and foreclosing on mortgages during the depressions of the early 1850s and 1870s. See Lampard, "The New York Metropolis," 54. Shortly before the dynasty's founder died in 1848, he is said to have expressed regrets: "Could I begin life again, knowing what I now know, and had money to invest, I would buy every foot of land on the island of Manhattan." Quoted by Marc Weiss in his entry on John Jacob Astor

in *The Encyclopedia of New York City,* ed. Kenneth Jackson (New Haven, Conn.: Yale University Press, 1995), 63.

27. Lampard, "The New York Metropolis," 55.

28. Ibid., 57; Jaher, *The Urban Establishment,* 200.

29. In the 1860s, women constituted one-fourth of the manufacturing labor force in Manhattan, concentrated in the garment industry. Most of these women, however, worked in sweatshops or in their homes, and most were recent immigrants.

30. See, for example, Patricia E. Malon, "The Growth of Manufacturing in Manhattan, 1860–1900: An Analysis of Factoral Changes and Urban Structure" (Ph.D. diss., Columbia University, 1981), esp. 394.

31. Ibid.

32. One of the most remarkable sources on the industrial establishments in New York in the early twentieth century is Edward Ewing Pratt, *Industrial Causes of Congestion of Population in New York City* (Columbia University Studies in History, Economics and Public Law, vol. 43, no. 1, whole no. 109) (New York: Columbia University, 1911). I discuss this source in greater detail in Chapter 4. The average number of workers per establishment in New York City in the late nineteenth and early twentieth centuries was still only eleven to twelve, whereas during the same period industrial establishments in Philadelphia and Chicago employed an average of two to four times that number.

33. Warner, *The Urban Wilderness,* 74, 75.

34. Pratt, *Industrial Causes of Congestion.*

35. Ira Rosenwaike, *Population History of New York City* (Syracuse, N.Y.: Syracuse University Press, 1972), 39. It was not until the New York State census of 1845 that information on place of birth was collected, although the censuses of 1825 and 1835 did ask about citizenship (38).

36. Ibid., 39, citing E. P. Hutchinson, "Notes on Immigration Statistics of the United States," *Journal of the American Statistical Association* 53 (December 1958): 963–1025.

37. The best books on this subject remain David Ward's *Cities and Immigrants: A Geography of Change in Nineteenth-Century America* (New York: Oxford University Press, 1971), and a companion volume, *Poverty, Ethnicity, and the American City, 1840–1925* (New York: Cambridge University Press, 1989).

38. See Rosenwaike, *Population History of New York City,* 42, Table 9.

39. Amy Bridges notes that the appearance of nativist parties in New York City closely correlated with recession dates. See her *A City in the Republic: Antebellum New York and the Origins of Machine Politics* (New York: Cambridge University Press, 1984), esp. the graph on 19. "Three nativist political parties were formed in New York City: Samuel Morse's Native American Democratic Association in 1836; the American Republican Party in 1844–45; and the Know Nothings in 1854–6" (29).

40. For more details, see Richard Plunz, *A History of Housing in New York City* (New York: Columbia University Press, 1990), 21–53.

41. Expansion according to the 1811 plan was slow. By 1839 the planned zone had reached only 35th Street; nevertheless, by 1874, subdivisions had been executed as far as 94th Street. See Boyer, *Manhattan Manners,* 9.

42. For details, see Roy Rosenzweig and Elizabeth Blackmar, *A History of Central Park: The Park and the People* (New York: Henry Holt, 1994), 65–77.

43. See Moses Yale Beach, *Wealth and Wealthy Citizens of New York City, Comprising an Alphabetical Arrangement of Persons Estimated to Be Worth $100,000, and Upwards* (New York: Sun Office, 1842).

44. Beckert, "The Making of New York City's Bourgeoisie," 29, citing Edward Pessen, *Riches, Class, and Power before the Civil War* (Lexington, Mass.: D. C. Heath, 1973), 34.

45. Beckert, "The Making of New York City's Bourgeoisie," 29, citing *Boyd's New York City Tax-Book* (New York: William Boyd, 1857).

46. Beckert, "The Making of New York City's Bourgeoisie," 32–33. Beckert drew a sample of almost five hundred names from those listed in *Boyd's New York City Tax-Book* as having wealth in excess of $10,000. He traced their occupations in various city directories and mapped their addresses, verifying and amplifying the information in the original schedules of the census of 1855 and in their obituaries. For his methodology, see 32–33 n. 6.

47. Ibid., 36, based on his own sample study.

48. Ibid., 39, citing Douglas T. Miller's *Jacksonian Aristocracy: Class and Democracy in New York, 1830–1860* (New York: Oxford University Press, 1967), 122; and also Glenn Porter and Harold C. Livesay, *Merchants and Manufacturers: Studies in the Changing Structure of Nineteenth-Century Marketing* (Baltimore: Johns Hopkins University Press, 1971), 73.

49. Jaher, *The Urban Establishment,* 205, Tables 4 and 5. Unfortunately, Jaher does not present similar information for the 1870s, when this social mobility began to decline. However, his Table 7 (254), which shows the geographic origins of the seven hundred New York millionaires in 1892 whose birthplaces could be identified, reveals that the foreign-born had declined to 18 percent, those from other states had decreased to 27 percent, and the New York–born had increased to 54 percent. By then, a third of all millionaires were at least "third-generation" wealthy, whereas the fortunes of another third were at least two generations old. (See Jaher's Table 6, p. 253, but see also a different figure in Table 8, p. 258, which suggests that by 1892 almost 80 percent of the millionaires represented "old money.")

50. In 1869 Junius Browne described "society" in New York as being subdivided into "circles within circles . . . segments and parts of segments." Quoted in Rosenzweig and Blackmar, *The History of Central Park,* 217. Such complexities intensified, so that by the 1890s these groups had, according to Hammack, formed even more distinctive networks. See David C. Hammack, *Power and Society: Greater New York at the Turn of the Century* (New York: Russell Sage Foundation, 1982).

51. Public works also, it must be noted, lined the pockets of the "bosses" of Tammany, which at about this time had been transformed from a relatively elite secret society of Protestants (founded by Aaron Burr after the Revolutionary War) to a wheeling and dealing montage of "ethnic operators," mostly Irish Catholic, who narrowly defeated the anticlerical Know-Nothings in significant mayoral races at midcentury and used the expanding need for public improvements and services as ways to award patronage jobs to disciplined party followers. This came to a head at the time of "Boss" Tweed.

52. Most poor lived in wooden shacks or in subdivided housing abandoned by their "betters." However, in 1850, Gotham Court in lower Manhattan was one of the first specifically constructed "tenements," a form of housing that would eventually spread all along both shores of the island. The central "ridge" of Fifth Avenue and adjacent avenues would gradually be preempted by the well-to-do in mansions and then French flats (multifamily housing for the middle class). See Chapter 4 for more details.

53. Philip Hone, *The Diary of Philip Hone, 1828–1851,* ed. Allen Nevins (New York: Dodd, Mead, 1927), 785. Hone, as mayor in 1821, officially opened the Erie Canal.

54. For more details on housing reformers, see, inter alia, Richard Plunz and Janet L. Abu-Lughod, "The Tenement as a Built Form," in Janet L. Abu-Lughod et al., *From Urban Village to East Village: The Battle for New York's Lower East Side* (Oxford: Blackwell, 1994): 63–79.

55. See Iver Bernstein, *The New York City Draft Riots: Their Significance for American Society and Politics in the Age of the Civil War* (New York: Oxford University Press, 1990), which paints a far more complex picture. In actual fact, only eleven of the more than one hundred killed in the rioting were blacks, but this was twice as high as their percentage in the population.

56. Beckert, "The Making of New York City's Bourgeoisie," 60–62. See Blackmar's discussion of growing class segregation in *Manhattan for Rent;* see also Bridges, *A City in the Republic.*

57. The best work on the invention and spread of apartment house living for the middle class in New York is Elizabeth Collins Cromley, *Alone Together: A History of New York's Early Apartments* (Ithaca, N.Y.: Cornell University Press, 1990); but see also Elizabeth Hawes, *New York, New York: How the Apartment House Transformed the Life of the City (1869–1930)* (New York: Owl/Holt, 1994).

58. Boyer, *Manhattan Manners,* 153–54.

59. Cromley, *Alone Together,* 209, emphasis added.

60. Boyer, *Manhattan Manners,* 36. See her Figure 23, p. 31, which shows the total number of building plans filed between 1868 and 1897, and her Figure 31, p. 36, showing the number of buildings erected in Manhattan between 1868 and 1880 by type of structure.

61. Ibid., 36.

62. Jaher, *The Urban Establishment,* 210.

63. Documentation of a scandalous but accurate nature can be found in Matthew P. Breen, *Thirty Years of New York Politics Up-to-Date* (New York: Arno, 1974 [1899]).

64. Although there is a large scholarly literature on Tammany, perhaps the most fascinating journalistic account can be found in Alfred Connable and Edward Silberfarb, *Tigers of Tammany: Nine Men Who Ran New York* (New York: Holt, Rinehart & Winston, 1967), which traces the major figures and changing rituals and roles of the society from its origin in the wake of the Revolution to its final demise under Carmen DeSapio in the 1960s. A fascinating set of documents of the era can be found in Breen, *Thirty Years of New York Politics.* Bridges's *A City in the Republic* is probably the best scholarly account of the transformation of New York's city government from the patriciate of the 1820s to the machine bosses of the post–Civil War era. In this process, "men of wealth withdrew from those leadership roles in which public and private were hardly differentiated, leaving charity to professionals and community to politics. . . . Later [i.e., just before the Civil War, the political resources of the working class] were used to demand that politicians endorse unionism, to protect (or assail) the civil liberties of immigrants and Catholics, and, perhaps most important, to gain welfare concessions from local government" (158–59).

65. Only a few tiny parcels had been left open in the gridiron plan of 1811, and of these, two were really fenced private parks accessible only to owners of adjacent dwellings. The most famous of the latter was Gramercy Park, privately deeded in 1831, along whose borders would live mayors, a governor (Tilden), George Templeton Strong, and that abstemious inventor, Peter Cooper. A fine study of the park and its residents is Carole Klein's *Gramercy Park: An American Bloomsbury* (Boston: Houghton Mifflin, 1987).

66. The unlikely account of how Olmsted gained the post of superintendent of construction from the politicians of the Common Council is told, possibly with tongue in cheek, by Olmsted himself in a fragment of an incomplete autobiography titled "Passages in the Life of an Unpractical Man," reproduced in *Landscape into Cityscape: Frederick Law Olmsted's Plans for a Greater New York City,* ed. Albert Fein (Ithaca, N.Y.: Cornell University Press, 1967), 50–62.

67. Rosenzweig and Blackmar, *The History of Central Park,* 160–61.

68. Ibid., 273. The authors quote from Martin Shefter's reprise of Tammany Hall

politics in *Political Crisis/Fiscal Crisis: The Collapse and Revival of New York City* (New York: Columbia University Press, 1992), chap. 2. Shefter demonstrates that the 1970s fiscal crisis had its parallels in the 1870s.

69. William Cronon, *Nature's Metropolis: Chicago and the Great West* (New York: W. W. Norton, 1991), 7–8, emphasis added.

70. Cronon, ibid., invokes these images through literature in his chapter subtitled "Cloud over Chicago" (see 9–19 in particular). It is significant that many of the novels written about Chicago begin with scenes of arrival into the inferno of a railroad station.

71. Irving Cutler, *Chicago: Metropolis of the Mid-Continent* (Dubuque, Iowa: Kendall/ Hunt, 1976), 17.

72. Peyton quoted in ibid.

73. Peyton quoted in ibid., 19. In 1847 the original McCormick plant was relocated north of the river, on the site where du Sable's cabin had once stood, and thus, unhappily, it was directly in the path of the Great Chicago Fire of 1871 and burned to the ground.

74. Cutler, *Chicago,* 19.

75. Cronon, *Nature's Metropolis,* 97.

76. Jaher, *The Urban Establishment,* 453–75, deals with Chicago. He notes that by midcentury "Chicago had become the largest primary grain, wheat, and lumber market in the country . . . and early in the Civil War it surpassed Cincinnati as the nation's premier meat-packing town" (454).

77. Ibid., 453, emphasis added (*parvenu* in italics in the original).

78. Ibid., 456.

79. Ibid., 461.

80. Before the Civil War, only a few industries were worth noting: meatpacking, iron-working and steelmaking, and agricultural implement production. McCormick started making the latter in 1848, Pullman organized his railcar business in 1859, and Crane started producing plumbing fixtures in 1855. See ibid., 460.

81. Cronon, *Nature's Metropolis,* 311.

82. Quoted, without full attribution, in Herman Kogan and Robert Cromie, *The Great Fire: Chicago 1871* (New York: G. P. Putnam's Sons, 1971), 9.

83. Ibid.

84. Ibid., 43. The strange and still extant water tower was the only structure in its neighborhood that remained intact after the fire.

85. Ibid., 49.

86. Despite attempts to discount as a myth the story that O'Leary's cow kicked over a kerosene lantern, which then ignited the straw and then the wooden barn, no evidence has ever been found that this was not exactly what happened.

87. Kogan and Cromie, *The Great Fire,* 113. The buildings destroyed included solidly built new commercial structures, the new courthouse, and many brick and stone churches.

88. The remarkable recovery of Chicago, not only physically but socially as well, is a story well told by Karen Sawislak, *Smoldering City: Chicagoans and the Great Fire, 1871–1874* (Chicago: University of Chicago Press, 1995).

89. Those include images of Chicago as the city of machine guns and the mob, the city of racial strife and labor strikes, and the city of industrial devolution in the present moment of rusting and deindustrialization.

90. Ross Miller, *The American Apocalypse: The Great Fire and the Myth of Chicago* (Chicago: University of Chicago Press, 1990), 12–13.

91. Ibid. Quotations from Miller reprinted by permission of The Wylie Agency.

92. Ibid., p. 17–18, emphasis added.

93. Howard Nelson, *The Los Angeles Metropolis* (Dubuque, Iowa: Kendall/Hunt, 1983), 135–40.

94. Ibid., 138.

95. The Mexican government, unable to protect its empire, "sold" New Mexico and California to the United States for fifteen million dollars. See Robert G. Cleland, *From Wilderness to Empire: A History of California, 1542–1900* (New York: Knopf, 1944), and John W. Caughey, *California* (New York: Prentice Hall, 1940), as cited in Robert M. Fogelson, *The Fragmented Metropolis: Los Angeles, 1850–1930* (Berkeley: University of California Press, 1993[1967]), 298 n. 19.

96. Nelson, *The Los Angeles Metropolis,* 143.

97. Carey McWilliams, *Southern California: An Island on the Land* (Salt Lake City: Peregrine Smith, 1990 [1946]), 50. This 1946 work remains one of the best books dealing with Los Angeles.

98. The "Spanish" elite were often indistinguishable, phenotypically, from the "mestizos" who were further down on the social ladder.

99. As paraphrased, without citation, in McWilliams, *Southern California,* 52. *Greaser,* the American racist term for Mexicans still in use, predated the conquest. McWilliams traces it back to the hide-and-tallow trade, when Mexican and Indian laborers were used to load the offending hides on clipper ships. "After the conquest, greaser became a synonym for Mexican, in fact, for any dark-skinned person" (57).

100. Ibid., 62, citing Hittell, but unspecified as to source or page. The parallels with land expropriations in European colonial imperial conquests are striking. The imposition of monetary taxes on a basically subsistence economy, the requirement that land titles be regularized and recorded in "foreign-language" registers governed by a different set of judicial laws, and the confiscation of communal lands by the new governing authority all served to alienate land from Mexican to Anglo owners. McWilliams is a harsh critic of this process. For a blander description, see Fogelson, *The Fragmented Metropolis* 13–14.

101. Nelson, *The Los Angeles Metropolis,* 141.

102. Ibid., 146–47.

II. THE ESTABLISHMENT OF THE TRIUMVIRATE

1. Significantly, European sources reserve the term *Great Depression* for the twenty-year slump between 1873 and 1893, whereas American sources use the same term to refer to the period that followed the crash of 1929.

2. *Restructuring* is a term currently in use that refers to moments of up to ten years when the international economy undergoes basic spatial reorientation and when the social and physical "technologies" of production and exchange undergo basic reorganization.

3. Eric Hobsbawm, *The Age of Extremes: A History of the World, 1914–1991* (New York: Pantheon, 1995), 86–87, emphasis added.

4. At this early stage, the term *globalization* is more accurately defined as including the Anglo-Atlantic powers and their colonial dependencies. In this, it must be distinguished from the current phase of "globalization" that encompasses much of the world.

5. Hobsbawm, *The Age of Extremes,* 88–89. Note that Hobsbawm's Eurocentric bias subtly changes the emphasis that Americans would place on the events.

6. A second and perhaps more satisfying explanation for why economic conditions were not identical in the Old and New Worlds is offered by Giovanni Arrighi in *The Long*

Twentieth Century: Money, Power, and the Origins of Our Times (London: Verso, 1994). He suggests that the European depression of 1873–93 was precipitated by a "switching crisis in British capitalism," when the capitalist profits of English investments were declining in their traditional outlets (see his discussion on 163–64). In contrast, the crisis that began in the United States in 1929 and then reverberated in Europe came from the opposite occurrence: a massive reduction in American overseas investments. A "domestic speculative boom or bust in the United States . . . result[ed] in a halt in [U.S.] foreign lending and in the collapse of the whole complex structure on which the restoration of world trade [after World War I] was based. . . . Towards the end of 1928, the boom on Wall Street began diverting funds from foreign lending to domestic speculation. As US banks recalled their European loans, the net export of capital from the United States—which had risen from less than $200 million in 1926 to over a billion in 1928—plunged to $200 million again in 1929. . . . Th[is] halt in US foreign lending was made permanent by the collapse of the Wall Street boom and the ensuing slump in the US economy" (274).

7. Isolationism has been much overstated; it may have been isolation from European entanglements, but it never was isolation from the hemisphere—witness the taking of California from Mexico at midcentury and, in 1898, the Spanish American War, which gained the United States its first "colonies" and protectorates in the Caribbean and the Pacific.

8. The current concern in the United States with "excessive" immigration of "unassimilable" foreigners has been foreshadowed twice in the country's history: during the 1840s and 1850s, when the influx of Irish (and, to a lesser extent, German) immigrants triggered anxieties about the loss of quality (and purity) and led to the brief popularity of the Know-Nothing Party, and again in the early 1900s, in the wake of the "great migrations" from eastern and southern Europe after 1880. Even before World War I (in 1911), a study of the problems engendered by such high levels of immigration had been commissioned. The multivolume study later provided the intellectual underpinnings for the drastic reduction in admissions after the war. The repatriation of Mexicans and the denial of benefits and publicly supported employment relief to aliens during the Depression of the 1930s foreshadowed the passage of Proposition 187 in California in 1994.

9. On a much smaller scale, a predominantly black zone began to appear in Los Angeles, with a cultural efflorescence on Central Avenue that paralleled but in no way matched the Harlem Renaissance.

10. It also led to a series of strikes throughout the country and a "Red Scare" that repressed radical labor movements.

11. Janet L. Abu-Lughod, *Changing Cities: Urban Sociology* (New York: HarperCollins, 1991), 104, based on Hilda Golden, *Urbanization and Cities* (Lexington, Mass.: D. C. Heath, 1981), 199, Table 8.3.

12. A computer library search for information on industries of Los Angeles during this period turned up almost exclusively publications on the movie industry.

13. This is not to claim that Los Angeles was entirely "free" of labor mobilizations or even periodic outbreaks of strikes and police repression, but these were minor in comparison with the labor unrest, in both urban and rural areas, that characterized Northern and Central California. It is significant that Kevin Starr devotes four lengthy chapters to labor movements in California before and during the Great Depression, but focuses primarily on San Francisco, where "the action" was. See *The Dream Endures: California Enters the 1940s* (New York: Oxford University Press, 1997).

14. Essentially, depoliticization reflected a desire to remove patronage and graft from new "bosses" who were busy building "machines" in New York and Chicago.

15. Whereas residues of earlier "arrangements" modified these changes in both New York and Chicago, the newness of Los Angeles, and the absence of an ethnically based "machine," meant that there was little to stand in the way of such innovative patterns of organization. See, for example, Raphael J. Sonenshein, *Politics in Black and White: Race and Power in Los Angeles* (Princeton, N.J.: Princeton University Press, 1993); see also several chapters in William Deverell and Tom Sitton, eds., *California Progressivism Revisited* (Berkeley: University of California Press, 1994).

16. Initially, the consolidation included Brooklyn (King's County), Queens County, and Staten Island (Richmond County), as well as the lower portions of Westchester County, constituted as the borough of the Bronx but earlier annexed to Manhattan and thus considered a part of New York County. It was not until 1914 that the Bronx became an officially designated separate county.

17. Three townships in the borough of Queens absolutely refused to join Greater New York City, forming instead the adjacent Long Island county of Nassau. As we shall see, this ostensible autonomy did not protect Long Island from the activities of Robert Moses, but forced the latter to operate from a state-based legal structure. This gave Republicans in New York City a somewhat greater strength in politics because even when Democrats routinely controlled city offices, coalitions with the state government in Albany, usually dominated by Republicans, were usually required.

18. The most noteworthy resistance was found in the townships of the upper-income suburbs of the North Shore. See Michael H. Ebner, *Creating Chicago's North Shore: A Suburban History* (Chicago: University of Chicago Press, 1988).

19. Ann Durkin Keating, *Building Chicago: Suburban Developers and the Creation of a Divided Metropolis* (Columbus: Ohio State University Press, 1988).

20. See Fred Viehe, "Black Gold Suburbs: The Influence of the Extractive Industry on the Suburbanization of Los Angeles, 1890–1930," *Journal of Urban History* 8, no. 1 (1981): 3–26.

21. See Gary J. Miller, *Cities by Contract: The Politics of Municipal Incorporation* (Cambridge: MIT Press, 1981). Miller tells the story of how resistance to annexation to Los Angeles started anew in 1954 with the Lakewood case and was followed by many other separate incorporations. "The book suggests that the primary purpose of the incorporation was the same as that of the Jarvis-Gann tax revolt of 1978: to limit the property tax burden on homeowners and businesses and to limit the expansion of governmental bureaucracies and social welfare programs. . . . Thus, in effect, as well as in motivation, the incorporation movement was analogous to Proposition 13" (viii).

22. The crown jewel of the Chrysler Building is the best example of the use of art deco in New York. In Chicago, examples were the Studebaker Building, the Diana Court, and the Carbon-Carbide Building (constructed at the request of its chief New York tenant). Regarding art deco in Los Angeles, see, for example, Carla Breeze, *L.A. Deco* (New York: Rizzoli, 1991); on New York, see Carla Breeze, *New York Deco* (New York: Rizzoli, 1991).

23. In 1868 the "profession" of architecture began with MIT's professional program. (See Christine Boyer, *Manhattan Manners: Architecture and Style, 1850–1900* (New York: Rizzoli, 1985), 7. Richard Morris Hunt was the first American architect to be trained at the Paris Ecole des Beaux-Arts and became an ardent advocate of classical architecture. Founder of the American Institute of Architects and Vanderbilt's personal architect, Hunt had visited the Philadelphia Fair and been appalled by how poorly the American buildings compared to the European contributions. He was a strong force in shifting American tastes toward the beaux arts tradition. Henry Hobson Richardson also studied with Viollet-le-Duc in Paris, but was a more individualistic artist, albeit not as successful financially as Hunt. His influence on

Chicago architecture was as important as Hunt's on New York architecture. For more details, see Christopher Tunnard, *The Modern American City* (Princeton, N.J.: Van Nostrand, 1968), esp. chaps. 3–5.

24. Existing uses that violated the new zoning laws were "grandfathered," that is, permitted to continue as nonconforming uses. Only in the still-growing "outer boroughs" could zoning and subdivision regulations have much effect.

4. NEW YORK SOLIDIFIES ITS CHARACTER

1. To this immigration must be added the natural increase of the "older immigrants." In 1890, "more than 406,000 New Yorkers had at least one Irish, and 426,000 one German, parent." Oscar Handlin, *The Newcomers: Negroes and Puerto Ricans in a Changing Metropolis* (Cambridge: Harvard University Press, 1959), 21.

2. Tenements displaced wooden shacks, and new buildings went up on the formerly swampy ground of Peter Stuyvesant's old estate there.

3. I define a caste as a group formed by the combination of common ethnicity/descent and occupation/class. In the United States, caste lines among whites have usually not been impermeable in subsequent generations, but have been stronger for racial minorities.

4. Although strictly speaking the term *outer boroughs* refers to all four counties that joined Manhattan in the 1898 confederation, because Staten Island (Richmond County) was so small, it is usually forgotten. When New Yorkers speak of the outer boroughs, they tend to mean only Brooklyn, Queens and the Bronx.

5. Zoning was extended especially after its legality was upheld by the Supreme Court in 1926 in the case of *Village of Euclid (Ohio) v. Ambler Realty.*

6. In 1880, there were only 13,411 residents of Manhattan and Brooklyn combined who had been born in Italy, and 4,760 who had been born in Russia. Ten years later, the number of Italian-born residents in the two boroughs was approaching 50,000, and the number of Russian-born had surpassed that mark. In the next decade, each group would triple in size. See, inter alia, Kenneth Jackson, ed., *The Encyclopedia of New York City* (New Haven, Conn.: Yale University Press, 1995), 584–85 .

7. By 1890, more than half of New York's Italians and an estimated three-quarters of Eastern European Jews and their children lived on the Lower East Side. See Ira Rosenwaike, *Population History of New York City* (Syracuse, N.Y.: Syracuse University Press, 1972), 84.

8. The population would gradually thin out as immigrants moved to areas of second settlement in the Bronx and Brooklyn in the 1920s and 1930s. By the 1930 census, the same district contained only a quarter of a million residents, of whom about half had been born abroad. See Jan Lin, "The Changing Economy of the Lower East Side," in Janet L. Abu-Lughod et al., *From Urban Village to East Village: The Battle for New York's Lower East Side* (Oxford: Blackwell, 1994), 54–55, Table 2.2. Lin's data are drawn from L. Durward Badgley and Homer Hoyt, *The Housing Demand of Workers in Manhattan* (New York: Corlears Hook Group for the F.H.A., 1939), 20.

9. Kenneth Jackson, "The Capital of Capitalism: The New York Metropolitan Region, 1890–1940," in *Metropolis 1890–1940,* ed. Anthony Sutcliffe (Chicago: University of Chicago Press, 1984), 323. Even today, when the proportion of foreign-born in the city has risen to 27 percent, far short of the 38 percent in Los Angeles, the range of diversity is far greater. Whereas half of Los Angeles's foreign population hails from Mexico, no single country contributes more than 10 percent to New York's foreign-born.

10. According to Rosenwaike, "This gain could not compare with that of almost

600,000 by Chicago, which with 1,100,000, superseded Philadelphia as the second largest American city at the 1890 census." *Population History of New York City,* 57.

11. I have calculated these percentages by combining figures from ibid., 63, Table 19, with borough breakdowns provided by Edward Ewing Pratt, *Industrial Causes of Congestion of Population in New York City* (Columbia University Studies in History, Economics and Public Law, vol. 43, no. 1, whole no. 109) (New York: Columbia University, 1911), whose work is reported in greater detail below. This was necessary because of an error in Rosenwaike's total population in 1890, where he reports a reconstructed five-borough total in place of the Manhattan figure.

12. One year later, Manhattan had its first telephone exchange, albeit with only 252 subscribers.

13. In 1860, some 39 percent of Brooklyn's population had been born abroad, contrasted with 47 percent of Manhattan's.

14. Brooklyn Bridge was opened in 1883. Hitherto, the two shores of the so-called East River (not a river but actually an inlet separating Long Island from both Manhattan and the southern coast of Connecticut) had been connected only by frequent ferry service and transport barges.

15. The two best demographic reconstructions are found in Pratt, *Industrial Causes of Congestion;* and Rosenwaike, *Population History of New York City.* I should point out, however, that these authors' numbers do not always agree, even though both claim to derive them from official censuses. In some cases I have tried to combine data from Pratt on reconstructed borough populations with data on borough-specific nativity figures provided by Rosenwaike. My figures are therefore only approximate. However, they are in general agreement with the independently generated figures compiled by James Bradley, "Immigration," in Jackson, *The Encyclopedia of New York City,* 582, a source that appeared after my own computations had been completed, and with the estimates for 1890 and 1900 shown in a table that appears in that volume's entry on population (921).

16. Pratt, *Industrial Causes of Congestion,* 26, Table 1, reconstructs (retrospectively) the populations of the five boroughs between 1790 and 1910, when the combined total rose from under 50,000 to well over 4.5 million. Manhattan's population increased from 33,000 in the earliest year to 2.33 million by 1910, Brooklyn's total increased from 4,500 to 1.634 million, the Bronx's grew from 1,781 to 430,980, and Queens's from 6,159 to 28,041. Smallest in extent, Staten Island's total increased from 3,855 to 85,969.

Pratt's figures clearly document the tendency, up to 1830, for the region's population to be increasingly concentrated within Manhattan (its proportion rose from 67 percent in 1790 to 84 percent in 1830), before the process of decentralization began. According to Pratt, Manhattan's share dropped monotonically—back to 80 percent in 1840, 74 percent in 1850, 69 percent in both 1855 and 1860, and then to 61 percent by 1870 (27, Table 2). After that, it settled down to the 50–60 percent range, before dropping to less than half by 1910. Conversely, Brooklyn's share increased from only 9 percent in 1790 to more than a third by 1910, with the largest increases occurring from the 1850s on. In contrast, the population living in what was to become the Bronx remained negligible until it began to rise around 1900, reaching 9 percent by 1910; a similarly delayed change occurred in Queens, but as late as 1910 that borough contained only 6 percent of the combined city's population.

17. Attempts to entice Nassau and Suffolk Counties on Long Island failed from the start, and of course the western half of the metropolitan region was in New Jersey, which precluded its annexation.

18. Pratt, *Industrial Causes of Congestion,* 27.

19. The enormous discrepancies between land values per square foot in Manhattan's

real estate market are shown in two maps in the first edition of Richard M. Hurd's *Principles of City Land Values* (New York: Real Estate Record Association, 1903), 157–58. As of 1903, the prices per square foot of (residential) properties adjacent to the east side of Central Park between 59th Street and 86th Street were averaging sixty to eighty dollars—the highest in Manhattan, with the exception of the financial and governmental center around Wall Street. (Wall Street had the highest average value: four hundred dollars per square foot.) In contrast, properties on the western perimeter of the park were with only one exception valued at sixteen dollars per square foot—not much higher than the per square foot values of four to eight dollars in the worst slums. See also Christine Boyer, *Manhattan Manners: Architecture and Style, 1850–1900* (New York: Rizzoli, 1985), 19. See especially her maps for the discrepancies of development east and west of the park. The one notable exception was the still extant Dakota apartment hotel (former home of ex-President Nixon and other "luminaries"), which was designed in 1882 and constructed on the western edge of Central Park. At the time it was built, it stood in isolated splendor in a sea of empty lots.

20. New York's first residential cooperative appeared there in 1884, setting in place a precedent that would significantly affect the financing of apartment houses in New York City to this day.

21. This would not be supplemented until twenty years later, when the Williamsburg Bridge was opened.

22. For details, see the clear graphic presentation by Edward O'Donnell showing the changing political structure of city government. It appears in Jackson, *The Encyclopedia of New York City,* 203–7.

23. This body had been initiated in the 1870s, when Manhattan's municipal functions expanded and, with them, the technical personnel to execute public works. The chief budget officer (the comptroller) was a central member.

24. These modifications included the revival of the bicameral system in 1924 and its later disappearance in 1938 when a single City Council was substituted.

25. See, inter alia, Joseph P. Viteritti, "The New Charter: Will It Make a Difference?" in *Urban Politics New York Style,* ed. Jewel Bellush and Dick Netzer (Armonk, N.Y.: M. E. Sharpe, 1990), 413–28. The ground for the finding of unconstitutionality was that, at least theoretically, the confederation of the five boroughs, which range widely in size, was to treat each borough as if it had "equal" power. Each was represented by its own president on the Board of Estimate, which was the body charged with overall city decision making. In actual practice, however, this was never the case. The board was dominated by the mayor (elected at large), his comptroller, the city's legal counsel, and, of course, Manhattan's borough president, a *primus inter pares.*

26. Jackson, "The Capital of Capitalism," 321–22. Jackson does not give a source, but he claims that New York State's per capita income was 60 percent higher than the nation's (349 n. 15).

27. See Clifton Hood, *722 Miles: The Building of the Subways and How They Transformed New York* (New York: Simon & Schuster, 1993). Hood is clearly enamored: "I think New York City's subway is magical. . . . I am more fascinated by it now than the day I began [to research it]" (11). The account that follows depends heavily on this enthusiastic and carefully researched book.

28. The false starts and the political controversies are well covered in ibid., 13–55.

29. See the discussion in David C. Hammack, *Power and Society: Greater New York at the Turn of the Century* (New York: Russell Sage Foundation, 1982): 230–58, which recounts the complicated and conflicting proposals and the important role played by the Chamber of

Commerce and Mayor Abram Hewitt in pressuring for the "subway solution." Hammack quotes from Hewitt's 1888 *Message on the Harbor, the Docks, the Streets (and street railways), Rapid Transit, the Annexed District, and the Tenement Houses* as follows: "Unless additional [rapid transit] facilities are provided, the population which ought to increase at the upper end of the city [then only Manhattan] will be driven to Long Island and New Jersey." Speaking in terms that are familiar to any municipal official concerned with fiscal matters, Hewitt continued, "Our rate of taxation depends upon the growth of the unoccupied portion of the city, particularly north of the Harlem River" (233).

30. Belmont, an immigrant from Germany, had changed his name to disassociate himself from the new Jewish business elite of New York, which, rejected by the older fortunes, had set up a parallel set of social institutions, just as was to happen in Los Angeles years later.

31. Hood, *722 Miles,* 71.

32. See ibid., 91, on the dedication. Hood notes that more than 110,000 users, many of whom had stood in line all day, entered when the doors were opened to the public at 7:00 p.m. "Some people spent the entire evening on the trains, going back and forth from 145th Street to city hall for hours" (95). Significantly, the opening of this line was soon followed by a strike of subway workers, a recurring pattern testifying to the centrality of the mass-transit system to the city's operation. On growth stimulated by the subway, as quoted, ibid., 113.

33. My calculations are assembled from various volumes of the *Census of Population and Housing,* 1990.

34. By the late 1890s, electricity was being supplied underground throughout Manhattan; as elevators became more common, building heights in the central business district rose dramatically. Manhattan's shift from blue- to white-collar jobs accompanied this growth in commerce and services. By 1910, Manhattan still contained some five hundred thousand industrial workers, but the number of white-collar workers had risen to three hundred thousand.

35. Jackson, "The Capital of Capitalism," 328, emphasis added. I have omitted Jackson's erroneous 1980 figure. The census of 1980 reported a Manhattan total of 1.428 million, which by 1990 had risen slightly, to 1.49 million. City Hall is now complemented by the "wedding cake" elaborate Municipal Building, constructed in 1905 according to plans provided by the dominant architectural firm of the city—McKim, Mead, and White. This firm had gained national prominence for its classic buildings at the Chicago's World's Fair of 1893.

36. Pratt, *Industrial Causes of Congestion,* 27.

37. See ibid., 40, Table 12, which shows the increase in establishments over time. Table 13 (41) is even more sensitive, showing changes in the number of establishments and workers for all boroughs except the Bronx. In this table, the continued overwhelming dominance of Manhattan as a site for industry is clear.

38. On the increasing scale of Philadelphia manufacturing, see Theodore Hershberg, ed., *Philadelphia: Work, Space, Family, and Group Experience in the 19th Century* (New York: Oxford University Press, 1981).

39. My calculations are based on Pratt's data in *Industrial Causes of Congestion.* Further, Pratt stresses that in 1910 "the great bulk of the manufacturing in Greater New York [was being] carried on in Manhattan below Fourteenth Street, on that small but immensely valuable one-hundredth of the city's total land area" (42). This can be largely attributed to the centrality of garment production in the city. In the early twentieth century, one-fifth of all the value produced in manufacturing in New York came from the garment industry, which indeed produced more than half of the ready-made clothing for the entire country (79). It was not until the

1920s that the garment industry relocated from the East Side below 14th Street to the new garment district in the 30s, after the construction of Pennsylvania Station at 34th Street.

40. Ibid., 114–15.

41. Jackson, "The Capital of Capitalism," 323. Jackson might also have added motion pictures. By 1910, when Greater New York's labor force accounted for only 5.6 percent of the U.S. total, it accounted for almost 13 percent of all editors and reporters. See Pratt, *Industrial Causes of Congestion,* 45, Table 2–5.

42. This tale is well told in Olivier Zunz, *Making America Corporate, 1870–1920* (Chicago: University of Chicago Press, 1990).

43. See Pratt, *Industrial Causes of Congestion,* 45, Table 2–5, which documents the extent to which certain professional and managerial occupations, such as bankers and brokers, authors and editors, architects, designers and engineers, and of course lawyers and insurance agents, were overrepresented in New York in 1890 and 1910.

44. Contrast this with labor agitations in "more typical" Chicago, where strikes began in the large and isolated Pullman sleeping car works, the steel mills on the southern fringes of the city, and the enormous stockyards, which constituted a world of their own. See Chapter 5 for a fuller discussion.

45. The owners had chained the doors in this loft shop to prevent workers from taking breaks; when the fire broke out, the women were trapped. Many leaped to their deaths in an attempt to escape the flames and smoke.

46. Although these two unions remained rivals to some extent, between them they managed to organize the entire industry and to pick up affiliates in other garment manufacturing cities as well. See Roger Waldinger, *Through the Eye of the Needle: Immigrants and Enterprise in New York's Garment Trades* (New York: New York University Press, 1986).

47. Pratt, *Industrial Causes of Congestion,* 99–100.

48. See, for example, Daniel Eli Bernstein, "Progressivism and Urban Crisis: The New York City Garbage Workers' Strike of 1907," *Journal of Urban History* 16 (August 1990): 386–423.

49. Later prohibited, strikes by municipal workers were not permitted until the 1950s.

50. The recent discovery of an African burial ground on a site being excavated for an extension of City Hall halted construction when an estimated ten to twenty thousand skeletons were found in this area, which had been beyond the city limits in the seventeenth and eighteenth centuries.

51. One of the earliest sociological sources on New York's black population is James Weldon Johnson's (1871–1938) *Black Manhattan* (New York: Atheneum, 1968 [1930]). This is the source, not adequately acknowledged, for much of early parts of Gilbert Osofsky, *Harlem: The Making of a Ghetto, Negro New York, 1890–1930,* 2d ed. (New York: Harper Torchbooks, 1971).

52. Johnson, *Black Manhattan,* 10–11.

53. Ibid., 13.

54. Ibid., 27.

55. See Sherrill Wilson, *New York City's African Slaveowners: A Social and Material Culture History* (New York: Garland, 1994). This book is based on Wilson's doctoral dissertation in anthropology at the New School for Social Research.

56. Johnson, *Black Manhattan,* 19, 39–44.

57. Even then, there was some overlap between black and foreign. Osofsky tells us that "some 5,000 [blacks] were foreign-born . . . primarily from the British West Indies. Although they represented an exceedingly small portion of the general population, there were more foreign-born Negroes in New York City than in any other city in America." *Harlem,* 3.

58. Johnson, *Black Manhattan,* 127.

59. Osofsky, *Harlem,* 46–52.

60. Fred Shapiro and James Sullivan, *Race Riots: New York 1964* (New York: Thomas Y. Crowell, 1964), 17.

61. Osofsky, *Harlem,* 71.

62. Ibid., 73.

63. Ibid., 75–76.

64. Ibid., 79–81.

65. Ibid., 82.

66. Osofsky, *Harlem,* 83–84. Seventeenth-century documents refer to slaves of the Dutch West India Company building roads and working on farms in Harlem.

67. Ibid., 87, quoting the *Real Estate Record and Builders' Guide* of 1904.

68. Ibid., 88. The usual stereotype of Harlem's early pioneers as acculturated German Jewish "strivers" escaping from the increasingly déclassé Russian Jewish community of the Lower East Side is considerably overdrawn. Not only was there greater ethnic diversity in early Harlem, but the range of classes and subcultures was wider than usually portrayed. See, for example, the discussion in Jeffrey S. Gurock, *When Harlem Was Jewish, 1870–1930* (New York: Columbia University Press, 1979).

69. Osofsky, *Harlem,* 90.

70. Ibid., 91–92.

71. As late as the 1910s, Harlem contained a Jewish community of more than one hundred thousand, and whites continued to outnumber blacks until well into the 1920s. See Gurock, *When Harlem Was Jewish,* 1.

72. Osofsky, *Harlem,* 105.

73. Johnson, *Black Harlem,* 151. Johnson reports that he himself witnessed one trainload of some twenty-five hundred workers from a single southern city.

74. Ibid., 152–53.

75. Ibid., 156.

76. Ibid., 157. I might add here that, in contrast to the case of Chicago, where blacks were being used in large-scale plants as scabs to break the backs of labor union actions, African Americans seldom served this function in New York's labor conflicts.

77. Ibid., 157–58.

78. Of course, Johnson was overly optimistic. He had no hint that there would be riots in 1935 and again in 1943, albeit ones that foreshadowed the ghetto uprisings of the 1960s. The clouds on his crystal ball are particularly evident in this passage: "It has often been stated as axiomatic that if Negroes were transported to the North in large numbers, the race problem with all its acuteness and inflexibility would be transferred with them. Well, more than two hundred thousand Negroes live in the heart of Manhattan . . . and do so without race friction . . . an integral part of New York citizenry. They have achieved political independence and without fear vote for either Republicans, Democrats, Socialists, or Communists. . . . Politically they have begun to fill important government posts and their artistic achievements have smashed stereotypes." Ibid., 281–82. The final page of Johnson's book is especially ironic: "The Negro in New York . . . still meets with discrimination and disadvantages. But New York guarantees her Negro citizens the fundamental rights of citizenship and protects them in the exercise of those rights. Possessing the basic rights, the Negro in New York ought to be able to work through the discriminations and disadvantages" (284). Unhappily, this "working through" of disadvantages has taken much longer than he anticipated, and indeed has met with significant setbacks in the "age of restructuring." Regarding the period of the Harlem Renaissance, see,

for example, Ann Douglas, *Terrible Honesty: Mongrel Manhattan in the 1920s* (New York: Farrar, Straus & Giroux, 1995), which is a remarkable reconstruction of that time and place in American history.

79. Osofsky, *Harlem,* 123, citing E. Franklin Frazier, "Negro Harlem: An Ecological Study," *American Journal of Sociology* 43 (July 1937): 72–88. But Osofsky might also have cited Johnson's *Black Manhattan,* which closely parallels this later publication. Johnson contrasts the beauty, centrality, and good housing of Harlem with the peripheral slums of other cities (146), and tells the familiar story of the overbuilding of Harlem, the crash, and the role of Negro realtors who bailed out landlords. He also notes that the "line" west of Lenox Avenue was "held" by redlining (148–49).

80. Osofsky, *Harlem,* 111.

81. Ibid., 128. See the table showing place of birth of non-New York blacks in the 1930 census (129). A surprisingly large number (54,750) were foreign-born, hailing mostly from the Caribbean. There is, however, an interesting footnote to history here. When the immigration restriction laws were passed in the early 1920s, they omitted mention of the West Indies, so there was relatively free movement, and even after quotas were belatedly imposed, they were seldom filled. Jamaicans favored New York almost exclusively. "There were ten times as many foreign-born Negroes in New York City as in any other American urban area. . . . About 25 percent of Harlem's population in the twenties was foreign-born" (131).

82. A classic rendition is found in Frederic Cople Jaher, *The Urban Establishment: Upper Strata in Boston, New York, Charleston, Chicago and Los Angeles* (Urbana: University of Illinois Press, 1982): "Older elites declined in New York politics . . . through loss of commercial eminence and displacement by urban machines who voiced the values, served the needs, and captured the votes of the immigrant masses" (260). A much more nuanced position is taken by Jon C. Teaford in his *The Unheralded Triumph: City Government in America, 1870–1900* (Baltimore: Johns Hopkins University Press, 1984), which is perhaps the best book on the development of municipal government in the United States during this period. Teaford points out that the standard critique, which blamed poor municipal government on the displacement of "good" (respectable) rulers by corrupt (immigrant) city bosses, came from a snobbish elite, including not only Lord Bryce, who gave it its most cogent expression, but local Protestant elites; they deplored the rise of ethnics not because they were losing all their power, but because they were losing their monopoly over power. But it was not only conservatives who critiqued the new "bosses." Henry George, running for mayor of New York in 1886 on a reform Labor Party ticket, suggested that the elite actually "used" the bosses for their own ends: "In all the great American cities there is to-day as clearly defined a ruling class as in the most aristocratic countries of the world. . . . Who are these men? The wise, the good, the learned—men who have earned the confidence of their fellow-citizens by the purity of their lives, the splendor of their talents, their probity in public trusts, their deep study of the problems of government. No, they are the gamblers, saloon-keepers, pugilists, or worse, who have made a trade of controlling votes, and of buying and selling offices and official acts. . . . It is through these men that rich corporations and powerful pecuniary interests can pack the Senate and the Bench with their creatures." See Hammack, *Power and Society,* 10, quoting Henry George, "Open Letter to the Hon. Abram S. Hewitt, Oct. 20, 1886." For the original source, see Louis F. Post and Fred C. Leubuscher, *Henry George's 1886 Campaign: An Account of the George-Hewitt Campaign in the New York Municipal Election of 1886* (New York: John W. Lovell, 1886).

83. Jaher's own data indicate that "55 percent of the millionaires [in New York in 1892] possessed relatively young fortunes," suggesting that multiple elite factions were already apparent. *The Urban Establishment,* 253–54.

84. Hammack, *Power and Society,* 27, emphasis added.

85. Teaford notes that although "throughout the United States city councils surrendered prerogatives during the last decades of the nineteenth century, . . . no council *suffered such a loss of power as occurred in . . . New York City.*" *The Unheralded Triumph,* 17, emphasis added.

86. The Croton reservoir and aqueduct projects were begun as early as 1830. A second Croton aqueduct was completed in 1893, together with the "new Croton Dam, the highest masonry dam in the world at the time of its completion. . . . By the 1890s New York City's reservoirs held 42 billion gallons of water, more than four times the capacity of the municipal system at the beginning of the 1880s." Ibid., 223–24.

87. Ironically, it had been Boss Tweed himself who had pressed for this change. See ibid., 17. Teaford notes with approval the fiscal reforms instituted after the Panic of 1873 to put municipalities on a more conservative path. Whereas municipalities foundered, along with businesses, in the Panic of 1873, "the panic of the 1890s was only a business depression. . . . No major city defaulted on its debt obligation between 1888 and 1900, and in the Panic of 1893 no municipality suffered . . . financial tribulations." In fact, "the annual cost of debt maintenance dropped sharply during the last two decades of the nineteenth century." Ibid., 289–90.

88. The city council therefore lost both power of the purse and power of patronage appointment. "By the 1880s and 1890s virtually the only formal power of significance left to New York's aldermen was . . . to regulate the use of city streets and sidewalks and to grant public utilities the rights of way along these thoroughfares" in their own wards. Ibid., 17. In 1880, a similar reform was extended to Brooklyn. "After 1882 Brooklyn's mayor had absolute power over appointments. . . . With little control over city finances and no role in the appointment of city officials, the Brooklyn Board survived as a minor element in the determination of city policy." Ibid., 19.

89. It also decreased the "voice" of neighborhoods and their ethnically based representatives, making New York's governance substantially different from Chicago's, where neighborhood representation remains significantly stronger to this day.

90. The drive for civil service reform was partially sparked by concern about corruption in the New York Police Department. In 1894, the Committee of Seventy (which grew out of a previous police corruption inquiry) was organized by religious reformer Charles Parkhurst to overthrow Tammany Hall. See Charles H. Parkhurst, *Our Fight with Tammany* (Freeport, N.Y.: Books for Libraries Press, 1970 [1895]). The committee issued a proclamation stating, in part, that "municipal government should be entirely divorced from party politics and from selfish personal ambition or gain. . . . We denounce as repugnant to the spirit and letter of our institutions any discriminations among citizens because of race or religious belief. We demand that the public service of this city be conducted upon a strictly non-partisan basis; that all subordinate appointments and promotions be based on Civil Service Examinations, and that all examinations, mental and physical, be placed under the control of the Civil Service Commission" (260–63). A more explicit statement of Progressive Era goals cannot be found.

91. This increased the "clout of a new breed of departmental bosses, functional lords who allowed little interference from lay persons and whose primary loyalty was to their profession and not to any particular political leader." Teaford, *The Unheralded Triumph,* 133.

92. Hammack, *Power and Society,* 110.

93. Teaford may be off by one year here, unless one dates the sweep of the Progressives from the time they took office rather than the time of the election and its campaign. It was in November 1894 that the Progressive coalition temporarily overthrew Tammany Hall, initiating, inter alia, significant changes in the city's educational system. For a detailed account of

this, see Sol Cohen, *Progressives and Urban School Reform: The Public Education Association of New York City, 1895–1954* (New York: Bureau of Publications, Teachers College, Columbia University, 1964).

94. Teaford, *The Unheralded Triumph,* 189–90.

95. "The bill provided that the commission consist of the mayor, the comptroller, the president of the Chamber of Commerce, and five citizens specifically named in the measure, four of whom were millionaire members of the chamber." Teaford, *The Unheralded Triumph,* 90.

96. "By the mid-1890s forty-four million passengers each year were taking the cable railway across the Brooklyn Bridge, and millions of others were crossing by foot or in wagons or carriages." Ibid., 233.

97. The following discussion is based on Richard Plunz and Janet L. Abu-Lughod, "The Tenement as a Built Form," in Janet L. Abu-Lughod et al., *From Urban Village to East Village: The Battle for New York's Lower East Side* (Oxford: Blackwell, 1994), 63–79, which in turn depends in part on Plunz's masterful *A History of Housing in New York* (New York: Columbia University Press, 1990).

98. Jacob Riis, *How the Other Half Lives* (New York: Scribner's, 1890). The material in this book had appeared in *Scribner's Magazine* a year before.

99. The commission's studies resulted in the remarkable work authored by Robert W. De Forest, *The Tenement House Problem,* 2 vols. (New York: Macmillan, [1903?]).

100. See Robert Hunter, *Tenement Conditions in Chicago: Report of the Investigating Committee of the City Homes Association* (Chicago: City Homes Association, 1901). For the connection between the New York and Chicago studies, see Peter Hall, *Cities of Tomorrow: An Intellectual History of Urban Planning and Design in the Twentieth Century* (Oxford: Blackwell, 1988), 44.

101. Earlier reforms had evidently failed. An 1879 "contest" for improved design had introduced the so-called dumbbell tenement, which required a center air shaft between adjacent structures; the "new-law" tenements were to be provided with small courtyards.

102. Hall, *Cities of Tomorrow,* 39.

103. Interestingly enough, Chicago and New York were the two final contenders for the fair's venue, and only the greater hustling ability of Chicago's new millionaires in guaranteeing the needed funds tipped the decision in favor of that city. As Christine Boyer puts it, "Not yet fifty years old, the city of Chicago, which pledged up to $10 million to subsidize the fair, was able to take the coveted prize away from New York. This was a great blow to the city and to the real estate interests especially." *Manhattan Manners,* 20. For details on the City Beautiful movement in the United States, see Christopher Tunnard, *The Modern American City* (Princeton, N.J.: D. Van Nostrand, 1968), chaps. 4, 5.

104. Louis Sullivan, one of the "fathers" of the Chicago school of architecture and guru to Frank Lloyd Wright, was one of the few Chicago-based architects to design a building for the fair, the remarkable Transportation Building. His criticisms of Burnham and the "classicists" he favored were scathing. Nancy Frazier, in her beautifully illustrated biography of Sullivan, *Louis Sullivan and the Chicago School* (London: Bison, 1991), attributes Sullivan's subsequent decline to his rift with the establishment over the decision to fill the fair with classical pillars and porticos (15–17).

105. Hall, *Cities of Tomorrow,* 525–26.

106. Jackson, "The Capital of Capitalism," 337. The plan received little support and was dismissed by the mayor.

107. Even before this, Californians had tried to control the spread of Chinese laundries through zoning, and from 1909 onward, Los Angeles was also developing comprehensive

land-use zoning. But the intent of these efforts was different from New York's, and they did not have the same influence. Hall, *Cities of Tomorrow,* 58–59.

108. In this connection, Jackson cites what he calls "a tedious, administrative history of municipal attempts to regulate residential density," John P. Comer's *New York City Building Control, 1800–1941* (New York: Columbia University Press, 1942), to which the reader can turn for more details. "The Capital of Capitalism," 350 n. 30.

109. Hall, *Cities of Tomorrow,* 58. McAneny was the Manhattan borough president and, as we shall see, was an important supporter of the Regional Plan Association (of New York), equally elite driven.

110. Ibid., 59.

111. Ibid., 60.

112. Carol Willis, *Form Follows Finance: Skyscrapers and Skylines in New York and Chicago* (New York: Princeton Architectural Press, 1995).

113. Ibid., 34, 67. Willis is not the first to point this out, although she has made it central. See her earlier articles "Zoning and Zeitgeist: The Skyscraper City in the 1920s," *Journal of the Society of Architectural Historians* (March 1986): 47–59; "A 3–D CBD: How the 1916 Zoning Law Shaped Manhattan's Central Business Districts," in *Planning and Zoning New York City, Yesterday, Today, and Tomorrow,* ed. Todd W. Bressi (New Brunswick, N.J.: Center for Urban Policy Research, Rutgers University, 1993), 3–26. Among her sources are S. J. Makielski Jr., *The Politics of Zoning: The New York Experience* (New York: Columbia University Press, 1966); and Seymour I. Toll, *Zoned American* (New York: Grossman, 1969). She also cites Marc Weiss, "Density and Intervention: New York's Planning Traditions," in *The Landscape of Modernity,* ed. David Ward and Olivier Zunz (New York: Russell Sage Foundation, 1992), 46–75.

114. Willis, *Form Follows Finance,* 40. But see also Romin Koebel, "The New York City Tower Coverage Provision as a Determinant of Urban Spatial Form," in *Proceedings of the 10th Annual Conference of the Environmental Design Research Association* (Buffalo, N.Y.: 1981); and Romin Koebel, "Incentive Zoning in New York City" (Ph.D. diss., Massachusetts Institute of Technology, 1973). Chicago, in marked contrast, enjoyed large block and lot sizes and, because of the fire, had significantly larger amounts of land on which to develop new skyscrapers. Although it also imposed a height limit, Chicago imposed no setback requirement, which meant that structures tended to square off at the top but required open cores for light and air. See my Chapter 5.

115. Hall, *Cities of Tomorrow,* 60–61.

116. The conflict between the RPAA and RPA approaches is well handled in Roy Lubove, *Community Planning in the 1920s: The Contribution of the Regional Planning Association of America* (Pittsburgh: University of Pittsburgh Press, 1963), chap. 7. Lubove clearly favors the "idealistic" approach to regional planning of the RPAA through a system of decentralized new-town "garden cities" (whose proponents were, inter alia, Lewis Mumford and Clarence Stein) based on the ideas of such British planners as Raymond Unwin and, of course, Ebenezer Howard. Outside of a few accomplishments in this genre (the Chicago suburb prototype of Riverside designed by Frederick Olmsted and three garden cities designed by Stein, which failed to become more than commuter dormitories), this approach was largely ineffective. In contrast, the opposing, more "practical," approach of the RPA of New York, with which the RPAA was in vigorous conflict, had a greater impact on New York. Supported by finance, utility, and real estate interests and funded by the Russell Sage Foundation at the urging of Charles Dyer Norton, the plan designed by English master planner Thomas Adams gained legitimacy through its association with McAneny, Rockefeller, and, later, Ford. A superb study

of the elite involvement in the RPA is provided by Forbes B. Hays, *Community Leadership: The Regional Plan Association of New York* (New York: Columbia University Press, 1965).

117. Much of the following information is based on the work of Hays, *Community Leadership,* chaps. 1, 2; and Jackson, "The Capital of Capitalism," 337–39.

118. Hall, *Cities of Tomorrow,* 156. Note that Hall's main sources are the two crucial studies cited in note 117, above.

119. Hays, *Community Leadership,* 12.

120. Adams was finally appointed director of plans and surveys in 1923, after Norton's death. Hall, *Cities of Tomorrow,* 156.

121. Ibid., 156–57.

122. These criticisms came largely from the competing RPAA. Attempts to use the state government as a regional planning mechanism were also being made at the same time, but with no greater success. Indeed, Clarence Stein, one of the leading figures in the RPAA, served "as the first and only chairman of the New York State Commission of Housing and Regional Planning (1923–26), a post he accepted on the explicit understanding that the commission would deal with regional planning as well as housing. Stein drew on the services of Mumford." Lubove, *Community Planning,* 71–72.

123. Hall, *Cities of Tomorrow,* 159.

124. In the United States in 1920 there were already nine million motor vehicles (cars, taxis, buses, and trucks) registered; by 1930, their number had tripled to almost twenty-seven million, even though the length of surfaced highways had grown only from 369,000 in 1920 to not even 700,000 by 1930. See Janet L. Abu-Lughod, *Changing Cities: Urban Sociology* (New York: HarperCollins, 1991), 129, Table 5.8, which is based on data from Hilda Golden, *Urbanization and Cities* (Lexington, Mass.: D. C. Heath, 1981), 311.

125. Abu-Lughod, *Changing Cities,* 128, Table 5.7. To some extent, however, this difference in growth rates was an artifact of political choice. New York and Chicago both expanded their boundaries to encompass large portions of their suburban rings in the late nineteenth century, so that peripheral growth was classified as center-city growth. After 1898 in New York and 1915 in Chicago, the option of annexation was effectively eliminated. Only Los Angeles, of the three cities, would continue to annex territory.

126. Hall, *Cities of Tomorrow,* 276.

127. Ibid., 276–77.

128. Hall reminds us that the first U.S. interstate expressway, the Pennsylvania Turnpike, opened only in 1940, the same year that Los Angeles finished building a short leg of its Arroyo Seco Parkway. By the end of the war, "Los Angeles had precisely 11 miles of freeway." Ibid., 282.

129. It would later be expanded through an interstate compact to coordinate port installations in New Jersey and New York.

130. In 1956, the RPA commissioned the Harvard University Graduate School of Public Administration to do a three-year restudy of the region. Nine substantive volumes and one summary were the results. These are discussed in greater detail in Chapter 7. See Robert C. Wood with Vladimir V. Almendinger, *1400 Governments: The Political Economy of the New York Metropolitan Region* (Cambridge: Harvard University Press, 1961).

131. Ibid., 1.

132. The first co-op thought to have been established in New York was built in 1857 at 15 West 10th Street for artists (with apartments, studios, and a gallery). "In the early 1900's, members of the Finnish community erected two dozen co-ops in Sunset Park, Brooklyn, and various labor unions also got into the co-op market. . . . During the roaring 20's, the 'white

glove' co-ops for the wealthy sprang up along Park Avenue and Fifth Avenue. Promoted by Douglas Ellman, a real estate broker, the buildings became the province of wealthy white Protestants, who were intent on keeping out 'undesirables'—namely blacks, Jews and Catholics. The onset of the Depression, however, toppled many co-ops and brought the movement to a standstill. . . . The acute need for housing for veterans returning from World War II rejuvenated the concept in the form of government-subsidized complexes. In time, thousands of apartments aimed at moderate-income tenants were also created under the state Mitchell-Lama program. . . . The pivotal years were the 1980's, when co-ops went mainstream. The easing of the rules for conversions in 1982, when the real-estate market was surging, stimulated an explosion in rental buildings' being transformed into co-ops. Driving the conversion was the desire of building owners to evade rent control. . . . When the stock market crashed in October 1987, the real-estate market began to come apart. . . . In the last few years, the number of co-ops has remained virtually unchanged." *New York Times,* October 30, 1995, B2. According to a graph produced by the city's Finance Division, the number of cooperative apartments in New York City rose from 83,732 in 1978 (including some publicly subsidized) to 416,003 by 1995. *New York Times,* October 30, 1995, 1. There are currently 8,080 co-op buildings in New York City, which is "more than half the co-ops in the nation. In contrast, there are just 1,040 condominium complexes, the less restrictive form of communal ownership more common in the rest of the country. Half of the city's co-op apartments are in Manhattan, with the largest and most expensive enclave lining the Upper East Side. And while New York remains emphatically a city of renters, roughly 15 percent of the population now lives in co-ops, though about 45 percent of those people rent the apartments from their owners." N. R. Kleinfield with Tracie Rozhon, "In Flat Market, Co-op Life Has Steep Ups and Downs," *New York Times,* October 30, 1995, B2. Maps accompanying this article show that most co-ops are on Manhattan Island, mostly on either side of Central Park, with another concentration in Queens.

133. Willis astutely points out that this was no accident of timing. She notes that "the tallest buildings generally appear just before the end of a boom" (*Form Follows Finance,* 155; but see also 166) and that pressures to limit the heights of commercial buildings are often associated with the "bust" portion of the real estate cycle (168).

5. CHICAGO BECOMES FORDIST

1. Ironically, although planned during years of a booming economy, the exposition's opening coincided with deep economic retrenchment, unemployment, and rising labor protests, as we shall see. This "bad timing" would be repeated with Chicago's next world's fair. The Century of Progress opened in 1934 in the midst of the worst depression ever experienced in the United States.

Concerning the metaphor of the phoenix—if any book or article written just after the fire did not invoke this image, I have not found it. I have been unable to trace the first time it was used. The icon is still in use: the recently completed Harold Washington Public Library sprouts copper phoenixes rising from its roofline.

2. When world's fairs became popular during the second half of the nineteenth century and the first several decades of the twentieth (before television and air travel made "foreign" scenes part of the imaginations of many), countries vied with one another to present themselves in the best light, although colonies were represented by metropole organizers to exploit their exotic qualities. Major cities in the United States competed for the privilege of hosting such fairs in part to show off their advantages to visitors and potential business investors. The

staging of a world fair was preceded by substantial investments in city improvements and infrastructure, on the assumption that visitors would not just be viewing the fair itself but would be judging the worthiness of its sponsors. Preparations often began three or four years in advance, and it was these preparations, even more than the actual fairgrounds themselves, that left lasting marks on urban forms. Today, now that world fairs have become passé, the parallel event is a city's hosting of the Olympic Games.

3. Hubert Howe Bancroft, *The Book of the Fair: An Historical and Descriptive Presentation Viewed through the Columbian Exposition at Chicago in 1893* (New York: Bounty, n.d.[1894]), 35–36.

4. See Lois Wille, *Forever Open, Clear, and Free: The Historic Struggle for Chicago's Lakefront* (Chicago: Regnery, 1972), xi, on the earliest history. Only much later would the eyesores of rail tracks be partially covered and bridges built to give access to new lakefront parks constructed on landfill.

5. Frederic Cople Jaher, *The Urban Establishment: Upper Strata in Boston, New York, Charleston, Chicago and Los Angeles* (Urbana: University of Illinois Press, 1982), 514. See Daniel H. Burnham and Edward H. Bennett, *Plan of Chicago* (New York: Da Capo, 1970 [1909]), who note: "Second only to Philadelphia in 1880, Chicago has now dropped to the seventh place in so far as park area is concerned; and when the relative density of population is taken into consideration this city occupies the thirty-second place!" (44).

6. Jon C. Teaford, *The Unheralded Triumph: City Government in America, 1870–1900* (Baltimore: Johns Hopkins University Press, 1984), 225, 217.

7. One can still see in certain older neighborhoods of Chicago frame houses whose entrances are gained by descending ten to fifteen steps below street level.

8. Not until the flow of the North Branch of the Chicago River was reversed would this situation be ameliorated.

9. See the more complete coverage in Teaford, *The Unheralded Triumph.*

10. There are several good sources on the development of Chicago's mass-transit system. The reader is referred to, inter alia, James Leslie Davis, *The Elevated System and the Growth of Northern Chicago* (Northwestern University Studies in Geography 10) (Evanston, Ill.: Northwestern University, 1965), which traces the evolution of the multiplex system from the Galena and Chicago Union Railroad, whose initial leg was built in 1848 to connect Chicago with the Desplaines River ten miles west of the city; to plank roads developed between 1848 and 1855; and then to horse railway lines, started in 1859 and expanding in the next ten years. Davis cites George W. Hilton, "Cable Railways of Chicago," *Electric Railway Historical Society Bulletin* 10 (1965), concerning details on the cable lines installed beginning in 1882 (59). Elevated railway lines were built between 1892 and 1900, the first of which connected the Loop with the fairgrounds to the south. A more complete source is Paul Barrett, *The Automobile and Urban Transit: The Formation of Public Policy in Chicago, 1900–1930* (Philadelphia: Temple University Press, 1983). Barrett argues that because industrial workers were too poor to pay the fares, "the horsecar systems—and the cable and electric lines which replaced them in the 1880s and 1890s—were paid out and developed as middle-class utilities serving the more affluent segments of the population" who worked downtown (12). Between 1892 and 1906, more than eighty miles of elevated railways were constructed and all cable-car powered lines had been converted to electricity (15). This was a considerable lag behind New York, where elevated service began in the 1870s in Manhattan and by 1885 in Brooklyn. "Though most viewed the elevated railroad as an aesthetic blot on the city, prior to the 1890s, it was generally regarded as the premier form of rapid transit." (Teaford, *The Unheralded Triumph,* 237). Subways of a limited nature would not come to Chicago until the 1940s, and

then only to traverse the CBD. See Irving Cutler, *Chicago: Metropolis of the Midcontinent* (Chicago: Geographical Society of Chicago, 1973), 88; but see also Chapter 8, this volume.

11. Harold M. Mayer and Richard C. Wade, *Chicago: Growth of a Metropolis* (Chicago: University of Chicago Press, 1969), 120. This lavishly illustrated volume is the most authoritative source on Chicago's geographic history. Perry Duis, *Chicago: Creating New Traditions* (Chicago: Chicago Historical Society, 1976), notes that the elevator, "a product of New York, was a rarity in the low buildings of pre-fire Chicago. However, elevator technology had attained a high degree of refinement by the 1870s, just when Chicagoans had begun to rebuild. . . . [and was thus widely employed. A]s late as 1890 the *Tribune* could boast that the city had elevators that were half again as fast as those in New York, and more numerous than in any city in the world."

12. See, inter alia, Carl Condit, *The Rise of the Skyscraper* (Chicago: University of Chicago Press, 1952), 14–15, for an explanation of why the higher and more famous (and still standing) Monadnock Building (1891–93) does not really qualify as representing the "new" form. Others have even questioned whether the Home Insurance Building qualifies. One might note that Louis Sullivan, fleeing the depression of 1873 that had the East in thrall, moved to Chicago, where he was hired by Jenney.

13. Carol Willis, *Form Follows Finance: Skyscrapers and Skylines in New York and Chicago* (New York: Princeton Architectural Press, 1995), says this "ceiling moved up and down several times in response to pressures from the real estate industry" (52). But it must be noted here that Chicago imposed no limit on the height of buildings before 1893.

14. See Daniel Bluestone, "'A City under One Roof': Skyscrapers, 1880–1895," in *Constructing Chicago* (New Haven, Conn.: Yale University Press, 1991), 104–51. Bluestone's book is copiously illustrated and filled with details of dates and architects. However, to appreciate the true genius of Chicago architecture, Louis Sullivan, whether engaged in designing skyscrapers or more "lowly" forms, the reader is urged to savor the color illustrations in Nancy Frazier, *Louis Sullivan and the Chicago School* (London: Bison, 1991), which better convey Bluestone's thesis that this was an aesthetic that belied the usual stereotype of Chicago as a money-grubbing, tasteless town.

15. This reversal was achieved through the excavation of a canal "across the drainage divide between Lake Michigan and the Mississippi Basin. . . . To carry on this work, the Illinois legislature created the Sanitary District of Chicago in 1889. . . . Completed in only a decade . . . it opened in January 1900." Mayer and Wade, *Chicago,* 274.

16. Even today, the air traveler recognizes the location of the Loop by its special cloud cover, even when the atmosphere is clear farther out.

17. Given the high costs of generating and distributing, only the Loop was really served by this new means. "The sheer density and diversity of activity in the Loop created a special need for artificial illumination even during the day. . . . Air pollution became a chronic nuisance during the winter months . . . [and] extra lighting was needed by 4:00 P.M. . . . By 1881 the problem had become so severe that the city council passed a smoke-abatement ordinance, but this was left unenforced, and the situation only became worse after the advent of the skyscraper. During the 1880s these tall buildings turned downtown streets into gloomy canyons filled with smoke from morning to night." Harold L. Platt, *The Electric City: Energy and the Growth of the Chicago Area, 1880–1930* (Chicago: University of Chicago Press, 1991), 27–28. Platt provides a detailed and thoughtful account of the transformation electricity brought about in Chicago.

18. London-born Insull began his career in the firm that represented Thomas Edison's electric and telephone interests in England. Arriving in the United States in 1881 as private

secretary to Edison, he was eventually put in full charge of the inventor's various corporations. Appointed president of Chicago Edison and Commonwealth Electric Company in 1892, he soon controlled the entire electrical lighting system in the city. Later, he also served as chairman of the board of the Chicago Elevated Railway Company.

19. The elite would soon begin to transfer their allegiance to the zone later called the Gold Coast, just north of the Chicago River, but such a move could not take place until the flow of the North Branch of the Chicago River had been reversed. This transformed an unattractive and odorous effluent from the industrial quarters along its banks into a clean stream drawing fresh waters from the lake. The relocation of the elite eventually opened space on the near South Side, which then could serve as a nucleus of Chicago's "Black Belt."

20. "Most visitors agreed that the 'wondrous enchantment of the night illumination' was the White City's greatest spectacle. Providing over ten times as much artificial illumination as the Paris show four years earlier, the 1893 fair used over 90,000 incandescent bulbs and 5,000 arc lights." Platt, *The Electric City,* 62.

21. Teaford, *The Unheralded Triumph,* 201.

22. Mayer and Wade, *Chicago,* 118, 120. Sullivan himself was drawn to Chicago by this chance for commissions. Sam Bass Warner Jr., *The Urban Wilderness: A History of the American City* (New York: Harper & Row, 1972) 108, notes that speculators rebuilt the downtown office quarter with funds from the East.

23. Mayer and Wade, *Chicago,* 176.

24. Only tiny additions would be made up to 1915, and none thereafter. The best account of this process and the development of suburban Chicago is Ann Durkin Keating, *Building Chicago: Suburban Developers and the Creation of a Divided Metropolis* (Columbus: Ohio State University Press, 1988), from which Maps 5.2 and 5.3 are reprinted. On the resistance to annexation from the northern suburbs, see Michael H. Ebner, *Creating Chicago's North Shore: A Suburban History* (Chicago: University of Chicago Press, 1988), esp. chap. 5.

25. See Jaher, *The Urban Establishment,* 457–58 on transport and 475–76 on finance.

26. Ibid., 480.

27. Ibid., 460.

28. McCormick began making agricultural implements in 1848, Pullman organized his rail car business in 1859, and Crane started making plumbing fixtures in 1855. These were all locally run and funded firms. By 1890, "Chicago was second to New York in value of industrial production [and] . . . ranked first in agricultural implements, meat packing, railroad car building, tinware, foundries and machine shops, piano and organ works, and furniture making, and second in leather tanning, railroad shop and construction work, clothing and cooperage." Ibid., 473.

29. Ibid., 486–87.

30. Ibid., 475, 481–82, 486, 490.

31. See also the fine discussion in James Gilbert, *Perfect Cities: Chicago's Utopias of 1893* (Chicago: University of Chicago Press, 1991), which I read after this chapter was essentially completed.

32. Bancroft, *The Book of the Fair,* 47.

33. Burnham and Bennett, *Plan of Chicago,* 120.

34. Jaher calls the 1850s "a milestone in upper-class maturity. In this decade emerged the historical society, the academy of sciences, the first public art show, the musical union, Northwestern University, the old University of Chicago . . . , several hospitals and shelters for the dependent, and the Relief and Aid Society." *The Urban Establishment,* 468.

35. See ibid., 493–97 for discussion, esp. tables 3 and 4, p. 493, and 5 and 6, p. 496.

36. Postmodernity, in the sense of an eclectic pastiche of historic styles, was well under way by the nineteenth century.

37. Louis Sullivan, *The Autobiography of an Idea* (New York: Dover, 1956[1924]), 322.

38. Ibid., 324–25. It is impossible to resist quoting more, as Sullivan pounds home the theme of contagion and virus time and again. Thus he satirizes the crowds who came and admired the fair and then returned to their homes, "each one of them . . . permeated by the most subtle and slow-acting of poisons" (321). Just after the last sentence quoted in the text, he refers to the fair's style as having "penetrated deep into the constitution of the American mind, effecting there lesions significant of dementia" (325).

39. This phrase is from the most frequently quoted part of Burnham's exhortation to "make no little plans," but with my commentary in brackets.

40. "The first germs of *The Plan of Chicago* followed shortly after the close of the Columbian Exhibition," when "Burnham prepared plans for the development of a series of islands along the lakefront not unlike those included in the published plan some fifteen years later." Wilbert Hasbrouck, "Introduction," in Burnham and Bennett, *Plan of Chicago,* vi. But the text of the *Plan* is explicit enough. "The origin of the plan of Chicago can be traced directly to the World's Columbian Exhibition." Burnham and Bennett, *Plan of Chicago,* 4.

41. Burnham and Bennett, *Plan of Chicago,* 36–37.

42. Ibid.

43. Between the fair and the Chicago Plan, Burnham had "cashed in" on his fame in entrepreneurial fashion by setting up an enormous consulting firm (employing a staff of a hundred), so he was well prepared for his new assignment. In New York, he is best known for having designed the Flatiron Building (1903).

44. Perhaps some scholar has already had the time and patience to analyze this list in full, but I have not found such a source. Sampling by alphabetical order rather than every *n*th name is permissible in cases where ethnic or class oversampling by letter is unlikely.

45. This estimate was provided by Bion Arnold, the electrical engineer mentioned above, and appears in Burnham and Bennett, *Plan of Chicago,* 33. On the same page, James J. Hill is quoted as predicting that Chicago will become the largest city in the world, once the population on the Pacific coast has reached twenty million. I might point out that even by 1990, the city itself had fewer than three million residents, Cook County including Chicago had six million, and there were only eight million persons living in the entire census-delimited consolidated metropolitan statistical area (CMSA) extending to portions of three states. One finds today an echo of this strange combination of boosterism and panic in some of the less measured writings about Los Angeles.

46. Ibid., 124, emphasis added. This is the final sentence of the plan.

47. Arthur Schlesinger, *The Rise of the City: 1878–1898* (New York: Macmillan, 1933), 426. Some of Schlesinger's lines are vivid: 1894 was when "the tramp of the unemployed from all parts of the country upon Washington" had begun, and when "Eugene V. Debs, jailed in Chicago in 1894 for his activities during the Pullman strike, was reading socialist tracts" (426).

48. Stead's speech was reprinted in a widely disseminated book. See William Thomas Stead, *If Christ Came to Chicago! A Plea for the Union of All Who Love in the Service of All Who Suffer* (Chicago: Laird & Lee, 1894).

49. Allan H. Spear, *Black Chicago: The Making of a Negro Ghetto, 1890–1920* (Chicago: University of Chicago Press, 1967), 130.

50. For much of the following I have depended upon two sources. See Thomas Lee Philpott, *The Slum and the Ghetto: Immigrants, Blacks, and Reformers in Chicago, 1880–1930* (Belmont, Calif.: Wadsworth, 1991[1978]), 6, Table 1.1. Philpott decomposes the sources of

Chicago's population increase between 1830 and 1900 (7, Table 1.2), citing as his source not only the census returns but Homer Hoyt's *One Hundred Years of Land Values in Chicago* (Chicago: University of Chicago Press, 1933), 284, Table 30. A second valuable source is Wesley Skogan, "Chicago since 1840: A Time-Series Data Handbook" (unpublished manuscript, University of Illinois Institute of Government and Public Affairs, 1976), 18–20, Table 1.

51. Until 1900, Chicago's black population accounted for less than 2 percent of the total.

52. During the depressed period of the 1870s there had been a relative reduction in foreign immigration, and the proportion of foreign-born had decreased to a low of 41 percent in 1880. After the burst in the mid-1880s, the proportion would recover to 47 percent.

53. Again, my figures are taken from Philpott, *The Slum and the Ghetto,* but it should be acknowledged that they do not quite add up, possibly because of rounding. The proportion of foreign-born dropped back to 41 percent by 1890, but that figure is an artifact of boundary changes that inflated the larger base with 80,000 to 90,000 native-born people who had already been living in the newly incorporated suburban zones. The figures after 1885 are therefore deceptive and cannot be used to evaluate the role that immigration played in Chicago's history.

54. This apparent reversal is clearly an artifact of boundary changes. See note 53, above.

55. James E. Vance Jr., *The Continuing City: Urban Morphology in Western Civilization* (Baltimore: Johns Hopkins University Press, 1990), 328–29.

56. Ibid., 331–35.

57. Warner, *The Urban Wilderness,* 85. Warner's chapter titled "The Segregated City" deals with Chicago; it is subtitled "Chicago 1870–1920: Factories, Railroads, and Skyscrapers."

58. Ibid., 86–88. "In 1916 (ironically the year in which federal aid was first granted to highways) the nation's rail network reached its apogee: 254,000 miles of tracks, 77 percent of the intercity freight tonnage, 98 percent of the intercity passengers" (89). Philadelphia also experienced sudden development, but there the large-scale industrialized sector, stimulated by rail connections to Pennsylvania coal mines that made steam power a bargain, was superimposed upon earlier models such as those that continued to prevail in New York.

59. Ibid., 94. Among other sources, Warner cites Alfred D. Chandler Jr., *Railroads, the Nation's First Big Business* (New York: Harcourt, Brace & World, 1965); and Chandler's "The Beginnings of 'Big Business' in American Industry," *Business History Review* 33 (Spring 1959); as well as his *Strategy and Structure: Chapters in the History of the American Industrial Enterprise* (Cambridge: MIT Press, 1962); and Oscar Anderson Jr., *Refrigeration in America* (Princeton, N.J.: Princeton University Press, 1953).

60. Philpott, *The Slum and the Ghetto,* 6. It is interesting to contrast this with another well-known slogan—"If a man could make it in New York, he could make it anywhere!"

61. Skogan, "Chicago since 1840," 24–26, Table 2, based on government records.

62. Warner, *The Urban Wilderness,* 92, makes a similar comparison, although his figures diverge from Skogan's more reliable data on Chicago and Pratt's better information on New York, presented in the previous chapter. Warner's Table 2 (93), contrasting the "average number of employees per manufacturing establishment," shows Chicago well ahead by 1870, with an average of twenty-five workers per manufacturing plant, as contrasted with twenty in New York and only nine in preindustrial Los Angeles. He alleges that by 1919 the Chicago average had increased to forty-eight, compared with twenty-five in New York and twenty-three in Los Angeles. These discrepancies among sources, however, do not invalidate my general point about an increase in scale.

63. These industries are well described by William Cronon in his *Nature's Metropolis: Chicago and the Great West* (New York: W. W. Norton, 1991).

64. Pullman's "utopian" community was hailed by "a London newspaper in 1883 . . .

[as] 'the most perfect city in the world,'" according to Mayer and Wade, *Chicago,* 192, but they do not give the source for this quotation. In a decade it would be the site of one of Chicago's bloodiest labor battles. See Stanley Buder, *Pullman: An Experiment in Industrial Order and Community Planning, 1880–1930* (New York: Oxford University Press, 1967).

65. "Chicago was the dominant meatpacking center of the United States even before the establishment of the Union Stock Yards, surpassing Cincinnati in the slaughter of hogs as early as 1861. During the Civil War, many plants left the war zones and moved to Chicago." Prior to 1865 meatpackers were scattered, with most along the North Branch of the Chicago River. In the Civil War era they relocated on the South Branch, especially after the Union Stock Yards was established. See Dominic A. Pacyga, *Polish Immigrants and Industrial Chicago: Workers on the South Side, 1880–1922* (Columbus: Ohio State University Press, 1991), 27. The definitive source on the stockyards is Louise Carroll Wade, *Chicago's Pride: The Stockyards, Packingtown, and Environs in the Nineteenth Century* (Urbana: University of Illinois Press, 1987), from which much of my account is drawn. See especially Wade's discussion of nuisance regulations (29), effects of the Civil War (32), and the establishment of the Union Stock Yard and Transit Company (48–49).

66. See, inter alia, Alma Herbst, *The Negro in the Slaughtering and Meat-Packing Industry in Chicago* (Boston: Houghton Mifflin, 1932), 5n, based primarily on Andreas's masterful three-volume history of Chicago. The Herbst book has provided much of the following information. But see also Wade, *Chicago's Pride,* and the books by Pacyga, *Polish Immigrants,* on the Polish community back of the yards in the late nineteenth century and early twentieth centuries, and Thomas J. Jablonsky, *Pride in the Jungle: Community and Everyday Life in Back of the Yards Chicago* (Baltimore: Johns Hopkins University Press, 1993). Jablonsky's first chapter summarizes details on the origin and site of the yards. Another excellent source, published after I completed work on this chapter, is Rick Halpern, *Down on the Killing Floor: Black and White Workers in Chicago's Packinghouses, 1904–54* (Urbana: University of Illinois Press, 1997).

67. Figures on meat, lumber, garments, and iron and steel come from Wade, *Chicago's Pride,* 61. By the end of the 1870s, Swift was sending large quantities of frozen beef to the East in the new refrigerator rail cars and had even initiated a transatlantic trade in dressed beef.

68. See Jaher, *The Urban Establishment,* 483. Refrigeration not only expanded the number of by-products that could be produced but also leveled some of the seasonal variations of work. See Wade, *Chicago's Pride,* 105.

69. Herbst, *The Negro,* 6–11, 13.

70. Herbst, *The Negro,* xvi. Deliveries came by train and could not be perfectly scheduled, and given the seasonalities of the "crop," there were fluctuations in the numbers of laborers needed and in the length of the workdays, with layoffs or only part-time work available during slack periods. The use of the word *manned* in this quote is accurate; according to Herbst, 85 percent of all workers in the stockyards were male.

71. Pacyga, *Polish Immigrants,* 30–31.

72. Ibid., 83.

73. By 1907, due to a public outcry, the companies were required to report "all accidents ending in death or in the loss of thirty or more workdays to the Illinois State Bureau of Labor Statistics." Ibid., 91.

74. Wade, *Chicago's Pride,* 145.

75. A reinforcing factor, at least with regard to the "back-of-the-yards" zone next to the stockyards, was cheap housing. Because this area lay outside city limits, the construction of cheap wooden structures was permissible. A number of developers made their fortunes providing jerry-built shacks to packinghouse workers.

76. I take a position somewhat different from that taken by Ira Katznelson in his book *City Trenches: Urban Politics and the Patterning of Class in the United States* (New York: Pantheon, 1981). Katznelson argues that residential neighborhoods organized by ethnicity in the nineteenth century undercut the possibility of class solidarities forged at workplaces. Perhaps because his study focuses on upper Manhattan, he reaches conclusions that not only do not fit Chicago but do not even necessarily apply to lower Manhattan.

77. The sordid conditions of work there, and the heartless confrontations between powerless immigrant workers and their "elite" factory owners, are portrayed graphically in Upton Sinclair's "novel," *The Jungle,* published in 1906. Ironically, Sinclair came to Chicago for only seven weeks to prepare to write an exposé of worker exploitation in the stockyards. His intent was to critique the class system, not unsanitary practices in meat preparation. His novel gave him instant notoriety and has been credited with contributing to the passage of the first Pure Food and Drug Act. No one was more surprised by this reaction than Sinclair, who has been quoted as having remarked, "I aimed at the public's heart, and by accident hit it in the stomach."

78. The 1910 strike was not the first labor action in Chicago's garment trade. Chicago garment workers had begun to organize as early as 1886, and by 1890 the Chicago Cloak Makers' Union was formally chartered in Illinois, which set in motion a series of important strikes. See Wilfred Carsel, *A History of the Chicago Ladies' Garment Workers' Union* (Chicago: Normandie House, 1940).

79. I am passing over here the labor actions of railroad workers, who in Chicago, as elsewhere in the world, were among the first workers to stage strikes. In 1877, for example, a ten-day railway workers' strike in Chicago was dispersed by the army with great loss of life (twenty to thirty-five dead), and in 1885, a six-day strike of city transit workers left many injured.

80. I have depended on Skogan, "Chicago since 1840," 101–4, App. A, for much of this information.

81. Pacyga, *Polish Immigrants,* 15–16, emphasis added. Poles were also crowding into the jerry-built frame houses that had been hastily thrown up near the yards.

82. In this regard, see the excellent book by Eric L. Hirsch, *Urban Revolt: Ethnic Politics in the Nineteenth-Century Chicago Labor Movement* (Berkeley: University of California Press, 1990).

83. The introduction of strikebreakers, protected by civil and military forces, led to the defeat of union efforts in the strikes of 1886, 1894, 1904, and 1921.

84. Herbst, *The Negro,* 24, 27, emphasis added. Herbst reports that fifty of the black strikebreakers brought in by train had been recruited by a single agent who was paid a dollar a head. It is testimony to basic racism that in the earlier strike of 1894, when most scabs were "Poles," it was the very few blacks who became the chief targets of picketers' wrath. See the discussion later in this chapter of racism in Chicago.

85. An account far more sympathetic to the plight of blacks vis-à-vis unions is to be found in James Grossman, "The White Man's Union: The Great Migration and the Resonances of Race and Class in Chicago, 1916–1922," in *The Great Migration in Historical Perspective: New Dimensions of Race, Class and Gender,* ed. Joe William Trotter Jr. (Bloomington: Indiana University Press, 1991), 83–105. Grossman acknowledges that blacks resisted unionization, but claims that was not true before 1919 among the "old" black workers, who tended to join unions at about the same rate as whites. He argues that it was the "new" black migrants from the South who were most resistant, because their prior experience with white craft unions in the South, which totally excluded them, had made them very suspicious of such efforts (89). Indeed, Grossman concludes: "Whatever the benefits of unions, they were . . . 'no good for the

colored man.' *They were white institutions*" (97, emphasis added). The black community did not condemn black strikebreakers, and news of strikes was not covered in the *Chicago Defender,* the leading newspaper of the black community, because black elites were unsympathetic to unions.

86. Herbst, *The Negro,* 45.

87. Ibid., introduction.

88. Pacyga, *Polish Immigrants,* 233.

89. Ibid., 238. The 1937 strike took place at Republic Steel. It lasted ninety days and resulted in ten killed by attacking police.

90. The "classic" work on this is John Allswang, *A House for All Peoples: Ethnic Politics in Chicago, 1890–1936* (Lexington: University Press of Kentucky, 1971).

91. Teaford, *The Unheralded Triumph,* 22, emphasis added.

92. Ibid., 181.

93. Jaher, *The Urban Establishment,* 503.

94. Ibid., 505. The conservatism of these reformers was patent. They had supported and funded the use of the militia to break strikes, had opposed the eight-hour day, and, being anti-union, took a hard line against the Haymarket prisoners (506–7).

95. In all fairness, the number of immigrants was so much larger than the number of blacks in 1889, when Jane Addams founded Hull House, that this concentration on "Americanization" is quite understandable.

96. Skogan, "Chicago since 1840," Table 1. See also Philpott, *The Slum and the Ghetto,* 117, Table 5.1, who gives more detailed figures: the total grew from fifty-three in 1840 to several hundred by 1850, when blacks constituted only 1 percent of the population, and then its growth generally paralleled that of the white population, so that the proportion of blacks in the population never exceeded 2 percent up to 1910. By 1920, the proportion had increased to 4.1 percent and approached 6.9 percent by 1930.

97. At least this is what Dorsey argues. He points out that southern Illinois is actually *in* the South (as far south as Maryland, Virginia, and the northern part of North Carolina), and is close to Missouri and Kentucky, and that the "socio-cultural values in the region were essentially southern." James Dorsey, *Up South: Blacks in Chicago's Suburbs, 1719–1983* (Bristol, Ind.: Wyndham Hall, 1986), chap. 4.

98. Dorsey summarizes the earliest history of blacks in the state. He notes that when the French conquered the Mississippi Valley in the seventeenth century, many of the first pioneers were black, albeit slaves legally recognized by the French government in the eighteenth century as real property (ibid., 6). When the French ceded their Illinois territory to the English in 1763, they sold their slaves before departing. In 1778 Illinois became a part of Virginia, but was ceded to the U.S. government in 1784. Even though the 1787 Northwest Ordinance prohibited slavery and involuntary servitude in the Northwest Territory, old settlers continued to hold slaves, although they were euphemistically called lifetime indentured servants (7). "When the Illinois Territory separated from Indiana in 1809 it adopted the regulations concerning indentured servitude stipulated by the Indiana Territory . . . [in legislation] of 1803, 1805 and 1807" (8), which permitted the indenture of Negro males for up to thirty-five years and females up to thirty-two years, although some indentures might last as long as ninety-nine years. The Illinois state constitution of 1818 prohibited slavery but did not speak to the status of existing slaves (8).

99. Ibid., 10.

100. Philpott, *The Slum and the Ghetto,* 118–19.

101. Dorsey, *Up South,* 24.

102. Philpott, *The Slum and the Ghetto,* 120–21.

103. Ibid., 121. "The Black Belt, as people were already calling it, stretched southward from the downtown railroad yards to another block of railway property just below 39th Street. The broad embankment of the Rock Island Railroad sealed it from the working-class immigrant communities to the west, and the South Side Elevated Railroad walled it off from 'the white belt of aristocracy and wealth' to the east . . . . The tracks were racial barricades, but only because there were white people on the other side to man them. It was the color line, not any railroad line, that checked the free movement of Negroes. A train track was simply a convenient place to draw the line. *The railways were merely instruments of folkways.*" Ibid., 147–48, emphasis added.

104. Pacyga, *Polish Immigrants,* 213.

105. Philpott, *The Slum and the Ghetto,* 120.

106. Spear, *Black Chicago,* 13–14, Table 2.

107. Ibid., 129–30. The 1919 race riot was the chief culprit.

108. These figures are from Spear, *Black Chicago,* 151. Women's occupations changed less; by 1920 some 64 percent were still engaged in domestic service, although 15 percent now worked in factories. See also Spear's Table 12 (152–54).

109. Ibid., 140, 146.

110. The best source on all of this is Chicago Commission on Race Relations, *The Negro in Chicago: A Study of Race Relations and a Race Riot* (Chicago: University of Chicago Press, 1922), which is the source cited by Philpott (*The Slum and the Ghetto*) and Spear (*Black Chicago*) as well. African American sociologist Charles S. Johnson, who was trained at the University of Chicago, is generally credited with being the chief researcher and author of the Chicago Commission report. But see also William Tuttle Jr., *Race Riot: Chicago in the Red Summer of 1919* (New York: Illini, 1996 [1970]).

111. *Border wars* is my term for what would come to characterize race relations in the city through the 1950s and 1960s.

112. Spear, *Black Chicago,* 158.

113. Pacyga, *Polish Immigrants,* 214.

114. Ibid., 215–217.

115. Bronzeville was the name adopted by St. Clair Drake and Horace A. Cayton in their famous work *Black Metropolis: A Study of Negro Life in a Northern City* (Chicago: University of Chicago Press, 1993 [1945]). Because their book deals with the evolution of the community in the 1930s and early 1940s, I reserve discussion of it to Chapter 8. Among the institutions that relocated in the black community was the press; the publishers of the *Chicago Defender* bought their own printing plant on the South Side after the riot cut them off from their printers.

116. Spear, *Black Chicago,* 187.

117. Ibid., 192.

118. Warner, *The Urban Wilderness,* 108.

119. I am reminded here of Peter Marcuse's discussion of contemporary New York not as a dual but a "quartered" city. See Peter Marcuse, "'Dual City': A Muddy Metaphor for a Quartered City," *International Journal of Urban and Regional Research* 13 (December 1989). If I may extend his usage, by the 1920s, Chicago was split six ways: front- and backstage, white and black, and city and suburb.

120. By 1915, statistics showed that single-family homes had fallen to 10.8 percent of all new construction within the city.

121. Skogan, "Chicago since 1840," Table 3, shows that by 1910 there were fewer than

13,000 cars registered in the city. This number increased to 90,000 by 1920, 142,000 by 1921, and climbed steadily thereafter to reach almost 420,000 by 1930. And note that this did not even include the cars registered in suburban Cook County.

122. Barrett, *The Automobile and Urban Transit,* 6, 7.

123. Ibid., 14. The street traction company interests of Charles Tyson Yerkes were opposed by the reform, anticorruption Municipal Voters' League (20), but a city council request for unification and public ownership of the mass-transit system failed (28–29).

124. See ibid., 37–45.

125. Ibid., 212.

126. The major source for the following discussion is Ann Durkin Keating's fascinating book *Building Chicago.*

127. Ibid., 65–66.

128. Ibid., 67–68.

129. Ibid., 70–77.

130. See Devereux Bowly Jr., *The Poorhouse: Subsidized Housing in Chicago, 1895–1976* (Carbondale: Southern Illinois University Press, 1978). Wright's two-story apartment building, constructed around a courtyard, was torn down in 1974, but Bowly includes a picture of it. The background of this building reveals some very interesting connections. The developer was Edward Waller, who lived in River Forest (a suburb designed by Olmsted) across from a house that Wright had designed and that Waller admired. Waller was a friend of Daniel Burnham and was also the manager of the Rookery, an office building designed by Burnham and Root; in 1905 Wright was commissioned to redesign the Rookery's lobby.

131. Ibid., 8–10.

132. Ibid., 12–16. By this time, Marshall Field III was actually living in New York.

133. Wright's Robie house was completed in 1909, and many of his prairie masterpieces in Oak Park date from early in the century. Sullivan's last masterpiece in Chicago, the Babson house in Riverside, was built in 1907.

134. Saarinin's exquisite art deco entry in the Tribune Tower competition of the 1920s, for example, was rejected in favor of wedding-cake gothic.

135. This quotation from Duncan's *Culture and Democracy* (52) appears in the feisty tribute to Chicago by Kenan Heise, *The Chicagoization of America, 1893–1917* (Evanston, Ill.: Chicago Historical Bookworks, 1990), 67. Heise goes even further, claiming that true democracy was a Chicago invention. See Hugh D. Duncan, *Culture and Democracy: The Struggle for Form in Society and Architecture in Chicago* (Totowa, N.J.: Bedminster, 1965), 52; as well as Duncan's *The Rise of Chicago as a Literary Center from 1885 to 1920: A Sociological Essay in American Culture* (Totowa, N.J.: Bedminster, 1964). In addition, see Dale Kramer, *Chicago Renaissance: The Literary Life in the Midwest, 1900–1930* (New York: Appleton-Century, 1966).

136. Regarding Dreiser, see, inter alia, the comments of Carl S. Smith in his *Chicago and the American Literary Imagination, 1880–1920* (Chicago: University of Chicago, 1984). Mr. Dooley, with his heavy brogue and biting Irish wit, was the creation of Chicago journalist Finley Peter Dunne at the turn of the century.

137. The most impressive product of their research was the remarkable collection, chiefly by Addams and Kelley, titled *Hull-House Maps and Papers: A Presentation of Nationalities and Wages in a Congested District of Chicago, by Residents of Hull House, a Social Settlement,* which is no. 5 of the Library of Economics and Politics, edited by land economist Richard T. Ely (New York: Thomas Y. Crowell, 1895).

138. The first attempt to outline a research agenda for sociologists of the city is acknowledged to have been Robert E. Park's essay "The City: Suggestions for the Investigation of

Human Behavior in the City Environment," *American Journal of Sociology* 20 (March 1915): 577–612. A more mature formulation of the Chicago school, collected after various studies had been conducted, can be found in Robert Park and Ernest Burgess (with the assistance of Roderick McKenzie), eds., *The City* (Chicago: University of Chicago Press, 1967 [1925]). There has been a recent efflorescence of secondary literature on the Chicago school. See, for example, Fred H. Matthews, *Quest for an American Sociology: Robert E. Park and the Chicago School* (Montreal: McGill-Queen's University Press, 1977); Winifred Rauschenbush, *Robert E. Park: Biography of a Sociologist* (Durham, N.C.: Duke University Press, 1979); and Martin Bulmer, *The Chicago School of Sociology: Institutionalization, Diversity, and the Rise of Sociological Research* (Chicago: University of Chicago Press, 1984). Readers are encouraged to examine the original sources, however, as well as the old but still relevant commentary by a direct heir, Robert E. Faris, *Chicago Sociology: 1920–1932* (Chicago: University of Chicago Press, 1970).

139. A significant correction to the conventional androcentric account has been made by Mary Jo Deegan in her *Jane Addams and the Men of the Chicago School, 1892–1918* (New Brunswick, N.J.: Transactions, 1988). Selections from some of the writings of these women can be found in Patricia Madoo Lengermann and Jill Niebrugge-Brantley, eds., *The Women Founders: Sociology and Social Theory, 1830–1930* (New York: McGraw-Hill, 1998), 229–75.

140. These generalizations appeared in Ernest Burgess's early essay "The Growth of the City: An Introduction to a Research Project," *Proceedings of the American Sociological Society* 18 (1923): 85–97, later reprinted in Park and Burgess, *The City,* and more fully developed in Burgess's "The Determination of Gradients in the Growth of a City," *Publications of the American Sociological Society* 21 (1927): 178–84.

141. The sole exception, of course, was Charles S. Johnson (unacknowledged author of *The Negro in Chicago*).

6. LOS ANGELES BECOMES "ANGLO"

1. John Russell Taylor, *Strangers in Paradise: The Hollywood Émigrés 1933–1950* (London: Faber & Faber, 1983), 33.

2. Morris Markey, *This Country of Yours* (Boston, 1932), as quoted in Robert M. Fogelson, *The Fragmented Metropolis: Los Angeles, 1850–1930* (Berkeley: University of California Press, 1993[1967]), 3.

3. Los Angeles-area ports handle some 13.5 million raw tons of imported ship-borne freight and more than 11 million raw tons of shipped exports, according to U.S. Army Corps of Engineers, Navigation Data Center, Waterborne Commerce Statistics Center, *Annuals* of 1991 and 1992. Whereas import tonnages are only a third of those entering New York's ports (excluding New Jersey), export tonnages far exceed those of New York.

4. As we shall see, this situation has changed drastically, and Anglos have now reverted to a "minority" (see Chapter 12). Only in the Southwest is the peculiar term *Anglo* in general usage, although its sociological referent is increasingly unclear. In its broadest usage today, it can refer to any non-Hispanic, nonblack person—even one whose native language is not English.

5. See Reyner Banham, *Los Angeles: The Architecture of Four Ecologies* (London: Penguin, 1971). "Autopia" (the freeways) is his fourth ecology. Edward W. Soja has suggested that for the contemporary period one must add the explosive inner city and "exopolis" (the "outermost" zones not encompassed by Banham's classificatory scheme). See Soja's "Los Angeles 1965–1992: The Six Geographies of Urban Restructuring," in *Thirdspace: Journeys to Los Angeles and Other Real-and-Imagined Places* (Cambridge, Mass.: Blackwell, 1996).

In a chapter titled "Los Angeles against the Mountain" in his book *The Control of Nature* (New York: Farrar Straus Giroux, 1989), 183–272, John McPhee deals with tensions between building on mountain slopes and the resultant land slides and floods. From the dust jacket copy: "Some of the more expensive real estate in Los Angeles is up against the mountains that are . . . disintegrating [from landslides] as rapidly as any in the world. . . . Plucking up trees and cars, bursting through doors and windows, filling up houses to their eaves, debris flows threaten the lives of people living in or near Los Angeles' famous canyons. At extraordinary expense the city has built a hundred and fifty stadium-like basins in a daring effort to catch the debris." The winter of 1995 gave ample proof of the failure of those efforts.

6. See Steven Erie, "The Local State and Economic Growth in Los Angeles, 1880–1932," *Urban Affairs Quarterly* 27, no. 4 (1992): 519–54. Erie notes that the "West's early embrace of . . . direct democracy made voters key actors in early-twentieth-century urban development policy" (524). The point is that voter referenda on policy issues were routinely held in western states, including California, although they were rare in the East and Midwest. This frequent recourse to direct democracy curtailed the power of elected legislators and executives, although, as we shall see, voters could still be manipulated by them.

7. Arthur Schlesinger, *The Rise of the City 1878–1898* (New York: Franklin Watts, 1975 [1933]), quotations extracted from 34–43.

8. "Under the provisions of the Homestead Act of 1862 a settler could acquire up to 160 acres of surveyed public domain. . . . The Desert Land Act of 1877 authorized the federal government to sell up to 320 acres of desert land to settlers at $1.25 an acre. In turn, settlers were obliged to irrigate their properties within three years. The Carey Land Act of 1894 authorized the federal government to turn over to each state up to one million acres of desert lands to be disposed of under the provisions of the Desert Land Act of 1877." Kevin Starr, *Material Dreams: Southern California through the 1920's* (New York: Oxford University Press, 1990), 25–26.

9. Erie, "The Local State and Economic Growth," 521.

10. "Before the New Deal, cities financed their public infrastructure and utilities almost exclusively with long-term general obligation bonds sold to Wall Street underwriters and investment syndicates. . . . Resource- and capital-poor western cities like Los Angeles were particularly dependent upon public financing for their infrastructures." Ibid., 522.

11. This chronology is based on material in Robert Mayer, ed., *Los Angeles: A Chronological and Documentary History, 1542–1976* (Dobbs Ferry, N.Y.: Oceana, 1978).

12. It seems that this applies only to the wealthiest landowners who had been given land grants from the Mexican government; most others owned no land but lived and worked on the ranches of the wealthy.

13. Howard Nelson, *The Los Angeles Metropolis* (Dubuque, Iowa: Kendall/Hunt, 1983), 146. This is a basic source on Los Angeles history.

14. Ibid., 146–47.

15. Ernest Marquez, *Port Los Angeles: A Phenomenon of the Railroad Era* (San Marino, Calif.: Golden West, 1975), 1. Here we see the "political economy" system of Los Angeles in clear view. After Banning was elected to the State Senate, he introduced the first railroad bill and "pushed through a Los Angeles bond issue to finance . . . the Los Angeles & San Pedro Railroad," in which he was one of the principal owners. He also used his influence to get the U.S. Army Corps of Engineers to survey San Pedro, which led to an appropriation of $200,000 used to remove the sandbar and to deepen the channel. See Charles Queenan, *The Port of Los Angeles: From Wilderness to World Port* (Los Angeles: Los Angeles Harbor Department, 1983), 30; see also John W. Robinson, *Southern California's First Railroad: The Los Angeles and San Pedro Railroad* (Los Angeles: Dawson's Bookstore, 1978).

16. The relationship between the county and city governments of Los Angeles is also deviant, because from the start the former exercised far more power than the governments of

most counties; the city, fully contained within the county but never becoming coterminous with it, was therefore only one of the players in the region's fate, although admittedly now more of an equal.

Queenan, *The Port of Los Angeles,* 33, actually calls the actions of the Southern Pacific "blackmail." Mike Davis tells this story with sarcastic elan in his *City of Quartz: Excavating the Future in Los Angeles* (New York: Vintage, 1992). There are interesting parallels between the political intrigues that led rail lines to favor Chicago over Galena as the terminus for rail lines at midcentury and the ones that selected Los Angeles over San Diego a generation later.

17. Marquez, *Port Los Angeles,* 1.

18. Ibid., 4, 7.

19. Ibid., 11, 14. On the very day the Los Angeles & Independence Railroad line was completed, the "Southern Pacific suddenly reduced its . . . shipping rates by half. The next day, when the new railroad opened for business, the Southern Pacific slashed its rates even more." Queenan, *The Port of Los Angeles,* 39.

20. Marquez, *Port Los Angeles,* 14–23. Ironically, at a later date the Southern Pacific would seek to exploit its access to Santa Monica by arguing that federal funds should be made available to create a central port there. But by then Southern Pacific's power had been broken, and local officials, who favored San Pedro (over which they could exercise greater control), won the coveted federal investment.

21. Erie, "The Local State and Economic Growth," 525, 527. But see also Davis, *City of Quartz,* 110–14, for a somewhat more complex treatment of the "ruling elite."

22. The full story of the San Diego–Los Angeles rivalry is well told in Fogelson, *The Fragmented Metropolis,* 43–62.

23. Ibid., 62.

24. Massive floods in the winter of 1861, followed by a prolonged several-season drought, had cut short an earlier real estate "boom." The new ranchers and farmers who had begun so hopefully went bankrupt, and the "possession of southern California's ranches passed to a few prominent Los Angeles and San Francisco capitalists." See ibid., 17. Nevertheless, after the Civil War, ranches were already being subdivided into building plots. "By 1877, according to the Los Angeles *Express,* there were 'but a few of the old ranches that have not been cut up' in Los Angeles and vicinity." Ibid., 19.

25. This figure comes from the U.S. Census of 1880, as reproduced in ibid., 21, Table 1. However, because of the still small perimeter of the city prior to the annexations that would expand it so dramatically in the twentieth century, there were twice as many residents living in the county outside those boundaries as in the city itself. The county population in 1880 was almost 33,400. In the discussion that follows I try to distinguish clearly between these two entities, which sources often tend to confuse.

26. Ibid., 39. See also Glenn S. Dumke, *The Boom of the Eighties in Southern California* (San Marino, Calif.: Huntington Library, 1944).

27. It may be a significant coincidence that large quantities of oil first began to flow in Los Angeles in that year.

28. See Fogelson, *The Fragmented Metropolis,* 79, Table 5, which is based on successive U.S. Censuses.

29. Fogelson indicates that 21.4 percent of the native-born residents of Los Angeles in 1890 hailed from the East North-Central states and another 12.6 percent from the West North-Central states. The Middle Atlantic states accounted for 12.4 percent, and no other regions made noteworthy contributions. Ibid., 81, Table 8. It should also be noted that before

1930, persons of Mexican descent were classified as "white" by the Census Bureau. The number of nonwhites was very small in 1890: only 1,250 "Negroes" and fewer than 2,000 Asians.

30. Nelson, *The Los Angeles Metropolis,* 155–57. Chicagoans will recognize the nostalgia that led Angelenos to name many streets and sections after streets and suburbs of that city. Thus there is a Highland Park, a Winnetka Avenue, and so on. But then there are also streets called Detroit and Genessee, and in Boyle Heights, now the heart of one Chicano zone, the main thoroughfare is called Brooklyn. These references to places of origin are randomly intermixed with the more common nomenclatures of Spanish origin.

31. Ibid., 158.

32. The California Building at the Chicago World's Fair of 1893 was a large and somewhat grotesque (postmodern?) composite of "mission" styles, but the propaganda contained in it seemed to be effective. See the photo in Fogelson, *The Fragmented Metropolis,* 71.

33. Ibid., 70; Fogelson's observations are based on Chamber of Commerce files.

34. For a harrowing account of one Ponzi scheme of speculative investments in oil, see Jules Tygiel's fascinating book *The Great Los Angeles Swindle: Oil, Stocks, and Scandal during the Roaring Twenties* (New York: Oxford University Press, 1994).

35. Marquez, *Port Los Angeles,* 26.

36. The relations between the United States and each of these "conquered" territories differed. Cuban independence was granted shortly after the war; Puerto Rico was governed for a long time by an American military governor; and the Philippines was treated as an American "trustee territory," slated for eventual independence.

37. Symbolic of California's central importance to the federal government, the signal to begin dumping the first bargeload of stone for the breakwater was given by President McKinley in Washington, D.C.; McKinley pushed a button at a prearranged time. Queenan, *The Port of Los Angeles,* 59.

38. Ibid., 77. The port facilities in the independent town of Long Beach still lagged behind (78), although it would eventually become the chief port for oil and a heavily industrialized zone.

39. Ibid., 81.

40. See also Clarence Matson, *Building a World Gateway: The Story of Los Angeles Harbor* (Los Angeles: 1945); Charles F. Queenan, *Long Beach and Los Angeles: A Tale of Two Ports* (Northridge, Calif.: Windsor, 1986).

41. Howard J. Nelson and William A. V. Clark, *The Los Angeles Metropolitan Experience: Uniqueness, Generality, and the Goal of the Good Life* (Cambridge, Mass.: Ballinger, 1976), 33.

42. Ibid., 34.

43. According to Table 6.1, which is based on Arthur G. Coons and Arjay Miller, "An Economic and Industrial Survey of the Los Angeles and San Diego Areas" (California State Planning Board, mimeo, 1941), the percentage of white native-born dropped in Los Angeles County from 80 percent in 1900 to 78 percent in 1910 and again in 1920, to 76 percent in 1930, but note how Mexicans were reclassified. Although there appears to have been a drop in the proportion of native-born whites by 1930, this drop is more than adequately accounted for by the reclassification of Mexicans. I would estimate that at no time during the first three decades of the twentieth century was the proportion of native-born whites lower than 75 percent, once those of Mexican descent are omitted. There is a discrepancy in Coons and Miller that I have not been able to resolve: they state that by 1930, 87 percent of the population in Los Angeles and its adjoining counties was white (both native-born and foreign-born), 9.1 percent were Mexican (both native and foreign-born), African Americans were 1.9 percent, and Japanese 1.5 percent (53).

44. Kern County, still largely agricultural and sparsely populated, was included in the Los Angeles CMSA in 1990 but has been omitted from the table.

45. Fogelson, *The Fragmented Metropolis,* 86.

46. Ibid., 89.

47. Scott L. Bottles, *Los Angeles and the Automobile: The Making of the Modern City* (Berkeley: University of California Press, 1987), 183. As Banham, *Los Angeles,* has pointed out, the routes determined, to a remarkable degree, the outlines of the future freeway system.

48. Marc A. Weiss, *The Rise of the Community Builders: The American Real Estate Industry and Urban Land Use Planning* (New York: Columbia University Press, 1987), 107–40, covers the development of subdivision regulations in California; see esp. 109–10.

49. Ibid., 18, 20.

50. Ibid., 80. See also Fogelson, *The Fragmented Metropolis,* 145–46, 200. Such deed restrictions were scarcely benign and were often used to exclude "undesirable" (read "minority") elements from the settlement. Indeed, the U.S. Supreme Court decision that made racially restrictive deeds unenforceable (*Shelley v. Kraemer,* 334 U.S. 1, 1948) grew out of a Los Angeles case. General zoning, of course, lay in the future, although some primitive experiments in prohibiting certain uses (hand laundries, for instance) succeeded in excluding certain people (Chinese, for example).

51. Weiss, *The Rise of the Community Builders,* 31–41.

52. See Fogelson, *The Fragmented Metropolis,* 146, Table 17. The preponderance of single-family homes was also a function of the city's recent development. As Bottles points out, "Fully 96 percent of . . . [its] housing stock was built after the turn of the century." *Los Angeles and the Automobile,* 187.

53. A traffic survey conducted in 1924 showed 1.2 million persons per day entering the CBD. Fogelson, *The Fragmented Metropolis,* 147.

54. Bottles, *Los Angeles and the Automobile,* 194–95. The main artery of this CBD was Broadway, which today caters to an almost exclusively "Mexican" clientele.

55. Ibid., 192–94.

56. Ibid., 194. Ten years later, the city center could claim only a 54 percent market share of department store revenue, and "by 1956, downtown department stores could muster only 23 percent of all department store sales in the county" (196).

57. See ibid., 196–97; Fogelson, *The Fragmented Metropolis,* 148.

58. See Starr, *Material Dreams,* 8–12. "By the late 1870s a comprehensive water plan encompassing both irrigation and flood control had clearly emerged as a necessity for California" (6). Efforts began in San Francisco. In the 1880s a massive multivolume study was made of the water resources and needs of the state. Titled *Physical Data and Statistics of California and Irrigation Development,* it was prepared under the direction of William Hammond Hall, but the focus was lost when Hall resigned in 1889 to join the U.S. Geological Survey.

59. Not until 1906 were legal problems cleared to secure the aqueduct's right of way.

60. The film *Chinatown* implanted the "noir" conspiratorial scenario in most novices' minds, but it has many inaccuracies. The most comprehensive and measured source on the aqueduct is William L. Kahrl, *Water and Power: The Conflict over Los Angeles' Water Supply in the Owens Valley* (Berkeley: University of California Press, 1982). Kahrl treads a careful line between two polarized positions: one emphasizes skullduggery and conspiracy and is favored by most critics, including Mike Davis; the other tends to whitewash the aqueduct decision makers and builders and is favored by civic boosters and Kevin Starr (who Davis dismisses simply as a "Whig" historian). Although Starr is devastatingly critical of developments in the Imperial Valley, he is more sympathetic to the achievement represented by the Los Angeles aqueduct.

(See Starr, *Material Dreams,* chap. 3, titled "Aqueduct Cities: Foundations of Urban Empire.") John Walton, *Western Times and Water Wars: State, Culture, and Rebellion in California* (Berkeley: University of California Press, 1991), in contrast, focuses somewhat sympathetically on the resistance of the people of the Owens Valley to the "theft" of their land/water rights. The most laudatory and intimate portrait of Mulholland is Margaret Leslie Davis's *Rivers in the Desert: William Mulholland and the Inventing of Los Angeles* (New York: HarperCollins, 1993). Her account paints Eaton as the villain (he bought up land in Owens Valley as a site for a reservoir and then asked such an outrageous price that the reservoir site had to be changed) and Mulholland as a solid citizen visionary and self-taught technocrat who ended in disgrace when the St. Francis Dam collapsed and he was held culpable; rumors were that it had been dynamited by disgruntled Owens Valleyites, but the jury's conclusion was inadequate engineering. Mulholland died a broken man.

61. Starr explains that "two-thirds of all precipitation fell in the northern third of the state. Only 11 percent of the rainfall fell south of the Tehachapis. Given the 65 percent loss rate [through evaporation by the sun or runoff into the sea], Southern California was left with a small percent of the state's natural water supply, and even this was endangered by frequent bouts of drought." *Material Dreams,* 1.

62. Ibid., 46.

63. Ibid., 46–47.

64. This was not the first: "Two private surveys performed in 1885 and 1891 . . . had shown it would be technically possible to construct a canal running 235 miles between the two regions [Owens Valley and Los Angeles] in which water would flow entirely by gravity." Kahrl, *Water and Power,* 47; Kahrl cites Mulholland's testimony before the Aqueduct Investigation Board as his source.

65. Ibid., 54–64; Starr, *Material Dreams,* 49–53.

66. Starr, *Material Dreams,* 51. It should be noted that as early as the 1930s, before the city reached this size, additional water would have to be tapped from the Hoover Dam across the Colorado River and transported over an even longer distance than that from Owens Valley to Los Angeles.

67. Ibid., 52.

68. Ibid., 53. By 1910, with a third of the project to go, the money ran out. It was eventually saved by a syndicate of New York financiers who agree to purchase new bonds.

69. Ibid., 58, 59.

70. Air service between Los Angeles and New York began in 1929; the journey took thirty-six hours and required an overnight stop. On the automotive, chemical, and trucking industries, see Fred W. Viehe, "Black Gold Suburbs: The Influence of the Extractive Industry on the Suburbanization of Los Angeles, 1890–1930," *Journal of Urban History* 8, no. 1 (1981): 3–26, esp. 13.

71. Queenan, *The Port of Los Angeles,* 77.

72. Ibid., 69. See ibid., 69–91, on the 1921–45 period.

73. Coons and Miller, "An Economic and Industrial Survey," xix.

74. Ibid., 86ff., Table 20, my calculations. A relatively low percentage of service sector employees were listed as domestic servants, but this may be due to their omission or undercounting.

75. The fascinating memoirs of an early cameraman can be found in Charles Clarke, *Early Film Making in Los Angeles* (Los Angeles: Dawson's Book Shop, 1976); see 9–10 for early history.

76. One of the first two films shown in that first theater was Edison's *Blizzard Scenes in New York.* See ibid., 13.

77. This was preceded by some shorts made in an amusement-park precursor of Disneyland—such exciting adventures as *The Pigeon Farm at Los Angeles,* followed by one showing an ostrich farm. Also filmed were a fiesta parade and the Santa Monica road races. Ibid., 17–18.

78. Ibid., 19.

79. Ibid., 22. But Griffith's real moneymaker came in 1915 with the release of *The Birth of a Nation,* twelve reels based on the novel *The Clansman* (see ibid., 46). This film is notorious for its antiblack racism.

80. Neal Gabler, *An Empire of Their Own: How the Jews Invented Hollywood* (New York: Crown, 1988), 1. It should be pointed out, however, that the first pioneers of the industry were mostly Anglo-Saxon. Only later, in the 1930s, did Jews gain prominence.

81. See, for example, Taylor's *Strangers in Paradise,* which concentrates on the importation of musical, writing, acting, and directing talent from Europe (especially from the 1930s on, when Hitler helped precipitate the flight of many, Jews and non-Jews alike) as well as on the communities these exiles formed and how they influenced American film culture. See also Otto Friedrich's *City of Nets: A Portrait of Hollywood in the 1940's* (New York: Harper & Row, 1986).

82. The 1912 figure is from Clarke, *Early Film Making,* 29; the 1939 figure is from Coons and Miller, "An Economic and Industrial Survey," xx.

83. Clarke, *Early Film Making,* 19–20.

84. Erie, "The Local State and Economic Growth," 539.

85. Viehe, "Black Gold Suburbs," 3, emphasis added.

86. Ibid., 6. "The presence of a nearby oil field usually increased a suburb's revenues and decreased its tax rate dramatically. . . . By the 1920s it was reported that 'Orange County practically lives off oil' [Viehe cites "Taxing Oil Properties," *Oil Age* (August 1919): 2, here]. . . . The obvious economic benefits provided by the presence of the oil industry encouraged the suburbs to incorporate and to include the oil fields within their boundaries" (7).

87. The case of Beverly Hills is particularly interesting because it illustrates almost all of the twists and turns of land history. Brendan Gill, in his "Reflections: The Horizontal City," *New Yorker,* September 15, 1980, 109–46, describes this "city of just under six square miles existing within the boundaries of Los Angeles but totally independent of it . . . as pretty and artificial as if it had been made out of spun sugar" (113). He claims that the "history of Beverly Hills amounts to a capsule history of the entire Los Angeles area" (113). Its original settler, Maria Rita Valdez, had an official land grant from the Mexican government to a ranch of more than four thousand acres, which she lost when American soldiers captured Los Angeles, broke into her home, and stole the trunk containing her deed. Although a U.S. court later restored Valdez's property to her, she soon sold it to Anglo land developers for very little money (113). The ranch then changed hands several times. When the railroads stimulated the building boom of the 1880s, "real estate speculators arranged for a train station to be built . . . with the intention of founding a town, Morocco . . . [but it] never got beyond being a fancy drawing on the speculators' office wall" (116). Finally, Burton Green, a director of the Amalgamated Oil Company, "called on a New York landscape architect named Wilbur Cook to lay out a model town [which he called Beverly Hills because he liked the name]. . . . The town was incorporated in 1914, with a population of five hundred and fifty . . . [and] prospered . . . thanks to the arrival of the so-called 'movie people' from adjacent Hollywood" (117).

88. Viehe, "Black Gold Suburbs," 11.

89. Donald Teruo Hata Jr. and Nadine Ishitani Hata, "Asian-Pacific Angelinos: Model Minorities and Indispensable Scapegoats," in *20th Century Los Angeles: Power, Promotion, and Social Conflict,* ed. Norman Klein and Martin J. Schiesl (Claremont, Calif.: Regina, 1990), 65.

90. Thomas Muller, *Immigrants and the American City* (New York: New York University Press, 1993), 35. Muller gives the high estimate of 150,000 (27), although Hata and Hata, "Asian-Pacific Angelinos," 68, suggest it was only around 75,000. I have not bothered to resolve this (unimportant for our purposes) inconsistency.

91. Hata and Hata, "Asian-Pacific Angelinos," 68.

92. Nelson and Clark, *The Los Angeles Metropolitan Experience,* 36.

93. The literature is weak on the early history of African Americans in the city. Some disappointing book-length histories of blacks in California exist, including Rudolph M. Lapp, *Afro-Americans in California,* 2d ed. (San Francisco: Boyd & Fraser, 1987), a thin account; and B. Gordon Wheeler, *Black California: The History of African-Americans in the Golden State* (New York: Hippocrene, 1993), which suffers from a dilemma common to the genre. By stressing that the "Mexican" settlers who exploited and destroyed the Indians were actually mostly blacks and mestizos, Wheeler is in the awkward position of "restoring" the reputation of this group at the same time that he associates it with the worst western practices. Several sociological studies of the black community in Los Angeles during the first half of the twentieth century exist, but none is as rich as the literature on the black community in either New York or Chicago. See, for example, two early unpublished theses: J. McFarline Ervin, "The Participation of the Negro in the Community Life of Los Angeles" (University of Southern California, 1931), which is thin and amateurish; and the far more sophisticated benchmark study by J. Max Bond, "The Negro in Los Angeles" (University of Southern California, 1936), on which subsequent writers have depended heavily. The post-1930 period is not much better served. Lawrence de Graaf's *Negro Migration to Los Angeles, 1930 to 1950* (San Francisco: R. & E. Research Associates, 1974), originally a 1962 doctoral dissertation at the University of California, Los Angeles, and de Graaf's classic article "The City of Black Angels: Emergence of the Los Angeles Ghetto, 1890–1930," *Pacific Historical Review* 39, no. 3 (1970): 323–52, are among the basic sources. His dissertation on migration was "updated" by Keith E. Collins in *Black Los Angeles: The Maturing of the Ghetto, 1940–1950* (Saratoga, Calif.: Century Twenty One Publishing, 1980). Most recently, the cultural "scene" on Central Avenue, Los Angeles's closest although miniature parallel to Harlem in the 1920s and 1930s, has been explored in Anthony Sweeting's dissertation, "The Dunbar Hotel and Central Avenue Renaissance" (Department of Theater Arts, University of California, Los Angeles, 1992). The sources mentioned copy freely from one another.

94. Bottles, *Los Angeles and the Automobile,* 182.

95. Nelson and Clark, *The Los Angeles Metropolitan Experience,* 36. The Supreme Court case that in 1948 would invalidate racial restrictive covenants centered on this Slauson Street "line."

96. Du Bois is quoted in Lonnie G. Bunch III, "A Past Is Not Necessarily a Prologue: The Afro-American in Los Angeles since 1900," in *20th Century Los Angeles: Power, Promotion, and Social Conflict,* ed. Norman Klein and Martin J. Schiesl (Claremont, Calif.: Regina, 1990), 101.

97. Ibid., 105.

98. Ervin, "The Participation of the Negro," 25–26.

99. The literature on Hispanics in Los Angeles, almost exclusively Mexican before the most recent era, is far richer than that for either Asians or blacks.

100. Bottles, *Los Angeles and the Automobile,* 182.

101. Armando Morales, *Ando Sangrando (I Am Bleeding): A Study of Mexican American–Police Conflict* (La Puente, Calif.: Perspectiva, 1972), 13–14. Morales faces a dilemma similar to that faced by black pride writers such as Wheeler, but he deplores the harm done to native peoples while distancing himself by referring to the early conquerors as "Spanish."

102. Gloria E. Miranda, "The Mexican Immigrant Family: Economic and Cultural

Survival in Los Angeles, 1900–1945," in *20th Century Los Angeles: Power, Promotion, and Social Conflict,* ed. Norman Klein and Martin J. Schiesl (Claremont, Calif.: Regina, 1990), 41. On the Pueblo, see, inter alia, Richard Griswold del Castillo, *The Los Angeles Barrio, 1850–1890* (Berkeley: University of California Press, 1979); and on East Los Angeles, see Ricardo Romo, *East Los Angeles: History of a Barrio* (Austin: University of Texas Press, 1983), although this source also contains valuable information on the Plaza core and other more decentralized enclaves, such as Watts.

103. I use the term Mexican to refer both to the original "Mexican" population and their descendants and post-1850 immigrants from Mexico and their descendants, whether legal, naturalized, or not. Although this is sloppy demography, for this early period it is defensible sociologically, because neither Anglos nor Mexicans seem to have made finer distinctions in their dealings with one another.

104. According to Carey McWilliams, *Southern California: An Island on the Land* (Salt Lake City: Peregrine Smith, 1990 [1946]), 57, the term *greaser* goes back to the old "hide and tallow" trade long before California was conquered, when New Englanders used it to refer to the "darker peoples" who loaded the loathsome hides onto their clipper ships. (McWilliams's book stands as the classic social history of Los Angeles, and has done so since its original publication in 1946.)

105. Morales, *Ando Sangrando,* 10–12.

106. Ibid., 15.

107. East Los Angeles, however, because it refused to annex to the city, did develop an independent power base for Chicanos that could later be directed to county politics.

108. Erie, "The Local State and Economic Growth."

109. Ibid., 519–20. It was not until the Depression that this strategy failed, because "plummeting property values reduced the city's bonding capacity." But by that time the New Deal and a shift to federally sponsored projects was occurring. Ibid., 549–50.

110. Ibid., 520.

111. In *City of Quartz,* Davis stresses the power of the Chandlers but does not draw this connection. I return to this issue in Chapter 9 when I examine Upton Sinclair's unsuccessful bid for the California governorship in 1934.

112. See McWilliams, *Southern California,* 274–83.

113. Erie, "The Local State and Economic Growth," 523.

114. Indeed, the political party became progressively less important over time, especially given that the number of elected officers was so small. Reappraisal of the Progressive Era in California is the subject of William Deverell and Tom Sitton, eds., *California Progressivism Revisited* (Berkeley: University of California Press, 1994).

115. Gill, "Reflections," 122.

116. The best source on the evolution of their style remains Randell L. Makinson, *Greene & Greene: Architecture as a Fine Art* (Salt Lake City: Peregrine Smith, 1977). Because, like Wright, Greene & Greene also designed interiors and built the furnishings, an essential companion volume is Randell L. Makinson, *Greene & Greene: Furniture and Related Designs* (Salt Lake City: Peregrine Smith, 1979). Although to the end the Greenes continued to work in wood, supplemented by brick and stone, Frank Lloyd Wright gradually abandoned these materials, which he had favored in his Midwest home, substituting concrete after he moved to Los Angeles in 1923. (See especially the Hollyhock, Millard, and Ennis houses.) Eventually, Wright's son, originally trained by the Olmsted brothers as a landscape architect, began designing on his own. Gill, "Reflections," 130–32.

117. For strict accuracy it must be stressed that Spanish influence predated the "mission

revival." According to an article that appeared in an issue of the *Los Angeles Times* in 1995, the Catholic Church was a continuing influence on architecture of the city: the finest example is St. Vibiana's Cathedral, which was dedicated in 1876. The cathedral's architect modeled St. Vibiana's on the Church of Puerto de San Miguel in Barcelona, Spain, the original home of Los Angeles's bishop.

118. At least one set of architectural historians connects Gill's work with both the arts and crafts movement and "modern" architecture. See David Gebhard and Robert Winter, *Architecture in Los Angeles* (Salt Lake City: Peregrine, 1985). They note sadly, "Unfortunately, Gill was almost a prophet without honor . . . and what has happened to most of his buildings forms a sorry chapter in the history of the destruction of the usable past" (16). I agree.

119. A number of these houses were moved to Echo Park, an otherwise largely working-class Mexican American area, when Bunker Hill was cleared to absorb the new governmental civic/cultural complex that now stands in soulless isolation on that height. In 1968 the "Angel's Flight" funicular that previously connected the Pueblo to Bunker Hill was boarded up (after sixty-eight years of operation) when the Bunker Hill urban renewal project began, with a promise that it would be reopened by 1972. It was not. Finally, in 1997–98, the short line was reconstructed.

120. The best source on art deco in Los Angeles is of course Carla Breeze's *L.A. Deco* (New York: Rizzoli, 1991), although much of what she calls art deco might better be called art nouveau or "moderne." Incidentally, there is a book on art deco architecture in Miami (which was growing at the same time as Los Angeles) that refers to that architecture as "tropical art deco," so perhaps a distinction needs to be made between low-rise stucco art deco (or nouveau) and skyscraper art deco. The acknowledged masterpiece of skyscraper art deco is the building that for years housed Bullocks Wilshire.

121. See Don Vlack, *Art Deco Architecture in New York 1920–1940* (New York: Harper & Row, 1974), especially the list by addresses, 151–74.

122. The explanation might look like this: Richardson, Sullivan, Holabird, Root, and others established a style of extremely "heavy" structures, even for skyscrapers, which did not so much "float" as "soar" from very solid bases. Their construction material was also "heavy"—mostly stone or stone-faced brick—although surface decorations were elaborate (Morris style, even though "modernized"—e.g., the Stock Exchange room as well as other structures designed by Sullivan). To this must be added "gothic," which was viewed as the alternative to "modern." The "kiss of death" to art deco possibilities in Chicago may have been given in the 1922 contest for the design of the Chicago Tribune Building. What is fascinating is that, although the design selected was a gothic wedding cake (much on the order of McKim's Municipal Building in New York), there was at least one design, submitted by Eliel Saarinen, that could be called art deco. Although clearly a masterpiece, it was rejected. Soon afterward, Frank Lloyd Wright submitted a design for the National Life Insurance Building at 830 North Michigan (project design 1924) that was also rejected. Other architects, aware of how such wonderful designs had been received, may have been discouraged from pursuing this style when they worked on other Chicago buildings. A good source on this subject is John Stamper, *Chicago's North Michigan Avenue: Planning and Development, 1900–1930* (Chicago: University of Chicago Press, 1991), which reproduces the unexecuted designs of Saarinen and Wright. In this copiously illustrated study of the buildings put up on North Michigan Avenue in the 1920s, only one comes close to art deco, namely, the building Holabird and Root did at 333 North Michigan Avenue, and it is a very modest effort. The only true art deco structure actually constructed was the Union Carbide and Carbon Building at 230 North Michigan, which Stamper calls the "last high-rise office building erected on North Michigan in the

1920s." It was designed by the Burnham brothers, but its acceptance as a design dates back to 1928, just after this New York–based company had already signed up as the major tenant. So perhaps it was because of different tastes in New York that this rare exception got built.

123. Frederic Cople Jaher, *The Urban Establishment: Upper Strata in Boston, New York, Charleston, Chicago and Los Angeles* (Urbana: University of Illinois Press, 1982), 526–27.

124. Gill, "Reflections," 133–34.

125. In part the Bradbury Building is famous as the scene of the gory but symbolically loaded struggle between good and evil in the film *Blade Runner.*

126. Charles Jencks calls this mixed tradition "hetero-architecture." See his chapter "Hetero-Architecture and the L.A. School," in *The City: Los Angeles and Urban Theory,* ed. Allen Scott and Edward Soja (Berkeley: University of California Press, 1996), 47–75.

127. In some ways, the county of Los Angeles *was* the region, so that its planning efforts substituted for a regional planning authority. In 1922, "the Board of Supervisors created the Los Angeles County Regional Planning Commission, with the power to plan for and regulate the use of land in all unincorporated areas of the huge county. The Commission, the first of its kind in the U.S., was also charged with coordinating its county land-use planning activities with the city planning commissions of Los Angeles, Pasadena, Long Beach, and the county's other incorporated cities." Weiss, *The Rise of the Community Builders,* 13. There are discussions of the L.A. County Planning Commission in Hugh Pomeroy, "Regional Planning in Practice," in *National Conference on City Planning Proceedings* (1924), 111–28, and in Hugh Pomeroy, "Two Years of Regional Planning in Los Angeles County," *City Planning* 1 (April 1925): 47–49. It was not until 1941 that a regional plan was released.

128. This plan only recently resurfaced in the 1990s, when many of the proposals it made for subways and commuter metro lines have been revived.

129. Weiss, *The Rise of the Community Builders,* 79, 80.

130. Ibid., 12.

131. Ibid., 84.

132. Ibid., 95–96.

133. Ibid., 104.

134. Ibid., 105.

135. Ibid., 139.

III. FROM THE DEPTHS OF THE DEPRESSION TO RESTRUCTURING, 1930–70

1. The direction was at least "different" after the U.S. monopoly was broken by the rise of rival economies, especially Germany and Japan, the "losers" in World War II.

2. There are, however, Cassandras who see the heated economy of the 1990s as merely a prelude to a real fall. Their predictions receive some support from the economic contractions in Asia, which might destabilize the world economy at the turn of the century.

3. The terms *Fordism* and *post-Fordism* are occasionally used in the literature to distinguish between the period treated in Part III and the post-1973 moments of restructuring that are covered in Part IV. See note 9 below for a more complete explanation of how I use the sometimes perplexing terms: *Fordist* and *post-Fordist.*

4. The conventional date is 1973–74, but, as I shall contend, the downturns in New York and Chicago really date from the late 1960s.

5. For a detailed discussion of the effects of the Depression and its antecedents in California, see Kevin Starr, *The Dream Endures: California Enters the 1940s* (New York: Oxford University Press, 1997). It is noteworthy that Starr concentrates heavily on San Francisco, in

contrast to Los Angeles, whose lesser degree of industrial development perhaps made it less vulnerable. The labor conflicts that Starr describes occurred primarily in that northern city; there were only mild repercussions in Southern California.

6. No less important were the jobs it created for unemployed writers, scholars, artists, photographers, and social researchers, who, in that decade, produced significant works on a scale that has never been duplicated.

7. An experimental model for the PWA (TERA) had already begun in New York State under Roosevelt's governorship.

8. The city had instituted its first municipally subsidized housing project, First Houses, even before public housing was written into national programs in 1937.

9. The concepts "Fordist" and "post-Fordist" are, of course, merely ideal types; they should not be expected to "fit" actual cases. Furthermore, like Kondratiev cycles, the terms are often used to *describe* conditions on which many analysts agree without indicating their consensus concerning *why* the changes have occurred. The clearest discussion I have found of the contrast between Fordism and post-Fordism is in the excellent collection edited by Ash Amin, *Post-Fordism: A Reader* (Oxford: Blackwell, 1994), especially Amin's chapter titled "Post-Fordism: Models, Fantasies and Phantoms of Transition." "The passing age, with its heyday in the 1950s and 1960s, has been named 'Fordism,' a term coined to reflect loosely the pioneering mass production methods and rules of management applied by Henry Ford in his car factories in America during the 1920s and 1930s. Fordism is summarized as the age of 'intensive accumulation' with 'monopolistic regulation' of the economy. . . . The driving force of Fordist 'intensive accumulation' is . . . the mass production dynamic, pioneered by the United States and reliant upon the intensification of work, the detailed division of tasks and mechanization to raise productivity, and various forms of monopolistic regulation to maintain this dynamic" (9).

Oddly enough, this Fordist model was first explicated, and even more surprisingly admired, by the Italian communist Antonio Gramsci, "who, in his prison notebooks at the beginning of the 1930s, introduced the notions of 'Americanism and Fordism' as shorthand for what he perceived as a new historical 'epoch' or 'passive revolution' which appeared to have the potential capacity to sweep away the last remnants of the 'Old Regime' in Europe." Mark Elam, "Puzzling Out the Post-Fordist Debate," in Amin, *Post-Fordism,* 63; Elam gives his source as Antonio Gramsci, *Selections from the Prison Notebooks,* ed. and trans. Quintin Hoare and Geoffrey Nowell Smith (New York: International, 1971), chap. 3. Later thinkers, however, have added numerous and not necessarily consistent elements to this basic definition, pointing out that especially in the post–World War II period, Fordism was more than simply a way to organize production; it was also a way to forge a collusive peace between powerful industrialists and powerful labor unions, thus enhancing profits and wages at the expense of excluded nonunionized workers and consumers. I shall return to these themes later and will hold until Part IV a discussion of the multiple meanings of post-Fordism.

Given the original meaning, however, it is clear that, of our three cities, Chicago between the 1920s and 1960s fits the ideal type most closely. New York never qualified as a "Fordist" city because of the smaller scale of its multiple industrial establishments and its heavy dependence upon the garment trade, which was simultaneously organized along both quintessentially pre-Fordist and post-Fordist patterns of flexible production and subcontracting. Applying the concept to Los Angeles is also difficult, because its labor movement was organized so late. Not until the 1950s could one call Los Angeles's economy Fordist in limited degree. But it may be, as Eric Hobsbawm has argued in *The Age of Extremes: A History of the World, 1914–1991* (New York: Pantheon, 1994), that although the "fordist peace" was always an overstatement, it did represent "more than a symbolic truth," especially when the prosperity, full employment, and mass consumption of the 1950s undermined the "conscious working-class cohesiveness" that had peaked "at the end of the Second World War" in western countries (305).

10. See Lizabeth Cohen, *Making a Deal: Industrial Workers in Chicago, 1919–1939* (Cambridge: Cambridge University Press, 1990), 241, Table 13. Cohen cites as the source of the table Grace Lee Maymor, "An Analysis of the United States Census Figures on Unemployment in Chicago, 1930 and 1931" (master's thesis, University of Chicago, 1934), 12.

11. Cohen, *Making a Deal,* 243, Table 14, based on Illinois Department of Labor figures, reprinted in Homer Hoyt, *One Hundred Years of Land Values in Chicago* (Chicago: University of Chicago Press, 1933), 269.

12. Harold Gosnell, *Machine Politics: Chicago Model* (New York: AMS, 1969 [1937]).

13. Chief among New York's liberal representatives were Fiorello La Guardia, who as the U.S. congressman representing East Harlem (before he became mayor) introduced labor protection legislation, and Robert F. Wagner Sr., who in his capacity as a senator from New York State from 1926 on, not only introduced the National Labor Relations Act of 1935 and the legislation that established Social Security, but also sponsored the Housing Act of 1937. His son would later serve as mayor of New York for three successive terms between 1953 and 1964.

14. See Ann Markusen, Peter Hall, Sabina Deitrich, and Scott Campbell, *The Rise of the Gunbelt: The Military Remapping of Industrial America* (New York: Oxford University Press, 1991).

15. During the Second World War, labor shortages induced the second "Great Migration" of blacks from the South, reproducing on an even larger scale the movement that had occurred during World War I. In 1890, only 20 percent of African Americans lived in cities. By 1940, about half of the black population lived in urban areas, a proportion that rose to 62 percent by 1950, to 72 percent by 1960, and to 81 percent by 1970, after which it stabilized. See Janet L. Abu-Lughod, *Changing Cities* (New York: HarperCollins, 1991), 120, Table 5.1. Although in the short run this internal migration immeasurably aided in raising the standard of living for most of the migrants, the rapid and enormous transfer of blacks from the rural South to the industrial cities of the North (and even into western cities such as Los Angeles, although at a lower order of magnitude) during and just after the war created overcrowded ghettos in all three cities.

16. The Detroit riot reads almost as a replay of the 1919 Chicago riot, triggered as it was by blacks presumably overstepping an invisible line in the segregated recreational facilities of the city. The label "zoot suit riots" is an absolute misnomer, given that the outbreaks were the result of attacks by "Anglo" sailors *against* young Mexican/Chicano males *who were not in uniform,* and may have been an expression of anger/jealousy, in much the same way that conscription-prone Irish vented their hostilities on conscription-exempt blacks in the New York Civil War riot of 1863. The 1943 Harlem riot was the first example of what later came to be known as "ghetto uprisings." A riot in Harlem in 1935 was transitional between the old and new types.

17. With later extensions, this became the infamous Cabrini-Green project, which has come to epitomize the "failure" of public housing.

18. In Los Angeles, the reverse occurred. Under the pressure of rising car ownership from the mid-1920s on, the rail/mass-transit system that had initially opened new areas for settlement was allowed to decay or, some say, was "killed off" by car interests. Ironically, its abandoned rights-of-way provided ideal routes for the new freeways on which postwar developments depended.

19. As we shall see, over time, Puerto Ricans in New York increasingly reported their

race as "white," which makes it impossible to determine from census figures exactly how much of New York's apparent "integration" was an artifact of the coalescence of Hispanic and African American residential quarters and the changing definitions of *Hispanic* in successive U.S. censuses. I explore this issue in greater detail in Chapters 7 and 10.

20. There was a small drop in the city's population between 1950 and 1960, but by 1970 it had recovered.

21. Among the other nonsouthern cities reporting interracial violence that year were Philadelphia and Cambridge, Maryland.

22. See National Advisory Commission on Civil Disorders, *Report of the National Advisory Commission on Civil Disorders* (New York: Bantam, March 1968).

23. The irony was that "separate and unequal" *had always been the case.*

24. It was not until 1983 that Chicago elected an antimachine black mayor, and that only because of a fluke created by a three-way race.

25. Although periodic eruptions of interracial and intercultural character recur regularly in New York, for the most part such "events" are confined to small specific neighborhoods; since 1964, none has triggered a citywide or even ghettowide uprising. The contention that New York was "going broke" as a result of its housing, health, and welfare allocations is the thesis of Ester R. Fuchs, *Mayors and Money: Fiscal Policy in New York and Chicago* (Chicago: University of Chicago Press, 1992). I treat this issue critically and in detail in Chapter 10.

26. See, inter alia, Raphael J. Sonenshein, *Politics in Black and White: Race and Power in Los Angeles* (Princeton, N.J.: Princeton University Press, 1993). This topic receives fuller treatment in Chapter 12.

7. A NEW YORK: A NEW DEAL

1. Lillian Brandt for the Welfare Council of New York City, *An Impressionistic View of the Winter of 1930–31 in New York City: Based on Statements from Some 900 Social Workers and Public Health Nurses* (New York: Welfare Council of New York City, 1932), v.

2. Thomas Kessner, *Fiorello H. La Guardia and the Making of Modern New York* (New York: McGraw-Hill, 1989), 216. The Emergency Work Bureau would serve as a model for the federal PWA (later the WPA). But it should be noted that even this temporary work engaged at best only 6 percent of the unemployed.

3. Brandt, *An Impressionistic View.* Although the Council's report was not published until 1932, it was evidently used by the council's director, William Hodson, in his pleas (demands?) to FDR.

4. Jimmy Walker, or "Beau James," a figure more noted for natty dress and glad hand than for brains or social conscience, later left office in disgrace amid charges of corruption.

5. Kessner, *Fiorello H. La Guardia,* 216.

6. Hopkins had earlier worked at the Christodora Settlement House on the Lower East Side and at New York's Association for Improving the Condition of the Poor. After Roosevelt was elected president, he appointed Hopkins to head the Federal Emergency Relief Administration and, eventually, the Public Works Administration.

7. In 1929, Republican La Guardia had failed in his bid for mayor when his rival on the Democratic ticket rode to victory on Roosevelt's coattails, but given the desperate conditions he was ready to try again in 1933, this time in a more winning Fusion combination. His unsuccessful rival in the Republican primary was none other than Robert Moses, who would later make a similarly unsuccessful bid for governor. See Robert A. Caro's masterful biography, *The Power Broker: Robert Moses and the Fall of New York* (New York: Knopf, 1974), chap. 21.

Unlike Chicago, where a disciplined Democratic Party eventually established long-term political dominance over the office of the city's mayor, New York's mayoral races from the post–Civil War period onward were often closely contested, and open not only to third and fourth parties, but also to coalitions of the most unlikely sort. In general, Democrats won these elections, even when that party was split among Tammany and other factions. But elections were close, and an occasional Republican could win, especially if a "Fusion" ticket, combining liberal Republicans with non-Tammany reform Democrats, could be organized. Thus Seth Low (sometime president of Columbia University) won the mayoralty on a Fusion ticket in 1903, as did Democrat John Mitchell in 1913. The outstanding examples, however, were Republican La Guardia, who carried the elections of 1933, 1937, and 1941 on various Fusion tickets, and John Lindsay in the mid-1960s.

The best book on La Guardia's early years is Arthur Mann's prize-winning biography, *La Guardia: A Fighter against His Times, 1882–1933* (Philadelphia: J. B. Lippincott, 1959). But see also Howard Zinn, *La Guardia in Congress* (Ithaca, N.Y.: Cornell University Press, 1959). Much of the following information has been drawn from Kessner, *Fiorello H. La Guardia.* La Guardia was a clear maverick in politics who began as a Republican "party man," first elected to Congress from Greenwich Village (which then had a large Italian population). He returned to New York City to fill a between-term vacated post as president of the Board of Aldermen on the promise the party would then nominate him for mayor. But his "progressive" views offended the conservatives who dropped their support. Eventually he was returned to Congress as a candidate of the Socialist Party representing East Harlem (then mostly Jewish and Italian). The American-born son of Italian immigrants who had lived in Europe and gained a wide knowledge of languages, he began his "career" in the United States as an interpreter at Ellis Island, and he consistently retained his deep sympathy with immigrants; it is not surprising, then, that in Congress he vigorously opposed the 1924 law restricting immigration.

8. Kessner, *Fiorello H. La Guardia,* 217–20. The "austerity" measures imposed by bankers to keep the city afloat were very similar to those that would be imposed by financiers in the 1975 fiscal crisis.

9. The personal relationship between FDR and La Guardia also greased the wheels for federal appropriations to New York. "'Our Mayor is the most appealing man I know,' said President Roosevelt of La Guardia. 'He comes to Washington and tells me a sad story. The tears run down my cheeks and the tears run down his cheeks and the first thing I know he's wangled another $50 million.'" Quoted in David H. Gelernter, *1939: The Lost World of the Fair* (New York: Free Press, 1995), 2; the original source is not specified.

10. See Mark Naison, "From Eviction Resistance to Rent Control: Tenant Activism in the Great Depression," in *The Tenant Movement in New York City, 1904–1984,* ed. Ronald Lawson and Mark Naison (New Brunswick, N.J.: Rutgers University Press, 1986), 101–18.

11. Peter Marcuse, "The Beginnings of Public Housing in New York," *Journal of Housing History* 12 (August 1986): 355–56. Marcuse cites Frances Fox Piven and Richard A. Cloward, *Poor People's Movements: Why They Succeed, How They Fail* (New York: Pantheon, 1977), 53–54, who in turn cite Richard O. Boyer and Herbert Morais, *Labor's Untold Story* (New York: Cameron, 1955) and a *New York Times* article dated February 2, 1932.

12. According to a detailed report of the New York City Housing Authority titled *Project Data: January 1, 1989,* by then the New York Housing Authority was supervising 316 operating projects containing a total of 179,045 dwelling units serving a population of 472,088 in 2,787 buildings, not including FHA-recovered and -resold houses. The overwhelming proportion of these projects were federally funded. It should be noted, however, that the official figures are gross underestimates of the population served, because of illegal doubling up.

13. First Houses was truly the first public housing project in the country. See, inter alia, the succinct account of Christopher Gray, "In the Beginning, New York Created First Houses," *New York Times,* September 24, 1995, real estate sec., p. 7. By December 1935, 122 families, selected from 3,800 applicants, moved into the "project." Among the more important sources on New York's public housing program are Marcuse, "The Beginnings of Public Housing"; and Anthony Jackson, *A Place Called Home: A History of Low-Cost Housing in Manhattan* (Cambridge: MIT Press, 1976). On the early period of housing reform, see Richard Plunz, *A History of Housing in New York City* (New York: Columbia University Press, 1990), chap. 1.

14. Marcuse tells the following story. The land and tenements (so deteriorated that they were about to be condemned) that yielded First Houses were sold to the city by Vincent Astor, who accepted payment in tax-free bonds payable over sixty years at 3.5 percent interest. The city agreed because it had no money. Although Harold Ickes of the Public Works Administration had promised twenty-five million dollars, the money had not yet arrived. Marcuse says that despite the fact that the project made no economic sense, the city did the rehabbing for "reasons of public relations." Nevertheless, the city had paid off the entire debt by 1944. "The Beginnings of Public Housing," 356–65.

15. Because organized labor objected to the use of free labor, the Housing Act of 1937 contained a provision that labor to construct public housing had to be paid the "going wage."

16. Many of the units under construction would be temporarily earmarked as emergency housing for war workers, once production geared up.

17. Marcuse, "The Beginnings of Public Housing," 354. Marcuse continues: "What was radical about the early public housing projects was precisely their similarity to their nonpublic housing contemporaries. *Public housing was not, at its outset, low-quality housing for lower-income people, but middle-class housing for working people*" (emphasis added).

18. See ibid., 365–70, for details. At that time government policy and "accepted usage" dictated that the "racial composition" of a neighborhood should be reproduced by future occupants. (A third project, Red Hook Houses, was built for whites. During wartime, defense workers received priority placements there.) In contrast to New York, as we shall see in Chapter 8, once federal policy was altered to require integration, Chicago virtually stopped building public housing. New York never did stop, although the level and types of federal funds available forced periodic shifts in approach and an overall retrenchment.

19. Ibid., 369. Marcuse cites *New York Times,* May 23, 1935.

20. Dominic J. Capeci Jr., *The Harlem Riot of 1943* (Philadelphia: Temple University Press, 1977), 3, emphasis added. Capeci's interpretation is somewhat at variance with that of Cheryl Greenberg, who argues that it was the *failure* of a well-organized political campaign to require white-owned stores in Harlem to hire blacks that led to the brief riot of 1935. See her "The Politics of Disorder: Reexamining Harlem's Riots of 1935 and 1943," *Journal of Urban History* 18 (August 1992): 395–441.

21. Capeci, *The Harlem Riot,* 4.

22. *The Complete Report of Mayor LaGuardia's Commission on the Harlem Riot of March 19, 1935* was never officially released and was apparently "lost" until 1968, when a 1935 clipping from the black newspaper the *Amsterdam News,* purporting to be a complete copy, was found in Columbia University's library files and published as part of a postriot series edited by Robert M. Fogelson and Richard E. Rubenstein under the general title of *Mass Violence in America* (New York: New York Times/Arno, 1969). Capeci, *The Harlem Riot,* cites E. Franklin Frazier, *The Negro Harlem: A Report on Social and Economic Conditions Responsible for the Outbreak of March 19, 1935,* but I have never found this source under this authorship

or title. Frazier did later publish a brief and rather conventional article on the ecology of Harlem, the only direct fruit of his labors. See E. Franklin Frazier, "Negro Harlem: An Ecological Study," *American Journal of Sociology* 43 (July 1937): 72–88.

23. Capeci, *The Harlem Riot,* 34–35.

24. "The Reverend John W. Robinson, chairman of the Permanent Committee for Better Schools in Harlem," pointed out how school districts had been gerrymandered to ensure segregation and how Harlem students were relegated to high schools "where the curriculum relegated them to a marginal economic status in society. . . . Robinson's committee found that almost four hundred books in the city's schools depicted blacks as slaves, 'lazy, shiftless.'" Ibid., 40.

25. Ibid., 41.

26. Ibid., 43. Only the phrase "in the midst of plenty" seems unwarranted.

27. Among other things, the commission recommended better handling of complaints against the police, which La Guardia unfortunately rejected. Had such a mechanism been in place, the 1943 Harlem riot might have followed a somewhat different course.

28. Capeci, *The Harlem Riot,* 7.

29. On Harlem Houses, see Marcuse, "The Beginnings of Public Housing," 369–75. "Forty-five percent of the construction costs was a grant; the balance was to be repaid to the federal government over a sixty-year period" (375).

30. The classic source on Robert Moses is, of course, Caro's *The Power Broker.* But see also the quirky book by Jerome Charyn, *Metropolis: New York as Myth, Marketplace and Magical Land* (New York: Penguin/Abacus, 1986). Moses has never been someone about whom people feel indifferent.

31. Peter Hall, *Cities of Tomorrow: An Intellectual History of Urban Planning and Design in the Twentieth Century* (Oxford: Blackwell, 1988), 159, calls this a program along pure RPAA lines, but, like many scholars, he has difficulty distinguishing between the Regional Plan Association of New York and the Regional Planning Association of America. It was the Regional Plan Association of New York that Delano actually headed after the death of Charles Norton. Hall is correct, however, in noting that (along with Charles Merriam and Wesley Mitchell) Delano was responsible for producing the 1937 report of the U.S. National Resources Research Committee on Urbanism, *Our Cities: Their Role in the National Economy,* which assumed the inevitability of massive decentralization (160–61).

32. In 1935, the CIO was formed inside the AFL, becoming independent three years later. (The two did not merge again until 1955.) Two other union giants (Amalgamated and ILGWU, both related to garments) initially established in New York City also picked up affiliates in other major garment-manufacturing cities. Although the two remained rivals, between them they did manage to organize the industry. See Roger Waldinger, *Through the Eye of the Needle: Immigrants and Enterprise in New York's Garment Trades* (New York: New York University Press, 1986). The degree of unionization is, of course, a major variable in yielding the different class structures in our three urbanized regions. As we have seen, the relatively small scale of enterprises in New York (primarily consumer and producer services, with only construction and transportation being larger-scale "industrial" types) and the service sectors that from the start dominated New York's economy did not lend themselves to confrontational union politics or to massive plant organizing; federations were essential to build up "scale." The garment trade in particular, which employed the largest number of "industrial" workers in Manhattan, but through small jobber plants and homework, was critical in developing techniques for organizing labor beyond single shop floors.

33. A detailed and well-reasoned history of the development of New York's municipal

unions and a critique of their use by city and union officials to maintain labor peace is Mark H. Maier's *City Unions: Managing Discontent in New York City* (New Brunswick, N.J.: Rutgers University Press, 1987). Maier recounts how, between 1954 and 1965, "Wagner moved the city toward full recognition of unions for its employees" (47). In some ways, Maier is describing the brief "Fordist" compact between management and labor within the governmental sphere.

34. Leonard Wallock, ed., *New York: Culture Capital of the World, 1940–1965* (New York: Rizzoli, 1988), 10–11.

35. See Carol Herselle Krinsky, "Architecture in New York City," in Wallock, *New York,* 89–121. Krinsky notes, "Two pavilions [at the fair] stood out . . . : that of Brazil (by Oscar Niemeyer), and that of Venezuela (designed by Gordon Bunshaft for the young American firm of Skidmore, Owings & Merrill). Brazil's pavilion was elevated on thin piers derived from Le Corbusier's *pilotis,* while Venezuela's had glass walls behind thin supports that sustained the ceiling and a canopy with a mural on its underside. These light and open structures contrasted markedly with" many of the clumsy or kitschy buildings at the fair (92).

36. Ibid. However, it would not be until the revision of New York's zoning laws in 1960 that the form of skyscrapers would be sufficiently "liberated" from the setback design to take full advantage of the straight lines of modern glass-coated constructions.

37. Ibid., 89–90.

38. Shaun O'Connell, *Remarkable, Unspeakable New York (A Literary History)* (Boston: Beacon, 1995), esp. 206–30.

39. There is an interesting contrast between this book and his quintessential novel of Los Angeles, written after West settled in that city in 1935. If *Miss Lonelyhearts* expresses suicidal depression, *The Day of the Locust* a decade later expresses Hollywood's "apocalyptic mood," a phrase used by Lionel Rolfe in his *Literary L.A.* (San Francisco: Chronicle, 1981) to describe what he calls a masterpiece. I see the nihilism of *The Day of the Locust* as foreshadowing the book that captures the city's despair in the prosperous 1980s, Brett Easton Ellis's *Less than Zero* (New York: Simon & Schuster, 1985). Significantly, the motif of *The Day of the Locust* is a painting of Los Angeles aflame.

40. The play is based on the 1934 taxi strike in New York. For more details on the initial response, see O'Connell, *Remarkable, Unspeakable New York,* 215–16.

41. I ignore here the vast literature of "growing up immigrant Jewish," which accounts for a significant proportion of New York's most famous novels of the period, just as "growing up Irish" is the preferred genre of this type in Chicago. Henry Roth's *Call It Sleep* may be the former's pinnacle, whereas James Farrell's Studs Lonnigan novels may represent a similar peroration on growing up Irish in Chicago.

42. William Grimes, "The Dark Side of a Noir City, in Black and White of Course," *New York Times,* November 18, 1994, C1, C27, emphasis added. In this extract, Grimes is quoting from Foster Hirsch's *Film Noir: The Dark Side of the Screen* (New York: Da Capo, 1981), which claims that the films "portray the city as enticing and dangerous, a place of neon, gloomy weather and impersonal crowds."

43. Federal Writers' Project, *WPA Guide to New York City: The Federal Writers' Project Guide to 1930s New York* (New York: Pantheon, 1982 [1939]).

44. At that time, Manhattan's population was approaching 1,689,000; Brooklyn had 2,800,000, the Bronx almost 1,500,000, Queens more than 1,340,000, and Staten Island only about 175,000.

45. Gelernter's *1939: The Lost World of the Fair* is the most recent book to evoke this event. It presents a particularly intimate and fascinating, if narrow, reconstruction, based largely on the (fictitious) preserved diary of a middle-class woman the author claims to have interviewed.

One of Gelernter's themes is the eschatological thrust of the entire enterprise, which he stresses in his article "Since the '39 World's Fair: Utopia Gained and Lost," *Los Angeles Times,* June 25, 1995, sec. M, pp. 1, 3. As Steve Erickson notes in a review of the book: "The Fair of 1939 was something like a biblical moment in what Gelernter calls the American religion, which was a faith not only in American destiny but its holy union with God's ultimate designs. . . . The American religion paraded its eschatological predictions and deep utopian faith most memorably and definitively at the 1939 New York World's Fair. . . . [Its planners] shared 'a fundamental conviction'—that the fair ought to deliver a 'powerful' and 'prophetic' message. . . . It was the mountaintop. Fair-goers ascended and looked out at the promised land." Steve Erickson, "From Here to Utopia: Looking Back at the Magic of the New York World's Fair of 1939," *Los Angeles Times,* June 25, 1995, Book Review sec., p. 2. New York would host another world's fair in 1965 on the same site in Queens, but it was a dim reflection of and had much less impact than the 1939 fair—perhaps the world's last "great" fair. Some suggest that the advent of television and air travel have vitiated the need for such "windows on the world."

46. Kohn had been one of the cofounders of the Regional Planning Association of America, along with Lewis Mumford. He had worked with Clarence Stein of "Garden City" fame and had been director of housing for the PWA. See Gelernter, *1939,* 25–26. Clarence Stein designed the few "greenbelt" (but dormitory) new towns ever built in the United States.

47. To our postmodern ears this sounds incredibly corny, and yet, as Gelernter discovered in interviewing people about their memories of the fair, it left lasting impressions on the viewers, often affecting their future life choices. I trace my own lifetime preoccupation with cities and their planning to the exhibits I saw as an impressionable youngster of eleven. Reading about them while preparing this book has triggered long-buried memories.

48. Federal Writers' Project, *WPA Guide,* 632.

49. The *WPA Guide* is mysteriously reticent about this exhibit, devoting considerable attention to the Chrysler and Ford buildings but only two sentences to Futurama (see 639). My account therefore depends more on other sources, including Gelernter, *1939.* Several books appeared at the time of the fair itself, including Frank Monaghan, *New York World's Fair 1939* (Chicago: Encyclopaedia Britannica, 1938), an oversize pictorial account of the fair; and Rebecca Rankin, *New York Advancing* (New York: Publishers Printing, 1939). Since then, the topic has been revisited by Richard Wurts in the heavily illustrated *The New York World's Fair, 1939–1940 in 155 Photographs* (New York: Dover, 1977); Larry Zim, Mel Lerner, and Herbert Rolfes, *The World of Tomorrow: The 1939 New York World's Fair* (New York: Harper & Row, 1988); and Rosemarie Haag Bletter et al., *Remembering the Future: The New York World's Fair from 1939 to 1964, with Essays by Rosemarie Haag Bletter and Others* (New York: Rizzoli, 1989).

50. Indeed, when the World's Fair was revitalized and reconstructed in 1964–65, Robert Moses was its new chairman. Interestingly enough, by then the Futurama exhibit had abandoned its old theme of cloverleafed highways, now found everywhere, and transported its visitors, instead, "across the surface of the moon, to the Antarctic, along the ocean floor, through the jungle, through a desert, and finally *past* the city of the future." See Bletter et al., *Remembering the Future,* 30.

51. Zim et al., *The World of Tomorrow,* 90. It is this exhibit, rather than the more pristine models of garden cities or superhighways, that made me an urbanist for the rest of my life.

52. See retrospective tables and charts in Port of New York Authority, *Foreign Trade at the Port of New York/1966* (New York: Port of New York Authority, 1967), esp. 2–3, 6–7, 8–9. These trends are updated to 1973 in the Port of New York–New Jersey Annual Report, *Foreign Trade During 1973 at the Port of New York–New Jersey: An Analysis of the Port's Position in*

the Handling of Oceanborne and Airborne Foreign Trade (New York: Port of New York–New Jersey, 1974).

53. David Hillyard compiled these figures for me. See his "Working Paper on the Port of New York" (unpublished manuscript, n.d.).

54. Robert C. Wood with Vladimir V. Almendinger, *1400 Governments: The Political Economy of the New York Metropolitan Region* (Cambridge: Harvard University Press, 1961), 3. Wood's chapter titled "The World of the Metropolitan Giants" has never been surpassed.

55. Ibid., 117 emphasis added.

56. See Robert Fitch, *The Assassination of New York* (London: Verso, 1993). Fitch ties together the political and economic power of the Rockefeller dynasty, the Port of New York Authority's power to raise public funds through bonds, Rockefeller's real estate interests in lower Manhattan, and the Regional Plan Association's conscious "decision" to deindustrialize New York City and to "destroy" its ports. Although his analysis has much merit (e.g., in that it draws explicit connections between the Port Authority's funding of the World Trade Center, which enhanced David Rockefeller's real estate fortunes invested in lower Manhattan, and Rockefeller's leadership of the Downtown Development Corporation), Fitch's preoccupation with "great" or, rather, "evil" men seems to treat deeper socioeconomic changes in New York as epiphenomena.

57. See Michael N. Danielson and Jameson W. Doig, *New York: The Politics of Urban Regional Development* (Berkeley: University of California Press, 1982), esp. 316–47.

58. The vulnerability to bombing of concentrated industrial facilities was a lesson learned in the European war theater. It is difficult for us today, in an age of atom- and hydrogen-bomb capabilities, to appreciate how seriously strategic planners then treated the argument for radical decentralization of factories.

59. See Edgar M. Hoover and Raymond Vernon, *Anatomy of a Metropolis: The Changing Distribution of People and Jobs within the New York Metropolitan Region* (Garden City, N.Y.: Doubleday Anchor, 1962 [1959]), 26, Table 3. In 1956, the Regional Plan Association of New York commissioned scholars at the Graduate School of Public Administration of Harvard University to undertake a study of developments in a twenty-two-county region and to project the future to 1985. Ten volumes resulted from their work, of which the most important are Hoover and Vernon's *Anatomy of a Metropolis* and Raymond Vernon's summary volume, *Metropolis 1985: An Interpretation of the Findings of the New York Metropolitan Region Study* (Cambridge: Harvard University Press, 1960).

60. In 1939 as well as in 1947, some 53 percent of all manufacturing jobs in the region were within New York City limits; by 1954 this had dropped to 51 percent. See Vernon, *Metropolis 1985,* 114, Table 14, and passim.

61. "Indeed, the state's civil rights legislation was the most advanced in the nation. As early as 1909, racial discrimination was forbidden in jury service, law practice, public school admissions, and some areas of public accommodations. Civil rights were extended to various fields of public employment, work relief, and public works projects during the Great Depression. By 1937, the legislature had created the Temporary Commission on the Condition of the Urban Colored Population. A year later, a constitutional provision forbade the denial of equal protection of state laws to any person 'because of race, color, creed, or religion.'" Capeci, *The Harlem Riot,* 31–32.

62. By the 1920s, the secondary "ghetto" of Brooklyn's Bedford-Stuyvesant had begun to form along the east-west thoroughfares of Fulton and Atlantic streets. For details, see Harold X. Connolly, *A Ghetto Grows in Brooklyn* (New York: New York University Press, 1977), esp. chap. 3. Italian and Hispanic families still lived in Harlem, although more than 80 percent of

the residents were native-born African Americans or had come from the Caribbean. During the 1940s, increased migration caused an expansion of black Harlem, north of 155th Street, south of 110th Street, and west across Amsterdam Avenue. By then, such Brooklyn sections as Bedford-Stuyvesant and Brownsville were becoming established as secondary settlements.

63. Capeci, *The Harlem Riot,* xii. La Guardia also fostered greater employment of blacks in municipal government, both in the civil service and at high-level appointments; he criticized racial discrimination and indeed drafted the text for Executive Order 8802, issued by President Roosevelt, which reaffirmed government's opposition to discrimination in employment and set up a mechanism of enforcement. La Guardia quickly adopted Executive Order 8802 as New York's official municipal policy, investigating discrimination within municipally funded programs and referring other complaints to Governor Lehman's recently established Committee on Discrimination in Employment and to the FEPC. See, inter alia, Capeci, *The Harlem Riot,* 8–13.

64. As was the case during World War I, there was an inverse relationship between international and internal labor recruitment. In 1940, white foreign-born residents in the five boroughs numbered more than 2 million. This total dropped to less than 1.8 million ten years later, largely because the older generation was dying off. In contrast, the number of native nonwhite (mostly black) residents rose from fewer than 419,000 in 1940 to almost 705,000 by 1950, whereas that of foreign-born nonwhites (mostly coming from the Caribbean) increased from 58,637 to 72,305 in the same period.

65. Capeci, *The Harlem Riot,* 69–70. Among the sources available on Detroit are Robert Shogan, *The Detroit Race Riot: A Study in Violence* (Philadelphia: Chilton, 1964); and the superb new book by Thomas J. Sugrue, *The Origins of the Urban Crisis: Race and Inequality in Postwar Detroit* (Princeton, N.J.: Princeton University Press, 1996).

66. Capeci, *The Harlem Riot,* 63.

67. For details, see ibid., chap. 4.

68. At that period, almost all stores in Harlem belonged to nonresident whites; a large proportion of the store owners were Jewish, so they bore the brunt of the anger.

69. Capeci, *The Harlem Riot,* xi, quotes Malcolm X's comment that "one could almost smell trouble ready to break out." One of the precipitating events may have been La Guardia's support for Robert Moses's plan to contract with the Metropolitan Life Insurance Company, known for its racially discriminatory policies, to construct quasi-public Stuyvesant Town on tenement-cleared land, over the objections of Adam Clayton Powell Jr. (see ibid., 13–14). The objections were legitimate: Stuyvesant Town did discriminate in tenant selection until well into the 1950s. For a description of the riot itself, see ibid., 99–108, from which the following account is condensed.

70. Ibid., 171.

71. One of the exceptions is Allen D. Grimshaw's dissertation-based article "Urban Racial Violence in the United States: Changing Ecological Considerations," *American Journal of Sociology* 64 (September 1960): 109–19, which was reprinted in Grimshaw's edited volume *Racial Violence in the United States* (Chicago: Aldine, 1969), 287–98. As we shall see in Chapter 12, this strategy could not be used in the more diffusely targeted Los Angeles riot of 1992, in what I shall call the first "drive-in" (or, more accurately, "drive-out") riot.

72. Capeci, *The Harlem Riot,* 104.

73. Ibid., 104–7.

74. In fact, although as in most riots participants were heavily "weighted" toward young males, the class range was too wide and participation too extensive for all those involved to be dismissed as hoodlums. Capeci notes that "once disorder occurred, class differences col-

lapsed as rioters shared the overwhelming commonality of black in a white society" and that "several observers recalled seeing 'solid citizens,' women, housewives, and children looting" (ibid., 122–23, 126).

75. Ibid., 115, emphasis added. Capeci's analysis appears in a chapter titled "Police, Hoodlums, Race, and Riot," 115–33.

76. Ibid., 158–59, emphasis added. It should be noted that New York remains one of the few cities in the country that has retained rent controls, albeit duly modified.

77. See Kenneth Jackson, *Crabgrass Frontier: The Suburbanization of the United States* (New York: Oxford University Press, 1985). Although Jackson explores at great length the early American precedents for suburbia, he devotes frustratingly little space to what even he calls "the Age of Subdivision" (see his 231–45), that is, the early postwar period.

78. Hall, *Cities of Tomorrow,* 277.

79. Jackson, *Crabgrass Frontier,* 233.

80. Special home-financing insurance programs rewarded veterans with impossible-to-resist low down payments and interest rates. In the pungent language of satirical novelist John Keats, in his *The Crack in the Picture Window* (Boston: Houghton Mifflin, 1956), "The real estate boys read the [VHA] Bill, looked at each other in happy amazement, and the dry, rasping noise they made rubbing their hands together could have been heard as far away as Tawi Tawi." (Quoted in Jackson, *Crabgrass Frontier,* 233).

81. New York University School of Education Center for Community and Field Services, *Levittown's Schools and the Future of the Community* (New York: New York University Press, 1954). Jackson credits the family of Abraham Levitt (large-scale builders of defense housing who eventually contributed more than 140,000 houses) with turning "a cottage industry into a major manufacturing process" after the war (*Crabgrass Frontier,* 234). There were three Levittowns: one on Long Island, one in New Jersey, and one in Pennsylvania. The Long Island Levittown was the largest of these, and, indeed, its eventual 17,400 houses made it "the largest housing development ever put up by a single builder" (235). Hall links its location to earlier highway construction: "The original Levittown [stood] just off an interchange on Moses's Wantagh State Parkway, built nearly twenty years earlier as one of the approaches to Jones Beach State Park" (*Cities of Tomorrow,* 278). It should be noted that the most famous sociological study of life in Levittown, Herbert Gans's *The Levittowners: Ways of Life and Politics in a New Suburban Community* (New York: Pantheon, 1967), deals not with the New York project or with the second community in Lower Bucks County, Pennsylvania, on the site of broccoli and spinach fields, but with a third settlement in New Jersey within commuting distance of Philadelphia.

82. The census is enjoined from collecting information on religious identity, which means that this distribution can only be approximate. The proportion of New York residents of Jewish belief/descent has been estimated as high as 25 percent; the three largest "old ethnic" descent groups—Irish, Italians, and Poles—are overwhelmingly Catholic. The Protestant "minority" is almost equally split between whites and blacks. Despite some debatable value positions the authors take, the best book on New York's "ethnics" for this period remains Nathan Glazer and Daniel Moynihan, *Beyond the Melting Pot: The Negroes, Puerto Ricans, Jews, Italians and Irish of New York City* (Cambridge: MIT Press, 1963); see 8–9 for some breakdowns by religion and national origin in 1960.

83. It was not until later (in the 1970s and 1980s) that the "complexion" of the city underwent its most dramatic shift. By 1980, whites still constituted 61 percent of the city's population, a proportion that had dropped to some 52 percent by 1990. Within Manhattan, the proportion of the population classified as "white" decreased and then stabilized at 59 percent

for 1980 and 1990. It was in Brooklyn and the Bronx that racial succession was the most dramatic during those decades. In 1980, Brooklyn's "white" proportion stood at 56 percent. Ten years later this had dropped to 47 percent. In 1980 a minority (47 percent) of the Bronx's residents were "white," but by 1990 the comparable figure had declined to 36 percent.

84. Nor were these the first such events. As the authors of the *Report of the National Advisory Commission on Civil Disorders* (often referred to as the Kerner Report) recount, as early as 1963 "serious disorders . . . broke out in Birmingham, Savannah, Cambridge, Md., Chicago, and Philadelphia [Pennsylvania]." By 1964, Jacksonville and St. Augustine, Florida, Cleveland, and Philadelphia, Mississippi, had been added to the list. In July, New York would join, as would several cities and towns in New Jersey. See National Advisory Commission on Civil Disorders, *Report of the National Advisory Commission on Civil Disorders* (New York: Bantam Books, 1968), 35–36.

85. The following account is based primarily on two sources: Fred C. Shapiro and James W. Sullivan, *Race Riots: New York 1964* (New York: Thomas Y. Crowell, 1964), chap. 6; and the fuller community study by Connolly, *A Ghetto Grows in Brooklyn.*

86. Shapiro and Sullivan, *Race Riots,* 108; see also Connolly, *A Ghetto Grows in Brooklyn,* 4–5. But in 1820, only some seven years before slaves were freed in New York State, half of the county's blacks were still in involuntary servitude. Connolly, *A Ghetto Grows in Brooklyn,* 6.

87. Shapiro and Sullivan, *Race Riots,* 109.

88. Ibid., 111. "The forties also saw the emergence of the area politically and socially. Although Harlemites might still slight Brooklyn Negroes by saying 'when a colored man can't afford to live in Harlem any longer, he moves to Bedford-Stuyvesant,' the truth was that prices in both areas by then were on a par, and a new social awareness was in the making in the minds of Bedford-Stuyvesant Negroes." Ibid., 112.

89. Ibid., 115.

90. Mayor's Commission on Black New Yorkers, *Report of the Mayor's Commission on Black New Yorkers* (New York: Mayor's Commission, November 14, 1988), Table I-A.

91. Ronald M. Denowitz, "Racial Succession in New York City, 1960–70," *Social Forces* 59, no. 2 (1980): 451.

92. Ibid., 452.

93. Interestingly enough, Denowitz avoided this problem by eliminating tracts containing substantial numbers of Puerto Ricans.

94. These are points legitimately emphasized in Glazer and Moynihan, *Beyond the Melting Pot.*

95. See Philip Kasinitz, *Caribbean New York: Black Immigrants and the Politics of Race* (Ithaca, N.Y.: Cornell University Press, 1992).

96. A marvelous account of this complexity can be found in the life history of a member of the "first black family" to settle in a Bronx neighborhood in the 1860s. See Judith Rollins, *All Is Never Said: The Narrative of Odette Harper Hines* (Philadelphia: Temple University Press, 1995). Members within this large extended clan of southern-origin "mixed bloods" ranged in appearance from blue-eyed blonds (the paterfamilias who bought his land and built his house, as well as an uncle who "passed," worked on Wall Street, and made secretly arranged visits "home") to those who more resembled their African-born ancestor, freed from slavery by her American Indian husband. This ambiguity of classification did not prevent the protagonist (who became chief publicist for the NAACP and later a civil rights activist) from full identification with black causes, just as Walter White's fair skin, blue eyes, and blond hair did not deter him from succeeding James Weldon Johnson as executive secretary of the NAACP in

1931. Although "passing" and light-skinned blacks are also found in Chicago's history, this seems to have been less common there than in New York or Philadelphia.

97. Probably the best book on the early history of this group is Virginia Sanchez Korrol, *From Colonia to Community: The History of Puerto Ricans in New York City, 1917–1948* (Westport, Conn.: Greenwood, 1983). See also her definitive compressed entry on Puerto Ricans in Kenneth Jackson, ed., *The Encyclopedia of New York City* (New Haven, Conn.: Yale University Press, 1995), 962–63. Glazer and Moynihan, *Beyond the Melting Pot,* 86–136, also discuss this group; their estimate of the Puerto Rican population is lower than Sanchez Korrol's. They give a figure of only 613,000 in 1960 of Puerto Rican birth or parentage, yielding some 8 percent of the total (see 94).

98. Glazer and Moynihan, *Beyond the Melting Pot,* 92–93.

99. Not only are the categories ambiguous and subject to individual choice, but they have been extremely "unstable" over time. Some of that instability can be attributed to the Bureau of the Census itself, which has tried, in vain, to impose greater "precision" by altering the terminologies and cross-classifications over time. But most has come from the refusal of Hispanics to "accept" American definitions of racial categories. This became clear in the 1990 census, when more than 90 percent of New York's "Hispanic" population refused to declare themselves either white or black, checking off the option of "other" instead. I return to this point in Part IV.

100. Christopher Mele, "Neighborhood 'Burn-Out,'" in Janet L. Abu-Lughod et al., *From Urban Village to East Village: The Battle for New York's Lower East Side* (Oxford: Blackwell, 1994), 132. Mele in turn cites Clara Rodriguez, *The Ethnic Queue in the United States: The Case of the Puerto Ricans* (San Francisco: R&E Associates, 1974), 121.

101. An excellent collection of studies on East Harlem over time, and therefore of the changing situation of Puerto Ricans concentrated there, is Judith Freidenberg, ed., "The Anthropology of Lower Income Urban Enclaves: The Case of East Harlem" *Annals of the New York Academy of Sciences* 749 (1995).

102. Kessner, *Fiorello H. La Guardia,* 134. Kessner cites the East Harlem Study, a 1937 WPA report of the Mayor's Committee on City Planning.

103. On the Lower East Side, large phalanxes of projects also replaced the tenements along the East River, and these, too, are now mostly occupied by Hispanics.

104. Martin Meyerson and Edward Banfield, *Politics, Planning and the Public Interest: The Case of Public Housing in Chicago* (Glencoe, Ill.: Free Press, 1955).

105. New York City Housing Authority, *Project Data: January 1, 1989.* The population figure of 472,088 is definitely an undercount, because of an acknowledged but unknown number of illegal subfamilies doubled up in legally resident households.

106. In 1989, the city had another seven projects under construction to provide 686 more apartments and was planning fifteen more projects designed to provide 1,621 more apartments serving an additional 6,200 persons.

107. Riis, Vladeck, and Wald projects on the Lower East Side, for example, preempted what might otherwise have been prime waterfront space overlooking the East River, although they were then insulated from the river by the FDR Drive (East River Drive) of Robert Moses.

108. In the discussion that follows I depend heavily on the account of Shapiro and Sullivan in *Race Riots,* although I disagree with some of their interpretations.

109. The young man was attending a summer remedial reading program at the Robert E. Wagner Sr. Junior High School, far from the Bronx Soundview housing project where he lived.

110. Shapiro and Sullivan, *Race Riots,* 1–2. Here I disagree somewhat with the role the riot played in touching off successive racial struggles. The causes were deep and pervasive—the

frustrated dreams of the civil rights movement, coupled with the beginnings of economic weakness.

111. Ibid., 12, 13. According to Shapiro and Sullivan, Black Muslims and Maoists also sought to "inflame" (i.e., work politically among) the demonstrators. CORE had good reason to want a civilian police review board. Later, a grand jury refused to indict the policeman. Ibid., 16.

112. "There is a definite correlation between heat and Negro Riots. If that day had been a cool one, there very likely would have been no riot. But it was a sizzler." Ibid., 43. This is certainly a suspect "theory," even though revolutions and uprisings of all kinds, including the American Revolution, have been more likely to occur in hot weather.

113. Ibid., 61.

114. Ibid., 62.

115. Shapiro and Sullivan quote what they call a lengthy and "almost logical analysis of the riot for the *Herald Tribune*" by Kenneth Clark, whom they identify as a psychology "teacher" at City College and a "director" of HARYOU. Shapiro and Sullivan cite HARYOU statistics on Harlem's high rates of homicide, drugs, juvenile delinquency, venereal disease, and poverty, and mostly black-on-black crime ignored by police. They also quote Clark as saying that black youth view police "as adversaries who are as zealous in seeking to maintain the racial status quo as the most ardent segregationists. . . . Each time a police officer shoots and kills a Negro teen-ager, that is an urban crime." Ibid., 68–69.

116. Ibid., 83.

117. Shapiro and Sullivan note that "the usual roar of Manhattan had dwindled. A dog could be heard barking in the distance, just as he could have been heard in a small town." Ibid., 90.

118. For details, see ibid., chap. 7 (titled "Tuesday, July 21"), and chap. 8 (titled "Wednesday, July 22").

119. Ibid., 159, emphasis added.

120. Ibid., 168–72.

121. Shapiro and Sullivan's analysis leaves much to be desired. They ask, rhetorically, "What stops a riot? Three days and nothing else. It is like a disease, apparently, that takes three days to check." Ibid., 193. However, Shapiro and Sullivan do advance an interesting "theory" about New York that links the city's short-lived and scattered rioting to the extent to which integration had proceeded in New York, as contrasted with Chicago or even Los Angeles, which leads to a spatial separation between leaders and looters. "Integration in the city of New York has progressed to the point where it is easier for a Negro leader to switch neighborhoods than fight. Most Bedford-Stuyvesant leaders live in integrated Crown Heights. Most Harlem leaders pack up at the end of the day and head for Queens or Westchester. It is worth noting that the house provided by the Black Muslims for Malcolm X . . . is in Queens. But the pluperfect example of absentee leadership is, of course, Adam Clayton Powell, who rules Harlem while commuting between his home in Puerto Rico and his office in Washington" (196).

8. FORDIST CHICAGO

1. Richard Wright, introduction to St. Clair Drake and Horace Cayton, *Black Metropolis: A Study of Negro Life in a Northern City,* rev. ed. (Chicago: University of Chicago Press, 1993[1945]), xvii. Wright points out that neither the authors nor he were native to Chicago: Drake migrated from the South, Cayton from the Northwest, and Wright from Mississippi. In that, they were "typical" Chicago African Americans.

Black Metropolis is considered an unparalleled guide to Chicago's African American community as it had evolved to the end of World War II. The original study was begun under the direction of Horace Cayton and W. Lloyd Warner and the auspices of the Works Progress Administration. Whereas it began as a study of juvenile delinquency on the South Side, it gradually evolved into a full-scale community study that took four years to complete and involved about twenty "research students." Earl Johnson and Louis Wirth were the academic sponsors, and the Julius Rosenwald Fund also helped to finance the study.

2. Lizabeth Cohen, *Making a New Deal: Industrial Workers in Chicago, 1919–1939* (New York: Cambridge University Press, 1990), 13.

3. See ibid., 14–15, Table 1, which is derived from the U.S. Department of Commerce, Bureau of the Census, *Biennial Census of Manufactures: 1923* (Washington, D.C.: U.S. Government Printing Office, 1926), 1400–1403.

4. The number of Mexicans employed in U.S. Steel's South Works fell from nineteen hundred in 1930 to only three hundred in 1932. See Cohen, *Making a New Deal,* 242. By 1933, minorities had been virtually eliminated from industrial employment, which was at a level of only half what it had been in 1929. Minorities were also the last to benefit from the war-generated recovery. As late as the 1940s, one-third of Chicago's black male workers remained unemployed.

5. Indeed, there was a certain irony in the dependence of immigrants on their own mutual-aid insurance and banking institutions; when these failed, as did the more universalist credit organizations and banks of the larger society, the betrayal seemed even more pernicious. Interestingly enough, the first bank to fail in the city was in the Black Belt. As Drake and Cayton note, "Chicago's banking structure broke at its weakest link—in the Black Belt. In July 1930, Binga's bank closed its doors, while mobs cried in the streets for their savings. Within a month every bank in Black Metropolis was closed." *Black Metropolis,* 84.

6. Cohen, *Making a New Deal,* 51.

7. Ibid., 63.

8. Harold E. Gosnell, *Machine Politics: Chicago Model* (Chicago: University of Chicago Press, 1968 [1937]), 2. Gosnell's study is the most astute examination of Chicago politics during the Depression era to date. As we shall see, this contrast between Democratic rule in Chicago and Cook County and periodic (Fusion/Republican) reform rule in New York has persisted to this day, which goes a long way in accounting for the different responses their city regimes have made to recent restructuring.

9. Blacks had enjoyed a certain bargaining power with long-time Republican mayor "Big Bill" Thompson. When he was defeated by Democrat Anton Cermak in the election of 1932, Chicago's African Americans had still not shifted their allegiance from the Republican to the Democratic Party, and thus lost political clout. In the election of 1932, fewer than a fourth of Chicago's black voters cast their ballot for FDR, which led to a "temporary eclipse in the influence of the Negro vote in Chicago." With the loss of patronage, the "machine" collapsed in the black wards. But by 1934, the black vote was swinging to Democrat and new ward organizations were getting started. The popularity of Roosevelt's New Deal transformed "a large proportion of Negro voters from staunch Republicans to zealous supporters of the Democratic ticket." Drake and Cayton, *Black Metropolis,* 352, 354. The WPA played a role in this popularity.

10. Cermak's term was to be brief. He was killed by an assassin's bullet intended for President Roosevelt.

11. Drake and Cayton, *Black Metropolis,* 88.

12. *Black Metropolis* and *Bronzeville* were terms applied by black social scientists who,

while not blind to the hardships of segregation, also tended to idealize certain aspects of "community" that such isolation engendered. The term *Black Belt,* usually employed by whites to designate the same South Side zone, emphasized the spatial pattern and overgeneralized to the generally negative social consequences.

13. To speak of New York's random crime is not to ignore the fame/notoriety of that city's crime syndicates. And noir films' depiction of the indifference of New Yorkers to victims of crime is mirrored in real life by such exemplars as the Kitty Genovese case, in which numerous neighbors observed her attack from their windows but none thought to call the police.

14. I searched in vain in film encyclopedias and over the Internet before reluctantly concluding that Chicago had not inspired imaginative dystopias on the order of either *Escape from New York* or *Blade Runner.*

15. It will be recalled that the efflorescence of New York noir films was in the 1940s through 1970s, set in the present, whereas Los Angeles's date primarily from the 1980s and are set in the future. In contrast, Chicago's are almost all set in the 1920s—the peak of the "age of gangsterism."

16. Shirley Miller Bartell, "The Chinese Bandit Novel and the American Gangster Film," *New Orleans Review* (Winter 1981): 102. Bartell compares the medieval classic Chinese bandit novel with classic American gangster films, noting that both popular art forms drew "upon an historical figure who was a rebel from his society at a time of great stress in that society." In addition, both the Chinese novel and Chicago gangster films develop a similar explanatory theme: a corrupt society that "causes" its own rebels. "Paradoxically, both portray the rebel indulging in criminal acts against the authorities . . . and yet he exemplified qualities or exhibits actions admired by that society. . . . the novel and films are explicit that not the rebels but the society and its institutions are corrupt" (102–3).

17. Although the stereotype places the Sicilian Mafia in a central role, it should be pointed out that New York Jews also were involved, suggesting that it was the intersection between recent immigrants and new "opportunity structures" that was decisive, rather than Sicilian "culture."

18. Thomas Kessner, *Fiorello H. La Guardia and the Making of Modern New York* (New York: McGraw-Hill, 1989), 114; Kessner in turn cites Humbert S. Nelli, *The Italians of Chicago, 1880–1930: A Study in Ethnic Mobility* (New York: Oxford University Press, 1970), 211–12. Although Nelli has an extended treatment of Italian crime in Chicago in the 1920s, I was not able to locate the information Kessner attributes to Nelli on the pages he indicates. Nelli does include some estimates of Capone's syndicate income on p. 219, but they are not the same figures presented by Kessner.

19. In the 1980s there was a brief flurry of interest in a safe alleged to have belonged to Al Capone; after a media campaign designed to build up suspense, the safe was ceremonially opened on television and found to be empty.

20. Drake and Cayton, *Black Metropolis,* 9. Their figures somewhat overstate the case, because the foreign-born were a much higher percentage of the population than were blacks. Perhaps one can gain a clearer picture of the same transformation by considering the fact that the years before the entry of the United States into World War I, when blacks constituted only 3 percent of the population, were the *last years* in which Chicago's foreign-born constituted as much as a third of the population. Thereafter, the trend lines diverged. By the time the United States entered World War II, only 20 percent of Chicago's population had been born abroad, whereas the proportion of African Americans had risen to almost 10 percent. By 1970, the positions of the two groups had been totally reversed: by then, one-third of the city's population was black, but only 11 percent had been born abroad. I have taken these figures from Wesley

Skogan, "Chicago since 1840: A Time-Series Data Handbook" (unpublished manuscript, University of Illinois, Institute of Government and Public Affairs, 1976), 18–20, Table 1.

21. The most notable of the Irish-themed stories were, of course, James T. Farrell's Studs Lonigan stories; see *Studs Lonigan: A Trilogy Containing Young Lonigan, The Young Manhood of Studs Lonigan, and Judgement Day* (Urbana: University of Illinois Press, 1993 [1934]). If Henry Roth's *Call It Sleep* (New York: Noonday, 1991 [1934]) is the classic "fictionalized" account of growing up Jewish on New York's Lower East Side, the Studs Lonigan trilogy offers the perfect parallel: growing up Irish in south Chicago. The contrasts, however, are probably more illuminating about the two cities than are the parallels.

Richard Wright's autobiography *Black Boy* (New York: HarperCollins, 1993 [1945]) and, of course, his fictionalized *Native Son* (New York: HarperCollins, 1997 [1940]), set in Chicago, come close to early accounts of the black experience in Chicago; these have now been joined by the life histories collected by social scientists.

22. Drake and Cayton, *Black Metropolis,* 88.

23. See James Grossman, *Land of Hope: Chicago, Black Southerners, and the Great Migration* (Chicago: University of Chicago Press, 1989).

24. See Peter Hall, "The City of Permanent Underclass: The Enduring Slum: Chicago, St. Louis, London, 1920–1987," in *Cities of Tomorrow: An Intellectual History of Urban Planning and Design in the Twentieth Century* (Oxford: Blackwell, 1988), 373. The basic source for all of this is *The Negro in Chicago: A Study of Race Relations,* the report of the Chicago Commission on Race Relations authored by black sociologist Charles S. Johnson (Chicago: University of Chicago Press, 1922). See also Allan H. Spear, *Black Chicago: The Making of a Negro Ghetto, 1890–1920* (Chicago: University of Chicago Press, 1967); and William Tuttle, *Race Riot: Chicago in the Red Summer of 1919* (New York: Atheneum, 1970). Even Drake and Cayton, in the more upbeat *Black Metropolis,* conclude that between "1935 and 1940 the Negro proletariat seemed doomed to become a *lumpen-proletariat*" (89).

25. This was a naive period in which the "best minds" believed that poor housing "caused" social pathologies, and that, therefore, rehousing could "cure" them. This was also a period in which reformers believed that citywide outbreaks of disease could be traced to slums as foyers of infection.

26. Harold M. Mayer and Richard C. Wade, *Chicago: Growth of a Metropolis* (Chicago: University of Chicago Press, 1969), 364–66, give the figure of five thousand, although other sources suggest it was more than seven thousand.

27. In the postwar period, before Chicago's public housing program ground to a halt over the contentious issue of integration, additions to this already massive project would be made.

28. Black workers were even granted "temporary" union cards to work on the project. For a discussion of the project, see Arnold Hirsch, *Making the Second Ghetto: Race and Class in Chicago, 1940–1960* (New York: Cambridge University Press, 1983), 10–12.

29. The Douglas C-54 transport planes and the aircraft engines produced by Pratt and Whitney were all made in Chicago.

30. Drake and Cayton, *Black Metropolis,* 9.

31. Ibid., 12.

32. According to Drake and Cayton, the city, concerned because of the Detroit and New York riots of 1943, mobilized to avert trouble via the Mayor's Committee on Race Relations, but what also helped was that blacks could no longer be used to break strikes (strikes were then outlawed) and, indeed, found employment in new plants where perhaps there were fewer ingrained animosities. Ibid., 92–93. I would add to this that during the war

the moratorium on new construction immobilized whites and blacks; as it was difficult for *anyone* to move, blacks were unable to expand the borders of the ghetto. Once they tried, in the postwar period, pent-up tensions bubbled to the surface.

33. In Harvey Zorbaugh's classic study of the North Side of Chicago in the 1920s, *The Gold Coast and the Slum: A Sociological Study of Chicago's Near North Side* (Chicago: University of Chicago Press, 1976 [1929]), Little Sicily was the slum.

34. Adamant neighborhood opposition prevented the CHA from assigning more than the agreed-upon 20 percent of the units to black families. Therefore, in the midst of a severe housing shortage, 140 apartments in the project were still unoccupied as late as 1943. See, inter alia, Hirsch, *Making the Second Ghetto,* 45–46.

35. Although "border wars" were common in many northern cities with large black minorities, none were as constant and characteristic as those in Chicago. Joseph Boskin, in his *Urban Racial Violence in the Twentieth Century* (Beverly Hills, Calif.: Glencoe, 1969), notes that "from the end of World War II until 1964 . . . [t]he most intense violence occurred when minority groups attempted to change the residential patterns. . . . Several urban racial clashes were instigated by Caucasians who resented attempts by Negroes to move into all-White neighborhoods." The most notable were the "Airport Homes violence in Chicago in November, 1946; the Fernwood Project violence in Chicago in August, 1947; . . . [and] the . . . Cicero, Illinois violence of 1951. . . . Between 1945 and 1948 there were more than a hundred attacks on the persons and property of Negroes who moved, or attempted to move, out of the Black ghettos into other areas." (64.)

36. Skogan, "Chicago since 1840," 28–29, Table 2.

37. Figure 8.1 is reproduced from Frank A. Randall, *The Development of Chicago Building Construction* (Urbana: University of Illinois, 1949), 297. If only Randall had continued his series into the 1950s and beyond, our exposition would have been deeply enriched.

38. One of the most famous articles ever written at the beginning of the field of urban sociology was Ernest Burgess's "The Growth of the City: An Introduction to a Research Project," *Proceedings of the American Sociological Society* 18 (1923): 178–84. The city, of course, was Chicago, and Burgess captured its pattern of concentric circles. Homer Hoyt, using economic data rather than demographic information, revealed Chicago's sectoral pattern. See his *One Hundred Years of Land Values in Chicago* (Chicago: University of Chicago Press, 1933). As I have already pointed out, the form of Chicago is a combination of rings and sectors.

39. See Brian Berry et al., *Chicago: Transformations of an Urban System* (Cambridge, Mass.: Ballinger, 1976), 44, Table 4.

40. Boskin, *Urban Racial Violence,* 64, emphasis added. The November 1946 attack on Airport Homes and the August 1947 attack on the Fernwood Project were against blacks who had been moved into outlying white-occupied public housing projects that were originally built for war workers.

41. As Drake and Cayton point out, even in the absence of any direct threat, fears persisted and reactions anticipated disaster. "Even during a period when the Belt is not expanding there is always the *possibility* that an invasion *may begin, and this is reflected in periodic 'scares,'*" with respect not only to residences but to businesses in border areas. *Black Metropolis,* 190, emphasis added.

42. Hirsch, *Making the Second Ghetto,* 52.

43. Drake and Cayton, *Black Metropolis,* 182.

44. Ibid., 184.

45. Eventually, another Chicago case (*Lee v. Hansberry*) reached the U.S. Supreme

Court, but the court declined to rule on "the constitutionality or legality of restriction agreements . . . nor the validity or sufficiency of the particular Washington Park restriction agreement before it in this case." Ibid., 187, quoting Woodlawn Association *Magazine.*

46. The Court made this ruling in *Shelley v. Kraemer.* Interestingly enough, this case originated not in Chicago, with its well-known racial antagonisms, but in Los Angeles, which considered its "race relations" more benign than Chicago's. The case involved restrictive covenants on Slauson Street, then the southern "border" of the growing black ghetto, which was advancing into the zone referred to today as "South-Central Los Angeles. (Details are presented in Chapter 9.)

47. The boom in suburban construction and the lack of rent controls that might otherwise have inhibited some mobility made the option of moving particularly attractive.

48. The best study of this phenomenon is Luigi Laurenti, *Property Values and Race: Studies in Seven Cities* (Berkeley: University of California Press, 1960). As Hirsch notes, however, even "the census figures for 1950 revealed not a city undergoing desegregation but one in the process of redefining racial borders after a period of relative stability. Black isolation was, in fact, increasing even as the Black Belt grew." *Making the Second Ghetto,* 5.

49. Hirsch, *Making the Second Ghetto,* 13–14.

50. Needless to say, redevelopment led to many controversies and scandals. First, it was not necessarily the worst slums that were selected; some areas declared "blighted" were those whose only fault was that their locations were coveted by private developers. And second, many of the replacement projects ended up with rents so high that none but the upper-middle class could afford them. Carl Sandburg Village, on the near North Side of Chicago, was among the latter.

51. Hall, "The City of Permanent Underclass," 383.

52. See Martin Meyerson and Edward Banfield, *Politics, Planning and the Public Interest: The Case of Public Housing in Chicago* (Glencoe, Ill.: Free Press, 1955). Both authors were young professors in the Department of Planning at the University of Chicago. Meyerson took a leave of absence to serve as director of planning for the CHA; he was appointed by Elizabeth Wood, then head of the Chicago Housing Authority. It is Meyerson's detailed descriptions of his interactions with members of the city council who had veto power over site selection, rather than Banfield's somewhat abstract theoretical discourses, that make this book an invaluable source.

53. Meyerson describes interminable bus trips with city council members to show them possible vacant sites, which they systematically rejected on NIMBY (not in my backyard) grounds (see ibid.). In New York, the less powerful aldermen were not involved in site selection at all; selections were made by the NYPHA, although city council approval after the fact was required. By scattering its sites throughout the boroughs, the NYPHA evidently forestalled the location games played in Chicago.

54. Hall, "The City of Permanent Underclass," 383–84. Hall depends heavily on Hirsch's *Making the Second Ghetto.*

55. Hirsch, *Making the Second Ghetto,* 63.

56. School desegregation on a metropoliswide basis has never been required, and it was not until 1976, in the *Hills v. Gautreaux* case originating in Chicago, that the U.S. Supreme Court ordered HUD to "administer federally subsidized housing programs throughout the six county Chicago metropolitan area to help remedy the effects of past racial bias in Chicago's public housing." Alexander Polikoff, *Housing the Poor: The Case for Heroism* (Cambridge, Mass.: Ballinger, 1978), xiii. (See Chapter 11 for more details.)

57. See Peter H. Rossi and Robert A. Dentler, *The Politics of Urban Renewal: The*

Chicago Findings (Glencoe, Ill.: Free Press, 1961), on Hyde Park; see also Harvey Molotch, "Racial Change in a Stable Community," *American Journal of Sociology* 75, no. 2 (1969): 226–38.

58. On the South Shore, see Harvey L. Molotch, *Managed Integration: Dilemmas of Doing Good in the City* (Berkeley: University of California Press, 1972).

59. Chicago was quick to take advantage of changes in the Urban Renewal Act that permitted replacement of slums by nonresidential uses. The near West Side, with its mixed population of blacks, Puerto Ricans, Mexicans, and (vestiges of the original) Italians, was cleared for the construction of the Chicago campus of the University of Illinois and eventually for an expansion of the Loop's commercial/office space. Minorities were thus "pushed" westward into Lawndale, which would be the prime site of Chicago's 1968 ghetto revolt. The early phases of the University of Illinois siting and neighborhood reaction are well covered in Gerald Suttles, *The Social Order of the Slum: Ethnicity and Territory in the Inner City* (Chicago: University of Chicago Press, 1968).

60. The growing poor population of blacks and Latinos in the West Side slum was increasingly trapped between the rock of downtown expansion from the east and the hard place of Cicero, a white ethnic industrial suburb to its west.

61. Skogan, "Chicago since 1840," appendix table.

62. Michael McCall, "Some Ecological Aspects of Negro Slum Riots (1968)," in *Protest, Reform, and Revolt: A Reader in Social Movements,* ed. Joseph R. Gusfield (New York: John Wiley, 1970), 350–51.

63. Skogan, "Chicago since 1840," appendix. Skogan depends upon the brief account of this "riot" presented in the Kerner Report. However, what the Kerner Report fails to mention is that this explosion occurred one day after Martin Luther King's rally for open housing, held in Soldier Field and attended by some twenty-five to fifty thousand persons, a rally that was the culmination of two years of demonstrations and marches for open housing in the city. See, inter alia, James R. Ralph Jr. *Northern Protest: Martin Luther King, Jr., Chicago, and the Civil Rights Movement* (Cambridge: Harvard University Press, 1993); and David Garrow, ed., *Chicago 1966: Open Housing Marches, Summit Negotiations, and Operation Breadbasket* (Brooklyn, N.Y.: Carlson, 1989). Housing, not hydrants, was the issue.

64. The younger Daley is sometimes referred to by pundits as R2D2. For an uncritical account of the "new" Daley, written on the eve of the 1996 Democratic Convention in Chicago (which stimulated a spate of "reminiscences" of the disastrous 1968 convention and its antiwar protests), see, inter alia, James Atlas, "The Daleys of Chicago," *New York Times Magazine,* August 25, 1996, 37–39, 52, 56–58.

65. Although scarcely a sociological variable, mortality has had an inordinate effect on Chicago politics. Richard Daley Sr., whom Royko refers to simply as "the Boss" in his fascinating biography, had a stranglehold on the office of mayor until his death in 1976. See Mike Royko, *Boss: Richard J. Daley of Chicago* (New York: New American Library, 1971). The lack of a powerful successor propelled Jane Byrne into a single term of office, after which she was defeated by Harold Washington. One must note, however, that the latter's election in 1983 was not so much a symptom of a change in the local power structure as it was the anomalous result of a three-way primary contest in which Jane Byrne ran against the son of Richard J. Daley, which split the "white" vote and allowed the black candidate to slip in through the breach. Washington died only seven months into his second term and was replaced temporarily by a black member of the Chicago City Council until new elections could be held. Significantly, this aberration was never repeated, and the younger Daley easily won the next election; as of 1999, he was still in office.

66. As Richard Keiser notes in his perceptive article "Explaining African-American Political Empowerment: Windy City Politics from 1900 to 1983," *Urban Affairs Quarterly* 29 (September 1993): "Early in the 20th century, Chicago was 'the seventh heaven' of political activity for African-Americans. In no city had African-American empowerment proceeded as far" (84). But instead of viewing "political machines [as] a 'ladder' for minority empowerment," Keiser argues that it was "electoral competition among white factions or parties [that] created the conditions under which African-American voters could determine electoral outcomes and African-American leaders could bargain for group empowerment" (84).

67. Drake and Cayton, *Black Metropolis,* 346.

68. Keiser, "Explaining African-American Political Empowerment," 84.

69. In the 1993 edition of Drake and Cayton's *Black Metropolis* there are two appended sections titled "Bronzeville 1961" (793–825) and "Postscript 1969" (826–36). In many ways, these two "updatings" say it all. The 1961 addition is full of hope and pride; by 1969, the tone had turned to despair. But even in the 1961 addendum, hints of problems appear: "With money in the bank and G.I. and F.H.A. loans available, Bronzeville's home owners have been lavishing attention upon their newly acquired properties. . . . Even the older parts of the Black Belt have a new look. Extensive slum-clearance and rebuilding have changed the face of the Black Belt's northern section while 'elbow grease,' paint and grass, storm windows and flowers, have eliminated much of the drab, run-down, depression look of yesteryears. *But unkempt neighborhoods and litter-laden alleys and streets have by no means disappeared; and Bronzeville's* masses *are still piled up on top of each other in cramped quarters to a greater extent than any other part of Midwest Metropolis*" (796, emphasis added).

70. Ibid., 806, emphasis added. The words "the masses" appear in italics in the original. Note the distancing of the authors from "the masses."

71. These events are chronicled in National Advisory Commission on Civil Disorders, *Report of the National Advisory Commission on Civil Disorders* (New York: Bantam, 1968). It is significant that this report, commonly referred to as the Kerner Report (after the designated chairman, Otto Kerner, then governor of Illinois), which details the increasing separation of the United States into two societies—one black and one white—was issued in March 1968, less than a month before King's assassination.

72. "Postscript 1969" in Drake and Cayton, *Black Metropolis,* 830–32, subsection headed "Violence—Spectre and Spur."

73. Ibid., 826, emphasis added.

74. Daley would eventually become head of the Cook County machine as well, thus further consolidating his control.

75. It is remarkable that one of the few detailed studies of Chicago's machine since Gosnell's classic study in the 1930s, Thomas M. Guterback's *Machine Politics in Transition: Party and Community in Chicago* (Chicago: University of Chicago Press, 1980), based on data collected in the early 1970s, virtually ignores race. But, in fairness, Guterback concentrates on a white ward.

76. See Ester R. Fuchs, *Mayors and Money: Fiscal Policy in New York and Chicago* (Chicago: University of Chicago Press, 1992); this volume is based on Fuchs's doctoral dissertation. Fuchs had served as a research assistant on a comparative statistical study of city finance conducted at the University of Chicago, which was stimulated by the 1975 fiscal crisis in New York. Although the larger comparative study found that by 1974 many cities in the United States were experiencing similar fiscal strains, only New York demonstrated this in exaggerated fashion. (The results of the larger study can be found in Terry Nichols Clark and Lorna Crowley Ferguson, *City Money: Political Processes, Fiscal Strain, and Retrenchment* [New York:

Columbia University Press, 1983].) Fuchs compares Chicago, which remained fiscally solvent, with New York, which had almost gone bankrupt. Her explanation draws on the theoretical typology of political cultures set forth in Clark and Ferguson's book. Studying the city budgets in the two cities, she found a growing discrepancy in per capita expenditures. Before 1960, New York's expenditures were routinely only a little higher than Chicago's. After that, the gap became increasingly wider, peaking in the mid-1970s, before the fiscal crisis forced a slight retrenchment. By that time, New York was spending some twelve hundred dollars per capita per year, whereas Chicago's expenditures per person had risen only to two hundred dollars. Unfortunately, Fuchs's study perpetuates the "boundary" problem inherent in the original analysis; she restricts her unit of analysis to the two cities (rather than metropolitan regions), as the larger study did. In Chapter 10, I revise Fuchs's analysis by comparing New York City's expenditures to those of Cook County and Los Angeles County, which removes most of the difference. See also Rowan A. Miranda, "Post-Machine Regimes and the Growth of Government: A Fiscal History of the City of Chicago, 1970–1990," *Urban Affairs Quarterly* 28 (March 1993): 397–422. Miranda responds to Fuchs's work by arguing that the differences can be traced to voter values, another hypothesis suggested by Clark and Ferguson.

77. I have not corrected these figures to account for the growing population of Hispanics, which was then still small.

78. Drake and Cayton, *Black Metropolis,* 180–90.

79. A third factor would be added as Latinos continued to migrate to the region and settle predominantly within the city limits.

80. Polikoff, *Housing the Poor,* xiii.

81. Their patterned locations were remarkably similar to those envisaged by the 1909 Burnham plan.

82. Ann Markusen and Karen McCurdy, "Chicago's Defense-Based High Technology: A Case Study of the 'Seedbeds of Innovation' Hypothesis," *Economic Development Quarterly* 3 (February 1989): 19, Table 1. Markusen and McCurdy develop an interesting index: "per capita prime contracts relative to the U.S. average," which is taken to be 100 for any given year. According to this, in 1951 the Illinois figure was only slightly below the average (index: 90), ranking eleventh of the eighteen states studied. By 1958 the Illinois index stood at only 50 (half the U.S. average, about even with New Hampshire and Virginia; only Wisconsin, with 30, ranked lower). In 1967, the Illinois index remained at 50 and, along with Wisconsin, ranked lowest in the eighteen states. By data year 1977 and again in 1984, the Illinois index had dropped to 20 and was the lowest rank in both years. (Wisconsin remained second lowest, with an index of 40.) The Northeast fared fairly well, starting the period with among the very highest and ending it with high ranks, even though the specific "positions" of the various states may have changed. (New York, for example, began with 190 and dropped to 100. New Jersey started with 160 and declined to 80, whereas Virginia started at 30 and rose to 160. Massachusetts started at 100 and increased to 230, and Maryland rose from 130 to 160. The biggest surprise was Connecticut, which was highest of all in 1951 with 440 contracts and was still highest in 1984 with 330.)

83. See Ann Markusen, Peter Hall, Sabina Dietrich, and Scott Campbell, *The Rise of the Gunbelt: The Military Remapping of Industrial America* (New York: Oxford University Press, 1991).

84. Ann Markusen and Virginia Carlson, "Losses in the Heartland: National Policies Will Decide the Fate of the Midwest Economy," *Northeast/Midwest Economic Review,* May 1, 1989, 8–13. A much fuller presentation appears in their "Deindustrialization in the American Midwest: Causes and Responses," in *Deindustrialization and Regional Economic Transformation:*

The Experience of the United States, ed. Lloyd Rodwin and Hidehiko Sazanami (Boston: Unwin Hyman, 1989), 29–59.

85. Markusen and Carlson, "Deindustrialization in the American Midwest." "At first sight, this bias is perplexing. The modern military-industrial complex was born in the midwestern industrial heartland. . . . Up through World War II, and to a lesser extent during the Korean and Vietnam periods, the industrial heartland hummed with factories devoted to the production of tanks, airplanes, ordnance, and other war materiel." Despite this lead and the existence of top engineering schools, a skilled workforce, and so on, the region lost out. "Decade by decade, especially after 1950, midwestern industrial cities lost ground to the emerging 'gunbelt'" (51–53).

"Both the state of Illinois and the Chicago area were bypassed by the cold war defense buildup. . . . When Chicago does sell to the Pentagon, sales are apt to take the form of bulk commodities on standardized parts and equipment . . . skewed toward the Army, while both city and state fall far behind in filling orders for the Air Force. . . . In contrast, California, one of the nation's major beneficiaries of the cold war buildup, has a far higher share of its orders originating from the Air Force" (70).

In the postwar period, the military-industrial complex rose in tandem with the Cold War, but it barely touched the Midwest. Markusen and Carlson argue for a political explanation: "Politicians beholden to new defense-oriented constituencies in states like Massachusetts, California, and Texas came to dominate the presidency and relevant congressional committees. . . . *as Donald Frey put it, '. . . the Midwest had no Fred Terman and no Tip O'Neill'*" (79, emphasis added).

86. Markusen and Carlson, "Losses in the Heartland," 10.

87. See James Vance, *The Continuing City: Urban Morphology in Western Civilization* (Baltimore: Johns Hopkins University Press, 1990), 486, Table 9.1.

88. Carol Willis, *Form Follows Finance: Skyscrapers and Skylines in New York and Chicago* (New York: Princeton Architectural Press, 1995), 181.

89. Before 1893, some of the early "skyscrapers" in the Loop rose as high as 200 feet above the sidewalk, and the city made no attempt to limit them. However, in the depression of 1893, there was a glut of office space. At the instigation of real estate interests concerned with reducing their vacancies, a cap on new building heights was placed at 130 feet. "In the thirty years before the city passed a zoning law [in 1923] that permitted towers, the maximum height moved up and down between 130 and 260 feet. At the same time, Manhattan towers stretched to 600 and 700 feet." Ibid., 50.

90. Ibid., 10.

91. Ibid.

92. Ibid., 128–29, 130.

9. LOS ANGELES BECOMES INDUSTRIAL

1. William H. Mullins, *The Depression and the Urban West Coast, 1929–1933: Los Angeles, San Francisco, Seattle, and Portland* (Bloomington: Indiana University Press, 1991), 10–11.

2. Ibid., 7.

3. Ibid., 12–14. Mullins cites Philip Neff and Anita Weifenbach, *Business Cycles in Selected Industrial Areas* (Berkeley: University of California Press for the Haynes Foundation, 1949), who demonstrate that "the Los Angeles economy turned for the worse at precisely the same time as the rest of the nation, September 1929" (66). A somewhat different position is taken by Kevin Starr, who claims that even though California was harshly affected during the

very early years of the Depression, because "agriculture [was] at the base of [the] economy, augmented by such Depression-resistant enterprises as motion pictures, defense, and federally subsidized shipping, Californians did not suffer the levels of visible turmoil and dislocations of more industrialized regions." See the third volume in his evolving history of California, *The Dream Endures: California Enters the 1940s* (New York: Oxford University Press, 1997), vii. Starr was very kind to allow me to read the galley proofs for this book (then under a different title); my quotations and cited page numbers refer to this preliminary version.

4. Whereas Los Angeles's leaders were reluctant supporters of the New Deal and rejected some of the assistance proffered by Washington, they did not hesitate to lobby for massive investments in infrastructural projects such as dams, port improvements, and irrigation.

5. More than the Depression held up this controversial project, because Chinatown would have been displaced by it. It was not until 1926 that voters finally agreed to support it, and then litigation held up execution through 1933. By then, however, the project was beyond the economic capacity of the city. Not until May 1939 was the station completed and opened to the public. See John D. Weaver, *Los Angeles: The Enormous Village 1781–1981* (Santa Barbara, Calif.: Capra, 1980), 215. (This book is a gold mine of little facts.) Restoration of this architectural gem did not take place until the 1990s.

6. This is a marked contrast with New York, where protestors were somewhat better accommodated after the 1935 Harlem riots. It should be pointed out that federal legislation in 1935 legitimated union activity, and this had its effects even in open-shop Los Angeles. Starr's *The Dream Endures* chronicles union activities and strife in California before and during the Depression; what is particularly significant is that his cases are drawn almost exclusively from San Francisco. Los Angeles's labor actions were minimal in contrast.

7. Also sometimes claiming exemption are "Californios." However, according to the careful demographic analysis of Frank D. Bean and Marta Tienda in *The Hispanic Population of the United States* (New York: Russell Sage Foundation, 1987), only a tiny percentage of current Mexican Americans can actually claim descent from pre-1850 territories, even though the land itself did belong to Mexico (107, 116). Whether accurately or not, Americans of Mexican descent tend to identify themselves with the "original settlers" and feel a certain sense of entitlement. Some of the conflicting attitudes are described by Peter Skerry in *Mexican Americans: The Ambivalent Minority* (Cambridge: Harvard University Press, 1993), chap. 1; Skerry also notes that Leo Grebler (see Grebler et al., *The Mexican-American People: The Nation's Second Largest Minority* [New York: Free Press, 1970]) had found a similar ambivalence a generation earlier. However, the book that best captures the sensibilities of Mexican immigrants toward California is George Sanchez's remarkable *Becoming Mexican American: Ethnicity, Culture and Identity in Chicano Los Angeles, 1900–1945* (New York: Oxford University Press, 1993).

8. This ambivalence was *not* present in relationship to the immigrants from northern Europe, especially those talented émigrés who fled Hitler's Germany. In the 1930s and even 1940s, many of these infused the high culture of Los Angeles through music (e.g., Arnold Schoenberg), art and architecture (inter alia, Richard Neutra), and literature (including Thomas Mann).

9. Unlike immigrants from Europe, the Mexican-origin population of the Southwest can theoretically claim an original "right" as emotionally powerful as that of the *Mayflower* descendants, even though that connection is mostly symbolic. That very few of today's Mexican American residents of Los Angeles would be able to trace their descent from the few pre-1850 Californios in no way eliminates the ambiguity surrounding claims and counterclaims. In some ways, one might characterize Chicano attitudes as flavored with "irredentism."

10. The institution of the "guest worker," well-known in Europe (see John Berger's bril-

liant *Seventh Man: Migrant Workers in Europe* [New York: Viking, 1975]) and most recently surfacing in the Middle East, not only in the Arabian Peninsula countries but in Israel, which now imports Asians as substitutes for the Palestinians it formerly used, creates grotesque anomalies by envaluing labor while denying rights. This disjuncture inevitably places guest workers in a position highly vulnerable to exploitation. Although the "theory" defines workers' sojourns as temporary, most importers of such labor have faced dilemmas about what to do with the offspring and spouses of workers. This phenomenon in the United States is found chiefly in the Southwest, with respect to Mexican nationals. Despite federal laws that have presumably outlawed this practice, exceptions have generally been made during periods of labor shortages. Neither New York nor Chicago needed or institutionalized this system, although on occasion each has mistreated aliens in ways that make the results comparable.

11. The 1917 Immigration Act was not applied uniformly. The Department of Labor, responding to pressures from growers' associations and large industrialists, granted exemptions from 1917 to 1920 "to [Mexican] recruits for the beet fields, railroad gangs, and other contracted labor." In this manner, some fifty thousand Mexican "guest workers" entered. "By the mid-twenties, most large American cities had their enclaves of Mexican nationals . . . [e.g., the] Ford motor company . . . in Detroit [and s]ignificant numbers . . . in Chicago." Abraham Hoffman, *Unwanted Mexican Americans in the Great Depression: Repatriation Pressures, 1929–1939* (Tucson: University of Arizona Press, 1974), 11–12.

12. Mary Anne Thatcher, *Immigrants and the 1930s: Ethnicity and Alienage in the Depression and the Coming War* (New York: Garland, 1990). More recent, see T. Almaguer and M.-K. Jung, "The Enduring Ambiguities of Race," in *Sociology for the Twenty-First Century,* ed. Janet Abu-Lughod (Chicago: University of Chicago Press, 1999).

13. The annual quotas, which were some 357,000 in 1921, were reduced to 165,000 in 1924. No quotas were imposed on immigrants from the Western Hemisphere, including Mexico.

14. Thatcher notes that between 1930 and 1940, only about a quarter of the available quota places were actually filled (*Immigrants and the 1930s,* 63 [diss. typescript]). Clearly, it was both more difficult to arrange travel and less attractive to do so, given the known economic problems that would face the immigrant upon arrival. Only prescient Jews fleeing the rise of Hitler constituted a countertrend.

15. Thatcher reports that in 1934 only 3 percent of persons receiving relief were aliens, even though in 1935 the unemployment rate for aliens was 65 percent, considerably higher than that for the native-born. In 1939 aliens were still ineligible for WPA work. The federal government had outlawed such discrimination, even including aliens in the Social Security Act of 1935, but local practices succeeded in excluding aliens even from programs to which they were legally entitled. See ibid.

16. Mullins, *The Depression and the Urban West Coast,* 18.

17. Ibid., 71. See also Carey McWilliams, "Getting Rid of the Mexican," *American Mercury* 28 (March 1933): 323; McWilliams claims that Los Angeles repatriated thirty-five thousand Mexicans in 1932 alone.

18. Armando Morales, *Ando Sangrando (I Am Bleeding): A Study of Mexican American–Police Conflict* (La Puente, Calif.: Perspectiva, 1972), 14.

19. According to Hoffman, 80,000 Mexicans were "repatriated" in 1929, 70,000 in 1930, 138,500 in 1931 (the peak year), 77,500 in 1932, and 33,500 in 1933. After that, the annual numbers declined gradually until they numbered only about 8,000 in 1937. *Unwanted Mexican Americans,* Appendix D. Bitter memories still linger of this cruel expulsion. Julian Nava (a university professor and the first Mexican American to serve on the Los

Angeles School Board), in his foreword to Hoffman's book, attributes "much of the feeling of alienation from Anglo-American society among Mexican-American adults today . . . [to] the belief that they are still not wanted except as they serve U.S. economic desires" (ix).

20. Ibid., 3. Outside of California and Texas (and to a lesser extent Arizona and Colorado), the only other places from which sizeable numbers of Mexicans were repatriated were Chicago and Detroit. See ibid., 118 ff.

21. Ibid., 43–44. Hoffman cites Robert K. Murray, *Red Scare: A Study in National Hysteria, 1919–1920* (Minneapolis: University of Minnesota Press, 1955).

22. Hoffman, *Unwanted Mexican Americans,* 49. At one point some four hundred persons were rounded up in the part of Los Angeles known as the Pueblo (59). The system was hardly efficient: "In order to capture the 389 aliens successfully prosecuted during . . . [one] period, [the authorities] had to round up and question somewhere between three thousand and four thousand people" (64–65).

23. See Mullins, *The Depression and the Urban West Coast,* 70.

24. Fred Viehe, "Black Gold Suburbs: The Influence of the Extractive Industry on the Suburbanization of Los Angeles, 1890–1930," *Journal of Urban History* 8 (November 1981): 18–19.

25. Mullins, *The Depression and the Urban West Coast,* 58, 92.

26. Viehe, "Black Gold Suburbs," 26.

27. Ibid., 99–100.

28. The books he published included *King Coal* in 1917, *Oil!* in 1927, and *Boston* (on the Sacco and Vanzetti case) in 1928—all "exposés." There is a very helpful literary criticism cum biography by William A. Bloodworth Jr., *Upton Sinclair* (Boston: G. K. Hall, 1977), which ties together Sinclair's writings and his life, although it deals only superficially with the EPIC campaign. It does, however, cite relevant writings often ignored by others. I have therefore depended heavily on this source.

29. The Democratic ticket was referred to, disparagingly, as "Uppie and Downey," the former being Sinclair's nickname and the latter the surname of his running mate.

30. Bloodworth, *Upton Sinclair,* 131–32.

31. This failure led quite naturally to a sequel volume, which he titled *I, Candidate for Governor, and How I Got Licked* (Pasadena, Calif.: Author, 1935).

32. Just before the election, Sinclair spent two hours with President Roosevelt, during which he presented his ideas about EPIC and his plan to substitute "use value" for "exchange value" (he actually used those terms); FDR apparently led him on by saying he would make an announcement in a few weeks in a fireside chat supporting some of Sinclair's ideas, but to Sinclair's despair, this never happened. During the same period, Sinclair also met with La Guardia at the Chicago World's Fair, where the two reformers aired their differences: Sinclair emphasized the importance of redistributing work and converting exchange to use value; La Guardia talked instead about redistributing wealth. On "dirty tricks," see Greg Mitchell, *The Campaign of the Century: Upton Sinclair's Race for Governor of California and the Birth of Media Politics* (New York: Random House, 1992).

33. Bloodworth, *Upton Sinclair,* 133.

34. For these totals, see Mel Scott, *Metropolitan Los Angeles: One Community* (Los Angeles: Haynes Foundation, 1949), 39. "In the 1930–1940 decade . . . [migration was] responsible for 87.6 percent of the increase." Arthur G. Coons and Arjay Miller, "An Economic and Industrial Survey of the Los Angeles and San Diego Areas" (California State Planning Board, mimeo, 1941), xv.

35. Scott, *Metropolitan Los Angeles,* 45. The city received a number of Europeans fleeing

from Hitler, and although their numbers may not have been large, their influence on Los Angeles culture was substantial. Musicians, writers, filmmakers, and architects, some of great repute, relocated in Los Angeles during the 1930s.

36. Ibid., 39. According to Thomas Muller: "Between 1935 and 1940, over 650,000 persons moved to California, primarily to the southern part of the state. The newcomers, who represented almost 10 percent of the state's population, increased the demand for housing, consumer goods and services, both private and public. The state also benefited from massive government projects to meet the tremendous demand of the mushrooming population for roads, bridges, and water, and to relieve unemployment. Throughout the 1930s, California outperformed the national economy in . . . housing, construction, per capita income, output per worker, and investment per worker." Thomas Muller, *Immigrants and the American City* (New York: New York University Press, 1993), 101.

37. Ann Markusen, Peter Hall, Sabina Deitrich, and Scott Campbell, "Aerospace Capital of the World: Los Angeles Takes Off," in *The Rise of the Gunbelt: The Military Remapping of Industrial America* (New York: Oxford University Press, 1991), see esp. 84. Automobile branch assembly plants had already been set up by the mid-1930s: Chrysler in 1931, Ford and Studebaker in 1935, and General Motors in 1936. These were located mostly in the old industrial zones of South Gate and South-Central. See John H. M. Laslett, "Historical Perspectives: The Rise of a Distinctive Urban Region," in *Ethnic Los Angeles,* ed. Roger Waldinger and Mehdi Bozorgmehr (New York: Russell Sage, 1997).

38. Coons and Miller, "Economic and Industrial Survey," xviii–xix; for details, see 1–33.

39. "By the close of 1939, aircraft employment accounted for two-thirds of the total increase in manufacturing employment, becoming the largest single source of employment in the spring of 1940. Shipbuilding was slower in getting under way. By December, 1941, aircraft employment was over 120,000 and shipbuilding employment was 25,000. . . . The backlog of major aircraft companies in the Area has expanded from $183,500,000 in January 1940 to $1,636,828,000 in October 1941. Payroll has increased from $3,815,000 to $20,269,743 in the same period." Ibid., xxii–xxiii. On the film industry, see Otto Friedrich, *City of Nets: A Portrait of Hollywood in the 1940s* (New York: Harper & Row, 1986); and John Russell Taylor, *Strangers in Paradise: The Hollywood Émigrés 1933–1950* (London: Faber & Faber, 1983), which concentrates on the importation of musical, writing, acting, and directing talent from Europe (especially from the 1930s on, when Hitler helped "cause" the flight of many, Jews and non-Jews alike), the communities these exiles formed, and their influence on American film culture. The best book by far, however, is Neal Gabler, *An Empire of Their Own: How the Jews Invented Hollywood* (New York: Doubleday Anchor, 1988).

40. The sequence of Los Angeles's expansion into aircraft and then aerospace is well chronicled in Markusen et al., "Aerospace Capital of the World."

41. The massive surge of Chicago's industrialization leveled off at the Depression and never really recovered its old momentum after World War II. By then, Los Angeles had become the new growth pole of the nation. Frederic Cople Jaher, *The Urban Establishment: Upper Strata in Boston, New York, Charleston, Chicago and Los Angeles* (Urbana: University of Illinois Press, 1982), 539–40. Of course, what Jaher does not recognize is that boundaries also played a role in magnifying apparent population losses. All cities experienced significant suburban growth after the war: such growth took place mostly outside city boundaries in New York City and Chicago; in Los Angeles, there was still room for "suburban expansion" *within* the city's limits.

42. Scott, *Metropolitan Los Angeles,* 39–40, emphasis added.

43. "The Iron and Steel Industry in Los Angeles County" (Board of Supervisors of

Los Angeles County and the Industrial Department of the Los Angeles County Chamber of Commerce, mimeo, [1945?]).

44. Ibid., 15. It is interesting to contrast this prediction with Mike Davis's account of the subsequent collapse of Kaiser Steel in Fontana. See the final chapter of his *City of Quartz: Excavating the Future in Los Angeles* (New York: Verso, 1990).

45. For information on changes in Los Angeles engendered by the war, see Arthur C. Verge, *Paradise Transformed: Los Angeles during the Second World War* (Dubuque, Iowa: Kendall, 1993).

46. Carey McWilliams, "Look What's Happened to California," *Harper's Magazine,* September 1949, 24–25.

47. Almost none of Los Angeles's blacks lived in the suburbs; in fact, in 1930, 70 percent lived in the increasingly black neighborhood around Central Avenue. Although their homes were thus close to industrial zones, few were employed in manufacturing. There are a number of important studies of this crucial period in the history of Los Angeles's black population. The benchmark remains J. Max Bond's doctoral dissertation "The Negro in Los Angeles" (University of Southern California, 1936), which includes extremely good material on the model of the "Chicago school" as well as interesting maps. Lawrence B. de Graaf has contributed two basic works: his "City of Black Angels: Emergence of the Los Angeles Ghetto, 1890–1930," *Pacific Historical Review* 39 (August 1970): 323–52; and his 1962 doctoral dissertation, "Negro Migration to Los Angeles, 1930 to 1950" (University of California, Los Angeles). A study that builds on those earlier works but focuses more directly on changes during the war years is Keith E. Collins, *Black Los Angeles: The Maturing of the Ghetto, 1940–1950* (San Francisco: Century Twenty One, 1980), originally also a dissertation. None of these sources, however, is as sophisticated as *Black Metropolis* on Chicago or the several classic studies of Harlem.

48. Figures for 1930, 1940, and 1950 are from successive decennial censuses. I have taken the 1944 and 1945–46 figures from Collins, *Black Los Angeles,* 40, Table IV. Collins cites various special census series publications that I have not consulted. Bernard Marchand, *The Emergence of Los Angeles: Population and Housing in the City of Los Angeles, 1940–1970* (London: Pion, 1986), gives somewhat different figures for the city, claiming that they are also based on successive U.S. Censuses. According to Marchand, the number of blacks rose from 66,889 in 1940 to more than 191,000 ten years later. The comparable figure for 1960 was 404,000, and for 1970, almost 650,000 (90, Table 4.1).

49. I have calculated these percentages from figures presented in Collins, *Black Los Angeles,* 41, Table V. Although Collins concludes that only half of the county's black community lived within the city in 1950 (42), his own table does not support this conclusion.

50. Ibid., 43–44. In fact, Watts was well located with respect to the major older industrial zones of Los Angeles, although mass-transit connections were admittedly deficient. Inaccessible, however, were the shipbuilding installations at the port and the new defense plants (aerospace factories) at peripheral locations.

51. The original Pueblo settlement at the Plaza expanded first by leaping over the largely Jewish areas of Brooklyn and Boyle Heights into the unincorporated area of Belvedere, although gradually it would sift westward to absorb those districts intervening between Belvedere and downtown Los Angeles. The best book on this subject is clearly Sanchez's *Becoming Mexican American.* Among the other good sources on "the barrio" are Ricardo Romo, *East Los Angeles: History of a Barrio* (Austin: University of Texas Press, 1983); and Rodolfo F. Acuña, *A Community under Siege: A Chronicle of Chicanos East of the Los Angeles River, 1945–1975,* Monograph 11 (Los Angeles: UCLA Chicano Studies Research Center, 1984). On the earliest

history of the Mexican settlements, see Richard Griswold del Castillo, *The Los Angeles Barrio, 1850–1890: A Social History* (Berkeley: University of California Press, 1979).

52. Through the Bracero Program's arrangement with the Mexican government, several hundred thousand Mexican farmworkers were brought into the Southwest between 1942 and 1963. See Ernesto Galarza, *Merchants of Labor: The Mexican Bracero Story* (Charlotte, Calif.: McNally & Loftin, 1964).

53. It is interesting that Peter Skerry, author of an otherwise fine book (despite its conservative sponsorship), leaves out any reference to the 1943 harassment of Chicanos and does not speculate on what role the navy and the police may have played in shaping the "ambivalence" of Mexican Americans. See his *Mexican Americans: The Ambivalent Minority* (Cambridge: Harvard University Press, 1993). Skerry, along with most other commentators, also ignores the 1970 demonstrations carried out by Chicano activists. In contrast, Morales (in *Ando Sangrando*) and Sanchez, both writing from a Chicano perspective, stress 1943 and 1970 as "defining moments" that intensified their "ambivalence," the title of part 4 of Sanchez's more nuanced book, *Becoming Mexican American.*

54. Morales, *Ando Sangrando,* 16–17. Morales and many others in the Mexican American community at the time attributed this persecution to racism against Mexicans, which had been endemic to Los Angeles for generations. But it should also be pointed out that few of the sailors were Angelenos or had much previous contact with Mexicans per se. A much more complicated analysis is offered by psychologist Mauricio Mazon in *The Zoot-Suit Riots: The Psychology of Symbolic Annihilation* (Austin: University of Texas Press, 1984). Despite his deceptive title, Mazon places the blame on wartime jingoism and "resentment" toward those who did not seem to be sacrificing themselves for the war effort. However, it must also be noted that local civilians participated in the attacks, and that it was the native Angelenos who fueled the anti-Japanese crusade that eventually resulted in one of the saddest chapters in American racism, the relocation of Japanese Americans to "concentration" camps. This deeper interpretation belies Mazon's superficial argument that the riots were a reaction against symbolic cultural traits such as costumes.

55. A June 1920 publication by the Interchurch World Movement of North America, prepared by G. Bromley Oxnam of the Los Angeles City Survey, had reported that Mexican residents were no more prone to commit crimes than the average resident of Los Angeles, even though their arrest rates were higher. Rather, they were far more subject to environmentally induced disease and suffered from extremely poor housing conditions. The report also predicted, quite accurately, that Mexicans would bear the brunt of displacement when the Union Station construction project was finally executed.

56. Quoted in Donald Teruo Hata Jr. and Nadine Ishitani Hata, "Asian-Pacific Angelinos: Model Minorities and Indispensable Scapegoats," in *20th Century Los Angeles: Power, Promotion, and Social Conflict,* ed. Norman Klein and Martin J. Schiesl (Claremont, Calif.: Regina, 1990), 77. For the role played by Los Angeles in pressuring for this precipitous act, see Roger Daniels, *The Decision to Relocate the Japanese Americans* (Philadelphia: J. B. Lippincott, 1975). For an early history and a critical discussion of life in one relocation camp, see Alexander Leighton, *The Governing of Men: General Principles and Recommendations Based on Experience at a Japanese Relocation Camp* (Princeton, N.J.: Princeton University Press, 1945).

57. Given that the Japanese-origin population was concentrated almost exclusively on the West Coast and Los Angeles had the largest number, it is not surprising that a third of all "detainees" during the war hailed from the Los Angeles area.

58. Hata and Hata, "Asian-Pacific Angelinos," 79.

59. Coons and Miller, "Economic and Industrial Survey," xxvi–xxvii.

60. McWilliams, "Look What's Happened to California," 23. Indeed, McWilliams accurately predicted that the growth of California's population would require a reapportionment of congressional seats, thus adding political strength to California at the expense of New York. The elections of favorite sons Nixon and Reagan confirm his prescience. McWilliams also noted that, "economically, the growth of West Coast industrial power, particularly the upsurge of California, has profound national significance. . . . California, with 10,000,000 people, represents quite a market . . . [and it] is not by chance . . . that the volume of north-south train, bus, and airline passenger traffic on the West Coast has begun to exceed in importance the volume of east-west traffic." Ibid., 28, 29.

61. Scott, *Metropolitan Los Angeles,* 40.

62. Between 1945 and 1948, 1,300 plants expanded and 850 new ones were built. "More new permanent jobs were created after the war than during the war." Ibid.

63. Sam Bass Warner Jr., "The New Freedom: Los Angeles 1920—Bureaucracy, Racism, and Automobiles," in *The Urban Wilderness* (New York: Harper & Row, 1972), 118–19.

64. See Markusen et al., "Aerospace Capital of the World."

65. Ibid., 93, Table 5.1. It was in the 1930s that California consolidated its claim to industry dominance. As late as 1925, of the forty-four major aircraft-producing firms in the country, by far the largest number (fifteen) were located in New York State; California ranked third with only four firms (just behind Ohio, which had five). However, by 1937, there were some ninety-two major firms in the country, of which twenty-four were in California. New York had dropped back to second place, with only seventeen. See Allen J. Scott, *Technopolis: High-Technology Industry and Regional Development in Southern California* (Berkeley: University of California Press, 1993), 57, Table 4.1

66. Markusen et al., "Aerospace Capital of the World," 104. This remarkable story will be told in Chapter 12. Allen J. Scott's undated paper "High-Technology Industry in the San Fernando Valley and Ventura County: Observations on Economic Growth and the Evolution of Urban Form" (unpublished manuscript, University of California, Los Angeles, n.d.), which later appeared as "High-Technology Industrial Development in the San Fernando Valley and Ventura County: Observations on Economic Growth and the Evolution of Urban Form," in *The City: Los Angeles and Urban Theory at the End of the Twentieth Century,* ed. Allen Scott and Edward Soja (Berkeley: University of California Press, 1996), 276–310, describes how the prewar industrial landscape of Los Angeles, originally a collar around the downtown with a few aircraft plants in suburban sites, had changed by the end of World War II. By then, two new districts had materialized: one to the west and southwest of the city (in places such as Santa Monica, Culver City, El Segundo, Hawthorne, and Inglewood) with firms such as Douglas, Northrup, North American Aviation, and Hughes Aircraft; and the second to the northwest of downtown (in Burbank, Glendale, and North Hollywood). It was only in the mid-1950s (i.e., after the Korean War) that high-tech industrial districts developed in Orange County.

67. Scott L. Bottles, *Los Angeles and the Automobile: The Making of the Modern City* (Berkeley: University of California Press, 1987), 187, 189. The later drop in the proportion of single-family houses is attributable to a densification within the city, as low apartment buildings and so-called dingbats (apartment structures set into single lots by building back deeply into the rear yard) replaced many single-family structures. The comparison with Chicago is somewhat unfair, because low-density two- and three-flats were concentrated toward the edges of the city, whereas single-family houses were located chiefly in suburban zones beyond the reaches of annexation. Only minor areas within the city, such as Evergreen Park, approximated the suburbs.

68. Ibid., 194.

69. Regarding the decline of downtown, Bottles notes that "by 1956, downtown department stores could muster only 23 percent of all department store sales in the county." Ibid., 196.

70. Ibid., 198–99.

71. Much of the following section depends on ibid., 211–34. As noted earlier, the same Automobile Club had earlier hired landscape architect Frederick Law Olmsted, planning consultant Harland Bartholomew, and Charles Cheney to produce the *Major Traffic Street Plan for Los Angeles,* delivered in 1924. See Martin Wachs, "The Evolution of Transportation Policy in Los Angeles," in *The City: Los Angeles and Urban Theory at the End of the Twentieth Century,* ed. Allen Scott and Edward Soja (Berkeley: University of California Press, 1996). I have drawn upon the prepublication typescript of Wachs's chapter. Olmsted had first suggested such parkways in 1930 and New York had already experimented with its freeway in 1936.

72. In the end, taxes on gasoline were earmarked for highway construction, and state highway funds became available when the freeways were declared to be part of the state highway system. See Bottles, *Los Angeles and the Automobile,* 232–33. The federal government eventually came to the rescue of all cities in 1956 by making highway construction funds available.

73. Ibid., 239. Many analysts of Los Angeles developments have posited a "conspiracy" on the part of automobile manufacturers to destroy their competitor, mass transit. Among these are not only Mike Davis in his *City of Quartz,* but the film *Who Framed Roger Rabbit,* in which the head of Cloverleaf Industries boasts that he has bought up the Red Car electric lines in order to dismantle them. However, at least one advocate of restoring street railways in Los Angeles has a more generous interpretation, while at the same time strongly opposing the subway alternative. See Robert C. Post, *Street Railways and the Growth of Los Angeles* (Los Angeles: Golden West, 1989); see also Post's article "The Myth behind the Streetcar Revival," *American Heritage,* May/June 1998, 95–100.

74. As David Brodsly notes, in his otherwise celebratory *L.A. Freeway: An Appreciative Essay* (Berkeley: University of California Press, 1981): "To keep right-of-way expenses under control, freeways were often routed through inexpensive property, with the result that a disproportionate number of those affected by relocation or disruption were poor, minority, or elderly—those least able to absorb uncompensated expenses, and those least served by the [transportation] projects" (39).

75. By 1938, when recovery was finally starting, loans of up to 90 percent of value were being offered at low interest and for an unprecedented amortization period of twenty-five years.

76. This was a practice called redlining, named for the red ink that blocked out areas not approved for insured lending.

77. Marc Weiss, *The Rise of the Community Builders* (New York: Columbia University Press, 1987), 155; a good summary can be found in Weiss's chap. 6.

78. Ibid., 147.

79. Remi A. Nadeau, "Supersubdivider," in *Los Angeles: Biography of a City,* ed. John and LaRee Caughey (Berkeley: University of California Press, 1977), 402. (This extract appeared originally in Nadeau's *Los Angeles from Mission to Modern City* [New York: Longman, Green, 1961].) For more details on Lakewood, see Gary J. Miller, *Cities by Contract: The Politics of Municipal Incorporation* (Cambridge: MIT Press, 1981).

80. Nadeau, "Supersubdivider," 403.

81. Some part of this was caused by the decisions of returning servicemen to relocate to a California they first saw in the service. Only 5 percent of armed service personnel were inducted from California, but 9 percent were discharged there. One should also note that internal migration of African Americans to the Los Angeles area also contributed to overall

population increase. By 1970, there were almost 642,000 black residents in the city of Los Angeles, which was more than three times their number in 1950, which in turn was three times higher than in 1940.

82. McWilliams, "Look What's Happened to California," 23.

83. Ibid., 26–27.

84. See Douglas Massey and B. Mullan, "Processes of Hispanic and Black Spatial Assimilation," *American Journal of Sociology* 89 (1984): 836–73. This is not to deny that there was also some "suburbanization" of the black population. An analysis of U.S. Census figures showed that in 1970 the "suburbs" of the Los Angeles SMSA contained more black residents than any other SMSA; many of these had moved there from the center city. See Francine Rabinowitz, "Minorities in the Suburbs: The Los Angeles Experience" (Working paper 31, MIT Harvard Joint Center for Urban Studies, 1975). But what should be borne in mind are the peculiar and arbitrary boundaries between center and suburb, to which I have alluded in Chapter 6 and to which I return in Chapter 12. The apparent suburbanization of the black population often involved a move from one "urban" area to an equally urbanized "suburb" that, because of the vagaries of irregular annexation, fell outside the irregular boundaries of the city.

85. Warner, *The Urban Wilderness,* 142, 144–45, emphasis added.

86. As late as 1970, black families in Los Angeles were even poorer than Spanish-surname families; in that year, "the median family income for blacks was $7,500; for Spanish-surname families, $8,900; and for white families, $11,400." Howard Nelson and William Clark, *Los Angeles: The Metropolitan Experience* (Cambridge, Mass.: Ballinger, 1976), 38.

87. Recall that the U.S. Supreme Court case that finally made racial restrictive covenants unenforceable in 1948 focused specifically on Slauson Street, long the southern "wall" of Los Angeles's spatial color line.

88. Nelson and Clark, *Los Angeles,* 37–38.

89. Charles Abrams, "Rats among the Palm Trees," *The Nation,* February 25, 1950, 177–78.

90. See Donald Craig Parson, "Urban Politics during the Cold War: Public Housing, Urban Renewal and Suburbanization in Los Angeles" (Ph.D. diss., Department of Urban Planning, University of California, Los Angeles, 1985), as well as an article by Parson that foreshadows his dissertation's main points: "The Development of Redevelopment: Public Housing and Urban Renewal in Los Angeles," *International Journal of Urban and Regional Research* 6 (1982): 393–413.

91. Parson, "The Development of Redevelopment," 395. Parson cites *United Progressive News,* October 25, 1937, as the source of his information.

92. Parson, "The Development of Redevelopment," 396.

93. Ibid., 397–98.

94. Ibid., 398.

95. "In the autumn of 1942, the HALA received 1795 applications for housing from blacks, 362 from whites, 238 from Mexicans, and 5 from other minority groups." Ibid.; Parson cites Collins, *Black Los Angeles,* 28.

96. Parson, "The Development of Redevelopment," 399. But public housing was not what the CRA had in mind.

97. Parson, "Urban Politics," 11.

98. Ibid., 84. Opposition to public housing had mobilized as early as 1942, when "the segregationist policy of the City Housing Authority (CHA)" was successfully challenged by the Citizen's Housing Association, but the coup de grâce did not come until ten years later,

when a public relations officer of the Housing Authority of Los Angeles, accused of being a communist, was "suspended and subsequently fired. A full scale investigation by the California State Un-American Activities Committee resulted in the dismissal of five Housing Authority employees and the cancellation of nearly half of the 10,000 unit public housing contract" (86). In 1950 "the city had just been awarded its first major contract under the 1949 Housing Act to build racially-integrated public housing projects throughout the city. Charges that public housing, especially that in Los Angeles, was communistic and socialistic were developed by City Councilmen in whose white and middle-income districts proposed projects were to be located, orchestrated by local newspapers, and financed by the real estate lobby in Southern California. Racism became apparent when representatives of the real estate lobby met with Housing Authority officials in the summer of 1952, offering to drop opposition to the program if the projects were sited in the inner city, black South-Central or the Chicano Eastside" (92–93).

Interestingly enough, in 1950 the city council had unanimously approved the original contract and even approved, by a margin of twelve to one, the sites that had been selected. But after conservatives came to power in the 1951 elections, the commitment to public housing disappeared. By December 1951 "the Council reversed its position and voted 8–7 against the federal contract," even though a ruling by the State Supreme Court in 1952 held that "the Council was legally bound to honor the federal contract" (97). That was when the battle was shifted to the new terrain of red-baiting, and "the California State Un-American Activities Committee and the House Committee on Government Operations came to Los Angeles to 'grill the reds' in the Housing Authority" (98). When the mayor, following court orders, proceeded to honor the contract, the press waged a vicious campaign that equated the mayor with public housing and with communism. In the election of 1953 he was defeated, and his successor reduced the commitment to only half of the units promised. See ibid., 99. Note the parallels to Upton Sinclair's bid for governor and Chicago's racially motivated public housing site wars.

99. Ibid., 107.

100. Ibid., 116.

101. Bunker Hill was a district of elegant Victorian structures, since transformed into "seedy" rooming houses and memorialized in Dashiel Hammett's detective novels. It contained a mixed population of about 9,500 low-income Chicanos and whites (mostly aged immigrants). The residents of Chavez Ravine were almost all Chicano.

102. Parson, "Urban Politics," 122.

103. Ibid., 127.

104. Ibid.

105. Ibid., 128–29.

106. Governor's Commission on the Los Angeles Riots, John A. McCone, Chair, *Violence in the City: An End or a Beginning?* (Los Angeles: Governor's Commission, 1965).

107. "Stunned" and "explosion" are recurring terms used in the report. The authors deny that what had occurred was a race riot. Rather, "what happened was an explosion—a formless, quite senseless, all but hopeless violent protest—engaged in by a few" (ibid., 4–5). The riot is referred to as a "nightmare," and the authors warn that unless the "expensive and burdensome" programs they are recommending are put into force, "the walls of segregation would rise ever higher," "the cost of police protection would increase," and "welfare costs would mount apace" (7). Yet the authors never recommend desegregation.

A content analysis of even the opening paragraphs of the report reveals the outraged emotions and the lacunae of understanding of this august investigating committee: "Negroes took to the streets in marauding bands," "caught up in an insensate rage of destruction," until "the spasm passed" (1). And later, "The lawlessness in this one segment . . . has terrified the entire county and its 6,000,000 citizens" (2).

108. Ibid., 4, emphasis added.

109. The major book summarizing many of these detailed studies is David O. Sears and John B. McConahay, *The Politics of Violence: The New Urban Blacks and the Watts Riot* (Boston: Houghton Mifflin, 1973). See also Nathan Cohen, ed., *The Los Angeles Riots: A Sociopsychological Study* (New York: Praeger, 1970). Cohen was research director for the UCLA study. Indeed, the Watts riot gave rise to a wide variety of books and studies, ranging from docudramas such as Robert Conot's *Rivers of Blood, Years of Darkness* (New York: Bantam, 1967) to illustrated day-by-day journalistic accounts, such as Spencer Crump's *Black Riot in Los Angeles: The Story of the Watts Tragedy* (Los Angeles: Trans-Anglo, 1966), to anecdotal interview accounts reported in Paul Bullock's *Watts: The Aftermath: An Inside View of the Ghetto* (New York: Grove, 1969), to scathing critiques of the McCone Report such as Robert Fogelson's "White on Black: A Critique of the McCone Commission Report on the Los Angeles Riots" (n.p., n.d.) and his later collection *The Los Angeles Riots* (New York: Arno, 1969), which includes his critical essay.

110. Sears and McConahay, *The Politics of Violence,* 9.

111. T. M. Tomlinson and David O. Sears, "Los Angeles Riot Study: Negro Attitudes toward the Riot" (UCLA Institute of Government and Public Affairs, mimeo, June 1967).

112. Of the 56 percent who said the riot had a purpose, 41 percent thought it would call attention to the problems Negroes face, 33 percent thought that it offered a catharsis for pent-up resentment, and 26 percent thought it could improve conditions by communicating with the power structure and thus bring discrimination to an end. Ibid., 14, Table 8.

113. Whereas 38 percent in the black sample thought the riot helped the "Negro's cause" and another 30 percent said they didn't know or that it made no difference, fully 75 percent of a sample of white residents outside the curfew zone thought the riot hurt the "Negro's cause." See ibid., 8, Table 3.

114. The Martin Luther King Jr. Hospital, which was built after the riots, now ironically serves a primarily Mexican American clientele.

115. In the aftermath of the riot, various "human relations commissions" were strengthened. In 1985, the county and city commissions held joint hearings to evaluate what had been achieved in following through the recommendations concerning employment, education, and housing made by the McCone Commission. The concluding paragraph of the report on these hearings is chilling: "Even though the intended emphasis of this hearing was on solutions, not surprisingly much of the testimony tended to focus on existing problems, *which for the most part are substantially the same as those in 1965.*" See "McCone Revisited: A Focus on Solutions to Continuing Problems in South Central Los Angeles" (Los Angeles County Commission on Human Relations and the Los Angeles City Human Relations Commission, mimeo, January 1985), n.p., emphasis added.

116. Nelson and Clark, *Los Angeles,* 33.

117. Ibid., 35–35. Fifteen years later, David Rieff, in his *Los Angeles: Capital of the Third World* (New York: Simon & Schuster, 1991), would emphasize a similar point.

118. This is not to minimize the difficulties Mexican Americans faced from discrimination in employment, rent gouging and fraud in housing, and political powerlessness in making their needs known. This horrendous story is told in detail by Acuña in *A Community under Siege.* Acuña discusses the impact on East Los Angeles of the Watts rebellion and why its discontents were ignored (109–11). Nor was the community complacent. On the growth of

Chicano consciousness, see Marguerite V. Marin, *Social Protest in an Urban Barrio: A Study of the Chicano Movement, 1966–1974* (Latham, Md.: University Press of America, 1991).

119. Recall that 1965 marked the first landing of marines for combat in Vietnam, that the Tet offensive of 1968 suggested that the cost in lives would be great in a possibly unwinnable war, and that 1970 marked the peak of war opposition and the shootings at Kent State. I have seen few discussions of "ghetto uprisings" that link them to the general violence of the times.

120. Morales, *Ando Sangrando.* Because very few sources on riots in general or in Los Angeles even mention these events, I treat them in more detail here in contrast to the better-known case of Watts.

121. Ibid., 91, emphasis added.

122. Ibid., 96–97. The following account is based largely on Morales's summary and analysis, but see also Acuña, *A Community under Siege,* 202 ff.

123. Morales, *Ando Sangrando,* 100.

124. Ibid.

125. Ibid., 107–8. For an account given by one parade monitor who was imprisoned and mercilessly mistreated, see 109–12.

126. According to Morales, Mexican Americans in Los Angeles constituted the largest proportion of persons (Mexican American community 58 percent, black community 24 percent, Anglo community 18 percent) arrested for "interfering with police" in episodes involving police malpractice. He cites a then-recent survey of sixty-four Mexican Americans in Fresno, San Jose, and Los Angeles; all respondents believed that the legal system was discriminatory toward Mexican Americans. He also makes reference to another study, made by the Western Center on Law and Poverty, that found that the average "judicial sentence *was harsher* for convicted felony defendants who were of Spanish surname or Blacks than for Anglos." Ibid. Morales gives inadequate information about these studies, so I was unable to verify his information.

127. "The central city's great expansion program closed in 1927 and has never been reinstituted, although relatively small additions continue to be made." Winston Crouch and Beatrice Dinerman, *Southern California Metropolis: A Study in Development of Government for a Metropolitan Area* (Berkeley: University of California Press, 1963), 179.

128. This fascinating story is told in Miller, *Cities by Contract.*

129. See League of Women Voters of Los Angeles, *Los Angeles: Structure of a City* (Los Angeles: League of Women Voters, 1976); chap. 1 gives a brief history of city government. An additional helpful source is Helen L. Jones and Robert F. Wilcox, *Metropolitan Los Angeles: Its Governments* (Los Angeles: Haynes Foundation, 1949), which goes into much greater detail. I have depended in part on Crouch and Dinerman, *Southern California Metropolis,* esp. 181 ff.

130. An example of such a special district is the Metropolitan Water District of Southern California.

131. In the early 1960s analysts thought that the county could logically serve as the agent for the metropolitan region. Thus Crouch and Dinerman complacently conclude that "the county is the one unit of local government in the metropolitan area that has jurisdiction over a sufficiently large portion of the territory to make it a potential metropolitan unit." Ibid., 180. Of course, what happened afterward was that the metropolitan region spilled over into so many adjacent counties that neither the city nor the county proved adequate in extent. None of these problems is recognized in the League of Women Voters, *Los Angeles,* although that publication's exposition of the functions of city and county is particularly clear.

132. It has often been noted that zoning ordinances can be (and are) used in the "beggar thy neighbor" game of intercommunity competition, in which each tries to maximize

resources (its tax base) and minimize social costs (its welfare bill) by attracting rich and repelling poor residents. A good description can be found in John R. Logan and Harvey L. Molotch, *Urban Fortunes: The Political Economy of Place* (Berkeley: University of California Press, 1987). We have already seen how oil towns resisted annexation; another good case is the so-called City of Industry, with fewer than a hundred residents but a tax base of numerous industrial firms. In Los Angeles, such "home-rule" prerogatives have been exercised invidiously (on the basis of market "power"), and the region has become a patchwork of ethnicity- and class-specific quarters. As noted above, especially after racially restrictive covenants were made illegal in 1948 and the 1954 *Brown* decision required school desegregation within cities (but failed the next step to require metropoliswide desegregation, including "suburbs"), the situation solidified.

133. State law in 1878, when Los Angeles still had a tiny population, established the fifteen-member city council, which was reduced to nine members under the home-rule charter of 1889. In 1925, a referendum to reduce the size to eleven and to elect councillors "at large" was defeated, and the current arrangement of fifteen members elected by ward was set into place, after a court case. See League of Women Voters, *Los Angeles,* 28–29. But what may have made sense in 1878 or even (though less so) in 1925 seems particularly unsuited to the present, at least for the representation of local interests. Skerry, *Mexican Americans,* 76–78 discusses how the Los Angeles political system, including "entrance fees" (i.e., high costs of campaigning), has made it very difficult for the large Mexican population to be properly represented. The same is true for the black minority, despite the city's election at large of a black mayor in 1973. See the discussion in Chapter 12.

134. An example is the defeat through a statewide referendum of an open housing law in 1964, at least temporarily, until it was overturned in the courts. At the present time, Proposition 13, by setting a ceiling on real estate tax rates at 1.25 percent of value, has crippled the provision of public services throughout California. In recent years, bankrupt Orange County could not even get voter approval for a sales tax hike. Los Angeles seems to be heading down the same road. But the most egregious use of the referendum was the recent passage of Proposition 187, which restricts social and health services and schooling to "legal" residents—a move that will have extremely deleterious effects on California's immigrants. But more of this in Chapter 12.

135. Prior to 1985, only one Mexican American had won a seat on the Los Angeles City Council (Roybal from East Los Angeles, who served between 1949 and 1962). The South-Central ward did manage to elect a black to the city council, and indeed, Tom Bradley, Los Angeles's first black mayor, who served between 1973 and 1993, used his positions on the police force and then as elected member of the city council representing South-Central as stepping-stones to that post. See Raphael J. Sonenshein, *Politics in Black and White: Race and Power in Los Angeles* (Princeton, N.J.: Princeton University Press, 1993).

136. Civil Service was introduced in 1903, and the present backlash against affirmative action in California seems to go back to that reasoning. On some of these points, see William Deverell and Tom Sitton, eds., *California Progressivism Revisited* (Berkeley: University of California Press, 1994).

137. Eric Hobsbawm, *The Age of Extremes: A History of the World, 1914–1991* (New York: Pantheon, 1995), 205.

138. Among the best of these books is Barry Bluestone and Bennett Harrison's *The Deindustrialization of America: Plant Closings, Community Abandonment, and the Dismantling of Basic Industry* (New York: Basic Books, 1982). Today, other pundits suggest a "reindustrialization," but in the rust/frost belt, this is often hard to perceive. See also Folker Froebel, Jürgen

Heinrichs, and Otto Kreye, *The New International Division of Labour,* trans. Pete Burgess (Cambridge: Cambridge University Press, 1980).

139. Hobsbawm, *The Age of Extremes,* 270.

140. The percentage of people employed in manufacturing began to decline from 1965 on in the United States. See ibid., 302.

141. It might not be out of order to review the history of this soon-forgotten war. The buildup of forces for Vietnam was begun in 1961 under President Kennedy; the first air strikes were ordered by President Johnson in 1964; the marines landed in 1965; and the Vietcong launched the Tet offensive in 1968, which is generally considered to be the "turning point." In 1973, the United States signed a peace accord and in 1975 the "North" captured Saigon, triggering an exodus of "refugees," many of whom settled in Los Angeles. A boxed table in the *Los Angeles Times* on July 12, 1995, gave the following statistics: for the World War I years of 1914–18, there were 116,516 U.S. deaths, and U.S. war costs were $19 billion; for the World War II years 1939–45, the respective figures were 405,399 and $263 billion; during the Korean War years 1950–53, the figures were 54,246 and $67 billion; and during the Vietnam War years 1959–1975, they were 58,000 and $150 billion.

IV. RESTRUCTURING THE GLOBAL ECONOMY

1. Perhaps the first systematic and theoretically informed studies of the early stages were Folker Froebel, Jürgen Heinrichs, and Otto Kreye, *The New International Division of Labour: Structural Unemployment in Industrial Countries* (London: Cambridge University Press, 1980), drawing primarily on German data; and Barry Bluestone and Bennett Harrison, *The Deindustrialization of America: Plant Closings, Community Abandonment, and the Dismantling of Basic Industries* (New York: Basic Books, 1982), based on U.S. data. In the early 1980s, the focus was on the "export" of production transnationally (which can be shorthanded by the gloss of "the global car"). Since then, other developments have superseded this as the basic trend, including the import of Third World labor and the international exchange of futures on money. For these, see, inter alia, Saskia Sassen, *The Mobility of Labor and Capital: A Study in International Investment and Labor Flow* (New York: Cambridge University Press, 1988).

2. The possible exception is Thierry J. Noyelle and Thomas Stanback Jr., *The Economic Transformation of American Cities* (Totowa, N.J.: Rowman & Allanheld, 1984), even though international causes play only a small role in their analysis of the changing urban hierarchy within the United States. Given that their data essentially end with 1977, perhaps one should not fault them for failing to predict what was just on the horizon.

3. Perhaps the first popular presentation of this view was Alvin Toffler's *The Third Wave* (New York: Morrow, 1980).

4. Urbanist Manuel Castells has gone so far as to call this revolution a shift to the informational mode of development. See his *The Informational City: Information Technology, Economic Restructuring, and the Urban-Regional Process* (Oxford: Blackwell, 1989). Of course, Melvin Webber anticipated Castells's thesis decades earlier; see his "The Urban Place and the Nonplace Urban Realm," in *Explorations into Urban Social Structure,* ed. M. Webber et al. (Philadelphia: University of Pennsylvania Press, 1964). Since this chapter was written, Manuel Castells has published a three-volume work under the general title *The Information Age: Economy, Society, and Culture* (Malden, Mass.: Basil Blackwell, 1996–98), in which he develops a complex theory of the relationship between the "network society" and the search for social identity and the self. See, inter alia, my review of the second volume of *The Information Age* in *Contemporary Sociology* 27 (March 1998): 163–64.

5. One can sympathize with the Luddites, who earlier feared that higher capitalization in production would ultimately displace workers in manufacturing, and one can now hope that the parallel displacement of workers in the services will prove only temporary. The most optimistic scenario would be if, as happened earlier in the case of industrial development, the workweek could be reduced without reducing consumer demand for the products created by this third "revolution." However, two factors cast doubt on the likelihood of this: first, the limited and narrow demand for the "product," and second, the tendency to export labor-intensive information-related jobs to parts of the world where labor costs are low (e.g., computer programming to India, data entry to the Caribbean).

6. In 1975, some $21 billion in monetary instruments circulated among the developed countries; by 1993 the total was on the order of $764 billion. *USA Today,* March 24, 1995, 4B.

7. Among the earliest authors to have spotted this trend are Noyelle and Stanback, in their *The Economic Transformation of American Cities.* Most recently, the Chicago Board of Trade had begun to forge an alliance with "Eurex, the all-electronic European exchange." See *London Financial Times,* March 19, 1998, 1.

8. Phil Patton, "The Virtual Office Becomes Reality," *New York Times,* October 28, 1993, C1, C6. These estimates were made by Link Resources, whose findings Patton cites. However, one may question how much "choice" there really is. The newest trend seems to be for "outsourcing" and "flexible production" to diffuse from manufacture, where the trend first began, to services and clerical work, which accounts for some of the apparent job losses in these areas. One of the chief consequences of "outsourcing" for workers is their loss of union protection and fringe benefits.

9. The growth of garment sweatshops in the centers of large cities of the industrial North and the relocation of mail- and telephone-order businesses to rural America and of high-tech electronics and space industries to lower-wage southern cities are all symptoms of this search for cost reductions.

10. These arguments are summarized by Jeffrey Madrick, "The End of Affluence," *New York Review of Books,* September 21, 1995, 13–14, 16–17, who in turn derives some of his conclusions from former OECD economist Angus Maddison, *Dynamic Forces in Capitalist Development: A Long-Run Comparative View* (New York: Oxford University Press, 1991), citing esp. 50–53. Madrick is the author of a book titled *The End of Affluence: The Causes and Consequences of America's Economic Dilemma* (New York: Random House, 1995) and is writing another about productivity. The counterargument, of course, is that the "fruits" of this transformation have just not yet shown up because of delays created by restructuring.

11. Madrick, "The End of Affluence," 13–14, citing Maddison, *Dynamic Forces.* Although downsizing began in the 1980s and stepped up in the 1990s and seemed to be resulting in improved productivity, as soon as the U.S. Department of Labor changed its way of calculating productivity, the annual gain decreased from an estimated 2.1 percent per year to an average of only 1.2 percent annually since the mid-1990s, "only slightly better than the recalculated 1 percent annual rate of improvement during a comparable period from 1979 to mid-1990." Louis Uchitelle, "In New Figures, Productivity Slows," *New York Times,* February 9, 1996, D3.

12. Madrick, "The End of Affluence," 14.

13. Ibid., 16. Among the causes Madrick lists as responsible for the drop in productivity are the enlargement of the markets of international competitors in Europe and Asia, the low wages in newly developing countries, and the shift to flexible production itself, because although the "proliferation of marginally-differentiated and rapidly changing products meant

heightened competition and greater risks from large-scale production," the shift to flexible production has resulted in lower profits. I have major doubts about his reasoning here.

14. These lines of argument surface in "Notes & Comments," *Atlantic Monthly,* September 1995. This editorial blames the stagnation in the American economy on the post-1973 shift from a "trading" to "raiding" nation, and on Reagan's policies of tax breaks to the rich and wild spending by the Pentagon. It blames current deficits on the Reagan-era "tax cuts, directed chiefly at the most affluent Americans, and the defense buildup," which, by requiring cuts in social spending and infrastructural investments while continuing war-related investments, may actually have depressed productivity even more (20, 22).

15. For arguments in support of immigration, see, for example, the Urban Land Institute's recent calculations and the more politically motivated pronouncements of elected officials in certain urban areas where demographic declines have been reversed by immigration. Both Mario Cuomo, former governor of New York, and New York City's mayor, Rudolph Giuliani, have consistently lauded the contributions of immigrants. Arguments against immigration have been most pronounced in California and to a lesser extent Texas, where Mexican and even Asian immigrants have been blamed for draining local coffers. The most obvious symptom of this has been the passage of Proposition 187 in California; this initiative sought to deprive illegal immigrants of social services, even though in practice it has been impossible to distinguish between legal and illegal newcomers. It must be stressed that the category "immigrant" conceals enormous variations in "human capital" by place of origin.

16. Lester Thurow, "Why Their World Might Crumble: How Much Inequality Can a Democracy Take?" *New York Times Magazine,* November 19, 1995, 78, emphasis added.

17. In late 1994, then economic adviser Robert Reich acknowledged that the gap had been "apparent for the better part of two decades." As reported in Jason DeParle, "Census Sees Falling Income and More Poor," *New York Times,* October 7, 1994, A16.

18. Census released figures cited in ibid., emphasis added.

19. Susan L. Fernandez, "Gap between the Very Rich and the Rest of Us Grows Wider," *Miami Herald,* June 20, 1996, 4A.

20. William W. Goldsmith and Edward J. Blakely, *Separate Societies: Poverty and Inequality in U.S. Cities* (Philadelphia: Temple University Press, 1992), 1.

21. Ibid., 20–21.

22. A secondary source summarizing the findings of this study is Keith Bradsher, "Widest Gap in Incomes? Study Covered Industrial Nations in 1980s," *New York Times,* October 27, 1995, D2.

23. The OECD study was conducted by Timothy M. Sneeding, director of the Luxembourg Income Study, and professors Lee Rainwater of Harvard University and Anthony B. Atkinson of Oxford University.

24. The basic measure was the ratio between the after-tax income of the person who barely made it into the top 10 percent and the after-tax income of the person who just slipped into the bottom 10 percent.

25. In applying this second measure, the researchers took the median per capita income after taxes (adjusted for differences in family size) in each country and then computed the incomes of the richest and poorest tenths as a percentage of the median.

26. In this analysis, "workers" were defined as those "who are dependent on selling their labor power or on receiving supplementary income from the welfare state." Anwar Shaikh, "The Welfare State and the Social Wage: A Multi-country Study" (unpublished manuscript, New School for Social Research, 1995), 9. I am grateful to Professor Shaikh for sharing this paper with me.

27. Shaikh distinguishes three postwar phases: a boom period from 1952 to 1969, when, although the net social wage ratio was negative (i.e., labor was subsidizing capital through government redistributions), "the security afforded by stable growth allow[ed] workers to improve their relative strength and gradually reduce the extent of their subsidy to capital"; the crisis time between 1969 and 1975, when government expenditures forced by growing unemployment and poverty rose somewhat to make the relative returns to labor and capital more equal; and the post-1975 period, when "the counterattack by capital and the state initiate[d] a dramatic secular decline in the net social wage." Ibid., 21.

28. Lawrence Mishel and David M. Frankel, *The State of Working America, 1990–91* (Armonk, N.Y.: M. E. Sharpe, 1991), exec. summary, 1.

29. Richard Barnet, "The End of Jobs: Employment Is One Thing the Global Economy Is *Not* Creating," *Harper's Magazine,* September 1993, 52. A report on the full study appears in Richard J. Barnet and John Cavanagh, *Global Dreams: Imperial Corporations and the New World Order* (New York: Simon & Schuster, 1994).

30. Louis Uchitelle, "1995 Was Good for Companies, and Great for a Lot of C.E.O.'s," *New York Times,* March 29, 1996, 1.

31. Ibid., D8.

32. The most important analysis of this situation is found in David M. Gordon's *Fat and Mean: The Corporate Squeeze of Working Americans and the Myth of Managerial "Downsizing"* (New York: Free Press, 1996). Gordon contends that as ordinary laborers have been increasingly demoralized and oppressed, corporations have had to increase the numbers of supervisors available to discipline their workers.

33. Goldsmith and Blakely, *Separate Societies,* 56.

34. Comparative data included in Gordon, *Fat and Mean,* confirm that between 1973 and 1993, real hourly compensation to workers employed in manufacturing within the United States remained relatively unchanged, whereas it increased in all other developed countries similarly affected by the general forces of globalization and restructuring. The internationalization of the economy, therefore, cannot account for American "exceptionalism."

35. Goldsmith and Blakely, *Separate Societies,* 56.

36. Ibid., 61. An even more recent trend has been toward mergers between American and European companies, which allow them the advantage of reporting profits where taxation is lowest.

37. Ibid., 63–70. For example, a recent strike against General Motors by a brake manufacturing unit was initially called to stop the company from "outsourcing" competitive supplies produced in subcontracted nonunion shops, but the settlement, although acceding to some demands for wage improvements and some limits on outsourcing, failed to prevent the latter.

38. Ibid., 71.

39. Quoted in Steven Greenhouse, "A Big Job for Labor: Rebirth of Unions Will Not Be Easy, *New York Times,* October 25, 1995, A28.

40. See Barbara Presley Noble, "Labor-Management Rorschach Test," *New York Times,* June 5, 1994, F21; this article summarizes the report issued by the Commission on the Future of Worker-Management Relations, headed by former Secretary of Labor John T. Dunlop.

41. Ibid.

42. Ibid. The graphic material that accompanied this article is attributed to the Service Employees International Union, which in turn depended upon figures from the Department of Labor and Citizens Tax Justice. I assume that these figures represent pretax income before transfer payments and that households include those headed by single mothers. If so, then some of the gap at the bottom may not reflect wage gaps per se but other trends in household composition.

43. Louis Uchitelle and N. R. Kleinfield, "On the Battlefields of Business, Millions of Casualties," *New York Times,* March 3, 1996, 27. This trend seems to have reversed somewhat by the late 1990s.

44. The *New York Times,* March 3–9, 1996, ran a remarkable series of seven daily articles under the general title "The Downsizing of America." I have depended heavily on the first article in this series and on the full page of graphic material that accompanied it. See ibid., 1, 26–29. The maps and pictographs appear on p. 27 and serve as the major source for my Table IV.1.

45. Ibid., 27.

46. Barnet, "The End of Jobs," 47. Indeed, this was the brilliant early insight of Karl Marx in *Das Capital.* Unfortunately, globalization appears to separate the costs of reproducing labor, which would ordinarily place a limit on the extraction of surplus profit, from the geographic base of the national economic unit, just as the global scale of imports and exports seems to deflect the national economic balance into an international trade deficit.

47. Ibid., 47–48.

48. Again, according to Barnet: "Multinational companies say that Indian programmers and Irish insurance examiners are usually more productive and reliable than workers in the home country. Metropolitan Life employs 150 workers in a village in County Cork to examine medical claims from all over the world. Irish workers cost 30 percent less than U.S. workers, and because work is so scarce in Ireland . . . there is not much turnover. The dimensions of what Marx called the reserve army of the unemployed are now staggering." Ibid., 49.

49. Ibid., 49–50.

50. Goldsmith and Blakely, *Separate Societies,* 53.

51. California's example was followed in 1979 when Massachusetts passed Proposition 2½, which similarly strangled municipal efforts to deliver expected services in that state.

10. THE NEW YORK REGION

1. See Robert D. Yaro and Tony Hiss, *A Region at Risk: The Third Regional Plan for the New York-New Jersey-Connecticut Metropolitan Area* (Washington, D.C.: Island Press for the Regional Plan Association, 1996).

2. Jean Gottmann, *Megalopolis: The Urbanized Northeastern Seaboard of the United States* (Cambridge: MIT Press, 1961).

3. Recently, the Bureau of the Census has added a county in Pennsylvania, making this CMSA a four-state unit.

4. Deyan Sudjic, *The 100 Mile City* (San Diego, Calif.: Harcourt Brace & Jovanovich, 1992). This is an imaginative and heavily illustrated work on the architectural and social characteristics of what Sudjic considers an urban revolution of the 1980s.

5. Ann R. Markusen and Vicky Gwiasda, "Multi-polarity and the Layering of Functions in World Cities: New York City's Struggle to Stay on Top" (working paper 55, Rutgers University Center for Urban Policy Research, 1993), 1–2. This paper was later published in the *International Journal of Urban and Regional Research* (June 1994). See also Saskia Sassen, *The Global City: New York, London, Tokyo* (Princeton, N.J.: Princeton University Press, 1991).

6. One extremely important and deleterious consequence of New York's failure to be the "national capital" is its perennial budget crisis. I argue this in "American Exceptionalism: The Global and the Local in the World Cities of New York, Chicago and Los Angeles" (paper presented at the biennial meeting of the International Sociological Association, Bielefeld, Germany, 1995), where I point out that national subventions help world-city capitals such as Paris and London to maintain their positions as symbols of their countries; in contrast, New

York City tends to send far more tax dollars to support the state and federal governments than it receives back in grants.

7. The last presidential candidate to run from New York was Thomas Dewey—and he lost. The last potentially viable candidate for nomination to the presidency was New York's Governor Mario Cuomo, who withdrew before the nominating convention.

8. In 1996 the college claimed to be celebrating its one hundredth anniversary, but that was stretching reality. Regarding the university's funding, see Ester R. Fuchs, *Mayors and Money: Fiscal Policy in New York and Chicago* (Chicago: University of Chicago Press, 1992), 191. Fuchs states that not until the 1975 fiscal crisis did New York State assume responsibility for the capital and operating budgets of the City University system.

9. Selma Berrolon, "City University of New York," in *The Encyclopedia of New York City,* ed. Kenneth Jackson (New Haven, Conn.: Yale University Press, 1995), 234.

10. See Harold Wechsler, "Colleges and Universities," in *The Encyclopedia of New York City,* ed. Kenneth Jackson (New Haven, Conn.: Yale University Press, 1995), 251–54.

11. Yaro and Hiss, *A Region at Risk,* 27.

12. Markusen and Gwiasda, "Multi-polarity," 9; these authors cite Port Authority of New York and New Jersey, *Regional Economy: Review 1990, Outlook for the New York-New Jersey Metropolitan Region* (New York: Port Authority, 1991), 30–31.

13. Yaro and Hiss, *A Region at Risk,* 27, Figure 7.

14. Some of the best economic analyses of New York's role in the international system have been done by Matthew Drennan. See his "The Decline and Rise of the New York Economy," in *The Dual City: Restructuring New York,* ed. John Mollenkopf and Manuel Castells (New York: Russell Sage Foundation, 1991), 25–42; as well as Drennan's "Gateway Cities: The Metropolitan Sources of US Producer Service Exports," *Urban Studies* 9 (1992): 217–35.

15. See Janet L. Abu-Lughod, "Comparing Chicago, New York, and Los Angeles: Testing Some World City Hypotheses," in *World Cities in a World-System,* ed. Paul L. Knox and Peter J. Taylor (Cambridge: Cambridge University Press, 1995), 179, Table 10.3. According to the U.S. Army Corps of Engineers Navigation Data Center, Waterborne Commerce Statistics Center, *Annuals of 1991 and 1992,* New York's ports received 47,121,436 raw tons of imports in 1989, in comparison to only 13,492,146 raw tons received by all Los Angeles region ports. Chicago, obviously because it could be reached from abroad only through the St. Lawrence Seaway, handled only some 3 million tons of imports. Given the growing markets in the Far East, however, the relative positions of New York and Los Angeles ports were reversed with respect to export tonnage, with the latter handling some 11 million raw tons to New York's 7 million. I suspect that if New Jersey's ports had been included, this apparent gap might have closed.

16. Regarding the silting of the harbor, see Andrew Revkin, "Curbs on Silt Disposal Threaten Port of New York," *New York Times,* March 18, 1996, 1, B4. The silting, of course, affects New Jersey as well as New York, which forces both governors to mute their competition to assure the region's comparative advantage. See also Andrew Revkin, "2 Governors Plan Cleanup for Harbor: Trying to Keep Shippers from Leaving New York," *New York Times,* October 6, 1996, 37–38.

In addition, there have been recent complaints of mismanagement lodged against the Port Authority, which is accused of slighting investments on the New York side. See John Sullivan, "Report Criticizes Port Authority," *New York Times,* May 23, 1996, B1; and Thomas J. Lueck, "Report on Port Authority Says It Favors New Jersey," *New York Times,* February 16, 1996, B5.

17. See Clifford J. Levy, "Port in a Storm: Planners Question the City's Maritime Future," *New York Times,* August 30, 1996, B1, B5. See also Douglas Martin, "State Panel to Announce Riverfront Plan," *New York Times,* June 6, 1996, B1.

18. See Abu-Lughod, "Comparing New York, Chicago and Los Angeles," 179, Table 10.4. According to the U.S. Department of Transportation, Federal Aviation Administration, Research and Special Programs, *Airport Activity Statistics of Certified Route Air Carriers,* annual reports of 1990 and 1991, the enplaned revenue tons of freight that passed through the airports of New York (including Newark), Los Angeles, and Chicago were more equal: more than 400,000 revenue tons from New York, about 360,000 revenue tons from Los Angeles (including Long Beach and Orange County), and about 300,000 revenue tons from Chicago. Unfortunately, it is impossible to distinguish between domestic and foreign destinations.

19. Neil MacFarquhar, "Newark Airport Is Pressing to Surpass Kennedy," *New York Times,* January 24, 1996, 1, B5. The city's politicians have long accused the Port Authority of New York-New Jersey of preferential treatment to New Jersey. It should be noted, however, that in order to retain its competitive edge, Kennedy Airport is now undergoing massive expansion of its passenger terminals as well as enhancing its accessibility through a long-overdue mass-transit connection to Manhattan.

20. Yaro and Hiss, *A Region at Risk,* esp. 27, Figure 7. The text is unclear here, but from the context it appears that these "service jobs" are *in addition* to the ones later identified more specifically. I therefore refer to them as "other miscellaneous services" or, in this instance, "undifferentiated."

21. Yaro and Hiss show that the category of services (which in 1995 accounted for 2.8 million jobs) does not include construction, transportation and public utilities, wholesale trade, retail trade, finance-insurance-real-estate (the famous FIRE sector), or government. Government jobs alone accounted for close to 1.5 million, whereas the FIRE sector accounted for many fewer than a million jobs. Ibid., 31, Figure 11.

22. See Tom Redburn, "New York Climbing Out of the Recession: Incomes Rising as Recovery Adds Jobs," *New York Times,* June 12, 1994, 1, 47. See also, for more recent confirmation, "Wall Street Leads a Recovery in New York," *New York Times,* October 21, 1996, 1, B6. Nevertheless, the rate of job creation in the New York region has continued to lag behind that of the country as a whole. The one bonanza attributable to the Wall Street boom that began in 1994, however, has been an unexpected rise in tax dollars at the disposal of the city and state administrations, which by the mid-1990s allowed a temporary respite from endemic fiscal crises.

23. Kirk Johnson, "U.S. Says New York Outdid Suburbs in '96 Job Growth," *New York Times,* January 23, 1997, B8.

24. Silicon Alley stretches southward from the Flatiron district to the tip of Manhattan. The city's fastest-growing business sector already employs some 18,000 workers in more than 1,100 companies. See *New York Observer,* August 3, 1996, 1.

25. Steve Lohr, "New York Area Is Forging Ahead in New Media," *New York Times,* April 15, 1996, D1, D4.

26. The sharpest and most visible contrast appears along Park Avenue on the East Side of Manhattan, at the breaking point of 96th Street, where submerged railway tracks suddenly rise to above ground. To the south of 96th Street is the neighborhood of Carnegie Hill, with the highest median incomes in the city; to the north begins the East Barrio, a neighborhood dominated by public housing projects. However, in the past few years, gentrification has been creeping slowly northward.

27. See Richard Harris, "The Geography of Employment and Residence in New York

since 1950," in *The Dual City: Restructuring New York,* ed. John Mollenkopf and Manuel Castells (New York: Russell Sage Foundation, 1991), 139, Figure 5.3. Note that the 1949 graph appeared originally in Raymond Vernon, *Metropolis 1985* (Cambridge: Harvard University Press for the Regional Plan of New York, 1960), 148. Harris does not identify his source for the 1979 graph.

28. See the maps reproduced in Sam Roberts, "Gap between Rich and Poor in New York City Grows Wide," *New York Times,* December 25, 1994, metro sec., 33. It should be pointed out that Roberts's emphasis is on Manhattan and that the unit of analysis in the study he reports is not the distribution of family incomes by borough or larger unit, but the average household income computed *within* individual census tracts. A comparison between the two data sets is therefore unwarranted.

29. Ibid., 33. The poorest families were more likely to be headed by a woman or a Hispanic and less likely to be working than in 1980. Far "fewer were employed in 1990 than in 1980—about 3 in 10, or slightly more than the proportion who were on welfare. In 1980, 8 in 10 of the poorest were working." Ibid., 34. Note that Roberts's income figures for the poor do not include noncash benefits and illegal or unreported income, or other sources of subsidy, such as public housing, rent control, and low-tuition colleges.

30. Ibid., 33.

31. "Among the poorest fifth, 13 percent of New York City households were receiving public assistance in 1980. By 1990, 28 percent of the poorest New York City households, but only 14 percent of those elsewhere in the region, were on welfare." Ibid., 34.

32. Strictly speaking, not all "blacks" are native-born, given that, as we have seen, New York's black population has always included a sizable proportion of "blacks" from the Caribbean and, now, even African nations, who were born abroad. I have been unable to disaggregate further, but have instead opted to utilize the "social definitions" most often employed by New Yorkers when they use the terms *black* and *Puerto Rican.* See the discussion in Chapter 7. Puerto Ricans, who have been classified in successive censuses as "Spanish surname," "Spanish speaker," and now "Hispanic," are not considered immigrants, according to the laws (Jones Act of 1919) that confer special privileges on the citizens of the semicolony of Puerto Rico.

33. Figures for Puerto Ricans have been generated out of successive censuses by David Hillyard. The numbers for blacks and Puerto Ricans should *not* be added together, because in the early census years some unknown proportion of persons reported as of Puerto Rican birth or descent may also be included in the category "black." For 1960, I have added those listed as of Puerto Rican origin to those born in Puerto Rico, regardless of race; and for 1970, I have used the figure of Puerto Rican birth or ancestry, again regardless of race. The figures for 1980 and 1990 have been extracted from the section on Hispanic origin. In the 1990 census, a very large percentage of Latinos in New York reported their race as "other."

34. The data in Table 10.3 are subject to the same reservations as those displayed in Table 10.2, from which the percentages have been computed.

35. I have not attempted to compare New York City with all nine "peripheral" counties identified as part of the region in the 1950–60.

36. Between 1960 and 1970, these counties all experienced high decennial growth rates. The population in inlying Nassau County increased by 9.8 percent in the decade and that of Westchester County grew by 10.5 percent. Farther out, in Rockland and Suffolk Counties, the decennial population increases were astronomical: each increased by 68 percent. However, by the 1970s and 1980s, Nassau and Westchester had already begun to experience net declines in population, while the decennial increases in Suffolk and Rockland Counties

tapered off to 14 and 12 percent, respectively, in the 1970s, and to only 3 and 2 percent, respectively, in the 1980s.

37. The image of "white flight" is again an inaccurate explanation of this "loss." Actually, the age distribution of the city's remaining white population is skewed toward older persons whose ranks are being decimated not by moves to the suburbs but by deaths or by relocation to southern retirement communities.

38. According to Ninna N. Sorenson, "Some Comments on the Anthropology of Lower Income Urban Enclaves: Dominican Newcomers in the City," in *The Anthropology of Lower Income Urban Enclaves: The Case of East Harlem,* ed. Judith Freidenberg (New York: New York Academy of Sciences, 1995), 213, estimates of the Dominican population range from two hundred thousand to a million, but the upper figure seems particularly unlikely to me. About half of the Dominicans have settled on Manhattan's Upper West Side (Washington Heights, Inwood, and Hamilton Heights), according to estimates made by the New York City Planning Department in 1992; the remainder are found chiefly in the Bronx, Brooklyn, and Queens, and on the Lower East Side of Manhattan. They are reputed to be "tough." In passing, Sorenson notes that a sign at her local coin laundry (in Washington Heights) reads: "Please remove coins, pencils, hairpins, nails, and bullets from clothes before filling in machines" (214). Sorenson notes: "Dominicans have been subjected to accusations of crime, violence, sexual promiscuity and so on. . . . Ironically, the accusations of drug-dealing may show up being a basis for ethnic organization in Washington Heights. When a Dominican youngster under suspicion of illegal weapon and drug possession was shot down on the street in the summer of 1992, a storm of protests arose from several layers of the New York based Dominican community. These protests became during autumn 1992 the basis on which claims for community houses, stronger political representation, and more Dominican police officers, were based" (215).

39. For the numbers and country origins of New York's immigrants between 1980 and 1990, see New York Department of City Planning, *The Newest New Yorkers: An Analysis of Immigration into New York City during the 1980s,* 2 vols. (New York: New York Department of City Planning, 1992). On Los Angeles, see Ashley Dunn, "In California, the Numbers Add Up to Anxiety," *New York Times,* October 30, 1994, E3. Dunn contrasts immigration to Los Angeles with that of New York. Details on Los Angeles will be presented in Chapter 12. Here I note merely that Mexican immigrants account for an overwhelming proportion of Los Angeles's population of foreign-born newcomers.

40. For an account of the deep persistence of negative images of immigrants, see Juan F. Perea, ed., *Immigrants Out! The New Nativism and the Anti-Immigrant Impulse in the United States* (New York: New York University Press, 1997). Significantly, Californians have always demonstrated more hostility to Mexican and "Oriental" immigrants than have New Yorkers.

41. Even some of the nearby "suburban" counties, such as Rockland with 14 percent and Westchester with 18 percent, contained higher proportions than Staten Island.

42. The reader may recall from Chapter 2 that this is exactly the same number of different languages spoken in Manhattan at its very beginning.

43. Quoted in "Immigrant Experiment Gets Rolling," *New York Times,* September 7, 1995, B4.

44. Since 1986, the numbers of immigrants to the New York metropolitan area have jumped from fewer than 120,000 per year between 1986 and 1988 to about 130,000 in 1989, then way up to almost 200,000 in 1990 and 1991, before dropping again to about 150,000 in 1992. However, the number of immigrants planning to remain in New York State did not rise commensurately. Many settle in New Jersey (up from slightly fewer than 40,000 in 1986 to

well over 40,000 between 1990 and 1992). The "net" number planning to stay in New York rose only from about 90,000 in the early year to about 115,000 by the later year. However, the *New York Times,* May 16, 1994, reported that immigration to the New York metropolitan area rose in the 1990s after a series of visa programs aimed at countries "adversely affected" by the stricter immigration controls were enacted in 1965. A so-called diversity immigrant visa lottery will select immigrants from the Bahamas, Latin America (except El Salvador, Mexico, and the Dominican Republic), the former Soviet Union, Africa, and Asian countries (except China, India, Vietnam, and Korea).

45. A report released in early January 1997 by the New York Department of City Planning estimated the overall increase in legal immigrants at 563,000. See New York Department of City Planning, *The Newest New Yorkers 1990–1994: An Analysis of Immigration to NYC in the Early 1990s* (New York: New York Department of City Planning, December 1996). A summary of the findings can be found in Celia Dugger, "City of Immigrants Becoming More So in 90's," *New York Times,* January 9, 1997, 1, B6, which was supplemented in the *Times,* January 12, 1997, 27, with a boxed insert map headed "For Half a Million, This Is Still the New World," which displays graphically and in tables the top forty places of origin of the 563,000 legal immigrants who came to New York City from some 150 countries between 1990 and 1994.

46. The problem of including only legal immigrants is apparent when one looks more closely at the figures. In the tally were fewer than thirty-five hundred persons from Mexico, which ranked only twenty-third among the sending countries. This clearly underestimates the number of Mexican immigrants, because the New York region is a preferred second-settlement move for Mexicans coming from Los Angeles.

47. See Saskia Sassen, *The Mobility of Labor and Capital: A Study in International Investment and Labor Flow* (New York: Cambridge University Press, 1988).

48. Roger Waldinger, *Still the Promised City? African-Americans and New Immigrants in Postindustrial New York* (Cambridge: Harvard University Press, 1996). For a similar use of the concept of ethnic niche, see Suzanne Model, "The Ethnic Niche and the Structure of Opportunity: Immigrants and Minorities in New York City," in *The "Underclass" Debate: Views from History,* ed. Michael B. Katz (Princeton, N.J.: Princeton University Press, 1993), 161–87. Model's analysis covers a longer time period (1910–80) and focuses on employed males in only five racial/ethnic groups in the city: Irish, Jews (Russians), Italians, Puerto Ricans, and African Americans, the same five groups that Nathan Glazer and Daniel Moynihan compare in their earlier *Beyond the Melting Pot: The Negroes, Puerto Ricans, Jews, Italians, and Irish of New York City* (Cambridge: MIT Press, 1963).

49. John D. Kasarda has been one of the strongest proponents of the "mismatch" hypothesis. See, inter alia, his "Economic Restructuring and America's Urban Dilemma," in *The Metropolis Era,* vol. 1, ed. Mattei Dogan and John D. Kasarda (Newbury Park, Calif.: Sage, 1988), 56–84.

50. See Waldinger, *Still the Promised City?* 54–55, Figures 2.5, 2.6.

51. U.S. Bureau of the Census, *Current Population Reports: Poverty in the United States* (Washington, D.C.: U.S. Government Printing Office, 1993). The poverty rate is the proportion of the population with incomes below the "poverty level" set in that year.

52. I am using the "standard" poverty line set by the government. In some ways, this standard underestimates the number of New York's poor because of the higher costs of living in the city. On the other hand, it does not take into account transfer payments and other social subsidies. If New York City did not extend these benefits, the situation of the poor would be even more precarious than it is.

53. See Terry J. Rosenberg, *Poverty in New York City, 1993: An Update* (New York: Community Service Society, 1994).

54. See Phillip Weitzman, *Worlds Apart: Housing, Race/Ethnicity and Income in New York City, 1978–1987* (New York: Community Service Society, 1989), 4, Table 1–2, and 11, Table 1.7. In 1987, Dominicans were the second largest group, accounting for some 19 percent of the city's Hispanics. The remaining nationality groups all made small proportional contributions: less than 5 percent of Hispanics were from Colombia, 4.4 percent were from Ecuador, and 3.5 percent from Mexico, although the latter is probably an underestimate and has been increasing in recent years. Since the late 1980s, the poverty rate among Dominican immigrants has continued to rise (up 8.6 percent between 1989 and 1996). See Mirta Ojito, "Dominicans, Scrabbling for Hope," *New York Times,* December 16, 1997, B1.

55. The reasons for the very low position of the Puerto Rican community of New York are complex. The disappearance of manufacturing jobs formerly filled by Puerto Rican workers is partially responsible for their high unemployment rate. Competition from new Hispanic immigrants willing to work for lower wages may also contribute. In addition, when men do not find jobs, they tend to return alone to Puerto Rico, leaving women with children in New York to take advantage of the various housing and welfare subsidies for which they can then qualify. Some evidence for this is that there are far more Puerto Rican women than men in the city.

56. Note, however, that these figures refer only to *private* employment. They are therefore an underestimate, given the high level of governmental employment in the city of New York and other central cities of the area. Excluded are all municipal, state, and federal employees as well as, of course, members of the armed forces. The figures are therefore not easily compared with those in other cities of the country, and over time they may alter whenever formerly public service activities are subcontracted to private firms.

57. See Yaro and Hiss, *A Region at Risk,* 69, Figure 37. The center cities included, in addition to the five boroughs of New York City, Mineola, Hicksville, Poughkeepsie, and White Plains in New York State; Jersey City, Trenton, New Brunswick, and Newark in New Jersey; and New Haven, Bridgeport, and Stamford in Connecticut.

58. See Jon C. Teaford, *The Rough Road to Renaissance: Urban Revitalization in America, 1940–1985* (Baltimore: Johns Hopkins University Press, 1990), 262, Table 20. For example, public employees in Chicago declined from about forty-seven thousand workers in 1977 to about forty-five thousand by 1985. Unfortunately, Teaford's table does not include information on Los Angeles.

59. Fuchs, *Mayors and Money,* 126.

60. It is interesting to note that in the wake of the city's fiscal crisis, the Twentieth Century Fund appointed a task force of prominent New Yorkers to evaluate "the state of the city" and to recommend policies for restabilizing growth. The lone dissenting voice when the report was issued by the task force was Andrew Biemiller, recently of the AFL-CIO, who deplored the neglect of unions and the report's tendency to "not pay proper attention to the concerns of human beings because it is concerned primarily with the problems of effete financial groups." See Masha Sinnreich for the Twentieth Century Fund Task Force on the Future of New York City, *New York—World City* (New York: Priority Press, 1980), 33–34. The task force seems not to have included any representation from municipal unions.

61. Fuchs, *Mayors and Money,* 124.

62. See Steven Greenhouse, "New York Again the Most Unionized State: Nearly Double U.S. Average, Due to Rise in Government Unions," *New York Times,* October 22, 1995, Metro sec., 38.

63. In the 1960s, New York was the first state in the country to pass legislation permitting

collective bargaining for public employees. Currently, about 73 percent of government employees are unionized, compared with 38.7 percent nationwide. Virtually all teachers and nonmanagerial municipal workers are in unions. See ibid.

64. California, with almost 2.2 million workers in unions (a greater number than New York State's 2 million) has a unionization rate of less than 18 percent. States with low rates are mostly in the South, and South Carolina, with less than 4 percent, has the lowest unionization rate in the country. Some companies have certainly continued to move their manufacturing operations to the South to take advantage of the nonunionized labor.

65. The fullest account of this dire situation, what gave rise to it, the mechanisms used to "rescue" the city, and the immediate consequences of the crisis can be found in Martin Shefter, *Political Crisis/Fiscal Crisis: The Collapse and Revival of New York City* (New York: Columbia University Press, 1992 [1985]), see esp. 128–37 on the mechanisms of the rescue.

66. Fuchs, *Mayors and Money,* 1.

67. Fairly sober evaluations of these economic changes can be found in J. Michael Finger and Thomas D. Willett, eds., "The Internationalization of the American Economy," *Annals of the American Academy of Political and Social Science* 460 (March 1982). Although the contributors to this issue are unequivocal about dating restructuring to 1973 (due to oil price increases and the end of the Bretton Woods Agreement), some authors of articles dealing with particular industries, such as steel, automobiles, and textiles, trace their decline to the 1960s.

68. See Barry Bluestone and Bennett Harrison, *The Deindustrialization of America: Plant Closings, Community Abandonment, and the Dismantling of Basic Industry* (New York: Basic Books, 1982).

69. In 1938, at the urging of Republican/Fusion mayor of New York, Fiorello La Guardia, the Committee on Social Welfare at the New York State Constitutional Convention approved an amendment to the state constitution, which was shortly thereafter ratified by voters in the state. Section 1 of Article 17 reads: "The aid, care and support of the needy are public concerns and shall be provided by the state and by any such of its subdivisions, in a manner and by such means, as the Legislature may from time to time determine."

70. Shefter, *Political Crisis/Fiscal Crisis,* 110, claims that it was more than the increased number of the poor that caused welfare costs to go up after 1964; rather, it was the political mobilization of the poor, in the context of liberal national policies, that led many more of the eligible families to apply for assistance. Certainly, political mobilization underlay the pressures to convert highly selective admissions policies in City College to open admissions, which drove costs up. According to Shefter's Table 5.1, p. 114, between 1961 and 1976, expenditures for welfare increased by 940 percent; those for hospitals increased 570 percent, those for higher education increased 1,224 percent, compared with increases in expenses for police of 278 percent, for fire protection of 217 percent, and for sanitation of 178 percent.

71. Cities, unlike the federal government, are not permitted to engage in deficit spending, and bond debt limits are strictly imposed by the overseeing state governments. When the passage of state and city budgets is delayed, as occurs routinely in New York, payrolls and current expenses must be paid by means of short-term loans that depend on the confidence of lenders. In 1975, these loans were denied by the banking community.

72. In *Mayors and Money,* Fuchs contrasts this with the Democratic Party control over Chicago and Cook County, which only had to repay support after elections, which cost less.

73. For an excellent history, see Charles Green and Basil Wilson, *The Struggle for Black Empowerment in New York City: Beyond the Politics of Pigmentation* (New York: Praeger, 1989).

74. There were certainly shades of La Guardia when, in 1968, Lindsay made shirtsleeve

appearances in predominantly black areas of New York and perhaps managed, by his actions, to cool tempers when other cities were "blowing."

75. As we shall see in Chapter 11, Chicago has been able to off-load many of these functions to Cook County, and thus tap the tax revenues of wealthier suburbanites, or has succeeded in setting up "special districts" in the metropolitan area with revenue-raising powers to handle individual functions. New York has been unable to follow such strategies because it is not contained within a larger "county" and its special-purpose districts must often straddle state boundaries.

76. One can travel the entire length of the subway system by paying a single fare of $1.50, whereas in a zoned-fare system, the price would vary with the distance traveled. On the other hand, only recently has the Metropolitan Transit Authority made available free transfers between its subway and bus systems.

77. Protests over the imposition of modest tuition fees for open-enrollment City College were rancorous, and each infrequent occasion when the Metropolitan Transit Authority has had to raise subway fares has drawn widespread protests.

78. Fuchs, *Mayors and Money.*

79. Ibid., 101.

80. See ibid., various charts. I will return to this issue in Chapter 11. It may be sufficient here to say that my own explanation for why Chicago could "afford" to ignore the needs of its poor turns on that city's "race problem."

81. I cannot understand why neither Shefter *(Political Crisis/Fiscal Crisis)* nor Fuchs *(Mayors and Money)* emphasizes this difference. Thus Shefter notes that the two large cities in the most precarious financial positions in the United States are New York and Washington, D.C., not recognizing what they have in common, namely, their need to be self-supporting.

82. See Terry N. Clark and Lorna C. Ferguson, *City Money: Political Processes, Fiscal Strain, and Retrenchment* (New York: Columbia University Press, 1983), 161, Table 6.5, which shows the average annual compensation per municipal employee in 1977. The entry for Chicago was $17,689; for Los Angeles, $16,425; and for New York, $17,636.

83. Twentieth Century Fund, *New York—World City,* 91, Table 4.5.

84. This was the case possibly because Los Angeles's poorest were Latino immigrants, both legal and undocumented, or were Asians classified as refugees, who received federal rather than local assistance.

85. The battles over the budget between the state and the city have been as acrimonious and as protracted as those between President Clinton and the federal legislative bodies. Short-term borrowing or other expediencies are required each year as negotiations over city expenditures are prolonged well beyond the start of the fiscal year.

86. Or rather, HUD took over Chicago's projects because of malfeasance and graft on the part of Chicago Housing Authority officials. For the scandalous details, see, inter alia, the discussion in Gerald D. Suttles, *The Man-Made City: The Land-Use Confidence Game in Chicago* (Chicago: University of Chicago Press, 1990).

87. In terms of capital investments, Chicago has been allowed by the state of Illinois to set up special authorities with debt capacities to do everything from public housing to public buildings (the Public Building Commission, set up in 1956), which reduces not only the city's capital outlays but also the expenses of debt service. In New York, these mechanisms have been restricted by the state. Interestingly enough, Los Angeles does its redevelopment through an authority—the CRA—that uses the public powers to condemn land and raise investment funds, and then monopolizes all the profits from these redevelopment projects.

88. As early as 1965, the *New York Herald Tribune* published a series of articles deploring

the deteriorating conditions of poor and minority New Yorkers and warning that the city would soon face fiscal disaster. See New York Herald Tribune, *New York City in Crisis* (New York: Pocket Books, 1965). Note that this was well in advance of the international economic crisis of 1973.

89. One reason for the low revenues from property taxes in New York City is that some 37 percent of the total assessed value of real estate in the city is "public" and therefore exempted from taxation. Fuchs, *Mayors and Money,* 185.

90. Twentieth Century Fund, *New York—World City,* 90.

91. These conclusions from a serious study conducted at the Kennedy School of Harvard University were reported in Robert Pear, "Federal Government Uses North's and Midwest's Dollars to Aid the South, Study Says," *New York Times,* October 8, 1996, A23. The article includes a table captioned "Imbalance Sheet: States: Some Pay More and Get Less."

92. See Peter Kilborn, "Welfare All Over the Map," *New York Times,* December 8, 1996, E3, which includes a table headed "The Tough-Love Index," which compares welfare expenditures and eligibility rules by state. New York City is far from having the largest proportion of its population actually on welfare. As of 1990, Detroit had the highest proportion (26.1 percent) on welfare, with Cleveland not far behind. In comparison, the city of Chicago had 14.4 percent, New York City had 13.1 percent, and Los Angeles only 10.7 percent. See the box captioned "Welfare Population in 15 Largest Cities," *New York Times,* August 25, 1996, 46.

93. See Raphael J. Sonenshein, *Politics in Black and White: Race and Power in Los Angeles* (Princeton, N.J.: Princeton University Press, 1993).

94. This is the problematic of Charles Green and Basil Wilson, *The Struggle for Black Empowerment in New York City: Beyond the Politics of Pigmentation* (New York: Praeger, 1989). One of their explanations is couched in the "diversity" concealed in New York's minority-majority. A second explanation they offer involves the long-standing "arrangements" to balance tickets by including Irish, Jewish, and Italian candidates; these coalitions are sufficient to assure election, without any particular efforts to include blacks.

95. "The electoral turnout rates of nonwhites in New York are among the lowest of any major city in the United States," according to Shefter. Only 32 percent of the black and Hispanic voters turned out for the Democratic primary, and even black voters, Farrell's chief supporters, were only 40 percent behind their "race" candidate; only 10 percent of Hispanic voters and 3 percent of white voters cast their ballots for Farrell. See Shefter, *Political Crisis/Fiscal Crisis,* xxi–xxii.

96. See the discussion in Green and Wilson, *The Struggle for Black Empowerment,* 119–37.

97. During Washington's "interregnum," redistributive expenditures increased in Chicago, but these have subsequently been cut back as control of the city has reverted to white leadership.

11. POSTAPOCALYPSE CHICAGO

1. For a description of the anti-Vietnam demonstration, see the Walker Report, *Rights in Conflict* (New York: Bantam, 1968). Memories are not eternal, however. In 1996 a peaceful "show" of a Democratic National Convention returned to that city, presided over by Mayor Richard J. Daley's son, Richard M. Daley.

2. One of the recent publications, among the many books on Chicago politics under Daley, is Roger Biles, *Richard J. Daley: Politics, Race, and the Governing of Chicago* (De Kalb: University of Northern Illinois Press, 1995).

3. Pierre Clavel and Wim Weiwel, "Introduction," in *Harold Washington and the Neighborhoods: Progressive City Government in Chicago, 1983–1987,* ed. Pierre Clavel and Wim Weiwel (New Brunswick, N.J.: Rutgers University Press, 1991), 19; these figures are based on data that appeared earlier in Wim Weiwel, *The State of the Economy and Economic Development in the Chicago Metropolitan Region* (Chicago: Metropolitan Planning Council, 1988), 4; and John F. McDonald, *Employment Location and Industrial Land Use in Metropolitan Chicago* (Champaign, Ill.: Stipes, 1984), 55–93.

4. The area's first steel mill was established on the banks of the Calumet River in 1875.

5. David Bensman and Roberta Lynch, *Rusted Dreams: Hard Times in a Steel Community* (New York: McGraw-Hill, 1987), 72. See this work generally for a discussion of the demise of the steel mills of southeast Chicago. For a description of this same community during an earlier period of stability/prosperity, see William Kornblum, *Blue Collar Community* (Chicago: University of Chicago Press, 1974).

6. Gregory Squires, Larry Bennett, Kathleen McCourt, and Philip Nyden, *Chicago: Race, Class, and the Response to Urban Decline* (Philadelphia: Temple University Press, 1987), 3; these authors cite Stanley Ziemba, "City Loses 123,500 Jobs, Study Shows," *Chicago Tribune,* June 12, 1983.

7. Squires et al., *Chicago,* 15, citing Robert G. Sheets, Russell L. Smith, and Kenneth P. Voytek, "Corporate Disinvestment and Metropolitan Manufacturing Job Loss," in *Report by Labor Market Information Service* (De Kalb: Center for Governmental Studies, Northern Illinois University, 1984).

8. Squires et al., *Chicago,* 4. Note that the figure they mention refers to manufacturing *plants,* not jobs.

9. These figures come from my own calculations based on data in the 1991 and 1992 editions of Illinois Department of Employment Security (IDES), *Where Workers Work in the Chicago Metropolitan Area,* appendix, Supplementary Statistical Tables 1 and 2.

10. See Richard D. Bingham and Randall W. Eberts, eds., *Economic Restructuring of the American Midwest* [Proceedings of the Midwest Economic Restructuring Conference of the Federal Reserve Bank of Cleveland] (Boston: Kluwer Academic, 1990).

11. See David Allardice, Wim Weiwel, and Wendy Wintermute, "Chicago, Illinois: Reaping the Benefits of Size and Diversity," in Bingham and Eberts, *Economic Restructuring,* 75–102. Allardice et al. contrast Chicago's industrial diversity with the one-industry city of Detroit, arguing that Chicago benefits from a solid level of producers' services, alleging that while "accurate data are hard to come by, it is clear that Chicago's financial, legal, accounting and consulting services export their services to the Midwest, the nation, and indeed the world" (75).

12. Ibid., 78.

13. Ibid., 99, emphasis added.

14. Ibid., 102, citing Ann Markusen and Karen McCurdy, "Chicago's Defense-Based High Technology: A Case Study of the 'Seedbeds of Innovation' Hypothesis," *Economic Development Quarterly* 3 (February 1989): 15–31. Markusen and McCurdy state their problematic: "By almost any measure, Chicago's stature as a center of innovation and high technology has been slipping dramatically in the postwar period. Thus it represents a striking anomaly to the seedbed metaphor. We develop a number of hypotheses about why Chicago has fared relatively poorly. Central to our interpretation is the role that military spending, especially on research and innovative weaponry, has played" (15). These points are developed more extensively in Ann Markusen and Virginia Carlson, "Deindustrialization in the American Midwest: Causes and Responses," in *Deindustrialization and Regional Economic Transformation: The*

Experience of the United States, ed. Lloyd Rodwin and Hidehiko Sazanami (Winchester, Mass.: Unwin Hyman, 1989), 29–59. A summary of this chapter appears in Markusen and Carlson, "Losses in the Heartland," *NE-MW Economic Review,* May 1, 1989, 8–13.

15. Markusen and McCurdy, "Chicago's Defense-Based High Technology," 19, Table 1. Only in terms of federal installations for the army, navy, and air force did Illinois and Chicago benefit from defense expenditures.

16. Ann Markusen, Peter Hall, Sabina Dietrich, and Scott Campbell, *The Rise of the Gunbelt: The Military Remapping of Industrial America* (New York: Oxford University Press, 1991), 52–53, emphasis added. The main themes of this book center on the relocation of the defense industries from the Midwest to the California coast and to Texas.

17. These figures come from my own calculations based on data from IDES, *Where Workers Work* (1991 and 1992 statistical appendices).

18. FIRE (finance, insurance, and real estate) is not a panacea because it creates too few jobs. See Chicagoland Chamber of Commerce, *Chicagoland Demographics,* December 1993, which gives the following information on the numbers of establishments in FIRE: 12,802 in Cook County (median size fifty to ninety-nine employees); 2,143 in DuPage County, almost all of them tiny; and 304 in McHenry, almost all with fewer than ten employees.

19. See John E. Silvia, "The Outlook for the Financial Services Industry in Chicagoland" (Chicagoland Chamber of Commerce, mimeo, March 7, 1994).

20. See Chicago Department of Planning and Development, *Chicago: The Crossroads of the Business World: A Statistical Profile* (Chicago: Department of Planning and Development, [1990?]). The purpose of this "report" is to attract business by demonstrating Chicago's "superiority" to "competitor cities." For its mention of *lower wages,* see 3; on *lack of congestion,* 6 (which shows Los Angeles the worst city with respect to highway congestion, New York ninth, and Chicago twenty-fifth); on Chicago's *lower average rent in downtown,* 11 ($30.83 average per square foot in New York, $25.24 in Los Angeles, and only $24.68 in Chicago); on *cheaper electric industrial rates,* 12 (Chicago at $6.17/KWH, compared to $7.24 for Los Angeles and $10.73 for New York). Not only are corporate taxes lower in Illinois than California and New York State, but the average state and local taxes per household are only $3,000 in Chicago, as contrasted with $3,800 in California and more than $6,000 in New York. Although these comparisons are not incorrect, they do permit my different interpretation.

21. It is, for example, conspicuously absent from the original list of world cities specified by John Friedmann and Goetz Wolfe in their "World City Formation: An Agenda for Research and Action," *International Journal of Urban and Regional Research* 6 (1982): 309–44.

22. Thierry J. Noyelle and Thomas Stanbeck Jr., in *The Economic Transformation of American Cities* (Totowa, N.J.: Rowman & Allenheld, 1984), identify *four* national "nodal" centers in the United States: New York, Chicago, Los Angeles, and San Francisco. By the end of the 1980s, of the 500 largest corporations in the United States (most of them with transnational connections), the New York metropolitan region was home headquarters for 138, Chicago occupied second place with 42, and Los Angeles ranked third with only 25. For more details and sources, see Janet L. Abu-Lughod, "Comparing Chicago, New York, and Los Angeles: Testing Some World City Hypotheses," in *World Cities in a World-System,* ed. Paul L. Knox and Peter J. Taylor (Cambridge: Cambridge University Press, 1995), esp. 178–80. For a study using other criteria that shows Chicago and Los Angeles as more equal, see Alex Schwartz, "Corporate Service Linkages in Large Metropolitan Areas: A Study of New York, Los Angeles, and Chicago," *Urban Affairs Quarterly* 28 (1989): 276–96.

23. For example, electronic money now flows through the former pig-farm area of Secaucus, New Jersey, just outside New York, where all ATM transactions are cleared. As Kirk

Johnson notes in "Where Electronic Money Talks as Fast as It Moves," *New York Times,* February 18, 1997: "Since the early 1990s, the Secaucus corridor has emerged as a national center for automated teller networks. . . . It has become the national capital of preprogrammed transfers. . . . When the Fed[eral Reserve Bank] completes the consolidation of its $1.4 trillion-a-day national interbank transfer system, Fedwire, in March 1998, the area's national presence will rise further still, enough to rival New York City for the first time in the volume of money moved" (B1). This development clearly illustrates the emergence of a "nonplace urban realm," as predicted by Melvin Webber in "The Urban Place and the Nonplace Urban Realm," in *Explorations into Urban Social Structure,* ed. Melvin Webber et al. (Philadelphia: University of Pennsylvania Press, 1964).

24. Much of the following account is drawn from Bob Tamarkin, *The MERC: The Emergence of a Global Financial Powerhouse* (New York: HarperCollins, 1993).

25. Ibid., dust jacket blurb.

26. Ibid., 160.

27. See ibid., 180–87, for a more complete explanation.

28. Squires et al., *Chicago,* 23–24.

29. Ibid., 24, emphasis added; see in general 23–60.

30. Nikolas C. Theodore and D. Garth Taylor, "The Geography of Opportunity: The Status of African Americans in the Chicago Area Economy" (Chicago Urban League Department of Research and Planning, March 1991), 2. This sophisticated and original study is central to my exposition, and I am grateful to the authors for making their original maps available.

31. Ibid., 3.

32. We can presume that it was African Americans and Hispanics who were more likely to be missed by the census. Therefore, the "real" proportion is probably higher.

33. Douglas S. Massey and Nancy A. Denton, *American Apartheid: Segregation and the Making of the Underclass* (Cambridge: Harvard University Press, 1993).

34. Ibid., 2–3, emphasis added.

35. As we shall see, the increase in the number of Hispanic residents could potentially yield greater collaboration with blacks for minorities to capture local government. However, it could also lead to greater competition among minorities for "a piece of the pie." Both have happened. A brief coalition formed between Hispanics and African Americans squeaked Harold Washington into the mayor's office in 1983 and reelected him in 1987, but more recently this unity has broken down.

36. Massey and Denton, *American Apartheid,* 9. They argue that segregation cannot be explained by class differences "because blacks are equally highly segregated at all levels of income" (11–12). After surveying the data, they reach three conclusions: "First, residential segregation continues unabated in the nation's largest metropolitan black communities, and this spatial isolation cannot be attributed to class. Second, although whites now accept open housing in principle, they have not yet come to terms with its implications in practice. . . . Third, discrimination against blacks is widespread and continues at very high levels in urban housing markets" (109).

37. See Douglas S. Massey and Nancy Denton, "Trends in the Residential Segregation of Blacks, Hispanics, and Asians: 1970–1980," *American Sociological Review* 52 (1980): 807–16. Massey and Denton identify the Chicago SMSA as the most racially segregated in the United States.

38. Theodore and Taylor, "The Geography of Opportunity."

39. Ibid. Theodore and Taylor do not include information on the collar counties, but this omission is not particularly significant because, as we have already seen, those counties

contain few black residents except those living in a handful of preexisting formerly industrial towns. For their analysis, Theodore and Taylor regroup the fifty-six zip code zones of the city into forty-seven contiguous "neighborhood areas."

40. One notable exception is the recently gentrified "Printer's Row" of converted industrial buildings just south of the Loop and around the reviving (but not for transportation) Dearborn train station. This was a speculators' (and downtown business interests') gamble linked to a plan to host the next world's fair on the track-laden lakefront land to its east. This venture would have paid owners off handsomely, had the plan not been opposed and then abandoned when Harold Washington assumed office.

41. Theodore and Taylor, "The Geography of Opportunity," i.

42. Squires et al., *Chicago,* 29–30.

43. Theodore and Taylor, "Geography of Opportunity," 9.

44. Ibid., 18.

45. In the late 1980s, East Chicago Heights (one of the most depressed of these black suburbs) changed its name to Ford Heights, a ploy, however, that failed to remove its stigma. According to the 1990 census, Ford Heights, with only about forty-two hundred residents, almost all black, was one of the poorest towns in the United States. With no jobs and little income to support town government, in October 1996 the town was the site of a major drug raid by the Cook County police for widespread corruption in which the poorly paid local police played important supporting roles.

46. Theodore and Taylor, "Geography of Opportunity," 18–19.

47. Ibid., 13–17.

48. As an aside, we might point out that William Julius Wilson's concept of the "underclass" (a term he has now rejected as pejorative) was generated almost exclusively out of his studies in Chicago, perhaps the most blatantly extreme case he could have chosen.

49. Theodore and Taylor, "Geography of Opportunity," 20.

50. See Douglas S. Massey, Andrew B. Gross, and Kumiko Shibuya, "Migration, Segregation, and the Concentration of Poverty," *American Sociological Review* 59 (June 1994): 425–45.

51. Ibid., 425–27. The purpose of their study was to test three hypotheses about the causes of this trend toward greater geographic concentration of poverty: Wilson's hypothesis about the selective departure of nonpoor middle- and working-class blacks from ghettos; Jargowsky and Bane's hypothesis about the decline of people into poverty caused by an increase in general poverty; and a hypothesis, formulated by Massey and his colleagues, that poverty became more concentrated in older U.S. cities in the Northeast and Midwest because a large and segregated group (African Americans and Puerto Ricans) experienced a sharp increase in poverty. They conclude: "The most important finding of this research is that geographically concentrated poverty ultimately stems from racially segregated U.S. housing markets." In contrast, selective out-migration of better-off blacks from poor ghetto areas had "little to do with the accumulation of poverty in black neighborhoods." In poor or very poor minority neighborhoods, the "poor were more likely to leave than those who were not" (442), and nonpoor blacks who left were likely to go to another poor neighborhood. *"Only nonpoor blacks already living outside poor black neighborhoods were relatively likely to migrate into nonpoor areas. To the extent that concentrated poverty is linked to the geographic moves of nonpoor African-Americans, therefore, it reflects a reluctance of those living outside of poor ghetto areas to move back in"* (443, emphasis added). Massey et al. conclude that "the concentration of black poverty arises from three mechanisms that grow out of the persistent segregation of American cities": (1) "the net in-migration of poor blacks into poor black neighborhoods"; (2) "the net downward socioeconomic mobility among blacks living in racially segregated neighborhoods"; and

(3) "most important, . . . the exclusion of blacks from white neighborhoods. . . . These segregational forces isolate blacks economically and socially and contribute directly and forcefully to the accumulation of poverty in black neighborhoods. . . . Unless racial discrimination in housing is eliminated, therefore, whatever improvements in black welfare are achieved through class-based interventions will tend to be overwhelmed by the disastrous neighborhood conditions that follow directly from residential segregation" (443). Therefore, in terms of policy, "strenuous efforts should be made to facilitate black residential mobility and to enhance the access of blacks to the full range of benefits and resources available in U.S. metropolitan housing markets" (444).

52. See, inter alia, the graphs contained in NIPC, *Vision 2020 Newsletter,* November 1993, 6, which present data from the 1990 census.

53. I suggest that Gerald D. Suttles's conclusion in *The Man-Made City: The Land-Use Confidence Game in Chicago* (Chicago: University of Chicago Press, 1990) that jobs have vanished from Chicago's predominantly black neighborhoods *because* black "ghetto culture" *makes* its occupants poor workers, has it backward. There is certainly no evidence that African Americans were "poor workers" when prospects for jobs were better. Rather, a combination of declining opportunities that can be attributed to economic collapse, together with employer preferences for nonblack workers (racism), has led, in turn, to alternate paths of survival and defensive "attitude" among many black males. At least, a more likely explanation lies in the interaction effects between the two, which constitute a proverbial vicious cycle.

Regarding lowered wages for employed blacks, Squires et al. point out that membership in private unions has collapsed with manufacturing. Only public sector unions have gained. But "Illinois was the last industrial state to pass legislation allowing government workers—state, county, and city employees—the right to organize and strike in non-essential service areas. . . . The law went into effect in July 1984. . . . These new unions are likely to become more powerful in Chicago, while older industrial and craft unions become weaker." *Chicago,* 45; see generally 39–45. Contrast this with the early recognition of municipal unions in New York City.

54. William Julius Wilson, *The Truly Disadvantaged: The Inner City, the Underclass, and Public Policy* (Chicago: University of Chicago Press, 1987). In 1970, Wilson identified sixteen poor communities in Chicago, a number that had increased to twenty-six ten years later (the number of communities with extremely high poverty rates increased from one to nine). This trend was occurring in other major cities as well. See also Paul A. Jargowsky and Mary Jo Bane, "Ghetto Poverty in the United States, 1970–80," in *The Urban Underclass,* ed. Christopher Jencks and Paul E. Peterson (Washington, D.C.: Brookings Institution, 1991), 235–73. Other works suggest that this trend continued into the 1980s and 1990s.

55. Squires et al., *Chicago,* 42. These conclusions follow from their Table 2.5, which incorporates an analysis by Art Lyons of the Institute on Taxation and Economic Policy in Chicago of unpublished U.S. Bureau of the Census data for 1959 and 1979. The table compares the percentages of families in low-, middle-, and upper-income classes in different parts of the metropolitan region. In 1959, 18 percent of Chicago families were classified as low income, 64 percent were middle, and 18 percent were high income. By 1979, 32.4 percent of Chicago's families were classified as having low incomes, whereas the proportion with middle incomes had dropped to 53 percent and that with high incomes had fallen to less than 15 percent. In contrast, in 1959 only 7.4 percent of families in suburban Cook County had low incomes, 62 percent had incomes in the middle, and almost 31 percent of the families were classified as having high incomes. Twenty years later, the proportion of families in suburban Cook County with low incomes had risen to 12 percent, and there were commensurate (but modest)

drops in the percentages with middle and upper incomes. The most radical changes were in the five collar counties beyond suburban Cook County, where the proportion of poor families dropped from 12.4 to 11.4 percent, the proportion with middle incomes dropped from 64.4 to 59.7 percent, and the proportion with high incomes increased from 23 to 29 percent.

56. For convenience, many of these figures have been taken from Chicago Department of Planning and Development, *Social and Economic Characteristics of Chicago's Population* (Chicago: Department of Planning and Development, December 1992), which gives limited information on the city as a whole and its seventy-seven Community Areas, based on the 1990 census. This source is, of course, much less useful than the local community fact books produced since the 1930s by social scientists, which compute indicators not only for community areas but their constituent census tracts and, as an innovation, on suburban areas as well.

57. These figures come from various reports issued by the Northeastern Illinois Planning Commission (assembled from its "Population and Household Forecast, 1980–2010"); the "Suburban Fact Book, 1979"; and the IDES 1990 report of *Where Workers Work.*

58. Many of these conclusions were foreseen by David J. Hartman in "Racial Change in the Chicago Area, 1980–1987," *Sociology and Social Research* 74 (April 1990): 168–73. Hartman analyzed changes in the six counties between 1970 and 1980 and projected these to 1987. He notes: "The metropolitan black population grew only 16% from 1970 to 1980 as compared to 38% from 1960 to 1970. In the city of Chicago the 1970 to 1980 increase was only nine percent, down from 36% for the preceding decade. . . . Since 1980 this trend has continued. Black net migration, reversing a long-time trend, slowed to nearly zero in the 1970s for the six-county metropolitan area, and was strongly negative for the city of Chicago" (168). Here he cites Donald Bogue, *Population Projections: Chicago SMSA, Chicago City, and Metropolitan Ring 1980–2000: By Age, Sex, and Race/Ethnicity* (Chicago: URLDAS, 1983), 51.

59. Hartman, "Racial Change," 169–70.

60. A particularly valuable source on NIPC is Barbara Page Fiske, ed., *Key to Government in Chicago and Suburban Cook County* (Chicago: University of Chicago Press, 1989), a volume prepared by volunteers from the League of Women Voters of Chicago, the League of Women Voters of Cook County, the Cook County Court Watchers, and the Citizens Information Service of Illinois. According to this publication, NIPC is governed by a commission made up of five local residents appointed by the governor, five appointed by the mayor (of whom three must be members of the city council), one member from each of the involved counties, and one representative each appointed by the Chicago Transit Authority (CTA), the Regional Transit Authority (RTA), the Metropolitan Sanitary District (MSD), the Illinois Association of Park Districts, and the Chicago Park District. "The other 7 commissioners are elected by an assembly of suburban mayors and village presidents" who must be municipal officials: two from Cook County (one from north and one from south of Roosevelt Road) and one from each of the other five counties. However, "NIPC has neither taxing authority nor any other assured sources of revenues; its funding comes from voluntary contributions or contracts for services." See pp. 4, 9, 12.

61. Ibid., 151. Although these data are somewhat old, because so little new housing has been added since 1985, I have not sought more current figures.

62. Suttles, *The Man-Made City,* 59–60. Suttles's work constitutes a virulent but detailed muckraking account of Chicago politics. In a footnote to this quotation, Suttles alleges that "by February 1982 the Chicago Housing Authority was the most heavily subsidized in the nation while HUD reported one month later that it was the worst run housing authority in the nation." He cites *Sun-Times,* March 21, 1982, as his source.

63. Fiske, *Key to Government in Chicago,* 154.

64. In 1985 this program stopped accepting applications because the waiting list was ten years behind: by then, forty thousand families and five thousand elderly were already on the waiting list.

65. Fiske, *Key to Government in Chicago,* 153.

66. Alexander Polikoff, *Housing the Poor: The Case for Heroism* (Cambridge, Mass.: Ballinger, 1978), xiii; this book is the best source on this case. The time lag between the initial case and its disposition by the Supreme Court ruling was almost obscene. In 1953, Dorothy Gautreaux (black head of a family of six) was assigned to a public housing project in a black neighborhood, an assignment she protested. Eleven years later, in 1964, Congress passed civil rights legislation outlawing discrimination in federally subsidized programs. The following year, "Dorothy Gautreaux and other CHA tenants asked the American Civil Liberties Union to try to halt another massive CHA project proposed for Chicago's west side black ghetto and to force a change in CHA site location polities" (xiv). Polikoff served voluntarily as head of the team of ACLU lawyers who took on the case. By the time the Supreme Court ruled in her favor in 1976, Gautreaux had been dead for many years, and the public housing program in Chicago was only slightly less moribund.

67. Details in Suttles, *The Man-Made City,* 60–61. Chicago had earlier experienced a crippling snowstorm that city hall (the "machine") proved unprepared to handle. This fiasco led to the election of Jane Byrne, Chicago's first (and so far only) woman mayor. She came from outside machine ranks.

68. Communities were supposed to have a voice this time through consultation with community-based organizations, rather than with elected aldermen who had obstructed site approvals in the 1950s. Race, however, remained the same bedrock issue.

69. Suttles, *The Man-Made City,* 66–67. But perhaps the most unreal moment was when Jane Byrne moved into the Cabrini-Green housing project for Christmas—an awkward moment captured by numerous political cartoons.

70. See Junerous Cook, "Public School Segregation, City of Chicago, 1963–1964 and 1964–1965" (Urban League, Chicago, mimeo, May 12, 1965), 1.

71. Ibid. Wholesale desertion of the public school system and/or of city residences by white families with children would eventually leave the residual enrollment in Chicago public schools so "minority-heavy" that little margin for desegregation would be left, without going beyond the city limits. However, as late as the mid-1960s, integration *could* have been achieved, given that in the 1963–64 school year, more than half of Chicago pupils were white, about 47 were Negro, and only 2.6 percent were "other," and in the 1964–65 school year, 48.6 percent of pupils were white, 48.8 percent were Negro, and 2.6 percent were "other." Ibid., 5 (the report uses the term *Negro*). A table in the same document's appendix (p. 27) gives somewhat different figures on the "head counts" taken on single days in the schools; it is based on official public school enrollment figures, so that an estimate of absentees has been added in. In 1963, in elementary grades, 51 percent of students (including those "absent") were Negro, 46 percent were white, and 3 percent were "other." One year later, 52 percent were Negro, 45 percent were white, and 2.8 percent were "other." White enrollment was even higher in secondary schools, where 64 percent of the students were white, 34 percent Negro, and only 1.7 percent "other"; one year later, it was 61 percent white, 37 percent Negro, and 1.8 percent "other."

72. In Chicago, with its fixation on the black/white split, Latinos are often ignored as "irrelevant," so it is hard to figure out what "other" meant to the analysts or to the Urban League. Latinos often resent their ambiguous (and excluded) position. As Kamasaki and Yzaguirre astutely recognize, "Tensions often arise when the two communities come together. Many blacks frequently see Hispanics as yet another 'white' immigrant group that has come in

at the bottom of the social and economic ladder and then overtaken them. Many Hispanics see blacks as an extension of the oppressive, 'Anglo' society." Charles Kamasaki and Raul Yzaguirre, "Black-Hispanic Tensions: One Perspective," *Journal of Intergroup Relations* 21 (winter 1994–5); 19–20.

73. Cook, "Public School Segregation," 3, emphasis added. The League used a minimal definition of "integration." A school was considered absolutely segregated if 100 percent of its students were of one race; it was considered effectively segregated if enrollment was 90–99.9 percent of a single race.

74. Marcia Turner Jones, "Chicago Area School Enrollment Trends, 1970–1982" (mimeo, n.d.), 2–3. Unfortunately, my copy of this report does not show its provenance.

75. The material that follows depends heavily on Marilyn Gittel, "School Reform in New York and Chicago: Revisiting the Ecology of Local Games," *Urban Affairs Quarterly* 30 (September 1994): 136–51. I certainly concur that her "comparative analysis of city school reform reveals significant differences in the two city cultures" (137), even though I disagree with some of her conclusions, and the recent rescinding of the Chicago decentralization plan refutes her optimistic projection.

76. See Don Terry, "One Fifth of Schools Put on Probation in Chicago," *New York Times,* October 1, 1996, A14. According to this article, the Chicago School Board "placed 109 of the city's lowest-scoring schools on academic probation," allowing the board to "replace principals and teachers" if these schools are unable to raise to 15 percent the proportion of its students who read at grade level—a modest goal indeed. "At 8 of the 38 high schools on probation, fewer than 4 percent of the students were reading at grade level. At one school, only 2.5 percent . . . were at grade level. . . . Probation in Chicago also allows the school board to remove a probationary school's local council. . . . The local councils were the backbone of Chicago's vast school reform plan of 1989, which embraced decentralization and greater parental control as the way to improve schools. But Mayor Daley's recent steps have changed that focus, giving him broader central control." A similar approach is now being followed in New York City under Mayor Giuliani.

77. Gittel, "School Reform," 139–40.

78. One important difference between the two cases was that New York's reforms were instituted *before* the public school system had become overwhelmingly minority dominated, whereas by the time the decentralization plan was approved in Chicago, the public schools already had very low white enrollments.

79. Gittel, "School Reform," 141–43.

80. Ibid., 147.

81. Ibid., 150.

82. In Chapter 8, I showed how neighborhood "self-determination" had largely been used to exclude blacks from white neighborhoods.

83. Squires et al., *Chicago,* 65.

84. Ibid., 69.

85. Ibid., 74.

86. Ibid., 80.

87. It was "electoral competition among white factions or parties [that] created the conditions under which African-American voters could determine electoral outcomes and African-American leaders could bargain for group empowerment." This was evidently still true at the time of Washington's initial victory. Richard A. Keiser, "Explaining African-American Political Empowerment: Windy City Politics from 1900 to 1983," *Urban Affairs Quarterly* 29 (September 1993): 84. See also Paul Kleppner, *Chicago Divided: The Making of a Black Mayor*

(De Kalb: Northern Illinois University Press, 1985); and Diane M. Pinderhughes, *Race and Ethnicity in Chicago Politics* (Urbana: University of Illinois Press, 1987). The latter book is a historically grounded analysis of black empowerment vis-à-vis older "white ethnics" and their temporary defection to a Republican candidate.

88. Doug Gills, "Chicago Politics and Community Development: A Social Movement Perspective," in *Harold Washington and the Neighborhoods: Progressive City Government in Chicago, 1983–1987,* ed. Pierre Clavel and Wim Weiwel (New Brunswick, N.J.: Rutgers University Press, 1991), 34. Gills was a neighborhood organizer and therefore, I think, tends to overemphasize the contributions of these groups and to minimize the remarkable voter registration drive in the black community and the linkages forged with Latinos.

89. Ibid., 37, emphasis added.

90. Ibid., 39. In the primary, Washington attracted 80 percent of the black vote, although 17 percent of his vote came from whites. "In the general election, Latinos provided the critical margin of victory. He was able to improve from 25 percent of the Latino vote in the primary to about 65 percent of the Latino vote in the general election. Washington garnered 75 percent of the Puerto Rican vote, 62 percent of the Mexican vote, and 52 percent of the Cuban vote." He also was aided by the neighborhood organizations and "his ability to gain at least nominal support of many of the locals in the Chicago Federation of Labor, and in the general election he got the nominal support of the Chicago Federation of Labor and the active support of many of the local unions" (52).

91. Larry Bennett, "Harold Washington and the Black Urban Regime," *Urban Affairs Quarterly* 28 (March 1993): 423, 425.

92. Ibid., 434.

93. Ibid., 436.

94. Robert P. Giloth and Robert Mier, "Spatial Change and Social Justice: Alternative Economic Development in Chicago," in *Economic Restructuring and Political Response,* ed. Robert A. Beauregard (Newbury Park, Calif.: Sage, 1989), 182–83. Giloth and Mier provide a good exposition of these local experiments.

95. The three cases that Giloth and Mier note as promising have in the end not borne fruit. They describe the Playskool toy factory retention plan (188–91); it is sobering to update this case. The "ghetto-located" factory received enormous subsidies to stay in the area and to hire local workers, but it left anyway and had to be sued; there was a settlement of sorts that focused on retraining Playskool workers, mostly for jobs as home health aids. The *1984 Development Plan* (see p. 185) was intended to work with the networks of development groups to chart a more responsive and equitable approach to development, balancing downtown and neighborhood needs as well as manufacturing and service industries, but here, too, results were disappointing. The second example Giloth and Mier give (see pp. 192–94) is the North River industrial corridor, including Goose Island, where industrial firms were actually outbid for factory buildings by a process of gentrification/loft conversions. The third case was the creation of special task forces to address the preservation of Chicago's steel and apparel industries (see pp. 197–99). As we have seen, steel has not recovered, and although the garment industry has revived somewhat, thanks to new Korean investors who employ cheap Mexican workers, this hardly fits the goal of replacing McDonald's-type jobs with those in heavy industry.

96. Ibid., 202.

97. See, inter alia, James Atlas, "The Daleys of Chicago," *New York Times Magazine,* August 25, 1996, 37–39, 52, 56–58.

98. See Rowan A. Miranda, "Post-machine Regimes and the Growth of Government: A Fiscal History of the City of Chicago, 1970–1990," *Urban Affairs Quarterly* 28 (March 1993):

397–422, esp. 417. Only during the brief interval of Washington's regime had the "fiscal conservatism" so admired by Fuchs and Miranda been "eased" to permit resources to flow to Chicago's neglected minority areas.

12. THE LOS ANGELES REGION TRANSFORMED

1. Deyan Sudjic, *The 100 Mile City* (San Diego, Calif.: Harcourt Brace & Company, 1992), 305.

2. It is not accidental that the frontispiece of Sudjic's book is a photo of smog-bound "downtown" Los Angeles, and that the accompanying caption identifies Los Angeles as "perhaps the clearest example of the hundred-mile city."

3. Italo Calvino, *Invisible Cities,* trans. William Weaver (San Diego, Calif.: Harcourt Brace Jovanovich, 1974), 10.

4. Reyner Banham, *Los Angeles: The Architecture of Four Ecologies* (London: Penguin, 1971).

5. Robert M. Fogelson, *The Fragmented Metropolis: Los Angeles, 1850–1930* (Berkeley: University of California Press, 1993[1967]).

6. In addition to Los Angeles County, the Los Angeles CMSA includes Ventura County to the north, San Bernardino and Riverside Counties to the east, and Orange County to the south. However, one could make an argument for considering San Diego County, to Orange County's south, a second "growth pole" in an almost continuously urbanized Southern California to the Mexican border. The Bureau of the Census, however, does not.

7. Mike Davis once taught a course titled "The Cannibal City," according to a bulletin board announcement posted at the University of California, Los Angeles, in 1995. And a graph that was published in the *Los Angeles Times,* February 17, 1995, A3, revealed how much agricultural land in Southern California has been lost to urban uses. Although the state of California lost only 12.5 percent of its farmland to urban developments between 1978 and 1992, Los Angeles County lost 50.3 percent; Orange County, 63.8 percent; San Bernardino County, 40.4 percent; and Riverside County, 19.5 percent. Thus far, the less developed (i.e., more agricultural) counties have experienced less land-use conversion. For example, Kern Country lost only 9.5 percent and Ventura only 5.8 percent.

8. Robert Glass Cleland, *The Irvine Ranch of Orange County, 1810–1950* (San Marino, Calif.: Huntington Library, 1952), 101.

9. Ibid, v.

10. Ibid., 4.

11. Ibid., 14.

12. Actually, James Irvine, the chief partner with Flint and Bixby, was not a "Yankee" at all, having fled his birthplace in Ireland during the great migration of 1848 and then headed westward during the 1849 gold rush, where he prospered in the grocery business. Ibid., 67, 75. The three partners bought at bargain price the hundred thousand acres of what became the Irvine Ranch in the drought of the mid-1860s. When their cattle died off for lack of water, the owners converted to sheep raising, which required less water, exporting their wool to New York and Boston via San Francisco; later they switched to the new harbor south of Los Angeles that Phineas Banning had built at Wilmington. Ibid., 66, 76, 79.

13. Ibid., 93, 95.

14. Ibid., 123–35.

15. The eight miles of ocean frontage and the ownership of several islands offshore made the Irvine Company a natural, if belated, developer. As Cleland wrote in 1950, "As of

this writing, The Irvine Company has a number of important subdivisions on Newport Bay . . . [and] extensive interests in the city of Laguna Beach. . . . The construction of the coastal highway in the mid-twenties for which The Irvine Company . . . gave the right-of-way through the ranch, stimulated the growth of numerous beach communities south of Newport Bay . . . [but] created a severe water problem. . . . Even with the [then new] large pipeline, the depletion of the water supply in the Santa Ana basin threatened to affect Laguna Beach. . . . As a result, the Coastal Municipal Water District was created." Ibid., 142–44.

16. Ibid., 147ff.

17. The details of the post-1950 period appear in Martin J. Schiesl, "Designing the Model Community: The Irvine Company and Suburban Development, 1950–88," *Postsuburban California: The Transformation of Orange County since World War II,* ed. Rob Kling, Spencer Olin, and Mark Poster (Berkeley: University of California Press, 1991), 55–91.

18. Rob Kling, Spencer Olin, and Mark Poster, "The Emergence of Postsuburbia: An Introduction," in *Postsuburban California: The Transformation of Orange County since World War II,* ed. Rob Kling, Spencer Olin, and Mark Poster (Berkeley: University of California Press, 1991), 1–2. The high-tech export business was so great that an export licensing office was opened in Newport Beach, "the first such branch outside of Washington, D.C."

19. Ibid., 5–7.

20. Edward W. Soja, "Inside Exopolis," in an early draft of *Third Space: Expanding the Geographical Imagination* (Oxford: Basil Blackwell, 1996). He takes his quotations from an advertisement for *Californians,* a travel guide published by the California Office of Tourism. Of course, the *real* theme park of Disneyland is located in Orange County in the town of Anaheim. I assume this material will appear in Soja's forthcoming book *Postmetropolis,* scheduled to be published by Blackwell in 1999.

21. Kling et al., "The Emergence of Postsuburbia," 8–9, emphasis added.

22. Schiesl, "Designing the Model Community," 58–59.

23. Kling et al., "The Emergence of Postsuburbia," 11.

24. Kling et al. may have derived the term *information capitalism* from articles that Manuel Castells published before the release of his *The Informational City* (New York: Basil Blackwell, 1989). "Kling and Turner calculate that about 58 percent of Orange County's work force is in the information sector . . . six times the size of its high tech force." "The Emergence of Postsuburbia," 12.

25. Ibid., 13, emphasis added.

26. For example, Kling et al. refer to McDonald's as participating in the "informational" economy because data analyses are required for mass ordering, inventories, management, and so on, in contrast to mom-and-pop greasy spoons (see ibid.). But most employees of McDonald's work in kitchens, mop floors, or work as cashiers; they are certainly *not* part of the informational economy, and, in California at least, they are largely of Mexican origin.

27. Allen J. Scott, *Metropolis: From the Division of Labor to Urban Form* (Berkeley: University of California Press, 1988), 1.

28. Ibid., 6. Scott argues convincingly that the concept of "postindustrial" society is wrong, especially with respect to the transcendence of capitalism by some "new information-processing mode of economic organization." Although it is true that the form of the new capitalism is different, there is no basic shift "away from the structure and logic of industrial capitalism" (7).

29. In 1980, almost 1.3 million of the jobs in the five-county region were in the industrial sector (the largest), which accounted for some 30 percent of all employment. In contrast, only 25 percent were in services and 18.5 percent in retail trade. All other sectors were small.

30. Edward W. Soja, Allan D. Heskin, and Marco Cenzatti, "Los Angeles: Through the Kaleidoscope of Urban Restructuring" (University of California, Los Angeles, Graduate School of Architecture and Urban Planning, pamphlet, 1985), 1.

31. Ibid., 13.

32. Although Soja has long used the term *exopolis,* perhaps his most explicit denotative definition can be found in his "Los Angeles, 1965–1992: From Crisis-Generated Restructuring to Restructuring-Generated Crisis," in *The City: Los Angeles and Urban Theory at the End of the Twentieth Century,* ed. Allen J. Scott and Edward W. Soja (Berkeley: University of California Press, 1996), 436–37.

33. The industrialization of the San Fernando Valley and, most recently, of certain districts in otherwise agricultural Ventura County is well covered in Allen Scott, "High-Technology Industrial Development in the San Fernando Valley and Ventura County: Observations on Economic Growth and the Evolution of Urban Form," in *The City: Los Angeles and Urban Theory at the End of the Twentieth Century,* ed. Allen J. Scott and Edward W. Soja (Berkeley: University of California Press, 1996), 276–310.

34. Soja, "Los Angeles, 1965–1992," 437.

35. Kling et al. acknowledge that "Orange County has been profoundly affected by the massive migration (most of it from Asia and Latin America) that has transformed the entire southern California area." "The Emergence of Postsuburbia," 15. In the 1970s, Hispanic residents increased by almost 150 percent to constitute some 15 percent of Orange County's population, and the Asian population increased by more than 370 percent to make up close to 5 percent. "Since the mid-1970s, Orange County's expanding service economy and its need for inexpensive blue-collar manual workers have combined to attract the nation's fourth largest permanent settlement of undocumented Mexican immigrants. Although they have customarily been perceived as agricultural labor, a significant number of Latinos and especially Asians are in fact employed in the industrial and high-tech sectors, where they often form the core of an army of assembly-line workers who construct computer and biomedical equipment and other products in the electronics and instrument industries" (15).

36. See Allen J. Scott, *Technopolis: High-Technology Industry and Regional Development in Southern California* (Berkeley: University of California Press, 1993), esp. 91, Table 5.1. Chapter 5 deals with the aircraft industry.

37. Ibid., 127, Figure 6.2; Scott's Chapter 6 examines missile and space-related industries.

38. Ibid., 141, Table 7.2.

39. There are almost no African Americans living in Orange County.

40. Scott, *Technopolis,* 195.

41. See, inter alia, the early studies of A. Saxenian, "Silicon Valley and Route 128: Regional Prototypes or Historic Exceptions" (paper presented at a conference on microelectronics, University of California, Santa Cruz, 1984); and Amy Glasmeier, "Spatial Differentiation of High Technology Industries: Implications for Planning" (Ph.D. diss., University of California, Berkeley, 1985).

42. Soja et al., *Los Angeles,* 2. The overwhelming proportion of workers in the garment industry are Latina, with some large but unknown percentage of them undocumented. See, inter alia, Edna Bonacich and Patricia Hanneman, "A Statistical Portrait of the Los Angeles Garment Industry" (unpublished manuscript, University of California, Riverside, Department of Sociology, 1992); and Edna Bonacich, "Asian and Latino Immigrants in the Los Angeles Garment Industry: An Exploration of the Relationship between Capitalism and Racial Oppression," in *Immigration and Entrepreneurship: Culture, Capital, and Ethnic Networks,* ed. Ivan Light and Parminder Bhachu (New Brunswick, N.J.: Transaction, 1993). See also Paul

Ong, Edna Bonacich, and Lucie Chang, eds., *The New Asian Immigration in Los Angeles and Global Restructuring* (Philadelphia: Temple University Press, 1994).

43. Some of this decline is attributable to downsizing, but some is due to the relocation of plants, especially in the aerospace industry, to lower-wage states such as Utah and Arizona. According to a paper by economics graduate student Marie Duggan, "Restructuring Los Angeles: The Case of Aerospace and Some Social Implications" (unpublished manuscript, New School for Social Research, 1994), the rate of profit in aerospace had already begun to decline in the 1970s, although downsizing and eventual restructuring and relocation had not hit their stride until the end of the 1980s and early part of the 1990s. Duggan's conclusions are derived, in part, from data contained in various issues of the industry's trade journal, *Aviation Week and Space Technology.*

44. See *Economic Report of the Governor 1992,* submitted by Pete Wilson to the California Legislature, 1991–92 Regular Session, esp. graphs on 17.

45. Ibid., 9, chart and graph.

46. Indeed, southern Los Angeles was in even more dire straits than it had been in 1965 at the time of the Watts riot. A special supplement to the *Los Angeles Times,* May 11, 1992, summarized and mapped findings from the U.S. Census of 1990. The accompanying text by Shawn Hubler, "South L.A.'s Poverty Rate Worse than '65," pointed out that Los Angeles was sitting on a keg of dynamite. Since the Watts riot of 1965, "joblessness, hopelessness and a crippling lack of skills and education" had grown even worse in the southern portion of the city. "Only the faces have changed. In 1965, the area was 81% black. By 1990, with more than double the population, half the people in South Los Angeles were Latino and the black community comprised 44.8%" (A1–A2).

47. Paul Ong was faculty director of a collective master's project in planning at UCLA titled "The Great Divide." The findings, duly updated, are summarized in Paul Ong and Evelyn Blumenfeld, "Income and Racial Inequality in Los Angeles," in *The City: Los Angeles and Urban Theory at the End of the Twentieth Century,* ed. Allen J. Scott and Edward W. Soja (Berkeley: University of California Press, 1996), 311–35.

48. Ibid., 315–16, emphasis added.

49. See ibid., 319, Table 10.3. However, this figure must be for the county, because within the city itself, the poverty rate had risen to 20 percent.

50. Ibid., 323, 325; for differential poverty rates by race and ethnicity, see 327, Table 10.6, which shows relative changes between 1969 and 1989. Whereas the poverty rate for blacks was substantially higher than that for Latinos in 1969, by 1989 the black poverty rate had dropped somewhat, whereas the Latino poverty rate had increased to above that of the black population.

51. The following data are taken from Center for Continuing Study of the California Economy, *California County Projections—1992,* Stephen Levy, chief economist (Palo Alto, Calif.: CCSCE, 1992), 7.

52. Ibid., 25.

53. Ibid., 26, table headed "Change in Manufacturing Jobs, May 1990–September 1992."

54. As Ann Markusen, Peter Hall, Sabina Dietrich, and Scott Campbell note in *The Rise of the Gunbelt: The Military Remapping of Industrial America* (New York: Oxford University Press, 1991), almost a quarter "of all prime aerospace contracts in any typical year go to California; and of these, well over one-half come to the Los Angeles Basin" (84–85). Markusen et al. have tried to evaluate why aerospace and other defense-related firms might leave California for other parts of the sun belt. They note that because California is now unionized, there is some temptation to move to lower labor cost areas, such as the "five 'slave

manufacturing plants' established by Hughes in the South." Furthermore, "Los Angeles contractors may be tempted to disperse outside California: *the political advantages of a broad geographic representation and, more specifically, to gain congressional support by putting a facility in a key representative's district.*" Nevertheless, they conclude that despite such temptations to move to other states, inertia, the existence of a developed regional complex, and a concentration of skilled workers should keep high-tech industry in Los Angeles. But Markusen et al. ask, "What impact will the end of the cold war have on Los Angeles?" They offer four reasons Los Angeles would not be devastated by these reductions: first, the peace dividends have thus far been relatively small; second, the cuts have been achieved primarily through the closing of military bases, which hits other places harder than it hits Los Angeles; third, "although Los Angeles may dominate American defense industries, defense does not wholly dominate Los Angeles"; finally, the workforce in Los Angeles is so skilled that it can easily turn its skills to peacetime activities. Markusen et al. conclude that "even if the 1990 thaw in Eastern Europe finally spreads to the military budget, Los Angeles may have irreversibly become the high-tech center of North America." (Quotations extracted from 110–17, with emphasis added.) However, their evaluation may have been too optimistic. By the early 1990s, cutbacks in military expenditures were already having a depressing effect. With hindsight, we can see that these effects have been more severe than Markusen et al. anticipated, perhaps because they have been compounded by other demographic and social changes and intensified by natural disasters.

55. This projection by the CCSCE, California County Projections, turned out to be low; by 1990, the county had 8,863,164 residents.

56. In contrast, Cook County, Illinois, grew by only 0.6 percent between 1980 and 1990, and in the New York region, gains were decidedly modest: the Bronx was up 4.7 percent; Manhattan, 5.7 percent; Brooklyn, 3.7 percent; Queens, 1.8 percent; Nassau was down by 0.3 percent, and Suffolk was up by 2.9 percent.

57. Georges Sabagh and Mehdi Bozorgmehr, "Population Change: Immigration and Ethnic Transformation," in *Ethnic Los Angeles,* ed. Roger Waldinger and Mehdi Bozorgmehr (New York: Russell Sage Foundation, 1994), 85.

58. Ibid., 86, citing 105 n. 14 of U.S. Bureau of the Census, *Gross Migration for Counties: 1975 to 1980* (Washington, D.C.: U.S. Government Printing Office, 1984).

59. Ibid., 85.

60. Ibid., 86. Sabagh and Bozorgmehr cite Manuel Moreno et al., "Impact of Undocumented Persons and Other Immigrants on Costs, Revenues and Services in Los Angeles County" (unpublished report 25, Los Angeles County Urban Research Section, 1992); see 105 n. 18.

61. Ibid., esp. 95–96, Table 3.2, from which my figures have been adapted.

62. Ashley Dunn, "In California, the Numbers Add Up to Anxiety," *New York Times,* October 30, 1994, E3. It is obvious from this title *whose* anxiety is being identified. In the *New York Times* series on California, see especially Robert Reinhold, "California's Welcome for Immigrants Turns to Resentment," *New York Times,* August 25, 1993, 1, A12.

63. Much smaller numbers hailed from El Salvador and other Central American countries. Undocumented immigrants, unless enumerated by the census, are not included in this count.

64. Between 1980 and 1990, New York added close to a million and a half residents through immigration. However, the top five sending countries (the Dominican Republic, China, Jamaica, Colombia, and Korea) accounted for only 28 percent of all immigrants. In marked contrast, 65 percent of the two million foreign immigrants to Los Angeles hailed from the top five sending countries, with Mexico by far the largest contributor.

65. For a fascinating account of the changes in Monterey Park, the largest "Asian city" in the United States, see John Horton, with the assistance of Jose Calderon, Mary Pardo, Leland Saito, Linda Shaw, and Yen-Fen Tseng, *The Politics of Diversity: Immigration, Resistance, and Change in Monterey Park, California* (Philadelphia: Temple University Press, 1995).

66. Howard J. Nelson and William A. V. Clark, *Los Angeles: The Metropolitan Experience: Uniqueness, Generality and the Goal of the Good Life* (Cambridge: Ballinger, 1976), 33.

67. David Rieff emphasizes the ways Anglos have benefited from Latino labor in *Los Angeles: Capital of the Third World* (New York: Simon & Schuster, 1991). Investors indeed continue to profit from the willingness of immigrants to work for low wages. Several decades of drop in real income from farm labor can be attributed to the failure of unionization, assisted by "crowding" of migrant laborers to the benefit of farm owners. The challenge to unionization of garment workers also comes from this source.

68. Ivan Light has been especially impressed with the way such Asian entrepreneurial skills have infused the local economy. See, inter alia, Ivan Light and Elizabeth Roach, "Self-Employment: Mobility Ladder or Economic Lifeboat?" in *Ethnic Los Angeles,* ed. Roger Waldinger and Mehdi Bozorgmehr (New York: Russell Sage Foundation, 1994), 193–213. For a somewhat less optimistic view, see in the same collection Lucie Cheng and Philip Q. Yang, "Asians: The 'Model Minority' Deconstructed," 305–44.

69. This might be called "*Blade Runner* panic," a syndrome to be treated later in this chapter.

70. Indeed, Peter Skerry, in *Mexican Americans: The Ambivalent Minority* (Cambridge: Harvard University Press, 1993), takes as one of his problematics the fact that in San Antonio, Texas, the Mexican American community has made substantial political headway in local government, whereas the equally proportional Mexican American community in Los Angeles has been essentially blocked from assuming power.

71. According to Waldinger and Bozorgmehr, the beneficiaries of the 1965 Hart-Celler Act were expected to be eastern and southern European immigrants, but "instead, the newcomers who took advantage of the newly liberalized system came from Asia, Latin America, and countries of the Caribbean." Roger Waldinger and Mehdi Bozorgmehr, "The Making of a Multicultural Metropolis," in *Ethnic Los Angeles,* ed. Roger Waldinger and Mehdi Bozorgmehr (New York: Russell Sage Foundation, 1994), 9.

72. This, indeed, is a general phenomenon in the United States, as the 1997 report by the Bureau of the Census ("Demographic State of the Nation") acknowledges. In 1996, non-Hispanics constituted more than 73 percent of the total population, a figure anticipated to drop to only 53 percent by the year 2050, due both to the aging of the non-Hispanic white population and the high rates of immigration and natural increase of Hispanics (most of them of Mexican origin). See, inter alia, Katherine Q. Seelye, "The New U.S.: Grayer and More Hispanic," *New York Times,* March 27, 1997, B16. In all of this, California is leading the way.

73. One presumes that most of the émigrés are native-born and white, although this is only an assumption.

74. Paul Jacobs, "Hitting the Road: Record Number of Drivers Join Exodus, DMV Says," *Los Angeles Times,* August 18, 1994, A3, A26. There is a certain time lag between the decision to move and actual relocation, and then an additional time lag until the driver's license is changed. Therefore, we can assume that the "dream" was already tarnishing before the riot and earthquake perhaps added the final incentive.

75. See Patrick Lee, "The Emigrants," *Los Angeles Times,* February 5, 1995, D6.

76. Ibid.

77. It will be recalled that the earliest Spanish "explorers" reported multiple earthquakes

along the Santa Ana River and a horrendous flood at the Los Angeles River. Furthermore, only two of the original eleven families sent from Mexico to settle Los Angeles were "Spanish," the rest being Negro, Indian, or of "mixed blood." Howard Nelson, *The Los Angeles Metropolis* (Dubuque, Iowa: Kendall/Hunt, 1983), 129–33.

78. See Jesus Sanchez, "Big Southland Population Jump Expected," *Los Angeles Times,* in 1995, n.d., D1, D11, who cites a study made by the CCSCE.

79. "A Welcome for Immigrants Turns to Resentment," *Los Angeles Times,* 1995, reports that "probably nowhere has the backlash been sharper than in Orange County, where . . . [t]here have been bitter disputes over street vendors, overcrowded apartments and bilingual teaching in the public schools. Santa Ana is more than two-thirds Hispanic." See also Robert Reinhold, "California's Welcome to Immigrants Turns to Resentment," *New York Times,* August 25, 1993, A1, A12.

80. Jess Carrillo, "The Process of School Desegregation: The Case of the Los Angeles Unified School District" (Ph.D. diss., University of California, Los Angeles, 1978), 11. My exposition depends heavily on this fine work.

81. Soon afterward, the judge was defeated for reelection by an antibusing candidate. See Raphael J. Sonenshein, *Politics in Black and White: Race and Power in Los Angeles* (Princeton, N.J.: Princeton University Press, 1993), 102.

82. For more details, see Carrillo, "The Process of School Desegregation," 59–61, on which the following summary depends.

83. Ibid., 60. The analysis that follows depends upon the data so collected.

84. Carrillo, "The Process of School Desegregation," 6.

85. Ibid., 215. Magnet schools are "schools within schools."

86. See ibid., 214–17.

87. These serial documents are the best sources of information on the lack of progress in desegregating Los Angeles schools. See the successive publications of the Los Angeles Unified School District, Information Technology Division, originally titled *Racial/Ethnic Survey* but later simplified to *Ethnic Survey Report.*

88. Los Angeles Unified School District, Information Technology Division, *Fall 1992 Ethnic Survey Report* (Publication 119) (Los Angeles: LAUSD, 1992), iii.

89. Enrollment would have declined due to both the older ages of whites and the tendency of whites with school-aged children to select residences in communities not included in the LAUSD.

90. California State Department of Education, *Report, 1990* (Sacramento: Department of Education, 1990).

91. California State Department of Finance, *Report of 1989* (Sacramento: Department of Finance, 1989).

92. See information included in "Tax Money Flowing Again, California Pares Class Size," *New York Times,* September 11, 1996, D18.

93. See Jim Newton and Matea Gold, "Latino Turnout a Breakthrough," *Los Angeles Times,* April 10, 1997, A1, A6. See also Amy Pyle and Lucille Renwick, "Schools Bask in the Glow of Bond Measure Approval," *Los Angeles Times,* April 10, 1997, B1, B3.

94. It must be noted that despite the fact that "Anglos" are now a minority of Los Angeles residents, they still constitute two-thirds of the electorate. See, for example, Susan Rasky, "Falling Off the Edge of the Dream," *The Nation,* March 23, 1993, 380–82. It should also be pointed out that not all legal aliens or native-born Hispanics in Los Angeles oppose efforts to reduce immigration, nor do all native-born or naturalized Hispanics oppose with-

drawing welfare assistance from aliens. The assumption of a radically politicized Latino community is, as we shall see, far from correct.

95. The Los Angeles Charter "imposes a limit of $1.25 per $100 of assessed property (assessed valuation represents approximately 25 percent of market value)." League of Women Voters of Los Angeles, *Los Angeles: Structure of a City,* ed. Irene Jerison (Los Angeles: League of Women Voters, 1976), 15.

96. Sonenshein, *Politics in Black and White,* 169. Sonenshein cites Ruth Ross, *The Impact of Federal Grants on the City of Los Angeles* (Federal Aid Case Studies Series Paper No. 8) (Washington, D.C.: Brookings Institution, 1980), as his source for these estimates.

97. Sonenshein, *Politics in Black and White,* 181, Table 11.6, calculated from figures from the County of Los Angeles, Registrar-Recorder, City Clerk, Election Division; see also 191.

98. It should be noted that support for the anti-immigrant proposition was also evidenced among black voters and among established older members of the Chicano community, both of whom had begun to view newcomers as threats who could displace them or erode prior gains in wages. A federal court ruled Proposition 187 invalid in 1997.

99. Laws that currently hold employers culpable for hiring undocumented workers have already had the perverse effect of making the hiring of Hispanic-appearing persons potentially risky; if employers are willing to take the risk, they are better off favoring undocumented workers who cost less and can be better controlled.

100. A recent change in Mexican nationality law that permits the holding of dual citizenship has freed some of those who were reluctant to give up their Mexican passports in order to become U.S. citizens.

101. Sam Howe Verhovek, "Immigrants' Anxieties Spur a Surge in Naturalizations," *New York Times,* September 13, 1997, 1, 16. This article, which carries a Houston, Texas, dateline, reports a rush of resident aliens to take the oath of citizenship.

102. There is even an economic incentive to change one's status. The INS now requires anyone who received a green card before 1979 to apply for a new one, which costs seventy-five dollars; it costs only twenty dollars more to apply for citizenship.

103. Verhovek, "Immigrants' Anxieties," 16.

104. David Firestone, "Giuliani Suit to Contest Cutoff of U.S. Benefits to Immigrants," *New York Times,* March 26, 1997, B3.

105. *Los Angeles Times,* July 22, 1995, 1, A26.

106. See, inter alia, Tim Golden, "Federal Appeals Court Upholds California's Ban on Preferences," *New York Times,* April 9, 1997, 1, B10.

107. On April 4, 1998, the *New York Times* ran an editorial reporting that black, Hispanic, and American Indian students will constitute only 10 percent of the University of California, Berkeley, freshman class in 1998–99, compared with 23 percent the year before. In the state's top professional schools, the situation was even worse: only one black will join the 268 first-year students in Berkeley's law school in 1998–99 (A12).

108. The deep-seated and long-standing animosities toward Mexicans in California are traced with unconcealed horror in Tomás Almaguer's recent book *Racial Fault Lines: The Historical Origins of White Supremacy in California* (Berkeley: University of California Press, 1994). A more "sympathetic" attempt to understand the dilemma of Anglo-Californians and the bases for their "panic" is found in Dale Maharidge, *The Coming White Minority: California's Eruptions and the Nation's Future* (New York: Random House/Times Books, 1996).

109. For a comparison of the New York and Los Angeles situations, see, inter alia, Roger Waldinger, *Still the Promised City? African-Americans and New Immigrants in Postindustrial New York* (Cambridge: Harvard University Press, 1996); and David M. Grant, Melvin Oliver,

and Angela D. James, "African Americans: Social and Economic Bifurcation," in *Ethnic Los Angeles,* ed. Roger Waldinger and Medhi Bozorgmehr (New York: Russell Sage Foundation, 1994), 379–411.

110. See Simmel's long essay "On the Significance of Numbers for Social Life," in *The Sociology of Georg Simmel,* trans. Kurt H. Wolff (Glencoe, Ill.: Free Press, 1950), esp. 145–69.

111. These cleavages, which resulted in New York City's experimentation with locally elected school boards, have never healed. But more important, they generated problems in the school system that disempowered superintendents and the chancellor of a system that now serves some 1.1 million students. In 1997, after a succession of failed chancellors, the system was "reformed" under a charismatic black chancellor. It is still too early to tell whether recent changes can turn the system around.

112. See Ester R. Fuchs, *Mayors and Money: Fiscal Policy in New York and Chicago* (Chicago: University of Chicago Press, 1992).

113. In the preface to *Politics in Black and White,* written in October 1992, Sonenshein avers: "I argue in this book that biracial coalitions between African-Americans and white liberals have been prematurely declared dead. And since biracial politics are still alive, I explore how biracial coalitions work—why they rise and why they fall" (xv).

114. Notably, I refer to Skerry's *Mexican Americans.* Although I may disagree with some of his conclusions, I have found this book, which compares Latino politics in San Antonio, Texas, and Los Angeles, very helpful to my own analysis.

115. Sonenshein claims that the key to the political success of the black population in Los Angeles "has been a durable alliance between Blacks and white liberals in general, and Blacks and Jews in particular. Over time the coalition has offered a major role to the business community and has expanded to include Latinos and Asian-Americans." *Politics in Black and White,* xvi. He contrasts the "success" of Los Angeles with what he calls New York's "vituperative race relations." "In both interests and leadership, New York City and Los Angeles stand worlds apart. I contend that a direct conflict of interest existed between Blacks and white liberals in New York City, while in Los Angeles they had common interests. In Los Angeles a strong biracial leadership network exploited that shared interest, while in New York City leaders failed to carry their communities across racial lines" (xvii).

116. Skerry, *Mexican Americans,* 75. But see also William Deverell and Tom Sitton, eds., *California Progressivism Revisited* (Berkeley: University of California Press, 1994), for a fuller interpretation of the earlier era.

117. What is remarkable is the relative constancy of these numbers, despite the hundredfold increase in population in the past hundred years. The current Los Angeles City Charter, passed in 1925, offered voters a choice between eleven or fifteen council districts, and the California Supreme Court settled the "controversy" by "giving the city its system of 15 members elected by district." For the early history and confirmation that no more than fifteen districts were ever proposed for the city, see League of Women Voters, *Los Angeles,* 28–29.

118. Skerry, *Mexican Americans,* 75.

119. In some mysterious fashion, campaign promises to change police chiefs and curtail the independence of the police department die out abruptly after mayors take office. Mayor Bradley attributed the reversal of his predecessor's position to blackmail—the "secret files" the department had on Mayor Yorty. But then one must ask whether Bradley, who also reversed his position once in office, did so for similar reasons. A structural explanation seems more compelling.

120. Skerry, *Mexican Americans,* 77.

121. Ibid., 76–77.

122. Perhaps the most vivid critique of the way centralized control over local politics has been consistently exercised by nonelected "leaders" is found in Mike Davis's hard-hitting *City of Quartz: Excavating the Future in Los Angeles* (New York: Verso, 1990). This wonderfully written book is in the best tradition of urban muckraking literature.

123. This district was known informally as "the Hispanic district," even though it contained almost equal numbers of black and Hispanic voters. Sonenshein, *Politics in Black and White,* 43.

124. Ibid., 44. It was not until 1985 that a Hispanic was elected as one of the five commissioners of Los Angeles County, and that was only after the county was districted, providing the Mexican Americans of East Los Angeles with some electoral strength.

125. In the 1965 postriot studies made by scholars, many respondents in the black community said that they thought some good might come out of the expressions of anger, even when they disapproved of violence and claimed they had not participated; in contrast, almost all whites interviewed said that their attitudes toward blacks had become more negative because of the riot. See the many mimeographed reports prepared by the UCLA Los Angeles Riot Study. The most germane is a report by T. M. Tomlinson and David O. Sears, "Los Angeles Riot Study: Negro Attitudes toward the Riot" (Report MR-97, UCLA Institute of Government and Public Affairs, mimeo, 1967). A synthetic account of the study's findings can be found in David O. Sears and John B. McConahay, *The Politics of Violence: The New Urban Blacks and the Watts Riot* (Boston: Houghton Mifflin, 1973).

126. Yorty had been elected in 1961 as a reform candidate who promised to rein in the power of Police Chief Parker and to assist poor Angelenos by taking advantage of the federal funds available through War on Poverty programs. According to Sonenshein, he did neither. The latter quotes Bradley's accusation that Parker "had the goods" on Yorty and therefore could not be dislodged. And federal agencies complained that Los Angeles refused to apply for the financial assistance then available. See Sonenshein, *Politics in Black and White,* 39–40, 71.

127. Sonenshein acknowledges this as a "good" thing. "My analysis confirms the importance of elite interracial networks. . . . I contend that a direct conflict of interest existed between Blacks and white liberals in New York City, while in Los Angeles they had common interests." Ibid., xvii. One of the questions I am raising is whether an important part of the "common interests" was the exclusion of Latinos. In any case, Sonenshein's analysis of why Bradley lost to Yorty in 1969 by 47 to 53 percent is that, in that early year, "Bradley's only real non-Black base was among Jews. . . . [Postelection analysis] suggested that Bradley was most preferred by Blacks, middle-to-upper-status Jews, and poorer Latinos. He would need to gain the support of more whites, a wider array of Jews, and upwardly mobile Latinos . . . [because a] majority of Latinos [had] voted for Yorty" (93–94).

128. League of Women Voters, *Los Angeles,* 112. This publication offers valuable information on the Community Redevelopment Agency.

129. Because the profits earned on CRA projects cannot be spent for anything outside the agency, the situation is reminiscent of the independent power Robert Moses amassed in New York through his access to toll revenues from various bridge and tunnel projects.

130. See Davis, *City of Quartz.*

131. See Paul A. Gilje, *Rioting in America* (Bloomington: Indiana University Press, 1996). Gilje traces some four thousand cases of "riots" (modestly defined) over several hundred years of American history.

132. Paul Chevigny, *Edge of the Knife: Police Violence in the Americas* (New York: New Press, 1995), 1–2, emphasis added. In some ways, his contrast between Los Angeles and New York parallels Kimeldorf's earlier characterization of East and West Coast ports, with "reds"

associated with San Francisco and "rackets" with New York. See Howard Kimeldorf, *Reds or Rackets? The Making of Radical and Conservative Unions on the Waterfront* (Berkeley: University of California Press, 1988).

133. Armando Morales, *Ando Sangrando (I Am Bleeding): A Study of Mexican American-Police Conflict* (La Puente, Calif.: Perspectiva, 1972), 11.

134. Ibid., 12.

135. See, inter alia, Marguerite V. Marin, *Social Protest in an Urban Barrio: A Study of the Chicano Movement, 1966–1974* (Lanham, Md.: University Press of America, 1991).

136. Morales, *Ando Sangrando,* 91ff. Details on the three riots can be found on 100–102, but see also the discussion in Chapter 9, above.

137. Ibid, 91, emphasis added.

138. Ibid., 93.

139. Ibid., 94. Morales claims that in the wake of the ghetto and antiwar riots of 1968, and "anticipating civil disorders in East Los Angeles, various city, county government and business leaders decided to build a $567,386 riot control center *in* East Los Angeles." And when a Special Enforcement Bureau was set up, "there were angry rumors in the Mexican American community that [it] was designed to be used against them" (96–97).

140. Alistair Rogers, "Ambiguous Boundaries and Urban Change: Blacks and Latinos in Los Angeles" (paper presented at the 26th meeting of the International Geographers Congress; typescript dated August 1988).

141. Details of the exit poll appeared in Jim Newton and Matea Gold, "Latino Turnout a Breakthrough," *Los Angeles Times* (Washington ed.), April 10, 1997, A1, A6; see esp. the table on A6.

142. This was the first time that Latinos exceeded black voters in the city's history. The increase in the Latino vote came from two sources: first, there was an increase in the number of potential voters, because of naturalization (see above); but second, a concerted effort was made to increase voter mobilization because an important referendum (a school bond issue) was also on the ballot. This was of particular importance to the Latino community because, by 1997, Latino children constituted some 80 percent of all children enrolled in the LAUSD public schools. However, the Latino vote on the bond issue merely strengthened existing support from other voters.

143. Of the voters who identified their political "ideology" in the exit poll, one-third of the 27 percent calling themselves "liberals" supported Riordan; the other two-thirds voted for Hayden.

144. This discussion ignores the Asian population, which tends to follow white voter patterns and, except for the poverty of a subset of refugees largely from Vietnam and Cambodia, tends to be at least equal to if not higher in economic and occupational status than whites. See Cheng and Yang, "Asians."

145. See Paul Ong and Abel Valenzuela Jr., "The Labor Market: Immigration Effects and Racial Disparities," in *Ethnic Los Angeles,* ed. Roger Waldinger and Mehdi Bozorgmehr (New York: Russell Sage Foundation, 1994), 165–91. This is one of the very best chapters in this generally important book.

146. Ibid., 178.

13. CONCLUSIONS AND A LOOK TO THE FUTURE

1. In the very early work of Godfrey Wilson and Monica Wilson on Africa, this increase in range is referred to as "increase in *scale.*" See their *The Analysis of Social Change Based on Observations in Central Africa* (London: Cambridge University Press, 1968[1945]). This

idea formed the conceptual basis for social area analysis, as explicated in Scott Greer, *The Emerging City* (New Brunswick, N.J.: Transaction, 1998[1962]).

2. See Leslie Sklair, *Sociology of the Global System* (Baltimore: Johns Hopkins University Press, 1991).

3. See, inter alia, the essays by Stuart Hall, Ulf Hannerz, and Janet L. Abu-Lughod in Anthony King, ed., *Culture, Globalization, and the World-System: Contemporary Conditions for the Representation of Identity* (Minneapolis: University of Minnesota Press, 1997). For a somewhat different view, see the discussion of the meaning of global as "globewide" in Bruce Mazlish and Ralph Buultjens, eds., *Conceptualizing Global History* (Boulder, Colo.: Westview, 1993). In my view, it would be a mistake to confine the analysis of globalization only to globewide conditions.

4. I am using the term *world system* here in a loose way, almost as a synonym for *the international system,* fully cognizant that in more technical literature it has a more specific meaning, associated with a "school" of sociology known as *world-systems analysis.*

5. I shall not address this question here. In an earlier article comparing New York and Cairo as global cities, I suggest that, despite many of their similarities as mixtures of "First" and "Third" World patterns (nested within each other), the deepest difference between them lies in their relationship to the international economy: one the controller, the other the controlled. See Janet L. Abu-Lughod, "New York and Cairo: A View from Street Level," *International Social Science Journal* 42 (1990): 307–18.

6. There has been a recent spate of collected volumes essaying the problematic of how globalization is affecting American cities, all of which have appeared after my text was written but predating it in time of publication. For examples, see David Wilson, ed., "Globalization and the Changing U.S. City," *Annals of the American Academy of Political and Social Science* 551 (May 1997); Peter Karl Kresl and Gary Gappert, eds., *North American Cities and the Global Economy* (Thousand Oaks, Calif.: Sage, 1995); and H. V. Savitch and Ronald Vogel, eds., *Regional Politics: America in a Post-City Age* (Thousand Oaks, Calif.: Sage, 1995). Although the topic is thus on the cutting age of debate, the deep theory remains unwritten, the somewhat accidentally selected and superficial case studies are no substitute for systematic comparisons, and in no case, to my knowledge, is the historical background given adequate attention.

7. To recapitulate, the variables identified in Chapter 1 are the strategic position of each city in a world system that is continually reshaped; the climate, resources, and terrain of their physical sites as these have been enhanced by human actions; the original economic functions, political sponsorships, and cultural patterns of their earliest settlers; the cohort moment of their greatest physical expansion, when the spatial template for the future city was established, including the technologies of transport during those phases when place-specific armatures of passage were established; the rates and special sources of their demographic increase over time, which helped to frame their evolving racial and ethnic compositions; and the specific governmental institutions and "political cultures" that evolved locally as mechanisms for adjudicating interests among groups with different class and ethnic characteristics.

8. This theory of urbanism is adumbrated, inter alia, in my book *Changing Cities: Urban Sociology* (New York: HarperCollins, 1991), chaps. 1–2.

9. The Phoenicians, in contrast, had moved westward into zones that the Roman Empire would absorb and combine with the Hellenistic region.

10. I trace this particular cycle in my book *Before European Hegemony: The World System A.D. 1250–1350* (New York: Oxford University Press, 1989).

11. There is always an irony about connectedness. Although it often enhances development, it also increases vulnerability. The diffusion of the Black Death followed the most heavily

traveled international trade routes, just as Japanese and Hong Kong currency difficulties in 1998 were more threatening to the economic health of the United States than were earlier, more severe crises in Indonesia and Malaysia.

12. This phase is covered in detail in Immanuel Wallerstein, *The Modern World-System,* vols. 1 and 2 (Orlando, Fla.: Academic Press, 1974 and 1980). It should be noted that Wallerstein and his followers use the term *world-system* in a highly restricted manner.

13. See Andre Gunder Frank's most recent book, *Re-Orient* (Berkeley: University of California Press, 1998), in which he makes the strongest case for the very long continuity of what he has termed the only "world-system" and the perpetual importance of Asia in it. See also Andre Gunder Frank and Barry K. Gills, eds., *The World System: Five Hundred Years or Five Thousand?* (London: Routledge, 1993).

14. A river valley minisystem along the Mississippi had long existed, sustained by First Nation tribes. The excavations in southern Illinois have revealed the extensive range and elaborate culture of that system. However, this system was fragmented at the time of the Civil War, and only in the twentieth century have the Southeast and South Central portions of the country begun to catch up and be drawn into the national and international system of production and distribution.

15. A fine-tuned study of the impact of World War II activities on various regions and cities of the United States is found in Gregory Hooks, "Regional Processes in the Hegemonic Nation: Political, Economic, and Military Influences on the Use of Space" (paper presented at the annual meeting of the American Sociological Association, Miami, Fla., August 1993). Hooks's maps showing the distribution of military installations and defense orders over time demonstrate the powerful role played by military investments. This study confirms arguments that Ann Markusen has made for the more recent period.

16. See John Broder, "Wide Open Once Again? Chicago Exchanges Seek to Loosen the Yoke of Regulation," *New York Times,* June 4, 1997, D1, D5.

17. I am grateful to Christopher Williams, who compiled much of the information in the tables that appear in this section. Some of the tables have already been published in Janet L. Abu-Lughod, "Comparing Chicago, New York, and Los Angeles: Testing Some World City Hypotheses," in *World Cities in a World-System,* ed. Paul L. Knox and Peter J. Taylor (Cambridge: Cambridge University Press, 1995).

18. One might predict that if the "axis" of U.S. trade is partially deflected from east-west to north-south under NAFTA, Chicago's role as a "border port" may expand.

19. Such figures are best used in time series for the same city, rather than for cross-city comparisons. Given the shift to containerization, it is probably useless to try to compare the pre– and post–Second World War periods.

20. The most recent acquisition of such a "trophy" property is the purchase by a German company of the advertising "tower" at the center of New York's now-gentrifying Times Square, at four times the price paid by the American seller only four years ago, which earned it first-page coverage. See Charles V. Bagli, "Tower in Times Sq., Billboards and All, Earns 400% Profit," *New York Times,* June 19, 1997, 1, B8.

21. See Matthew Drennan, "The Decline and Rise of the New York Economy," in *Dual City: Restructuring New York,* ed. John Mollenkopf and Manuel Castells (New York: Russell Sage Foundation, 1991), 37.

22. Alex Schwartz, "Corporate Service Linkages in Large Metropolitan Areas: A Study of New York, Los Angeles, and Chicago," *Urban Affairs Quarterly* 28 (1992): 276–96. Schwartz analyzes data from the *Corporate Finance Bluebook* (serial since 1983), an annual directory of major U.S. companies.

23. Median sales volume of city-located firms and the median number of employees per city firm were almost twice as high as in suburban-located firms. Schwartz, "Corporate Service Linkages," 283.

24. See Saskia Sassen, *The Global City: New York, London, Tokyo* (Princeton, N.J.: Princeton University Press, 1991).

25. Recently, scholars have begun to reemphasize the importance of local as distinguished from global forces, restoring a balance between the two through detailed studies of different kinds of economic activities—from the most locally embedded to the most footloose. A collection of excellent case studies is found in Kevin Cox, ed., *Spaces of Globalization: Reasserting the Power of the Local* (New York: Guilford, 1997).

26. An apparent reversal of the trend of out-migration from the Great Plains has recently been noted, but it seems to represent a reversed migration of some white residents from large metropolitan areas who are seeking an escape from the increased "minority" populations there.

27. It should be noted that underenumeration of the foreign-born, especially of undocumented residents, makes these figures an absolute minimum; the real proportions may be considerably higher.

28. For example, from 1990 to 1994 (the most recent period for which we have data), immigrants from the former Soviet Union constituted only 6 percent of all immigrants to the United States but almost 12 percent of all immigrants to the city of New York. Some 54 percent of immigrants to New York City were drawn from the Caribbean region, even though such sending countries accounted for only 11 percent of all such immigrants to the United States. See New York City Department of City Planning, *The Newest New Yorkers, 1990–1994: An Analysis of Immigration to NYC in the Early 1990s* (New York: Department of City Planning, December 1996), 12, Table 2.4; my own calculations.

29. Taken cumulatively, the work of Roger Waldinger illuminates how immigrants have found distinctive "niches" in the economies of New York and Los Angeles. On New York, see his *Still the Promised City? African-Americans and New Immigrants in Postindustrial New York* (Cambridge: Harvard University Press, 1996); on Los Angeles, see his volume edited with Mehdi Bozorgmehr, *Ethnic Los Angeles* (New York: Russell Sage Foundation, 1994). I have not found a comparable study on Chicago.

30. On the earlier development of the network of Korean delis in New York, see Ilsoo Kim, *New Urban Immigrants: The Korean Community in New York* (Princeton, N.J.: Princeton University Press, 1980). For the same period in Los Angeles, see, inter alia, Edna Bonacich, Ivan Light, and Charles Choy Wong, "Korean Immigrants: Small Business in Los Angeles," in *Sourcebook on the New Immigration: Implications for the United States and the International Community*, ed. Roy Simon Bryce-Laporte (New Brunswick, N.J.: Transaction, 1980), 167–84; and a fuller treatment in Ivan Light and Edna Bonacich, *Immigrant Entrepreneurs: Koreans in Los Angeles 1965–1982* (Berkeley: University of California Press, 1988). One can contrast the consequences of these differential insertions in the two cities in later years by comparing two sources: Paul Ong and Suzanne Hee, "Losses in the Los Angeles Civil Unrest, April 29–May 1, 1992: Lists of Damaged Properties and the L.A. Riot/Rebellion and Korean Merchants" (University of California, Los Angeles, Center for Pacific Rim Studies, mimeo, 1993); and Claire Jean Kim, "Cracks in the 'Gorgeous Mosaic': Black-Korean Conflict and Racial Mobilization in New York City" (Ph.D. diss., Yale University, December 1996). In Los Angeles, absentee-owned Korean convenience and liquor stores concentrated in South-Central were the generalized objects of attack; in New York, scattered Korean-operated delis in various "minority" zones have become the targets of specifically generated offenses, both real and perceived, by the businesses' owners, but these actions, no matter how widely publicized, do not spread.

31. Data cited here are from the Immigration and Naturalization Service, graphed in Robert Reinhold, "California's Welcome to Immigrants Turns into Resentment," *New York Times,* August 25, 1993, A1.

32. New York and Chicago city councils also have such powers, but they have exercised them to make only marginal, if hardly uncontroversial, adjustments; in Los Angeles, ward boundaries are extremely unstable and appear capricious.

33. In a presentation I recently made in Peter Marcuse's course on global cities at Columbia University, Marcuse caught me unawares by asking what proportion of the variance in the cities I thought could be attributed directly to international forces. I answered, without thinking, "About 10 percent at most." This was a shot in the dark at a question that is, in the last analysis, not subject to verification or denial. Much turns on how one distinguishes "direct" from "indirect" effects.

34. Of course, there is massive slippage between this theory and actual practice. In fact, the federal level has increasingly shaped what can be done at more local levels. However, the tensions are always there. On the one hand, states complain about federal mandates that are handed down without adequate resources to meet them; and on the other hand, there has been a resurgence in pressure to substitute block grants to the states for federally set and funded specific programs, especially in welfare and housing.

35. I explore some of these issues in "American Exceptionalism: The Global and the Local in the World Cities of New York, Chicago, and Los Angeles" (paper presented at the biennial meeting of the International Sociological Association, Bielefeld, Germany, 1994).

36. The burning down of 63rd Street (the important commercial thoroughfare to its south) in the course of the 1968 "riot" completed this process.

37. This was the old term used within the black community (with good reason) for Chicago's earlier schemes of urban redevelopment and renewal.

38. This remains somewhat controversial, and there are counterstudies that suggest that the city might be the net loser. To my knowledge, however, no one has calculated the costs and benefits of a city-state that would incorporate the relevant portions of the states of New York, New Jersey, Connecticut, and Pennsylvania. See below.

39. See Ester R. Fuchs, *Mayors and Money: Fiscal Policy in New York and Chicago* (Chicago: University of Chicago Press, 1992).

40. Recall that Robert Wood's fourteen hundred governments have now proliferated to some two thousand. See Robert C. Wood with Vladimir V. Amendinger, *1400 Governments: The Political Economy of the New York Metropolitan Region* (Cambridge: Harvard University Press, 1961).

41. Mayor Guiliani has claimed that "the city would be in the black if only it could shake free of expensive state (not to mention Federal) mandates." Quoted in Clyde Haberman, "Time Again for an Old Idea: 51st State?" *New York Times,* December 17, 1996, B1.

42. Ibid.

43. John Friedmann and Goetz Wolff, "World City Formation: An Agenda for Research and Action," *International Journal of Urban and Regional Research* 6, no. 2 (1982).

44. Ibid.

45. Kirk Johnson, "Wall Street Leads, but New York's Economy Doesn't Follow," *New York Times,* March 7, 1997, B1, B6. The State Comptroller's office reported that between 1989 and 1995, when real wages for New York City's 3.2 million workers went up 8.4 percent, adjusted for inflation, most of this gain came from one place: Wall Street.

46. Joseph Giovannini, "I Love New York and L.A., Too," *New York Times Magazine,* September 11, 1983, 147.

47. Ibid., 148. Giovannini obviously never ventured into the outer boroughs or more distant suburbs.

48. Ibid.

49. Ibid.; these quotations are extracted from 144, 147–49.

50. Ibid., 149.

Index

JANET L. ABU-LUGHOD, professor emerita of sociology of Northwestern University and the Graduate Faculty of the New School for Social Research, has been writing about and studying cities for more than fifty years. Her books include *From Urban Village to East Village: The Battle for New York's Lower East Side; Changing Cities: Urban Sociology; Before European Hegemony: The World System A.D. 1250–1350; Rabat: Urban Apartheid in Morocco;* and *Cairo: 1001 Years of the City Victorious,* among many other publications. In 1999 she received the Robert and Helen Lynd Award (American Sociological Association, Section on Community and Urban Sociology) for distinguished lifetime contributions to the study of cities.